C000115596

RTMENT OF THE BISHOPRIC.

The
**rganized Church of Jesus Christ
of Latter Day Saints.**

Organized April 6, 1830.

W. Rowell, Librarian

Berkeley, Cal

Dear Sir:-

Noticing your
warding books of the Re
have forwarded such in
atters of the society.
It is our wis
the true positions of t
people may read and judg
be that you at any ti
library you can notify.
catalogue.

Herald Pub- lishing House

....and

Bookbindery

Catalogue and
Price List of
Publications and
Books . . . .

Lamoni, Decatur Co
Iowa

HISTORY

OF THE

CHURCH OF JESUS CHRIST

Of Latter Day Saints.

1805–1835.

WRITTEN AND COMPILED BY

PRESIDENT JOSEPH SMITH

AND

APOSTLE HEMAN C. SMITH,

Of the Reorganized Church.

VOLUME 1

LIBRARY OF THE UNIVERSITY OF CALIFORNIA

LAMONI, IOWA:
PUBLISHED BY THE BOARD OF PUBLICATION OF THE
REORGANIZED CHURCH OF JESUS CHRIST
OF LATTER DAY SAINTS.
1897.

BX1611
.S58
V.1.

· Copyrighted by the BOARD OF PUBLICATION of the Reorgan-
ized Church of Jesus Christ of Latter Day Saints. Publishers and
Proprietors, in the year 1896, in the office of the Librarian of
Congress at Washington, D. C.

77260α.

HERALD PUBLISHING HOUSE AND BOOKBINDERY,
LAMONI, IOWA.

LIBRARY
OF THE
UNIVERSITY
OF CALIFORNIA

PUBLISHER'S PREFACE.

THE demand for an authentic history of the church together with the remarkable events which culminated in its organization, April 6, A. D. 1830, has greatly increased with the extension of the church work, both from within and without the association, and to be able to supply this demand the Board of Publication in its report to the General Conference in 1892, presented the following statement:—

"It is the sense of the Board that an authentic history of the rise and progress of the church should be compiled and published, and we therefore recommend that the Conference of the church shall now take action authorizing the Board to cause such compilation and publication to be made."

This was duly considered and approved by the conference and a committee of "examination and revision" was appointed consisting of Joseph Smith, W. H. Kelley, Charles Derry, and Joseph R. Lambert in connection with the Board of Publication, with power to act when the manuscript was ready.

At the time it was the design of the Board to enlist the services of a number of prominent writers who were known to be conversant with the history and work of the church, and arrange among them the work of preparation in equal periods, according to time and importance of events; but the meager encouragement received by the Board under this proposition led to the determination to arrange with competent writers who could and would give close and constant attention to the work until its completion.

At its regular meeting May 1, 1896, the Board selected President Joseph Smith and Apostle Heman C. Smith for the work, the latter being able to so arrange his regular missionary charge, as to devote his entire time to the preparation of the history till its completion; and the result has been most satisfactory.

In the final examination and review, however, the Board has been deprived of the services of one of its members, President W. W. Blair, deceased, and the special committee appointed by the conference has been compelled to act in great part without the aid of Elders W. H. Kelley and Charles Derry, other work precluding the attendance of these members at the councils of the committee.

But, whatever the difficulties and magnitude of the task of writing a history approximating correctness, covering a period of more than ninety years, of a work and people having part in some of the most wonderful and stirring events of the nineteenth century, the undertaking is no longer an experiment but a fact. The first volume we now place before the public and the second is ready for the printer.

In the preparation it has not been the effort to exhaust the subject, but to give such clear and concise narration of the general facts touching all the principal occurrences and events as would give the candid reader a proper comprehension and understanding of the policies, doctrine, and work of the church from the beginning, and the grounds and manner of work of its opposers so far as relative to the occurring events. The Board does not claim for it infallibility; but that it is worthy a careful and considerate reading by every lover of truth, and invites honorable and fair criticism from all without regard to fear or favor, having had from the beginning the object and purpose of discovering and revealing the truth.

THE BOARD OF PUBLICATION.

Lamoni, Iowa, November 24, 1896.

your Husband until death

Joseph Smith Jr

(From a portrait painted in his thirty-eighth year.)

CONTENTS.

CHAPTER 1.

CHAPTER 2.

1805–1828.

CHAPTER 3.

1828–1829.

CHAPTER 4.
1829.

CHAPTER 5.
1829.

CHAPTER 6.
1830.

CHAPTER 7.
1830.

CHAPTER 11.

1832–1833.

CHAPTER 12.

1833.

CHAPTER 13.

1833.

CHAPTER 19.

1834.

CHAPTER 20.

1834.

CHAPTER 21.

1835.

CHAPTER 22.

1835.

CHAPTER 23.

1835.

CONTENTS.

Hyrum Smith

(From a portrait painted in his forty-fourth year.)

LIBRARY OF THE UNIVERSITY OF CALIFORNIA

CHAPTER 1.

HISTORY OF JOSEPH SMITH AND THE CHURCH UNIQUE —ANTAGO-
NISM TO BE EXPECTED—CLAIMS WORTHY OF INVESTIGATION
—IN HARMONY WITH REFORMERS—COMING OF AN ELIAS—
LUTHER IN THE SPIRIT OF ELIAS — JOHN WESLEY ON THE
LATTER-DAY GLORY, AND THE KINGDOM—PROTESTANTS SHOULD
PATIENTLY HEAR—HON. JOSIAH QUINCY ON JOSEPH SMITH—
REV. MR. PRIOR ON JOSEPH SMITH—SMUCKER ON JOSEPH
SMITH'S CHARACTER.

THE history of Joseph Smith and the work to the establishment of which he gave his life must ever be a strange and unique chapter in the history of his genera·tion. The claims he made were not only new and strange, but in positive conflict with the traditions and settled convictions of his time.

Unique feature.

For a man to claim that he was intrusted with a divine appointment to restore to a Christian nation what they supposed they already possessed and richly enjoyed, would naturally create bitter antagonism, and we are not surprised that the conflict still continues; nor do we blame men for refusing to accept the claims of the Latter Day Saints until good reasons are shown for so doing, but we are quite anxious that the world should patiently hear and investigate, assured that our claims will bear all the light that can be thrown upon them.

Antagonism expected.

Worthy of in-vestigation.

The supposed extraordinary claims of Joseph Smith seem to harmonize with the spirit and feelings of some of the Reformers who preceded him. The claim that one should come in the spirit and power of Elias, as a "restorer," now seems strange and new; yet Martin Luther said:—

Harmony with Re-formers.

"I cannot tell what to say of myself. Perhaps I am

Philip's (Melancthon's) forerunner. I am preparing the way
Coming of
Elias. for him, like Elias, in spirit and in power."—D'Au-
bigné's History of the Reformation, vol. 2, p. 105.

It is evident from these words that Luther felt that he
was laboring in the spirit and power of Elias, as a restorer;
Luther in the
spi it of
Elias. and that he was the forerunner of one who was
to do a greater work than he. He thought it might
be Philip Melancthon, but did not know.

The claim of Joseph Smith that Elias did come to
restore all things is but a testimony of the consummation of
an event that Martin Luther felt would come, and for which
he ardently hoped, zealously labored, and fervently prayed.

The famous John Wesley also believed in the ushering
in of a latter-day dispensation and the establishing of God's
kingdom on the earth. He says:—

"The times which we have reason to believe are at hand,
(if they are not already begun,) are what many pious men
John Wesley
on the Latter-
Day Glory. have termed, the time of 'the latter-day glory';—
meaning, the time wherein God would gloriously
display his power and love, in the fulfillment of his
gracious promise that 'the knowledge of the Lord shall
cover the earth, as the waters cover the sea.'"

Again, he says:—

"What could God have done which he hath not done, to
convince you that the day is coming, that the time is at hand,
when he will fulfill his glorious promises; when he will arise
to maintain his own cause, and to set up his kingdom over
all the earth?"—Wesley's Sermons, vol. 2, sermon 71.

Are not the claims of Joseph Smith regarding the
glorious display of God's power, the "latter-day glory," and
the setting up of God's kingdom, if true, a remarkable
fulfillment of what Wesley said would come?

You Protestant lovers of the Reformation, will you not
Protestants
should pa-
tiently hear. then patiently hear us while we relate the thrilling
experiences, the wonderful testimonies, and the
remarkable work of this strange man, and invite
your investigation of the work accomplished or begun by him?

Already some of the most astute minds of the age have
paid their tribute of respect to the man and his work. In a

ordinary persons of his time, a man of rude genius, who

accomplished a much greater work than he

Smucker on Joseph Smith's character. knew; and whose name, whatever he may have been

whilst living, will take its place among the notabilities of the world."—Smucker, p. 183.

Reader, do you not think it wiser to investigate the work of this remarkable character than to ignorantly hurl unsavory epithets at his memory? If you do, we ask the privilege of submitting historical facts for your consideration.

CHAPTER 2.

1805-1828.

THE events of the early life of this remarkable man can best be told in his own language, published in *Times and Seasons*, volume 3:—

"I was born in the year of our Lord one thousand eight hundred and five, on the twenty-third day of December, in the town of Sharon, Windsor County, State of Vermont. My father, Joseph Smith, Senior, left the State of Vermont, and moved to Palmyra, Ontario (now Wayne) County, in the State of New York, when I was in my tenth year. In about four years after my father's arrival at Palmyra, he moved with his family into Manchester, in the same county of Ontario. His family, consisting of eleven souls; namely: My father, Joseph Smith, my mother, Lucy Smith (whose name, previous to her marriage was Mack, daughter of Solomon Mack), my brothers, Alvin (who is now dead), Hyrum, myself, Samuel Harrison, William, Don Carlos, and my sisters, Sophronia, Catharine, and Lucy.[1]

Early history of Joseph Smith.

His father's family.

---

[1] Lucy Smith, in her history of Joseph Smith, gives the date of Lucy's birth July 18, 1821. See p. 43.

"Sometime in the second year after our removal to Manchester, there was in the place where we lived an unusual excitement on the subject of religion. It commenced with the Methodists, but soon became general among all the sects in that region of country; indeed the whole district of country seemed affected by it, and great multitudes united themselves to the different religious parties, which created no small stir and division amongst the people, some crying, "lo, here," and some, "lo, there;" some were contending for the Methodist faith, some for the Presbyterian, and some for the Baptists. For, notwithstanding the great love which the converts for these different faiths expressed at the time of their conversion, and the great zeal manifested by the respective clergy, who were active in getting up and promoting this extraordinary scene of religious feeling, in order to have everybody 'converted,' as they were pleased to call it, let them join what sect they pleased; yet, when the converts began to file off, some to one party, and some to another, it was seen that the seemingly good feelings of both the priests and the converts were more pretended than real; for a scene of great confusion and bad feeling ensued, priest contending against priest, and convert against convert, so that all the good feelings, one for another, if they ever had any, were entirely lost in a strife of words, and a contest about opinions.

Religious revival.

"I was at this time in my fifteenth year. My father's family was proselyted to the Presbyterian faith, and four of them joined that church; namely, my mother Lucy, my brothers Hyrum, Samuel Harrison, and my sister Sophronia.

"During this time of great excitement my mind was called up to serious reflection and great uneasiness; but though my feelings were deep and often pungent, still I kept myself aloof from all those parties, though I attended their several meetings as often as occasion would permit; but in process of time my mind became somewhat partial to the Methodist sect, and I felt some desire to be united with them, but so great was the confusion and strife among the different denominations that it was impossible for a person young as I was and so unacquainted

Greatly exercised on religious subjects.

with men and things to come to any certain conclusion who was right, and who was wrong. My mind at different times was greatly excited, the cry and tumult was so great and incessant. The Presbyterians were most decided against the Baptists and Methodists, and used all their powers of either reason or sophistry to prove their errors, or at least to make the people think they were in error; on the other hand the Baptists and Methodists in their turn were equally zealous to establish their own tenets, and disprove all others.

"In the midst of this war of words and tumult of opinions, I often said to myself, What is to be done? Who of all these parties are right? Or, are they all wrong together? If any one of them be right, which is it, and how shall I know it?

"While I was laboring under the extreme difficulties caused by the contests of these parties of religionists, I was one day reading the epistle of James, first chapter and fifth verse, which reads: 'If any of you lack wisdom, let him ask of God, that giveth to all men liberally, and upbraideth not; and it shall be given him.' Never did any passage of scripture come with more power to the heart of man than this did at this time to mine. It seemed to enter with great force into every feeling of my heart. I reflected on it again and again, knowing that if any person needed wisdom from God I did, for how to act I did not know, and unless I could get more wisdom than I then had would never know; for the teachers of religion of the different sects understood the same passage so differently as to destroy all confidence in settling the question by an appeal to the Bible. At length I came to the conclusion that I must either remain in darkness and confusion, or else I must do as James directs; that is, ask of God. I at length came to the determination to 'ask of God,' concluding that if he gave wisdom to them that lacked wisdom and would give liberally, and not upbraid, I might venture. So in accordance with this my determination, to ask of God, I retired to the woods to make the attempt. It was on the morning of a beautiful clear day, early in the spring of eighteen hundred and twenty. It was the first time in my

[sidenote: Is encouraged by reading the epistle of the Apostle James.]

[sidenote: Retires to the woods to pray.]

life that I had made such an attempt, for amidst all my anxieties I had never as yet made the attempt to pray vocally.

"After I had retired into the place where I had previously designed to go, having looked around me and finding myself alone, I kneeled down and began to offer up the desires of my heart to God. I had scarcely done so when immediately I was seized upon by some power which entirely overcame me, and had such astonishing influence over me as to bind my tongue so that I could not speak. Thick darkness gathered around me, and it seemed to me for a time as if I were doomed to sudden destruction. But exerting all my powers to call upon God to deliver me out of the power of this enemy which had seized upon me, and at the very moment when I was ready to sink into despair and abandon myself to destruction, (not to an imaginary ruin, but to the power of some actual being from the unseen world who had such a marvelous power as I had never before felt in my being,) just at this moment of great alarm, I saw a pillar of light exactly over my head, above the brightness of the sun; which descended gradually until it fell upon me. It no sooner appeared than I found myself delivered from the enemy which held me bound. When the light rested upon me I saw two personages (whose brightness and glory defy all description) standing above me in the air. One of them spake unto me, calling me by name, and said, (pointing to the other,) 'This is my beloved Son, hear him.'

Sees a vision.

"My object in going to inquire of the Lord was to know which of all the sects was right, that I might know which to join. No sooner therefore did I get possession of myself, so as to be able to speak, than I asked the personages who stood above me in the light, which of all the sects was right, (for at this time it had never entered into my heart that all were wrong,) and which I should join. I was answered that I must join none of them, for they were all wrong, and the personage who addressed me said that all their creeds were an abomination in his sight; that those professors were all corrupt; 'they draw near to me with their lips, but their hearts are far from me; they teach for doctrine the commandments of men, having a form of godliness, but they deny the power thereof.' He again forbade me to join with any of them: and many other things did he say unto me which I cannot write at this time. When I came to myself again I found myself lying on my back, looking up into heaven.

"Some few days after I had this vision I happened to be in company with one of the Methodist preachers who was very active in the before-mentioned religious

Relates the vision to a minister. excitement, and conversing with him on the subject of religion I took occasion to give him an account of the vision which I had had. I was greatly surprised at his behavior; he treated my communication not only lightly,

Is repulsed. but with great contempt, saying it was all of the Devil; that there was no such thing as visions or revelations in these days; that all such things had ceased with the apostles, and that there never would be any more of them. I soon found, however, that my telling the story had excited a great deal of prejudice against me among professors of religion, and was the cause of great persecution, which continued to increase; and though I was an obscure boy only between fourteen and fifteen years of age, and my circumstances in life such as to make a boy of no consequence in the world, yet men of high standing would take notice sufficient to excite the public mind against me, and create a hot persecution; and this was common among all the sects; all united to persecute me. It has often caused me serious reflection both then and since, how very strange it was that an obscure boy of a little over fourteen years of age, and one too who was doomed to the necessity of obtaining a scanty maintenance by his daily labor, should be thought a character of sufficient importance to attract the attention of the great ones of the most popular sects of the day, so as to create in them a spirit of the hottest persecution and reviling. But strange or not, so it was, and was often cause of great sorrow to myself. However, it was nevertheless a fact that I had had a vision. I have thought since that I felt much like Paul when he made his defense before King Agrippa and related the account of the vision he had when he 'saw a light and heard a voice,' but still there were but few who believed him; some said he was dishonest, others said he was mad; and he was ridiculed and reviled; but all this did not destroy the reality of his vision. He had seen a vision, he knew he had, and all the persecution under heaven could not make it otherwise; and though they should persecute him unto death, yet he knew and would know unto his latest breath, that he had both seen a light, and heard a voice speaking to him, and all the world could not make him think or believe otherwise. So it was with me. I had actually seen a light, and in the midst of that light I saw two personages, and they did in reality speak unto me, or one of them did; and though I was hated and persecuted for saying that I had seen a vision, yet it was true; and while they were persecuting me, reviling me, and speaking all manner of evil against me falsely for so saying, I was led to say in my heart, Why persecute for telling the truth? I have actually seen a vision, and 'Who am I that I can withstand God,' or why does the world think to make me deny what I have actually seen; for I had seen a vision; I knew it, and I knew that God knew it, and I could not deny it, neither dare I do it; at least I knew that by so doing I would offend God and come under condemnation.

"I had now got my mind satisfied so far as the sectarian world was concerned, that it was not my duty to join with any of them, but continue as I was until further directed; I had found the testimony of James to be true, that a man who lacked wisdom might ask of God, and obtain and not be upbraided. I continued to pursue my common avocations in life until the twenty-first of September, one thousand eight hundred and twenty-three, all the time suffering severe persecution at the hands of all classes of men, both religious and irreligious, because I continued to affirm that I had seen a vision. During the space of time which inter-
Yields to
weaknesses. vened between the time I had the vision, and the year eighteen hundred and twenty-three, having been forbidden to join any of the religious sects of the day, and being of very tender years, and persecuted by those who ought to have been my friends, and to have treated me

kindly, and if they supposed me to be deluded to have endeavored in a proper and affectionate manner to have reclaimed me, I was left to all kinds of temptations, and mingling with all kinds of society, I frequently fell into many foolish errors and displayed the weakness of youth and the corruption of human nature, which I am sorry to say led me into divers temptations, to the gratification of many appetites offensive in the sight of God.   In consequence of these things I often felt condemned for my weakness and imperfections; when on the evening of the above-mentioned twenty-first of September, after I had retired to my bed for the night, I betook myself to prayer and supplication to Almighty God for forgiveness of all my sins and follies, and also for a manifestation to me, that I might know of my state and standing before him; for I had full confidence in obtaining a divine manifestation as I had previously had one.

"While I was thus in the act of calling upon God I discovered a light appearing in the room, which continued to increase until the room was lighter than at noon-day, when immediately a personage appeared at my bedside standing in the air, for his feet did not touch the floor.   He had on a loose robe of most exquisite whiteness. It was a whiteness beyond anything earthly I had ever seen; nor do I believe that any earthly thing could be made to appear so exceedingly white and brilliant; his hands were naked, and his arms also a little above the wrist.   So also were his feet naked, as were his legs a little above the ankles.   His head and neck were also bare.   I could discover that he had no other clothing on but this robe, as it was open so that I could see into his bosom.   Not only was his robe exceedingly white, but his whole person was glorious beyond description, and his countenance truly like lightning.   The room was exceedingly light, but not so very bright as immediately around his person.   When I first looked upon him I was afraid, but the fear soon left me.   He called me by name, and said unto me that he was a messenger sent from the presence of God to me, and that his name was Nephi.[2]   That God had a work for me to do, and that my

An angel appears.

---

[2] This name is given "Moroni" in Doctrine and Covenants 26:2 and 110:20.

name should be had for good and evil, among all nations, kindreds, and tongues; or that it should be both good and Is told of the plates. evil spoken of among all people. He said there was a book deposited written upon gold plates, giving an account of the former inhabitants of this continent, and the source from whence they sprang. He also said that the fullness of the everlasting gospel was contained in it, as delivered by the Savior to the ancient inhabitants. Also that there were two stones in silver bows, and these stones fastened to a breastplate constituted what is called the Urim and Thummim, deposited with the plates, and the possession and use of these stones was what constituted seers in ancient or former times, and that God had prepared them for the Much instruction given. purpose of translating the book. After telling me these things he commenced quoting the prophecies of the Old Testament. He first quoted part of the third chapter of Malachi; and he quoted also the fourth or last chapter of the same prophecy, though with a little variation from the way it reads in our Bibles. Instead of quoting the first verse as it reads in our books, he quoted it thus: 'For behold the day cometh that shall burn as an oven, and all the proud, yea, and all that do wickedly shall burn as stubble, for they that cometh shall burn them saith the Lord of hosts, that it shall leave them neither root nor branch.' And again he quoted the fifth verse thus: 'Behold, I will reveal unto you the priesthood by the hand of Elijah the prophet before the coming of the great and dreadful day of the Lord.' He also quoted the next verse differently: 'And he shall plant in the hearts of the children the promises made to the fathers, and the hearts of the children shall turn to their fathers; if it were not so the whole earth would be utterly wasted at his coming.' In addition to these he quoted the eleventh chapter of Isaiah, saying that it was about to be fulfilled. He quoted also the third chapter of Acts, twenty-second and twenty-third verses, precisely as they stand in our New Testament. He said that that prophet was Christ, but the day had not yet come when 'they who would not hear his voice should be cut off from among the people,' but soon would come.

"He also quoted the second chapter of Joel from the twenty-eighth to the last verse. He also said that this was not yet fulfilled, but was soon to be. And he further stated the fullness of the Gentiles was soon to come in. He quoted many other passages of scripture and offered many explanations which cannot be mentioned here. Again he told me that when I got those plates of which he had spoken (for the time that they should be obtained was not yet fulfilled) I should not show them to any person, neither the Breastplate with the Urim and Thummim, only to those to whom I should be commanded to show them, if I did I should be destroyed. While he was conversing with me about the plates the vision was opened to my mind that I could see the place where the plates were deposited, and that so clearly and distinctly that I knew the place again when I visited it.

"After this communication I saw the light in the room begin to gather immediately around the person of him who had been speaking to me, and it continued to do so until the room was again left dark except just around him, when instantly I saw as it were a conduit open right up into heaven, and he ascended up till he entirely disappeared and the room was left as it had been before this heavenly light had made its appearance.

"I lay musing on the singularity of the scene and marveling greatly at what had been told me by this extraordinary messenger, when in the midst of my meditation I suddenly discovered that my room was again beginning to get lighted, and in an instant, as it were, the same heavenly messenger was again by my bedside. He commenced and again related the very same things which he had done at his first visit without the least variation, which having done, he informed me of great judgments which were coming upon the earth, with great desolations by famine, sword, and pestilence, and that these grievous judgments would come on the earth in this generation.. Having related these things he again ascended as he had done before.

The angel repeats the visitation.

"By this time so deep were the impressions made on my mind that sleep had fled from my eyes and I lay overwhelmed in astonishment at what I had both seen and heard; but what was my surprise when again I beheld the same messenger at my bedside, and heard him rehearse or repeat over again to me the same things as before, and added a caution to me, telling me that Satan would try to tempt me (in consequence of the indigent circumstances of my father's family) to get the plates for the purpose of getting rich. This he forbade me, saying that I must have no other object in view in getting the plates but to glorify God, and must not be influenced by any other motive but that of building his kingdom, otherwise I could not get them. After this third visit he again ascended up into heaven as before and I was again left to ponder on the strangeness of what I had just experienced, when almost immediately after the heavenly messenger had ascended from me the third time, the cock crew, and I found that day was approaching, so that our interviews must have occupied the whole of that night. I shortly after arose from my bed, and as usual went to the necessary labors of the day; but in attempting to labor as at other times, I found my strength so exhausted as rendered me entirely unable. My father who was laboring along with me discovered something to be wrong with me and told me to go home. I started with the intention of going to the house, but in attempting to cross the fence out of the field where we were, my strength entirely failed me and I fell helpless on the ground and for a time was quite unconscious of anything. The first thing that I can recollect was a voice speaking unto me calling me by name. I looked up and beheld the same messenger standing over my head surrounded by light as before. He then again related unto me all that he had related to me the previous night, and commanded me to go to my father and tell him of the vision and commandments which I had received.

"I obeyed, I returned back to my father in the field and rehearsed the whole matter to him. He replied to me that it was of God, and to go and do as commanded by the messenger. I left the field and went to the place where the messenger had told me the plates were deposited; and owing to the distinctness of the vision which

Relates the vision to his father.

I had had concerning it, I knew the place the instant that I arrived there.   Convenient to the village of Manchester, Ontario County, New York, stands a hill of considerable size, and the most elevated of any in the neighborhood.   On the west side of this hill, not far from the top, under a stone of considerable size, lay the plates deposited in a stone box. This stone was thick and rounding in the middle on the upper side, and thinner towards the edges, so that the middle part of it was visible above the ground, but the edge all round was covered with earth.   Having removed the earth and obtained a lever which I got fixed under the edge of the stone and with a little exertion raised it up, I looked in and there indeed did I behold the plates, the Urim and Thummim, and the Breast-plate, as stated by the messenger.   The box in which they lay was formed by laying stones together in some kind of cement; in the bottom of the box were laid two stones crossways of the box, and on these stones lay the plates and the other things with them.

Obtains a view of the plates.

"I made an attempt to take them out, but was forbidden by the messenger and was again informed that the time for bringing them forth had not yet arrived, neither would until four years from that time; but he told me that I should come to that place precisely in one year from that time, and that he would there meet with me, and that I should continue to do so until the time should come for obtaining the plates. Accordingly as I had been commanded I went at the end of each year, and at each time I found the same messenger there, and received instruction and intelligence from him at each of our interviews respecting what the Lord was going to do and how and in what manner his kingdom was to be conducted in the last days.

"As my father's worldly circumstances were very limited, we were under the necessity of laboring with our hands, hiring by day's works and otherwise as we could get opportunity.   Sometimes we were at home and sometimes abroad, and by continued labor were enabled to get a comfortable maintenance.

"In the year eighteen hundred and twenty-four my

father's family met with a great affliction by the death of my
Alvin's death. eldest brother Alvin. In the month of October,
eighteen hundred and twenty-five, I hired with an
old gentleman, by the name of Josiah Stoal, who lived in
Chenango County, State of New York. He had heard
Labors for Mr. Stoal. something of a silver mine having been opened by
the Spaniards in Harmony, Susquehanna County,
State of Pennsylvania, and had previous to my hiring with
him been digging in order if possible to discover the mine.
After I went to live with him he took me among the rest of
his hands to dig for the silver mine, at which I continued to
work for nearly a month without success in our undertaking,
and finally I prevailed with the old gentleman to cease
digging after it. Hence arose the very prevalent story of
my having been a money digger.

"During the time that I was thus employed I was put to
Boards at Mr. Hale's. board with a Mr. Isaac Hale of that place; it was
there that I first saw my wife (his daughter) Emma
Marries Miss Emma Hale. Hale. On the eighteenth of January, eighteen
hundred and twenty-seven, we were married while
yet I was employed in the service of Mr. Stoal.

"Owing to my still continuing to assert that I had seen a
vision persecution still followed me, and my wife's father's
family were very much opposed to our being married. I
was therefore under the necessity of taking her elsewhere,
so we went and were married at the house of Squire Tarbill,
in South Bainbridge, Chenango County, New York. Immediately after my marriage I left Mr. Stoal's and went to my
father's and farmed with him that season.

"At length the time arrived for obtaining the plates, the
Urim and Thummim, and the Breastplate. On the twenty-
Receiving the plates. second day of September, one thousand eight
hundred and twenty-seven, having went as usual
at the end of another year to the place where they were
deposited, the same heavenly messenger delivered them
up to me, with this charge that I should be responsible
for them; that if I should let them go carelessly or through
any neglect of mine, I should be cut off; but that if I would
use all my endeavors to preserve them, until he the

messenger should call for them, they should be protected.

"I soon found out the reason why I had received such strict charges to keep them safe, and why it was that the messenger had said that when I had done what was required at my hand, he would call for them; for no sooner was it known that I had them than the most strenuous exertions were used to get them from me. Every stratagem that could be invented was resorted to for that purpose. The persecution became more bitter and severe than before, and multitudes were on the alert continually to get them from me if possible; but by the wisdom of God they remained safe in my hands until I had accomplished by them what was required at my hand. when according to arrangements the messenger called for them, I delivered them up to him, and he has them in his charge until this day, being the second day of May, one thousand eight hundred and thirty-eight.

"The excitement, however, still continued, and rumor with her thousand tongues was all the time employed in circulating tales about my father's family, and about myself. If I were to relate a thousandth part of them Mr. Harris befriends him. it would fill up volumes. The persecution, however, became so intolerable that I was under the necessity of leaving Manchester, and going with my wife to Susquehanna County in the State of Pennsylvania. While preparing to start, (being very poor and the persecution so heavy upon us that there was no probability that we would ever be otherwise,) in the midst of our afflictions we found a friend in a gentleman by the name of Martin Harris, who came to us and gave me fifty dollars to assist us in our afflictions. Mr. Harris was a resident of Palmyra Township, Wayne County, in the State of New York, and a farmer of Removes to Harmony, Pennsylvania. respectability. By this timely aid was I enabled to reach the place of my destination in Pennsylvania, and immediately after my arrival there I commenced copying the characters of the plates. I copied a considerable number of them, and by means of the Urim and Thummim I translated some of them, which I did between the time I arrived at the house of my wife's father in the month of December, and the February following.

"Sometime in this month of February the aforementioned Mr. Martin Harris came to our place, got the characters
Mr. Harris visits Dr. Mitchill and Prof. Anthon. which I had drawn off the plates, and started with them to the city of New York. For what took place relative to him and the characters, I refer to his own account of the circumstances as he related them to me after his return, which was as follows: 'I went to the city of New York and presented the characters which had been translated, with the translation thereof, to Professor Anthon, a gentleman celebrated for his literary attainments. Professor Anthon stated that the translation was correct, more so than any he had before seen translated from the Egyptian. I then showed him those which were not yet translated, and he said that they were Egyptian, Chaldaic, Assyriac, and Arabic, and he said that they were the true characters. He gave me a certificate certifying to the people of Palmyra that they were true characters, and that the translation of such of them as had been translated was also correct. I took the certificate and put it into my pocket, and was just leaving the house, when Mr. Anthon called me back, and asked me how the young man found out that there were gold plates in the place where he found them. I answered that an angel of God had revealed it unto him.

"'He then said to me, "Let me see that certificate." I accordingly took it out of my pocket and gave it to him, when he took it and tore it to pieces, saying that there was no such thing now as ministering of angels, and that if I would bring the plates to him, he would translate them. I informed him that part of the plates were sealed, and that I was forbidden to bring them. He replied, "I cannot read a sealed book." I left him and went to Dr. Mitchill, who sanctioned what Professor Anthon had said respecting both the characters and the translation.'"

This testimony was related to hundreds of people before it was written in 1838, as many witnesses now living can testify, and was adhered to, and often reaffirmed without variation, to the time of his death, in June, 1844. Strange though the claims contained in this testimony are, yet it would be stranger still to think he could suffer as he did for

the sake of establishing what he knew to be false. There
was absolutely no inducement for him to do so. Neither
wealth, fame, nor ease came to him as a result of his thus
unflinchingly maintaining this unpopular cause. Thoughtful
men who choose to believe his work a delusion, are compelled to admit his sincerity.

The following statement of Mr. Smucker is a case in
point:—

"If he were an impostor, deliberately and coolly inventing,
and pertinaciously propagating a falsehood, there is this

Smucker on
Joseph's
sincerity.
much to be said, that never was an impostor more
cruelly punished than he was, from the first moment of his appearance as a prophet to the last.
Joseph Smith, in consequence of his pretensions to be a seer
and prophet of God, lived a life of continual misery and persecution. He endured every kind of hardship, contumely,
and suffering. He was derided, assaulted, and imprisoned.
His life was one long scene of peril and distress, scarcely
brightened by the brief beam of comparative repose which
he enjoyed in his own city of Nauvoo. In the contempt
showered upon his head his whole family shared. Father
and mother, and brothers, wife, and friends, were alike
involved in the ignominy of his pretensions, and the sufferings that resulted. He lived for fourteen years amid vindictive enemies, who never missed an opportunity to vilify,
to harass, and to destroy him; and he died at last an
untimely and miserable death, involving in his fate a
brother to whom he was tenderly attached. If anything
can tend to encourage the supposition that Joseph Smith
was a sincere enthusiast, maddened with religious frenzies,
as many have been before and will be after him—and that he
had strong and invincible faith in his own high pretensions
and divine mission, it is the probability that unless supported
by such feelings, he would have renounced the unprofitable
and ungrateful task, and sought refuge from persecution
and misery in private life and honorable industry."—
Smucker, pp. 182-183.

This reasoning seems to be good. If it is weak at all it is
in this: that Joseph Smith could be sincere and his testi-

mony not true. Was his testimony of that character that he could be deceived regarding it? When his sincerity is admitted (and surely Mr. Smucker gives good reasons why we should admit it), is it not virtually admitting the truth of his testimony?

It appears that Professor Anthon has written two letters concerning this matter, and his connection therewith. One Professor Anthon writes two letters. was written to E. D. Howe, of Painesville, Ohio, February 17, 1834, a copy of which is found on pages 37-39 of Smucker's work; the other was written in 1841 to an Episcopal minister, of New Rochelle, New York, extracts of which are found in O. Pratt's writings, where reference is made to a periodical called "*The Church Record*, vol. 1, No. 22."

In both of these letters he admits that a man whom he describes as "a plain, apparently simple hearted farmer," "a plain looking countryman," etc., called on him with a copy of characters, which he requested him to decipher.

In the letter of 1834 the Professor says:—

"The whole story about my pronouncing the Mormonite inscription to be 'Reformed Egyptian hieroglyphics,' is perfectly false."

The reader will observe that Martin Harris does not represent the Professor as pronouncing them "*Reformed* Egyptian," Howe misrepresents. etc. This is doubtless the language of Howe to Professor Anthon, and is a misrepresentation of the claim made by Martin Harris, hence the denial has no force.

In the letter of 1834 the Professor describes the paper as follows:—

"This paper, in question, was in fact a singular scroll. It consisted of all kinds of crooked characters, disposed in Anthon describes the characters. columns, and had evidently been prepared by some person who had before him at the time a book containing various alphabets. Greek and Hebrew letters, crosses, and flourishes; Roman letters inverted or placed sideways, were arranged and placed in perpendicular columns; and the whole ended in a rude delineation of a circle, divided into various compartments,

decked with various strange marks, and evidently copied
after the Mexican Calendar, given by Humboldt, but copied
in such a way as not to betray the source whence it was
derived."

In the 1841 letter he says:—

"The characters were arranged in columns, like the
Chinese mode of writing, and presented the most singular
medley that I ever beheld. Greek, Hebrew, and all sorts of
letters, more or less distorted, either through unskillfulness
or from actual designs, were intermingled with sundry de-
lineations of half moons, stars, and other natural objects,
and the whole ended in a rude representation of the Mexican
zodiac."

Though the Professor gives it as his opinion "that it was
a mere hoax, and a very clumsy one too," it will be seen
that he corroborates the testimony of Martin Harris on
the most important points; and though differing from him
in opinion, agrees with him as to the events happening.

In 1870 Mr. Harris in his declining years renewed his
testimony in a letter written to Mrs. H. B. Emerson, of New
Richmond, Ohio. He writes from Smithfield, Utah, November 23, 1870, and says:—

"I do say that the angel did show to me the plates containing the Book of Mormon. Further, the translation that I
carried to Professor Anthon was copied from
these same plates; also, that the Professor did
testify to it being a correct translation."— *Saints'
Herald*, vol. 22, p. 630.

<small>Harris re-
news his
testimony.</small>

The paper containing the characters (not translated) which
Martin Harris carried to Professor Anthon was carefully
preserved, copied, and photographed. We have
examined them when in the hands of the late
David Whitmer. Without further comment we herewith
present a facsimile, from a plate used in Presidency and
Priesthood by W. H. Kelley. The reader can examine
them, compare them with Professor Anthon's statements,
examine the evidence, and form conclusions accordingly.

<small>Facsimile of
character.</small>

Characters

CHAPTER 3.

1828–1829.

MR. HARRIS returned home and arranged his business affairs, then went to Harmony, Pennsylvania, where Joseph was, and began writing for him. He commenced writing about April 12, 1828, and continued until June 14, when he had written one hundred and sixteen pages of foolscap.

M. Harris writes for Joseph.

He then became very solicitous for permission to show the manuscript to his family and friends. He gained this permission, after much importuning, on conditions that he was to show it to none except his brother, his own wife, his father and mother, and a Mrs. Cobb, a sister to his wife.

Desires and obtains permission to show manuscript.

He placed himself under solemn covenant to Joseph Smith to observe these conditions, but when he had gained possession of the manuscript, through anxiety and zeal to promulgate the record, or for other reasons, he took the liberty to show it to others, contrary to his obligation. In some way some of his supposed friends got the manuscript from him, and it was never recovered.

Violates obligations.

For this breach of trust he was severely rebuked, and he humbled himself in much sorrow and contrition of spirit. Joseph Smith was also rebuked for trusting him, and for repeatedly entreating the Lord for his consent after having been denied.

Joseph and Harris rebuked.

He lost his gift, the Urim and Thummim, also the plates
were taken from him for a time. He was in con-
Urim and
Thummim and sequence of this punishment greatly troubled in
gift taken
from Joseph. mind. Finally they were restored to him. He
then inquired of the Lord and received a communication and partial direction as to the proper procedure. [1]

[1] 1. The works, and the designs, and the purposes of God, cannot be
frustrated, neither can they come to nought, for God doth not walk in
crooked paths; neither doth he turn to the right hand nor to the left;
neither doth he vary from that which he hath said; therefore his paths
are straight and his course is one eternal round.

2. Remember, remember, that it is not the work of God that is frustrated, but the work of men; for although a man may have many
revelations, and have power to do many mighty works, yet, if he boasts
in his own strength, and sets at nought the counsels of God, and follows
after the dictates of his own will, and carnal desires, he must fall and
incur the vengeance of a just God upon him.

3. Behold, you have been intrusted with these things, but how strict
were your commandments; and remember, also, the promises which
were made unto you, if you did not transgress them; and, behold, how oft
you have transgressed the commandments and the laws of God, and have
gone on in the persuasions of men: for, behold, you should not have
feared man more than God, although men set at nought the counsels of
God, and despise his words, yet you should have been faithful and he
would have extended his arm, and supported you against all the fiery
darts of the adversary; and he would have been with you in every time
of trouble.

4. Behold, thou art Joseph, and thou wast chosen to do the work of the
Lord, but because of transgression, if thou art not aware thou wilt fall,
but remember God is merciful; therefore, repent of that which thou hast
done, which is contrary to the commandment which I gave you, and
thou art still chosen, and art again called to the work; except thou
do this, thou shalt be delivered up and become as other men, and have
no more gift.

5. And when thou deliveredst up that which God had given thee sight
and power to translate, thou deliveredst up that which was sacred, into
the hands of a wicked man, who has set at nought the counsels of God,
and has broken the most sacred promises, which were made before God,
and has depended upon his own judgment, and boasted in his own
wisdom, and this is the reason that thou hast lost thy privileges for a
season, for thou hast suffered the counsel of thy director to be trampled
upon from the beginning.

6. Nevertheless, my work shall go forth, for, inasmuch as the knowledge of a Savior has come unto the world, through the testimony of the
Jews, even so shall the knowledge of a Savior come unto my people, and
to the Nephites, and the Jacobites, and the Josephites, and the Zoram-
ites, through the testimony of their fathers; and this testimony shall
come to the knowledge of the Lamanites, and the Lemuelites, and the
Ishmaelites, who dwindled in unbelief because of the iniquity of their
fathers, whom the Lord has suffered to destroy their brethren the
Nephites, because of their iniquities and their abominations; and for
this very purpose are these plates preserved which contain these records,
that the promises of the Lord might be fulfilled, which he made to his
people; and that the Lamanites might come to the knowledge of their

Then the Urim and Thummim and plates were again taken from him, and after a time again restored. A further revelation was then received giving instruction how to proceed in the emergency.[a] The objector has sought to make capital out of the policy adopted in this revelation; viz., to abandon the record from which the one hundred and

Another record substituted.

sixteen pages were translated, and the substituting of another and a fuller account. The claim is made that this was frustrating the purposes of God—that he attempted to bring forth one record and being hindered by the designs of men he was compelled to substitute another. It is answered that it was the evident design of God to give

fathers, and that they might know the promises of the Lord, and that they may believe the gospel and rely upon the merits of Jesus Christ, and be glorified through faith in his name, and that through their repentance they might be saved. Amen.

[a] 1. Now, behold, I say unto you, that because you delivered up those writings which you had power given unto you to translate, by the means of the Urim and Thummim, into the hands of a wicked man, you have lost them; and you also lost your gift at the same time, and your mind became darkened; nevertheless, it is now restored unto you again, therefore see that you are faithful and continue on unto the finishing of the remainder of the work of translation as you have begun. Do not run faster, or labor more than you have strength and means provided to enable you to translate; but be diligent unto the end; pray always, that you may come off conqueror; yea, that you may conquer Satan, and that you may escape the hands of the servants of Satan, that do uphold his work. Behold, they have sought to destroy you; yea, even the man in whom you have trusted, has sought to destroy you. And for this cause I said, that he is a wicked man, for he has sought to take away the things wherewith you have been intrusted; and he has also sought to destroy your gift, and because you have delivered the writings into his hands, behold, wicked men have taken them from you; therefore, you have delivered them up; yea, that which was sacred unto wickedness. And, behold, Satan has put it into their hearts to alter the words which you have caused to be written, or which you have translated, which have gone out of your hands; and, behold, I say unto you, that because they have altered the words, they read contrary from that which you translated and caused to be written; and on this wise the Devil has sought to lay a cunning plan, that he may destroy this work; for he has put it into their hearts to do this, that by lying they may say they have caught you in the words which you have pretended to translate.

2. Verily I say unto you, that I will not suffer that Satan shall accomplish his evil design in this thing, for, behold, he has put it into their hearts to get thee to tempt the Lord thy God, in asking to translate it over again; and then, behold, they say and think in their hearts, We will see if God has given him power to translate, if so, he will also give him power again; and if God giveth him power again, or if he translate again, or in other words, if he bringeth forth the same words, behold, we have the same with us, and we have altered them; therefore, they will not

to the world the record that was finally given, and that the
other was intrusted to Joseph Smith that he might practically learn the lesson not to trust in man; and further, that
he might learn how sacred was the trust reposed in him.

Whatever may have been the purpose in this, however, it
is not without its parallel, hence Bible believers cannot consistently find fault. It is related in the thirty-sixth chapter
of Jeremiah that a prophecy of Jeremiah's was burned by
King Jehoiakim, and that it was not only restored, but as in

agree, and we will say that he has lied in his words, and that he has no
gift, and that he has no power; therefore, we will destroy him, and also
the work, and we will do this that we may not be ashamed in the end,
and that we may get glory of the world.

3. Verily, verily I say unto you, that Satan has great hold upon their
hearts; he stirreth them up to iniquity against that which is good, and
their hearts are corrupt, and full of wickedness and abominations, and
they love darkness rather than light, because their deeds are evil; therefore they will not ask of me. Satan stirreth them up, that he may lead
their souls to destruction. And thus he has laid a cunning plan, thinking
to destroy the work of God, but I will require this at their hands, and it
shall turn to their shame and condemnation in the day of judgment; yea,
he stirreth up their hearts to anger against this work; yea, he saith unto
them, Deceive and lie in wait to catch, that ye may destroy; behold, this
is no harm, and thus he flattereth them, and telleth them that it is no
sin to lie, that they may catch a man in a lie, that they may destroy
him, and thus he flattereth them, and leadeth them along until he drag-
geth their souls down to hell; and thus he causeth them to catch themselves in their own snare; and thus he goeth up and down, to and fro in
the earth, seeking to destroy the souls of men.

4. Verily, verily I say unto you, Woe be unto him that lieth to deceive,
because he supposes that another lieth to deceive, for such are not
exempt from the justice of God.

5. Now, behold, they have altered those words, because Satan saith unto
them, He hath deceived you; and thus he flattereth them away to do
iniquity, to get thee to tempt the Lord thy God.

6. Behold, I say unto you, that you shall not translate again those
words which have gone forth out of your hands; for, behold, they shall
not accomplish their evil designs in lying against those words. For,
behold, if you should bring forth the same words they will say that you
have lied; that you have pretended to translate, but that you have contradicted yourself; and, behold, they will publish this, and Satan will
harden the hearts of the people to stir them up to anger against you, that
they will not believe my words. Thus Satan thinketh to overpower
your testimony in this generation, that the work may not come forth in
this generation; but, behold, here is wisdom, and because I show unto you
wisdom, and give you commandments concerning these things, what you
shall do, show it not unto the world until you have accomplished the
work of translation.

7. Marvel not that I said unto you, Here is wisdom, show it not unto
the world, for I said, Show it not unto the world, that you may be preserved. Behold, I do not say that you shall not show it unto the righteous; but as you cannot always judge the righteous, or as you cannot

the other case, it was made more full. Here is the account:—

"Then took Jeremiah another roll, and gave it to Baruch the scribe, the son of Neriah; who wrote therein from the mouth of Jeremiah all the words of the book which Jehoiakim king of Judah had burned in the fire: and there were added besides unto them many like words."—Jer. 36: 32.

The pecuniary circumstances of Joseph Smith would not

always tell the wicked from the righteous; therefore, I say unto you, Hold your peace until I shall see fit to make all things known unto the world concerning the matter.

8. And now, verily I say unto you, that an account of those things that you have written, which have gone out of your hands, are engraven upon the plates of Nephi; yea, and you remember, it was said in those writings, that a more particular account was given of these things upon the plates of Nephi.

9. And now, because the account which is engraven upon the plates of Nephi, is more particular concerning the things which in my wisdom I would bring to the knowledge of the people in this account, therefore, you shall translate the engravings which are on the plates of Nephi, down even till you come to the reign of King Benjamin, or until you come to that which you have translated, which you have retained; and, behold, you shall publish it as the record of Nephi, and thus I will confound those who have altered my words. I will not suffer that they shall destroy my work; yea, I will show unto them that my wisdom is greater than the cunning of the Devil.

10. Behold, they have only got a part, or an abridgment of the account of Nephi. Behold, there are many things engraven on the plates of Nephi, which do throw greater views upon my gospel; therefore, it is wisdom in me, that you should translate this first part of the engravings of Nephi, and send forth in this work. And, behold, all the remainder of this work, does contain all those parts of my gospel which my holy prophets, yea, and also my disciples, desired in their prayers, should come forth unto this people. And I said unto them, that it should be granted unto them according to their faith in their prayers; yea, and this was their faith, that my gospel which I gave unto them, that they might preach in their days, might come unto their brethren, the Lamanites, and also, all that had become Lamanites, because of their dissensions.

11. Now this is not all, their faith in their prayers was, that this gospel should be made known also, if it were possible that other nations should possess this land; and thus they did leave a blessing upon this land in their prayers, that whosoever should believe in this gospel, in this land, might have eternal life; yea, that it might be free unto all of whatsoever nation, kindred, tongue, or people, they may be.

12. And now, behold, according to their faith in their prayers, will I bring this part of my gospel to the knowledge of my people. Behold, I do not bring it to destroy that which they have received, but to build it up.

13. And for this cause have I said, If this generation harden not their hearts, I will establish my church among them. Now I do not say this to destroy my church, but I say this to build up my church; therefore, whosoever belongeth to my church need not fear, for such shall inherit

permit him to engage in the work of translation immediately. He says:—

"I did not however go immediately to translating, but went to laboring with my hands upon a small farm which I Translation delayed. had purchased of my wife's father, in order to provide for my family. In the month of February, eighteen hundred and twenty-nine, my father came to visit us, at which time I received the following revelation for him."[3]

the kingdom of heaven; but it is they who do not fear me, neither keep my commandments, but build up churches unto themselves, to get gain; yea, and all those that do wickedly, and build up the kingdom of the Devil; yea, verily, verily I say unto you, that it is they that I will disturb, and cause to tremble and shake to the center.

14. Behold, I am Jesus Christ, the Son of God. I came unto my own, and my own received me not. I am the light which shineth in darkness, and the darkness comprehendeth it not. I am he who said, Other sheep have I which are not of this fold, unto my disciples, and many there were that understood me not.

15. And I will show unto this people, that I had other sheep, and that they were a branch of the house of Jacob; and I will bring to light their marvelous works, which they did in my name; yea, and I will also bring to light my gospel, which was ministered unto them, and behold they shall not deny that which you have received, but they shall build it up, and shall bring to light the true points of my doctrine; yea, and the only doctrine which is in me; and this I do, that I may establish my gospel, that there may not be so much contention; yea, Satan doth stir up the hearts of the people to contention, concerning the points of my doctrine; and in these things they do err, for they do wrest the scriptures, and do not understand them; therefore, I will unfold unto them this great mystery; for, behold, I will gather them as a hen gathereth her chickens under her wings, if they will not harden their hearts; yea, if they will come, they may, and partake of the waters of life freely.

16. Behold, this is my doctrine: Whosoever repenteth and cometh unto me, the same is my church; whosoever declareth more or less than this, the same is not of me, but is against me; therefore, he is not of my church.

17. And now, behold, whosoever is of my church, and endureth of my church to the end, him will I establish upon my Rock, and the gates of hell shall not prevail against him.

18. And now, remember the words of him who is the life and the light of the world, your Redeemer, your Lord, and your God. Amen.

[3] 1. Now, behold, a marvelous work is about to come forth among the children of men, therefore, O ye that embark in the service of God, see that ye serve him with all your heart, might, mind, and strength, that ye may stand blameless before God at the last day; therefore, if ye have desires to serve God, ye are called to the work, for, behold, the field is white already to harvest, and lo, he that thrusteth in his sickle with his might, the same layeth up in store that he perish not, but bringeth salvation to his soul; and faith, hope, charity, and love, with an eye single to the glory of God, qualifies him for the work.

2. Remember, faith, virtue, knowledge, temperance, patience, broth-

In March, 1829, at the request of Martin Harris Joseph inquired and received the will of the Lord concerning him. [4]

Joseph Smith's history, published in *Times and Seasons*, volume 3, page 832, states that Oliver Cowdery came to his house Wednesday. April 15, 1829, and on the 17th they resumed the work of translation, Oliver Cowdery acting as scribe for Joseph. (Oliver Cowdery gives the date of his arrival as Sunday, April 5, and

Oliver Cowdery comes to Joseph.

erly kindness, godliness, charity, humility, diligence. Ask and ye shall receive, knock and it shall be opened unto you. Amen.

[4] 1. Behold, I say unto you, that as my servant Martin Harris has desired a witness at my hand, that you, my servant Joseph Smith, Jr., have got the plates of which you have testified and borne record that you have received of me; and now, behold, this shall you say unto him: He who spake unto you said unto you, I, the Lord, am God, and have given these things unto you, my servant Joseph Smith, Jr., and have commanded you that you should stand as a witness of these things, and I have caused you that you should enter into a covenant with me, that you should not show them except to those persons to whom I command you; and you have no power over them except I grant it unto you. And you have a gift to translate the plates, and this is the first gift that I bestowed upon you, and I have commanded that you should pretend to no other gift until my purpose is fulfilled in this; for I will grant unto you no other gift until it is finished.

2. Verily, I say unto you, that woe shall come unto the inhabitants of the earth if they will not hearken unto my words; for hereafter you shall be ordained and go forth and deliver my words unto the children of men. Behold, if they will not believe my words, they would not believe you, my servant Joseph, if it were possible that you could show them all these things which I have committed unto you. O, this unbelieving and stiff-necked generation, mine anger is kindled against them!

3. Behold, verily, I say unto you, I have reserved those things which I have intrusted unto you, my servant Joseph, for a wise purpose in me, and it shall be made known unto future generations; but this generation shall have my word through you; and in addition to your testimony, the testimony of three of my servants, whom I shall call and ordain, unto whom I will show these things; and they shall go forth with my words that are given through you; yea, they shall know of a surety that these things are true; for from heaven will I declare it unto them; I will give them power that they may behold and view these things as they are; and to none else will I grant this power, to receive this same testimony, among this generation, in this, the beginning of the rising up, and the coming forth of my church out of the wilderness; clear as the moon and fair as the sun, and terrible as an army with banners. And the testimony of three witnesses will I send forth of my word; and, behold, whosoever believeth on my words, them will I visit with the manifestation of my Spirit, and they shall be born of me, even of water and of the Spirit. And you must wait yet a little while, for ye are not yet ordained; and their testimony shall also go forth unto the condemnation of this generation, if they harden their hearts against them; for a desolating scourge shall go forth among the inhabitants of the earth, and shall continue to be poured out, from time to time, if they repent not, until the

the date of their beginning their work as Tuesday, the 7th. See *Messenger and Advocate*, vol. 1, p. 14.)

They received a revelation about this time.[5] This seems to be an intimate trust for so short an acquaintance; but each claims to have had spiritual instruction before they met

.

earth is empty, and the inhabitants thereof are consumed away, and utterly destroyed by the brightness of my coming. Behold, I tell you these things even as I also told the people of the destruction of Jerusalem, and my word shall be verified at this time as it hath hitherto been verified.

4. And now I command you, my servant Joseph, to repent and walk more uprightly before me, and yield to the persuasions of men no more; and that you be firm in keeping the commandments wherewith I have commanded you, and if you do this, behold, I grant unto you eternal life, even if you should be slain.

5. And now again I speak unto you, my servant Joseph, concerning the man that desires the witness: Behold, I say unto him, he exalts himself and does not humble himself sufficiently before me; but if he will bow down before me, and humble himself in mighty prayer and faith, in the sincerity of his heart, then will I grant unto him a view of the things which he desires to see. And then he shall say unto the people of this generation, Behold, I have seen the things which the Lord has shown unto Joseph Smith, Jr., and I know of a surety that they are true, for I have seen them; for they have been shown unto me by the power of God and not of man. And I, the Lord, command him, my servant Martin Harris, that he shall say no more unto them concerning these things, except he shall say, I have seen them, and they have been shown unto me by the power of God, and these are the words which he shall say; but if he deny this he will break the covenant which he has before covenanted with me, and behold he is condemned. And now, except he humble himself and acknowledge unto me the things that he has done which are wrong, and covenant with me that he will keep my commandments, and exercise faith in me, behold, I say unto him, he shall have no such views; for I will grant unto him no views of the things of which I have spoken. And if this be the case, I command you, my servant Joseph, that you shall say unto him, that he shall do no more, nor trouble me any more concerning this matter.

6. And if this be the case, behold, I say unto thee, Joseph, When thou hast translated a few more pages thou shalt stop for a season, even until I command thee again; then thou mayest translate again. And except thou do this, behold, thou shalt have no more gift, and I will take away the things which I have intrusted with thee. And now, because I foresee the lying in wait to destroy thee; yea, I foresee that if my servant Martin Harris humbleth not himself, and receive a witness from my hand, that he will fall into transgression; and there are many that lie in wait to destroy thee from off the face of the earth; and for this cause, that thy days may be prolonged, I have given unto thee these commandments; yea, for this cause I have said, Stop and stand still until I command thee, and I will provide means whereby thou mayest accomplish the thing which I have commanded thee; and if thou art faithful in keeping my commandments, thou shalt be lifted up at the last day. Amen.

[5] 1. A great and marvelous work is about to come forth unto the children of men: behold, I am God, and give heed unto my word, which is quick

regarding the work in which they were jointly to engage. Oliver Cowdery boarded at Joseph Smith's father's in Man-

Becomes his scribe.

chester, New York, while teaching school in the neighborhood, and Lucy Smith (Joseph's mother) in her history says of him, that shortly after receiving information concerning the plates "he told Mr. Smith that he was highly delighted with what he had heard, that he had

and powerful, sharper than a two-edged sword, to the dividing asunder of both joints and marrow: therefore, give heed unto my words.

2. Behold, the field is white already to harvest, therefore, whoso desireth to reap, let him thrust in his sickle with his might, and reap while the day lasts, that he may treasure up for his soul everlasting salvation in the kingdom of God: yea, whosoever will thrust in his sickle and reap, the same is called of God; therefore, if you will ask of me you shall receive; if you will knock it shall be opened unto you.

3. Now, as you have asked, behold, I say unto you, Keep my commandments, and seek to bring forth and establish the cause of Zion: seek not for riches but for wisdom; and, behold, the mysteries of God shall be unfolded unto you, and then shall you be made rich. Behold, he that hath eternal life is rich.

4. Verily, verily I say unto you, Even as you desire of me, so shall it be unto you; and if you desire, you shall be the means of doing much good in this generation. Say nothing but repentance unto this generation: keep my commandments, and assist to bring forth my work according to my commandments, and you shall be blessed.

5. Behold, thou hast a gift, and blessed art thou because of thy gift. Remember it is sacred and cometh from above: and if thou wilt inquire, thou shalt know mysteries which are great and marvelous; therefore, thou shalt exercise thy gift, that thou mayest find out mysteries, that thou mayest bring many to the knowledge of the truth; yea, convince them of the error of their ways. Make not thy gift known unto any, save it be those who are of thy faith. Trifle not with sacred things. If thou wilt do good, yea, and hold out faithful to the end, thou shalt be saved in the kingdom of God, which is the greatest of all the gifts of God; for there is no gift greater than the gift of salvation.

6. Verily, verily I say unto thee, Blessed art thou for what thou hast done, for thou hast inquired of me, and, behold, as often as thou hast inquired, thou hast received instruction of my Spirit. If it had not been so, thou wouldst not have come to the place where thou art at this time.

7. Behold, thou knowest that thou hast inquired of me, and I did enlighten thy mind; and now I tell thee these things, that thou mayest know that thou hast been enlightened by the Spirit of truth; yea, I tell thee, that thou mayest know that there is none else save God, that knowest thy thoughts and the intents of thy heart. I tell thee these things as a witness unto thee, that the words or the work which thou hast been writing is true.

8. Therefore be diligent, stand by my servant Joseph faithfully in whatsoever difficult circumstances he may be, for the word's sake. Admonish him in his faults and also receive admonition of him. Be patient; be sober; be temperate: have patience, faith, hope, and charity.

9. Behold, thou art Oliver, and I have spoken unto thee because of thy desires; therefore, treasure up these words in thy heart. Be faithful and diligent in keeping the commandments of God, and I will encircle thee in the arms of my love.

been in a deep study upon the subject all day, and that it was impressed upon his mind, that he should yet have the privilege of writing for Joseph." (See p. 136.)

Further he says: "I have made it a subject of prayer, and I firmly believe it is the will of the Lord that I should go."—Ibid. p. 137.

Of Joseph she says: "Joseph had been so hurried with his secular affairs, that he could not proceed with his spiritual concerns so fast as was necessary for the speedy completion of the work; there was also another disadvan-

10. Behold, I am Jesus Christ, the Son of God. I am the same that came unto my own and my own received me not. I am the light which shineth in darkness, and the darkness comprehendeth it not.

11. Verily, verily I say unto you, If you desire a further witness, cast your mind upon the night that you cried unto me in your heart, that you might know concerning the truth of these things; did I not speak peace to your mind concerning the matter? What greater witness can you have than from God? And now, behold, you have received a witness, for if I have told you things which no man knoweth, have you not received a witness? And, behold, I grant unto you a gift, if you desire of me, to translate even as my servant Joseph.

12. Verily, verily I say unto you, that there are records which contain much of my gospel, which have been kept back because of the wickedness of the people; and now I command you, that if you have good desires, a desire to lay up treasures for yourself in heaven, then shall you assist in bringing to light, with your gift, those parts of my scriptures which have been hidden because of iniquity.

13. And now, behold, I give unto you, and also unto my servant Joseph, the keys of this gift, which shall bring to light this ministry; and in the mouth of two or three witnesses, shall every word be established.

14. Verily, verily I say unto you, If they reject my words, and this part of my gospel and ministry, blessed are ye, for they can do no more unto you than unto me; and if they do unto you, even as they have done unto me, blessed are ye, for you shall dwell with me in glory: but if they reject not my words, which shall be established by the testimony which shall be given, blessed are they; and then shall ye have joy in the fruit of your labors.

15. Verily, verily I say unto you, as I said unto my disciples, Where two or three are gathered together in my name, as touching one thing, behold, there will I be in the midst of them: even so am I in the midst of you. Fear not to do good, my sons, for whatsoever ye sow, that shall ye also reap: therefore, if ye sow good, ye shall also reap good for your reward:

16. Therefore fear not, little flock, do good, let earth and hell combine against you, for if ye are built upon my Rock, they cannot prevail. Behold, I do not condemn you, go your ways and sin no more: perform with soberness the work which I have commanded you; look unto me in every thought, doubt not, fear not: behold the wounds which pierced my side, and also the prints of the nails in my hands and feet; be faithful; keep my commandments, and ye shall inherit the kingdom of heaven. Amen.

tage under which he labored. his wife had so much of her time taken up with the care of her house, that she could write for him but a small portion of the time. On account of these embarrassments, Joseph called upon the Lord, three days prior to the arrival of Samuel and Oliver, to send him a scribe, according to the promise of the angel; and he was informed that the same should be forthcoming in a few days. Accordingly, when Mr. Cowdery told him the business that he had come upon, Joseph was not at all surprised."—Pp. 138, 139.

During the month of April the translation continued with little delay. Of this experience Oliver Cowdery says:—

"These were days never to be forgotten—to sit under the sound of a voice dictated by the inspiration of heaven, Describes his awakened the utmost gratitude of this bosom! experience. Day after day I continued, uninterrupted, to write from his mouth, as he translated, with the Urim and Thummim, or, as the Nephites would have said, 'Interpreters,' the history, or record, called 'The Book of Mormon.'"— *Messenger and Advocate*, vol. 1, p. 14.

From the amount of work accomplished we think it probable that the date of commencement given by Oliver Cowdery; viz., April 7, is correct.

The point as to the day they commenced we do not, however, consider a material one, as the error is probably typographical. We give both simply because there is a discrepancy, and we wish to give the reader the benefit of it, that he may form his own conclusions.

Joseph says:—

"A difference of opinion arising between us about the account of John the Apostle, mentioned in the New Testa-John the ment, John, twenty-first chapter and twenty-Apostle. second verse, whether he died or whether he continued—we mutually agreed to settle it by the Urim and Thummim."

This was the occasion of the receiving of a revelation.[*]

---

[*] 1. And the Lord said unto me, John, my beloved, what desirest thou? For if ye shall ask, what you will, it shall be granted unto you. And I said unto him, Lord, give unto me power over death, that I may live

Two other revelations were also given during April.[7]

The work of translation continued without any other extraordinary event transpiring until Friday, May 15, when the

Aaronic priesthood conferred.

Aaronic priesthood was conferred upon them through the instrumentality of John the Baptist. On this point we allow Joseph Smith and Oliver Cowdery to relate the circumstance.

Joseph Smith says:—

"We still continued the work of translation, when in the ensuing month (May, eighteen hundred and twenty-nine) we on a certain day went into the woods to pray and inquire of the Lord respecting baptism for the remission of sins, as we found mentioned in the translation of the plates. While we were thus employed, praying, and calling upon the Lord, a messenger from heaven descended in a cloud of light, and having laid his hands upon us, he ordained us, saying unto us, 'Upon you, my fellow servants, in the name of Messiah,

and bring souls unto thee. And the Lord said unto me, Verily, verily I say unto thee, because thou desirest this thou shalt tarry until I come in my glory, and shall prophesy before nations, kindreds, tongues, and people.

2. And for this cause the Lord said unto Peter, If I will that he tarry till I come, what is that to thee? For he desiredst of me that he might bring souls unto me; but thou desiredst that thou might speedily come unto me in my kingdom. I say unto thee, Peter, this was a good desire, but my beloved has desired that he might do more, or a greater work yet among men, than what he has before done; yea, he has undertaken a greater work; therefore, I will make him as flaming fire, and a ministering angel; he shall minister for those who shall be heirs of salvation who dwell on the earth; and I will make thee to minister for him and for thy brother James; and unto you three I will give this power and the keys of this ministry until I come.

3. Verily I say unto you, Ye shall both have according to your desires, for ye both joy in that which ye have desired.

[7] 1. Oliver Cowdery, verily, verily I say unto you, that assuredly as the Lord liveth, who is your God and your Redeemer, even so sure shall you receive a knowledge of whatsoever things you shall ask in faith, with an honest heart, believing that you shall receive a knowledge concerning the engravings of the old records, which are ancient, which contain those parts of my scripture of which have been spoken, by the manifestation of my Spirit; yea, behold, I will tell you in your mind and in your heart by the Holy Ghost, which shall come upon you, and which shall dwell in your heart.

2. Now, behold, this is the Spirit of revelation; behold, this is the Spirit by which Moses brought the children of Israel through the Red Sea on dry ground; therefore this is thy gift; apply unto it and blessed art thou, for it shall deliver you out of the hands of your enemies, when, if it were not so, they would slay you, and bring your soul to destruction.

I confer the priesthood of Aaron, which holds the keys of the ministering of angels, and of the gospel of repentance, and of baptism by immersion, for the remission of sins; and this shall never be taken again from the earth, until the sons of Levi do offer again an offering unto the Lord in righteous-

3. O, remember these words, and keep my commandments! Remember this is your gift. Now this is not all thy gift, for you have another gift, which is the gift of Aaron; behold, it has told you many things; behold, there is no other power save the power of God that can cause this gift of Aaron to be with you; therefore doubt not, for it is the gift of God, and you shall hold it in your hands, and do marvelous works; and no power shall be able to take it away out of your hands, for it is the work of God. And, therefore, whatsoever you shall ask me to tell you by that means, that will I grant unto you, and you shall have knowledge concerning it; remember, that without faith you can do nothing. Therefore, ask in faith. Trifle not with these things; do not ask for that which you ought not; ask that you may know the mysteries of God, and that you may translate and receive knowledge from all those ancient records which have been hid up, that are sacred, and according to your faith shall it be done unto you. Behold, it is I that have spoken it; and I am the same who spake unto you from the beginning. Amen.

1. Behold, I say unto you, my son, that because you did not translate according to that which you desired of me, and did commence again to write for my servant Joseph Smith, Jr., even so I would that you should continue until you have finished this record, which I have intrusted unto him; and then, behold, other records have I, that I will give unto you power that you may assist to translate.

2. Be patient, my son, for it is wisdom in me, and it is not expedient that you should translate at this present time. Behold, the work which you are called to do is to write for my servant Joseph; and, behold, it is because that you did not continue as you commenced, when you began to translate, that I have taken away this privilege from you. Do not murmur, my son, for it is wisdom in me that I have dealt with you after this manner.

3. Behold, you have not understood; you have supposed that I would give it unto you, when you took no thought, save it was to ask me; but, behold, I say unto you, that you must study it out in your mind; then you must ask me if it be right, and if it is right, I will cause that your bosom shall burn within you; therefore, you shall feel that it is right; but if it be not right, you shall have no such feelings, but you shall have a stupor of thought, that shall cause you to forget the thing which is wrong; therefore, you cannot write that which is sacred, save it be given you from me.

4. Now, if you had known this, you could have translated; nevertheless, it is not expedient that you should translate now. Behold, it was expedient when you commenced, but you feared, and the time is past, and it is not expedient now; for, do you not behold that I have given unto my servant Joseph sufficient strength, whereby it is made up, and neither of you have I condemned?

5. Do this thing which I have commanded you, and you shall prosper. Be faithful, and yield to no temptation. Stand fast in the work wherewith I have called you, and a hair of your head shall not be lost, and you shall be lifted up at the last day. Amen.

ness.' He said this Aaronic priesthood had not the power of laying on of hands, for the gift of the Holy Ghost, but that this should be conferred on us hereafter; and he commanded us to go and be baptized, and gave us directions that I should baptize Oliver Cowdery, and afterwards that he should baptize me.

"Accordingly we went and were baptized, I baptized him first, and afterwards he baptized me, after which I laid my hands upon his head and ordained him to the A: ronic priesthood, and afterwards he laid his hands on me and ordained me to the same priesthood, for so we were commanded.

"The messenger who visited us on this occasion, and conferred this priesthood upon us, said that his name was John, the same that is called John the Baptist, in the New Testament, and that he acted under the direction of Peter, James, and John, who held the keys of the priesthood of Melchisedec, which priesthood he said should in due time be conferred on us—and that I should be called the first elder, and he the second. It was on the fifteenth day of May, eighteen hundred and twenty-nine, that we were baptized and ordained under the hand of the messenger.

"Immediately upon our coming up out of the water, after we had been baptized, we experienced great and glorious blessings from our heavenly Father. No sooner had I baptized Oliver Cowdery than the Holy Ghost fell upon him and he stood up and prophesied many things which should shortly come to pass. And again, so soon as I had been baptized by him, I also had the spirit of prophecy, when, standing up, I prophesied concerning the rise of the church, and many other things connected with the church, and this generation of the children of men. We were filled with the Holy Ghost, and rejoiced in the God of our salvation.

"Our minds being now enlightened, we began to have the Scriptures laid open to our understandings, and the true meaning of their more mysterious passages revealed unto us, in a manner which we never could attain to previously, nor ever before had thought of. In the meantime we were forced to keep secret the circumstances of our having been baptized, and having received the priesthood, owing to a spirit of persecution which had already manifested itself in the neighborhood. We had been threatened with being mobbed, from time to time, and this too by professors of religion. And their intentions of mobbing us were only counteracted by the influence of my wife's father's family, (under Divine Providence,) who had become very friendly to me, and were opposed to mobs, and were willing that I should be allowed to continue the work of translation without interruption; and therefore offered and promised us protection from all unlawful proceedings as far as in them lay.

"After a few days, however, feeling it to be our duty, we commenced to reason out of the Scriptures, with our acquaintances and friends, as we happened to meet with them. About this time my brother Samuel H. Smith came to visit us. We informed him of what the Lord was about to do for the children of men; and to reason with him out of the Bible. We also showed him that part of the work which we had translated, and labored to persuade him concerning the gospel of Jesus Christ which was now about to be revealed in its fullness. He was not, however, very easily persuaded of these things, but after much inquiry and explanation, he retired to the woods, in order that by secret and fervent prayer he might obtain of a merciful God, wisdom to enable him to judge for himself. The result was that he obtained revelations for himself sufficient to convince him of the truth of our assertions to him, and on the fifteenth day of that same month in which we had been baptized and ordained, Oliver Cowdery baptized him; and he returned to his father's house greatly glorifying and praising God, being filled with the Holy Spirit."—*Times and Seasons*, vol. 3, pp. 865, 866.

Oliver Cowdery says:—

"This was not long desired before it was realized. The Lord, who is rich in mercy, and ever willing to answer the consistent prayer of the humble, after we had called upon him in a fervent manner, aside from the abodes of men, condescended to manifest to us his will. On a sudden, as from the midst of eternity, the voice of the Redeemer spake peace to us, while the vail was parted and the angel of God came down clothed with glory, and delivered the anxiously looked for message, and the keys of the gospel of repentance! What joy! what wonder! what amazement! While the world was racked and distracted—while millions were groping as the blind for the wall, and while all men were resting upon uncertainty, as a general mass, our eyes beheld—our ears heard. As in the 'blaze of day;' yes, more—above the glitter of the May sunbeam, which then shed its brilliancy over the face of nature! Then his voice, though mild, pierced to the center, and his words, 'I am thy fellow-servant,' dispelled every fear. We listened—we gazed—we admired! 'Twas the voice of the angel from glory—'twas a message from the Most High! and as we heard we rejoiced, while his love enkindled upon our souls, and we were rapt in the vision of the Almighty! Where was room for doubt? Nowhere: uncertainty had fled, doubt had sunk, no more to rise, while fiction and deception had fled forever!

"But, dear brother, think, further think for a moment, what joy filled our hearts and with what surprise we must have bowed, (for who would not have bowed the knee for such a blessing?) when we received under his hand the holy priesthood, as he said, 'Upon you my fellow-servants, in the name of Messiah, I confer this priesthood and this authority, which shall remain upon earth, that the sons of Levi may yet offer an offering unto the Lord in righteousness!'

"I shall not attempt to paint to you the feelings of this heart, nor the majestic beauty and glory which surrounded us on this occasion; but you will believe me when I say, that earth, nor men, with the eloquence of time, cannot begin to clothe language in as interesting and sublime a manner as this holy personage. No; nor has this earth power to give the joy, to bestow the peace, or comprehend the wisdom which was contained in each sentence as they were delivered by the power of the Holy Spirit! Man may deceive his fellow-man; deception may follow deception, and the children of the wicked one may have power to seduce the foolish and untaught, till naught but fiction feeds the many, and the fruit of falsehood carries in its current the giddy to the grave; but one touch with the finger of his love, yes, one ray of glory from the upper world, or one word from the mouth of the Savior, from the bosom of eternity, strikes it *all* into insignificance, and blots it forever from the mind! The assurance that we were in the presence of an angel; the certainty that we heard the voice of Jesus, and the truth unsullied as it flowed from a pure personage, dictated by the will of God, is to me, past description, and I shall ever look upon this expression of the Savior's goodness with wonder and thanksgiving while I am permitted to tarry, and in those mansions where perfection dwells and sin never comes, I hope to adore in that day which shall never cease!"—*Messenger and Advocate*, vol. 1, pages 15, 16.

The testimony of Oliver Cowdery, graphic and beautiful as it is, does not go as far with the history of the events as does Joseph Smith's, but it is gratifying to note such complete harmony in these two accounts of this, one of the most important epochs in the history of the latter-day work.

With the accounts of these two men,—the leading actors in the introduction of the work,—we leave this matter, as no words of ours would add to the clearness or importance of the wonderful transactions here presented.

About this time a revelation was given to Hyrum Smith.[s]

---

[s] 1. A great and marvelous work is about to come forth among the children of men. Behold, I am God, and give heed to my word, which is quick and powerful, sharper than a two-edged sword, to the dividing asunder of both joints and marrow; therefore, give heed unto my word.

2. Behold, the field is white already to harvest, therefore, whoso desireth to reap, let him thrust in his sickle with his might, and reap while the day lasts, that he may treasure up for his soul everlasting salvation in the kingdom of God; yea, whosoever will thrust in his sickle and reap, the same is called of God; therefore, if you will ask of me, you shall receive; if you will knock, it shall be opened unto you.

3. Now as you have asked, behold, I say unto you, Keep my commandments, and seek to bring forth and establish the cause of Zion. Seek not for riches, but for wisdom, and, behold, the mysteries of God shall be unfolded unto you, and then shall you be made rich; behold, he that hath eternal life is rich.

4. Verily, verily I say unto you, Even as you desire of me, so shall it be done unto you; and, if you desire you shall be the means of doing much good in this generation. Say nothing but repentance unto this generation. Keep my commandments, and assist to bring forth my work according to my commandments, and you shall be blessed.

5. Behold, thou hast a gift, or thou shalt have a gift if thou wilt desire of me in faith, with an honest heart, believing in the power of Jesus

Christ, or in my power which speaketh unto thee; for, behold, it is I that speaketh; behold, I am the light which shineth in darkness, and by my power I give these words unto thee.

6. And now, verily, verily I say unto thee, Put your trust in that Spirit which leadeth to do good; yea, to do justly, to walk humbly, to judge righteously, and this is my Spirit.

7. Verily, verily I say unto you, I will impart unto you of my Spirit, which shall enlighten your mind, which shall fill your soul with joy, and then shall ye know, or by this shall you know, all things whatsoever you desire of me, which is pertaining unto things of righteousness, in faith believing in me that you shall receive.

8. Behold, I command you, that you need not suppose that you are called to preach until you are called: wait a little longer, until you shall have my word, my rock, my church, and my gospel, that you may know of a surety my doctrine; and then, behold, according to your desires, yea, even according to your faith, shall it be done unto you.

9. Keep my commandments; hold your peace; appeal unto my Spirit; yea, cleave unto me with all your heart, that you may assist in bringing to light those things of which have been spoken; yea, the translation of my work; be patient until you shall accomplish it.

10. Behold, this is your work, to keep my commandments; yea, with all your might, mind, and strength; seek not to declare my word, but first seek to obtain my word, and then shall your tongue be loosed; then, if you desire, you shall have my Spirit, and my word; yea, the power of God unto the convincing of men; but now hold your peace; study my word which hath gone forth among the children of men, and also study my word which shall come forth among the children of men, or that which is now translating; yea, until you have obtained all which I shall grant unto the children of men in this generation; and then shall all things be added thereunto.

11. Behold, thou art Hyrum, my son; seek the kingdom of God, and all things shall be added according to that which is just. Build upon my rock, which is my gospel; deny not the Spirit of revelation, nor the Spirit of prophecy, for woe unto him that denieth these things; therefore, treasure up in your hearts until the time which is in my wisdom that you shall go forth: behold, I speak unto all who have good desires, and have thrust in their sickles to reap.

12. Behold, I am Jesus Christ, the Son of God. I am the life and the light of the world. I am the same who came unto my own, and my own received me not; but verily, verily I say unto you, that as many as receiveth me, them will I give power to become the sons of God, even to them that believe on my name. Amen.

CHAPTER 4.

1829.

ONE thing which peculiarly impresses the mind of the investigator is that in every emergency some one seemed
Emergencies always supplied. ready to meet it, and move the work along. To be sure it was a time when men were largely governed by the impulse of the moment, but what seems peculiar is, that notwithstanding the bitter and vindictive opposition, there was always, in time of need, some one moved to stand in the breach, to succor or protect the work struggling for existence. A case in point is mentioned by Joseph Smith about this time. It is well known that Joseph Smith was a very poor man, and it was often a serious question while his time was occupied with spiritual concerns as to where needed sustenance was to come from. While, assisted by Oliver Cowdery, he was bending every energy to forward the work of translation, he was in a very unexpected way supplied. He says:—

"About the same time came an old gentleman to visit us, of whose name I wish to make honorable mention; Mr. Joseph Knight, Sen., of Colesville, Broome County, New York, who, having heard of the manner in which we were occupying our time, very kindly and considerately brought us a quantity of provisions, in order that we might not be interrupted in the work of translation, by the want of such necessaries of life; and I would just mention here (as in duty bound) that he several times brought us supplies (a distance of at least thirty miles) which enabled us to continue the work which otherwise we must have relinquished for a season.

"Being very anxious to know his duty as to this work, I inquired of the Lord for him."[1]—*Times and Seasons*, vol. 3, p. 884.

Another remarkable instance of the same nature is related by him, as follows:—

"Shortly after commencing to translate, I became acquainted with Mr. Peter Whitmer, of Fayette, Seneca County, New York, and also with some of his family. In the beginning of the month of June his son David Whitmer came to the place where we were residing, and brought with him a two horse wagon, for the purpose of having us accompany him to his father's place and there remain until we should finish the work. He proposed that we should have our board free of charge, and the assistance of one of his brothers to write for me, as also his own assistance when convenient.

"Having much need of such timely aid in an undertaking so arduous, and being informed that the people of the neighborhood were anxiously awaiting the opportunity to inquire into these things, we accepted the invitation, and accompanied Mr. Whitmer to his father's house, and there resided until the translation was

They remove to Fayette, New York.

[1] 1. A great and marvelous work is about to come forth among the children of men. Behold, I am God, and give heed to my word, which is quick and powerful, sharper than a two-edged sword, to the dividing asunder of both joints and marrow; therefore, give heed unto my word.

2. Behold, the field is white already to harvest, therefore, whoso desireth to reap, let him thrust in his sickle with his might, and reap while the day lasts, that he may treasure up for his soul everlasting salvation in the kingdom of God; yea, whosoever will thrust in his sickle and reap, the same is called of God; therefore, if you will ask of me you shall receive, if you will knock it shall be opened unto you.

3. Now, as you have asked, behold, I say unto you, Keep my commandments, and seek to bring forth and establish the cause of Zion.

4. Behold, I speak unto you, and also to all those who have desires to bring forth and establish this work; and no one can assist in this work, except he shall be humble and full of love, having faith, hope, and charity, being temperate in all things whatsoever shall be intrusted to his care.

5. Behold, I am the light and the life of the world, that speaketh these words; therefore, give heed with your might, and then you are called. Amen.

finished, and the copyright secured. Upon our arrival, we found Mr. Whitmer's family very anxious concerning the work, and very friendly towards ourselves. They continued so, boarded and lodged us according to proposal, and John Whitmer, in particular, assisted us very much in writing during the remainder of the work.

"In the meantime, David, John, and Peter Whitmer, Jr., became our zealous friends and assistants in the work," etc. — *Times and Seasons*, vol. 3, pp. 884, 885.

During this time several revelations were given.[2]

[2] 1. A great and marvelous work is about to come forth unto the children of men. Behold, I am God, and give heed to my word, which is quick and powerful, sharper than a two-edged sword, to the dividing asunder of both joints and marrow; therefore, give heed unto my word.

2. Behold, the field is white already to harvest, therefore, whoso desireth to reap, let him thrust in his sickle with his might, and reap while the day lasts, that he may treasure up for his soul everlasting salvation in the kingdom of God; yea, whosoever will thrust in his sickle and reap, the same is called of God; therefore, if you will ask of me you shall receive, if you will knock it shall be opened unto you.

3. Seek to bring forth and establish my Zion. Keep my commandments in all things; and if you keep my commandments and endure to the end, you shall have eternal life; which gift is the greatest of all the gifts of God.

4. And it shall come to pass, that if you shall ask the Father in my name, in faith believing, you shall receive the Holy Ghost, which giveth utterance, that you may stand as a witness of the things of which you shall both hear and see; and also, that you may declare repentance unto this generation.

5. Behold, I am Jesus Christ the Son of the living God, who created the heavens and the earth; a light which cannot be hid in darkness; wherefore, I must bring forth the fullness of my gospel from the Gentiles unto the house of Israel. And, behold, thou art David, and thou art called to assist; which thing if ye do, and are faithful, ye shall be blessed both spiritually and temporally, and great shall be your reward. Amen.

1. Hearken, my servant John, and listen to the words of Jesus Christ, your Lord and your Redeemer, for, behold, I speak unto you with sharpness and with power, for mine arm is over all the earth, and I will tell you that which no man knoweth save me and thee alone; for many times you have desired of me to know that which would be of the most worth unto you.

2. Behold, blessed are you for this thing, and for speaking my words which I have given you, according to my commandments.

3. And now, behold, I say unto you, that the thing which will be of the most worth unto you, will be to declare repentance unto this people, that you may bring souls unto me, that you may rest with them in the kingdom of my Father. Amen.

1. Hearken, my servant Peter, and listen to the words of Jesus Christ, your Lord and your Redeemer, for, behold, I speak unto you with sharpness and with power, for mine arm is over all the earth, and I will tell you that which no man knoweth save me and thee alone; for many times

While at Mr. Whitmer's, engaged in translation, occurred another of the most wonderful and confirming events connected with the introduction of the Book of Mormon and the establishment of the work. Joseph was no longer to be the sole witness of the existence of the plates and the correctness of their translation. How joyful must have been his feelings as he realized that the burden which before he had borne alone was now to be shared by others. No wonder that he exclaimed when the wonderful vision had been concluded, "Father, Mother, you do not know how happy I am; the Lord has now caused the plates to be shown to three more besides myself. They have seen an angel, who has testified to them, and they will have to bear witness to the truth of what I have said, for now they know for themselves that I do not go about to deceive the people, and I feel as if I was relieved of a burden which was almost too heavy for me to bear, and it rejoices my soul that I am not any longer to be entirely alone in the world." —Lucy Smith's History, p. 147.

Three witnesses view the plates.

The relation of these remarkable events we here present in the words of Joseph Smith:—

"We found the people of Seneca County in general friendly and disposed to inquire into the truth of these strange matters which now began to be noised abroad: many opened their houses to us in order that we might have an opportunity of meeting with our friends for the purposes of instruction and explanation. We met with many from time to time, who were willing to hear us, and wishful to find out the truth as it is in Christ Jesus, and apparently willing to obey the gospel when once fairly convinced and satisfied in their own minds; and in this same month of June, my brother Hyrum Smith, David Whitmer, and Peter Whitmer, Jr., were bap-

---

you have desired of me to know that which would be of the most worth unto you.

2. Behold, blessed are you for this thing, and for speaking my words, which I have given unto you, according to my commandments.

3. And now, behold, I say unto you, that the thing which will be of the most worth unto you, will be to declare repentance unto this people, that you may bring souls unto me, that you may rest with them in the kingdom of my Father. Amen.

tized in Seneca Lake, the two former by myself, the latter by Oliver Cowdery. From this time forth many became believers, and were baptized, whilst we continued to instruct and persuade as many as applied for information.

"In the course of the work of translation we ascertained that three special witnesses were to be provided by the Lord, to whom he would grant that they should see the plates from which this work (the Book of Mormon) should be translated, and that these witnesses should bear record of the same; as will be found recorded. . . .

"Almost immediately after we had made this discovery, it occurred to Oliver Cowdery, David Whitmer, and the aforementioned Martin Harris (who had come to inquire after our progress in the work) that they would have me inquire of the Lord, to know if they might not obtain of him to be these three special witnesses; and finally they became so very solicitous, and teased me so much, that at length I complied, and through the Urim and Thummim, I obtained of the Lord for them the following revelation[3]:—

"Not many days after the above commandment was given, we four; viz.: Martin Harris, David Whitmer, Oliver Cowdery, and myself, agreed to retire into the woods, and try to

[3] 1. Behold, I say unto you, that you must rely upon my word, which if you do, with full purpose of heart, you shall have a view of the plates, and also of the breastplate, the sword of Laban, the Urim and Thummim, which were given to the brother of Jared upon the mount, when he talked with the Lord face to face, and the miraculous directors which were given to Lehi while in the wilderness, on the borders of the Red Sea; and it is by your faith that you shall obtain a view of them, even by that faith which was had by the prophets of old.

2. And after that you have obtained faith, and have seen them with your eyes, you shall testify of them, by the power of God; and this you shall do that my servant Joseph Smith, Jr., may not be destroyed, that I may bring about my righteous purposes unto the children of men, in this work. And ye shall testify that you have seen them, even as my servant Joseph Smith, Jr., has seen them, for it is by my power that he has seen them, and it is because he had faith; and he has translated the book, even that part which I have commanded him, and as your Lord and your God liveth, it is true.

3. Wherefore you have received the same power, and the same faith, and the same gift like unto him; and if you do these last commandments of mine, which I have given you, the gates of hell shall not prevail against you; for my grace is sufficient for you; and you shall be lifted up at the last day. And I, Jesus Christ, your Lord and your God, have spoken it unto you, that I might bring about my righteous purposes unto the children of men. Amen.

obtain, by fervent and humble prayer, the fulfillment of the
promises given in the revelation; that they should have a
view of the plates, etc. We accordingly made choice of a
piece of woods convenient to Mr. Whitmer's house, to which
we retired, and having knelt down we began to pray in much
faith, to Almighty God, to bestow upon us a realization of
these promises. According to previous arrangements I commenced, by vocal prayer to our heavenly Father, and was
followed by each of the rest in succession. We did not yet,
however, obtain any answer, or manifestation of the divine
favor in our behalf. We again observed the same order of
prayer, each calling on and praying fervently to God in rota-
tion; but with the same result as before. Upon this our second
failure, Martin Harris proposed that he would withdraw
himself from us, believing as he expressed himself that his
presence was the cause of our not obtaining what we wished
for. He accordingly withdrew from us, and we knelt down
again, and had not been many minutes engaged in prayer,
when presently we beheld a light above us in the air of exceeding brightness, and behold, an angel stood before us. In
his hands he held the plates which we had been praying for
these to have a view of. He turned over the leaves one by
one, so that we could see them, and discover the engravings
thereon distinctly. He addressed himself to David Whitmer,
and said: 'David, blessed is the Lord, and he that keeps
his commandments.' When immediately afterwards, we
heard a voice from out of the bright light above us, saying,
'These plates have been revealed by the power of God, and
they have been translated by the power of God; the translation of them which you have seen is correct, and I command
you to bear record of what you now see and hear.'

"I now left David and Oliver, and went in pursuit of Martin Harris, whom I found at a considerable distance, fervently
engaged in prayer. He soon told me, however, that he had
not yet prevailed with the Lord, and earnestly requested me
to join him in prayer, that he also might realize the same
blessings which we had just received. We accordingly
joined in prayer, and ultimately obtained our desires, for
before we had yet finished, the same vision was opened to

our view; at least it was again to me, and I once more beheld, and heard the same things; whilst at the same moment Martin Harris cried out, apparently in ecstacy of joy, "'Tis enough; mine eyes have beheld,' and jumping up he shouted, Hosanah, blessing God, and otherwise rejoiced exceedingly.

"Having thus, through the mercy of God, obtained these manifestations, it now remained for these three individuals to fulfill the commandment which they had received; viz.: to bear record of these things, in order to accomplish which, they drew up and subscribed the following document:—

" 'THE TESTIMONY OF THREE WITNESSES.

" 'Be it known unto all nations, kindreds, tongues, and people, unto whom this work shall come, that we, through the grace of God the Father, and our Lord Jesus Christ, have seen the plates which contain this record, which is a record of the people of Nephi, and also of the Lamanites, their brethren, and also of the people of Jared, who came from the tower of which hath been spoken; and we also know that they have been translated by the gift and power of God, for his voice hath declared it unto us: wherefore we know of a surety, that the work is true. And we also testify that we have seen the engravings which are upon the plates; and they have been shown unto us by the power of God, and not of man. And we declare with words of soberness, that an angel of God came down from heaven, and he brought and laid before our eyes, that we beheld and saw the plates, and the engravings thereon; and we know that it is by the grace of God the Father, and our Lord Jesus Christ, that we beheld and bear record that these things are true; and it is marvelous in our eyes, nevertheless, the voice of the Lord commanded us that we should bear record of it; wherefore, to be obedient unto the commandments of God, we bear testimony of these things. And we know that if we are faithful in Christ we shall rid our garments of the blood of all men, and be found spotless before the judgment seat of Christ, and shall dwell with him eternally in the heavens. And the honor be to the Father, and to the Son, and to the Holy Ghost, which is one God. Amen.

"'OLIVER COWDERY.
"'DAVID WHITMER.
"'MARTIN HARRIS.'

"Soon after these things had transpired, the following additional testimony was obtained:—

"'AND ALSO THE TESTIMONY OF EIGHT WITNESSES.

"'Be it known unto all nations, kindreds, tongues, and people, unto whom this work shall come, that Joseph Smith, Jr., the translator of this work, has shown unto us the plates of which hath been spoken, which have the appearance of gold; and as many of the leaves as the said Smith has translated, we did handle with our hands: and we also saw the engravings thereon, all of which has the appearance of ancient work, and of curious workmanship. And this we bear record with words of soberness, that the said Smith has shown unto us, for we have seen and hefted, and know of a surety, that the said Smith has got the plates of which we have spoken. And we give our names unto the world to witness unto the world that which we have seen; and we lie not, God bearing witness of it.

Eight other witnesses.

"'CHRISTIAN WHITMER.
"'JACOB WHITMER.
"'PETER WHITMER, JR.
"'JOHN WHITMER. ·
"'HIRAM PAGE.
"'JOSEPH SMITH, SEN.
"'HYRUM SMITH.
"'SAMUEL H. SMITH.'"

—*Times and Seasons*, vol. 3, pp. 897-899.

The testimony of these witnesses is plain, and of a nature to preclude the possibility of their having been deceived. They could not have been mistaken, hence their testimony is true, or they are liars. What inducement could have been offered them to lie? The cause was unpopular; yes, bitterly and violently persecuted. They had every reason to believe that contumely, persecution, and ostracism would be their portion if they thus publicly espoused this cause. Joseph Smith had neither wealth, emolument, nor positions of honor to offer them.

By some careless writers it has been stated that some of them denied or renounced their testimony in after years, but

Witnesses have not renounced their testimony. no authenticated denial or renouncement exists to our knowledge; at least none has been produced, though often publicly demanded. We suppose that this report has obtained through a misunderstanding of their attitude.

It is true that some of them became disaffected during the troublesome times in Missouri, and that differences arose between them and Joseph Smith; but these differences did not occur on account of the Book of Mormon or the testimonies before published. Their contention arose from other causes, real or supposed, and did not in any sense affect their attitude towards the book.

It is not our province to discuss these differences, or to say which was right, if either. There may have been unwise actions and unwise sayings on both sides; but the fact of their estrangement only makes their former testimony stronger when we reflect that neither party during their differences and contention accused the other of fraud in these testimonies. There were no exposures, no confessions, but all went to their graves unwaveringly maintaining the truth of their testimony. Some strong and perhaps harsh statements were made during this controversy, but this only argues that they were not afraid of retaliation by way of exposure of previous frauds.

Some of these witnesses have left on record no further testimony than that found in the document to which they subscribed in 1829.

The three witnesses, whose testimony is most important,
The three witnesses reaffirm. have reaffirmed it, however; so also has John Whitmer, the last surviving one of the eight.

To each of the writers of this history David Whitmer said, in the presence of witnesses and at his home in Richmond,
Oliver Cowdery. Missouri, that he attended Oliver Cowdery, who died at Richmond, Missouri, Sunday, March 3, 1850, on his deathbed, and that during his last sickness Oliver admonished him to be faithful to his testimony for it was true. "It is recorded in the American Cyclopedia and

the Encyclopedia Britannica, that I, David Whitmer, have denied my testimony as one of the three witnesses to the divinity of the Book of Mormon; and that the other two witnesses, Oliver Cowdery and Martin Harris, denied their testimony to that book. I will say once more to all mankind, that I have never at any time denied that testimony or any part thereof. I also testify to the world, that neither Oliver Cowdery or Martin Harris ever at any time denied their testimony. They both died reaffirming the truth of the divine authenticity of the Book of Mormon. I was present at the deathbed of Oliver Cowdery, and his last words were, 'Brother David, be true to your testimony to the Book of Mormon.' He died here in Richmond, Missouri, on March 3, 1850. Many witnesses yet live in Richmond, who will testify to the truth of these facts, as well as to the good character of Oliver Cowdery."— David Whitmer's "Address," p. 8.

George Reynolds in his "Myth of the Manuscript Found,"[4] pages 79 and 80, relates the testimony of Cowdery in 1848 in harmony with the foregoing. He quotes from the *Deseret News*.

Martin Harris, who died at Clarkston, Cache County, Utah, Saturday, July 10, 1875, wrote from Smithfield, Utah, to Mrs. H. B. Emerson, of New Richmond, Ohio, in Martin Harris November, 1870, and in January, 1871, and bears a renewed testimony.[5]

---

[4] At a special conference at Council Bluffs, Iowa, held on the 21st of October, in the year 1848, Bro. Oliver Cowdery, one of the three important witnesses to the truth of the Book of Mormon, and who had been absent from the church, through disaffection, for a number of years, and had been engaged in the practice of law, was present and made the remarks here annexed. . . .

"Friends and brethren, my name is Cowdery—Oliver Cowdery. In the early history of this church I stood identified with her, and one in her councils. True it is that the gifts and callings of God are without repentance. Not because I was better than the rest of mankind was I called; but, to fulfill the purposes of God, he called me to a high and holy calling. I wrote, with my own pen, the entire Book of Mormon (save a few pages), as it fell from the lips of the Prophet Joseph Smith, as he translated it by the gift and power of God, by the means of the Urim and Thummim, or, as it is called by that book, 'holy interpreters.' *I beheld with my eyes and handled with my hands the gold plates from which it was translated.* I also saw with my eyes and handled with my hands the 'holy interpreters.' That book is *true*. Sidney Rigdon did not write it. Mr. Spalding did not write it. I wrote it myself as it fell from the lips of the Prophet."

[5] SMITHFIELD, Utah, Nov. 23, 1870.

Mr. Emerson; Sir:—I received your favor. In reply I will say con-

We here insert a letter of D. B. Dille as published in the "Myth of the Manuscript Found," pages 88, 89, which takes it from the *Millennial Star:*—

"SEPTEMBER 15, 1853.

"Be it known to all whom this may concern that I, David B. Dille, of Ogden City, Weber County, Salt Lake, enroute to Great Britain, having business with one Martin Harris, formerly of the Church of Latter Day Saints, and residing at Kirtland, Lake County, Ohio, did personally wait upon him at his residence, and found him sick in bed; and was informed by the said Martin Harris that he had not been able to take any nourishment for the space of three days. This, together with his advanced age, had completely prostrated him. After making my business known to Mr. Harris, and some little conversation with him, the said Martin Harris started up in bed, and, after particularly inquiring concerning the prosperity of the church, made the following declaration:—

"'I feel that a spirit has come across me—the old spirit of Mormonism; and I begin to feel as I used to feel; and I will not say—"I won't go to the valley." Then addressing himself to his wife, he said—'I don't know but that, if you will get me some breakfast, I will get up and eat it.' . . .

"I afterwards put the following questions to Mr. Harris, to which he severally replied with the greatest cheerfulness: 'What do you think of the Book of Mormon? Is it a divine record?'

cerning the plates: I do say that the angel did show to me the plates containing the Book of Mormon. Further, the translation that I carried to Prof. Anthon was copied from these same plates; also, that the Professor did testify to it being a correct translation. . . .

SMITHFIELD, Cache Co., U. T., January, 1871.

To H. Emerson; Dear Sir:—Your second letter, dated December, 1870, came duly to hand. I am truly glad to see a spirit of inquiry manifested therein. I reply by a borrowed hand, as my sight has failed me too much to write myself. Your questions: Question 1, "Did you go to England to lecture against 'Mormonism'?"

Answer. I answer emphatically, No, I did not;—no man ever heard me in any way deny the truth of the Book of Mormon, the administration of the angel that showed me the plates; nor the organization of the Church of Jesus Christ of Latter Day Saints, under the administration of Joseph Smith, Jr., the prophet whom the Lord raised up for that purpose, in these the latter days, that he may show forth his power and glory. . . .—*Saints' Herald*, vol. 22, p. 630.

"Mr. Harris replied: 'I was the right hand man of Joseph Smith, and I know that he was a prophet of God. I know the Book of Mormon is true—*and you know that I know that it is true.* I know that the plates have been translated by the gift and power of God, for his voice declared it unto us; therefore I know of a surety that the work is true; *for did I not at one time hold the plates on my knee an hour and a half,* while in conversation with Joseph, when we went to bury them in the woods, that the enemy might not obtain them? Yes, I did. *And as many of the plates as Joseph Smith translated, I handled with my hands, plate after plate.*' Then, describing their dimensions, he pointed with one of the fingers of his left hand to the back of his right hand and said: 'I should think they were so long,' or about eight inches, 'and about so thick,' or about four inches; 'and each of the plates was thicker than the thickest tin.'

"I then asked Mr. Harris if he ever lost three thousand dollars by the publishing of the Book of Mormon?

"Mr. Harris said, 'I never lost one cent. Mr. Smith paid me all that I advanced, and more too.' As much as to say he received a portion of the profits accruing from the sale of the books.

"Mr. Harris further said: 'I took a transcript of the characters of the plates to Dr. Anthon, of New York. When I arrived at the house of Professor Anthon, I found him in his office and alone, and presented the transcript to him, and asked him to read it. He said if I would bring the plates, he would assist in the translation. I told him I could not, for they were sealed. Professor Anthon then gave me a certificate certifying that the characters were Arabic, Chaldaic, and Egyptian. I then left Dr. Anthon, and was near the door, when he said, 'How did the young man know the plates were there?' I said an angel had shown them to him. Professor Anthon then said, 'Let me see the certificate!' Upon which, I took it from my waistcoat pocket and unsuspectingly gave it to him. He then tore it up in anger, saying there was no such things as angels now, it was all a hoax. I then went to Dr. Mitchill with the transcript, and he confirmed what Professor Anthon had said.'

"Mr. Harris is about fifty-eight years old, and is on a valuable farm of ninety acres, beautifully situated at Kirtland, Lake County, Ohio."—*Millennial Star.*

We also insert a statement made by Simon Smith concerning his visit to the deathbed of Martin Harris:—

"We had the opportunity, this morning, to interview Elder Simon Smith, of Cameron, Missouri, (the gentleman referred to yesterday who visited Martin Harris before his death,) and asked the following questions, which were answered without hesitancy:—

" 'Did you know Martin Harris, one of the three witnesses of the Book of Mormon?' 'Yes, sir.'

" 'When did you first make his acquaintance?' 'I am not certain, but I think in 1873.'

" 'Were you intimately acquainted with him?' 'Yes.'

" 'How long were you acquainted with him?' 'About two years.'

" 'What are your convictions of his character as regards veracity?' 'He was a truthful and reliable man so far as my acquaintance with him is concerned.'

" 'What was his reputation in this regard?' 'Good. He was considered reliable by all who were acquainted with him.'

" 'Did you ever hear him refer to his testimony in connection with the Book of Mormon?' 'Yes, sir.'

" 'Did he deny it?' 'No, sir.'

" 'Were you present when he died?' 'I was not present at the last moment, but was with him while he was on his death-bed, and his son told me that the last words he spoke which were understood by them were in testimony of the angel and the Book of Mormon.'

" 'How long before his death did you see him last?' 'About four days.'

" 'At the time you saw him last did he say anything in regard to his testimony?' 'Yes; he certified to me that his testimony in connection with the Book of Mormon was true, and added, "I tell you these things that you may tell others. I cannot and dare not deny it lest the power of God should consume me."' "

" 'Did he seem to be sensible of his approaching death?'
'Yes; as I entered the room he held out his hand to me and
said, "Bishop, I am going to leave you now."'

" 'Did he appear to be in proper possession of his faculties,
or was his mind wandering?' 'He had full control of his
faculties.'

" 'It has been reported that a body of ministers visited his
deathbed, and to them he denied his testimony. Do you
know anything of this?' 'I was the only minister who visited
him. In fact, there were no ministers of other denominations in the town.'

" 'How far did you live from where he died?' 'About two
blocks.'

" 'Were you intimate with the family after his death?'
'Yes, sir.'

" 'Did you ever hear them speak of such a visit?' 'No,
sir, not them or anyone else. The first I heard of it was
here in Stewartsville, yesterday.'

" 'Where did he die?' 'At Clarkston, Cache County, Utah.'

" 'Did he indorse polygamy?' 'No, sir, I asked him the
question and he answered, No. I asked him if Joseph Smith
taught it, and he answered, No, nor was it a doctrine of the
church in his life. It is Brigham Young's doctrine.'"—St.
Joseph, Missouri, *Herald*, April 16, 1884.

David Whitmer, the last surviving one of the three, who
died at his home, Richmond, Missouri, Wednesday, January
25, 1888, reaffirmed his testimony many times
during the last years of his life. We select a few
of his reaffirmations. On the top of the humble marble that
marks his resting place in Richmond cemetery may be seen
to-day the chiseled figure of the Bible, upon which lies one
of the Book of Mormon, while underneath are inscribed
some of his last words as follows:—

"The Record of the Jews, and the Record of the Nephites
are one. Truth is Eternal."

We visited the tomb and copied the inscription on Wednesday, June 24, 1896.

James Caffall, of Council Bluffs, Iowa, visited him in
August, 1874. He says:—

"Before I bade him good-bye, I said to him, 'Can I, Father Whitmer, say, I this day have seen a living witness to the Book of Mormon?' whereupon he raised his eyes heavenward, and said: 'AS MY TESTIMONY STANDS, SO IT IS; I HAVE NOT, NOR WILL I DENY IT.'"—*Saints' Herald*, vol. 21, p. 564.

We received a letter from him in 1876 which is quite positive and to the point.[5]

John Whitmer, one of the eight witnesses, when leaving the editorial chair of the *Messenger and Advocate*, in 1836, in an address published in March issue of that year, said:—

John Whitmer.

"It may not be amiss in this place to give a statement to the world concerning the work of the Lord, as I have been a member of this church of Latter Day Saints from its begin-

---

[5] RICHMOND, Ray Co., Mo., December 5, 1876.

Heman C. Smith; Dear Sir:—As concerning the Book of Mormon, and its contents, and my views, for which you inquire: I can say the book and its contents are true, and my testimony in connection with the book is also true.

In his "Address to All Believers in Christ," pages 8, 9, 10, he makes this statement:—

"A PROCLAMATION.

"Unto all nations, kindred, tongues, and people, unto whom these presents shall come:—

"It having been represented by one John Murphy, of Polo, Caldwell County, Missouri, that I, in a conversation with him last summer, denied my testimony as one of the three witnesses to the 'Book of Mormon.'

"To the end, therefore, that he may understand me now, if he did not then; and that the world may know the truth, I wish now, standing as it were, in the very sunset of life, and in the fear of God, once for all to make this public statement:—

"That I have never at any time denied that testimony or any part thereof, which has so long since been published with that book, as one of the three witnesses. Those who know me best, well know that I have always adhered to that testimony. And that no man may be misled or doubt my present views in regard to the same, I do again affirm the truth of all of my statements, as then made and published.

"'He that hath an ear to hear, let him hear;' it was no delusion! What is written is written, and he that readeth let him understand.

"And that no one may be deceived or misled by this statement, I wish here to state: that I do not indorse polygamy or spiritual wifeism. It is a great evil, shocking to the moral sense, and the more so, because practiced in the name of religion. It is of man and not of God, and is especially forbidden in the Book of Mormon itself.

"I do not indorse the change of the name of the church, for as the wife takes the name of her husband so should the Church of the Lamb of God take the name of its head, even Christ himself. It is the Church of Christ.

ning. To say that the Book of Mormon is a revelation from God, I have no hesitancy; but with all confidence have signed my name to it as such; and I hope that my patrons will indulge me in speaking freely on this subject, as I am about

"As to the high priesthood, Jesus Christ himself is the last Great High Priest, this too after the order of Melchisedec, as I understand the Holy Scriptures.

"Finally, I do not indorse any of the teachings of the so-called Mormons, of Latter Day Saints, which are in conflict with the gospel of our Lord and Savior Jesus Christ, as taught in the Bible and Book of Mormon; for the same gospel is plainly taught in both of these books as I understand the word of God.

"And if any man doubt should he not carefully and honestly read and understand the same, before presuming to sit in judgment and condemning the light, which shineth in darkness, and showeth the way of eternal life as pointed out by the unerring hand of God.

"In the spirit of Christ who hath said: 'Follow thou me, for I am the life, the light, and the way,' I submit this statement to the world. God in whom I trust being my judge as to the sincerity of my motives and the faith and hope that is in me of eternal life.

"My sincere desire is that the world may be benefited by this plain and simple statement of the truth.

"And all the honor be to the Father, the Son, and the Holy Ghost, which is one God. Amen.   DAVID WHITMER.

"RICHMOND, Missouri, March 19, 1881.

"We, the undersigned citizens of Richmond, Ray County, Missouri, where David Whitmer has resided since the year A. D. 1838, certify that we have been long and intimately acquainted with him and know him to be a man of the highest integrity, and of undoubted truth and veracity.

"Given at Richmond, Missouri, this March 19, A. D. 1881.

"Gen. Alexander W. Doniphan.
"Hon. George W. Dunn, Judge of the Fifth Judicial Circuit.
"Thos. D. Woodson, President of Ray County Savings Bank.
"J. T. Child, Editor of *Conservator*.
"H. C. Garner, Cashier of Ray County Savings Bank.
"L. C. Cantwell, Postmaster, Richmond.
"George I. Wasson, Mayor.
"James A. Davis, County Collector.
"C. J. Hughes, Probate Judge and Presiding Justice of Ray County Court.
"George W. Trigg, County Clerk.
"W. W. Mosby, M. D.
"W. A. Holman, County Treasurer.
"J. S. Hughes, Banker, Richmond.
"James Hughes, Banker, Richmond.
"D. P. Whitmer, Attorney at Law.
"Hon. James W. Black, Attorney at Law.
"Thomas McGinnis, Ex-Sheriff Ray County.
"J. P. Quesenberry, Merchant.
"W. R. Holman, Furniture Merchant.
"Lewis Slaughter, Recorder of Deeds.
"George W. Buchanan, M. D.
"A. K. Reyburn.

"From the Richmond (Missouri), *Conservator*, March 24, 1881:—

"AN EXPLANATION.

"Elsewhere we publish a letter from David Whitmer, an old and well-know citizen of Ray, as well as an indorsement of his standing as a man, signed by a number of the leading citizens of this community, in reply to some unwarranted aspersions made upon him.

leaving the editorial department. Therefore I desire to testify to all that will come to the knowledge of this address that I have most assuredly seen the plates from whence the Book of Mormon is translated, and that I have handled these plates, and know of a surety that Joseph Smith, Jr., has translated the Book of Mormon by the gift and power of God, and in this thing the wisdom of the wise most assuredly has perished: therefore, know ye, O ye inhabitants of the earth, wherever this address may come, that I have in this thing freed my garments of your blood, whether you believe or disbelieve the statements of your unworthy friend and well-wisher."—*Messenger and Advocate*, vol. 2, pp. 286, 287.

To us he wrote in 1876, in harmony with the foregoing.*

The testimonies, given at various times by the very men who report says denied their testimony, lead us to believe that said reports are not true, hence have no rightful place in history, especially so when we consider that no statement from them confirming the rumor has ever been authenticated.

"There is no doubt that Mr. Whitmer, who was one of the three witnesses of the authenticity of the gold plates, from which he asserts that Joseph Smith translated the Book of Mormon (a facsimile of the characters he now has in his possession with the original records), is firmly convinced of its divine origin, and while he makes no effort to obtrude his views or beliefs, he simply wants the world to know that so far as he is concerned there is no 'variableness or shadow of turning.' Having resided here for near a half of a century, it is with no little pride that he points to his past record with the consciousness that he has done nothing derogatory to his character as a citizen and a believer in the Son of Mary, to warrant such an attack on him, come from what source it may, and now with the lilies of seventy-five winters crowning him like an aureole, and his pilgrimage on earth well-nigh ended, he reiterates his former statements, and will leave futurity to solve the problem that he was but a passing witness to its fulfillment. His attacks on the vileness that has sprung up with the Utah Church, must have a salutary effect upon those bigamists who have made adultery the corner-stone in the edifice of their belief."

* FAR WEST, Caldwell Co., Mo., December 11, 1876.

H. C. Smith; Dear Sir:—Your letter came to hand—your request considered. First, as for giving all particulars that I know of the Book of Mormon, cannot be written on one sheet of paper; therefore permit me to be brief. From what you have written I conclude you have read the Book of Mormon, together with the testimonies that are thereto attached, in which testimonies you read my name subscribed as one of the eight witnesses to said book. *That testimony was, is, and will be true, henceforth and forever.* Respectfully yours,

JOHN WHITMER.

Their testimony then stands unretracted and unimpeached. The reader can examine it, together with the circumstances under which it was given, and form his own conclusion as he expects to answer for that conclusion at the bar of God.

Their testimony unretracted and unimpeached.

CHAPTER 5.

1829.

AFTER the thrilling events related in the last chapter
occurred another of the most important events of this dispensation; viz., a provision for receiving the office
of elder in the higher or Melchisedec priesthood;

Provision for conferring the office of elder.

which priesthood, according to a subsequent revelation, holds "the keys of all the spiritual blessings of the church; to have the privilege of receiving the
mysteries of the kingdom of heaven; to have the heavens
opened unto them; to commune with the general assembly
and church of the firstborn; and to enjoy the communion and
presence of God the Father, and Jesus the Mediator of the
new covenant."—Doctrine and Covenants 104: 9.

What transports of peace, what exultant praise, what overwhelming joy must have filled their souls, if they realized
the import of all the promises enumerated here! But probably they did not; but few men, if any, ever do. It furnishes
food for a lifetime of careful thought. It gives occasion for
a lifetime of the most triumphant joy that the mind of
humanity can experience. It causes man to feel that heaven
is nearer, and earth more blessed. It gives him a higher
regard for honor and purity; and yet it admonishes him to
be virtuous and humble, lest he be unworthy of such exalted
and desirable privileges.

Let us again hear Joseph while he relates this remarkable
event:—

"Meantime we continued to translate, at intervals, when not necessitated to attend to the numerous inquirers, that now began to visit us; some for the sake of finding the truth, others for the purpose of putting hard questions, and trying to confound us. Among the latter class were several learned priests who generally came for the purpose of disputation: however the Lord continued to pour out upon us his Holy Spirit, and as often as we had need, he gave us in that moment what to say; so that although unlearned, and inexperienced in religious controversies, yet were we able to confound those learned Rabbis of the day, whilst at the same time, we were enabled to convince the honest in heart, that we had obtained (through the mercy of God) to the true and everlasting gospel of Jesus Christ, so that almost daily we administered the ordinance of baptism for the remission of sins, to such as believed. We now became anxious to have that promise realized to us, which the angel that conferred upon us the Aaronic priesthood had given us; viz., that provided we continued faithful we should also have the Melchisedec priesthood, which holds the authority of the laying on of hands for the gift of the Holy Ghost. We had for some time made this matter a subject of humble prayer, and at length we got together in the chamber of Mr. Whitmer's house in order more particularly to seek of the Lord what we now so earnestly desired: and here to our unspeakable satisfaction did we realize the truth of the Savior's promise; 'Ask, and you shall receive, seek, and you shall find, knock, and it shall be opened unto you;' for we had not long been engaged in solemn and fervent prayer when the word of the Lord came unto us in the chamber, commanding us that I should ordain Oliver Cowdery to be an elder in the Church of Jesus Christ, and that he also should ordain me to the same office, and then to ordain others as it should be made known unto us, from time to time: we were, however, commanded to defer this our ordination until such times as it should be practicable to have our brethren, who had been and who should be baptized, assembled together, when we must have their sanction to our thus proceeding to ordain each other, and have them decide by vote whether they were willing to accept us as spiritual teachers, or not, when also we were commanded to bless bread and break it with them, and to take wine, bless it, and drink it with them, afterward proceed to ordain each other according to commandment, then call out such men as the Spirit should dictate, and ordain them, and then attend to the laying on of hands for the gift of the Holy Ghost upon all those whom we had previously baptized; doing all things in the name of the Lord."—*Times and Seasons*, vol. 3, p. 915.

On this occasion was received the revelation providing for the choosing of twelve apostles. [1]

One provision mentioned in the above instruction is of peculiar importance. Notwithstanding the Lord appoints these men to a high and responsible position, he recognizes the rights of the people, and shows no disposition to force

[1] 1. Now, behold, because of the thing which you, my servant Oliver Cowdery, have desired to know of me, I give unto you these words: Behold, I have manifested unto you, by my Spirit in many instances, that the things which you have written are true; wherefore you know that they are true; and if you know that they are true, behold, I give unto you a commandment, that you rely upon the things which are written; for in them are all things written concerning the foundation of my church, my gospel, and my rock; wherefore, if you shall build up my church upon the foundation of my gospel and my rock, the gates of hell shall not prevail against you.

2. Behold, the world is ripening in iniquity, and it must needs be that the children of men are stirred up unto repentance, both the Gentiles, and also the house of Israel; wherefore, as thou hast been baptized by the hand of my servant, Joseph Smith, Jr., according to that which I have commanded him, he hath fulfilled the thing which I commanded him. And now marvel not that I have called him unto mine own purpose, which purpose is known in me; wherefore, if he shall be diligent in keeping my commandments, he shall be blessed unto eternal life, and his name is Joseph.

3. And now, Oliver Cowdery, I speak unto you, and also unto David Whitmer, by the way of commandment; for, behold, I command all men everywhere to repent, and I speak unto you, even as unto Paul mine apostle, for you are called even with that same calling with which he was called. Remember the worth of souls is great in the sight of God; for, behold, the Lord your Redeemer suffered death in the flesh; wherefore he suffered the pain of all men, that all men might repent and come unto him. And he hath risen again from the dead, that he might bring all men unto him on conditions of repentance. And how great is his joy in the soul that repenteth. Wherefore you are called to cry repentance unto this people. And if it so be that you should labor all your days, in crying repentance unto this people, and bring save it be one soul unto me, how great shall be your joy with him in the kingdom of my Father!

4. And now, if your joy will be great with one soul that you have brought unto me into the kingdom of my Father, how great will be your joy, if you should bring many souls unto me! Behold, you have my gos-

upon them a man not indorsed by them. He instructs them not to carry out his direction until they present the same before their brethren for indorsement. Is not this a grand condescension upon the part of God, that having called men Rights of the body. to be colaborers he recognizes their right to a voice in the things done? But he is just, and this is justice. This principle, if true, ought to admonish men who aspire to be coworkers "together with God" that it is necessary to work in the same spirit in which he works, and with the same motives to purify and bless mankind; otherwise they will not be worthy to retain their standing, and, in harmony with the inexorable laws of justice, must fall. Further; they should be admonished that as God recognizes

pel before you, and my rock, and my salvation. Ask the Father in my name, in faith believing that you shall receive, and you shall have the Holy Ghost which manifesteth all things, which is expedient unto the children of men. And if you have not faith, hope, and charity, you can do nothing. Contend against no church, save it be the church of the Devil. Take upon you the name of Christ, and speak the truth in soberness, and as many as repent, and are baptized in my name, which is Jesus Christ, and endure to the end, the same shall be saved. Behold, Jesus Christ is the name which is given of the Father, and there is none other name given whereby man can be saved; wherefore, all men must take upon them the name which is given of the Father, for in that name shall they be called at the last day; wherefore, if they know not the name by which they are called, they cannot have place in the kingdom of my Father.

5. And now, behold, there are others who are called to declare my gospel, both unto Gentile and unto Jew; yea, even twelve; and the twelve shall be my disciples, and they shall take upon them my name; and the twelve are they who shall desire to take upon them my name, with full purpose of heart; and if they desire to take upon them my name, with full purpose of heart, they are called to go into all the world to preach my gospel unto every creature; and they are they who are ordained of me to baptize in my name, according to that which is written; and you have that which is written before you; wherefore you must perform it according to the words which are written. And now I speak unto the twelve: Behold, my grace is sufficient for you; you must walk uprightly before me and sin not. And, behold, you are they who are ordained of me to ordain priests and teachers to declare my gospel, according to the power of the Holy Ghost which is in you, and according to the callings and gifts of God unto men; and I, Jesus Christ, your Lord and your God, have spoken it. These words are not of men, nor of man, but of me; wherefore, you shall testify they are of me, and not of man; for it is my voice which speaketh them unto you; for they are given by my Spirit unto you; and by my power you can read them one to another, and save it were by my power, you could not have them; wherefore you can testify that you have heard my voice, and know my words.

6. And now, behold, I give unto you, Oliver Cowdery, and also unto David Whitmer, that you shall search out the twelve who shall have the

them, and their rights of voice and vote, they should recognize their brethren. Again; as God permits man the privilege of ratifying his choice, is it not disrespectful for men to God's right to direct select and ordain, without consulting him and obtaining his will? Another indorsement of this principle is found in the Book of Doctrine and Covenants, section 107, paragraph 46, where, after giving names for all the important offices of the church, it is said:—

"I give unto you that you should fill all these offices and approve of those names which I have mentioned or else disapprove of them at my general conference," etc.

Of course, as God is always right, it would be disastrous to reject his counsel; but is it not right that the body should have the right to invite disastrous consequences if it choose?

But, reader, is it not inconsistent to charge a man with seeking to be a dictator and an arbitrary ruler, who Charge of arbitrary ruling inconsistent. revealed the principle that the right was inherent in the body to even reject the revelations of God himself, if they so choose, subject, of course, to the consequences of such rejection?

Another thing worthy of note, and especial consideration, in the above quotation, is the manner of ordaining. Some Manner of ordaining. have concluded from the language found in Doctrine and Covenants 26:8, "And also with Peter, and James, and John, whom I have sent unto you, by whom I have ordained you and confirmed you to be apostles and Two ordinations without proof. especial witnesses of my name," etc., that Peter, James, and John literally laid their own hands on the heads of Joseph and Oliver. But this commandment was to the effect that they should ordain

desires of which I have spoken; and by their desires and their works, you shall know them; and when you have found them you shall show these things unto them. And you shall fall down and worship the Father in my name; and you must preach unto the world, saying, You must repent and be baptized in the name of Jesus Christ; for all men must repent and be baptized, and not only men, but women; and children who have arrived to the years of accountability.

7. And now, after that you have received this, you must keep my commandments in all things; and by your hands I will work a marvelous work among the children of men, unto the convincing of many of their sins, that they may come unto repentance, and that they may come unto the kingdom of my Father; wherefore, the blessings which I give unto

each other. This they afterwards did, as Joseph Smith
relates in his history. (See *Times and Seasons*, vol. 3, p.
945.) In regard to this event Oliver Cowdery is reported
by George Reynolds in his "Myth of the Manuscript Found,"
page 80 (before referred to), as saying:—

"I was also present with Joseph when the higher or
Melchisedec priesthood was conferred by the holy angel
from on high. This priesthood was then conferred on each
other, by the will and commandment of God."

Joseph and Oliver agree as to their being commanded of
God to ordain each other; also as to the fact that they did so
ordain. Joseph states in an epistle written at Nauvoo, September 6, 1842, that he heard the voice of Peter, James,
and John, but says nothing of such an event as their laying
hands on them. His statement is as follows:—

"And again, what do we hear? Glad tidings of Cumorah!
Moroni, an angel from heaven, declaring the fulfillment of
the prophets—the book to be revealed. A voice of the Lord
in the wilderness of Fayette, Seneca County, declaring the
three witnesses to bear record of the book. The voice of
Michael on the banks of the Susquehanna, detecting the
Devil when he appeared as an angel of light. The voice of
Peter, James, and John, in the wilderness between Harmony,
Susquehanna County, and Colesville, Broome County, on
the Susquehanna River, declaring themselves as possessing
the keys of the kingdom, and of the dispensation of the fullness of times. And again, the voice of God in the chamber
of old Father Whitmer, in Fayette, Seneca County," etc.—
Doctrine and Covenants 110: 20, 21.   (See also *Times and
Seasons*, vol. 3, pp. 935, 936.)

Some have supposed that they received two ordinations;
one under the hands of Peter, James, and John, and one by
each other; but it is scarcely supposable that they would
fail to mention so important an item. There is no historical
evidence of such an event. Nor is there any evidence that

you are above all things. And after that you have received this, if you
keep not my commandments, you cannot be saved in the kingdom of my
Father. Behold, I, Jesus Christ, your Lord and your God, and your Redeemer, by the power of my Spirit, have spoken it. Amen.

Peter, James, and John were present, either when the

Peter, James, and John not present.

instruction was given to ordain or when the ordination actually took place. The only historical account of their appearance is in the epistle quoted from above, and the place of that appearance is definitely given as between Harmony, Susquehanna County (Pennsylvania), and Colesville, Broome County (New York), while the place of instruction concerning ordination, as also the ordination itself, was at Fayette, Seneca County (New York). It is not safe then to write historically that Joseph Smith and Oliver Cowdery were ever ordained literally under the hands of Peter, James, and John. He who does so writes recklessly and without sufficient evidence upon which to base his conclusion.

The words of the revelation, "by whom I have ordained you," do not furnish the proof; to claim that they do would

Definit on of the word "ordain."

be putting a strained construction on the word "ordained." To be sure, if they did lay their hands on them it would have been an ordination, but there are other meanings to the word "ordained," and hence to say they ordained, is no evidence they did so by the imposition of their own hands. Webster defines ordain:—

"1. To set in order; to arrange according to rule; to regulate; to set; to establish.

"2. To regulate, or establish. by appointment, decree, or law; to constitute; to decree; to appoint; to institute.

"3. To set apart for an office; to appoint.

"4. (*Eccl.*) To invest with ministerial or sacerdotal functions; to introduce into the office of the Christian ministry, by the laying on of hands, or other forms; to set apart by the ceremony of ordination."

Hence Peter, James, and John could have ordained by holding and exercising the power to direct, set in order, arrange, regulate, establish, appoint. decree. enact, or institute, etc. In the absence of any evidence that Peter, James, and John ordained according to Webster's fourth definition, we are not justified as historians in saying that Joseph and Oliver were so ordained. It is fair to presume that they were not, for the reason that so important an event certainly would have been mentioned by the parties concerned. It establishes the principle that a command of God is sufficient authority for any man to perform the ordinance of ordination.

It is evident that the inherent right to the priesthood by virtue of their lives being "hid with Christ in God," was recognized; and because of this they were authorized by command to do the work.

Inherent right to the priesthood.

CHAPTER 6.

1830.

AFTER the events heretofore recorded the instruction given seems to be by way of preparation for the grand event of setting up or organizing the Church of God upon earth. This marks another important epoch in the history of this generation. What strikes the reader with peculiar emphasis is that notwithstanding the events and experiences related are of thrilling interest and importance, Joseph makes no effort at display or embellishment, but relates his narrative in a plain, unvarnished way, as though conscious of the strength of his position, and recognizing no need of a special effort to bolster it up.

Simple manner of recording events.

He writes:—

"In this manner did the Lord continue to give us instructions from time to time, concerning the duties which now devolved upon us, and among many other things of the kind, we obtained of him the following, by the Spirit of prophecy and revelation; which not only gave us much information, but also pointed out to us the precise day upon which, according to his will and commandment, we should proceed to organize his church once again here upon the earth:—

"The rise of the Church of Christ in these last days,

being one thousand eight hundred and thirty years since the coming of our Lord and Savior Jesus Christ in the flesh, it being regularly organized and established agreea- bly to the laws of our country, by the will and commandments of God in the fourth month, and on the sixth day of the month which is called April; which commandments were given to Joseph Smith, Jr., who was called of God and ordained an apostle of Jesus Christ, to be the first elder of this church; and to Oliver Cowdery, who was also called of God an apostle of Jesus Christ, to be the second elder of this chuich. and ordained under his hand: and this according to the grace of our Lord and Savior Jesus Christ, to whom be all the glory both now and forever. Amen.

A revelation containing important provisions.

"After it was truly manifested unto this first elder that he had received a remission of his sins, he was entangled again in the vanities of the world; but after repenting, and humbling himself, sincerely, through faith, God ministered unto him by an holy angel whose countenance was as light- ning, and whose garments were pure and white above all other whiteness, and gave unto him commandments which inspired him, and gave him power from on high, by the means which were before prepared, to translate the Book of Mor- mon, which contains a record of a fallen people, and the full- ness of the gospel of Jesus Christ to the Gentiles, and to the Jews also, which was given by inspiration, and is confirmed to others by the ministering of angels, and is declared unto the world by them, proving to the world that the Holy Scrip- tures are true, and that God does inspire men and call them to his holy work in this age and generation, as well as in generations of old, thereby showing that he is the same God yesterday, to-day, and forever. Amen.

"Therefore, having so great witnesses, by them shall the world be judged, even as many as shall hereafter come to a knowledge of this work; and those who receive it in faith and work righteousness, shall receive a crown of eter- nal life; but those who harden their hearts in unbelief and reject it, it shall turn to their own condemnation, for the Lord God has spoken it; and we, the elders of the church, have heard and bear witness to the words of the glorious Majesty on high, to whom be glory forever and ever. Amen.

"By these things we know that there is a God in heaven who is infinite and eternal, from everlasting to everlasting the same unchangeable God, the framer of heaven and earth and all things which are in them, and that he created man male and female; after his own image and in his own likeness created he them, and gave unto them commandments that they should love and serve him the only living and true God, and that he should be the only being whom they should worship. But by the transgression of these holy laws, man became sensual and devilish, and became fallen man.

"Wherefore the almighty God gave his only begotten Son, as it is written in those scriptures which have been given of him: he suffered temptations but gave no heed unto them; he was crucified, died, and rose again the third day; and ascended into heaven to sit down on the right hand of the Father, to reign with almighty power according to the will of the Father, that as many as would believe and be baptized, in his holy name, and endure in faith to the end, should be saved: not only those who believed after he came in the meridian of time in the flesh, but all those from the beginning, even as many as were before he came, who believed in the words of the holy prophets, who spake as they were inspired by the gift of the Holy Ghost, who truly testified of him in all things, should have eternal life, as well as those who should come after, who should believe in the gifts and callings of God by the Holy Ghost, which beareth record of the Father, and of the Son, which Father, Son, and Holy Ghost are one God, infinite and eternal, without end. Amen.

"And we know that all men must repent and believe on the name of Jesus Christ and worship the Father in his name, and endure in faith on his name to the end, or they cannot be saved in the kingdom of God. And we know that justification through the grace of our Lord and Savior Jesus Christ, is just and true; and we know, also, that sanctification through the grace of our Lord and Savior Jesus Christ, is just and true, to all those who love and serve God with all their mights, minds, and strength; but there is a possibility that man may fall from grace and depart from the living God. Therefore let the church take heed and pray always, lest they fall into temptations; yea, and even let those who are sanctified, take heed also.   And we know that these things are true and according to the revelations of John, neither adding to, nor diminishing from the prophecy of his book, the Holy Scriptures, or the revelations of God which shall come hereafter by the gift and power of the Holy Ghost, the voice of God, or the ministering of angels: and the Lord God has spoken it; and honor, power, and glory, be rendered to his holy name, both now and ever.   Amen.

"*And again by way of commandment to the church concerning the manner of baptism:—*

"All those who humble themselves before God and desire to be baptized, and come forth with broken hearts and contrite spirits, and witness before the church that they have truly repented of all their sins, and are willing to take upon them the name of Jesus Christ, having a determination to serve him to the end, and truly manifest by their works that they have received of the Spirit of Christ unto the remission of their sins, shall be received by baptism into his church.

"*The duty of the elders, priests, teachers, deacons, and members of the Church of Christ:—*

"An apostle is an elder, and it is his calling to baptize, and to ordain other elders, priests, teachers, and deacons, and to administer bread and wine—the emblems of the flesh and blood of Christ—and to confirm those who are baptized into the church, by the laying on of hands for the baptism of fire and the Holy Ghost, according to the scriptures; and to teach, expound, exhort, baptize, and watch over the church; and to confirm the church by the laying on of the hands, and the giving of the Holy Ghost, and to take the lead of all meetings.

"The elders are to conduct the meetings as they are led by the Holy Ghost, according to the commandments and revelations of God.

"The priest's duty is to preach, teach, expound, exhort, and baptize, and administer the sacrament, and visit the house of each member, and exhort them to pray vocally and in secret, and attend to all family duties: and he may also ordain other priests, teachers, and deacons; and he is to take the lead of meetings when there is no elder present, but when there is an elder present he is only to preach, teach, expound, exhort, and baptize, and visit the house of each member, exhorting them to pray vocally and in secret, and attend to all family duties. In all these duties the priest is to assist the elder if occasion requires.

"The teacher's duty is to watch over the church always, and be with, and strengthen them, and see that there is no iniquity in the church, neither hardness with each other; neither lying, backbiting, nor evil speaking; and see that the church meet together often, and also see that all the members do their duty, and he is to take the lead of meetings in the absence of the elder or priest, and is to be assisted always, in all his duties in the church, by the deacons, if occasion requires; but neither teachers nor deacons have authority to baptize, administer the sacrament, or lay on hands; they are, however, to warn, expound, exhort, and teach, and invite all to come unto Christ.

"Every elder, priest, teacher, or deacon, is to be ordained according to the gifts and callings of God unto him; and he is to be ordained by the power of the Holy Ghost which is in the one who ordains him.

"The several elders composing this Church of Christ are to meet in conference once in three months, or from time to time, as said conferences shall direct or appoint; and said conferences are to do whatever church business is necessary to be done at the time.

"The elders are to receive their licenses from other elders, by vote of the church to which they belong, or from the conferences.

"Each priest, teacher, or deacon, who is ordained by a priest, may take a certificate from him at the time, which certificate, when presented to an elder, shall entitle him to a license, which shall authorize him to perform the duties of his calling; or he may receive it from a conference.

"No person is to be ordained to any office in this church,

where there is a regularly organized branch of the same, without the vote of that church; but the presiding elders, traveling bishops, high counselors, high priests, and elders, may have the privilege of ordaining, where there is no branch of the church, that a vote may be called.

"Every president of the high priesthood (or presiding elder), bishop, high counselor, and high priest, is to be ordained by the direction of a high council, or general conference.

"The duty of the members after they are received by baptism:—

"The elders or priests are to have a sufficient time to expound all things concerning the Church of Christ to their understanding, previous to their partaking of the sacrament, and being confirmed by the laying on of the hands of the elders; so that all things may be done in order. And the members shall manifest before the church, and also before the elders, by a godly walk and conversation, that they are worthy of it, that there may be works and faith agreeable to the Holy Scriptures, walking in holiness before the Lord.

"Every member of the Church of Christ having children, is to bring them unto the elders before the church, who are to lay their hands upon them in the name of Jesus Christ, and bless them in his name.

"No one can be received into the Church of Christ unless he has arrived unto the years of accountability before God, and is capable of repentance.

"Baptism is to be administered in the following manner unto all those who repent: The person who is called of God and has authority from Jesus Christ to baptize, shall go down into the water with the person who has presented him or herself for baptism, and shall say, calling him or her by name: Having been commissioned of Jesus Christ, I baptize you in the name of the Father, and of the Son, and of the Holy Ghost, Amen. Then shall he immerse him or her in the water, and come forth again out of the water.

. "It is expedient that the church meet together often to partake of bread and wine in remembrance of the Lord Jesus; and the elder or priest shall administer it; and after this manner shall he administer it: He shall kneel with the

church and call upon the Father in solemn prayer, saying,
O God, the eternal Father, we ask thee in the name of thy
Son Jesus Christ, to bless and sanctify this bread to the
souls of all those who partake of it, that they may eat in
remembrance of the body of thy Son, and witness unto thee,
O God, the eternal Father, that they are willing to take upon
them the name of thy Son, and always remember him and
keep his commandments which he has given them, that they
may always have his Spirit to be with them.   Amen.

"The manner of administering the wine: He shall take
the cup also, and say: O God, the eternal Father, we ask
thee in the name of thy Son Jesus Christ, to bless and sanctify this wine to the souls of all those who drink of it, that
they may do it in remembrance of the blood of thy Son
which was shed for them, that they may witness unto thee,
O God, the eternal Father, that they do always remember
him, that they may have his Spirit to be with them.   Amen.

"Any member of the Church of Christ transgressing, or
being overtaken in a fault, shall be dealt with as the scriptures direct.

"It shall be the duty of the several churches composing
the Church of Christ to send one or more of their teachers to
attend the several conferences, held by the elders of the
church, with a list of the names of the several members
uniting themselves with the church since the last conference,
or send by the hand of some priest, so that a regular list of
all the names of the whole church may be kept in a book, by
one of the elders, whoever the other elders shall appoint
from time to time, and also if any have been expelled from
the church, so that their names may be blotted out of the
general church record of names.

"All members removing from the church where they
reside, if going to a church where they are not known, may
take a letter certifying that they are regular members and
in good standing, which certificate may be signed by any
elder or priest, if the member receiving the letter is personally acquainted with the elder or priest, or it may be signed
by the teachers or deacons of the church.

"Meantime our translation drawing to a close, we went to

Palmyra, Wayne County, New York, secured the copyright, and agreed with Mr. Egbert Grandin to print five thousand copies, for the sum of three thousand dollars.

"I wish also to mention here, that the title page of the Book of Mormon is a literal translation, taken from the very last leaf, on the left hand side of the collection or book of plates, which contained the record which has been translated; the language of the whole running the same as all Hebrew writing in general; and that said title page is not by any means a modern composition either of mine or of any other man's who has lived or does live in this generation. Therefore, in order to correct an error which generally exists concerning it, I give below that part of the title page of the English version of the Book of Mormon, which is a genuine and literal translation of the title page of the original Book of Mormon, as recorded on the plates.

"'THE BOOK OF MORMON.

"'An account written by the hand of Mormon, upon plates, taken from the plates of Nephi.

"'Wherefore it is an abridgement of the record of the people of Nephi, and also of the Lamanites; written to the Lamanites, who are a remnant of the house of Israel; and also to Jew and Gentile: written by way of commandment, and also by the Spirit of prophecy and of revelation.

Title page of the B ok of Mormon.

"'Written, and sealed up, and hid up unto the Lord, that they might not be destroyed; to come forth by the gift and power of God unto the interpretation thereof: sealed by the hand of Moroni, and hid up unto the Lord, to come forth in due time by the way of Gentile; the interpretation thereof by the gift of God.

"'An abridgement taken from the Book of Ether, also; which is a record of the people of Jared: who were scattered at the time the Lord confounded the language of the people when they were building a tower to get to heaven: which is to show unto the remnant of the house of Israel what great things the Lord hath done for their fathers; and that they may know the covenants of the Lord, that they are not cast off forever; and also to the convincing of the Jew and Gentile that Jesus is the Christ, the eternal God, manifesting himself unto all nations. And now if there are faults, they are the mistakes of men; wherefore condemn not the things of God, that ye may be found spotless at the judgment seat of Christ.'

"The remainder of the title page is, of course, modern."
—*Times and Seasons*, vol. 3, pp. 928–931, 943.

About this time a revelation to Martin Harris was received. [1]

---

[1] 1. I am Alpha and Omega, Christ the Lord; yea, even I am He, the beginning and the end, the Redeemer of the world: I having accomplished and finished the will of him whose I am, even the Father, concerning me; having done this, that I might subdue all things unto myself; retaining all power, even to the destroying of Satan and his works at the end of the world, and the last great day of judgment, which I shall pass upon the inhabitants thereof, judging every man according to his works, and the deeds which he has done. And surely every man must repent or suffer, for I God am endless; wherefore, I revoke not the judgments which I shall pass, but woes shall go forth, weeping, wailing, and gnashing of teeth; yea, to those who are found on my left hand; nevertheless, it is not written that there shall be no end to this torment; but it is written endless torment.

2. Again, it is written eternal damnation; wherefore it is more express than other scriptures, that it might work upon the hearts of the children of men, altogether for my name's glory; wherefore, I will explain unto you this mystery, for it is meet unto you to know even as mine apostles. I speak unto you that are chosen in this thing, even as one, that you may enter into my rest; for, behold, the mystery of Godliness, how great is it? For, behold, I am endless, and the punishment which is given from my hand is endless punishment, for Endless is my name; wherefore—

Eternal punishment is God's punishment.

Endless punishment is God's punishment.

Wherefore, I command you to repent, and keep the commandments which you have received by the hand of my servant Joseph Smith, Jr., in my name; and it is by my almighty power that you have received them; therefore I command you to repent—repent, lest I smite you by the rod of my mouth, and by my wrath, and by my anger, and your sufferings be sore—how sore you know not! how exquisite you know not! yea, how hard to bear you know not! For, behold, I, God, have suffered these things for all, that they might not suffer, if they would repent; but if they would not repent, they must suffer even as I; which suffering caused myself, even God, the greatest of all, to tremble because of pain, and to bleed at every pore, and to suffer both body and spirit, and would that I might not drink the bitter cup, and shrink; nevertheless, glory be to the Father, and I partook and finished my preparations unto the children of men; wherefore, I command you again to repent, lest I humble you with my almighty power, and that you confess your sins, lest you suffer these punishments of which I have spoken, of which in the smallest, yea, even in the least degree, you have tasted at the time I withdrew my Spirit. And I command you that you preach naught but repentance, and show not these things unto the world until it is wisdom in me; for they cannot bear meat now, but milk they must receive; wherefore, they

Joseph resumes his narrative as follows:—

"Whilst the Book of Mormon was in the hands of the printer, we still continued to bear testimony and give infor- Organization mation, as far as we had opportunity; and also of the church. made known to our brethren that we had received commandment to organize the church, and accordingly we met together for that purpose, at the house of the above-mentioned Mr. Whitmer (being six in number) on Tuesday, the sixth day of April, A. D. one thousand eight hundred and thirty.

"Having opened the meeting by solemn prayer to our heavenly Father we proceeded (according to previous com-

---

must not know these things, lest they perish. Learn of me, and listen to my words; walk in the meekness of my Spirit and you shall have peace in me. I am Jesus Christ; I came by the will of the Father, and I do his will.

3. And again, I command thee that thou shalt not covet thy neighbor's wife; nor seek thy neighbor's life. And again, I command thee that thou shalt not covet thine own property, but impart it freely to the printing of the Book of Mormon, which contains the truth and the word of God, which is my word to the Gentile, that soon it may go to the Jew, of whom the Lamanites are a remnant, that they may believe the gospel, and look not for a Messiah to come who has already come.

4. And again, I command thee that thou shalt pray vocally as well as in thy heart; yea, before the world as well as in secret; in public as well as in private. And thou shalt declare glad tidings; yea, publish it upon the mountains, and upon every high place, and among every people that thou shalt be permitted to see. And thou shalt do it with all humility, trusting in me, reviling not against revilers. And of tenets thou shalt not talk, but thou shalt declare repentance and faith on the Savior, and remission of sins by baptism and by fire; yea, even the Holy Ghost.

5. Behold, this is a great, and the last commandment which I shall give unto you concerning this matter; for this shall suffice for thy daily walk even unto the end of thy life. And misery thou shalt receive, if thou wilt slight these counsels; yea, even the destruction of thyself and property. Impart a portion of thy property; yea, even part of thy lands, and all save the support of thy family. Pay the debt thou hast contracted with the printer. Release thyself from bondage. Leave thy house and home, except when thou shalt desire to see thy family; and speak freely to all; yea, preach, exhort, declare the truth, even with a loud voice; with a sound of rejoicing, crying Hosanna! hosanna! blessed be the name of the Lord God!

6. Pray always and I will pour out my Spirit upon you, and great shall be your blessing; yea, even more than if you should obtain treasures of earth and corruptibleness to the extent thereof. Behold, canst thou read this without rejoicing and lifting up thy heart for gladness; or canst thou run about longer as a blind guide; or canst thou be humble and meek and conduct thyself wisely before me; yea, come unto me thy Savior. Amen.

andment) to call on our brethren to know whether they
accepted us as their teachers in the things of the kingdom of
God, and whether they were satisfied that we should proceed and be organized as a church according to said commandment which we had received. To these they consented
a unanimous vote. I then laid my hands upon Oliver
Cowdery and ordained him an elder of the 'Church of Jesus
Christ of Latter Day Saints,' after which he ordained me
to the office of an elder of said church. We then took
bread, blessed it, and brake it with them, also wine, blessed
it and drank it with them. We then laid our hands on each
individual member of the church present that they might receive the gift of the Holy Ghost, and be confirmed members
of the Church of Christ. The Holy Ghost was poured out
upon us to a very great degree. Some prophesied, whilst
all praised the Lord and rejoiced exceedingly."—*Times*
and Seasons, vol. 3, pp. 944, 945.

Thus in a few plain, simple words is chronicled the history
of the organization of the Church of Jesus Christ, at Fayette,
Seneca County, New York, on Tuesday, April 6,
1830, with only six members; a partial organization to be sure, but provision had already been
for a complete organization. Revelation had been
providing for a quorum of apostles, for elders, priests,
and deacons, and the duties of each defined. Provision had been made for a president of the
high priesthood, bishop, high counselor, high
priest, and general church recorder. Provision
had been made for local churches; the transfer-
membership from one church to another; for the
calling of conferences. Instruction was given regarding
ordination, the granting of licenses, the instruction of
those baptized, the blessing of children, manner of baptism,
administering the sacrament, and other essential features of
church government. This appears from the fact that the
revelation (section 17) was given some time before the organization effected April 6, 1830; for by it, according to the
foregoing history, they learned the exact day on which the
organization was to take place. Was Joseph Smith making

provision for all this stupendous organization and its pr
tical workings by his own wisdom and cunning? If so,
was taking desperate chances on being able to find the req
site material—the men to fill the places provided for the
Yet as time moved on, men who had not known of the ex
ence of Joseph Smith when the provision was made, ca

Men found
to fill places
provided.

forward one by one, dropped into line, took
positions provided for them, subscribed to the
fraud, if fraud it was, and cheerfully suffered persecution, violence, and death for the cause. And still, aft r
more than half a century has elapsed, men of talent a
moral influence are leaving positions of wealth and honor
accept positions in the ranks of that great army, provis
for which was made ere the material for its organization
found.

Reader, you have your choice between believing that
a series of events could have been provided for by
sagacity of Joseph Smith, or of believing his claim that
was inspired of God to lay the foundation and provide for t
unfolding of God's plan and the development of his chur
As historians we do no more than to record these fact
your consideration.

Joseph continues as follows:—

"We now proceeded to call out and ordain some others
the brethren to different offices of the priesthood, accordi

More ordi-
nations.

as the Spirit manifested unto us; and after a hap
time spent in witnessing and feeling for ourselv
the powers and the blessings of the Holy Ghost, through t
grace of God bestowed upon us, we dismissed with the plea
ing knowledge that we were now individually members
and acknowledged of God, 'The Church of Jesus Chris
organized in accordance with commandments and revelatio
given by him to ourselves in the last days, as well as accor.
ing to the order of the church as recorded in the New Test
ment.

"Several persons who had attended the above meeting a
got convinced of the truth, came forward shortly after, a
were received into the church, among the rest, my ow
father and mother were baptized to my great joy and con

on, and about the same time Martin Harris and A.
well."—*Times and Seasons*, vol. 4, p. 12.

ore separating on this memorable sixth of April further
was received.

After instruction was given concerning those who
wished to unite with the church on baptisms
received in other churches.

the same month was also received a revelation to
Cowdery, Hyrum Smith, Samuel H. Smith, Joseph
Sr., and Joseph Knight, Sr., in answer to their

uld, there shall be a record kept among you, and in it thou
called a seer, a translator, a prophet, an apostle of Jesus Christ,
of the church through the will of God the Father, and the grace
Lord Jesus Christ; being inspired of the Holy Ghost to lay the
thereof, and to build it up unto the most holy faith; which
was organized and established, in the year of your Lord eighteen
and thirty, in the fourth month, and on the sixth day of the
which is called April.

fore, meaning the church, thou shalt give heed unto all his
commandments, which he shall give unto you, as he receiv-
alking in all holiness before me; for his word ye shall receive,
mine own mouth, in all patience and faith; for by doing these
gates of hell shall not prevail against you; yea, and the Lord
disperse the powers of darkness from before you, and cause the
to shake for your good, and his name's glory. For thus saith
him have I inspired to move the cause of Zion in mighty
good; and his diligence I know, and his prayers I have heard:
weeping for Zion I have seen, and I will cause that he shall
er no longer, for his days of rejoicing are come unto the re-
of his sins, and the manifestations of my blessings upon his

hold, I will bless all those who labor in my vineyard, with a
sing, and they shall believe on his words, which are given
me, by the Comforter, which manifesteth that Jesus was
sinful men for the sins of the world; yea, for the remission
to the contrite heart. Wherefore, it behooveth me, that he
ordained by you, Oliver Cowdery, mine apostle; this being an
unto you, that you are an elder under his hand, he being the
you, that you might be an elder unto this Church of Christ,
name; and the first preacher of this church, unto the church,
the world; yea, before the Gentiles; yea, and thus saith the
lo! to the Jews, also. Amen.

I say unto you, that all old covenants have I caused to be done
thing, and this is a new and an everlasting covenant; even
as from the beginning. Wherefore, although a man should
hundred times, it availeth him nothing; for you cannot
straight gate by the law of Moses, neither by your dead
is because of your dead works, that I have caused this last
this church to be built up unto me; even as in days of old.
enter ye in at the gate, as I have commanded, and seek not
our God. Amen.

request to know their respective duties in relation to the work.[4]

A few facts regarding the publication of the Book of Mormon may be of value.   Joseph Smith does not state in his history what day the translation was finished.   We learn from the certificate of the clerk of the court that the title page was deposited in the office on June 11, 1829.

Date of completing translation.

Here is the certificate as published in the first edition:

"*Northern District of New-York, to wit:*

"BE IT REMEMBERED, That on the eleventh day of June in the fifty-third year of the Independence of the United States of America, A. D. 1829, JOSEPH SMITH, JUN. of the said District, hath deposited in this office the title of a Book, the right whereof he claims as author, in the words following, to wit: 'The Book of Mormon: an account written by the hand of Mormon, upon plates taken from the plates of Nephi.   Wherefore, it is an abridgment of the Record of the People of Nephi;' and also of the Lamanites;   written to the Lamanites, who are a remnant of the House of Israel; and also to Jew and Gentile.

Clerk's certificate.

---

[4] 1. Behold, I speak unto you, Oliver, a few words.   Behold, thou art blessed, and art under no condemnation.   But beware of pride, lest thou shouldst enter into temptation.   Make known thy calling unto the church, and also before the world; and thy heart shall be opened to preach the truth from henceforth and forever.   Amen.

2. Behold, I speak unto you, Hyrum, a few words, for thou also art under no condemnation, and thy heart is opened, and thy tongue loosed; and thy calling is to exhortation, and to strengthen the church continually.   Wherefore thy duty is unto the church forever; and this because of thy family.   Amen.

3. Behold, I speak a few words unto you, Samuel, for thou also art under no condemnation, and thy calling is to exhortation, and to strengthen the church.   And thou art not as yet called to preach before the world.   Amen.

4. Behold, I speak a few words unto you, Joseph; for thou also art under no condemnation and thy calling also is to exhortation, and to strengthen the church.   And this is thy duty from henceforth and forever.   Amen.

5. Behold, I manifest unto you, Joseph Knight, by these words, that you must take up your cross, in the which you must pray vocally before the world, as well as in secret, and in your family, and among your friends, and in all places.   And, behold, it is your duty to unite with the true church, and give your language to exhortation continually, that you may receive the reward of the laborer.   Amen.

written by way of commandment, and also by the spirit of Prophecy and of Revelation. Written, and sealed up, and hid up unto the Lord, that they might not be destroyed; to come forth by the gift and power of God, unto the interpretation thereof; sealed by the hand of Moroni, and hid up unto the Lord, to come forth in due time by the way of Gentile; the interpretation thereof by the gift of God; an abridgment taken from the Book of Ether. Also, which is a Record of the People of Jared, which were scattered at the time the Lord confounded the language of the people when they were building a tower to get to Heaven: which is to shew unto the remnant of the House of Israel, how great things the Lord hath done for their fathers; and that they may know the covenants of the Lord, that they are not cast off forever: and also to the convincing of the Jew and Gentile, that Jesus is the Christ, the Eternal God, manifesting Himself unto all nations. And now if there be fault, it be the mistake of men; wherefore condemn not the things of God, that ye may be found spotless at the judgment seat of Christ.—By Joseph Smith, Jun. Author and Proprietor.'

"In conformity to the act of the Congress of the United States, entitled, 'An act for the encouragement of learning, by securing the copies of Maps, Charts, and Books, to the authors and proprietors of such copies, during the times therein mentioned;' and also the act, entitled, 'An act supplementary to an act, entitled, "An act for the encouragement of learning, by securing the copies of Maps, Charts, and Books, to the authors and proprietors of such copies, during the times therein mentioned, and extending the benefits thereof to the arts of designing, engraving, and etching historical and other prints.' R. R. LANSING,

"Clerk of the Northern District of New-York."

Mr. John H. Gilbert, of Palmyra, New York, who claims Gilbert on dates. to have set the type for the Book of Mormon, was interviewed at his residence by Elders W. H. and E. L. Kelley, on March 5, 1881. To them he said:—

"The manuscript was put in our hands in August, 1829, and all printed by March, 1830." — *Saints' Herald*, vol. 28, p. 166.

From the best information we can obtain we are confident that these dates are approximately if not exactly correct.

As will be seen in the foregoing extracts, Joseph Smith tells us how much of the title page was taken from the plates, and how much is modern. We here insert the title page of the Palmyra edition, which please read in connection with Joseph Smith's description heretofore given:—

Title page.

THE

BOOK OF MORMON:

AN ACCOUNT WRITTEN BY THE HAND OF MOR-MON, UPON PLATES TAKEN FROM THE PLATES OF NEPHI.

Wherefore it is an abridgment of the Record of the People of Nephi; and also of the Lamanites; written to the Lamanites, which are a remnant of the House of Israel; and also to Jew and Gentile; written by way of commandment, and also by the spirit of Prophecy and of Revelation. Written, and sealed up, and hid up unto the LORD, that they might not be destroyed; to come forth by the gift and power of GOD unto the interpretation thereof; sealed by the hand of Moroni, and hid up unto the LORD, to come forth in due time by the way of Gentile; the interpretation thereof by the gift of GOD; an abridgment taken from the Book of Ether.

Also, which is a Record of the People of Jared, which were scattered at the time the LORD confounded the language of the people when they were building a tower to get to Heaven: which is to shew unto the remnant of the House of Israel how great things the LORD hath done for their fathers; and that they may know the covenants of the LORD, that they are not cast off forever; and also to the convincing of the Jew and Gentile that JESUS is the CHRIST, the ETERNAL GOD, manifesting Himself unto all nations. And now if there be fault, it be the mistake of men; wherefore condemn not the things of GOD, that ye may be found spotless at the judgment seat of CHRIST.

BY JOSEPH SMITH, JUNIOR,
AUTHOR AND PROPRIETOR.

PALMYRA:
PRINTED BY E. B. GRANDIN, FOR THE AUTHOR.
1830.

It will be seen that the words, of which so much has been
said by critics; viz., "By Joseph Smith, Junior,
Author and Proprietor," are not a part of the
record found on the plates, but are a modern addition.

Author and
proprietor.

The reason he is called the "author" is, doubtless, as set
forth in the clerk's certificate quoted above, that he might be
entitled to the rights of an author under the law.
Observe the words of the clerk: "Be it remembered, That on the eleventh day of June, in the fifty-third
year of the Independence of the United States of America,
A. D. 1829, Joseph Smith, Jun. of the said District, hath
deposited in this office the title of a Book, *the right whereof
he claims as author*," etc.

His protection
under the law.

This was his protection under the law, and by being known
in law as the author, he was entitled to the rights of an
author; and yet there was no deception, for in his "preface"
to the book, which is given below, he fully explains what
the work was and his relation to it. No one who reads should
misunderstand his claim:—

"PREFACE.

"TO THE READER—

"As many false reports have been circulated respecting
the following work, and also many unlawful measures taken
by evil designing persons to destroy me, and also
the work, I would inform you that I translated,
by the gift and power of God, and caused to be written,
one hundred and sixteen pages, the which I took from
the Book of Lehi, which was an account abridged from
the plates of Lehi, by the hand of Mormon; which said
account, some person or persons have stolen and kept from
me, notwithstanding my utmost exertions to recover it again
—and being commanded of the Lord that I should not translate the same over again, for Satan had put it into their
hearts to tempt the Lord their God, by altering the words,
that they did read contrary from that which I translated and
caused to be written; and if I should bring forth the same
words again, or, in other words, if I should translate the
same over again, they would publish that which they had
stolen, and Satan would stir up the hearts of this genera-

Preface to Pal-
myra edition.

tion. that they might not receive this work: but behold, the Lord said unto me, I will not suffer that Satan shall accomplish his evil design in this thing: therefore thou shalt translate from the plates of Nephi, until ye come to that which ye have translated, which ye have retained; and behold ye shall publish it as the record of Nephi; and thus I will confound those who have altered my words.   I will not suffer that they shall destroy my work; yea, I will shew unto them.that my wisdom is greater than the cunning of the Devil. Wherefore, to be obedient unto the commandments of God, I have, through his grace and mercy, accomplished that which he hath commanded me respecting this thing. I would also inform you that the plates of which hath been spoken, were found in the township of Manchester, Ontario county, New York.   THE AUTHOR."

The work was zealously and vigorously pushed by its adherents. Accessions were constantly being made. With Obstacles met. confidence in final triumph they met every species of opposition, including slander, personal violence, and abuse, but were cheered, comforted, and strengthened by manifestations of power not known or comprehended by the religious world. Since the very hour of its introduction to the public "Mormonism" (so-called) has presented a problem to the world which has not yet been solved to the satisfaction of all. Each writer and speaker has his theory, but the only ones whose solution seems to satify even themselves are those who accept its claims as being true. In every place where it has been promulgated these testify with calm yet earnest conviction of complete satisfaction.

Let us hear the statement of the prophet concerning the preaching and baptisms, also of the first miracle peiformed in the church:—

"On Sunday, April 11, 1830, Oliver Cowdery preached the first public discourse that was delivered by any of our First miracle. number. Our meeting was held by previous appointment at the house of Mr. Whitmer, [in] Fayette. Large numbers of people attended, and the same day the following were baptized; viz.: Hyrum Page, Katharine Page, Christian Whitmer, Anne Whitmer, Jacob Whitmer, Elizabeth

Whitmer; and on the 18th day Peter Whitmer, Sr., Mary Whitmer, William Jolly, Elizabeth Jolly, Vincent Jolly, Richard Z. Peterson, and Elizabeth Anne Whitmer, all by Oliver Cowdery in Seneca Lake.

"During this month of April I went on a visit to the residence of Mr. Joseph Knight, of Colesville, Broome County, New York, with whom and his family I had been previously acquainted, and of whose name I have above mentioned as having been so kind and thoughtful towards us, while translating the Book of Mormon. Mr. Knight and his family were Universalists, but were willing to reason with me upon my religious views, and were as usual friendly and hospitable. We held several meetings in the neighborhood; we had many friends, and some enemies. Our meetings were well attended, and many began to pray fervently to Almighty God, that he would give them wisdom to understand the truth. Amongst those who attended our meetings regularly was Newel Knight, son to Joseph Knight. He and I had many and serious conversations on the important subject of man's eternal salvation: we had got into the habit of praying much at our meetings and Newel had said that he would try and take up his cross, and pray vocally during meeting; but when we again met together he rather excused himself; I tried to prevail upon him making use of the figure, supposing that he should get into a mudhole would he not try to help himself out? and that we were willing now to help him out of the mudhole. He replied that provided he had got into a mudhole through carelessness, he would rather wait and get out himself than have others to help him, and so he would wait until he should get into the woods by himself, and there he would pray. Accordingly he deferred praying until next morning, when he retired into the woods; where (according to his own account afterwards) he made several attempts to pray but could scarcely do so, feeling that he had not done his duty, but that he should have prayed in the presence of others. He began to feel uneasy, and continued to feel worse both in mind and body, until upon reaching his own house, his appearance was such as to alarm his wife very much. He requested her to go and bring me to him. I went and found him suffering very much in his mind, and his body acted upon in a very strange manner. His visage and limbs distorted and twisted in every shape and appearance possible to imagine; and finally he was caught up off the floor of the apartment and tossed about most fearfully. His situation was soon made known to his neighbors and relatives, and in a short time as many as eight or nine grown persons had got together to witness the scene. After he had thus suffered for a time, I succeeded in getting hold of him by the hand, when almost immediately he spoke to me, and with great earnestness requested of me that I should cast the devil out of him, saying that he knew he was in him, and that he also knew that I could cast him out. I replied, 'If you know that I can it shall be done,' and then almost unconsciously I rebuked the devil; and commanded him in the name of Jesus Christ to depart from him; when immediately Newel spoke out and said that he saw the devil leave him and vanish from his sight.

"This was the first miracle which was done in this church or by any member of it, and it was done not by man nor by the power of man, but it was done by God, and by the power of godliness: therefore let the honor and the praise, the dominion and the glory be ascribed to the Father, Son, and Holy Spirit forever and ever. Amen.

"The scene was now entirely changed, for as soon as the devil had departed from our friend, his countenance became natural, his distortions of body ceased, and almost immediately the Spirit of the Lord descended upon him, and the visions of eternity were opened to his view. He afterwards related his experience as follows: 'I now began to feel a most pleasing sensation resting upon me, and immediately the visions of heaven were opened to my view. I felt myself attracted upward, and remained for some time enwrapt in contemplation, insomuch that I knew not what was going on in the room. By and by I felt some weight pressing upon my shoulder and the side of my head; which served to recall me to a sense of my situation, and I found that the Spirit of the Lord had actually caught me up off the floor, and that my shoulder and head were pressing against the beams.'

"All this was witnessed by many, to their great astonishment and satisfaction, when they saw the devil thus cast out; and the power of God and his Holy Spirit thus made manifest. So soon as consciousness returned, his bodily weakness was such that we were obliged to lay him upon his bed and wait upon him for some time. As may be expected, such a scene as this contributed much to make believers of those who witnessed it, and finally, the greater part of them became members of the church.

"Soon after this occurrence I returned to Fayette, Seneca County. The Book of Mormon ('The stick of Joseph in the hands of Ephraim') had now been published for some time, and as the ancient prophet had predicted of it, 'It was accounted as a strange thing.' No small stir was created by its appearance; great opposition and much persecution followed the believers of its authenticity; but it had now come to pass that truth had sprung out of the earth, and righteousness had looked down from heaven; so we feared not our opponents, knowing that we had both truth and righteousness on our side; that we had both the Father and the Son, because we had the doctrines of Christ, and abided in them; and therefore we continued to preach, and to give information to all who were willing to hear.

"During the last week in May, the above-mentioned Newel Knight came to visit us, at Fayette, and was baptized by David Whitmer.

"On the first day of June, 1830, we held our first conference as an organized church. Our numbers were about thirty, besides whom many assembled with us, who were either believers, or anxious to learn.

"Having opened by singing and prayer, we partook together of the emblems of the body and blood of our Lord Jesus Christ. We then proceeded to confirm several who had lately been baptized, after which we called out and ordained several to the various offices of the priesthood. Much exhortation and instruction was given, and the Holy Ghost was poured out upon us in a miraculous manner:—many of our number prophesied, whilst others had the heavens opened to their view, and were so overcome that we had to lay them on beds, or other convenient places. Among the rest was brother Newel Knight, who had to be placed on a bed, being unable to help himself. By his own account of the transaction he could not understand why we should lay him on the bed, as he felt no sensibility of weakness. He felt his heart filled with love, with glory and pleasure unspeakable, and could discern all that was going on in the room; when, all of a sudden, a vision of futurity burst upon him. He saw there represented the great work which through my instrumentality was yet to be accomplished. He saw heaven opened, and beheld the Lord Jesus Christ seated at the right hand of the Majesty on high, and had it made plain to his understanding that the time would come when he would be admitted into his presence, to enjoy his society forever and ever. When their bodily strength was restored to these brethren, they shouted 'Hosannas to God and the Lamb,' and rehearsed the glorious things which they had seen and felt, whilst they were yet in the Spirit.

"Such scenes as these were calculated to inspire our hearts with joy unspeakable, and fill us with awe and reverence for that almighty Being by whose grace we had been called to be instrumental in bringing about for the children of men the enjoyment of such glorious blessings as were now poured out upon us. To find ourselves engaged in the very same order of things as observed by the holy apostles of old; to realize the importance and solemnity of such proceedings, and to witness and feel with our own natural senses the like glorious manifestations of the power of the priesthood; the gifts and blessings of the Holy Ghost; and the goodness and condescension of a merciful God, unto such as obey the everlasting gospel of our Lord Jesus Christ; combined to create within us sensations of rapturous gratitude, and inspire us with fresh zeal and energy in the cause of truth.

"Shortly after this conference David Whitmer baptized the following persons in Seneca Lake; viz.: John Poorman, John Jolly, Jerusha Smith, Katharine Smith, William Smith, Don C. Smith, Peter Rockwell, Caroline Rockwell, and Electa Rockwell.

"Immediately after this conference I returned to my own

house, and from thence (accompanied by my wife, Oliver
Cowdery, John Whitmer, and David Whitmer)
journeyed again on a visit to Mr. Knight's, of
Colesville, Broome County. We found a number in the
neighborhood still believing and anxious to be baptized.

Visits
Colesville.

"We appointed a meeting for the Sabbath, and on the afternoon of Saturday we erected a dam across a stream of water
which was convenient, for the purpose of there attending to
the ordinance; but during the night a mob collected and tore
down our dam, which hindered us of attending to the baptism on the Sabbath.

"We afterward found out that this mob had been instigated
to this act of molestation by certain sectarian priests of the
neighborhood, who began to consider their craft in danger,
and took this plan to stop the progress of the truth, and the
sequel will show how determinedly they prosecuted their
opposition, as well as to how little purpose in the end.

"The Sabbath arrived and we held our meeting. Oliver
Cowdery preached, and others of us bore testimony to the
truth of the Book of Mormon, the doctrince of repentance,
baptism for the remission of sins, and laying on of hands for
the gift of the Holy Ghost, etc., etc. Amongst our audience
were those who had torn down our dam, and who seemed
wishful to give us trouble, but did not until after the meeting was dismissed, when they immediately commenced talking to those whom they considered our friends, to try to turn
them against us and our doctrines."—*Times and Seasons*, vol.
4, pp. 12, 13, 22, 23.

These blessings and manifestations were strange in those
days, for most Christians had concluded that since the
apostles fell asleep revelations and miracles had
ceased. They are yet esteemed by many to be
unworthy of credence, yet some noted men of the
past have understood that Christians were entitled to them
if worthy. John Wesley says, in regard to their ceasing to
be enjoyed, "The cause of this was not, (as has
been vulgarly supposed,) 'because there was no
more occasion for them,' because all the world
was become Christians. This is a miserable mistake:

Blessings
considered
strange.

Wesley on
extraordi-
nary gifts.

not a twentieth part of it was then nominally Christians. The real cause was, 'the love of many,' almost of all Christians, so-called, was 'waxed cold.' The Christians had no more of the Spirit of Christ, than the other heathens. The Son of man, when he came to examine his church, could hardly 'find faith upon earth.' This was the real cause, why the extraordinary gifts of the Holy Ghost were no longer to be found in the Christian church; because the Christians were turned heathens again, and had only a dead form left."—Wesley's Sermons, vol. 2, ser. 94.

Alexander Campbell wrote:—

"We want the old gospel back, and sustained by the ancient order of things: and this alone, by the blessing of the Divine Spirit, is all that we do want, or can expect, to reform and save the world. And if this gospel, as proclaimed and enforced on Pentecost, cannot do this, vain are the hopes, and disappointed must be the expectations, of the so-called Christian world."—Christian System, pp. 234, 235; (also St. Louis edition of 1890, p. 250.)

A. Campbell on ancient order.

Joseph Smith, then, was not alone in seeing the necessity and in recognizing the possibility of a restoration of the gospel, "sustained by the ancient order of things," the enjoyment of the Holy Spirit, together with its extraordinary gifts. History records the fact, as we have seen, that others held similar views on this subject. However, he did claim more than they, so far as realization is concerned, as in the instance of the healing of Mr. Knight, as recorded above. If in this claim he bore false witness, he should be condemned and the fraud exposed. His claim seems to be remarkably verified, however, by creditable witnesses not of his religious faith.

We give a few out of the many on record as examples of this testimony:—

"Whatever we may say of the moral character of the author of Mormonism, it cannot be denied that Joseph Smith was a man of remarkable power—over others. Added to the stupendous claim of supernatural power, conferred by the direct gift of God, he exercised an almost mag-

Hayden's testimony.

netic power—an irresistible fascination—over those with whom he came in contact. Ezra Booth, of Mantua, a Methodist preacher of much more than ordinary culture, and with strong natural abilities, in company with his wife, Mr. and Mrs. Johnson, and some other citizens of this place, visited Smith at his home in Kirtland, in 1831. Mrs. Johnson had been afflicted for some time with a lame arm, and was not at the time of the visit able to lift her hand to her head. The party visited Smith partly out of curiosity, and partly to see for themselves what there might be in the new doctrine. During the interview, the conversation turned on the subject of supernatural gifts, such as were conferred in the days of the apostles. Some one said, 'Here is Mrs. Johnson with a lame arm; has God given any power to men now on earth to cure her?' A few moments later, when the conversation had turned in another direction, Smith rose, and walking across the room, taking Mrs. Johnson by the hand, said in the most solemn and impressive manner: '*Woman, in the name of the Lord Jesus Christ, I command thee to be whole*,' and immediately left the room.

"The company were awe-stricken at the infinite presumption of the man, and the calm assurance with which he spoke. The sudden mental and moral shock—I know not how better to explain the well-attested fact—electrified the rheumatic arm—Mrs. Johnson at once lifted it up with ease, and on her return home the next day she was able to do her washing without difficulty or pain."—Hayden's History of "The Western Reserve," pp. 249, 250.

"In the San Francisco *Weekly Chronicle*, November 28, 1882, in an article entitled 'Stalwarts Rebuked,' signed Garfield's 'Gath,' he in treating of the late President Garstatement. field relates that the latter said to him, 'There is a corner in my character which makes everything of a supernatural or mystical sort very fascinating to me.' Gath further says: 'He then told me a number of tales, all original and peculiar. For instance, he related that in his district, at a place called Kirtland, Joseph Smith, the Mormon, had gathered his first congregation, and there was a person brought to Smith, apparently possessed of a devil, with something that made the man froth, or bark. Smith, whom General Garfield described to be a fine man physically, with abundant magnetism, put the subject under his control, and finally raising his hands, shouted with a powerful voice, "I command that you come out of him!" And the General said that it was in testimony that the man behaved like one in his right mind after that.'"—*Saints' Herald*, vol. 85, p. 779.

"The testimony of Mr. Garfield is surprising only in the fact that it came from him. That Joseph Smith did, by the power of God, cast out devils, is a matter well authenticated and thoroughly believed in by the saints, though stoutly denied by his enemies, and imputed by Mr. Garfield to magnetism. Magnetism is one thing, and the Holy Spirit is another and very different thing. Joseph Smith wrought by the latter, which is the highest and greatest of all powers." (*Saints' Herald.* Editorial comment.)

We have selected these two out of many hundreds because of the prominence of the persons. Mr. A. S. Hayden was a prominent minister and author in the "Christian Church." Of the lamented President James A. Garfield, we need say nothing. The facts are clearly stated and, in one case at least, said to be well attested. True, both Mr. Garfield and Mr. Hayden seek to attribute these results to the effect of magnetism, but this is rather a hasty way of disposing of a "well-attested fact." Similar Bible facts could be disposed of in a similar way, but Christians would not be satisfied, they would demand a closer investigation. Why not give these well-attested facts a fuller consideration?

Joseph Smith not only claimed to receive the power of God, as in the case of Mr. Knight, given above, but as early as December, 1830, the promise was given through him that all who believed should receive blessings wrought by the power of God. He states:—

Spiritual blessings promised.

"And it shall come to pass, that there shall be a great work in the land, even among the Gentiles, for their folly and their abominations shall be made manifest, in the eyes of all people; for I am God, and mine arm is not shortened, and I will show miracles, signs and wonders, unto all those who believe on my name. And whoso shall ask it in my name, in faith, they shall cast out devils; they shall heal the sick; they shall cause the blind to receive their sight, and the deaf to hear, and the dumb to speak, and the lame to walk: and the time speedily cometh that great things are to be shown forth unto the children of men; but without faith shall not anything be shown forth except desolations upon Babylon, the same which has made all nations drink of the wine of the wrath of her fornication. And there are none that doeth good except those who are ready to receive the fullness of my gospel, which I have sent forth unto this generation."—Doctrine and Covenants 34: 3.

These promises have been so generally fulfilled and these blessings so universally enjoyed that wherever the reader may find a representative of the work a witness will be found; and so we refer you to them wherever found for further evidence on this great and important subject.

CHAPTER 7.

1830.

IN this chapter we give quite fully the account written by
Joseph Smith of some of his early persecutions, including

Persecutions.   the first two efforts made by his enemies to convict him of crime before the courts. We present
this in detail because so much has been said about fraud and

Trials before   immorality that we wish the reader to know, so
the courts.   far as possible, the facts concerning him, as
brought out on trial. He writes:—

"Amongst the many present at this meeting was one
Emily Coburn, sister to the wife of Newel Knight. The
Rev. Mr. Shearer, a divine of the Presbyterian faith, who
had considered himself her pastor, came to understand that
she was likely to believe our doctrine, and had, a short time
previous to this our meeting, come to labor with her; but
having spent some time with her without being able to persuade her against us, he endeavored to have her leave her
sister's house, and go with him to her father's, who lived at
a distance of at least ten miles off. For this purpose he had
recourse to stratagem: he told her that one of her brothers

was waiting at a certain place, wishful to have her go home with him. He succeeded thus to get her a little distance from the house, when, seeing that her brother was not in waiting for her, she refused to go any further with him, upon which he got hold of her by the arm to force her along; but her sister was soon with them; the two women were too many for him, and he was forced to sneak off without his errand, after all his labor and ingenuity. Nothing daunted, however, he went to her father, represented to him something or other, which induced the old gentleman to give him a power of attorney, which, as soon as our meeting was over, on the above-named Sunday evening, he immediately served upon her and carried her off to her father's residence, by open violence, against her will. All his labor was in vain, however, for the said Emily Coburn, in a short time afterwards, was baptized and confirmed a member of the 'Church of Jesus Christ of Latter Day Saints.'

"However, early on Monday morning we were on the alert, and before our enemies were aware we had repaired the dam, and proceeded to baptize, when the following thirteen persons were baptized under the hands of Oliver Cowdery; viz.: Emma Smith, Hezekiah Peck and wife, Joseph Knight and wife, William Stringham and wife, Joseph Knight, Jr., Aaron Culver and wife, Levi Hall, Polly Knight, and Julia Stringham. Before the baptism was entirely finished, the mob began again to collect, and shortly after we had retired, they amounted to about fifty men. They surrounded the house of Mr. Knight (where we had retired to), raging with anger and apparently wishful to commit violence upon us. Some asked us questions, others threatened us, so that we thought it wisdom to leave and go to the house of Newel Knight.

"There also they followed us, and it was only by the exercise of great prudence on our part, and reliance on our heavenly Father that they were kept from laying violent hands upon us, and so long as they chose to stay we were obliged to answer them various unprofitable questions, and bear with insults and threatenings without number.

"We had appointed a meeting for this evening, for the

purpose of attending to the confirmation of those who had been the same morning baptized. The time appointed had arrived, and our friends had nearly all collected together, when to my surprise I was visited by a constable, and arrested by him on a warrant, on charge of being a disorderly person; of setting the country in an uproar by preaching the Book of Mormon, etc., etc. The constable informed me (soon after I had been arrested) that the plan of those who had got out the warrant was to get me into the hands of the mob, who were now lying in ambush for me; but that he was determined to save me from them, as he had found me to be a different sort of person from what I had been represented to him. I soon found that he had told me the truth in this matter, for not far from Mr. Knight's house the wagon in which we had set out was surrounded by the mob, who seemed only to await some signal from the constable; but to their great disappointment he gave the horse the whip and drove me out of their reach. Whilst driving along pretty quickly one of the wagon wheels came off, which left us, once more, very nearly surrounded by them, as they had come on, in close pursuit. However, we managed to get the wheel on again and again left them behind us. He drove on to the town of South Bainbridge, Chenango County, where he lodged me for the time being, in an upper room of a tavern, and in order that all might be right with himself and with me also, he slept during the night with his feet against the door and a loaded musket by his side, whilst I occupied a bed which was in the room, he having declared that if we were interrupted unlawfully, that he would fight for me and defend me as far as in his power.

"On the day following a court was convened for the purpose of investigating those charges which had been preferred against me. A great excitement prevailed on account of the scandalous falsehoods which had been circulated, the nature of which will come out in the sequel.

"In the meantime my friend, Joseph Knight, had repaired to two of his neighbors, viz.: James Davidson and John Reed, Esqrs., (respectable farmers, men renowned for their integrity, and well versed in the laws of their country,) and retained them on my behalf during my trial. At length the trial commenced amidst a multitude of spectators, who in general evinced a belief that I was guilty of all that had been reported concerning me, and of course were very zealous that I should be punished according to my crimes. Among many witnesses called up against me was Mr. Josiah Stoal (of whom I have made mention, as having worked for him some time) and examined to the following effect. *Q.* Did not the prisoner, Joseph Smith, have a horse of you? *Ans.* Yes. *Q.* Did not he go to you and tell you that an angel had appeared unto him, and authorized him to get the horse from you? *Ans.* No, he told me no such story. *Q.* Well; how had he the horse of you? *Ans.* He bought him of me, as another man would do. *Q.* Have you had your pay? *Ans.* That is not your business.—The question being again put, the witness replied, 'I hold his note for the price of the horse, which I consider as good as the pay; for I am well acquainted with Joseph Smith, Jr., and know him to be an honest man; and if he wishes I am ready to let him have another horse on the same terms.'

"Mr. Jonathan Thompson was next called up, and examined. *Q.* Has not the prisoner, Joseph Smith, Jr., had a yoke of oxen of you? *Ans.* Yes. *Q.* Did he not obtain them of you by telling you that he had a revelation to the effect that he was to have them? *Ans.* No, he did not mention a word of the kind concerning the oxen, he purchased them the same as another man would.

"After a few more such attempts, the court was detained for a time, in order that two young women, (daughters to Mr. Stoal,) with whom I had at times kept company, might be sent for, in order, if possible, to elicit something from them which might be made a pretext against me. The young ladies arrived and were severally examined touching my character and conduct in general, but particularly as to my behavior towards them both in public and private, when they both bore such testimony in my favor as left my enemies without a pretext on their account. Several attempts were now made to prove something against me, and even circumstances which were alleged to have taken place in

Broome County were brought forward; but these my lawyers would not here admit of against me, in consequence of
which. my persecutors managed to detain the court, until
they had succeeded in obtaining a warrant from Broome
County, and which warrant they served upon me, at the
very moment in which I had been acquitted by this court.

"The constable who served this second warrant upon me
had no sooner arrested me than he began to abuse and insult
me, and so unfeeling was he with me, that although I had been
kept all the day in court, without anything to eat since the
morning, yet he hurried me off to Broome County, a distance of about fifteen miles, before he allowed me any kind
of food whatever. He took me to a tavern and gathered in
a number of men, who used every means to abuse, ridicule,
and insult me. They spat upon me, pointed their fingers at
me, saying Prophesy, prophesy; and thus did they imitate
those who crucified the Savior of mankind, not knowing
what they did. We were at this time not far distant from
my own house. I wished to be allowed the privilege of
spending the night with my wife, at home, offering any
wished-for security for my appearance, but this was denied
me. I applied for something to eat. The constable ordered
me some crusts of bread, and water, which was the only
fare I that night received. At length we retired to bed; the
constable made me lie next the wall. He then laid himself
down by me, and put his arm around me; and upon my moving in the least would clench me fast, fearing that I intended
to escape from him; and in this not very agreeable manner
did we pass the night. Next day I was brought before the
Magistrates' court, of Colesville, Broome County, and put
upon my trial. My former faithful friends and lawyers
were again at my side; my former persecutors were arrayed
against me. Many witnesses were again called forward and
examined, some of whom swore to the most palpable falsehoods, and like to the false witnesses which had appeared
against me the day previous, they contradicted themselves
so plainly that the court would not admit their testimony.
Others were called, who showed by their zeal that they were
willing enough to prove something against me; but all they

could do was to tell some things which somebody else had told them. In this 'frivolous and vexatious' manner did they proceed for a considerable time, when finally, Newel Knight was called up and examined, by lawyer Seymour, who had been especially sent for on this occasion. One, lawyer Burch, also was on the side of the prosecution; but Mr. Seymour seemed to be a more zealous Presbyterian, and appeared very anxious and determined that the people should not be deluded by anyone professing the power of Godliness; and not 'denying the power thereof.'

"So soon as Mr. Knight had been sworn, Mr. Seymour proceeded to interrogate him as follows: Q. Did the prisoner, Joseph Smith, Jr., cast the devil out of you? Ans. No sir. Q. Why, have not you had the devil cast out of you? A. Yes sir. Q. And had not Joe Smith some hand in its being done? A. Yes sir. Q. And did not he cast him out of you? A. No sir; it was done by the power of God, and Joseph Smith was the instrument in the hands of God, on the occasion. He commanded him out of me in the name of Jesus Christ. Q. And are you sure that it was the devil? A. Yes sir. Q. Did you see him, after he was cast out of you? A. Yes sir, I saw him. Q. Pray, what did he look like? (Here one of my lawyers informed the witness that he need not answer the question.) The witness replied, I believe I need not answer your last question, but I will do it provided I be allowed to ask you one question, first, and you answer me; viz.: Do you, Mr. Seymour, understand the things of the spirit? No, answered Mr. Seymour, I do not pretend to such big things. Well then, replied Knight, it would be of no use to tell you what the devil looked like, for it was a spiritual sight, and spiritually discerned; and of course you would not understand it, were I to tell you of it. The lawyer dropped his head, whilst the loud laugh of the audience proclaimed his discomfiture. Mr. Seymour now addressed the court, and in a long and violent harangue endeavored to blacken my character and bring me in guilty of the charges which had been brought against me. Among other things, he brought up the story of my having been a money digger; and in this manner proceeded, in hopes to influence the court and the people against me. Mr. Davidson and Mr. Reed followed on my behalf. They held forth in true colors the nature of the prosecution, the malignancy of intention, and the apparent disposition to persecute their client, rather than to afford him justice. They took up the different arguments which had been brought by the lawyers for the prosecution, and having shown their utter futility and misapplication, then proceeded to scrutinize the evidence which had been adduced, and each in his turn thanked God that he had been engaged in so good a cause as that of defending a man whose character stood so well the test of such a strict investigation. In fact, these men, although not regular lawyers, were upon this occasion able to put to silence their opponents, and convince the court that I was innocent. They spoke like men inspired of God, whilst those who were arrayed against me trembled under the sound of their voices, and quailed before them like criminals before a bar of justice.

"The majority of the assembled multitude had now began to find that nothing could be sustained against me: even the constable who arrested me, and treated me so badly, now came and apologized to me, and asked my forgiveness of his behavior towards me: and so far was he changed that he informed me that the mob were determined that if the court acquitted me that they would *have* me, and rail ride me, and tar and feather me; and further, that he was willing to favor me, and lead me out in safety by a private way.

"The court finding the charges against me not sustained, I was accordingly acquitted, to the great satisfaction of my friends, and vexation of my enemies, who were still determined upon molesting me; but through the instrumentality of my new friend, the constable, I was enabled to escape them and make my way in safety to my wife's sister's house, where I found my wife awaiting with much anxiety the issue of those ungodly proceedings; and with her in company next day, arrived in safety at my own house.

"After a few days, however, I again returned to Colesville, in company with Oliver Cowdery, for the purpose of confirming those whom we had thus been forced to abandon for a time. We had scarcely arrived at Mr. Knight's, when the mob was seen collecting together to oppose us, and we considered it wisdom to leave for home, which we did, without even waiting for any refreshment. Our enemies pursued us, and it was oftentimes as much as we could do to elude them; however, we managed to get home, after having traveled all night, except a short time, during which we were forced to rest ourselves under a large tree by the wayside, sleeping and watching alternately. And thus were we persecuted on account of our religious faith, in a country the constitution of which guarantees to every man the indefeasible right to worship God according to the dictates of his own conscience; and by men too who were professors of religion, and who were not backward to maintain this privilege for themselves, though they thus wantonly could deny it to us. For instance; Cyrus M'Master, a Presbyterian of high standing in his church, was one of the chief instigators of these persecutions; and he at one time told me personally that he considered me guilty, without judge or jury. The celebrated Doctor Boyington, also a Presbyterian, was another instigator to these deeds of outrage; whilst a young man named Benton, of the same religious faith, swore out the first warrant against me. I could mention many others also, but for brevity's sake will make these suffice for the present."—*Times and Seasons*, vol. 4, pp. 39-41, 61, 62.

This account is verified by the testimony of Mr. Reed, one of his counsel in the trials referred to. Mr. Reed was never Statement of Attorney Reed. a member of the church, but was ever after a friend of Joseph Smith. At a State convention held in Nauvoo, Illinois, in 1844, he said:—

"Those bigots soon made up a false accusation against him and had him arraigned before Joseph Chamberlain, a justice of the peace, a man that was always ready to deal out justice to all, and a man of great discernment of mind. The case came on about ten o'clock a. m. I was called upon to defend the prisoner. The prosecutors employed the best counsel they could get, and ransacked the town of Bainbridge and county of Chenango for witnesses that would swear hard enough to convict the prisoner; but they entirely failed.

Yes sir, let me say to you that not one blemish nor spot was found against his character. He came from that trial, notwithstanding the mighty efforts that were made to convict him of crime by his vigilant persecutors, with his character unstained by even the appearance of guilt. The trial closed about twelve o'clock at night. After a few moments deliberation, the court pronounced the words 'not guilty,' and the prisoner was discharged. But alas! the Devil not satisfied with his defeat, stirred up a man not unlike himself, who was more fit to dwell among the fiends of hell than to belong to the human family, to go to Colesville and get another writ, and take him to Broome County for another trial. They were sure they could send that boy to hell, or to Texas, they did not care which; and in half an hour after he was discharged by the court he was arrested again and on the way to Colesville for another trial. I was again called upon by his friends to defend him against his malignant persecutors, and clear him from the false charges they had preferred against him. I made every reasonable excuse I could, as I was nearly worn down through fatigue and want of sleep, as I had been engaged in lawsuits for two days and nearly the whole of two nights. But I saw the persecution was great against him. And here let me say, Mr. Chairman, singular as it may seem, while Mr. Knight was pleading with me to go, a peculiar impression or thought struck my mind, that I must go and defend him, for he was the Lord's anointed. I did not know what it meant, but thought I must go and clear the Lord's anointed. I said I would go; and started with as much faith as the apostles had when they could remove mountains, accompanied by Father Knight, who was like the old patriarchs that followed the ark of God to the city of David. We rode on until we came to the house of Hezekiah Peck, where a number of Mormon women had assembled, as I was informed, for the purpose of praying for the deliverance of the prophet of the Lord. The women came out to our wagon, and Mrs. Smith among the rest. O my God, sir; what were my feelings when I saw that woman who had but a few days before given herself, heart and hand, to be a consort for life, and that so soon her crimson cheeks must be wet with tears that came streaming from her eyes. Yes sir, it seemed that her very heartstrings would be broken with grief. My feelings, sir, were moved with pity and sorrow for the afflicted; and on the other hand they were wrought up to the highest pitch of indignation against those fiends of hell who had thus caused the innocent to suffer.

"The next morning about ten o'clock the court was organ-ized. The prisoner was to be tried by three justices of the peace, that his departure out of the county might be made sure. Neither talents nor money were wanting to insure them success. They employed the ablest lawyer in that county, and introduced twenty or thirty witnesses before dark, but proved nothing. They then sent out runners and ransacked the hills and vales, grog shops and ditches, and gathered together a company that looked as if they had come from hell and had been whipped by the soot boy thereof, which they brought forward to testify one after another, but with no better success than before, although they wrung and twisted into every shape, in trying to tell something that would criminate the prisoner. Nothing was proven against him whatever. Having got through with the examination of their witnesses about two o'clock, in the morning, the case was argued about two hours. There was not one particle of testimony against the prisoner. No sir, he came out like the three children from the fiery furnace, without the smell of fire upon his garments. The court delib-erated upon the case for half an hour with closed doors, and then we were called in. The court arraigned the prisoner and said: 'Mr. Smith, we have had your case under consid-eration, examined the testimony and find nothing to condemn you, and therefore you are discharged.' "—*Times and Seasons*, vol. 5, pp. 550, 551.

Shortly after this a revelation was received.[1]

[1] 1. The words of God which he spake unto Moses, at a time when Moses was caught up into an exceeding high mountain, and he saw God face to face, and he talked with him, and the glory of God was upon Moses; therefore Moses could endure his presence.

2. And God spake unto Moses, saying, Behold, I am the Lord God Almighty, and endless is my name, for I am without beginning of days or end of years; and is not this endless?

3. And, behold, thou art my son, wherefore look, and I will show thee

Persecution is no new thing, especially religious persecution. Bad men and impostors have been persecuted, but not
Persecution   more so than worthy reformers, honest men—men
no new thing. of God.   Then while vile reports and unrelenting
persecution are not conclusive evidence of the truth of Joseph

the workmanship of mine hands, but not all; for my works are without
end, and also my words, for they never cease; wherefore, no man can
behold all my works except he behold all my glory; and no man can behold all my glory, and afterwards remain in the flesh, on the earth.

4. And I have a work for thee, Moses, my son; and thou art in the
similitude of mine Only Begotten; and my Only Begotten is and shall be
the Savior, for he is full of grace and truth; but there is no God beside
me; and all things are present with me, for I know them all.

5. And now, behold, this one thing I show unto thee, Moses, my son;
for thou art in the world, and now I show it unto thee.

6. And it came to pass, that Moses looked and beheld the world upon
which he was created.   And as Moses beheld the world, and the ends
thereof, and all the children of men, which are and which were created;
of the same he greatly marveled, and wondered.   And the presence of
God withdrew from Moses, that his glory was not upon Moses; and
Moses was left unto himself; and as he was left unto himself, he fell unto
the earth.

7. And it came to pass, that it was for the space of many hours before
Moses did again receive his natural strength like unto man; and he said
unto himself, Now, for this cause, I know that man is nothing, which
thing I never had supposed; but now mine eyes have beheld God; but
not mine natural but my spiritual eyes, for mine natural eyes could not
have beheld, for I should have withered and died in his presence; but his
glory was upon me, and I beheld his face, for I was transfigured before
him.

8. And now it came to pass, that when Moses had said these words,
behold, Satan came tempting him, saying, Moses, son of man, worship
me.   And it came to pass that Moses looked upon Satan, and said, Who
art thou, for, behold, I am a son of God, in the similitude of his Only Begotten; and where is thy glory, that I should worship thee?   For, behold,
I could not look upon God except his glory should come upon me, and I
were transfigured before him.   But I can look upon thee in the natural
man.   Is it not so surely?

9. Blessed be the name of my God, for his Spirit hath not altogether
withdrawn from me; or else where is thy glory, for it is darkness unto
me, and I can judge between thee and God; for God said unto me, Worship God, for him only shalt thou serve.   Get thee hence, Satan, deceive
me not; for God said unto me, Thou art after the similitude of mine
Only Begotten.

10. And he also gave unto me commandment, when he called unto
me out of the burning bush, saying, Call upon God in the name of mine
Only Begotten, and worship me.

11. And again, Moses said, I will not cease to call upon God. I have
other things to inquire of him; for his glory has been upon me, and it is
glory unto me; wherefore, I can judge between him and thee.   Depart
hence, Satan.

12. And now, when Moses had said these words, Satan cried with a
loud voice, and went upon the earth, and commanded, saying, I am the
Only Begotten, worship me.

13. And it came to pass, that Moses began to fear exceedingly; and as

Smith's claims, they should not be received as sufficient evidence of his guilt.

We need not remind you that Jesus Christ and the prophets and apostles were bitterly maligned; that they suffered

Christ, prophets, and apostles persecuted. violence, abuse, and sometimes death, by legal decree or otherwise, at the hands of their relentless enemies; evidence of which is found in the Sacred Volume, and elsewhere. Never has there been such shocking stories told of Joseph Smith or the Latter Day Saints as were told (falsely no doubt) of the early Christians.

he began to fear, he saw the bitterness of hell; nevertheless, calling upon God he received strength, and he commanded, saying, Depart hence, Satan; for this one God only will I worship, which is the God of glory.

14. And now, Satan began to tremble, and the earth shook, and Moses received strength and called upon God in the name of the Only Begotten, saying to Satan, Depart hence.

15. And it came to pass, that Satan cried with a loud voice, with weeping, and wailing, and gnashing of teeth, and departed hence; yea, from the presence of Moses, that he beheld him not.

16. And now, of this thing Moses bore record; but because of wickedness, it is not had among the children of men.

17. And it came to pass, that when Satan had departed from the presence of Moses, that Moses lifted up his eyes unto heaven, being filled with the Holy Ghost, which beareth record of the Father and the Son; and calling upon the name of God, he beheld again his glory; for it rested upon him, and he heard a voice, saying, Blessed art thou, Moses, for I, the Almighty, have chosen thee, and thou shalt be made stronger than many waters; for they shall obey thy command even as if thou wert God.

18. And lo, I am with thee, even unto the end of thy days, for thou shalt deliver my people from bondage; even Israel my chosen.

19. And it came to pass, as the voice was still speaking, he cast his eyes and beheld the earth; yea, even all the face of it; and there was not a particle of it which he did not behold, discerning it by the Spirit of God. And he beheld also the inhabitants thereof, and there was not a soul which he beheld not, and he discerned them by the Spirit of God, and their numbers were great, even as numberless as the sand upon the sea shore. And he beheld many lands, and each land was called earth; and there were inhabitants on the face thereof.

20. And it came to pass, that Moses called upon God, saying, Tell me, I pray thee, why these things are so, and by what thou madest them? And, behold, the glory of God was upon Moses, so that Moses stood in the presence of God, and he talked with him face to face.

21. And the Lord God said unto Moses, For mine own purpose have I made these things. Here is wisdom, and it remaineth in me. And by the word of my power have I created them, which is mine Only Begotten Son, who is full of grace and truth. And worlds without number have I created, and I also created them for mine own purpose; and by the Son I created them, which is mine Only Begotten. And the first man of all men have I called Adam, which is many. But only an account of this earth, and the inhabitants thereof, give I unto you; for, behold, there are many worlds which have passed away by the word of my power; and there are many also which now stand, and numberless are they unto man;

4

Gibbon in his "Decline and Fall of the Roman Empire" relates the following:—

"These obscure teachers (such was the charge of malice and infidelity) are as mute in public as they are loquacious Gibbon on persecution. and dogmatical in private. Whilst they cautiously avoid the dangerous encounter of philosophers, they mingle with the rude and illiterate crowd, and insinuate themselves into those minds, whom their age, their sex, or their education, has the best disposed to receive the impression of superstitious terrors."—Vol. 1, p. 584, six vol. edition of 1850.

Again:—

"Those among them who condescended to mention the Christians, consider them only as obstinate and perverse enthusiasts, who exacted an implicit submission to their mysterious doctrines, without being able to produce a single argument that could engage the attention of men of sense and learning."—Ibid., p. 587.

"By embracing the faith of the gospel, the Christians incurred the supposed guilt of an unnatural and unpardonable offense. They dissolved the sacred ties of custom and education, violated the religious institutions of their country, and presumptuously despised whatever their fathers had

but all things are numbered unto me; for they are mine, and I know them.

22. And it came to pass, that Moses spake unto the Lord, saying, Be merciful unto thy servant, O God, and tell me concerning this earth, and the inhabitants thereof; and also the heavens, and then thy servant will be content.

23. And the Lord God spake unto Moses, saying, The heavens, they are many and they cannot be numbered unto man, but they are numbered unto me, for they are mine; and as one earth shall pass away, and the heavens thereof, even so shall another come; and there is no end to my works, neither to my words; for this is my work and my glory, to bring to pass the immortality, and eternal life of man.

24. And now, Moses, my son, I will speak unto you concerning this earth upon which you stand; and you shall write the things which I shall speak. And in a day when the children of men shall esteem my words as naught, and take many of them from the book which you shall write, behold, I will raise up another like unto you, and they shall be had again among the children of men, among even as many as shall believe.

25. These words were spoken unto Moses in the mount, the name of which shall not be known among the children of men. And now they are spoken unto you. Amen.—"Preface" to "The Holy Scriptures, Translated and Corrected by the Spirit of Revelation, by Joseph Smith, Jr., the Seer," pp. 7–9.

believed as true, or had reverenced as sacred."—Ibid., vol. 2, p. 6.

"The new converts seemed to renounce their family and country, that they might connect themselves in an indissoluble band of union with a peculiar society, which everywhere assumed a different character from the rest of mankind. Their gloomy and austere aspect, their abhorrence of the common business and pleasures of life, and their frequent predictions of impending calamities, inspired the Pagans with the apprehension of some danger, which would arise from the new sect, the more alarming as it was the more obscure. 'Whatever,' says Pliny, 'may be the principle of their conduct, their inflexible obstinacy appeared deserving of punishment.'

"The precautions with which the disciples of Christ performed the offices of religion were at first dictated by fear and necessity; but they were continued from choice. By imitating the awful secrecy which reigned in the Eleusinian mysteries, the Christians had flattered themselves that they should render their sacred institutions more respectable in the eyes of the Pagan world. But the event, as it often happens to the operations of subtle policy, deceived their wishes and their expectations. It was concluded, that they only concealed what they would have blushed to disclose. Their mistaken prudence afforded an opportunity for malice to invent, and for suspicious credulity to believe, the horrid tales which described the Christians as the most wicked of human kind, who practiced in their dark recesses every abomination that a depraved fancy could suggest, and who solicited the favor of their unknown God by the sacrifice of every moral virtue. There were many who pretended to confess or to relate the ceremonies of this abhorred society. It was asserted, 'that a newborn infant, entirely covered over with flour, was presented, like some mystic symbol of initiation, to the knife of the proselyte, who unknowingly inflicted many a secret and mortal wound on the innocent victim of his error; that as soon as the cruel deed was perpetrated, the sectaries drank up the blood, greedily tore asunder the quivering members, and pledged themselves to eternal secrecy, by a mutual consciousness of guilt. It was as confidently affirmed, that this inhuman sacrifice was succeeded by a suitable entertainment, in which intemperance served as a provocative to brutal lust; till, at the appointed moment, the lights were suddenly extinguished, shame was banished, nature was forgotten; and, as accident might direct, the darkness of the night was polluted by the incestuous commerce of sisters and brothers, of sons and of mothers.'"—Ibid., vol. 2, pp. 10, 11.

These things are almost too shocking to relate, yet such were the stories related of the early Christians by their persecutors. Satisfied as we are that these things are untrue, and slanders upon an innocent and virtuous people, we should not be deterred from an honest and thorough investigation by reports of similar nature told against other professed followers of the meek and lowly One.

Nor is this disposition to abuse, slander, and violently maltreat, confined to past ages. We are all historically acquainted with cruelties practiced under Puritan rules in our own boasted land of freedom. And subsequently men have maliciously misrepresented their coreligionists. As late as 1837 the *Baptist Banner* had this to say of Alexander Campbell:—

Modern persecution.

A. Campbell persecuted.

"But to be serious, we cannot believe that any good will follow this debate. But too much excitement is attempted to be gotten up against the Roman Catholics—an excitement bordering on intolerance. Could we feel assured, either from his course in this instance or from a retrospect of his past life, that Mr. Campbell sought this discussion solely to vindicate truth and expose error, and not ostentatiously to exhibit his tact in debate and to reap a pecuniary harvest by a new publication, we might feel less distrust of consequences, and should have some faint hope that probably good would ensue; but credulous, nay, stupid must be the man, who in looking over the circumstances which have concurred in originating this debate, can suppose that any religious or commendable motive prompted him to throw the gauntlet and provoke the controversy. In looking over his past career, a love of truth and a desire to promote the

peace and prosperity of Zion, have not been the prominent
traits which have marked his character and rendered conspicuous his course. We do not speak for other places, but
in Kentucky he has caused more serious injury to the cause
of religion, more disturbance, more wrangling, collision, and
division in society, in a few years, than in our humble judgment, the Catholics can ever do. But we forbear. The
debate will take place. The Campbellites will sip delicious
wisdom from the lips of their leader. A new impulse will
be given to their now drooping state. They will again
wage his high claims to competency to reform religion and
introduce the Millennium. And Mr. Campbell will have the
proud satisfaction of rendering great good—to himself by
the sale of another book! This will be about all that will
result from this discussion."—P. 59 of Campbell and Purcell
Debate, published by J. A. James & Co., Cincinnati, 1837.

John Wesley suffered relentless and bitter persecution in
his work of reformation. Canon Farrar says:—

"We might think it strange that the desire to preach the
gospel of Christ should invoke such deadly opposition, alike
John Wesley of the so-called respectable and religious classes,
persecu ed. and of the rude and ignorant multitude. Yet so
it was. . . . Every form of opposition, we are told, was tried
against him. 'Milldams were let out; church bells were
jangled; drunken fiddlers and ballad singers were hired;
organs pealed forth; drums were beaten;' street-venders,
clowns, drunken fops, and Papists were hired, and incited to
brawl or blow horns, so as to drown his voice. He was
struck in the face with sticks, he was cursed and groaned at,
pelted with stones, beaten to the ground, threatened with
murder, dragged and hustled hither and thither by drink-
ing, cursing, swearing, riotous mobs, who acted the part of
judge, jury, and executioner. 'Knock him down and kill
him at once,' was the shout of the brutal roughs who assaulted him at Wednesbury. On more than one occasion, a
mad or a baited bull was driven into the midst of his assemblies; the windows of the houses in which he stayed were
broken, and rioters burst their way even into his private
rooms. 'The men,' says Dr. Taylor, 'who commenced and

continued this arduous service—and they were scholars and gentleman—displayed a courage far surpassing that which carries the soldier through the hailstorm of the battlefield. Ten thousand might more easily be found who would confront a battery than two, who, with the sensitiveness of education about them, could (in that day) mount a table by the roadside, give out a Psalm, and gather a mob.'

"To face all this, and to face it day after day, and year by year, in England, in Scotland, in Wales, in Cornwall, in Ireland, required a supreme bravery, and persistence. Yet it needed even greater courage to meet hurricanes of abuse, and tornadoes of slander. Wesley had to face this also on all sides. The most popular actors of the day held him up to odium and ridicule in lewd comedies. Reams of calumny were written against him; shoals of pamphlets, full of virulence and falsehood, were poured forth from the press. The most simple, the most innocent, the most generous of men, he was called a smuggler, a liar, an immoral and designing intriguer, a Pope, a Jesuit, a swindler, the most notorious hypocrite living. The clergy, I grieve to say, led the way. Rowland Hill called Wesley 'a lying apostle, a designing wolf, a dealer in stolen wares,' and said that he was 'as unprincipled as a rook, and as silly as a jackdaw, first pilfering his neighbor's plumage, and then going proudly forth to display it to a laughing world.' Augustus Toplady said, among floods of other and worse abuse, that 'for thirty years he had been endeavoring to palm on his credulous followers his pernicious doctrines, with all the sophistry of a Jesuit, and the dictatorial authority of a Pope;' and described him as 'the most rancorous hater of the gospel system that ever appeared in England.' Bishop Lavington, of Exeter, denounced the Methodists as a dangerous and presumptuous sect, animated with an enthusiastical and fanatical spirit, and said that they were 'either innocent madmen or infamous cheats.'" — Archdeacon Farrar, D. D., in *The Contemporary Review.*—"From Palmyra to Independence," pp. 302-304.

Thus we see that to judge of a man, a people, or a cause, by reports, is unreliable, and should be unsatisfactory to all right-minded people. We only call attention to these things

historically to show the unreliability of this mode of judging, and not to reflect upon the parties referred
to. The reader will agree with us that in each
case referred to injustice was done by resorting to
foul slander and unhallowed persecution to accomplish what'
fair means and honorable controversy could not accomplish.
Such a course, to put it mildly, is a mistaken one. Allow us
to suggest that the opposition met by Joseph Smith and his
associates may have been caused by a like mistake.

Persecution a mistaken policy.

Joseph continues as follows:—

"Meantime, notwithstanding all the rage of our enemies,
still we had much consolation, and many things occurred to
strengthen our faith and cheer our hearts. After our return
from Colesville, the church there were. as might be expected, very anxious concerning our again visiting them,
during which time Sister Knight (wife of Newel Knight) had
a dream, which enabled her to say that we would visit them
that day, which really came to pass, for a few hours afterwards we arrived; and thus was our faith much strengthened, concerning dreams and visions in the last days,
foretold by the ancient prophet, Joel; and although we this
time were forced to seek safety from our enemies by flight,
yet did we feel confident that eventually we should come off
victorious, if we only continued faithful to him who had
called us forth from darkness into the marvelous light of the
everlasting gospel of our Lord Jesus Christ."—*Times and
Seasons,* vol. 4, p. 92.

After returning home a revelation was given to Joseph
Smith and Oliver Cowdery;[2] one to Emma Smith setting forth

---

[2] 1. Behold, thou wast called and chosen to write the Book of Mormon,
and to my ministry; and I have lifted thee up out of thy afflictions, and
have counseled thee, that thou hast been delivered from all thine enemies,
and thou hast been delivered from the powers of Satan, and from darkness! Nevertheless, thou art not excusable in thy transgressions; nevertheless go thy way and sin no more.

2. Magnify thine office; and after thou hast sowed thy fields and
secured them, go speedily unto the church which is in Colesville, Fayette, and Manchester, and they shall support thee; and I will bless them
both spiritually and temporally; but if they receive thee not, I will send
upon them a cursing instead of a blessing.

3. And thou shalt continue in calling upon God in my name, and writing the things which shall be given thee by the Comforter, and expound.

her office and calling and directing her to make a selection
of sacred hymns for use in the church;[3] also a revelation

ing all scriptures unto the church, and it shall be given thee, in the very
moment, what thou shalt speak and write; and they shall hear it, or I
will send unto them a cursing instead of a blessing.

4. For thou shalt devote all thy service in Zion. And in this thou
shalt have strength. Be patient in afflictions, for thou shalt have many;
but endure them, for lo, I am with you, even unto the end of thy days.
And in temporal labors thou shalt not have strength, for this is not thy
calling. Attend to thy calling and thou shalt have wherewith to magnify thine office, and to expound all scriptures. And continue in laying
on of the hands, and confirming the churches.

5. And thy brother Oliver shall continue in bearing my name before
the world, and also to the church. And he shall not suppose that he can
say enough in my cause; and lo, I am with him to the end. In me he
shall have glory, and not of himself, whether in weakness or in strength,
whether in bonds or free. And at all times and in all places, he shall
open his mouth and declare my gospel as with the voice of a trump, both
day and night. And I will give unto him strength such as is not known
among men.

6. Require not miracles, except I shall command you; except casting
out devils; healing the sick; and against poisonous serpents; and against
deadly poisons; and these things ye shall not do, except it be required of
you by them who desire it, that the scriptures might be fulfilled, for ye
shall do according to that which is written. And in whatsoever place ye
shall enter, and they receive you not, in my name, ye shall leave a cursing
instead of a blessing, by casting off the dust of your feet against them as
a testimony, and cleansing your feet by the wayside.

7. And it shall come to pass, that whosoever shall lay their hands upon
you by violence, ye shall command to be smitten in my name, and behold I will smite them according to your words, in mine own due time.
And whosoever shall go to law with thee shall be cursed by the law.
And thou shalt take no purse, nor scrip, neither staves, neither two coats,
for the church shall give unto thee in the very hour what thou needest
for food, and for raiment, and for shoes, and for money, and for scrip;
for thou art called to prune my vineyard with a mighty pruning, yea,
even for the last time. Yea, and also, all those whom thou hast ordained.
And they shall do even according to this pattern. Amen.

[3] 1. Hearken unto the voice of the Lord your God, while I speak unto
you, Emma Smith, my daughter, for verily I say unto you, All those who
receive my gospel are sons and daughters in my kingdom. A revelation
I give unto you concerning my will, and if thou art faithful and walk in
the paths of virtue before me, I will preserve thy life, and thou shalt receive an inheritance in Zion. Behold, thy sins are forgiven thee, and
thou art an elect lady, whom I have called. Murmur not because of the
things which thou hast not seen, for they are withheld from thee, and
from the world, which is wisdom in me in a time to come.

2. And the office of thy calling shall be for a comfort unto my servant
Joseph Smith, Jr., thy husband, in his afflictions, with consoling words,
in the spirit of meekness. And thou shalt go with him at the time of
his going, and be unto him for a scribe, while there is no one to
be a scribe for him, that I may send my servant Oliver Cowdery whithersoever I will. And thou shalt be ordained under his hand to expound
scriptures, and to exhort the church, according as it shall be given
thee by my Spirit; for he shall lay his hands upon thee, and thou shalt

to Joseph Smith, Oliver Cowdery, and John Whitmer.[4]

Joseph further writes:—

"Shortly after . . . Oliver Cowdery returned to Mr. Whitmer's, and I began to arrange and copy the revelations *Joseph copies revelations.* which we had received from time to time; in which I was assisted by John Whitmer, who now resided with me. Whilst thus (and otherwise at intervals) employed in the work appointed me, by my heavenly Father, I received a letter from Oliver Cowdery, the contents of which gave me both sorrow and uneasiness. Not *Receives letter from O. Cowdery.* having that letter now in my possession, I cannot, of course, give it here in full, but merely an extract of the most prominent parts, which I can yet, and expect long to remember. He wrote to inform me that he had discovered an error in one of the commandments: . . . 'And truly manifested by their works that they have received of the Spirit of Christ unto the remission of their sins.' The above quotation, he said, was erroneous, and added, I command you in the name of God to erase these words, that no priestcraft be amongst us!! I immediately wrote to him in reply, in which I asked him by

receive the Holy Ghost, and thy time shall be given to writing, and to learning much. And thou needest not fear, for thy husband shall support thee in the church; for unto them is his calling, that all things might be revealed unto them, whatsoever I will, according to their faith.

3. And verily I say unto thee, that thou shalt lay aside the things of this world, and seek for the things of a better. And it shall be given thee, also, to make a selection of sacred hymns, as it shall be given thee, which is pleasing unto me, to be had in my church; for my soul delighteth in the song of the heart; yea, the song of the righteous is a prayer unto me. And it shall be answered with a blessing upon their heads. Wherefore, lift up thy heart and rejoice, and cleave unto the covenants which thou hast made.

4. Continue in the spirit of meekness, and beware of pride. Let thy soul delight in thy husband, and the glory which shall come upon him. Keep my commandments continually, and a crown of righteousness thou shalt receive. And except thou do this, where I am you cannot come. And verily, verily I say unto you, that this is my voice unto all. Amen.

[4] 1. Behold, I say unto you, that you shall let your time be devoted to the studying of the scriptures, and to preaching, and to confirming the church at Colesville; and to performing your labors on the land, such as is required, until after you shall go to the west, to hold the next conference; and then it shall be made known what you shall do. And all things shall be done by common consent in the church, by much prayer and faith; for all things you shall receive by faith. Amen.

what authority he took upon him to command me to alter or erase, to add or diminish to or from a revelation or commandment from Almighty God. In a few days afterwards I visited him and Mr. Whitmer's family, where I found the family, in general, of his opinion concerning the words above quoted; and it was not without both labor and perseverance that I could prevail with any of them to reason calmly on the subject. However Christian Whitmer at length got convinced that it was reasonable, and according to scripture, and, finally, with his assistance, I succeeded in bringing, not only the Whitmer family, but also Oliver Cowdery, to acknowledge they had been in error, and that the sentence in dispute was in accordance with the rest of the commandments. And thus was their error rooted out, which having its rise in presumption and rash judgment, was the more particularly calculated (when once fairly understood) to teach each and all of us the necessity of humility and meekness before the Lord, that he might teach us of his ways, that we might walk in his paths, and live by every word that proceedeth forth from his mouth."—*Times and Seasons,* vol. 4, p. 108.

This little sketch of history is important as showing that at this early time they not only had their external, but also internal trials. It is valuable also as evidence that the men associated with Joseph Smith in that early time were not man worshipers under the absolute control of Joseph Smith, as has so often been asserted. They thought for themselves and dared express their thoughts. Though in this instance Oliver Cowdery's manner of expressing his convictions was rash, and calculated to wound, it does not appear that Joseph exhibited anything but a kindly spirit towards him; and when an understanding finally was reached, with commendable humility he confessed that the trial could be made useful to all in teaching a lesson of meekness and humility. There was no exhibition of that threatening, domineering spirit to be found in tyrants and oppressors. Neither was there that disposition to yield, for policy's sake, which sometimes characterizes the diplomat. It is a time to try his integrity and

Joseph's attitude in a peculiar trial.

courage. Through many severe trials and dangers, friends tried and true have stood by him, and showed by their unselfish sacrifices that they loved both himself and the cause in which he was engaged. Now some among the most faithful and devoted of these friends demand a concession. Shall it be granted? If not, will not his friends desert him? Will he not need henceforth to stand alone and alone meet the bitter and cruel denunciations of relentless persecutors? Not much is demanded—only erase one sentence and peace will be restored. If it is all a fraud this will not detract much from it. Why not erase it? Surely its loss will not be so much to his scheme as the loss of Cowdery and the Whitmers. But if he ever faltered he never betrayed it He was sorrowful and uneasy, but if he was angry he did not express it. Kindly, bravely, resolutely, he faced the situation. Foes were on the alert seeking to destroy his prospects, his character, aye, his life; and in addition to this there was a prospect of losing his friends—he can retain them by a concession. Realizing this situation more keenly than anyone without his experience can, he never faltered, but with a courage born of conviction and devotion to principle he declared this to be a part of a revelation from God. If friends should desert him and he be required to stand alone, still he would avow it. Friends, we submit for your consideration, Was his the act of an impostor, a coward, a sycophant, a hypocrite? or was it the act of a brave and true man, conscious of the truth of his position, and aware that the God whom he served would be with him, and stand for his defense?

The account given by Joseph continues:—

"Early in the month of August, Newel Knight and his wife paid us a visit, at my place, at Harmony, Pennsylvania, and as neither his wife nor himself had been as yet confirmed, it was proposed that we should confirm them, and partake together of the sacrament, before he and his wife should leave us. In order to prepare for this, I set out to go to procure some wine for the occasion, but had gone only a short distance when I was met by a heavenly messenger, and received the following revela-

Instruction on the sacrament.

tion; the first paragraph of which was written at this time.[s]

"In obedience to the above commandment we prepared some wine of our own make, and held our meeting, consisting only of five; viz., Newel Knight and his wife, myself and my wife, and John Whitmer. We partook together of the sac-

[s] 1. Listen to the voice of Jesus Christ, your Lord, your God, and your Redeemer, whose word is quick and powerful. For, behold, I say unto you, that it mattereth not what ye shall eat, or what ye shall drink, when ye partake of the sacrament, if it so be that ye do it with an eye single to my glory; remembering unto the Father my body which was laid down for you, and my blood which was shed for the remission of your sins; wherefore a commandment I give unto you, that you shall not purchase wine, neither strong drink of your enemies; wherefore you shall partake of none, except it is made new among you; yea, in this my Father's kingdom which shall be built up on the earth.

2. Behold, this is wisdom in me; wherefore marvel not, for the hour cometh that I will drink of the fruit of the vine with you on the earth, and with Moroni, whom I have sent unto you to reveal the Book of Mormon, containing the fullness of my everlasting gospel; to whom I have committed the keys of the record of the stick of Ephraim; and also with Elias, to whom I have committed the keys of bringing to pass the restoration of all things, or the restorer of all things spoken by the mouth of all the holy prophets since the world began, concerning the last days; and also John the son of Zacharias, which Zacharias he (Elias) visited and gave promise that he should have a son, and his name should be John, and he should be filled with the spirit of Elias; which John I have sent unto you, my servants, Joseph Smith, Jr., and Oliver Cowdery, to ordain you unto this first priesthood which you have received, that you might be called and ordained even as Aaron; and also Elijah, unto whom I have committed the keys of the power of turning the hearts of the fathers to the children and the hearts of the children to the fathers, that the whole earth may not be smitten with a curse; and also, with Joseph, and Jacob, and Isaac, and Abraham, your fathers; by whom the promises remain; and also with Michael, or Adam, the father of all, the prince of all, the ancient of days.

3. And also with Peter, and James, and John, whom I have sent unto you, by whom I have ordained you and confirmed you to be apostles and especial witnesses of my name, and bear the keys of your ministry; and of the same things which I revealed unto them; unto whom I have committed the keys of my kingdom, and a dispensation of the gospel for the last times; and for the fullness of times, in the which I will gather together in one all things, both which are in heaven and which are on earth; and also with all those whom my Father hath given me out of the world; wherefore lift up your hearts and rejoice, and gird up your loins, and take upon you my whole armor, that ye may be able to withstand the evil day, having done all ye may be able to stand. Stand, therefore, having your loins girt about with truth, having on the breastplate of righteousness, and your feet shod with the preparation of the gospel of peace, which I have sent mine angels to commit unto you, taking the shield of faith wherewith ye shall be able to quench all the fiery darts of the wicked; and take the helmet of salvation, and the sword of my Spirit, which I will pour out upon you, and my word which I reveal unto you, and be agreed as touching all things whatsoever ye ask of me, and be faithful until I come, and ye shall be caught up, that where I am ye shall be also. Amen.

rament, after which we confirmed these two sisters [persons] into the church, and spent the evening in a glorious manner. The Spirit of the Lord was poured out upon us; we praised the Lord God, and rejoiced exceedingly. About this time a

Joseph's wife's family turned against them. spirit of persecution began again to manifest itself against us in the neighborhood where I now resided, which was commenced by a man of the Methodist persuasion, who professed to be a minister of God, and whose name was ———. This man came to understand that my father-in-law and his family had promised us protection, and were friendly; and inquiring into the work, and knowing that if he could get him turned against me, my friends in that place would be but few, he accordingly went to visit my father-in-law, and told him falsehoods concerning me, of the most shameful nature, which turned the old gentleman and this family so much against us that they would no longer promise us protection nor believe our doctrines. Towards the latter end of August I (in company with John and David Whitmer, and my brother Hyrum Smith) visited the church at Colesville, New York. Well knowing the determined hostilities of our enemies in that quarter, and also knowing that it was our duty to visit the church, we had called upon our heavenly Father, in mighty prayer, that he would grant us an opportunity of meeting with them; that he would blind the eyes of our enemies, so that they would not know us, and that we might, on this occasion, return unmolested.

"Our prayers were not in vain, for when within a little distance of Mr. Knight's place we encountered a large com-

Enemies on the alert. pany at work upon the public road, amongst whom were several of our most bitter enemies. They looked earnestly at us, but not knowing us, we passed on without interruption. We that evening assembled the church, and confirmed them, partook of the sacrament, and held a happy meeting, having much reason to rejoice in the God of our salvation and sing hosannas to his holy name. Next morning we set out on our return home, and although our enemies had offered a reward of five dollars to anyone who would give them information of our arrival, yet did we get clear out of the neighborhood, without the least annoyance, and arrived at home in safety. Some few days afterwards, however, Newel Knight came to my place, and from him we learned that very shortly after our departure the mob had come to know of our having been there, when they immediately collected together and had threatened the brethren and very much annoyed them during all that day. Meantime Brother Knight had come with his wagon, prepared to move my family, etc., etc., to Fayette, New York. Mr. Whitmer having heard of the persecutions which had been gotten up against us at Harmony, Pennsylvania, had invited us to go and live with him; and during the last week of August we arrived at Fayette, amidst the congratulations of our brethren and friends. To our great grief, however, we soon found that Satan had been lying in wait to deceive,

Hiram Page deceived by a seer stone
and seeking whom he might devour. Brother Hiram Page had got in his possession a certain stone, by which he had obtained to certain revelations, concerning the upbuilding of Zion, the order of the church, etc., etc., all of which were entirely at variance with the order of God's house, as laid down in the New Testament, as well as in our late revelations. As a conference meeting had been appointed for the first day of September, I thought it wisdom not to do much more than to converse with the brethren on the subject, until the conference should meet. Finding, however, that many, (especially the Whitmer family and Oliver Cowdery,) were believing much in the thing set forth by this stone, we thought best to inquire of the Lord, concerning so important a matter."—*Times and Seasons*, vol. 4, pp. 117–119.

In answer to this inquiry a revelation was received.[*] It will be seen that in the above revelation provision is made

Mission to the West.
for extending the borders of the church into the western country, the presenting of the record of their fathers to the Lamanites (Indians), and the building of

---

[*] 1. Behold, I say unto thee, Oliver, that it shall be given unto thee that thou shalt be heard by the church in all things whatsoever thou shalt teach them by the Comforter, concerning the revelations and commandments which I have given.

the city of Zion somewhere in the West. Each of these is an event of great importance and will receive attention in appropriate time and place.

Joseph's wife's family had now been turned against them, and she was henceforth to be a stranger in her father's Revelation to house, and to follow the fortunes of her husband Emma Smith. through dangers sufficient to appall the stoutest heart. How opportune was the revelation given a short time before to fortify her for this, to her, unforeseen event! When we consider that this revelation was given to a young woman so soon to be banished from the home of her youth, Its peculiar whose tender heart was to be almost broken by significance. being ruthlessly banished from the arms and the love of parents, brothers, and sisters, how appropriate are

2. But, behold, verily, verily I say unto thee, No one shall be appointed to receive commandments and revelations in this church excepting my servant Joseph Smith, Jr., for he receiveth them even as Moses; and thou shalt be obedient unto the things which I shall give unto him, even as Aaron, to declare faithfully the commandments and revelations, with power and authority unto the church. And if thou art led at any time by the Comforter to speak or teach, or at all times by the way of commandment unto the church, thou mayest do it. But thou shalt not write by way of commandment, but by wisdom; and thou shalt not command him who is at thy head, and at the head of the church, for I have given him the keys of the mysteries and the revelations, which are sealed, until I shall appoint unto them another in his stead.

3. And now, behold, I say unto you that you shall go unto the Lamanites, and preach my gospel unto them; and inasmuch as they receive thy teachings, thou shalt cause my church to be established among them, and thou shalt have revelations, but write them not by way of commandment. And now, behold, I say unto you, that it is not revealed, and no man knoweth where the city shall be built, but it shall be given hereafter. Behold, I say unto you that it shall be on the borders by the Lamanites.

4. Thou shalt not leave this place until after the conference, and my servant Joseph shall be appointed to preside over the conference by the voice of it, and what he saith to thee thou shalt tell. And again, thou shalt take thy brother Hiram Page between him and thee alone, and tell him that those things which he hath written from that stone are not of me, and Satan deceiveth him; for, behold, these things have not been appointed unto him; neither shall anything be appointed unto any of this church contrary to the church covenants, for all things must be done in order and by common consent in the church, by the prayer of faith.

5. And thou shalt assist to settle all these things, according to the covenants of the church, before thou shalt take thy journey among the Lamanites. And it shall be given thee from the time thou shalt go, until the time thou shalt return, what thou shalt do. And thou must open thy mouth at all times, declaring my gospel with the sound of rejoicing. Amen.

the words, "And thou needest not fear, for thy husband shall support thee in the church;" "Let thy soul delight in thy husband, and the glory which shall come upon him"!

The event of his going and her duty in the emergency are clearly pointed out in the following: "And thou shalt go with him at the time of his going," etc.

That this noble woman faithfully fulfilled her obligations and duties towards her husband is attested by John Taylor,

John Taylor's tribute.

who knew her long and well. In an editorial, in the *Times and Seasons*, January 15, 1845, he wrote:—

"Suppose we say a word concerning the 'prophet's wife,' Mrs. Emma Smith; she honored her husband while living, and she will never knowingly dishonor his good name while his martyred blood mingles with mother earth!"

This also from History of Joseph Smith, in *Millennial Star*, volume 19, pages 695, 696, language used by him dur-

Joseph's words of praise for his wife.

ing his forced absence from home during the trouble of 1842, pays a touching and fitting tribute to the faithfulness of this noble woman and affectionate wife:—

"How glorious were my feelings when I met that faithful and friendly band, on the night of the eleventh, on Thursday, on the island at the mouth of the slough, between Zarahemla and Nauvoo: with what unspeakable delight, and what transports of joy swelled my bosom, when I took by the hand, on that night, my beloved Emma—she that was my wife, even the wife of my youth, and the choice of my heart. Many were the revibrations of my mind when I contemplated for a moment the many scenes we had been called to pass through, the fatigues and the toils, the sorrows and sufferings, and the joys and consolations, from time to time, which had strewed our paths and crowned our board. Oh what a commingling of thought filled my mind for the moment, again she is here, even in the seventh trouble—undaunted, firm, and unwavering—unchangeable, affectionate Emma."

We record these tributes of praise to the honored memory of Emma Smith here in connection with the event that exiled her from her father's house because we believe her

Your mother

Emma Smith

(From a portrait taken in her seventieth year.)

to have been worthy of all commendation and praise, and ~~Emma 'mith's worthiness.~~ because her name has been traduced by those who should have been her friends, but against whose dishonorable acts her very existence was a living protest.

In her youth she gave her heart and hand to a poor, illiterate young man. By this act she invited the displeasure of ~~Incidents of her life.~~ her family. For a brief season they received her back, then turned from her again, and she accompanied her husband to the western wilds. They resided for a season in Ohio, then farther west we see her standing side by side with her companion while surrounded by a hostile foe. Again we behold her, as in tears and bitter anguish she sees her husband torn from her by a ruthless mob and dragged away to prison and prospective death. She is left in poverty and distress, and being no longer able to remain near her husband because of the cruel edict of an inhuman executive, she turns her face eastward and with her little children faces the pitiless winter storm. On foot she crosses the ice of the Father of Waters, her two youngest children in her arms, the other two clinging to her dress. Then in anguish and suspense she awaits tidings from her husband, whom she has left in a dungeon surrounded by cruel foes. If in all this she ever murmured or faltered in her devotion we know it not. At length he joins her and a brief season of repose is granted them, during which she sees her husband rise to eminence and distinction, and she, as she was commanded, delights in the glory that came upon him. But alas! this is only the calm before the storm. Again the heavy, cruel hand of persecution is upon them, and upon a calm summer day they bear to her home the mutilated body of her murdered husband. Thousands pass the bier, and look for the last time on the face of the honored dead. Then she gathers her children around that silent form, and looks upon those calm lips which had in time of trouble pronounced those words so full of pathos and love, "My beloved Emma —she that was my wife, even the wife of my youth, and the choice of my heart. . . . Again she is here, even in the seventh trouble—undaunted, firm, and unwavering—unchangeable, affectionate Emma;" and from her full heart cries, "My husband, Oh! my husband; have they taken you from me, at last!" Shall this noble woman, this faithful wife, this loving mother, this devoted and humble saint, be denied an honorable mention in history, especially since an effort has been made by the vile traducer of the pure and the good to tarnish her fair name? Not while a sense of justice wields the pen, or there remains in the human breast a love for the good and the brave. Was it not her loving hand, her consoling and comforting words, her unswerving integrity, fidelity, and devotion, her wise counsel, that assisted to make this latterday work a success? If God raised up a Joseph as a prophet and a restorer of gospel truth, then did he also raise up an Emma as an help meet for him.

Noble woman! rest in peace! When you meet your traducers at the bar of God, justice will be triumphant. Then, if not till then, will your virtuous name be honored, and proper credit be given for your unselfish sacrifice and your labor of love!

During the month of August there was another revelation given.[7]

[7] 1. Listen to the voice of Jesus Christ, your Redeemer, the great I AM, whose arm of mercy hath atoned for your sins, who will gather his people even as a hen gathereth her chickens under her wings, even as many as will hearken to my voice, and humble themselves before me, and call upon me in mighty prayer. Behold, verily, verily I say unto you, that at this time your sins are forgiven you, therefore ye receive these things; but remember to sin no more, lest perils shall come upon you.

2. Verily I say unto you, that ye are chosen out of the world to declare my gospel with the sound of rejoicing, as with the voice of a trump; lift up your hearts and be glad, for I am in your midst, and am your advocate with the Father; and it is his good will to give you the kingdom; and as it is written, Whatsoever ye shall ask in faith, being united in prayer according to my command, ye shall receive; and ye are called to bring to pass the gathering of mine elect, for mine elect hear my voice and harden not their hearts; wherefore the decree hath gone forth from the Father that they shall be gathered in unto one place, upon the face of this land, to prepare their hearts, and be prepared in all things, against the day when tribulation and desolation are sent forth upon the wicked; for the hour is nigh, and the day soon at hand, when the earth is ripe; and all the proud, and they that do wickedly, shall be as stubble, and I will burn them up, saith the Lord of Hosts, that wickedness shall not be upon the earth; for the hour is nigh, and that which was spoken by mine apostles must be fulfilled; for as they spoke, so shall it come to pass; for I will reveal myself from heaven with power and great glory, with all the hosts thereof, and dwell in righteousness with men on earth a thousand years, and the wicked shall not stand.

On September 1 the conference before referred to met and
Conference. the difficulty occasioned by Hiram Page being
deceived by a seer stone was adjusted to the satisfaction of all. Of this Joseph writes:—

"At length our conference assembled; the subject of the

3. And again, verily, verily I say unto you, and it hath gone forth in a
firm decree, by the will of the Father, that mine apostles, the twelve
which were with me in my ministry at Jerusalem, shall stand at my
right hand, at the day of my coming, in a pillar of fire, being clothed
with robes of righteousness, with crowns upon their heads, in glory even
as I am, to judge the whole house of Israel, even as many as have loved
me and kept my commandments, and none else; for a trump shall sound,
both long and loud, even as upon Mount Sinai, and all the earth shall
quake, and they shall come forth, yea, even the dead which died in me,
to receive a crown of righteousness, and to be clothed upon, even as I
am, to be with me, that we may be one.

4. But, behold, I say unto you, that before this great day shall come,
the sun shall be darkened, and the moon shall be turned into blood, and
the stars shall fall from heaven; and there shall be greater signs in
heaven above, and in the earth beneath; and there shall be weeping and
wailing among the hosts of men; and there shall be a great hailstorm
sent forth to destroy the crops of the earth; and it shall come to pass,
because of the wickedness of the world, that I will take vengeance upon
the wicked, for they will not repent; for the cup of mine indignation is
full; for, behold, my blood shall not cleanse them if they hear me not.

5. Wherefore, I, the Lord God, will send forth flies upon the face of
the earth, which shall take hold of the inhabitants thereof, and shall eat
their flesh, and shall cause maggots to come in upon them, and their
tongues shall be stayed that they shall not utter against me, and their
flesh shall fall from off their bones, and their eyes from their sockets;
and it shall come to pass that the beasts of the forests and the fowls of
the air shall devour them up; and that great and abominable church,
which is the whore of all the earth, shall be cast down by devouring fire,
according as it is spoken by the mouth of Ezekiel the prophet, which
spoke of these things, which have not come to pass, but surely must, as I
live, for abomination shall not reign.

6. And again, verily, verily I say unto you, that when the thousand
years are ended, and men again begin to deny their God, then will I
spare the earth but for a little season; and the end shall come, and the
heaven and the earth shall be consumed, and pass away, and there shall
be a new heaven and a new earth; for all old things shall pass away, and
all things shall become new, even the heaven and the earth, and all the
fullness thereof, both men and beasts, the fowls of the air, and the fishes
of the sea; and not one hair, neither mote, shall be lost, for it is the
workmanship of mine hand.

7. But, behold, verily I say unto you, Before the earth shall pass
away, Michael, mine archangel, shall sound his trump, and then shall all
the dead awake, for their graves shall be opened, and they shall come
forth; yea, even all; and the righteous shall be gathered on my right
hand unto eternal life; and the wicked on my left hand will I be
ashamed to own before the Father; wherefore I will say unto them,
Depart from me ye cursed into everlasting fire, prepared for the Devil
and his angels.

8. And now, behold, I say unto you, Never at any time, have I declared

stone mentioned in a previous number, was discussed, and
Hiram Page
matter ad-
justed. after considerable investigation, Brother Page, as
well as the whole church, who were present, re-
nounced the said stone, and all things connected
therewith, much to our mutual satisfaction and happiness.

"We now partook of the sacrament, confirmed and

from my own mouth that they should return, for where I am they cannot come, for they have no power; but remember that all my judgments
are not given unto men; and as the words have gone forth out of my
mouth, even so shall they be fulfilled; that the first shall be last, and that
the last shall be first in all things, whatsoever I have created by the word
of my power, which is the power of my Spirit; for by the power of my
Spirit, created I them; yea, all things both spiritual and temporal:
firstly spiritual, secondly temporal, which is the beginning of my work;
and again, firstly temporal, and secondly spiritual, which is the last of
my work; speaking unto you that you may naturally understand, but
unto myself my works have no end, neither beginning; but it is given
unto you that ye may understand, because ye have asked it of me and
are agreed.

9. Wherefore, verily I say unto you, that all things unto me are spiritual, and not at any time have I given unto you a law which was temporal,
neither any man, nor the children of men; neither Adam your father,
whom I created; behold, I gave unto him that he should be an agent
unto himself; and I gave unto him commandment, but no temporal commandment gave I unto him; for my commandments are spiritual; they
are not natural, nor temporal, neither carnal nor sensual.

10. And it came to pass, that Adam being tempted of the Devil, for,
behold, the Devil was before Adam, for he rebelled against me, saying,
Give me thine honor, which is my power; and also a third part of the
hosts of heaven turned he away from me because of their agency; and
they were thrust down, and thus became the Devil and his angels; and,
behold, there is a place prepared for them from the beginning, which
place is hell; and it must needs be that the Devil should tempt the children of men, or they could not be agents unto themselves, for if they
never should have bitter, they could not know the sweet.

11. Wherefore, it came to pass, that the Devil tempted Adam and he
partook the forbidden fruit, and transgressed the commandment, wherein
he became subject to the will of the Devil, because he yielded unto
temptation; wherefore, I the Lord God caused that he should be cast
out from the garden of Eden, from my presence, because of his transgression; wherein he became spiritually dead; which is the first death,
even that same death, which is the last death, which is spiritual, which
shall be pronounced upon the wicked when I shall say, Depart ye cursed.

12. But, behold, I say unto you, that I, the Lord God, gave unto Adam
and unto his seed, that they should not die as to the temporal death,
until I, the Lord God, should send forth angels to declare unto them repentance and redemption through faith on the name of mine only
begotten Son; and thus did I, the Lord God, appoint unto man the days
of his probation; that by his natural death, he might be raised in
immortality unto eternal life, even as many as would believe, and they
that believe not, unto eternal damnation; for they cannot be redeemed
from their spiritual fall, because they repent not, for they will love darkness rather than light, and their deeds are evil, and they receive their
wages of whom they list to obey.

ordained many, and attended to a great variety of church business on that and the following day, during which time we had much of the power of God manifested amongst us; the Holy Ghost came upon us, and filled us with joy unspeakable; and peace, and faith, and hope, and charity abounded in our midst.

"During the conference, which contin e l three days, the utmost harmony prevailed, and all things were settled satisfactory to all present, and a desire was manifested by all the saints to go forward and labor with all their powers to spread the great and glorious principles of truth, which had been revealed by our heavenly Father. A number were baptized during the conference and the work of the Lord spread and prevailed. At this time a great desire was manifested by several of the elders respecting the remnants of the house of Joseph, the Lamanites, residing in the West; knowing that the purposes of God were great to that people, and hoping that the time had come when the promises of the Almighty in regard to that people were about to be accomplished, and that they would receive the gospel and enjoy its blessings."—*Times and Seasons*, vol. 4, pp. 146, 172.

Before separating another revelation was received,[8] and

13. But, behold, I say unto you, that little children are redeemed from the foundation of the world, through mine Only Begotten; wherefore they cannot sin, for power is not given unto Satan to tempt little children, until they begin to become accountable before me; for it is given unto them even as I will, according to mine own pleasure, that great things may be required at the hand of their fathers.

14. And again I say unto you, that whoso having knowledge, have I not commanded to repent? and he that hath no understanding, it remaineth in me to do according as it is written. And now, I declare no more unto you at this time. Amen.

8 1. Behold, I say unto you, David, that you have feared man and have not relied on me for strength, as you ought; but your mind has been on the things of the earth more than on the things of me, your Maker, and the ministry whereunto you have been called; and you have not given heed unto my Spirit, and to those who were set over you, but have been persuaded by those whom I have not commanded; wherefore, you are left to inquire for yourself, at my hand, and ponder upon the things which you have received. And your home shall be at your father's house, until I give unto you further commandments. And you shall attend to the ministry in the church, and before the world, and in the regions round about. Amen.

2. Behold, I say unto you, Peter, that you shall take your journey with your brother Oliver, for the time has come, that it is expedient in me,

soon after a revelation was also received for Thomas B. Marsh. [9]

In October a revelation was given appointing P. P. Pratt and Z. Peterson to accompany O. Cowdery west. [10]

that you shall open your mouth to declare my gospel; therefore, fear not but give heed unto the words and advice of your brother, which he shall give you. And be you afflicted in all his afflictions, ever lifting up your heart unto me in prayer, and faith, for his and your deliverance; for I have given unto him power to build up my church among the Lamanites; and none have I appointed to be his counselor, over him, in the church, concerning church matters, except it is his brother Joseph Smith, Jr. Wherefore, give heed unto these things, and be diligent in keeping my commandments, and you shall be blessed unto eternal life. Amen.

3. Behold, I say unto you, my servant John, that thou shalt commence from this time forth to proclaim my gospel, as with the voice of a trump. And your labor shall be at your brother Philip Burrough's, and in that region round about; yea, wherever you can be heard, until I command you to go from hence. And your whole labor shall be in Zion, with all your soul, from henceforth; yea, you shall ever open your mouth in my cause, not fearing what man can do, for I am with you. Amen.

[9] 1. Thomas, my son, blessed are you because of your faith in my work. Behold, you have had many afflictions because of your family: nevertheless I will bless you, and your family; yea, your little ones, and the day cometh that they will believe and know the truth and be one with you in my church.

2. Lift up your heart and rejoice, for the hour of your mission is come; and your tongue shall be loosed, and you shall declare glad tidings of great joy unto this generation. You shall declare the things which have been revealed to my servant Joseph Smith, Jr. You shall begin to preach from this time forth; yea, to reap in the field which is white already to be burned; therefore, thrust in your sickle with all your soul; and your sins are forgiven you; and you shall be laden with sheaves upon your back, for the laborer is worthy of his hire. Wherefore your family shall live.

3. Behold, verily I say unto you, Go from them only for a little time, and declare my word, and I will prepare a place for them; yea, I will open the hearts of the people and they will receive you. And I will establish a church by your hand; and you shall strengthen them and prepare them against the time when they shall be gathered. Be patient in afflictions, revile not against those that revile. Govern your house in meekness, and be steadfast.

4. Behold, I say unto you, that you shall be a physician unto the church, but not unto the world, for they will not receive you. Go your way whithersoever I will, and it shall be given you by the Comforter what you shall do, and whither you shall go. Pray always, lest you enter into temptation, and lose your reward. Be faithful unto the end, and lo, I am with you. These words are not of man nor of men, but of me, even Jesus Christ, your Redeemer, by the will of the Father. Amen.

[10] 1. And now concerning my servant Parley P. Pratt, behold, I say unto him, that as I live I will that he shall declare my gospel and learn of me, and be meek and lowly of heart; and that which I have appointed unto him, is that he shall go with my servants Oliver Cowdery and

Peter Whitmer, Jr., into the wilderness, among the Lamanites; and Ziba Peterson, also, shall go with them, and I myself will go with them and be in their midst: and I am their Advocate with the Father, and nothing shall prevail. And they shall give heed to that which is written and pretend to no other revelation, and they shall pray always that I may unfold them to their understanding; and they shall give heed unto these words and trifle not, and I will bless them. Amen.

CHAPTER 8.

1830.

THIS mission to the West was one of the most important events in the early history of the church. It resulted in the establishment of the church in Kirtland, Ohio, where some of the most thrilling events of the age transpired, and where yet the Temple stands as a monument to their faithfulness and patient endurance. Here the leading quorums of the church were organized; and here were found some of the men who were destined to become prominent in the church and her councils. Here in Northern Ohio were found, among others who were afterwards identified with the history of the church, Sidney Rigdon, Frederick G. Williams, Orson Hyde, Lyman Wight, Luke S. and Lyman E. Johnson, Edward Partridge, and Newel K. Whitney.

Importance of the mission to the West.

The missionaries also proceeded west as far as Independence, Missouri, and into the Territory of Kansas, preaching by the way to many, including some tribes of Indians.

Of this mission Joseph Smith writes:—

"Immediately on receiving this revelation, preparations were made for the journey of the brethren therein designated, to the borders of the Lamanites, and a copy of the revelation was given them. Having got ready for their journey, they bade adieu to their brethren and friends, and commenced their journey, preaching by the

Missionaries start West.

way, and leaving a sealing testimony behind them, lifting up their voice like a trump in the different villages through which they passed.   They continued their journey until they came to Kirtland, Ohio, where they tarried some time, there being quite a number in that place who believed their testimony and came forward and obeyed the gospel.   Among the number was Elder Sidney Rigdon, and a large portion of the church over which he presided.

Arrive at Kirtland.

Present their testimony to S. Rigdon and others.

"As there has been a great rumor, and many false statements have been given to the world respecting Elder Rigdon's connection with the Church of Jesus Christ, it is necessary that a correct account of the same be given, so that the public mind may be disabused on the subject.   I shall therefore proceed to give a brief history of his life down, from authentic sources, as also an account of his connection with the church of Christ.

Sketch of the life of Rigdon.

"Sidney Rigdon was born in Saint Clair Township, Allegheny County, State of Pennsylvania, on the 19th of February, A. D. 1793, and was the youngest son of William and Nancy Rigdon.   William Rigdon, his father, was a native of Hartford County, State of Maryland; was born A. D. 1743, and died May 26, A. D. 1810, in the sixty-second [seventh] year of his age.   William Rigdon was the son of Thomas Baker and Ann Lucy Rigdon.   Thomas Baker Rigdon was a native of the State of Maryland, and was the son of Thomas Baker Rigdon, who came from Great Britain.

"Ann Lucy Rigdon, grandmother of Sidney Rigdon, was a native of Ireland, and emigrated to the city of Boston, Massachusetts, and was there married to Thomas Baker Rigdon.   Nancy Rigdon's mother was a native of Freehold, Monmouth County, New Jersey; was born March 16, 1759, and died October 3, 1839, and was the eldest daughter of Bryant Gallaher, who was a native of Ireland.   Elizabeth Gallaher, mother to the said Nancy Rigdon, was the second wife of the said Bryant Gallaher, and whose maiden name was Reed, and who was a native of Monmouth County, New Jersey.   Their parents were natives of Scotland.

"His father, William Rigdon, was a farmer, and he removed from the State of Maryland some time prior to his
marriage; to the State of Pennsylvania; and his mother had
removed some time prior to that, from the State of New
Jersey to the same State; where they were married, and
continued to follow agricultural pursuits.   They had four
children; viz., three sons, and one daughter.   The eldest,
sons, were called Carvil, Loami, and Sidney, the subject of
this brief history.   The fourth, a daughter, named Lucy.

"Nothing very remarkable took place in the youthful days
of Elder Rigdon; suffice it to say that he continued at home
with his parents, following the occupation of a farmer until
he was seventeen years of age, when his father died; after
which event he continued on the same farm with his mother,
until he was twenty-six years of age.   In his twenty-fifth
year he connected himself with a society which in that country was called Regular Baptists.   The church he united with
was at that time under the charge of the Rev. David Phillips,
a clergyman from Wales.   The year following he left the
farm and went to reside with the Rev. Andrew Clark, a minister of the same order.   During his continuance with him
he received a license to preach in that society, and commenced from that time to preach, and returned to farming
occupations no more.   This was in March, 1819.

"In the month of May, of the same year, he left the State
of Pennsylvania and went to Trumbull County, State of
Ohio, and took up his residence at the house of Adamson
Bentley, a preacher of the same faith.   This was in July of
same year.   While there he became acquainted with Phebe
Brook, to whom he was married on the 12th of June, A. D.
1820.   She was a native of the State of New Jersey, Bridge-
town, Cumberland County, and had previously removed to
Trumbull County, Ohio.   After his marriage he continued
to preach in that district of country until November, 1821,
when he was requested by the First Baptist Church of the
city of Pittsburg to take the pastoral charge of said church,
which invitation he accepted, and in February, A. D. 1822,
he left Warren, Trumbull County, and removed to that city
and entered immediately upon his pastoral duties, and con-

tinued to preach to that church with considerable success. At the time he commenced his labors in that church, and for some time before, the church was in a very low state and much confusion existed in consequence of the conduct of their former pastor. However, soon after Elder Rigdon commenced his labors there was a pleasing change effected, for by his incessant labors and his peculiar style of preaching the church was crowded with anxious listeners. The number of members rapidly increased, and it soon became one of the most respectable churches in that city. He was now a popular minister, and was much respected in that city, and all classes and persuasions sought his society. After he had been in that place some time, his mind was troubled and much perplexed with the idea that the doctrines maintained by that society were not altogether in accordance with the Scriptures. This thing continued to agitate his mind, more and more, and his reflections on these occasions were peculiarly trying; for according to his views of the word of God no other church that he was acquainted with was right, or with whom he could associate; consequently, if he was to disavow the doctrine of the church with whom he was then associated, he knew of no other way of obtaining a livelihood except by mental [manual?] labor, and at that time had a wife and three children to support.

"On the one hand was wealth, popularity, and honor; on the other appeared nothing but poverty and hard labor. But notwithstanding his great ministerial success and the prospect of ease and affluence, (which frequently swerve the mind, and have an undue influence on too many who wear the sacred garb of religion, who for the sake of popularity and of wealth can calm and lull to rest their conscientious scruples, and succumb to the popular church,) yet his mind rose superior to all these considerations. Truth was his pursuit, and for truth he was prepared to make every sacrifice in his power. After mature deliberation, deep reflection, and solemn prayer to his heavenly Father, the resolve was made and the important step was taken; and in the month of August, A. D. 1824, after laboring among that people two years and six months, he made known his determination, to withdraw from the church, as he could no longer uphold the doctrines taught and maintained by it. This announcement was like a clap of thunder. Amazement seized the congregation, which was then collected, which at last gave way in a flood of tears. It would be in vain to attempt to describe the feelings of the church on that occasion, who were zealously attached to their beloved pastor, or the feelings of their minister. On his part it was indeed a struggle of principle over affection and kindness.

"There was at the time of his separation from that church a gentleman of the name of Alexander Campbell, who was formerly from Ireland, and who has since obtained considerable notoriety in the religious world, who was then a member of the same association, and who afterwards separated from it. There was also another gentleman, by the name of Walter Scott, a Scotchman by birth, who was a member of the Scandinavian Church, in that city, and who separated from the same about that time.

"Prior to these separations, Mr. Campbell resided in Bethany, Brook County, Virginia, where he published a monthly periodical, called the 'Christian Baptist.' After they had separated from the different churches these gentlemen were on terms of the greatest friendship, and frequently met together to discuss the subject of religion, being yet undetermined respecting the principles of the doctrine of Christ, or what course to pursue. However, from this connection sprung up a new church in the world, known by the name of 'Campbellites;' they call themselves 'Disciples.' The reason why they were called Campbellites was in consequence of Mr. Campbell's publishing the periodical above mentioned, and it being the means through which they communicated their sentiments to the world. Other than this, Mr. Campbell was no more the originator of that sect than Elder Rigdon.

"Having now retired from the ministry, and having no way by which to sustain his family besides his own industry, he was necessitated to find other employment in order to provide for his maintenance, and for this purpose he engaged in the humble capacity of a journeyman tanner, in that city, and followed his new employment, without murmuring, for two years, during which time he both saw and experienced that by resigning his pastoral vocations in that city and engaging in the humble occupation of a tanner he had lost many who once professed the greatest friendship, and who manifested the greatest love for his society; that when he was seen by them in the garb suited to the employment of a tanner, there was no longer that freedom, courtesy, and friendship manifested; that many of his former friends became estranged and looked upon him with coolness and indifference too obvious to admit of deception. To a well-regulated and enlightened mind—to one who soars above the arbitrary and vain lines of distinction which pride or envy may draw, such conduct appears ridiculous, while at the same time it cannot but cause feelings of a peculiar nature in those who for their honesty and integrity of heart have brought themselves into situations to be made the subjects of it.

"These things, however, did not affect his mind so as to change his purpose. He had counted the cost before his separation, and had made his mind known to his wife, who cheerfully shared his sorrow and humiliation, believing that all things would work together for their good, being conscious that what they had done was for conscience' sake and in the fear of the Lord.

"After laboring for two years as a tanner, he removed to Bainbridge, Geauga County, Ohio, where it was known that he had been a preacher, and had gained considerable distinction as a public speaker, and the people soliciting him to preach, he complied with their request. From this time forward, he devoted himself to the work of the ministry, confining himself to no creed, but held up the Bible as the rule of faith, and advocating those doctrines which had been the subject of his, and Mr. Campbell's investigations; viz.: Repentance and baptism, for the remission of sins.

"He continued to labor in that vicinity one year, and during that time, his former success attended his labors. Large numbers invariably attended his meetings. While he labored in that neighborhood, he was instrumental in building up a large and respectable church, in the town of Mantua, Portage County, Ohio. The doctrines which he advanced being new, public attention was awakened, and great excitement pervaded throughout that whole section of country, and frequently the congregations which he addressed, were so large that it was impossible to make himself audible to all. The subjects he proposed were presented in such an impressive manner to the congregations, that those who were unbiased by bigotry and prejudice, had to exclaim, 'we never heard it in this manner before.' There were some, however, that opposed the doctrines which he advanced, but not with that opposition which ever ought to characterize the noble and ingenious. Those by whom he was opposed, well knew that an honorable and public investigation, would inevitably discover the weakness and fatality of their doctrines; consequently they shunned it, and endeavored, by ridiculing the doctrines which he promulgated, to suppress them.

"This, however, did not turn him from the path which he felt to be his duty; for he continued to set forth the doctrines of repentance, and baptism for remission of sins, and the gift of the Holy Ghost, according to the teachings of Peter, on the day of Pentecost, exhorting his hearers in the meantime, to throw away their creeds of faith — to take the Bible as their standard, and search its sacred pages — to learn to live by every word that proceedeth from the mouth of the Lord, and to rise above every sectarian sentiment, and the traditions of the age, and explore the wide and glorious fields of truth which the scriptures holds out to them.

"After laboring in that neighborhood one year, he received a very pressing invitation to remove to the town of Mentor, in the same county, about thirty miles from Bainbridge, and within a few miles from Lake Erie, which he some time afterwards complied with. The persons by whom he was more particularly requested to move to that place were the remnants of a Baptist church, which was nearly broken up, the members of which had become attached to the doctrines promulgated by Elder Rigdon.

"The town of Mentor was settled by wealthy and enterprising individuals, who had by their industry and good management made that township one of the most delightful in that country, or probably in the Western Reserve. Its advantages for agricultural purposes could hardly be surpassed, while the splendid farms, fertile fields, and stately mansions made it particularly attractive to the eye of the traveler, and gives evidence of enterprise and wealth. In that beautiful location he took up his residence, and immediately commenced his labors, with that zeal and assiduity which had formerly characterized him.

"But being a stranger, and many reports being put in circulation of a character calculated to lessen him in the estimation of the people, and consequently destroy his influence, some persons were even wicked enough to retail those slanderous reports which were promulgated, and endeavored to stir up persecution against him; consequently many of the citizens were jealous, and did not extend to him that confidence which he might otherwise have expected.

"His path was not strewed with flowers, but the thorns of persecution beset him, and he had to contend against much prejudice and opposition, whose swollen waves might have sunk one less courageous, resolute, and determined; yet notwithstanding these unfavorable circumstances, he continued to meet the storm, to stem the torrent, and bear up under the reproach for some time.

"At length the storm subsided, for after laboring in that neighborhood about eight months, he so wrought upon the feelings of the people by his consistent walk and conversation—his sociability, combined with his overwhelming eloquence, that a perfect calm succeeded; their evil apprehensions and surmisings were allayed, their prejudices gave way, and the man whom they had looked upon with jealousy was now their theme of praise, and their welcome guest. Those who had been most hostile now became his warmest admirers and most constant friends.

"The churches in which he preached, which had heretofore been filled with anxious hearers, were now filled to overflowing; the poor flocked to the services, and the rich thronged the assemblies.

"The doctrines he advanced were new, but at the same

time were elucidated with such clearness and enforced with an eloquence altogether superior to what they had listened to before that those whose sectarian prejudices were not too deeply rooted, who listened to the deep and searching discourses which he delivered from time to time, could not fail of being greatly affected and convinced that the principles he advanced were true and in accordance with the Scriptures. Nor were his labors and success confined to that township alone, but calls were made in every direction for him to preach, which he complied with as much as he possibly could, until his labors became very extensive, and spread over a vast extent of country.

"Wherever he went the same success attended his ministry, and he was everywhere received with kindness and welcomed by persons of all classes. Prejudice after prejudice gave way on every hand; opposition after opposition was broken down, and bigotry was rooted from its strongholds. The truths he advanced were received with gladness, and the doctrines he taught had a glorious ascendency wherever he had the opportunity of promulgating them.

"His fame as an orator and deep reasoner in the Scriptures continued to spread far and wide, and he soon gained a popularity and an elevation which has fallen to the lot of but few, consequently thousands flocked to hear his eloquent discourses.

"When it was known where he was going to preach there might be seen long before the appointed time, persons of all classes, sects, and denominations, flocking like doves to their windows, from a considerable distance. The humble pedestrian, and the rich in their splendid equipages might be seen crowding the roads.

"The churches in the different places where he preached were now no longer large enough to contain the vast assemblies which congregated from time to time, so that he had to repair to the widespread canopy of heaven, and in the woods and in the groves he addressed the multitudes which flocked to hear him. Nor was his preaching in vain. It was not empty sound that so closely engaged the attention of his audiences and with which they were so deeply interested, but it was the truths which were imparted, the intelligence which was conveyed, and the duties which were enforced.

"Not only did the writings of the New Testament occupy his attention, but occasionally those of the ancient prophets, particularly those prophecies which had reference to the present and to the future, were brought up to review and treated in a manner entirely new and deeply interesting. No longer did he follow the old beaten track, which had been traveled for ages by the religious world, but he dared to enter upon new grounds; called in question the opinions of uninspired men; showed the foolish ideas of many commentators on the sacred Scriptures—exposed their ignorance and contradictions—threw new light on the sacred volume, particularly those prophecies which so deeply interest this generation, and which had been entirely overlooked, or mystified by the religious world—cleared up scriptures which had heretofore appeared inexplicable, and delighted his astonished audience with things 'new and old' -- proved to a demonstration the literal fulfillment of prophecy, the gathering of Israel in the last days, to their ancient inheritances, with their ultimate splendor and glory; the situation of the world at the coming of the Son of Man —the judgments which Almighty God would pour out upon the ungodly prior to that event, and the reign of Christ with his saints on the earth, in the millennium.

"These important subjects could not fail to have their weight on the minds of his hearers, who clearly discerned the situation in which they were placed, by the sound and logical arguments which he adduced; and soon numbers felt the importance of obeying that form of doctrine which had been delivered them; so that they might be accounted worthy to escape those things which were coming on the . earth, and many came forward desiring to be baptized for the remission of sins. He accordingly commenced to baptize, and like John of old, there flocked to him people from all the region round about—persons of all ranks and standings in society—the rich, the poor, the noble and the brave, flocked to be baptized of him. Nor was this desire confined to individuals, or families, but whole societies threw away their creeds and articles of faith and became obedient to the faith he promulgated, and he soon had large and flourishing societies throughout that whole region of country.

"He now was a welcome visitor wherever he traveled—his society was courted by the learned, and intelligent, and the highest encomiums were bestowed upon him for his biblical lore and his eloquence.

"The work of the ministry engaged all his time and attention; he felt deeply for the salvation of his fellow man, and for the attainment of which he labored with unceasing diligence.

"During this state of unexampled success, the prospect of wealth and affluence was fairly open before him; but he looked upon it with indifference, and made everything subservient to the promotion of correct principles; and having food and raiment, he learned therewith to be content. As a proof of this his family were in no better circumstances, and made no greater appearance in the world, than when he labored at the occupation of tanning. His family consisted of his wife and six children, and lived in a very small, unfinished frame house, hardly capable of making a family comfortable; which affords a clear proof that his affections were not set upon things of a worldly nature, or secular aggrandizement.

"After he had labored in that vicinity some time, and having received but little pecuniary aid, the members of the church which he had built up, held a meeting to take his circumstances into consideration, and provide for his wants, and place him in a situation suitable to the high and important office which he sustained in the church. They resolved upon erecting him a suitable residence, where he could make his family comfortable, and accommodate his numerous friends, who visited him. A committee was appointed to make a purchase of land, and to erect such buildings as were necessary. The committee soon made a purchase of a farm in a beautiful situation in that township, made contracts for erecting a suitable dwelling house, stable, barn, etc., and soon made a commencement on the house, and had a quantity of the building materials on the spot. He being held in the highest respect by that people, they entered the work with pleasure, and seemed to vie with each other in their labors of love, believing it a duty to make their beloved pastor and his family comfortable. His prospects, with regard to temporal things, were now brighter than they ever had been; and he felt happy in the midst of a people who had every disposition to promote his welfare.

"Under these pleasing circumstances, and enjoying this full tide of prosperity, he hardly thought that, for his attachment to truth, he would soon see the prospect blasted, and himself and family reduced to a more humble situation than before.

"At this time, it being in the fall of A. D. 1830, Elders Parley P. Pratt, Ziba Peterson, Oliver Cowdery, and Peter Whitmer, called at that town on their way to the western boundary of the State of Missouri, testifying to the truth of the 'Book of Mormon,' and that the Lord had raised up a prophet, and restored the priesthood. Previous to this, Elder Parley Pratt had been a preacher in the same church with Elder Rigdon, and resided in the town of Amherst, Lorain County, in that State, and had been sent into the State of New York, on a mission, where he became acquainted with the circumstances of the coming forth of the Book of Mormon, and was introduced to Joseph Smith, Jr., and others of the Church of Latter Day Saints. After listening to the testimony of the 'witnesses,' and reading the 'Book,' he became convinced that it was of God, and that the principles which they taught, were the principles of truth. He was then baptized, and shortly after was ordained an elder, and began to preach, and from that time became a strenuous advocate of the truth.

"Believing there were many in the church with whom he had formerly been united, who were honest seekers after truth, induced him, while on his journey to the West, to call upon his friends, and make known the great things which the Lord had brought to pass. The first house at which they called was Elder Rigdon's; and after the usual salutations, presented him with the Book of Mormon—stating that

it was a revelation from God. This being the first time he
had ever heard of or seen the Book of Mormon, he felt very
much prejudiced at the assertion; and replied that, 'he had
one Bible which he believed was a revelation from God, and
with which he pretended to have some acquaintance; but
with respect to the book they had presented him he must
say that he had considerable doubt.' Upon which they
expressed a desire to investigate the subject, and argue the
matter; but he replied, 'No, young gentlemen, you must not
argue with me on the subject; but I will read your book,
and see what claim it has upon my faith, and will endeavor
to ascertain whether it be a revelation from God or not.'
After some further conversation on the subject, they expressed a desire to lay the subject before the people, and
requested the privilege of preaching in Elder Rigdon's
church, to which he readily consented.   The appointment
was accordingly published, and a large and respectable
congregation assembled.   Oliver Cowdery and Parley P.
Pratt severally addressed the meeting.   At the conclusion,
Elder Rigdon arose and stated to the congregation that the
information they had that evening received was of an extraordinary character, and certainly demanded their most serious consideration: and as the apostle advised his brethren
'to prove all things, and hold fast that which is good,' so he
would exhort his brethren to do likewise, and give the matter a careful investigation; and not turn against it, without
being fully convinced of its being an imposition, lest they
should, possibly, resist the truth.

"This was, indeed, generous on the part of Elder Rigdon,
and gave evidence of his entire freedom from any sectarian
bias; but allowing his mind full scope to range, untram-
meled, through the scriptures, embracing every principle of
truth, and rejecting error, under whatever guise it should
appear. He was perfectly willing to allow his members the
same privilege. Having received great light on the Scriptures, he felt desirous to receive more, from whatever quarter it should come. This was his prevailing characteristic;
and if any sentiment was advanced by anyone, that was new,
or tended to throw light on the Scriptures, or the dealings of

God with the children of men, it was always gladly received, and treasured up in his mind. After the meeting broke up, the brethren returned home with Elder Rigdon, and conversed upon the important things which they had proclaimed. He informed them that he should read the Book of Mormon, give it a full investigation, and then would frankly tell them his mind and feelings on the subject—told them they were welcome to abide at his house until he had opportunity of reading it.

"About two miles from Elder Rigdon's, at the town of Kirtland, were a number of the members of his church, who lived together, and had all things common—from which circumstance has arisen the idea that this was the case with the Church of Jesus Christ—to which place they immediately repaired, and proclaimed the gospel to them, with some considerable success; for their testimony was received by many of the people, and seventeen came forward in obedience to the gospel.

"While thus engaged, they visited Elder Rigdon occasionally, and found him very earnestly engaged in reading the 'Book of Mormon,'—praying to the Lord for direction, and meditating on the things he heard and read; and after a fortnight from the time the book was put in his hands, he was fully convinced of the truth of the work, by a revelation from Jesus Christ, which was made known to him in a remarkable manner, so that he could exclaim 'flesh and blood hath not revealed it unto me, but my Father which is in heaven.'

"Being now fully satisfied in his own mind of the truth of the work, and the necessity of obedience thereto, he informed his wife of the same, and was happy to find that she was not only diligently investigating the subject, but was believing with all her heart, and was desirous of obeying the truth, which, undoubtedly, was a great satisfaction to his mind.

"The consequence of obeying the truth, and embracing a system of religion so unpopular as that of the Church of Jesus Christ, presented itself in the strongest possible light.

"At present, the honors and applause of the world were

showered down upon him, his wants were abundantly supplied, and were anticipated.   He was respected by the entire community, and his name was a tower of strength.   His counsel was sought for, respected and esteemed.   But if he should unite with the Church of Christ, his prospects of wealth and affluence would vanish; his family dependent upon him for support must necessarily share his humiliation and poverty.   He was aware that his character and his reputation must suffer in the estimation of the community.

"Aware of all these things, there must have been feelings of no ordinary kind, agitate his bosom at that particular crisis; but yet they did not deter him from the path of duty. He had formerly made a sacrifice for truth and conscience' :sake, and had been sustained; consequently, he felt great confidence in the Lord, believing that if he pursued the path of duty, no good thing would be withheld from him.

"Although he felt great confidence in the Lord, yet he felt it a trial of some magnitude, when he avowed.his determination to his beloved companion, who had before shared in his poverty, and who had cheerfully struggled through it without murmuring or repining.   He informed her what the consequences would undoubtedly be respecting their worldly circumstances if they obeyed the gospel; and then said: 'my dear, you have once followed me into poverty, are you again willing to do the same?'   She then said: 'I have weighed the matter, I have contemplated on the circumstances in which we may be placed; I have counted the cost, and I am perfectly satisfied to follow you; it is my desire to do the will of God, come life or come death.'   Accordingly, they were both baptized into the Church of Jesus Christ; and, together with those who had been previously admitted to baptism, made a little branch in this section of Ohio, of about twenty members, whom the brethren, bound for the borders of the Lamanites. after adding to their number one of their converts, Dr. Frederick G. Williams, bade an affectionate farewell, and went on their way rejoicing."—*Times and Seasons*, vol. 4, pp. 172, 177, 178, 193, 194, 209, 210, 289, 290, 305.

The above extract gives quite a full account of the former life of Sidney Rigdon and his connection with the Latter

Day Saints. We reproduce it here, believing it will be found to be correct. But an effort has been made to show that he had

Story of the Manuscript Found. acquaintance with Joseph Smith before the publication of the Book of Mormon, and that he in fact furnished the basis of it by supplying him with a copy of the "Spalding Story" or "Manuscript Found," written at New Salem, Ohio, by one Solomon Spalding, who was, it is claimed, a graduate of Dartmouth College. This was written about the year 1812, and was read to many of his neighbors. After its completion Mr. Spalding removed to Pittsburg, Pennsylvania, where he exhibited it to a Mr. Patterson, who borrowed it for perusal, "retained it for a long time," then made a proposition to Mr. Spalding to publish it on certain conditions. These conditions were not accepted. The manuscript was returned to the author, who removed to Amity, Washington County, Pennsylvania, and died there in 1816. On this latter point the widow of Mr. Spalding states:—

"At length the manuscript was returned to its author, and soon after we removed to Amity, Washington County, etc., where Mr. Spalding deceased in 1816. The manuscript then fell into my hands, and was carefully preserved."

It is further claimed that the manuscript was in the possession of Mrs. Spalding until after the Book of Mormon was published, and that it was delivered into the hands of Dr. P. Hurlbut in 1834. If Rigdon had access to this manuscript it was before 1816.

Coming more particularly to dates, on page 282 of E. D. Howe's "History of Mormonism," published at Painesville, Ohio, in 1840, we find a statement by Henry Lake in which he states:—

"Spalding left here [Conneaut, Ohio] in 1812, and I furnished him the means to carry him to Pittsburg, where he said he would get the book printed, and pay me."

On page 287 of the same book we find this:—

"A messenger was dispatched to look up the widow of Spalding, who was found residing in Massachusetts. From her we learned that Spalding resided in Pittsburg, about two years," etc.

Then he left Pittsburg in 1814, and, as we have seen, took the manuscript with him.   So if Rigdon had access to it, it was before 1814.

But it is claimed that he copied it while at the publishing house of Patterson, in Pittsburg.   We think this theory untenable for several reasons:—

First.   Sidney Rigdon being born in 1793 was only twenty or twenty-one years of age at the time.   It is not likely that a boy of that age would conceive of such a scheme; besides, the testimony shows that during this period and for years after he was at home on his father's farm.

The story untenable.

Second.   It has not been shown that he resided in Pittsburg until 1822, eight years after the manuscript had left there.

Third.   It has never been shown that he was associated with Joseph Smith in any way until December, 1830, and the Book of Mormon was delivered to the printer in August, 1829, and the printing all done by March, 1830.

Fourth.   This theory assumes without proof that Joseph Smith, Sidney Rigdon, Oliver Cowdery, P. P. Pratt, and others were all guilty of lying, perjury, and deceit; which is not only contemptibly unfair, but has no warrant in law, nor in practice among men of honor, hence should receive no countenance by the historian.

Joseph Smith's version of the matter has already been given.

Sidney Rigdon stated, in a communication to the *Boston Journal*, from Commerce, Illinois, May 27, 1839:—

"In your paper of the 18th instant, I see a letter signed by somebody calling herself Maltilda Davison, pretending to give the origin of Mormonism, as she is pleased to call it, by relating a moonshine story about a certain Solomon Spalding, a creature with the knowledge of whose earthly existence I am entirely indebted to this production; for surely, until Dr. Philastus Hurlbut informed me that such a being lived, at some former period, I had not the most distant knowledge of his existence. . . . . It is only necessary to say, in relation to the whole story about Spald-

Rigdon speaks.

ing's writings being in the hands of Mr. Patterson, who was in Pittsburg, and who is said to have kept a printing office, and my saying that I was concerned in the said office, etc., etc., is the most base of lies, without even the shadow of truth."

This is rather harsh and forcible language to be sure, but we do not expect humanity to be always calm when accused of stealing, lying, and fraud.

Oliver Cowdery, as we have seen, stated in 1848:—

"I wrote, with my own pen, the entire Book of Mormon (save a few pages), as it fell from the lips of the Prophet Cowdery's statement. Joseph Smith, as he translated it by the gift and power of God. . . . *I beheld with my eyes and handled with my hands the gold plates from which it was translated.* . . . That book is *true.* Sidney Rigdon did not write it. Mr. Spalding did not write it. I wrote it myself as it fell from the lips of the Prophet."

P. P. Pratt writes to the *New Era,* from New York, November 27, 1839, as follows:—

"Mr. Rigdon embraced the doctrine through my instrumentality. I first presented the Book of Mormon to him. I Pratt makes a statement. stood upon the bank of the stream while he was baptized, and assisted to officiate in his ordination, and I myself was unacquainted with the system until some months after its organization, which was on the 6th of April, 1830."

The life of Sidney Rigdon was that of an active minister, and his whereabouts can be determined by public records so Rigdon's record. frequently as to make it impossible that he could have made the long and tedious journeys to New York (which this story makes necessary) for the purpose of conspiring with Joseph Smith in those days of slow transportation.

The following is a list of events and dates collected, verified, and arranged by Elder E. L. Kelley, while His whereabouts located. a resident of Kirtland, Ohio:—

Times and places definitely settled by positive and undisputed evidence as to the whereabouts, occupation, and business of Elder Sidney Rigdon from November 1, 1826, to January 1, 1831, inclusive.

FIRST, BY COURT RECORDS.

1.

STATE OF OHIO,
Geauga County.

This is to certify that I solemnized the marriage contract between John G. Smith and Julia Giles, on the second of November, 1826, agreeable to license obtained from court of said county.

SIDNEY RIGDON.

Recorded the 13th Dec., 1826.

EDWARD PAINE, JUN., Clerk Com. Pleas.

2.

STATE OF OHIO,
Geauga County.

This is to certify that on the fifth of June, 1827, in the village of Painesville, I solemnized the marriage contract between Theron Freeman and Elizabeth Waterman, agreeable to license obtained from the clerk of the court of said county.

SIDNEY RIGDON.

Recorded June 7th, 1827.   ED. PAINE, JUN., Clerk Com. Pleas.

3.

STATE OF OHIO,
Geauga County.

This is to certify that I solemnized the marriage contract between James Gray and Mary Kerr, in township of Mentor, on the 3d of July, 1827.

SIDNEY RIGDON.

Recorded July 12, 1827. EDWARD PAINE, JUN., Clerk Com. Pleas.

4.

STATE OF OHIO,
Geauga County.

This is to certify that on the 19th of July, 1827, I solemnized the marriage contract in the township of Kirtland, between Alden Snow and Ruth Parker, agreeably to license obtained from the clerk of the court of the said county.

SIDNEY RIGDON.

Recorded August 10th, 1827.   ED. PAINE, JUN., Clerk Com. Pleas.

5.

STATE OF OHIO,
Geauga County.

This is to certify that I solemnized the marriage contract, on the 9th of October, 1827, in the town-

ship of Mentor, between Stephen Sherman and Wealthy Mathews, agreeably to license obtained from the clerk of the court of the said county.

SIDNEY RIGDON.

Recorded October 27, 1827. ED. PAINE, JUN., Clerk Com. Pleas.

6.

STATE OF OHIO, }
Geauga County. }

This is to certify that I solemnized the marriage contract between Alvin Wait and Sophia Gunn, on the 6th of Dec., 1827, in the township of Kirtland, agreeably to license obtained from the clerk of the court of said county.

SIDNEY RIGDON.

Recorded December 12th, 1827.

EDWARD PAINE, JUN., Clerk Com. Pleas.

7.

STATE OF OHIO, }
Geauga County. }

This is to certify that I solemnized the marriage contract between Roswell D. Cottrell and Matilda Olds, in the township of Concord, on the 13th day of December, 1827, agreeably to license obtained from the clerk of the court of said county.

SIDNEY RIGDON.

Recorded January 8th, 1828. EDWARD PAINE, JUN., Clerk Com. Pleas.

8.

STATE OF OHIO, }
Geauga County. }

This is to certify that I solemnized the marriage contract between Otis Herrington and Lyma Corning, in the township of Mentor, on the 14th of February, 1828, agreeably to license obtained from the clerk of the court of said county.

SIDNEY RIGDON.

Recorded March 31st, 1828. EDWARD PAINE, JUN., Clerk Com. Pleas.

9.

STATE OF OHIO, }
Geauga County. }

This is to certify that I solemnized the marriage contract between Luther Dille and Clarissa Kent, in the township of Mentor, on the 7th day of September, 1828, agreeably to license obtained from the clerk of the court of said county.

SIDNEY RIGDON.

Recorded October 13, 1828. D. D. AIKEN, Clerk Com. Pleas

10.

STATE OF OHIO, }
 Geauga County. }

   This is to certify that I solemnized the marriage contract between Nachor Corning and Phebe E. Willson, in the township of Mentor, on the 18th day of September, 1828, agreeably to license obtained from the clerk of the court of said county.

SIDNEY RIGDON.

Recorded Oct. 13, 1828.   D. D. AIKEN, Clerk Com. Pleas.

11.

STATE OF OHIO, }
 Geauga County. }

   This is to certify that I solemnized the marriage contract between Erastus Root and Rebecca Tuttle, on the 1st day of Feb., 1829, in the township of Mentor, agreeably to a license obtained from clerk of court of said county.

SIDNEY RIGDON.

Recorded February 12th, 1829. D. D. AIKEN, Clerk Com. Pleas.

12.

STATE OF OHIO, }
 Geauga County. }

   This is to certify that I solemnized the marriage contract between Albert Churchill and Anna Fosdick on the 1st of Jan., 1829, in the township of Concord, agreeably to license obtained from clerk of court of said county.

SIDNEY RIGDON.

Recorded February 12, 1829. D. D. AIKEN, Clerk. Com. Pleas.

13.

STATE OF OHIO, }
 Geauga County. }

   This is to certify that I solemnized the marriage contract between John Strong and Ann Eliza More, on the 13th of Aug., 1829, in the township of Kirtland, agreeably to license obtained from clerk of the court of said county.

SIDNEY RIGDON.

Recorded September 14, 1829. D. D. AIKEN, Clerk Com. Pleas.

14.

STATE OF OHIO, }
 Geauga County. }

   This is to certify that I solemnized the marriage contract between Darwin Atwater and Harriett

Clapp, on the 14th day of September, 1829, in the township of Mentor, agreeably to license obtained from clerk of said county.

SIDNEY RIGDON.

Recorded October 7, 1829.   D. D. AIKEN, Clerk Com. Pleas.

15.

STATE OF OHIO, }
Geauga County. }

This is to certify that I solemnized the marriage contract between Joel Roberts and Relief Bates, on the 1st of Oct., 1829, in the Township of Perry, agreeably to license obtained from clerk of court of said county.

SIDNEY RIGDON.

Recorded October 7, 1829.   D. D. AIKEN, Clerk Com. Pleas.

16.

STATE OF OHIO, }
Geauga County. }

This certifies that I married Lewis B. Wood to Laura Cleaveland in Kirtland Township, on the 4th of November, 1830.

SIDNEY RIGDON.

Recorded November 11, 1830.   D. D. AIKEN, Clerk Com. Pleas.

STATE OF OHIO, } ss.—PROBATE COURT;
Geauga County, }

I, H. K. Smith, Judge of the Probate Court in and for said County, hereby certify that the above and foregoing certificates numbering from one to sixteen were truly taken and copied from the record of marriages in this county preserved in this office where the same by law are required to be kept. In testimony whereof I have hereunto set my hand and affixed the seal of said Court at Chardon, this 27th day of April, A. D., 1891.

H. K. SMITH,

[Seal.]   Probate Judge.

17.

STATE OF OHIO, } David Chandler and Polly Johnson.
Cuyahoga Co. }

This certifies that I solemnized the marriage contract between David Chandler and Polly Johnson in the township of Chagrin on the 31st day of December, one thousand eight hundred and twenty-nine, agreeably to license obtained from the clerk of the court of said County.

SIDNEY RIGDON.
Pastor Baptist
Church in Mentor,

Filed and Recorded January 12, 1830.   Geauga Co., Ohio.

STATE OF OHIO, } ss.—In the Probate Court.
  Cuyahoga Co. }

I, Henry C. White, Judge of said Court, do hereby certify that the foregoing is a true and correct transcript taken from the Marriage Records in this office, where the same is by law required to be kept.

[Seal.]
                    HENRY C. WHITE, Probate Judge.
                    BY H. A. SCHWAB, Dep. Clerk.

SECOND, BY HISTORICAL AND PERSONAL TESTIMONY.

18. January, 1827. Elder Rigdon held public meetings in Mantua, Ohio. (Hayden's Hist. of the Disciples of the Western Reserve, page 237.)

19. February, 1827. Preached funeral discourse of Hannah Tanner, Chester, Ohio. (Authenticated by Henry Tanner.)

20. March and April, 1827. Held protracted meetings at Mentor, Ohio; baptizing Nancy M. Sanford, William Dunson and wife, and others. (Evidence by Nancy M. Sanford, Mantua, Ohio.)

21. June 15, 1827. Baptized Thomas Clapp, and others, Mentor, Ohio. (Personal testimony of Henry H. Clapp, Mentor, Ohio.)

22. August 23, 1827. Elder Rigdon met with the Ministerial Association of the Western Reserve at New Lisbon, Ohio. (Hist. Dis. W. Res., pages 55-57.)

23. October 20, 1827. A member of the Ministerial Council at Warren, Ohio. (Hist. Dis., page 137.)

24. November, 1827. Held series of meetings at New Lisbon, Ohio. (Hist. Dis., pages 72-75.)

25. March, 1828. Instructor of a class in theology at Mentor, Ohio; and also held series of meetings at Mentor and Warren, Ohio. Zebulon Rudolph, afterwards an Elder in the Disciple Church, was a member of this class in theology, with others. He became a man of note in the Western Reserve. (Hist. Dis., page 198.)

26. April, 1828. Elder Rigdon conducted a great religious revival at Kirtland, Ohio. (Hist. Dis., page 194.)

27. May, 1828. He meets with Alexander Campbell at Shalersville, Ohio, and held a protracted meeting at that place. (Hist. Dis., page 155.)

28. June, 1828. Elder Rigdon baptized Henry H. Clapp at Mentor, Ohio. (Testimony by Mr. Clapp, himself.)

29. August, 1828. Attended great yearly Association at Warren, Ohio. (See Hayden's Hist., page 163.)

30. March, 1829. Protracted meeting, Mentor, Ohio. (Authenticated by Rev. Zebulon Rudolph.)

31. April 12, 1829. Protracted meeting at Kirtland, Ohio.

32. July 1, 1829. Organized church at Perry, Ohio. (Hist. Dis., page 346.)

33. September, 1829. Series of meetings at Mentor, Ohio; baptizing J. J. Moss, who was afterwards Disciple minister of some note. (Evidence Rev. J. J. Moss; "Braden and Kelley Debate, page 387.)

34. October, 1829. At Perry, Ohio. (Hist. Dis., pages 207 and 409.)

35. November, 1829. Held meeting at Wait Hill, Ohio; baptizing Alvin Wait. (Hist. Dis., pages 204–207.)

36. March, 1830. At Mentor, Ohio. (Evidence Henry Clapp.)

37. June 1 to 30. At Mentor, Ohio. (*Millennial Harbinger*, page 389.)

38. July, 1830. Protracted meeting at Pleasant Valley, Ohio; baptized 45. (Evidence Reuben P. Harmon, Kirtland, Ohio.)

39. August, 1830. With Alexander Campbell at Austintown, Ohio. (Hist. Dis., page 209.)

40. December, 1830. Attended meetings held by P. P. Pratt and Oliver Cowdery and others at Mentor and also Kirtland, Ohio: and united with the Church of Jesus Christ, afterwards also known as Latter Day Saints. (Testimony, Reuben P. Harmon, "Braden and Kelley Debate," page 392.)

In addition to these items we find the following matters of record:—

Lyman Wight in his private journal, the manuscript of which is now before us, writes:—

"I resided in this place [Warrensville, Ohio] till 1829, about the month of *May*, when I heard Sidney Rigdon preach what was then called the Rigdonite doctrine. After hearing him go through the principle of baptism for the remission of sins I went forward and was baptized by his hands."

Again he writes.—

"August [same year] my wife was baptized together with John Murdock and many others by S. Rigdon."

The above dates and events are so thoroughly in accord with the statements of Joseph Smith above quoted that we feel safe in presenting the sketch of Rigdon's life by Joseph as historically correct.

The reputation of Sidney Rigdon will hardly justify one in believing him guilty of such deceit as his enemies accuse Rigdon's him of during his successful career as a minister reputation. in Northern Ohio. A. S. Hayden, one of his fellow ministers in the Christian or Disciple Church during Hayden's those times, who subsequently bitterly opposed testimony. the faith which he (Rigdon) afterwards espoused, said of Rigdon:—

"Whatever may be justly said of him after he had surrendered himself a victim and a leader of the Mormon delusion, it would scarcely be just to deny sincerity and candor to him, previous to the time when his bright star became permanently eclipsed under that dark cloud."—"History of the Disciples in the Western Reserve," p. 192.

The following extract from the journal of Lyman Wight, who was at the time identified with the new movement Lyman Wight under Sidney Rigdon, Alexander Campbell, and confirms the account of Jo- Walter Scott, confirms the account of Joseph seph Smith. Smith in two important particulars; viz.: as to who was responsible for the teaching and practice of the principle of "all things common" at Kirtland, Ohio, and in regard to the date of the arrival at Mentor and Kirtland of the missionaries. He writes:—

"I now began to look at the doctrine of the apostles pretty closely, and especially that part contained in the second chapter of the Acts of the Apostles, where they had all things common. In consideration of this doctrine I went to Kirtland, about twenty miles, to see Bro. I. Morley and — Billings, after some conversation on the subject we entered into a covenant to make our interests one as anciently. In conformity to this covenant I moved the next February [1830] to Kirtland, into the house with Bro. Morley. We commenced our labors together with great peace and union. We were soon joined by eight other families. Our labors were united both in farming and mechanism, all of which was prosecuted with great vigor. We truly began to feel as if the millennium was close at hand.

"Everything moved smoothly on till about the first of November. About this time five families concluded to join us in the town of Mayfield, about seven miles up the river. They owning each a good farm and mills, it was concluded best to establish a branch there; accordingly I was appointed to go and take the charge of the same.

"When I had my goods about half loaded, there came along four men; namely, P. Pratt, O. Cowdery, P. Whitmer, and Ziba Peterson, and brought with them the Book of Mormon, which they wished to introduce to us. I desired they would hold on till I got away, as my business was of vital importance, and I did not wish to be troubled with romances nor idle speculators. But nothing daunted they were not to be put off, but were as good-natured as you please. Curiosity got uppermost, and I concluded to stop for a short time. We called meeting and one testified that he had seen angels, and another that he had seen the plates, and that the gifts were back in the church again, etc. The meeting became so interesting withal that I did not get away till the sun was about an hour high at night, and it was dark before I arrived at my new home. But I amused myself by thinking that the trouble was over, and that I should not see them again for a long time, supposing they would start the next morning for the western boundary of the State of Missouri; but in this I was very much disappointed. But to describe the scenes of the next seven weeks, [in] which one scene would be as interesting as another, would fill quite a large volume. I shall therefore content myself by saying, that they brought the Book of Mormon to bear upon us, and the whole of the common stock family was baptized. And during the seven weeks they tarried they succeeded in building

up a church of one hundred and thirty members.   Myself
and family were baptized by P. Pratt on the 14th of November, 1830, in Shageen [Chagrin] River, at Kirtland, Ohio.   I
was confirmed on the 18th by O. Cowdery, and on the 20th
ordained an elder by the same."

The widow of Lyman Wight states that she remembers
distinctly that Rigdon was baptized the sam da; they were,
so this fixes the date of Rigdon's baptism to be November
14, 1830.

These testimonies are also corroborated by Parley P.
Pratt in his autobiography:—

"It was now October, 1830.   A revelation had been given
through the mouth of this Prophet, Seer, and Translator, in
P. P. Pratt's which Elders Oliver Cowdery, Peter Whitmer,
account. Ziba Peterson, and myself were appointed to go
into the wilderness, through the Western States, and to
the Indian Territory.   Making arrangements for my wife in
the family of the Whitmers, we took leave of our friends and
the church late in October, and started on foot.

"After traveling for some days we called on an Indian
nation at or near Buffalo; and spent part of a day with them,
instructing them in the knowledge of the record of their
forefathers.   We were kindly received, and much interest
was manifested by them on hearing this news.   We made a
present of two copies of the Book of Mormon to certain of
them who could read, and repaired to Buffalo.   Thence we
continued our journey, for about two hundred miles, and at
length called on Mr. Rigdon, my former friend and instructor, in the Reformed Baptist Society.   He received us
cordially and entertained us with hospitality.

"We soon presented him with a Book of Mormon, and related to him the history of the same.   He was much interested, and promised a thorough perusal of the book.

"We tarried in this region for some time, and devoted our
time to the ministry, and visiting from house to house.

"At length Mr. Rigdon and many others became convinced
that they had no authority to minister in the ordinances of
God; and that they had not been legally baptized and ordained.   They, therefore, came forward and were baptized

by us, and received the gift of the Holy Ghost by the laying on of hands, and prayer in the name of Jesus Christ.

"The news of our coming was soon noised abroad, and the news of the discovery of the Book of Mormon and the marvelous events connected with it. The interest and excitement now became general in Kirtland, and in all the region round about. The people thronged us night and day, insomuch that we had no time for rest or retirement. Meetings were convened in different neighborhoods, and multitudes came together soliciting our attendance; while thousands flocked about us daily; some to be taught, some for curiosity, some to obey the gospel, and some to dispute or resist it.

"In two or three weeks from our arrival in the neighborhood with the news, we had baptized one hundred and twenty-seven souls, and this number soon increased to one thousand. The disciples were filled with joy and gladness, while rage and lying was abundantly manifested by gainsayers; faith was strong, joy was great, and persecution heavy.

"We proceeded to ordain Sidney Rigdon, Isaac Morley, John Murdock, Lyman Wight, Edward Partridge, and many others to the ministry; and, leaving them to take care of the churches and to minister the gospel, we took leave of the saints and continued our journey."—Autobiography of Parley P. Pratt, pp. 49, 50.

CHAPTER 9.

1830-1831.

RESUMING the thread of history as furnished us by Joseph
Smith we find that a revelation was given in October, 1830,
to Ezra Thayre and Northrop Sweet.[1]

[1] 1. Behold, I say unto you, my servants Ezra and Northrop, Open ye
your ears and hearken to the voice of the Lord your God, whose word is
quick and powerful, sharper than a two-edged sword, to the dividing
asunder of the joints and marrow, soul and spirit; and is a discerner of the
thoughts and intents of the heart. For verily, verily I say unto you, that
ye are called to lift up your voices as with the sound of a trump, to declare my gospel unto a crooked and a perverse generation: for, behold,
the field is white already to harvest; and it is the eleventh hour, and for
the last time that I shall call laborers into my vineyard. And my vineyard has become corrupted every whit; and there is none which doeth
good save it be a few; and they err in many instances, because of priest-
crafts, all having corrupt minds.
2. And verily, verily I say unto you, that this church have I established and called forth out of the wilderness; and even so will I gather
mine elect from the four quarters of the earth, even as many as will
believe in me, and hearken unto my voice; yea, verily, verily I say unto
you, that the field is white already to harvest; wherefore, thrust in your
sickles, and reap with all your might, mind, and strength. Open your

Early in November a young man, who afterwards became a leading and influential man in the church, came to Joseph to inquire what his duty was. This young man was Orson Pratt, who had been baptized on his nineteenth birthday, on the nineteenth of the previous September, by his brother, Parley P., whose name has been prominently mentioned in the foregoing pages. For this young man Joseph inquired of the Lord and received instruction.[2]

Orson Pratt.

mouths and they shall be filled; and you shall become even as Nephi of old, who journeyed from Jerusalem in the wilderness; yea, open your mouths and spare not, and you shall be laden with sheaves upon your backs, for lo, I am with you; yea, open your mouths and they shall be filled, saying, Repent, repent and prepare ye the way of the Lord, and make his paths straight; for the kingdom of heaven is at hand; yea, repent and be baptized every one of you, for the remission of your sins; yea, be baptized even by water, and then cometh the baptism of fire and the Holy Ghost.

3. Behold, verily, verily I say unto you, This is my gospel, and remember that they shall have faith in me, or they can in nowise be saved; and upon this Rock I will build my church; yea, upon this rock ye are built, and if ye continue, the gates of hell shall not prevail against you; and ye shall remember the church articles and covenants to keep them; and whoso having faith you shall confirm in my church, by the laying on of the hands, and I will bestow the gift of the Holy Ghost upon them. And the Book of Mormon, and the Holy Scriptures, are given of me for your instruction; and the power of my Spirit quickeneth all things; wherefore, be faithful, praying always, having your lamps trimmed and burning, and oil with you, that you may be ready at the coming of the Bridegroom; for, behold, verily, verily I say unto you, that I come quickly; even so. Amen.

[2] 1. My son Orson, hearken and hear and behold what I, the Lord God, shall say unto you, even Jesus Christ your Redeemer, the light and the life of the world; a light which shineth in darkness and the darkness comprehendeth it not; who so loved the world that he gave his own life, that as many as would believe might become the sons of God; wherefore you are my son, and blessed are you because you have believed, and more blessed are you because you are called of me to preach my gospel; to lift up your voice as with the sound of a trump, both long and loud, and cry repentance unto a crooked and perverse generation; preparing the way of the Lord for his second coming; for behold, verily, verily I say unto you, The time is soon at hand, that I shall come in a cloud with power and great glory, and it shall be a great day at the time of my coming, for all nations shall tremble.

2. But before that great day shall come, the sun shall be darkened, and the moon be turned into blood, and the stars shall refuse their shining, and some shall fall, and great destructions await the wicked; wherefore lift up your voice and spare not, for the Lord God hath spoken. Therefore prophesy and it shall be given by the power of the Holy Ghost; and if you are faithful, behold, I am with you until I come; and verily, verily I say unto you, I come quickly. I am your Lord and your Redeemer. Even so. Amen.

Joseph continues:—

"It was in December that Elder Sidney Rigdon, a sketch of whose history I have before mentioned, came to inquire of the Lord, and with him came that man, (of **Sidney Rigdon and Edward Partr dge visit the prophet.** whom I will hereafter speak more fully,) named Edward Partridge. He was a pattern of piety, and one of the Lord's great men, known by his steadfastness, and patient endurance to the end."—*Times and Seasons*, vol. 4, p. 320.

Soon after the arrival of these men two more revelations were given.[a]

[a] 1. Listen to the voice of the Lord your God, even Alpha and Omega, the beginning and the end, whose course is one eternal round, the same to-day as yesterday and forever. I am Jesus Christ, the Son of God, who was crucified for the sins of the world, even as many as will believe on my name, that they may become the sons of God, even one in me as I am in the Father, as the Father is one in me, that we may be one.

2. Behold, verily, verily I say unto my servant Sidney, I have looked upon thee and thy works. I have heard thy prayers and prepared thee for a greater work. Thou art blessed, for thou shalt do great things. Behold, thou wast sent forth even as John, to prepare the way before me, and before Elijah which should come, and thou knew it not. Thou didst baptize by water unto repentance, but they received not the Holy Ghost; but now I give unto thee a commandment, that thou shalt baptize by water, and they shall receive the Holy Ghost by the laying on of the hands, even as the apostles of old.

3. And it shall come to pass, that there shall be a great work in the land, even among the Gentiles, for their folly and their abominations shall be made manifest, in the eyes of all people; for I am God, and mine arm is not shortened, and I will show miracles, signs and wonders, unto all those who believe on my name. And whoso shall ask it in my name, in faith, they shall cast out devils; they shall heal the sick; they shall cause the blind to receive their sight, and the deaf to hear, and the dumb to speak, and the lame to walk: and the time speedily cometh that great things are to be shown forth unto the children of men; but without faith shall not anything be shown forth except desolations upon Babylon, the same which has made all nations drink of the wine of the wrath of her fornication. And there are none that doeth good except those who are ready to receive the fullness of my gospel, which I have sent forth unto this generation.

4. Wherefore, I have called upon the weak things of the world, those who are unlearned and despised, to thresh the nations by the power of my Spirit; and their arm shall be my arm, and I will be their shield and their buckler, and I will gird up their loins, and they shall fight manfully for me; and their enemies shall be under their feet; and I will let fall the sword in their behalf; and by the fire of mine indignation will I preserve them. And the poor and the meek shall have the gospel preached unto them, and they shall be looking forth for the time of my coming, for it is nigh at hand; and they shall learn the parable of the fig tree; for even now already summer is nigh, and I have sent forth the fullness of my gospel by the hand of my servant Joseph; and in weakness have I blessed him, and I have given unto him the keys of the mystery of those

We have omitted to mention that about June, 1830, Joseph, as directed by inspiration, began a translation of the Jewish **Inspired** Scriptures, which work he did by the Spirit of **Translation.** revelation. The necessity for this was clearly shown by the revelation of June, 1830. (Doctrine and Covenants, section 22.) According to this revelation the Lord said unto Moses, "In a day when the children of men shall esteem my words as naught, and take many of them from

things which have been sealed, even things which were from the foundation of the world, and the things which shall come from this time until the time of my coming, if he abide in me, and if not, another will I plant in his stead.

5. Wherefore watch over him that his faith fail not, and it shall be given by the Comforter, the Holy Ghost, that knoweth all things; and a commandment I give unto thee, that thou shalt write for him; and the scriptures shall be given even as they are in mine own bosom, to the salvation of mine own elect; for they will hear my voice, and shall see me, and shall not be asleep, and shall abide the day of my coming, for they shall be purified even as I am pure. And now I say unto you, Tarry with him and he shall journey with you; forsake him not and surely these things shall be fulfilled. And inasmuch as ye do not write, behold, it shall be given unto him to prophesy; and thou shalt preach my gospel; and call on the holy prophets to prove his words, as they shall be given him.

6. Keep all the commandments and covenants by which ye are bound, and I will cause the heavens to shake for your good, and Satan shall tremble, and Zion shall rejoice upon the hills, and flourish; and Israel shall be saved in mine own due time. And by the keys which I have given shall they be led, and no more be confounded at all. Lift up your hearts and be glad; your redemption draweth nigh. Fear not, little flock, the kingdom is yours until I come. Behold, I come quickly. Even so. Amen.

1. Thus saith the Lord God, the Mighty One of Israel, Behold, I say unto you, my servant Edward, that you are blessed, and your sins are forgiven you, and you are called to preach my gospel as with the voice of a trump; and I will lay my hand upon you by the hand of my servant Sidney Rigdon, and you shall receive my Spirit, the Holy Ghost, even the Comforter, which shall teach you the peaceable things of the kingdom; and you shall declare it with a loud voice, saying, Hosanna, blessed be the name of the most high God.

2. And now this calling and commandment give I unto you concerning all men, that as many as shall come before my servants Sidney Rigdon and Joseph Smith, Jr., embracing this calling and commandment, shall be ordained and sent forth to preach the everlasting gospel among the nations, crying repentance, saying, Save yourselves from this untoward generation, and come forth out of the fire, hating even the garments spotted with the flesh.

3. And this commandment shall be given unto the elders of my church, that every man which will embrace it with singleness of heart, may be ordained and sent forth, even as I have spoken. I am Jesus Christ, the Son of God; wherefore gird up your loins and I will suddenly come to my temple. Even so. Amen.

the book which you shall write, behold, I will raise up another
like unto you, and they shall be had again among the children
of men," etc.   The purpose of this revision was doubtless to
restore these things.   Joseph had been engaged at this work
Rigdon as-   as opportunity offered, and when Sidney Rigdon
sists Joseph.   came, he rendered Joseph valuable assistance.   It
was while engaged in this work in December, 1830, that they
received by revelation an extract from the Prophecy of
Enoch.[4]   The circumstances attending the receiving of this
revelation are described by Joseph as follows:—

"It may be well to observe here that the Lord greatly
encouraged and strengthened the faith of his little flock,

---

[4] 1. And it came to pass, that Enoch continued his speech, saying,
Behold, our father Adam taught these things, and many have believed,
and become the sons of God; and many have believed not, and have perished in their sins, and are looking forth with fear, in torment, for the
fiery indignation of the wrath of God to be poured out upon them.

2. And from that time forth, Enoch began to prophesy, saying unto
the people, that, as I was journeying, and stood in the place Mahujah,
and cried unto the Lord, there came a voice out of heaven, saying, Turn
ye and get ye upon the mount Simeon.

3. And it came to pass, that I turned and went up on the mount; and
as I stood upon the mount, I beheld the heavens open, and I was clothed
upon with glory.

4. And I saw the Lord, and he stood before my face, and he talked with
me, even as a man talketh one with another, face to face; and he said
unto me, Look, and I will show unto thee the world for the space of
many generations.

5. And it came to pass, that I beheld in the valley of Shum, and, lo! a
great people which dwelt in tents, which were the people of Shum.

6. And again the Lord said unto me, Look, and I looked towards the
north, and I beheld the people of Cainan, which dwelt in tents.

7. And the Lord said unto me, Prophesy; and I prophesied, saying,

8. Behold, the people of Cainan which are numerous, shall go forth in
battle array against the people of Shum, and shall slay them, that they
shall be utterly destroyed.

9. And the people of Cainan shall divide themselves in the land, and
the land shall be barren and unfruitful, and none other people shall
dwell there, but the people of Cainan; for, behold, the Lord shall curse
the land with much heat, and the barrenness thereof shall go forth for
ever.

10. And there was a blackness came upon all the children of Cainan,
that they were despised among all people.

11. And it came to pass, that the Lord said unto me, Look, and I
looked, and I beheld the land of Sharon, and the land of Enoch, and the
land of Omner, and the land of Heni, and the land of Shem, and the land
of Haner, and the land of Hanannihah, and all the inhabitants thereof.

12. And the Lord said unto me, Go forth to this people, and say unto
them, Repent; lest I come out and smite them with a curse, and they
die.

13. And he gave unto me a commandment, that I should baptize in the

which had embraced the fullness of the everlasting gospel, as revealed to them in the Book of Mormon, by giving some

name of the Father, and of the Son, who is full of grace and truth, and the Holy Ghost which beareth record of the Father and the Son.

14. And it came to pass, that Enoch continued to call upon all the people, save it were the people of Cainan, to repent.

15. And so great was the faith of Enoch, that he led the people of God, and their enemies came to battle against them, and he spake the word of the Lord, and the earth trembled, and the mountains fled, even according to his command.

16. And the rivers of water were turned out of their course, and the roar of the lions was heard out of the wilderness.

17. And all nations feared greatly, so powerful was the word of Enoch, and so great was the power of the language which God had given him.

18. There also came up a land out of the depths of the sea; and so great was the fear of the enemies of the people of God, that they fled and stood afar off, and went upon the land which came up out of the depths of the sea.

19. And the giants of the land also stood afar off; and there went forth a curse upon all the people which fought against God.

20. And from that time forth, there were wars and bloodshed among them; but the Lord came and dwelt with his people, and they dwelt in righteousness.

21. And the fear of the Lord was upon all nations, so great was the glory of the Lord which was upon his people.

22. And the Lord blessed the land, and they were blessed upon the mountains, and upon the high places, and did flourish.

23. And the Lord called his people, Zion; because they were of one heart and one mind, and dwelt in righteousness; and there was no poor among them.

24. And Enoch continued his preaching in righteousness unto the people of God.

25. And it came to pass in his days, that he built a city that was called the city of Holiness, even Zion.

26. And it came to pass, that Enoch talked with the Lord, and he said unto the Lord, Surely, Zion shall dwell in safety for ever. But the Lord said unto Enoch, Zion have I blessed, but the residue of the people have I cursed.

27. And it came to pass, that the Lord showed unto Enoch all the inhabitants of the earth, and he beheld, and lo! Zion in process of time was taken up into heaven.

28. And the Lord said unto Enoch, Behold mine abode for ever.

29. And Enoch also beheld the residue of the people which were the sons of Adam, and they were a mixture of all the seed of Adam, save it were the seed of Cain; for the seed of Cain were black, and had not place among them.

30. And after that Zion was taken up into heaven, Enoch beheld, and lo, all the nations of the earth were before him; and there came generation upon generation.

31. And Enoch was high and lifted up, even in the bosom of the Father, (and the Son of Man;) and, behold, the powers of Satan were upon all the face of the earth; and he saw angels descending out of heaven, and he heard a loud voice, saying, Woe! woe! be unto the inhabitants of the earth!

32. And he beheld Satan, and he had a great chain in his hand, and it veiled the whole face of the earth with darkness; and he looked up and laughed, and his angels rejoiced.

more extended information upon the Scriptures, a translation of which had already commenced.

"Much conjecture and conversation frequently occurred among the saints concerning the books mentioned, and

33. And Enoch beheld angels descending out of heaven, bearing testimony of the Father, and of the Son.

34. And the Holy Ghost fell on many, and they were caught up by the power of heaven into Zion.

35. And it came to pass, that the God of heaven looked upon the residue of the people, and wept; and Enoch bore record of it, saying, How is it that the heavens weep, and shed forth their tears as the rain upon the mountains? And Enoch said unto the Lord, How is it that thou canst weep, seeing thou art holy, and from all eternity to all eternity?

36. And were it possible that man could number the particles of the earth, yea, and millions of earths like this, it would not be a beginning to the number of thy creations;

37. And thy curtains are stretched out still, and thou art there, and thy bosom is there; and also, thou art just, thou art merciful and kind for ever;

38. Thou hast taken Zion to thine own bosom, from all thy creations, from all eternity to all eternity; and naught but peace, justice, and truth is the habitation of thy throne; and mercy shall go before thy face and have no end. How is it that thou canst weep?

39. The Lord said unto Enoch, Behold, these thy brethren, they are the workmanship of mine own hands, and I gave unto them their knowledge in the day that I created them.

40. And in the garden of Eden gave I unto man his agency; and unto thy brethren have I said, and also gave commandment, that they should love one another; and that they should choose me their Father.

41. But, behold, they are without affection, and they hate their own blood; and the fire of mine indignation is kindled against them; and in my hot displeasure will I send in the floods upon them; for my fierce anger is kindled against them.

42. Behold, I am God; Man of Holiness is my name; Man of Council is my name; and Endless and Eternal is my name also. Wherefore I can stretch forth my hands and hold all the creations which I have made, and mine eye can pierce them also.

43. And among all the workmanship of my hands there has not been so great wickedness as among thy brethren; but, behold, their sins shall be upon the heads of their fathers; Satan shall be their father, and misery shall be their doom; and the whole heavens shall weep over them, even all the workmanship of my hands.

44. Wherefore should not the heavens weep, seeing these shall suffer? But, behold, these which thine eyes are upon shall perish in the floods; and, behold, I will shut them up; a prison have I prepared for them, and that which I have chosen has plead before my face;

45. Wherefore he suffereth for their sins, inasmuch as they will repent, in the day that my chosen shall return unto me; and until that day they shall be in torment.

46. Wherefore for this shall the heavens weep, yea, and all the workmanship of my hands.

47. And it came to pass, that the Lord spake unto Enoch, and told Enoch all the doings of the children of men.

48. Wherefore Enoch knew and looked upon their wickedness, and their misery; and wept, and stretched forth his arms, and his heart

referred to in various places in the Old and New Testaments, which were now nowhere to be found. The common remark was, they were *lost books;* but it seems the apostolic churches had some of these writings, as Jude mentions or

swelled wide as eternity, and his bowels yearned, and all eternity shook.

49. And Enoch saw Noah also, and his family, that the posterity of all the sons of Noah should be saved with a temporal salvation.

50. Wherefore Enoch saw that Noah built an ark, and the Lord smiled upon it, and held it in his own hand; but upon the residue of the wicked came the floods and swallowed them up.

51. And as Enoch saw thus, he had bitterness of soul, and wept over his brethren, and said unto the heavens, I will refuse to be comforted.

52. But the Lord said unto Enoch, Lift up your heart and be glad, and look. And it came to pass, that Enoch looked, and from Noah he beheld all the families of the earth; and he cried unto the Lord, saying, When shall the day of the Lord come? When shall the blood of the righteous be shed, that all they that mourn may be sanctified, and have eternal life?

53. And the Lord said, It shall be in the meridian of time; in the days of wickedness and vengeance.

54. And, behold, Enoch saw the day of the coming of the Son of Man, even in the flesh; and his soul rejoiced, saying, The righteous is lifted up; and the Lamb is slain from the foundation of the world; and through faith I am in the bosom of the Father; and behold, Zion is with me!

55. And it came to pass, that Enoch looked upon the earth, and he heard a voice from the bowels thereof, saying, Woe! woe! is me, the mother of men! I am pained, I am weary, because of the wickedness of my children! When shall I rest, and be cleansed from the filthiness which has gone forth out of me? When will my Creator sanctify me, that I may rest, and righteousness for a season abide upon my face.

56. And when Enoch heard the earth mourn, he wept, and cried unto the Lord, saying, O Lord, wilt thou not have compassion upon the earth? wilt thou not bless the children of Noah?

57. And it came to pass, that Enoch continued his cry unto the Lord, saying, I ask thee, O Lord, in the name of thine Only Begotten, even Jesus Christ, that thou wilt have mercy upon Noah, and his seed, that the earth might never more be covered by the floods.

58. And the Lord could not withhold; and he covenanted with Enoch, and sware unto him with an oath, that he would stay the floods; that he would call upon the children of Noah; and he sent forth an unalterable decree, that a remnant of his seed should always be found among all nations, while the earth should stand.

59. And the Lord said, Blessed is he through whose seed Messiah shall come; for he saith, I am Messiah, the King of Zion, the Rock of heaven, which is broad as eternity; and whoso cometh in at the gate, and climbeth up by me shall never fall. And wherefore blessed are they of whom I have spoken, for they shall

60. Wherefore blessed are they of whom I have spoken, for they shall come forth with songs of everlasting joy.

61. And it came to pass, that Enoch cried unto the Lord, saying, When the Son of Man cometh in the flesh shall the earth rest? I pray thee show me these things.

62. And the Lord said unto Enoch, Look; and he looked, and beheld the Son of Man lifted up on the cross, after the manner of men.

63. And he heard a loud voice, and the heavens were veiled; and all the creations of God mourned, and the earth groaned; and the rocks were

quotes the prophecy of Enoch, the seventh from Adam.   To
the joy of the flock, which in all, from Colesville to Canan-

rent; and the saints arose, and were crowned at the right hand of the
Son of Man, with crowns of glory.

64. And as many of the spirits as were in prison came forth and stood
on the right hand of God.   And the remainder were reserved in chains
of darkness until the judgment of the great day.

65. And again Enoch wept, and cried unto the Lord, saying, When
shall the earth rest?

66. And Enoch beheld the Son of Man ascend up unto the Father; and
he called unto the Lord, saying, Wilt thou not come again upon the
earth? for inasmuch as thou art God, and I know thee, and thou hast
sworn unto me, and commanded me that I should ask in the name of
thine Only Begotten; thou hast made me, and given me a right to thy
throne, and not of myself, but through thine own grace; wherefore I ask
thee if thou wilt not come again on the earth?

67. And the Lord said unto Enoch, As I live, even so will I come in the
last days, in the days of wickedness and vengeance, to fulfill the oath
which I made unto you concerning the children of Noah.

68. And the day shall come that the earth shall rest.   But before that
day the heavens shall be darkened, and a veil of darkness shall cover the
earth; and the heavens shall shake, and also the earth.

69. And great tribulations shall be among the children of men, but my
people will I preserve; and righteousness will I send down out of heaven,
and truth will I send forth out of the earth, to bear testimony of mine
Only Begotten; his resurrection from the dead; yea, and also the resurrection of all men.

70. And righteousness and truth will I cause to sweep the earth as with
a flood, to gather out mine own elect from the four quarters of the earth,
unto a place which I shall prepare: an holy city, that my people may
gird up their loins, and be looking forth for the time of my coming; for
there shall be my tabernacle, and it shall be called Zion; a New Jerusalem.

71. And the Lord said unto Enoch, Then shalt thou and all thy city
meet them there; and we will receive them into our bosom; and they
shall see us, and we will fall upon their necks, and they shall fall upon
our necks, and we will kiss each other;

72. And there shall be mine abode, and it shall be Zion, which shall
come forth out of all the creations which I have made; and for the space
of a thousand years shall the earth rest.

73. And it came to pass, that Enoch saw the day of the coming of the
Son of Man, in the last days, to dwell on the earth, in righteousness, for
the space of a thousand years.

74. But before that day, he saw great tribulation among the wicked;
and he also saw the sea, that it was troubled, and men's hearts failing
them, looking forth with fear for the judgment of the Almighty God,
which should come upon the wicked.

75. And the Lord showed Enoch all things, even unto the end of the
world.   And he saw the day of the righteous, the hour of their redemption, and received a fullness of joy.

76. And all the days of Zion, in the days of Enoch, were three hundred and sixty-five years.

77. And Enoch and all his people walked with God, and he dwelt in
the midst of Zion

78. And it came to pass, that Zion was not, for God received it up into
his own bosom; and from thence went forth the saying, Zion is fled.

daigua, New York, numbered about seventy members, did the Lord reveal the following doings of olden times, from the prophecy of Enoch."—*Times and Seasons*, vol. 4, p. 336.

In December, 1830, there was also a revelation given Directed to directing them to translate no more until they had go to Ohio. removed to Ohio.[5] Thus ended the eventful year of 1830.

This year had seen the Book of Mormon given to the world, the church organized, several branches built up in Events New York and Pennsylvania, the work firmly of 1830. planted in Ohio, where many influential men had been added to the faith, and its adherents in the Western Reserve numbering its hundreds; and as the closing hours of the year were passing away five zealous missionaries were pushing their work farther west among both the Indians and the whites. The translation of the Bible had also been begun and many important revelations had been given. The Melchisedec priesthood had been restored and many glorious blessings, including the extraordinary gifts of the Holy Spirit, enjoyed.

Joseph says: "The year [1831] opened with a prospect great and glorious for the welfare of the kingdom."

A conference convened at Fayette, New York, Sunday, January 2, 1831, at which time a further revelation was Conference given commanding them to go to the Ohio, and at Fayette. promising them a great endowment there; also A promise and warning them that in secret chambers something a warning. was had to bring about their destruction in process of time.[6]

---

[6] 1. Behold, I say unto you, that it is not expedient in me that ye should translate any more until ye shall go to the Ohio; and this because of the enemy and for your sakes. And again, I say unto you, that ye shall not go until ye have preached my gospel in those parts, and have strengthened up the church whithersoever it is found, and more especially in Colesville; for, behold, they pray unto me in much faith.

2. And again a commandment I give unto the church, that it is expedient in me that they should assemble together at the Ohio, against the time that my servant Oliver Cowdery shall return unto them. Behold, here is wisdom, and let every man choose for himself until I come. Even so. Amen.

[6] 1. Thus saith the Lord your God, even Jesus Christ, the great I AM, Alpha and Omega, the beginning and the end, the same which looked

upon the wide expanse of eternity, and all the seraphic hosts of heaven, before the world was made; the same which knoweth all things, for all things are present before mine eyes: I am the same which spake and the world was made, and all things came by me: I am the same which have taken the Zion of Enoch into mine own bosom; and verily I say, even as many as have believed on my name, for I am Christ, and in mine own name. by the virtue of the blood which I have spilt, have I plead before the Father for them: but, behold, the residue of the wicked have I kept in chains of darkness until the judgment of the great day, which shall come at the end of the earth; and even so will I cause the wicked to be kept, that will not hear my voice but harden their hearts, and woe, woe, woe is their doom.

2. But, behold, verily, verily I say unto you, that mine eyes are upon you: I am in your midst and ye cannot see me, but the day soon cometh that ye shall see me and know that I am; for the veil of darkness shall soon be rent, and he that is not purified shall not abide the day: wherefore, gird up your loins and be prepared. Behold, the kingdom is yours and the enemy shall not overcome.

3. Verily I say unto you, Ye are clean but not all; and there is none else with whom I am well pleased, for all flesh is corruptible before me, and the powers of darkness prevail upon the earth, among the children of men, in the presence of all the hosts of heaven, which causeth silence to reign, and all eternity is pained, and the angels are waiting the great command to reap down the earth, to gather the tares that they may be burned; and, behold, the enemy is combined.

4. And now I show unto you a mystery, a thing which is had in secret chambers, to bring to pass even your destruction, in process of time, and ye knew it not, but now I tell it unto you, and ye are blessed, not because of your iniquity, neither your hearts of unbelief, for verily some of you are guilty before me; but I will be merciful unto your weakness. Therefore, be ye strong from henceforth; fear not for the kingdom is yours: and for your salvation I give unto you a commandment, for I have heard your prayers, and the poor have complained before me, and the rich have I made, and all flesh is mine, and I am no respecter of persons. And I have made the earth rich, and, behold, it is my footstool: wherefore, again I will stand upon it; and I hold forth and deign to give unto you greater riches, even a land of promise; a land flowing with milk and honey, upon which there shall be no curse when the Lord cometh; and I will give it unto you for the land of your inheritance, if you seek it with all your hearts: and this shall be my covenant with you, Ye shall have it for the land of your inheritance, and for the inheritance of your children forever, while the earth shall stand; and ye shall possess it again in eternity, no more to pass away.

5. But verily I say unto you, that, in time, ye shall have no king nor ruler, for I will be your king and watch over you. Wherefore, hear my voice and follow me, and you shall be a free people, and ye shall have no laws but my laws, when I come, for I am your lawgiver, and what can stay my hand? But verily I say unto you, Teach one another according to the office wherewith I have appointed you, and let every man esteem his brother as himself, and practice virtue and holiness before me. And again I say unto you, Let every man esteem his brother as himself: for what man among you having twelve sons, and is no respecter to them, and they serve him obediently, and he saith unto the one, Be thou clothed in robes and sit thou here; and to the other, Be thou clothed in rags and sit thou there, and looketh upon his sons and saith, I am just.

6. Behold, this I have given unto you a parable, and it is even as I am: I say unto you, Be one; and if ye are not one, ye are not mine. And

Shortly after this conference there came to Joseph a man whose name was James Covill, who had been a Baptist minister. The word of the Lord came to him through Joseph, but he rejected it and returned to his former principles and people. [1]

James Covill.

---

again I say unto you, that the enemy in the secret chambers seeketh your lives. Ye hear of wars in far countries, and you say that there will soon be great wars in far countries, but ye know not the hearts of men in your own land. I tell you these things because of your prayers; wherefore, treasure up wisdom in your bosoms, lest the wickedness of men reveal these things unto you, by their wickedness, in a manner that shall speak in your ears, with a voice louder than that which shall shake the earth: but if ye are prepared, ye shall not fear.

7. And that ye might escape the power of the enemy, and be gathered unto me a righteous people, without spot and blameless: wherefore, for this cause I gave unto you the commandment, that ye should go to the Ohio; and there I will give unto you my law; and there you shall be endowed with power from on high, and from thence, whomsoever I will, shall go forth among all nations, and it shall be told them what they shall do; for I have a great work laid up in store, for Israel shall be saved, and I will lead them whithersoever I will, and no power shall stay my hand.

8. And now I give unto the church in these parts, a commandment, that certain men among them shall be appointed, and they shall be appointed by the voice of the church; and they shall look to the poor and the needy, and administer to their relief, that they shall not suffer; and send them forth to the place which I have commanded them; and this shall be their work, to govern the affairs of the property of this church. And they that have farms that cannot be sold, let them be left or rented as seemeth them good. See that all things are preserved, and when men are endowed with power from on high, and sent forth, all these things shall be gathered unto the bosom of the church.

9. And if ye seek the riches which it is the will of the Father to give unto you, ye shall be the richest of all people; for ye shall have the riches of eternity; and it must needs be that the riches of the earth are mine to give: but beware of pride, lest ye become as the Nephites of old. And again I say unto you, I give unto you a commandment, that every man, both elder, priest, teacher, and also member, go to with his might, with the labor of his hands, to prepare and accomplish the things which I have commanded. And let your preaching be the warning voice, every man to his neighbor, in mildness and in meekness. And go ye out from among the wicked. Save yourselves. Be ye clean that bear the vessels of the Lord. Even so. Amen.

[1] 1. Hearken and listen to the voice of him who is from all eternity to all eternity, the great I AM, even Jesus Christ, the light and the life of the world; a light which shineth in darkness, and the darkness comprehendeth it not; the same which came in the meridian of time unto my own, and my own received me not; but to as many as received me, gave I power to become my sons, and even so will I give unto as many as will receive me, power to become my sons.

2. And verily, verily I say unto you, He that receiveth my gospel, receiveth me; and he that receiveth not my gospel, receiveth not me. And this is my gospel: repentance and baptism by water, and then cometh

In the latter part of January Joseph and his wife accompanied Sidney Rigdon and Edward Partridge to
Kirtland, Ohio.   A brief history of this move and
of his reception in Kirtland is given by Joseph as follows:—

"The latter part of January, in company with Brothers
Sidney Rigdon and Edward Partridge, I started with my

the baptism of fire and the Holy Ghost, even the Comforter, which showeth all things, and teacheth the peaceable things of the kingdom.

3. And now, behold, I say unto you, my servant James, I have looked
upon thy works, and I know thee; and verily I say unto thee, Thine heart
is now right before me at this time, and, behold, I have bestowed great
blessings upon thy head; nevertheless thou hast seen great sorrow, for
thou hast rejected me many times because of pride, and the cares of the
world; but, behold, the days of thy deliverance are come, if thou wilt
hearken to my voice, which saith unto thee, Arise and be baptized, and
wash away your sins, calling on my name, and you shall receive my
Spirit, and a blessing so great as you never have known. And if thou
do this, I have prepared thee for a greater work. Thou shalt preach the
fullness of my gospel which I have sent forth in these last days; the covenant which I have sent forth to recover my people, which are of the
house of Israel.

4. And it shall come to pass that power shall rest upon thee; thou shalt
have great faith and I will be with thee and go before thy face. Thou
art called to labor in my vineyard, and to build up my church, and to
bring forth Zion, that it my rejoice upon the hills and flourish. Behold,
verily, verily I say unto thee, Thou art not called to go into the eastern
countries, but thou art called to go to the Ohio. And inasmuch as my
people shall assemble themselves to the Ohio, I have kept in store a blessing such as is not known among the children of men, and it shall be
poured forth upon their heads. And from thence men shall go forth into
all nations.

5. Behold, verily, verily I say unto you, that the people in Ohio call
upon me in much faith, thinking I will stay my hand in judgment upon
the nations, but I cannot deny my word; wherefore lay to with your
might and call faithful laborers into my vineyard, that it may be pruned
for the last time. And inasmuch as they do repent and receive the fullness of my gospel, and become sanctified, I will stay mine hand in judgment; wherefore, go forth, crying with a loud voice, saying, The kingdom
of heaven is at hand; crying, Hosanna! blessed be the name of the most
high God. Go forth baptizing with water, preparing the way before my
face, for the time of my coming; for the time is at hand; the day nor
the hour no man knoweth; but it surely shall come, and he that receiveth
these things receiveth me; and they shall be gathered unto me in time
and in eternity.

6. And again, it shall come to pass, that on as many as ye shall baptize
with water, ye shall lay your hands, and they shall receive the gift of the
Holy Ghost, and shall be looking forth for the signs of my coming, and
shall know me. Behold, I come quickly. Even so. Amen.

1. Behold, verily I say unto you, that the heart of my servant James
Covill was right before me, for he covenanted with me, that he would
obey my word. And he received the word with gladness, but straightway
Satan tempted him; and the fear of persecution, and the cares of the
world, caused him to reject the word; wherefore he broke my covenant,
and it remaineth with me to do with him as seemeth me good. Amen.

wife for Kirtland, Ohio, where we arrived about the first of February, and were kindly received and welcomed into the house of Brother N. K. Whitney. I and my wife lived in the family of Brother Whitney several weeks, and received every kindness and attention which could be expected, and especially from Sister Whitney. The branch of the church in this part of the Lord's vineyard, which had increased to nearly one hundred [this evidently should read one thousand] members, were striving to do the will of God, so far as they knew it, though some strange notions and false spirits had crept in among them. With a little caution and some wisdom I soon assisted the brethren and sisters to overcome them. The plan of 'common stock,' which had existed in what was called 'the family,' whose members generally had embraced the everlasting gospel, was readily abandoned for the more perfect law of the Lord: and the false spirits were easily discerned and rejected by the light of revelation."—*Times and Seasons*, vol. 4, p. 368.

On Friday, February 4, 1831, a revelation was given promising, on conditions of their assembling with prayer **Promised a law.** and faith, that a law should be given "that ye may know how to govern my church, and have all things right before me."

In this revelation provision is made for the financial department of the work by the call of the first bishop of the **Bishop called.** church, whose duties were to be subsequently defined. They were also told that the law which they were to receive was "to be answered upon your souls **Law not to be abrogated.** in the day of judgment;" teaching as plainly as words can that it was not to be abrogated in time, but would be in force until the judgment. The reader will please remember this point, for we may refer to it again.[s]

* 1. Hearken and hear, O ye my people, saith the Lord and your God, ye whom I delight to bless with the greatest blessings; ye that hear me: and ye that hear me not will I curse, that have professed my name, with the heaviest of all cursings. Hearken, O ye elders of my church whom I have called: behold, I give unto you a commandment, that ye shall assemble yourselves together to agree upon my word, and by the prayer of your faith ye shall receive my law, that ye may know how to govern my church, and have all things right before me.

2. And I will be your Ruler when I come; and, behold, I come quickly;

The bishop called in this revelation was Edward Partridge, of whom Joseph writes:—

"As Edward Partridge now appears, by revelation, as one of the heads of the church, I will give a sketch of his **Edward** history. He was born in Pittsfield, Berkshire **Partridge.** County, Massachusetts, on the 27th of August, 1793, of William and Jemima Partridge. His father's ancestor emigrated from Berwick, in Scotland, during the seventeenth century, and settled at Hadley, Massachusetts, on Connecticut River. Nothing worthy of note transpired in his youth, with this exception, that he remembers (though the precise time he cannot recollect) that the Spirit of the Lord strove with him a number of times, insomuch that his heart was made tender, and he went and wept, and that sometimes he went silently and poured the effusions of his soul to God in prayer. At the age of sixteen he went to learn the hatting trade, and continued as an apprentice for about four years. At the age of twenty he had become disgusted with the religious world. He saw no beauty, comeliness, or loveliness in the character of the God that was preached up by the sects. He, however, heard a universal restorationer preach upon the love of God; this sermon gave him exalted opinions of God, and he concluded that universal restoration was right according to the Bible. He continued in this belief till 1828, when he and his wife

and ye shall see that my law is kept. He that receiveth my law and doeth it the same is my disciple; and he that saith he receiveth it and doeth it not, the same is not my disciple, and shall be cast out from among you; for it is not meet that the things which belong to the children of the kingdom, should be given to them that are not worthy, or to dogs, or the pearls to be cast before swine.

3. And again, it is meet that my servant Joseph Smith, Jr., should have a house built, in which to live and translate. And again, it is meet that my servant Sidney Rigdon should live as seemeth him good, inasmuch as he keepeth my commandments. And again, I have called my servant Edward Partridge, and give a commandment, that he should be appointed by the voice of the church, and ordained a bishop unto the church, to leave his merchandise and to spend all his time in the labors of the church; to see to all things as it shall be appointed unto him in my laws, in the day that I shall give them. And this because his heart is pure before me, for he is like unto Nathaniel of old, in whom there is no guile. These words are given unto you, and they are pure before me; wherefore, beware how you hold them, for they are to be answered upon your souls in the day of judgment. Even so. Amen.

were baptized into the Campbellite Church, by Elder Sidney
Rigdon, in Mentor, though they resided in Painesville, Ohio.
He continued a member of this church, though doubting at
times its being the true one, till P. P. Pratt, O. Cowdery, P.
Whitmer, and Z. Peterson came along with the Book of
Mormon, when he began to investigate the subject of reli-
gion anew; went with Sidney Rigdon to Fayette, New York,
where, on the 11th of December, I baptized him in the Seneca
River. Other incidents of his life will be noticed in their
time and place."—*Times and Seasons*, vol. 4, pp. 368, 369.

On Wednesday, February 9, the revelation containing
_{Promised} the law, which was before promised, was given,
_{law given.} in the presence of twelve elders. *

* 1. Hearken, O ye elders of my church, who have assembled yourselves together, in my name, even Jesus Christ, the Son of the living
God, the Savior of the world; inasmuch as they believe on my name and
keep my commandments; again I say unto you, Hearken and hear and
obey the law which I shall give unto you; for verily I say, As ye have
assembled yourselves together according to the commandment wherewith I commanded you, and are agreed as touching this one thing, and
have asked the Father in my name, even so ye shall receive.

2. Behold, verily I say unto you, I give unto you this first commandment, that ye shall go forth in my name, every one of you, excepting my
servants Joseph Smith, Jr., and Sidney Rigdon. And I give unto them
a commandment that they shall go forth for a little season, and it shall
be given by the power of my Spirit when they shall return; and ye shall
go forth in the power of my Spirit, preaching my gospel, two by two, in
my name. lifting up your voices as with the voice of a trump, declaring
my word like unto angels of God; and ye shall go forth baptizing with
water, saying, Repent ye, repent ye, for the kingdom of heaven is at
hand.

3. And from this place ye shall go forth into the regions westward;
and inasmuch as ye shall find them that will receive you, ye shall build
up my church in every region, until the time shall come when it shall be
revealed unto you from on high, when the city of the New Jerusalem
shall be prepared, that ye may be gathered in one, that ye may be my
people, and I will be your God. And again, I say unto you, that my
servant Edward Partridge shall stand in the office wherewith I have
appointed him. And it shall come to pass that if he transgress, another
shall be appointed in his stead. Even so. Amen.

4. Again I say unto you that it shall not be given to anyone to go
forth to preach my gospel, or to build up my church, except he be ordained by some one who hath authority, and it is known to the church
that he has authority, and has been regularly ordained by the heads of
the church.

5. And again, the elders, priests, and teachers of this church shall
teach the principles of my gospel which are in the Bible and the Book of
Mormon in the which is the fullness of the gospel; and they shall observe the covenants and church articles to do them, and these shall be
their teachings, as they shall be directed by the Spirit; and the Spirit
shall be given unto you by the prayer of faith, and if ye receive not the

He who will carefully read it will discover that if the
church had heeded it, all the shame and confusion she has
Its impor-
tance.   since experienced would have been avoided.   In
        the government of the church thus. all things
would have been right before God.   Killing, stealing, lying,

Spirit ye shall not teach.   And all this ye shall observe to do as I have
commanded concerning your teaching, until the fullness of my scriptures are given.   And as ye shall lift up your voices by the Comforter,
ye shall speak and prophesy as seemeth me good; for, behold, the Comforter knoweth all things, and beareth record of the Father and of the
Son.

6. And now, behold, I speak unto the church.   Thou shalt not kill;
and he that kills shall not have forgiveness in this world, nor in the
world to come.

7. And again, I say, Thou shalt not kill; but he that killeth shall die.
Thou shalt not steal; and he that stealeth and will not repent, shall be
cast out.   Thou shalt not lie; he that lieth and will not repent, shall be
cast out.   Thou shalt love thy wife with all thy heart, and shall cleave
unto her and none else; and he that looketh upon a woman to lust after
her, shall deny the faith, and shall not have the Spirit; and if he repents
not, he shall be cast out.   Thou shalt not commit adultery; and he that
committeth adultery and repenteth not, shall be cast out; but he that
has committed adultery and repents with all his heart, and forsaketh it,
and doeth it no more, thou shalt forgive; but if he doeth it again, he
shall not be forgiven, but shall be cast out.   Thou shalt not speak evil of
thy neighbor, nor do him any harm.   Thou knowest my laws concerning these things are given in my scriptures; he that sinneth and repenteth not, shall be cast out.

8. If thou lovest me, thou shalt serve me and keep all my commandments.   And, behold, thou wilt remember the poor, and consecrate of
thy properties for their support, that which thou hast to impart unto
them, with a covenant and a deed which cannot be broken; and inasmuch as ye impart of your substance unto the poor, ye will do it unto
me, and they shall be laid before the bishop of my church and his counselors, two of the elders, or high priests, such as he shall or has appointed
and set apart for that purpose.

9. And it shall come to pass that after they are laid before the bishop
of my church, and after that he has received these testimonies concerning the consecration of the properties of my church, that they cannot be
taken from the church, agreeably to my commandments; every man
shall be made accountable unto me, a steward over his own property, or
that which he has received by consecration, inasmuch as is sufficient for
himself and family.

10. And again, if there shall be properties in the hands of the church,
or any individuals of it, more than is necessary for their support, after
this first consecration, which is a residue, to be consecrated unto the
bishop, it shall be kept to administer unto those who have not, from
time to time, that every man who has need may be amply supplied, and
receive according to his wants.   Therefore, the residue shall be kept in
my storehouse, to administer to the poor and the needy, as shall be appointed by the high council of the church, and the bishop and his council, and for the purpose of purchasing lands for the public benefit of the
church. and building houses of worship, and building up of the New
Jerusalem which is hereafter to be revealed, that my covenant people

polygamy, adultery, speaking evil of a neighbor or doing
him harm, pride, with all manner of wickedness, are positively
forbidden; and for the grossest of these crimes the penalty
was expulsion from the church and the guilty member to be

may be gathered in one, in that day when I shall come to my temple.
And this I do for the salvation of my people.

11. And it shall come to pass that he that sinneth and repenteth not,
shall be cast out of the church, and shall not receive again that which
he has consecrated unto the poor and the needy of my church, or, in
other words, unto me; for inasmuch as ye do it unto the least of these,
ye do it unto me; for it shall come to pass that which I spake by the
mouths of my prophets shall be fulfilled; for I will consecrate of the
riches of those who embrace my gospel, among the Gentiles, unto the
poor of my people who are of the house of Israel.

12. And again, thou shalt not be proud in thy heart; let all thy garments be plain, and their beauty the beauty of the work of thine own
hands, and let all things be done in cleanliness before me. Thou shalt
not be idle; for he that is idle shall not eat the bread nor wear the garments of the laborer. And whosoever among you are sick, and have not
faith to be healed, but believe, shall be nourished with all tenderness
with herbs and mild food, and that not by the hand of an enemy. And
the elders of the church, two or more, shall be called, and shall pray for,
and lay their hands upon them in my name; and if they die, they shall
die unto me, and if they live, they shall live unto me. Thou shalt live
together in love, insomuch that thou shalt weep for the loss of them that
die, and more especially for those that have not hope of a glorious resurrection. And it shall come to pass that those that die in me shall not
taste of death, for it shall be sweet unto them; and they that die not in
me, woe unto them, for their death is bitter.

13. And again, it shall come to pass, that he that hath faith in me to be
healed, and is not appointed unto death, shall be healed; he who hath
faith to see shall see; he who hath faith to hear shall hear; the lame who
hath faith to leap shall leap; and they who have not faith to do these
things, but believe in me, have power to become my sons; and inasmuch
as they break not my laws, thou shalt bear their infirmities.

14. Thou shalt stand in the place of thy stewardship; thou shalt not
take thy brother's garment; thou shalt pay for that which thou shalt receive of thy brother; and if thou obtainest more than that which would
be for thy support, thou shalt give it unto my storehouse, that all things
may be done according to that which I have said.

15. Thou shalt ask, and my scriptures shall be given as I have appointed, and they shall be preserved in safety; and it is expedient that
thou shouldst hold thy peace concerning them, and not teach them until
ye have received them in full. And I give unto you a commandment,
that then ye shall teach them unto all men; for they shall be taught
unto all nations, kindreds, tongues, and people.

16. Thou shalt take the things which thou hast received, which have
been given unto thee in my scriptures for a law, to be my law, to govern
my church; and he that doth according to these things, shall be saved,
and he that doeth them not shall be damned, if he continues.

17. If thou shalt ask, thou shalt receive revelation upon revelation,
knowledge upon knowledge, that thou mayest know the mysteries, and
peaceable things; that which bringeth joy, that which bringeth life eternal. Thou shalt ask, and it shall be revealed unto you in mine own due
time, where the New Jerusalem shall be built.

delivered up to the law of the land.   A pure law of morality
is laid down, while the priesthood is also admonished to
teach the principles of the gospel as found in the Bible and
the Book of Mormon.   Instruction is given to make dili-

18. And, behold, it shall come to pass, that my servants shall be sent
forth to the east, and to the west, to the north, and to the south; and
even now, let him that goeth to the east, teach them that shall be converted to flee to the west; and this in consequence of that which is coming on the earth, and of secret combinations.   Behold, thou shalt observe
all these things, and great shall be thy reward; for unto you it is given to
know the mysteries of the kingdom, but unto the world it is not given
to know them.   Ye shall observe the laws which ye have received, and be
faithful.   And ye shall hereafter receive church covenants, such as shall
be sufficient to establish you, both here, and in the New Jerusalem.
Therefore, he that lacketh wisdom, let him ask of me, and I will give
him liberally, and upbraid him not.   Lift up your hearts and rejoice,
for unto you the kingdom, or in other words, the keys of the church,
have been given.   Even so.   Amen.

19. The priests and teachers shall have their stewardships, even as
the members, and the elders, or high priests who are appointed to assist
the bishop as counselors, in all things are to have their families supported out of the property which is consecrated to the bishop, for the
good of the poor, and for other purposes, as before-mentioned, or they
are to receive a just remuneration for all their services; either a stewardship, or otherwise, as may be thought best, or decided by the counselors and bishop.   And the bishop also, shall receive his support, or a just
remuneration for all his services, in the church.

20. Behold, verily I say unto you, that whatever persons among you
having put away their companions for the cause of fornication, or in
other words, if they shall testify before you in all lowliness of heart that
this is the case, ye shall not cast them out from among you; but if ye
shall find that any persons have left their companions for the sake of
adultery, and they themselves are the offenders, and their companions
are living, they shall be cast out from among you.   And again I
say unto you, that ye shall be watchful and careful, with all inquiry,
that ye receive none such among you if they are married, and if they are
not married, they shall repent of all their sins, or ye shall not receive
them.

21. And again, every person who belongeth to this Church of Christ
shall observe to keep all the commandments and covenants of the
church.   And it shall come to pass, that if any persons among you shall
kill, they shall be delivered up and dealt with according to the laws of
the land; for remember that he hath no forgiveness; and it shall be
proven according to the laws of the land.

22. And if any man or woman shall commit adultery, he or she shall
be tried before two elders of the church or more, and every word shall be
established against him or her by two witnesses of the church, and not
of the enemy; but if there are more than two witnesses it is better; but
he or she shall be condemned by the mouth of two witnesses, and the
elders shall lay the case before the church, and the church shall lift up
their hands against him or her, that they may be dealt with according
to the law of God.   And if it can be, it is necessary that the bishop is
present also.   And thus ye shall do in all cases which shall come before
you.   And if a man or woman shall rob, he or she shall be delivered up
unto the law of the land.   And if he or she shall steal, he or she shall be

gent inquiry to avoid receiving those living in transgression, and how to deal with members who violate the law of God.

As before promised, instruction was given respecting the bishop's duty, and the duty of the church towards him as a Instruction to representative of the financial department of the the Bishop. church. Altogether it is one of the most important documents ever given to the church, and should be carefully studied by all.

Soon after this revelation was given a woman came pretending to give revelations and commandments to the A woman gives church; and as she, like all others of great prerevelations. tensions, found sympathizers, Joseph inquired and received a revelation on the subject.[10]

---

delivered up unto the law of the land. And if he or she shall lie, he or she shall be delivered up unto the law of the land. If he or she do any manner of iniquity, he or she shall be delivered up unto the law, even that of God.

23. And if thy brother or sister offend thee, thou shalt take him or her between him or her and thee alone; and if he or she confess, thou shalt be reconciled. And if he or she confess not, thou shalt deliver him or her up unto the church, not to the members, but to the elders. And it shall be done in a meeting, and that not before the world. And if thy brother or sister offend many, he or she shall be chastened before many. And if anyone offend openly, he or she shall be rebuked openly, that he or she may be ashamed. And if he or she confess not, he or she shall be delivered up unto the law of God. If any shall offend in secret, he or she shall be rebuked in secret, that he or she may have opportunity to confess in secret to him or her whom he or she has offended, and to God, that the church may not speak reproachfully of him or her. And thus shall ye conduct in all things.

[10] 1. O hearken, ye elders of my church, and give ear to the words which I shall speak unto you: for, behold, verily, verily I say unto you, that ye have received a commandment for a law unto my church, through him whom I have appointed unto you, to receive commandments and revelations from my hand. And this ye shall know assuredly, that there is none other appointed unto you to receive commandments and revelations until he be taken, if he abide in me.

2. But verily, verily I say unto you, that none else shall be appointed unto this gift except it be through him, for if it be taken from him he shall not have power, except to appoint another in his stead; and this shall be a law unto you, that ye receive not the teachings of any that shall come before you as revelations, or commandments; and this I give unto you, that you may not be deceived, that you may know they are not of me. For verily I say unto you, that he that is ordained of me, shall come in at the gate and be ordained as I have told you before, to teach those revelations which you have received, and shall receive through him whom I have appointed.

3. And now, behold, I give unto you a commandment, that when ye are assembled together, ye shall instruct and edify each other, that ye may know how to act and direct my church how to act upon the points

This circumstance will explain why the positive statement was made, "Ye shall know assuredly, that there is none other appointed unto you to receive commandments and revelations until he be taken, if he abide in me."

of my law and commandments, which I have given; and thus ye shall become instructed in the law of my church, and be sanctified by that which ye have received, and ye shall bind yourselves to act in all holiness before me, that inasmuch as ye do this, glory shall be added to the kingdom which ye have received. Inasmuch as ye do it not, it shall be taken, even that which ye have received. Purge ye out the iniquity which is among you; sanctify yourselves before me, and if ye desire the glories of the kingdom, appoint ye my servant Joseph Smith, Jr., and uphold him before me by the prayer of faith. And again, I say unto you, that if ye desire the mysteries of the kingdom, provide for him food and raiment and whatsoever thing he needeth to accomplish the work, wherewith I have commanded him; and if ye do it not, he shall remain unto them that have received him, that I may reserve unto myself a pure people before me.

4. Again I say, hearken ye elders of my church whom I have appointed: ye are not sent forth to be taught, but to teach the children of men the things which I have put into your hands by the power of my Spirit; and ye are to be taught from on high. Sanctify yourselves and ye shall be endowed with power, that ye may give even as I have spoken.

5. Hearken ye, for, behold, the great day of the Lord is nigh at hand. For the day cometh that the Lord shall utter his voice out of heaven; the heavens shall shake and the earth shall tremble, and the trump of God shall sound both long and loud, and shall say to the sleeping nations: Ye saints arise and live: Ye sinners stay and sleep until I shall call again: wherefore gird up your loins, lest ye be found among the wicked. Lift up your voices and spare not. Call upon the nations to repent, both old and young, both bond and free; saying, Prepare yourselves for the great day of the Lord: for if I, who am a man, do lift up my voice and call upon you to repent, and ye hate me, what will ye say when the day cometh when the thunders shall utter their voices from the ends of the earth, speaking to the ears of all that live, saying: Repent, and prepare for the great day of the Lord; yea, and again, when the lightnings shall streak forth from the east unto the west, and shall utter forth their voices unto all that live, and make the ears of all tingle, that hear, saying these words: Repent ye, for the great day of the Lord is come.

6. And again, the Lord shall utter his voice out of heaven, saying: Hearken, O ye nations of the earth, and hear the words of that God who made you. O, ye nations of the earth, how often would I have gathered you together as a hen gathereth her chickens under her wings, but ye would not? How oft have I called upon you by the mouth of my servants, and by the ministering of angels, and by mine own voice, and by the voice of thunderings, and by the voice of lightnings, and by the voice of tempests, and by the voice of earthquakes, and great hailstorms, and by the voice of famines and pestilences of every kind, and by the great sound of a trump, and by the voice of judgment, and by the voice of mercy all the day long, and by the voice of glory and honor, and the riches of eternal life, and would have saved you with an everlasting salvation, but ye would not? Behold, the day has come, when the cup of the wrath of mine indignation is full.

7. Behold, verily I say unto you, that these are the words of the Lord your God; wherefore, labor ye, labor ye in my vineyard for the last time:

Here also is an intimation to the church that Joseph would at some time be taken away; and in connection with it pro-

Joseph's successor. vision was made for the selection of his successor, and the people warned to be not deceived. It was also said that this successor should "teach those revelations which you *have received*, and *shall receive* through him whom I have appointed;" thus forewarning the church that after Joseph should be taken away revelations would be presented not consistent with the former ones; and in such a case they were in this warned to be not deceived, for the true successor would teach nothing that did not harmonize with former revelations, hence could consistently teach both.

Soon after this, another revelation was given which provided for the calling of a General Conference.[11]

This conference was called to meet early in June. There is a little discrepancy in accounts regarding the exact day, of which more will be said hereafter.

---

for the last time call upon the inhabitants of the earth, for in my own due time will I come upon the earth in judgment; and my people shall be redeemed and shall reign with me on earth; for the great Millennial, which I have spoken by the mouth of my servants, shall come; for Satan shall be bound; and when he is loosed again, he shall only reign for a little season, and then cometh the end of the earth; and he that liveth in righteousness, shall be changed in the twinkling of an eye; and the earth shall pass away so as by fire; and the wicked shall go away into unquenchable fire; and their end no man knoweth, on earth, nor ever shall know, until they come before me in judgment.

8. Hearken ye to these words; behold, I am Jesus Christ, the Savior of the world. Treasure these things up in your hearts, and let the solemnities of eternity rest upon your minds. Be sober. Keep all my commandments. Even so. Amen.

[11] 1. Behold, thus saith the Lord unto you, my servants, it is expedient in me that the elders of my church should be called together, from the east, and from the west, and from the north, and from the south, by letter, or some other way.

2. And it shall come to pass, that inasmuch as they are faithful, and exercise faith in me, I will pour out my Spirit upon them in the day that they assemble themselves together. And it shall come to pass that they shall go forth into the regions round about, and preach repentance unto the people; and many shall be converted, insomuch that ye shall obtain power to organize yourselves according to the laws of man, that your enemies may not have power over you, that you may be preserved in all things, that you may be enabled to keep my laws, that every band may be broken wherewith the enemy seeketh to destroy my people.

3. Behold, I say unto you, that ye must visit the poor and the needy, and administer to their relief, that they may be kept until all things may be done according to my law, which ye have received. Amen.

About this time many strange, foolish, and false stories
Slanderous reports. went the rounds of the newspapers about "the
Mormons." Some of these were forgotten in
time, but some are yet related by the ignorant and profane.

While these scenes were being enacted in Kirtland, the
word was being preached in other parts, and many were
obedient to the message. An extract from P. P. Pratt's
Mission among the Ind ans. account of their mission among the Indians may
prove interesting. In his autobiography he
writes:—

"In the beginning of 1831 we renewed our journey; and,
passing through St. Louis and St. Charles, we traveled on
foot for three hundred miles through vast prairies and
through trackless wilds of snow—no beaten road; houses
few and far between; and the bleak northwest wind always
blowing in our faces with a keenness which would almost
take the skin off the face. We traveled for whole days,
from morning till night, without a house or fire, wading in
snow to the knees at every step, and the cold so intense that
the snow did not melt on the south side of the houses, even
in the midday sun, for nearly six weeks. We carried on
our backs our changes of clothing, several books, and corn
bread and raw pork. We often eat [ate] our frozen bread
and pork by the way, when the bread would be so frozen
that we could not bite or penetrate any part of it but the
outside crust.

"After much fatigue and some suffering we all arrived in
Independence, in the county of Jackson, on the extreme
western frontiers of Missouri, and of the United States.

"This was about fifteen hundred miles from where we
started, and we had performed most of the journey on foot,
through a wilderness country, in the worst season of the
year, occupying about four months, during which we had
preached the gospel to tens of thousands of Gentiles and
two nations of Indians; baptizing, confirming, and organizing many hundreds of people into churches of Latter Day
Saints.

"This was the first mission performed by the elders of the
church in any of the States west of New York, and we were

the first members of the same which were ever on this frontier.

"Two of our number now commenced work as tailors in the village of Independence, while the others crossed the frontier line and commenced a mission among the Lamanites, or Indians.

"Passing through the tribe of Shawnees we tarried one night with them, and the next day crossed the Kansas River and entered among the Delawares. We immediately inquired for the residence of the principal chief, and were soon introduced to an aged and venerable looking man, who had long stood at the head of the Delawares, and been looked up to as the Great Grandfather, or Sachem of ten nations or tribes.

"He was seated on a sofa of furs, skins, and blankets, before a fire in the center of his lodge; which was a comfortable cabin, consisting of two large rooms.

"His wives were neatly dressed, partly in calicoes and partly in skins; and wore a vast amount of silver ornaments. As we entered his cabin he took us by the hand with a hearty welcome, and then motioned us to be seated on a pleasant seat of blankets, or robes. His wives, at his bidding, set before us a tin pan full of beans and corn boiled up together, which proved to be good eating; although three of us made use alternately of the same wooden spoon.

"There was an interpreter present and through him we commenced to make known our errand, and to tell him of the Book of Mormon. We asked him to call the council of his nation together and give us a hearing in full. He promised to consider on it till next day, in the meantime recommending us to a certain Mr. Pool for entertainment; this was their blacksmith, employed by government.

"The man entertained us kindly and comfortably. Next morning we again called on Mr. Anderson, the old chief, and explained to him something of the Book. He was at first unwilling to call his council; made several excuses, and finally refused; as he had ever been opposed to the introduction of missionaries among his tribe.

"We continued the conversation a little longer, till he at

last began to understand the nature of the Book. He then changed his mind; became suddenly interested, and requested us to proceed no further with our conversation till he could call a council. He despatched a messenger, and in about an hour had some forty men collected around us in his lodge, who, after shaking us by the hand, were seated in silence; and in a grave and dignified manner awaited the announcement of what we had to offer. The chief then requested us to proceed; or rather, begin where we began before, and to complete our communication. Elder Cowdery then commenced as follows:—

" 'Aged Chief and Venerable Council of the Delaware nation; we are glad of this opportunity to address you as our red brethren and friends. We have traveled a long distance from towards the rising sun to bring you glad news; we have traveled the wilderness, crossed the deep and wide rivers, and waded in the deep snows, and in the face of the storms of winter, to communicate to you great knowledge which has lately come to our ears and hearts; and which will do the red man good as well as the pale face.

" 'Once the red men were many; they occupied the country from sea to sea—from the rising to the setting sun; the whole land was theirs; the Great Spirit gave it to them, and no pale faces dwelt among them. But now they are few in numbers; their possessions are small, and the pale faces are many.

" 'Thousands of moons ago, when the red men's forefathers dwelt in peace and possessed this whole land, the Great Spirit talked with them, and revealed His law and His will, and much knowledge to their wise men and prophets. This they wrote in a Book; together with their history, and the things which should befall their children in the latter days.

" 'This Book was written on plates of gold, and handed down from father to son for many ages and generations.

" 'It was then that the people prospered, and were strong and mighty; they cultivated the earth; built buildings and cities, and abounded in all good things, as the pale faces now do.

" 'But they became wicked; they killed one another and shed much blood; they killed their prophets and wise men, and sought to destroy the Book. The Great Spirit became angry, and would speak to them no more; they had no more good and wise dreams; no more visions; no more angels sent among them by the Great Spirit; and the Lord commanded Mormon and Moroni, their last wise men and prophets, to hide the Book in the earth, that it might be preserved in safety, and be found and made known in the latter day to the pale faces who should possess the land; that they might again make it known to the red man; in order to restore them to the knowledge of the will of the Great Spirit and to His favor. And if the red man would then receive this Book and learn the things written in it, and do according thereunto, they should be restored to all their rights and privileges; should cease to fight and kill one another; should become one people; cultivate the earth in peace, in common with the pale faces, who were willing to believe and obey the same book, and be good men and live in peace.

" 'Then should the red men become great, and have plenty to eat and good clothes to wear, and should be in favor with the Great Spirit and be his children, while he would be their Great Father, and talk with them, and raise up prophets and wise and good men amongst them again, who should teach them many things.

" 'This Book, which contained these things, was hid in the earth by Moroni, in a hill called by him, Cumorah, which hill is now in the State of New York, near the village of Palmyra, in Ontario County.

" 'In that neighborhood there lived a young man named Joseph Smith, who prayed to the Great Spirit much, in order that he might know the truth; and the Great Spirit sent an angel to him, and told him where this Book was hid by Moroni; and commanded him to go and get it. He accordingly went to the place, and dug in the earth, and found the Book written on golden plates.

" 'But it was written in the language of the forefathers of the red man; therefore this young man, being a pale face, could not understand it; but the angel told him and showed him, and gave him knowledge of the language, and how to interpret the Book. So he interpreted it into the language of the pale faces, and wrote it on paper, and caused it to be printed, and published thousands of copies of it among them; and then sent us to the red men to bring some copies of it to them, and to tell them this news. So we have now come from him, and here is a copy of the Book, which we now present to our red friend, the chief of the Delawares, and which we hope he will cause to be read and known among his tribe; it will do them good.'

"We then presented him with a Book of Mormon.

"There was a pause in the council, and some conversation in their own tongue, after which the chief made the following reply:—

" 'We feel truly thankful to our white friends who have come so far, and been at such pains to tell us good news, and especially this new news concerning the Book of our forefathers; it makes us glad in here'—placing his hand on his heart.

" 'It is now winter, we are new settlers in this place; the snow is deep, our cattle and horses are dying, our wigwams are poor; we have much to do in the spring –to build houses, and fence and make farms; but we will build a council house, and meet together, and you shall read to us and teach us more concerning the Book of our fathers and the will of the Great Spirit.'

"We again lodged at Mr. Pool's, told him of the Book, had a very pleasant interview with him, and he became a believer and advocate for the Book, and served as an interpreter.

"We continued for several days to instruct the old chief and many of his tribe. The interest became more and more intense on their part, from day to day, until at length nearly the whole tribe began to feel a spirit of inquiry and excitement on the subject.

"We found several among them who could read, and to them we gave copies of the Book, explaining to them that it was the Book of their forefathers.

"Some began to rejoice exceedingly, and took great pains to tell the news to others, in their own language.

"The excitement now reached the frontier settlements in Missouri, and stirred up the jealousy and envy of the Indian agents and sectarian missionaries to that degree that we were soon ordered out of the Indian country as disturbers of the peace; and even threatened with the military in case of non-compliance.

"We accordingly departed from the Indian country, and came over the line, and commenced laboring in Jackson County, Missouri, among the whites. We were well received, and listened to by many; and some were baptized and added to the church.

"Thus ended our first Indian Mission, in which we had preached the gospel in its fullness, and distributed the record of their forefathers among three tribes, viz.: the Catteraugus Indians, near Buffalo, New York, the Wyandots of Ohio, and the Delawares west of Missouri.

"We trust that at some future day, when the servants of God go forth in power to the remnant of Joseph, some precious seed will be found growing in their hearts, which was sown by us in that early day."—Autobiography of Parley P. Pratt, pp. 54–61.

Orson Pratt, early in 1831, had walked from New York to
O. Pratt's labors. Kirtland, Ohio, preaching by the way, and was zealously laboring with success in Northern Ohio.

Lyman Wight records in his journal that from the date of his ordination, November 20, 1830, to June 14, 1831, he trav-
Labors of Lyman Wight. eled six hundred miles in Ohio and Pennsylvania, baptized three hundred and ninety-three persons, and organized eight churches. Several others were doing missionary work, but we have not the items.

On Monday, March 7, 1831, another revelation was received, in which the people were commanded to gather out
Gather out of eastern lands. of the eastern lands, and the elders were commanded to go to western countries with the gospel message.[12]

---

[12] 1. Hearken, O ye people of my church, to whom the kingdom has been given, hearken ye, and give ear to him who laid the foundation of the earth, who made the heavens and all the hosts thereof, and by whom all things were made which live and move and have a being. And again I say, Hearken unto my voice, lest death shall overtake you; in an hour

when ye think not, the summer shall be past, and the harvest ended, and your souls not saved.   Listen to him who is the Advocate with the Father, who is pleading your cause before him, saying, Father, behold the sufferings and death of him who did no sin, in whom thou wast well pleased; behold the blood of thy Son which was shed, the blood of him whom thou gavest that thyself might be glorified; wherefore, Father, spare these my brethren that believe on my name, that they may come unto me and have everlasting life.

2. Hearken, O ye people of my church, and ye elders, listen together, and hear my voice, while it is called to-day, and harden not your hearts; for verily I say unto you that I am Alpha and Omega, the beginning and the end, the light and the life of the world; a light that shineth in darkness, and the darkness comprehendeth it not.   I came unto my own, and my own received me not; but unto as many as received me gave I power to do miracles and to become the sons of God, and even unto them that believed on my name gave I power to obtain eternal life.   And even so I have sent mine everlasting covenant into the world, to be a light to the world, and to be a standard for my people and for the Gentiles to seek to it, and to be a messenger before my face to prepare the way before me. Wherefore come ye unto it; and with him that cometh I will reason as with men in days of old, and I will show unto you my strong reasoning: wherefore hearken ye together, and let me show it unto you, even my wisdom, the wisdom of him whom you say is the God of Enoch and his brethren, who were separated from the earth, and were received unto myself; a city reserved until a day of righteousness shall come: a day which was sought for by all holy men, and they found it not, because of wickedness and abominations, and confessed that they were strangers and pilgrims on the earth, but obtained a promise that they should find it, and see it in their flesh.   Wherefore hearken, and I will reason with you, and I will speak unto you and prophesy, as unto men in days of old; and I will show it plainly, as I showed it unto my disciples, as I stood before them in the flesh, and spake unto them, saying, As ye have asked of me concerning the signs of my coming, in the day when I shall come in my glory in the clouds of heaven, to fulfill the promises that I have made unto your fathers; for as ye have looked upon the long absence of your spirits from your bodies to be a bondage, I will show unto you how the day of redemption shall come, and also the restoration of the scattered Israel.

3. And now ye behold this temple which is in Jerusalem, which ye call the house of God, and your enemies say that this house shall never fall.   But verily I say unto you that desolation shall come upon this generation as a thief in the night, and this people shall be destroyed and scattered among all nations.   And this temple which ye now see shall be thrown down, that there shall not be left one stone upon another.   And it shall come to pass that this generation of Jews shall not pass away until every desolation which I have told you concerning them shall come to pass.   Ye say that ye know that the end of the world cometh; ye say, also, that ye know that the heavens and the earth shall pass away; and in this ye say truly, for so it is; but these things which I have told you shall not pass away until all shall be fulfilled.   And this I have told you concerning Jerusalem; and when that day shall come, shall a remnant be scattered among all nations, but they shall be gathered again; but they shall remain until the times of the Gentiles be fulfilled.

4. And in that day shall be heard of wars and rumors of wars, and the whole earth shall be in commotion, and men's hearts shall fail them, and they shall say that Christ delayeth his coming until the end of the earth. And the love of men shall wax cold, and iniquity shall abound; and when the time of the Gentiles is come in, a light shall break forth among them

that sit in darkness, and it shall be the fullness of my gospel; but they receive it not, for they perceive not the light, and they turn their hearts from me because of the precepts of men; and in that generation shall the times of the Gentiles be fulfilled; and there shall be men standing in that generation that shall not pass, until they shall see an overflowing scourge, for a desolating sickness shall come over the land; but my disciples shall stand in holy places, and shall not be moved; but among the wicked, men shall lift up their voices and curse God, and die. And there shall be earthquakes, also, in divers places, and many desolations; yet men will harden their hearts against me, and they will take up the sword one against another, and they will kill one another.

5. And now, when I the Lord had spoken these words unto my disciples, they were troubled; and I said unto them, Be not troubled, for when all these things come to pass, ye may know that the promises which have been made unto you shall be fulfilled; and when the light shall begin to break forth, it shall be with them like unto a parable which I shall show you; ye look and behold the fig trees, and ye see them with your eyes, and ye say, when they begin to shoot forth and their leaves are yet tender, that summer is now nigh at hand; even so it shall be in that day, when they shall see all these things, then shall they know that the hour is nigh.

6. And it shall come to pass that he that feareth me shall be looking forth for the great day of the Lord to come, even for the signs of the coming of the Son of Man; and they shall see signs and wonders, for they shall be shown forth in the heavens above, and in the earth beneath; and they shall behold blood and fire, and vapors of smoke; and before the day of the Lord shall come, the sun shall be darkened, and the moon be turned into blood, and stars fall from heaven; and the remnant shall be gathered unto this place; and then they shall look for me, and behold I will come; and they shall see me in the clouds of heaven, clothed with power and great glory, with all the holy angels; and he that watches not for me shall be cut off.

7. But before the arm of the Lord shall fall, an angel shall sound his trump, and the saints that have slept, shall come forth to meet me in the cloud; wherefore if ye have slept in peace, blessed are you, for as you now behold me and know that I am, even so shall ye come unto me and your souls shall live, and your redemption shall be perfected, and the saints shall come forth from the four quarters of the earth.

8. Then shall the arm of the Lord fall upon all nations, and then shall the Lord set his foot upon this mount, and it shall cleave in twain, and the earth shall tremble and reel to and fro; and the heavens also shall shake, and the Lord shall utter his voice and all the ends of the earth shall hear it, and the nations of the earth shall mourn, and they that have laughed shall see their folly, and calamity shall cover the mocker, and the scorner shall be consumed, and they that have watched for iniquity, shall be hewn down and cast into the fire.

9. And then shall the Jews look upon me and say, What are these wounds in thy hands, and in thy feet? Then shall they know that I am the Lord; for I will say unto them, These wounds are the wounds with which I was wounded in the house of my friends. I am he who was lifted up. I am Jesus that was crucified. I am the Son of God. And then shall they weep because of their iniquities; then shall they lament because they persecuted their King.

10. And then shall the heathen nations be redeemed, and they that knew no law shall have part in the first resurrection; and it shall be tolerable for them; and Satan shall be bound that he shall have no place in the hearts of the children of men. And at that day when I shall come in my glory, shall the parable be fulfilled which I spake concerning the ten virgins; for they that are wise and have received the truth,

During the month of March much valuable information was given by revelation.[13]

and have taken the Holy Spirit for their guide, and have not been deceived, verily I say unto you, They shall not be hewn down and cast into the fire, but shall abide the day, and the earth shall be given unto them for an inheritance; and they shall multiply and wax strong, and their children shall grow up without sin unto salvation, for the Lord shall be in their midst, and his glory shall be upon them, and he will be their King and their law-giver.

11. And now, behold, I say unto you, It shall not be given unto you to know any further concerning this chapter, until the New Testament be translated, and in it all these things shall be made known; wherefore I give unto you that you may now translate it, that ye may be prepared for the things to come; for verily I say unto you, that great things await you; ye hear of wars in foreign lands, but, behold, I say unto you, They are nigh, even at your doors, and not many years hence ye shall hear of wars in your own lands.

12. Wherefore, I the Lord have said, Gather ye out from the eastern lands, assemble ye yourselves together ye elders of my church; go ye forth unto the western countries, call upon the inhabitants to repent, and inasmuch as they do repent, build up churches unto me; and with one heart and with one mind, gather up your riches that ye may purchase an inheritance which shall hereafter be appointed unto you, and it shall be called the New Jerusalem, a land of peace, a city of refuge, a place of safety for the saints of the most high God; and the glory of the Lord shall be there, and the terror of the Lord also shall be there, insomuch that the wicked will not come unto it; and it shall be called Zion.

13. And it shall come to pass, among the wicked, that every man that will not take his sword against his neighbor, must needs flee unto Zion for safety. And there shall be gathered unto it out of every nation under heaven; and it shall be the only people that shall not be at war one with another. And it shall be said among the wicked, Let us not go up to battle against Zion, for the inhabitants of Zion are terrible, wherefore we cannot stand.

14. And it shall come to pass that the righteous shall be gathered out from among all nations, and shall come to Zion singing, with songs of everlasting joy.

15. And now I say unto you, Keep these things from going abroad unto the world, until it is expedient in me, that ye may accomplish this work in the eyes of the people and in the eyes of your enemies, that they may not know your works until ye have accomplished the thing which I have commanded you; that when they shall know it, that they may consider these things, for when the Lord shall appear he shall be terrible unto them, that fear may seize upon them, and they shall stand afar off and tremble; and all nations shall be afraid because of the terror of the Lord, and the power of his might. Even so. Amen.

[13] 1. Hearken, O ye people of my church, for verily I say unto you, that these things were spoken unto you for your profit and learning; but notwithstanding those things which are written, it always has been given to the elders of my church, from the beginning, and ever shall be, to conduct all meetings as they are directed and guided by the Holy Spirit; nevertheless, ye are commanded never to cast anyone out from your public meetings, which are held before the world. Ye are also commanded not to cast anyone, who belongeth to the church, out of your sacrament meetings; nevertheless, if any have trespassed, let him not partake until he makes reconciliation.

2. And again I say unto you, Ye shall not cast anyone out of your sacrament meetings, who is earnestly seeking the kingdom: I speak this concerning those who are not of the church.

3. And again I say unto you, concerning your confirmation meetings, that if there be any that is not of the church, that is earnestly seeking after the kingdom, ye shall not cast them out; but ye are commanded in all things to ask of God, who giveth liberally, and that which the Spirit testifies unto you, even so I would that ye should do in all holiness of heart, walking uprightly before me, considering the end of your salvation, doing all things with prayer and thanksgiving, that ye may not be seduced by evil spirits, or doctrines of devils, or the commandments of men, for some are of men, and others of devils.

4. Wherefore, beware, lest ye are deceived, and that ye may not be deceived, seek ye earnestly the best gifts, always remembering for what they are given; for verily I say unto you, They are given for the benefit of those who love me and keep all my commandments, and him that seeketh so to do, that all may be benefited, that seeketh or that asketh of me, that asketh and not for a sign that he may consume it upon his lusts.

5. And again, verily I say unto you, I would that ye should always remember, and always retain in your minds what those gifts are, that are given unto the church, for all have not every gift given unto them; for there are many gifts, and to every man is given a gift by the Spirit of God: to some it is given one, and to some is given another, that all may be profited thereby; to some it is given by the Holy Ghost to know that Jesus Christ is the Son of God, and that he was crucified for the sins of the world; to others it is given to believe on their words, that they also might have eternal life, if they continue faithful.

6. And again, to some it is given by the Holy Ghost to know the differences of administration, as it will be pleasing unto the same Lord, according as the Lord will, suiting his mercies according to the conditions of the children of men. And again, it is given by the Holy Ghost to some to know the diversities of operations, whether it be of God, that the manifestation of the Spirit may be given to every man to profit withal.

7. And again, verily I say unto you, To some it is given, by the Spirit of God, the word of wisdom; to another it is given the word of knowledge, that all may be taught to be wise and to have knowledge. And again, to some it is given to have faith to be healed, and to others it is given to have faith to heal. And again, to some it is given the working of miracles; and to others it is given to prophesy, and to others the discerning of spirits. And again, it is given to some to speak with tongues, and to another it is given the interpretation of tongues: and all these gifts cometh from God, for the benefit of the children of God. And unto the bishop of the church, and unto such as God shall appoint and ordain to watch over the church, and to be elders unto the church, are to have it given unto them to discern all those gifts, lest there shall be any among you professing and yet be not of God.

8. And it shall come to pass that he that asketh in spirit shall receive in spirit; that unto some it may be given to have all those gifts, that there may be a head, in order that every member may be profited thereby: he that asketh in the spirit, asketh according to the will of God, wherefore it is done even as he asketh.

9. And again I say unto you, All things must be done in the name of Christ, whatsoever you do in the spirit; and ye must give thanks unto God in the spirit for whatsoever blessing ye are blessed with; and ye must practice virtue and holiness before me continually. Even so. Amen.

About this time there united with the church a gentleman
by the name of Lemon Copley, who was formerly a member
Shakers.   of the society of Shakers, and who still believed
          the Shakers were right in some particulars.
Joseph therefore inquired of the Lord and obtained information.[14]

1. Behold, it is expedient in me that my servant John should write
and keep a regular history, and assist you, my servant Joseph, in transcribing all things which shall be given you, until he is called to further
duties. Again, verily I say unto you, that he can also lift up his voice
in meetings, whenever it shall be expedient.

2. And again, I say unto you, that it shall be appointed unto him to
keep the church record and history continually, for Oliver Cowdery I
have appointed to another office. Wherefore, it shall be given him,
inasmuch as he is faithful, by the Comforter, to write these things.
Even so. Amen.

1. It is necessary that ye should remain, for the present time, in your
places of abode, as it shall be suitable to your circumstances; and inasmuch as ye have lands, ye shall impart to the eastern brethren; and
inasmuch as ye have not lands, let them buy for the present time in
those regions round about as seemeth them good, for it must needs be
necessary that they have places to live for the present time.

2. It must needs be necessary, that ye save all the money that ye can,
and that ye obtain all that ye can in righteousness, that in time ye may
be enabled to purchase lands for an inheritance, even the city. The
place is not yet to be revealed, but after your brethren come from the
east, there are to be certain men appointed, and to them it shall be given
to know the place, or to them it shall be revealed; and they shall be
appointed to purchase the lands, and to make a commencement, to lay
the foundation of the city; and then ye shall begin to be gathered with
your families, every man according to his family, according to his circumstances, and as is appointed to him by the presidency and the bishop
of the church, according to the laws and commandments, which ye have
received, and which ye shall hereafter receive. Even so. Amen.

[14] 1. Hearken unto my word, my servants Sidney, and Parley, and
Lemon, for, behold, verily I say unto you, that I give unto you a commandment, that you shall go and preach my gospel, which ye have
received, even as ye have received it, unto the Shakers. Behold, I say
unto you, that they desire to know the truth in part, but not all, for they
are not right before me, and must needs repent; wherefore I send you, my
servants Sidney and Parley, to preach the gospel unto them; and my
servant Lemon shall be ordained unto this work, that he may reason
with them, not according to that which he has received of them, but according to that which shall be taught him by you, my servants, and by
so doing I will bless him, otherwise he shall not prosper: thus saith the
Lord, for I am God and have sent mine only begotten Son into the world,
for the redemption of the world, and have decreed that he that receiveth
him shall be saved, and he that receiveth him not shall be damned.

2. And they have done unto the Son of Man even as they listed; and he
has taken his power on the right hand of his glory, and now reigneth in
the heavens, and will reign till he descends on the earth to put all
enemies under his feet; which time is nigh at hand: I, the Lord God,

In one of the revelations before cited John Whitmer was appointed Church Historian that the record of events might be kept,—a very necessary and important work. Thus, one by one, things were put into shape for complete and orderly work.

Historian appointed.

During the month of April Joseph was engaged on the work of translating the Scriptures as before referred to.

have spoken it; but the hour and the day no man knoweth, neither the angels in heaven, nor shall they know until he comes; wherefore I will that all men shall repent, for all are under sin, except them which I have reserved unto myself, holy men that ye know not of; wherefore I say unto you, that I have sent unto you mine everlasting covenant, even that which was from the beginning, and that which I have promised I have so fulfilled, and the nations of the earth shall bow to it; and, if not of themselves, they shall come down, for that which is now exalted of itself, shall be laid low of power; wherefore I give unto you a commandment that ye go among this people and say unto them, like unto mine apostle of old, whose name was Peter: Believe on the name of the Lord Jesus, who was on the earth, and is to come, the beginning and the end; repent and be baptized in the name of Jesus Christ, according to the holy commandment, for the remission of sins; and whoso doeth this, shall receive the gift of the Holy Ghost, by the laying on of the hands of the elders of this church.

3. And again, I say unto you, that whoso forbiddeth to marry, is not ordained of God, for marriage is ordained of God unto man; wherefore it is lawful that he should have one wife, and they twain shall be one flesh, and all this that the earth might answer the end of its creation; and that it might be filled with the measure of man, according to his creation before the world was made. And whoso forbiddeth to abstain from meats, that man should not eat the same, is not ordained of God; for, behold, the beasts of the field, and the fowls of the air, and that which cometh of the earth, is ordained for the use of man, for food, and for raiment, and that he might have it in abundance, but it is not given that one man should possess that which is above another; wherefore the world lieth in sin; and woe be unto man that sheddeth blood or that wasteth flesh and hath no need.

4. And again, verily I say unto you, that the Son of Man cometh not in the form of a woman, neither of a man traveling on the earth; wherefore be not deceived, but continue in steadfastness, looking forth for the heavens to be shaken; and the earth to tremble, and to reel to and fro as a drunken man; and for the valleys to be exalted; and for the mountains to be made low; and for the rough places to become smooth; and all this when the angel shall sound his trumpet.

5. But before the great day of the Lord shall come, Jacob shall flourish in the wilderness; and the Lamanites shall blossom as the rose. Zion shall flourish upon the hills, and rejoice upon the mountains, and shall be assembled together unto the place which I have appointed. Behold, I say unto you, Go forth as I have commanded you; repent of all your sins; ask and ye shall receive; knock and it shall be opened unto you: behold, I will go before you, and be your rearward; and I will be in your midst, and you shall not be confounded; behold, I am Jesus Christ, and I come quickly. Even so. Amen.

In May there arose some misunderstanding among the
Spirit mani- elders regarding the different spirit manifestations
festations. in the world.   In consequence of this, instruction
was given on the subject. [16]

[16] 1. Hearken, O ye elders of my church, and give ear to the voice of
the living God; and attend to the words of wisdom which shall be given
unto you, according as ye have asked and are agreed as touching the
church, and the spirits which have gone abroad in the earth.   Behold,
verily I say unto you, that there are many spirits which are false spirits,
which have gone forth in the earth, deceiving the world: and also Satan
hath sought to deceive you, that he might overthrow you.

2. Behold, I the Lord have looked upon you, and have seen abominations in the church, that profess my name; but blessed are they who are
faithful and endure, whether in life or in death, for they shall inherit
eternal life.   But woe unto them that are deceivers, and hypocrites, for
thus saith the Lord, I will bring them to judgment.

3. Behold, verily I say unto you, There are hypocrites among you,
and have deceived some, which has given the adversary power, but.
behold, such shall be reclaimed; but the hypocrites shall be detected
and shall be cut off, either in life or in death, even as I will, and woe
unto them who are cut off from my church, for the same are overcome
of the world; wherefore, let every man beware lest he do that. which is
not in truth and righteousness before me.

4. And now come, saith the Lord, by the Spirit, unto the elders of his
church, and let us reason together, that ye may understand: let us reason even as a man reasoneth one with another face to face: now when a
man reasoneth, he is understood of man, because he reasoneth as a man;
even so will I, the Lord, reason with you that you may understand:
wherefore I, the Lord, asketh you this question, Unto what were ye
ordained?   To preach my gospel by the Spirit, even the Comforter,
which was sent forth to teach the truth: and then received ye spirits
which ye could not understand, and received them to be of God, and in
this are ye justified?   Behold, ye shall answer this question yourselves,
nevertheless I will be merciful unto you; he that is weak among you
hereafter shall be made strong.

5. Verily I say unto you, He that is ordained of me and sent forth to
preach the word of truth by the Comforter, in the Spirit of truth, doth
he preach it by the Spirit of truth, or some other way? and if it be by
some other way, it be not of God.   And again, he that receiveth the
word of truth, doth he receive it by the Spirit of truth, or some other
way? if it be some other way, it be not of God: therefore, why is it that
ye cannot understand and know that he that receiveth the word by the
Spirit of truth, receiveth it as it is preached by the Spirit of truth?

6. Wherefore, he that preacheth and he that receiveth, understandeth
one another, and both are edified and rejoice together; and that which
doth not edify, is not of God, and is darkness: that which is of God is
light, and he that receiveth light and continueth in God, receiveth more
light, and that light groweth brighter and brighter, until the perfect
day.   And again, verily I say unto you, and I say it that you may know
the truth, that you may chase darkness from among you, for he that is
ordained of God and sent forth, the same is appointed to be the greatest,
notwithstanding he is least, and the servant of all: wherefore, he is possessor of all things, for all things are subject unto him, both in heaven
and on the earth, the life, and the light, the spirit, and the power, sent
forth by the will of the Father, through Jesus Christ, his Son; but no

Not long after this, the saints from the East began to arrive in companies, by families and individuals, and in consequence of the need created by their being unsettled, instruction was given.[16]

Inheritances.

man is possessor of all things, except he be purified and cleansed from all sin; and if ye are purified and cleansed from all sin, ye shall ask whatsoever you will in the name of Jesus, and it shall be done: but know this, it shall be given you what you shall' ask, and as ye are appointed to the head, the spirits shall be subject unto you.

7. Wherefore, it shall come to pass, that if you behold a spirit manifested that you cannot understand, and you receive not that spirit, ye shall ask of the Father, in the name of Jesus, and if he give not unto you that spirit, that you may know that it is not of God; and it shall be given unto you power over that spirit, and you shall proclaim against that spirit with a loud voice, that it is not of God; not with railing accusation, that ye be not overcome; neither with boasting, nor rejoicing, lest you be seized therewith: he that receiveth of God, let him account it of God, and let him rejoice that he is accounted of God worthy to receive, and by giving heed and doing these things which ye have received, and which ye shall hereafter receive; and the kingdom is given you of the Father, and power to overcome all things, which is not ordained of him; and, behold, verily I say unto you, Blessed are you who are now hearing these words of mine from the mouth of my servant, for your sins are forgiven you.

8. Let my servant Joseph Wakefield, in whom I am well pleased, and my servant Parley P Pratt, go forth among the churches and strengthen them by the word of exhortation; and also my servant John Corrill, or as many of my servants as are ordained unto this office, and let them labor in the vineyard; and let no man hinder them of doing that which I have appointed unto them: wherefore in this thing my servant Edward Partridge, is not justified, nevertheless let him repent and he shall be forgiven. Behold, ye are little children, and ye cannot bear all things now; ye must grow in grace and in the knowledge of the truth. Fear not, little children, for you are mine, and I have overcome the world, and you are of them that my Father hath given me; and none of them that my Father hath given me shall be lost; and the Father and I are one; I am in the Father and the Father in me; and inasmuch as ye have received me, ye are in me, and I in you; wherefore I am in your midst; and I am the good Shepherd (and the stone of Israel: he that buildeth upon this rock shall never fall), and the day cometh that you shall hear my voice and see me, and know that I am. Watch, therefore, that ye may be ready. Even so. Amen.

[16] 1. Hearken unto me, saith the Lord your God, and I will speak unto my servant Edward Partridge, and give unto him directions; for it must needs be that he receive directions how to organize this people, for it must needs be that they are organized according to my laws, if otherwise, they will be cut off; wherefore let my servant Edward Partridge, and those whom he has chosen, in whom I am well pleased, appoint unto this people their portion, every man equal according to their families, according to their circumstances, and their wants and needs; and let my servant Edward Partridge, when he shall appoint a man his portion, give unto him a writing that shall secure unto him his portion, that he shall hold it, even this right and this inheritance in the church, until he transgresses and is not accounted worthy by the voice of the

LIBRARY OF THE UNIVERSITY

Joseph in his account of the conference held in June, says:—

"On the sixth of June the elders from the various parts of the country where they were laboring came in, and the conference before appointed convened, in Kirtland, and the Lord displayed his power in a manner that could not be mistaken. The man of sin was revealed, and the authority of the Melchisedec priesthood was manifested, and conferred for the first time upon several of the elders. It was clearly evident that the Lord gave us power in proportion to the work to be done, and strength according to the race set before us; and grace and help as our needs required. Great harmony prevailed; several were ordained; faith was strengthened; and humility, so necessary for the blessing of God to follow prayer, characterized the saints."—*Times and Seasons*, vol. 5, p. 416.

June conference.

church, according to the laws and covenants of the church, to belong to the church; and if he shall transgress, and is not accounted worthy to belong to the church, he shall not have power to claim that portion which he has consecrated unto the bishop for the poor and the needy of my church; therefore he shall not retain the gift, but shall only have claim on that portion that is deeded unto him. And thus all things shall be made sure according to the laws of the land.

2. And let that which belongs to this people be appointed unto this people; and the money which is left unto this people, let there be an agent appointed unto this people to take the money, to provide food and raiment, according to the wants of this people. And let every man deal honestly, and be alike among this people, and receive alike, that ye may be one, even as I have commanded you.

3. And let that which belongeth to this people not be taken and given unto that of another church; wherefore, if another church would receive money of this church, let them pay unto this church again, according as they shall agree; and this shall be done through the bishop or the agent, which shall be appointed by the voice of the church.

4. And again, let the bishop appoint a storehouse unto this church, and let all things, both in money and in meat, which is more than is needful for the want of this people, be kept in the hands of the bishop. And let him also reserve unto himself, for his own wants, and for the wants of his family, as he shall be employed in doing this business. And thus I grant unto this people a privilege of organizing themselves according to my laws; and I consecrate unto them this land for a little season, until I, the Lord, shall provide for them otherwise, and command them to go hence; and the hour and the day is not given unto them; wherefore let them a: t upon this land as for years, and this shall turn unto them for their good

5. Behold, this shall be an example unto my servant Edward Partridge, in other places, in all churches. And whoso is found a faithful, a just, and a wise steward, shall enter into the joy of his Lord, and shall inherit eternal life. Verily, I say unto you, I am Jesus Christ, who cometh quickly, in an hour you think not. Even so. Amen.

There is one thing in the above which seems peculiar in connection with the account previously given, where Joseph Smith and Oliver Cowdery were commanded to and did ordain each other to the Melchisedec priesthood. He here says:—

Melch sedec priesthood conferred for the first time.

"The man of sin was revealed, and the authority of the Melchisedec priesthood was manifested, and conferred for the *first time* upon several of the elders."

The reader will doubtless inquire, "How could this be the *first time*, if they were ordained to the office of elder over a year previous?" The thought here expressed by Joseph is also found in Lyman Wight's account. as recorded in his journal, as follows:—

"On the fourth of June, 1831, a conference was held at Kirtland, Ohio, represented by all the above-named branches. Joseph Smith, our modern prophet, presided. Here for the first time I saw the visible manifestation of the power of God, as plain as could have been on the day of Pentecost; and here for the *first time* I saw the Melchisedec priesthood introduced into the Church of Jesus Christ, as anciently, whereunto I was ordained under the hands of Joseph Smith, and I then ordained sixteen others, such as he chose, unto the same priesthood."

Lyman Wight had been ordained an *elder* on November 20, 1830. If he was then ordained he receiv:d a further ordination. To what office could he have been ordained?

David Whitmer states in his "Address," page 64, as follows:—

"In Kirtland. Ohio, in June, 1831, at a conference of the church, the first high priests were ordained into the church."

High Priests ordained.

Taking these testimonies together it is evident that both Joseph Smith and Lyman Wight had reference to the *fullness* of the Melchisedec priesthood being bestowed for the *first time* in June, 1831, recognizing the fact as afterwards explained by revelation (D. C. 83:5) that, "the office of elder and bishop are necessary *appendages* belonging unto the high priesthood."

Explanation.

To this testimony and our conclusion P. P. Pratt agrees:—

"On the sixth of June, 1831, a General Conference was convened at Kirtland, consisting of all the elders, far and near, who could be got together. In this conference much instruction was given by President Smith, who spake in great power, as he was moved by the Holy Ghost; and the spirit of power and of testimony rested down upon the elders in a marvelous manner. Here also were some strange manifestations of false spirits, which were immediately rebuked.

"Several were then selected by revelation, through President Smith, and ordained to the High Priesthood after the order of the Son of God; which is after the order of Melchisedec. This was the first occasion in which this priesthood had been revealed and conferred upon the elders in this dispensation, although the office of an elder is the same in a certain degree, but not in the fullness. On this occasion I was ordained to this holy ordinance and calling by President Smith."—Autobiography of Parley P. Pratt, p. 72.

It will be observed that in the accounts given above there is a discrepancy of two days in dates; one, giving the date of the convening of the conference as June 4, the other two, as June 6. The exact date is not important, only as it concerns the correctness of history. The difference could easily occur through a mistake of either the scribe or the typographer. June 4, of 1831, fell on Saturday, and the sixth on Monday. According to the custom which has since obtained the conference would be the more likely to meet on Saturday, yet it may have been on Monday.

The next day after the conference a revelation was given providing that the next conference should be held in Missouri, and several of the elders were called to go, two by two, by different routes, and meet in Missouri, there to hold the conference.[17]

Next conference to meet in Missouri.

---

[17] 1. Behold, thus saith the Lord unto the elders whom he hath called and chosen, in these last days, by the voice of his Spirit, saying, I, the Lord, will make known unto you what I will that ye shall do from this time until the next conference, which shall be held in Missouri, upon the land which I will consecrate unto my people, which are a remnant of Jacob, and those who are heirs according to the covenant.

2. Wherefore, verily I say unto you, Let my servant Joseph Smith, Jr., and Sidney Rigdon, take their journey as soon as preparations can

Immediately after this, three of these elders; viz., Jacob Scott, Edson Fuller, and William Carter, apostatized, hence refused to go. Wheeler Baldwin, being thus deprived of his companion, remained behind, laboring among the churches.

be made to leave their homes, and journey to the land of Missouri. And inasmuch as they are faithful unto me, it shall be made known unto them what they shall do; and it shall also, inasmuch as they are faithful, be made known unto them the land of your inheritance. And inasmuch as they are not faithful, they shall be cut off, even as I will, as seemeth me good.

3. And again, verily I say unto you, Let my servant Lyman Wight, and my servant John Corrill, take their journey speedily; and also my servant John Murdock, and my servant Hyrum Smith, take their journey unto the same place, by the way of Detroit. And let them journey from thence, preaching the word by the way, saying none other things than that which the prophets and apostles have written, and that which is taught them by the Comforter, through the prayer of faith. Let them go two by two, and thus let them preach by the way in every congregation, baptizing by water, and the laying on of the hands by the water's side; for thus saith the Lord, I will cut my work short in right-eousness, for the days cometh that I will send forth judgment unto victory. And let my servant Lyman Wight beware, for Satan desireth to sift him as chaff.

4. And, behold, he that is faithful shall be made ruler over many things. And again, I will give unto you a pattern in all things, that ye may not be deceived; for Satan is abroad in the land, and he goeth forth deceiving the nations; wherefore he that prayeth whose spirit is contrite, the same is accepted of me, if he obey mine ordinances. He that speaketh, whose spirit is contrite, whose language is meek, and edifieth, the same is of God, if he obey mine ordinances. And again, he that trembleth under my power shall be made strong, and shall bring forth fruits of praise, and wisdom, according to the revelations and truths which I have given you.

5. And again, he that is overcome and bringeth not forth fruits, even according to this pattern, is not of me; wherefore by this pattern ye shall know the spirits in all cases, under the whole heavens. And the days have come, according to men's faith it shall be done unto them. Behold, this commandment is given unto all the elders whom I have chosen. And again, verily I say unto you, Let my servant Thomas B. Marsh, and my servant Ezra Thayre, take their journey also, preaching the word by the way, unto this same land. And again, let my servant Isaac Morley, and my servant Ezra Booth, take their journey, also preaching the word by the way, unto the same land.

6. And again, let my servants Edward Partridge and Martin Harris take their journey with my servants Sidney Rigdon and Joseph Smith, Jr. Let my servants David Whitmer and Harvey Whitlock also take their journey, and preach by the way, unto this same land. Let my servants Parley P. Pratt and Orson Pratt take their journey, and preach by the way, even unto this same land. And let my servants Solomon Hancock and Simeon Carter also take their journey unto this same land, and preach by the way. Let my servants Edson Fuller and Jacob Scott also take their journey. Let my servants Levi Hancock and Zebedee Coltrin also take their journey. Let my servants Reynolds Cahoon and Samuel H. Smith also take their journey. Let my servants Wheeler Baldwin and William Carter also take their journey.

The others named started upon this long and tedious journey in full faith of accomplishing what they were directed to do. In the month of June revelations were given to Sidney Gilbert and Newel Knight.[18]

7. And let my servants Newel Knight and Selah J. Griffin both be ordained and also take their journey: yea, verily I say, Let all these take their journey unto one place, in their several courses, and one man shall not build upon another's foundation, neither journey in another's track. He that is faithful, the same shall be kept and blessed with much fruit.

8. And again, I say unto you, Let my servants Joseph Wakefield and Solomon Humphrey take their journey into the eastern lands. Let them labor with their families, declaring none other things than the prophets and apostles, that which they have seen, and heard, and most assuredly believe, that the prophesies may be fulfilled. In consequence of transgression, let that which was bestowed upon Heman Basset, be taken from him, and placed upon the head of Simonds Rider.

9. And again, verily I say unto you, Let Jared Carter be ordained a priest, and also George James be ordained a priest. Let the residue of the elders watch over the churches, and declare the word in the regions among them. And let them labor with their own hands, that there be no idolatry nor wickedness practiced. And remember in all things, the poor and the needy, the sick and the afflicted, for he that doeth not these things, the same is not my disciple. And again, let my servants Joseph Smith, Jr., and Sidney Rigdon, and Edward Partridge, take with them a recommend from the church. And let there be one obtained for my servant Oliver Cowdery also; and thus, even as I have said, if ye are faithful, ye shall assemble yourselves together to rejoice upon the land of Missouri, which is the land of your inheritance, which is now the land of your enemies. But, behold, I the Lord, will hasten the city in its time, and will crown the faithful with joy and with rejoicing. Behold, I am Jesus Christ the Son of God, and I will lift them up at the last day. Even so. Amen.

[19]1. Behold, I say unto you, my servant Sidney Gilbert, that I have heard your prayers, and you have called upon me, that it should be made known unto you, of the Lord your God, concerning your calling, and election in this church, which I, the Lord, have raised up in these last days.

2. Behold, I, the Lord, who was crucified for the sins of the world, giveth unto you a commandment, that you shall forsake the world. Take upon you mine ordinances, even that of an elder, to preach faith and repentance, and remission of sins, according to my word, and the reception of the Holy Spirit by the laying on of hands. And also to be an agent unto this church in the place which shall be appointed by the bishop, according to commandments which shall be given hereafter.

3. And again, verily I say unto you, You shall take your journey with my servants Joseph Smith, Jr., and Sidney Rigdon. Behold, these are the first ordinances which you shall receive; and the residue shall be made known in a time to come, according to your labor in my vineyard. And again, I would that ye should learn that it is he only who is saved, that endureth unto the end. Even so. Amen.

1. Behold, thus saith the Lord, even Alpha and Omega, the beginning and the end, even he who was crucified for the sins of the world. Behold, verily, verily I say unto you, my servant Newel Knight, You shall stand fast in the office wherewith I have appointed you; and if your

While the elders were departing for the West, according to
Cowdery's
letter. the commandment, Joseph received a letter from
Oliver Cowdery, of which he writes as follows:—

"The elders now began to go to the western country, two
and two, according to the previous word of the Lord. From
P. P. Pratt, who had returned from the expedition of last
fall, during the spring we had verbal information; and from
letters from the still remaining elders we had written intelligence; and as this was the most important subject which
then engrossed the attention of the saints, I will here insert
the copy of a letter received about this time, from that section, dated

" 'KAW TOWNSHIP, Missouri, May 7, 1831.

" 'Our Dearly Beloved Brethren:—I have nothing particular to write as concerning the Lamanites, and because of a
short journey which I have just returned from, in consequence of which I have not written to you since the sixteenth of last month. I and brother Ziba went into the
county east, which is Lafayette, and is about forty miles;
and in the name of Jesus we called on the people to repent;
many of whom are, I believe, earnestly searching for truth,
and if sincerely, I pray they may find that precious treasure.
. . . The letter we received from you informed us that the
opposition was great against you. Now our beloved brethren, we verily believe that we also can rejoice that we are
counted worthy to suffer shame for His name; for almost
the whole country, which consists of Universalists, Atheists,

brethren desire to escape their enemies let them repent of all their sins,
and become truly humble before me and contrite; and as the covenant
which they made unto me, has been broken, even so it has become void
and of none effect; and woe to him by whom this offense cometh, for it
had been better for him that he had been drowned in the depth of the
sea; but blessed are they who have kept the covenant, and observed the
commandment, for they shall obtain mercy.

2. Wherefore, go to now and flee the land, lest your enemies come upon
you; and take your journey, and appoint whom you will to be your
leader, and to pay moneys for you. And thus you shall take your journey into the regions westward, unto the land of Missouri, unto the borders of the Lamanites. And after you have done journeying, behold, I
say unto you, Seek ye a living like unto men, until I prepare a place for
you.

3. And again, be patient in tribulation until I come; and, behold, I
come quickly, and my reward is with me, and they who have sought me
early shall find rest to their souls. Even so. Amen.

Deists, Presbyterians, Methodists, Baptists, and professed Christians, priests and people, with all the devils from the infernal pit, are united and foaming out their own shame. God forbid that I should bring a railing accusation against them, for vengeance belongeth to Him who is able to repay: and herein brethren we confide.

"'I am informed of another tribe of Lamanites lately, who have abundance of flocks of the best kinds of sheep and cattle, and they manufacture blankets of a superior quality. The tribe is very numerous; they live three hundred miles west of Santa Fe, and are called Navajoes. Why I mention this tribe is, because I feel under obligations to communicate to my brethren every information concerning the Lamanites that I meet with in my labors and travels, believing as I do that much is expected from me in the cause of our Lord; and doubting not but I am daily remembered in your prayers before the throne of the Most High by all of my brethren, as well by those who have not seen my face in the flesh as those who have.

"'We begin to expect our brother Pratt, soon; we have heard from him only when he was at St. Louis. We are all well (bless the Lord) and preach the gospel we will if earth and hell oppose our way and we dwell in the midst of scorpions; for in Jesus we trust. Grace be with you all. Amen.

"'P. S. I beseech brother Whitney to remember and write; and direct to me, Independence, Jackson County, Missouri.   OLIVER COWDERY.'"

—*Times and Seasons*, vol. 5, pp. 432, 433.

While Joseph and those who were to accompany him were preparing for their journey, a gentleman by the name of W. W. Phelps arrived at Kirtland with his family. He desired to know the will of God concerning himself, and in answer to petition received instruction directing him that he was called to the ministry, and also to assist in literary concerns.[19]

W. W. Phelps arrives.

----

[19] 1. Behold, thus saith the Lord unto you, my servant William; yea, even the Lord of the whole earth, Thou art called and chosen, and after thou hast been baptized by water, which if you do with an eye single to my glory, you shall have a remission of your sins, and a reception of the

As Ezra Thayre, the companion of Thomas B. Marsh, could not get ready as soon as Elder Marsh wished to go, he inquired of the Lord for direction and was given another companion.[20]

Holy Spirit, by the laying on of hands. And then thou shalt be ordained by the hand of my servant Joseph Smith, Jr., to be an elder unto this church, to preach repentance and remission of sins by way of baptism in the name of Jesus Christ, the Son of the living God; and on whomsoever you shall lay your hands, if they are contrite before me, you shall have power to give the Holy Spirit.

2. And again, you shall be ordained to assist my servant Oliver Cowdery to do the work of printing, and of selecting, and writing books for schools, in this church, that little children also may receive instruction before me as is pleasing unto me. And again, verily I say unto you, For this cause you shall take your journey with my servants Joseph Smith, Jr., and Sidney Rigdon, that you may be planted in the land of your inheritance. to do this work.

3. And again let my servant Joseph Coe also take his journey with them. The residue shall be made known hereafter; even as I will. Amen.

[20] 1. Hearken, O ye people who profess my name, saith the Lord your God, for, behold, mine anger is kindled against the rebellious, and they shall know mine arm and mine indignation in the day of visitation and of wrath upon the nations. And he that will not take up his cross and follow me, and keep my commandments, the same shall not be saved.

2. Behold, I the Lord commandeth, and he that will not obey shall be cut off in mine own due time; and after that I have commanded and the commandment is broken, wherefore I the Lord command and revoke, as it seemeth me good: and all this to be answered upon the heads of the rebellious saith the Lord; wherefore I revoke the commandment which was given unto my servants Thomas B. Marsh and Ezra Thayre, and give a new commandment unto my servant Thomas, that he shall take up his journey speedily to the land of Missouri; and my servant Selah J Griffin shall also go with him: for, behold, I revoke the commandment which was given unto my servants Selah J. Griffin and Newel Knight. in consequence of the stiff-neckedness of my people which are in Thompson: and their rebellions: wherefore let my servant Newel Knight remain with them, and as many as will go, may go, that are contrite before me, and be led by him to the land which I have appointed.

3. And again, verily I say unto you, that my servant Ezra Thayre must repent of his pride and of his selfishness, and obey the former commandment which I have given him concerning the place upon which he lives; and if he will do this, as there shall be no divisions made upon the land, he shall be appointed still to go to the land of Missouri; otherwise he shall receive the money which he has paid. and shall leave the place, and shall be cut off out of my church, saith the Lord God of hosts; and though the heaven and the earth pass away, these words shall not pass away, but shall be fulfilled.

4. And if my servant Joseph Smith, Jr, must needs pay the money, behold, I, the Lord. will pay it unto him again in the land of Missouri, that those of whom he shall receive may be rewarded again, according to that which they do. For according to that which they do, they shall receive; even in lands for their inheritance. Behold, thus saith the Lord unto my people, You have many things to do, and to repent of; for, behold, your sins have come up unto me, and are not pardoned, because

you seek to counsel in your own ways.   And your hearts are not satisfied. And ye obey not the truth, but have pleasure in unrighteousness.

5. Woe unto you rich men, that will not give your substance to the poor, for your riches will canker your souls; and this shall be your lamentation in the day of visitation, and of judgment, and of indignation: The harvest is past, the summer is ended, and my soul is not saved! Woe unto you poor men, whose hearts are not broken, whose spirits are not contrite, and whose bellies are not satisfied, and whose hands are not stayed from laying hold upon other men's goods, whose eyes are full of greediness, who will not labor with their own hands!

6. But blessed are the poor, who are pure in heart, whose hearts are broken, and whose spirits are contrite, for they shall see the kingdom of God coming in power and great glory unto their deliverance; for the fatness of the earth shall be theirs; for. behold, the Lord shall come, and his recompense shall be with him, and he shall reward every man, and the poor shall rejoice; and their generations shall inherit the earth from generation to generation, forever and ever.   And now I make an end of speaking unto you.   Even so.   Amen.

CHAPTER 10.

1831-1832.

JOSEPH AND COMPANY LEAVE KIRTLAND—LYMAN WIGHT'S ACCOUNT
—TEMPLE LOT POINTED OUT—W. W. PHELPS PREACHES IN MIS-
SOURI—SIDNEY RIGDON AND OTHERS ARRIVE IN MISSOURI—
REVELATION CONCERNING ZION—FIRST LOG LAID FOR HOUSE IN
ZION—DESCRIPTION OF ZION—SPOT FOR TEMPLE DEDICATED—
THE SABBATH—INSTRUCTION ON RETURNING EAST—JOSEPH AND
TEN OTHERS START EAST—INCIDENTS BY THE WAY—PURCHAS-
ING LAND—PREPARES TO REMOVE TO HIRAM—FURTHER INFOR-
MATION CONCERNING ZION—PREPARE TO ESTABLISH A PRESS IN
MISSOURI—TRANSLATION RESUMED—PREFACE TO BOOK OF COM-
MANDMENTS—SOME MURMUR CONCERNING LANGUAGE IN REVE-
LATIONS—JOSEPH SMITH TO ARRANGE REVELATIONS—OLIVER
COWDERY TO CARRY THEM TO MISSOURI—THE APPENDIX—JOHN
WHITMER TO ACCOMPANY OLIVER COWDERY—COWDERY AND
WHITMER START FOR THE WEST—COUNCIL IN KIRTLAND—
BISHOP N. K. WHITNEY CALLED—MISSIONARY TRIP—TRANSLA-
TION RESUMED—CONFERENCE HELD AT AMHERST, OHIO—RE-
MARKABLE VISION—JOSEPH SMITH AND SIDNEY RIGDON MOBBED
—JOURNEY TO MISSOURI—COUNCIL CALLED—THE PROPHET AC-
KNOWLEDGED AS PRESIDENT OF THE HIGH PRIESTHOOD—ORDI-
NATION CONSIDERED—BOOK OF COMMANDMENTS AND HYMN BOOK
—JOURNEY TO KIRTLAND—INCIDENTS BY THE WAY—"EVENING
AND MORNING STAR"—"COMMON SCHOOLS"—REVELATION ON
PRIESTHOOD.

JOSEPH and the brethren who were to accompany him left
Kirtland on the nineteenth of June and were among the first

Leave
Kirtland.

to arrive at Independence. But few of the details
of the travels of the several elders who went to
Missouri have been preserved. They would doubtless be
very interesting, but we must be content with such as we
have. Joseph's account of so long, and doubtless so eventful a journey, is very short. It is as follows:—

"On the 19th of June, in company with Sidney Rigdon,
Martin Harris, Edward Partridge, W. W. Phelps, Joseph
Coe, A. S. Gilbert and his wife, I started from Kirtland,
Ohio, for the land of Missouri, agreeable to the commandment before received, wherein it was promised that if we
were faithful, the land of our inheritance, even the place
for the city of the New Jerusalem, should be revealed. We

went by wagon, canal boats, and stages to Cincinnati, where I had an interview with the Rev. Walter Scott, one of the fathers of the Campbellites, or Newlight Church. Before the close of our interview, he manifested one of the bitterest spirits against the doctrine of the New Testament ('that these signs should follow them that believe,' as recorded in the 16th chapter of the Gospel according to St. Mark) that I ever witnessed among men. We left Cincinnati in a steamer, and landed at Louisville, Kentucky, where we were detained three days in waiting for a steamer to convey us to St. Louis. At St. Louis, myself, Brethren Harris, Phelps, Partridge, and Coe, went on foot by land, to Independence, Jackson County, Missouri, where we arrived about the middle of July; and the residue of the company came by water a few days after. Notwithstanding the corruptions and abominations of the times, and the evil spirits manifested towards us on account of our belief in the Book of Mormon, at many places and among various persons, yet the Lord continued his watchful care and loving kindness to us day by day: and we made it a rule, wherever there was an opportunity, to read a chapter in the Bible, and pray; and these seasons of worship gave us great consolation. The meeting of our brethren, who had long waited our arrival, was a glorious one, and moistened with many tears. It seemed good and pleasant for brethren to meet together in unity. But our reflections were great, coming as we had from a highly cultivated state of society in the East, and standing now upon the confines or western limits of the United States, and looking into the vast wilderness of those that sat in darkness. How natural it was to observe the degradation, leanness of intellect, ferocity and jealousy, of a people that were nearly a century behind the time, and to feel for those who roamed about without the benefit of civilization, refinement, or religion! Yea, and exclaim in the language of the prophets, 'When will the wilderness blossom as a rose? when will Zion be built up in her glory? and where will Thy temple stand unto which all nations shall come in the last days.' "—*Times and Seasons*, vol. 5, p. 434.

Lyman Wight kept a daily account of the journey and ex-

periences of himself and John Murdock, but it is too long for
Wight's account. insertion here. They baptized many, among whom
we notice the historical names of James Emmett
and Morris Phelps. Lyman Wight arrived at Independence,
August 12, leaving his companion fifty miles behind, sick.
Here he procured a horse and went back for him, and brought
him in on the horse, while he walked by his side, supporting
him. We only mention this as an instance of the zeal,
energy, courage, and devotion with which these early de-
fenders of the cause met the hardships and sacrifices incident to the arduous work of establishing the church in the
West. Doubtless many if not all of those who went on that
perilous mission passed through like experiences. It would
be interesting if all had been preserved.

In July, 1831, there was a revelation given at Independ-
Temple Lot pointed out. ence pointing out the spot for the building of the
Temple and giving instruction on other important
matters.[1]

---

[1] 1. Hearken, O ye elders of my church, saith the Lord your God, who
have assembled yourselves together, according to my commandments, in
this land which is the land of Missouri, which is the land which I have
appointed and consecrated for the gathering of the saints: wherefore
this is the land of promise, and the place for the city of Zion. And thus
saith the Lord your God, If you will receive wisdom here is wisdom.
Behold, the place which is now called Independence, is the center place,
and the spot for the temple is lying westward upon a lot which is not far
from the courthouse; wherefore it is wisdom that the land should be
purchased by the saints; and also every tract lying westward, even unto
the line running directly between Jew and Gentile. And also every
tract bordering by the prairies, inasmuch as my disciples are enabled to
buy lands. Behold, this is wisdom, that they may obtain it for an everlasting inheritance.

2. And let my servant Sidney Gilbert, stand in the office which I have
appointed him, to receive moneys, to be an agent unto the church, to
buy land in all the regions round about, inasmuch as can be in righteousness, and as wisdom shall direct.

3. And let my servant Edward Partridge, stand in the office which I
have appointed him, to divide the saints their inheritance, even as I
have commanded; and also those whom he has appointed to assist him.

4. And again, verily I say unto you, Let my servant Sidney Gilbert
plant himself in this place, and establish a store, that he may sell goods
without fraud, that he may obtain money to buy lands for the good of
the saints, and that he may obtain whatsoever things the disciples may
need to plant them in their inheritance. And also let my servant Sidney
Gilbert obtain a license (behold, here is wisdom, and whoso readeth let
him understand), that he may send goods also unto the people, even by
whom he will as clerks, employed in his service, and thus provide for
my saints, that my gospel may be preached unto those who sit in darkness and in the region and shadow of death.

On the first Sunday after the arrival of Joseph and party in Jackson County, Missouri, W. W. Phelps preached to a mixed audience of white pioneers, negroes, and Indians, and on the same day two were baptized.

Phelps preaches in Missouri.

The following week the Colesville branch (from Colesville, New York), Sidney Rigdon and wife, and Elders Morley and Booth arrived.

Rigdon arrives.

About the same time another revelation was given containing additional instruction concerning Zion and the duties of certain officers of the church. [2]

Revelation on Zion.

5. And again, verily I say unto you, Let my servant William W. Phelps be planted in this place, and be established as a printer unto the church; and lo, if the world receiveth his writings (behold, here is wisdom), let him obtain whatsoever he can obtain in righteousness, for the good of the saints. And let my servant Oliver Cowdery assist him, even as I have commanded, in whatsoever place I shall appoint unto him, to copy, and to correct, and select, that all things may be right before me, as it shall be proved by the Spirit through him. And thus let those of whom I have spoken, be planted in the land of Zion, as speedily as can be, with their families, to do those things even as I have spoken.

6. And now concerning the gathering, let the bishop and the agent make preparations for those families which have been commanded to come to this land, as soon as possible, and plant them in their inheritance. And unto the residue of both elders and members, further directions shall be given hereafter. Even so. Amen.

[2] 1. Hearken, O ye elders of my church, and give ear to my word, and learn of me what I will concerning this land unto which I have sent you; for verily I say unto you, Blessed is he that keepeth my commandments, whether in life or in death; and he that is faithful in tribulation, the reward of the same is greater in the kingdom of heaven.

2. Ye cannot behold with your natural eyes, for the present time, the design of your God concerning those things which shall come hereafter, and the glory which shall follow, after much tribulation. For after much tribulation cometh the blessings. Wherefore the day cometh that ye shall be crowned with much glory; the hour is not yet, but is nigh at hand.

3. Remember this which I tell you before, that you may lay it to heart, and receive that which shall follow. Behold, verily I say unto you, For this cause I have sent you that you might be obedient, and that your hearts might be prepared to bear testimony of the things which are to come; and also that you might be honored of laying the foundation, and of bearing record of the land upon which the Zion of God shall stand; and also that a feast of fat things might be prepared for the poor; yea, a feast of fat things, of wine on the lees well refined, that the earth may know that the mouths of the prophets shall not fail; yea, a supper of the house of the Lord, well prepared, unto which all nations shall be invited. Firstly, the rich and the learned, the wise and the noble; and after that cometh the day of my power; then shall the poor, the lame, and the

For a description of the land of Zion in 1831 and of the dedication of the Temple Lot, we here reproduce the words of Joseph Smith:—

"On the second day of August I assisted the Colesville

blind, and the deaf, come in unto the marriage of the Lamb, and partake of the supper of the Lord, prepared for the great day to come. Behold, I, the Lord, have spoken it.

4. And that the testimony might go forth from Zion; yea, from the mouth of the city of the heritage of God; yea, for this cause I have sent you hither, and have selected my servant Edward Partridge, and have appointed unto him his mission in this land; but if he repent not of his sins, which are unbelief and blindness of heart, let him take heed lest he fall. Behold, his mission is given unto him, and it shall not be given again. And whoso standeth in this mission is appointed to be a judge in Israel, like as it was in ancient days, to divide the lands of the heritage of God unto his children, and to judge his people by the testimony of the just, and by the assistance of his counselors, according to the laws of the kingdom which are given by the prophets of God; for verily I say unto you, My law shall be kept on this land.

5. Let no man think that he is ruler, but let God rule him that judgeth, according to the counsel of his own will; or, in other words, him that counseleth or sitteth upon the judgment seat. Let no man break the laws of the land, for he that keepeth the laws of God hath no need to break the laws of the land; wherefore be subject to the powers that be, until He reigns whose right it is to reign, and subdues all enemies under his feet. Behold, the laws which ye have received from my hand are the laws of the church, and in this light ye shall hold them forth. Behold, here is wisdom.

6. And now, as I spake concerning my servant Edward Partridge, this land is the land of his residence, and those whom he has appointed for his counselors, and also the land of the residence of him whom I have appointed to keep my storehouse; wherefore let them bring their families to this land, as they shall counsel between themselves and me; for, behold, it is not meet that I should command in all things, for he that is compelled in all things, the same is a slothful and not a wise servant; wherefore he receiveth no reward. Verily I say, Men should be anxiously engaged in a good cause, and do many things of their own free will, and bring to pass much righteousness; for the power is in them, wherein they are agents unto themselves. And inasmuch as men do good, they shall in nowise lose their reward. But he that doeth not anything until he is commanded, and receiveth a commandment with doubtful heart, and keepeth it with slothfulness, the same is damned. Who am I that made man, saith the Lord, that will hold him guiltless that obeys not my commandments? Who am I, saith the Lord, that have promised and have not fulfilled? I command and a man obeys not, I revoke and they receive not the blessing; then they say in their hearts, This is not the work of the Lord, for his promises are not fulfilled. But woe unto such, for their reward lurketh beneath, and not from above.

7. And now I give unto you further directions concerning this land. It is wisdom in me that my servant Martin Harris should be an example unto the church, in laying his moneys before the bishop of the church. And, also, this is a law unto every man that cometh unto this land, to receive an inheritance, and he shall do with his moneys according as the law directs. And it is wisdom, also, that there should be lands pur-

branch of the church to lay the first log, for a house, as a
First log laid foundation for Zion in Kaw Township, twelve
for house in   miles west of Independence. The log was carried
Zion.   and placed by twelve men, in honor of the twelve
tribes of Israel. At the same time, through prayer, the
land of Zion was consecrated and dedicated for the gather-

chased in Independence, for the place of the storehouse, and also for
the house of the printing.

8. And other directions, concerning my servant Martin Harris, shall
be given him of the Spirit, that he may receive his inheritance as
seemeth him good. And let him repent of his sins, for he seeketh the
praise of the world.

9. And also let my servant William W. Phelps stand in the office which
I have appointed him, and receive his inheritance in the land. And,
also, he hath need to repent, for I, the Lord, am not well pleased with him,
for he seeketh to excel, and he is not sufficiently meek before me. Behold, he who has repented of his sins, the same is forgiven, and I, the
Lord, remembereth them no more. By this ye may know if a man
repenteth of his sins. Behold, he will confess them and forsake them.
And now, verily I say, concerning the residue of the elders of my church,
The time has not yet come, for many years, for them to receive their
inheritance in this land, except they desire it through the prayer of faith,
only as it shall be appointed unto them of the Lord. For, behold, they
shall push the people together from the ends of the earth; wherefore
assemble yourselves together, and they who are not appointed to stay in
this land, let them preach the gospel in the regions round about; and
after that, let them return to their homes. Let them preach by the way,
and bear testimony of the truth in all places, and call upon the rich, the
high, and the low, and the poor, to repent; and let them build up
churches, inasmuch as the inhabitants of the earth will repent.

10. And let there be an agent appointed by the voice of the church,
unto the church in Ohio, to receive moneys to purchase lands in Zion.

11. And I give unto my servant Sidney Rigdon a commandment that
he shall write a description of the land of Zion, and a statement of the
will of God, as it shall be made known by the Spirit, unto him; and an
epistle and subscription, to be presented unto all the churches, to obtain
moneys, to be put into the hands of the bishop, to purchase lands for an
inheritance for the children of God, of himself or the agent, as seemeth
him good, or as he shall direct. For, behold, verily I say unto you, The
Lord willeth that the disciples, and the children of men, should open
their hearts even to purchase this whole region of country, as soon as
time will permit. Behold, here is wisdom; let them do this lest they
receive none inheritance, save it be by the shedding of blood.

12. And again, inasmuch as there is land obtained, let there be workmen sent forth, of all kinds, unto this land, to labor for the saints of God.
Let all these things be done in order. And let the privileges of the lands
be made known, from time to time, by the bishop, or the agent of the
church; and let the work of the gathering be not in haste, nor by flight,
but let it be done as it shall be counseled by the elders of the church at
the conferences, according to the knowledge which they receive from
time to time.

13. And let my servant Sidney Rigdon consecrate and dedicate this
land, and the spot of the temple, unto the Lord. And let a conference
meeting be called, and after that let my servants Sidney Rigdon and

ing of the saints, by Elder Rigdon; and it was a season of joy
to those present, and afforded a glimpse of the future, which
time will yet unfold to the satisfaction of the faithful.   As
we had received a commandment for Elder Rigdon to write
a description of the land of Zion, we sought for all the in-
Descrip-   formation necessary to accomplish so desirable an
tion of Zion. object.   Unlike the timbered States in the East,
except upon the rivers and water courses, which were
verdantly dotted with trees from one to three miles wide, as
far as the eye can glance, the beautiful rolling prairies lay
spread around like a sea of meadows.   The timber is a mixture of oak, hickory, black walnut, elm, cherry, honey locust,
mulberry, coffee bean, hackberry, box elder, and basswood,
together with the addition of cottonwood, buttonwood, pecan,
soft and hard maple, upon the bottoms.   The shrubbery was
beautiful, and consisted in part of plums, grapes, crab apples,
and persimmons.   The prairies were decorated with a growth
of flowers that seemed as gorgeous and grand as the brilliancy
of stars in the heavens, and exceed description.   The soil is
rich and fertile, from three to ten feet deep, and generally
composed of rich black mold, intermingled with clay and
sand.   It produces in abundance, wheat, corn, and many
other commodities, together with sweet potatoes and cotton.
Horses, cattle, and hogs, though of an inferior breed, are
tolerably plenty, and seem nearly to raise themselves by

Joseph Smith, Jr., return, and also Oliver Cowdery with them, to
accomplish the residue of the work which I have appointed unto them
in their own land, and the residue as shall be ruled by the conferences.

14. And let no man return from this land, except he bear record, by
the way, of that which he knows and most assuredly believes. Let that
which has been bestowed upon Ziba Peterson be taken from him, and let
him stand as a member in the church, and labor with his own hands,
with the brethren, until he is sufficiently chastened for all his sins, for
he confesseth them not, and he thinketh to hide them.

15. Let the residue of the elders of this church, who are coming to this
land, some of whom are exceedingly blessed, even above measure, also
hold a conference upon this land. And let my servant Edward Partridge direct the conference which shall be held by them. And let them
also return, preaching the gospel by the way, bearing record of the
things which are revealed unto them; for, verily, the sound must go
forth from this place into all the world; and unto the uttermost parts
of the earth, the gospel must be preached unto every creature, with
signs following them that believe. And, behold, the Son of Man cometh.
Amen.

grazing in the vast prairie range in summer, and feeding upon the bottoms in winter. The wild game is less plenty where man has commenced the cultivation of the soil than it is a little distance farther in the wild prairies. Buffalo, elk, deer, bear, wolves, beaver, and many lesser animals roam at pleasure. Turkeys, geese, swans, ducks, yea, a variety of the feathered race are among the rich abundance that graces the delightful regions of this goodly land of the heritage of the children of God. Nothing is more fruitful, or a richer stock-holder in the blooming prairies, than the honey bee; honey is but about twenty-five cents per gallon.

"The season is mild and delightful nearly three quarters of the year, and as the land of Zion, situated at about equal distances from the Atlantic and Pacific oceans, as well as from the Allegheny and Rocky Mountains, in the thirty-ninth degree of north latitude, and between the tenth and seventeenth degrees of west longitude.[3] It bids fair to become one of the most blessed places on the globe, when the curse is taken from the land, if not before. The winters are milder than in the Atlantic States, of the same parallel of latitude; and the weather is more agreeable, so that were the virtues of the inhabitants only equal to the blessings of the Lord, which he permits to crown the industry and efforts of those inhabitants, there would be a measure of the good things of life, for the benefit of the saints, full, pressed down and running over, even an hundredfold. The disadvantages here, like all new countries, are self-evident, lack of mills and schools, together with the natural privations and inconveniences, which the hand of industry and the refinement of society with the polish of science overcome. But all these impediments vanish when it is recollected that the prophets have said concerning Zion in the last days how the glory of Lebanon is to come upon her; the fir tree, the pine tree, and the box together, to beautify the place of his sanctuary, that he may make the place of his feet glorious; where for brass he will bring gold, and for iron he will bring silver, and for wood brass, and for stones iron; and where the feast of fat things will be given to the ·just;" yea, when the splen-

[3] From Washington.

dor of the Lord is brought to one consideration, for the good of his people; the calculations of men and the vain glory of the world vanishes; and we exclaim: God will shine — the perfection of beauty out of Zion.

"On the third day of August the spot for the Temple, a little west of Independence, was dedicated in presence of Spot for Temple dedicated. eight men, among whom were myself, Sidney Rigdon, Edward Partridge, W. W. Phelps, Oliver Cowdery, Martin Harris, and Joseph Coe. The eighty-seventh Psalm was read, and the scene was solemn and impressive. On the 4th I attended the first conference in the land of Zion. It was held at the house of Brother Joshua Lewis, in Kaw Township, in presence of the Colesville branch of the church. The Spirit of the Lord was there. On the 7th, I attended the funeral of Sister Polly Knight, the wife of Joseph Knight, Sen. This was the first death in the church in this land, and I can say a worthy member sleeps in Jesus till the resurrection."—*Times and Seasons*, vol. 5, p. 450.

On Sunday, August 7, another revelation was given instructing the inhabitants of Zion regarding moral The Sabbath. conduct, the keeping of the Lord's holy day, and other matters. [4]

[4] 1. Behold, blessed, saith the Lord, are they who have come up unto this land with an eye single to my glory, according to my commandments; for them that live shall inherit the earth, and them that die shall rest from all their labors, and their works shall follow them, and they shall receive a crown in the mansions of my Father, which I have prepared for them; yea, blessed are they whose feet stand upon the land of Zion, who have obeyed my gospel, for they shall receive for their reward the good things of the earth; and it shall bring forth in its strength; and they shall also be crowned with blessings from above; yea, and with commandments not a few, and with revelations in their time; they that are faithful and diligent before me.

2. Wherefore I give unto them a commandment, saying thus: Thou shalt love the Lord thy God, with all thy heart, with all thy might, mind, and strength; and in the name of Jesus Christ thou shalt serve him. Thou shalt love thy neighbor as thyself. Thou shalt not steal; neither commit adultery, nor kill, nor do anything like unto it. Thou shalt thank the Lord thy God in all things. Thou shalt offer a sacrifice unto the Lord thy God in righteousness; even that of a broken heart and a contrite spirit. And that thou mayest more fully keep thyself unspotted from the world, thou shalt go to the house of prayer and offer up thy sacraments upon my holy day; for verily this is a day appointed unto you to rest from your labors, and to pay thy devotions unto the Most High; nevertheless thy vows shall be offered up in righteousness on all days, and at all times; but remember that on this, the Lord's day,

On Monday, the 8th, a revelation was given in-
Instruction on structing the elders concerning their return to
returning East. the East. [5]

thou shalt offer thine oblations, and thy sacraments, unto the Most High,
confessing thy sins unto thy brethren, and before the Lord.

3. And on this day thou shalt do none other thing, only let thy food be
prepared with singleness of heart, that thy fasting may be perfect; or in
other words, that thy joy may be full. Verily this is fasting and prayer;
or, in other words, rejoicing and prayer.

4. And inasmuch as ye do these things, with thanksgiving, with cheerful hearts, and countenances; not with much laughter, for this is sin,
but with a glad heart and a cheerful countenance; verily I say, that
inasmuch as ye do this the fullness of the earth is yours: the beasts
of the fields, and the fowls of the air, and that which climbeth upon
the trees, and walketh upon the earth; yea, and the herb, and the good
things which cometh of the earth, whether for food or for raiment, or
for houses or for barns, or for orchards, or for gardens, or for vineyards;
yea, all things which cometh of the earth, in the season thereof, are
made for the benefit and the use of man, both to please the eye, and to
gladden the heart; yea, for food and for raiment, for taste and for smell,
to strengthen the body, and to enliven the soul.

5. And it pleaseth God that he hath given all these things unto man;
for unto this end were they made, to be used with judgment, not to excess, neither by extortion: and in nothing doth man offend God, or
against none is his wrath kindled. save those who confess not his hand
in all things, and obey not his commandments. Behold, this is according to the law and the prophets: wherefore trouble me no more concerning this matter, but learn that he who doeth the works of righteousness,
shall receive his reward, even peace in this world, and eternal life in the
world to come. I, the Lord, have spoken it and the Spirit beareth record. Amen.

[5] 1. Behold, thus saith the Lord unto the elders of his church, who are
to return speedily to the land from whence they came. Behold, it pleaseth me, that you have come up hither; but with some I am not well
pleased, for they will not open their mouths, but hide the talent which I
have given unto them, because of the fear of man. Woe unto such, for
mine anger is kindled against them.

2. And it shall come to pass, if they are not more faithful unto me, it
shall be taken away, even that which they have, for I, the Lord, ruleth
in the heavens above, and among the armies of the earth; and in the day
when I shall make up my jewels, all men shall know what it is that
bespeaketh the power of God. But verily I will speak unto you concerning your journey unto the land from whence you came. Let there be a
craft made, or bought, as seemeth you good, it mattereth not unto me,
and take your journey speedily for the place which is called St. Louis.
And from thence let my servants Sidney Rigdon, and Joseph Smith, Jr.,
and Oliver Cowdery, take their journey for Cincinnati: and in this place
let them lift up their voice, and declare my word with loud voices, without wrath or doubting, lifting up holy hands upon them. For I am able
to make you holy, and your sins are forgiven you.

3. And let the residue take their journey from St. Louis, two by two,
and preach the word, not in haste, among the congregations of the
wicked, until they return to the churches from whence they came. And
all this for the good of the churches; for this intent have I sent them.
And let my servant Edward Partridge impart of the money which I have

On Tuesday, August 9, in company with ten elders, Joseph started for Kirtland. They left Independence Landing in canoes, and went the first day as far as Fort Osage.

Joseph starts East.

The night of the third day they encamped on the bank of the river, at McIlwain's Bend, and the next morning (Friday, the 12th) after prayer Joseph received another revelation.[6]

Incidents by the way.

given him, a portion unto mine elders, who are commanded to return; and he that is able, let him return it by the way of the agent, and he that is not, of him it is not required. And now I speak of the residue who are to come unto this land. Behold, they have been sent to preach my gospel among the congregations of the wicked; wherefore, I give unto them a commandment thus: Thou shalt not idle away thy time; neither shalt thou bury thy talent that it may not be known.

4. And after thou hast come up unto the land of Zion, and hast proclaimed my word, thou shalt speedily return, proclaiming my word among the congregations of the wicked. Not in haste, neither in wrath nor with strife; and shake off the dust of thy feet against those who receive thee not, not in their presence, lest thou provoke them, but in secret, and wash thy feet as a testimony against them in the day of judgment. Behold, this is sufficient for you, and the will of him who hath sent you. And by the mouth of my servant Joseph Smith, Jr., it shall be made known concerning Sidney Rigdon and Oliver Cowdery, the residue hereafter. Even so. Amen.

[6] 1. Behold, and hearken unto the voice of him who has all power, who is from everlasting to everlasting, even Alpha and Omega, the beginning and the end. Behold, verily thus saith the Lord unto you, O ye elders of my church, who are assembled upon this spot, whose sins are now forgiven you, for I the Lord forgiveth sins, and am merciful unto those who confess their sins with humble hearts; but verily I say unto you, that it is not needful for this whole company of mine elders, to be moving swiftly upon the waters, whilst the inhabitants on either side are perishing in unbelief; nevertheless, I suffered it that ye might bear record; behold, there are many dangers upon the waters and more especially hereafter, for I the Lord have decreed, in mine anger, many destructions upon the waters; yea, and especially upon these waters; nevertheless, all flesh is in mine hand, and he that is faithful among you, shall not perish by the waters.

2. Wherefore it is expedient that my servant Sidney Gilbert, and my servant William W. Phelps, be in haste upon their errand and mission; nevertheless I would not suffer that ye should part until you are chastened for all your sins, that you might be one; that you might not perish in wickedness; but now verily I say, It behooveth me that ye should part; wherefore let my servants Sidney Gilbert and William W. Phelps, take their former company, and let them take their journey in haste that they may fill their mission, and through faith they shall overcome; and inasmuch as they are faithful, they shall be preserved, and I, the Lord, will be with them. And let the residue take that which is needful for clothing. Let my servant Sidney Gilbert take that which is not needful with him, as you shall agree. And now, behold, for your good, I gave unto you a commandment concerning these things; and I, the Lord, will reason with you as with men in days of old.

The next day (Saturday, the 13th) they met several of the
elders who were on their way to the land of Zion, and joyful

3. Behold, I, the Lord, in the beginning, blessed the waters, but in the
last days by the mouth of my servant John, I cursed the waters; wherefore, the days will come that no flesh shall be safe upon the waters, and it
shall be said in days to come, that none is able to go up to the land of Zion,
upon the waters, but he that is upright in heart. And, as I, the Lord,
in the beginning cursed the land, even so in the last days have I blessed
it, in its time, for the use of my saints, that they may partake the fatness thereof. And now I give unto you a commandment, and what I
say unto one I say unto all, that you shall forewarn your brethren concerning these waters, that they come not in journeying upon them, lest
their faith fail, and they are caught in her snares; I, the Lord, have
decreed, and the destroyer rideth upon the face thereof, and I revoke
not the decree; I, the Lord, was angry with you yesterday, but to-day
mine anger is turned away. Wherefore let those concerning whom I
have spoken, that should take their journey in haste—again I say unto
you, Let them take their journey in haste, and it mattereth not unto me,
after a little, if it so be that they fill their mission, whether they go by
water or by land; let this be as it is made known unto them according to
their judgments hereafter.

4. And now, concerning my servants Sidney Rigdon, and Joseph Smith,
Jr., and Oliver Cowdery, let them come not again upon the waters, save
it be upon the canal, while journeying unto their homes, or, in other
words, they shall not come upon the waters to journey, save upon the
canal. Behold, I, the Lord, have appointed a way for the journeying of
my saints, and, behold, this is the way; that after they leave the canal,
they shall journey by land, inasmuch as they are commanded to journey
and go up unto the land of Zion; and they shall do like unto the children
of Israel, pitching their tents by the way.

5. And, behold, this commandment you shall give unto all your brethren; nevertheless unto whom it is given power to command the waters,
unto him it is given by the Spirit to know all his ways; wherefore let him
do as the Spirit of the living God commandeth him, whether upon the
land or upon the waters, as it remaineth with me to do hereafter; and
unto you it is given the course for the saints, or the way for the saints of
the camp of the Lord, to journey. And again, verily I say unto you,
My servants Sidney Rigdon, and Joseph Smith, Jr., and Oliver Cowdery,
shall not open their mouths in the congregations of the wicked, until
they arrive at Cincinnati; and in that place they shall lift up their voices
unto God against that people; yea, unto him whose anger is kindled
against their wickedness; a people who are well-nigh ripened for destruction; and from thence let them journey for the congregations of their
brethren, for their labors, even now, are wanted more abundantly among
them, than among the congregations of the wicked.

6. And now concerning the residue, let them journey and declare the
word among the congregations of the wicked, inasmuch as it is given,
and inasmuch as they do this they shall rid their garments, and they
shall be spotless before me; and let them journey together, or two by
two, as seemeth them good, only let my servant Reynolds Cahoon, and
my servant Samuel H. Smith, with whom I am well pleased, be not
separated until they return to their homes, and this for a wise purpose
in me. And now verily I say unto you, and what I say unto one I say
unto all, Be of good cheer, little children, for I am in your midst, and
I have not forsaken you, and inasmuch as you have humbled yourselves before me, the blessings of the kingdom are yours. Gird up your

were their salutations. On this occasion Joseph received a revelation.[7]

Joseph writes of the remainder of his journey as follows:—

"After this little meeting of the elders, myself, and Sidney Rigdon, and Oliver Cowdery continued our journey by land to St. Louis, where we overtook Brothers Phelps and Gilbert. From this place we took stage, and they went by water to Kirtland, where we arrived safe and well, on the 27th. Many things transpired upon this journey to strengthen our faith, and displayed the goodness of God in such a marvelous manner that we could not help beholding the exertions of Satan to blind the eyes of the people, so as to hide the true light that lights every man that comes into the world. In these infant days of the church there was a great anxiety to obtain the word of the Lord upon Purchasing land. every subject that in any way concerned our salvation; and as 'the land of Zion' was now the most important temporal object in view, I inquired of the Lord for further information upon the gathering of the saints and the pur-

loins and be watchful, and be sober, looking forth for the coming of the Son of Man, for he cometh in an hour you think not. Pray always that you enter not into temptation, that you may abide the day of his coming, whether in life or in death. Even so. Amen.

[7] 1. Behold, and hearken, O ye elders of my church, saith the Lord your God; even Jesus Christ, your Advocate; who knoweth the weakness of man and how to succor them who are tempted; and verily mine eyes are upon those who have not as yet gone up unto the land of Zion; wherefore your mission is not yet full; nevertheless ye are blessed, for the testimony which ye have borne is recorded in heaven for the angels to look upon, and they rejoice over you, and your sins are forgiven you.

2. And now continue your journey. Assemble yourselves upon the land of Zion, and hold a meeting and rejoice together, and offer a sacrament unto the Most High; and then you may return to bear record; yea, even all together, or two by two, as seemeth you good; it mattereth not unto me, only be faithful, and declare glad tidings unto the inhabitants of the earth, or among the congregations of the wicked. Behold, I, the Lord, have brought you together that the promise might be fulfilled, that the faithful among you should be preserved and rejoice together in the land of Missouri. I, the Lord, promised the faithful and cannot lie.

3. I, the Lord, am willing, if any among you desireth to ride upon horses, or upon mules, or in chariots, he shall receive this blessing, if he receive it from the hand of the Lord, with a thankful heart in all things. These things remain with you to do according to judgment and the directions of the Spirit. Behold, the kingdom is yours. And, behold, and lo, I am with the faithful always. Even so. Amen.

chase of the land and other matters."—*Times and Seasons*, vol. 5, p. 465.

· On this occasion and in answer to this petition he received a revelation. [a]

[a] 1. Hearken, O ye people, and open your hearts, and give ear from afar; and listen, you that call yourselves the people of the Lord, and hear the word of the Lord, and his will concerning you; yea, verily, I say, Hear the word of him whose anger is kindled against the wicked and rebellious; who willeth to take even them whom he will take, and preserveth in life them whom he will preserve; who buildeth up at his own will and pleasure; and destroyeth when he pleases, and is able to cast the soul down to hell.

2. Behold, I, the Lord, utter my voice, and it shall be obeyed. Wherefore, verily I say, Let the wicked take heed, and let the rebellious fear and tremble; and let the unbelieving hold their lips, for the day of wrath shall come upon them as a whirlwind, and all flesh shall know that I am God. And he that seeketh signs shall see signs, but not unto salvation.

3. Verily, I say unto you, There are those among you who seek signs, and there have been such even from the beginning; but, behold, faith cometh not by signs, but signs follow those that believe. Yea, signs cometh by faith, not by the will of men, nor as they please, but by the will of God. Yea, signs cometh by faith, unto mighty works, for without faith no man pleaseth God: and with whom God is angry he is not well pleased: wherefore, unto such he showeth no signs, only in wrath unto their condemnation.

4. Wherefore, I, the Lord, am not pleased with those among you, who have sought after signs and wonders for faith, and not for the good of men unto my glory; nevertheless, I gave commandments and many have turned away from my commandments and have not kept them. There were among you adulterers and adulteresses; some of whom have turned away from you, and others remain with you, that hereafter shall be revealed. Let such beware and repent speedily, lest judgment shall come upon them as a snare, and their folly shall be made manifest, and their works shall follow them in the eyes of the people.

5. And verily I say unto you, as I have said before, He that looketh on a woman to lust after her, or if any shall commit adultery in their hearts, they shall not have the Spirit, but shall deny the faith and shall fear: wherefore, I, the Lord, have said that the fearful, and the unbelieving, and all liars, and whosoever loveth and maketh a lie, and the whoremonger, and the sorcerer, shall have their part in that lake which burneth with fire and brimstone, which is the second death. Verily I say, that they shall not have part in the first resurrection.

6. And now, behold, I, the Lord, saith unto you, that ye are not justified because these things are among you; nevertheless he that endureth in faith and doeth my will, the same shall overcome, and shall receive an inheritance upon the earth, when the day of transfiguration shall come; when the earth shall be transfigured, even according to the pattern which was shown unto mine apostles upon the mount; of which account the fullness ye have not yet received.

7. And now, verily I say unto you, that as I said that I would make known my will unto you, behold, I will make it known unto you, not by the way of commandment, for there are many who observe not to keep my commandments; but unto him that keepeth my commandments, I will give the mysteries of my kingdom, and the same shall be in him a well of living water, springing up unto everlasting life.

The early part of September, 1831, was spent by Joseph in preparing to remove to the town of Hiram for the purpose of engaging in the translation of the Bible Some brethren had been selected according to the last revelation to go up to Zion, and they were busily engaged in getting ready to start in October.

Prepares to remove to Hiram.

8. And now, behold, this is the will of the Lord your God concerning his saints, that they should assemble themselves together unto the land of Zion, not in haste, lest there should be confusion, which bringeth pestilence. Behold, the land of Zion, I, the Lord, holdeth it in mine own hands; nevertheless, I, the Lord, rendereth unto Cæsar the things which are Cæsar's: wherefore, I, the Lord, willeth, that you should purchase the lands, that you may have advantage of the world, that you may have claim on the world, that they may not be stirred up unto anger; for Satan putteth it into their hearts to anger against you, and to the shedding of blood; wherefore the land of Zion shall not be obtained but by purchase, or by blood, otherwise there is none inheritance for you. And if by purchase, behold, you are blessed; and if by blood, as you are forbidden to shed blood, lo, your enemies are upon you, and ye shall be scourged from city to city, and from synagogue to synagogue, and but few shall stand to receive an inheritance.

9. I, the Lord, am angry with the wicked; I am holding my Spirit from the inhabitants of the earth. I have sworn in my wrath and decreed wars upon the face of the earth, and the wicked shall slay the wicked, and fear shall come upon every man, and the saints also shall hardly escape; nevertheless, I, the Lord, am with them, and will come down in heaven from the presence of my Father, and consume the wicked with unquenchable fire. And, behold, this is not yet, but by and by; wherefore seeing that I, the Lord, have decreed all these things upon the face of the earth, I willeth that my saints should be assembled upon the land of Zion; and that every man should take righteousness in his hands, and faithfulness upon his loins, and lift a warning voice unto the inhabitants of the earth; and declare both by word and by flight, that desolation shall come upon the wicked. Wherefore let my disciples in Kirtland arrange their temporal concerns, which dwell upon this farm.

10. Let my servant Titus Billings, who has the care thereof, dispose of the land, that he may be prepared in the coming spring, to take his journey up unto the land of Zion, with those that dwell upon the face thereof, excepting those whom I shall reserve unto myself, that shall not go until I shall command them. And let all the moneys which can be spared, it mattereth not unto me whether it be little or much, be sent up unto the land of Zion, unto them whom I have appointed to receive.

11. Behold, I, the Lord, will give unto my servant Joseph Smith, Jr., power that he shall be enabled to discern by the Spirit those who shall go up unto the land of Zion, and those of my disciples who shall tarry.

12. Let my servant Newel K. Whitney retain his store, or, in other words, the store yet for a little season. Nevertheless let him impart all the money which he can impart, to be sent up unto the land of Zion. Behold, these things are in his own hands, let him do according to wisdom. Verily I say, Let him be ordained as an agent unto the disciples that shall tarry, and let him be ordained unto this power; and now speedily visit the churches, expounding these things unto them, with my servant Oliver Cowdery. Behold, this is my will, obtaining moneys even as I have directed.

On Sunday, the 11th of September, a revelation was received concerning the duties of certain individuals, and containing some further items concerning Zion, also some instruction concerning repentance. *

On Zion.

13. He that is faithful and endureth shall overcome the world. He that sendeth up treasures unto the land of Zion, shall receive an inheritance in this world, and his works shall follow him; and also a reward in the world to come: yea, and blessed are the dead that die in the Lord from henceforth, when the Lord shall come, and old things shall pass away, and all things become new, they shall rise from the dead and shall not die after, and shall receive an inheritance before the Lord, in the holy city, and he that liveth when the Lord shall come, and has kept the faith, blessed is he; nevertheless it is appointed to him to die at the age of man; wherefore children shall grow up until they become old, old men shall die; but they shall not sleep in the dust, but they shall be changed in the twinkling of an eye; wherefore, for this cause preached the apostles unto the world the resurrection of the dead: these things are the things that ye must look for, and speaking after the manner of the Lord, they are now nigh at hand; and in a time to come, even in the day of the coming of the Son of Man, and until that hour, there will be foolish virgins among the wise, and at that hour cometh an entire separation of the righteous and the wicked; and in that day will I send mine angels, to pluck out the wicked, and cast them into unquenchable fire.

14. And now, behold, verily I say unto you, I, the Lord, am not pleased with my servant Sidney Rigdon, he exalted himself in his heart, and received not counsel, but grieved the Spirit; wherefore his writing is not acceptable unto the Lord, and he shall make another, and if the Lord receive it not, behold, he standeth no longer in the office which I have appointed him.

15. And again, verily I say unto you, Those who desire in their hearts, in meekness, to warn sinners to repentance, let them be ordained unto this power; for this is a day of warning, and not a day of many words. For I, the Lord, am not to be mocked in the last days. Behold, I am from above, and my power lieth beneath. I am over all, and in all, and through all, and searcheth all things; and the day cometh that all things shall be subject unto me. Behold, I am Alpha and Omega, even Jesus Christ. Wherefore let all men beware how they take my name in their lips; for, behold, verily I say, that many there be who are under this condemnation; who useth the name of the Lord, and useth it in vain, having not authority. Wherefore, let the church repent of their sins, and I, the Lord, will own them, otherwise they shall be cut off.

16. Remember that that which cometh from above is sacred, and must be spoken with care, and by constraint of the Spirit, and in this there is no condemnation; and ye receive the Spirit through prayer; wherefore, without this there remaineth condemnation. Let my servants Joseph Smith, Jr., and Sidney Rigdon, seek them a home as they are taught through prayer, by the Spirit. These things remain to overcome, through patience, that such may receive a more exceeding and eternal weight of glory; otherwise, a greater condemnation. Amen.

* 1. Behold, thus saith the Lord your God unto you, O ye elders of my church, Hearken ye, and hear, and receive my will concerning you; for verily I say unto you, I will that ye should overcome the world; wherefore I will have compassion upon you. There are those among you who have sinned; but verily I say, For this once, for mine own glory, and for the salvation of souls, I have forgiven you your sins.

Provision was made about this time for the establishment of a printing press in Jackson County, Missouri. Joseph writes:—

"On the 12th of September I removed with my family to the township of Hiram, and commenced living with John Johnson. Hiram was in Portage County and about thirty

2. I will be merciful unto you, for I have given unto you the kingdom; and the keys of the mysteries of the kingdom, shall not be taken from my servant Joseph Smith, Jr., through the means I have appointed, while he liveth, inasmuch as he obeyeth mine ordinances. There are those who have sought occasion against him without cause; nevertheless he has sinned, but verily I say unto you, I, the Lord, forgiveth sins unto those who confess their sins before me, and ask forgiveness, who have not sinned unto death. My disciples, in days of old, sought occasion against one another, and forgave not one another in their hearts, and for this evil they were afflicted, and sorely chastened; wherefore I say unto you, that ye ought to forgive one another, for he that forgiveth not his brother his trespasses, standeth condemned before the Lord, for there remaineth in him the greater sin. I, the Lord, will forgive whom I will forgive, but of you it is required to forgive all men; and ye ought to say in your hearts, Let God judge between me and thee, and reward thee according to thy deeds. And he that repenteth not of his sins, and confesseth them not, then ye shall bring him before the church, and do with him as the scriptures saith unto you, either by commandment, or by revelation. And this ye shall do that God might be glorified, not because ye forgive not, having not compassion, but that ye may be justified in the eyes of the law, that ye may not offend him who is your Lawgiver.

3. Verily I say, For this cause ye shall do these things. Behold, I, the Lord, was angry with him who was my servant Ezra Booth; and also my servant Isaac Morley; for they kept not the law, neither the commandments; they sought evil in their hearts, and I the Lord, withheld my Spirit. They condemned for evil, that thing in which there was no evil; nevertheless, I have forgiven my servant Isaac Morley. And also my servant Edward Partridge, behold, he hath sinned, and Satan seeketh to destroy his soul; but when these things are made known unto them, they repent of the evil, and they shall be forgiven.

4. And now, verily I say, that it is expedient in me that my servant Sidney Gilbert, after a few weeks, should return upon his business, and to his agency in the land of Zion; and that which he hath seen and heard may be made known unto my disciples, that they perish not. And for this cause have I spoken these things. And again, I say unto you, that my servant Isaac Morley may not be tempted above that which he is able to bear, and counsel wrongfully to your hurt, I gave commandment that his farm should be sold. I willeth not that my servant Frederick G. Williams should sell his farm, for I, the Lord, willeth to retain a strong hold in the land of Kirtland, for the space of five years, in the which I will not overthrow the wicked, that thereby I may save some; and after that day, I, the Lord, will not hold any guilty that shall go, with an open heart, up to the land of Zion; for I, the Lord, requireth the hearts of the children of men.

5. Behold, now it is called to-day (until the coming of the Son of Man), and verily it is a day of sacrifice, and a day for the tithing of my people; for he that is tithed shall not be burned (at his coming); for after to-day cometh the burning: this is speaking after the manner of the Lord; for

miles southeasterly from Kirtland.   From this time until
the fore part of October I did little more than to prepare to
recommence the translation of the Bible.   About this time
Ezra Booth came out as an apostate.   He came into the
church upon seeing a person healed of an infirmity of many
years standing.   He had been a Methodist priest for some
time previous to his embracing the fullness of the gospel as
developed in the Book of Mormon, and upon his admission
into the church he was ordained an elder, as will be seen by
the foregoing revelations.   He went up to Missouri as a
companion of Elder Morley, but when he actually learned
that faith, humility, patience, and tribulation, were before
blessing; and that God brought low before he exalted; that
instead of 'the Savior's granting him power to smite men,
and make them believe' (as he said he wanted God to do
him), he found he must become all things to all men that he
might peradventure save some, and that too by all diligence,
by perils by sea and land; as was the case in the days of

verily I say, To-morrow all the proud and they that do wickedly shall be
as stubble; and I will burn them up, for I am the Lord of hosts; and I
will not spare any that remaineth in Babylon.   Wherefore, if ye believe
me, ye will labor while it is called to-day.   And it is not meet that my
servants Newel K. Whitney and Sidney Gilbert should sell their store,
and their possessions here, for this is not wisdom until the residue of the
church, which remaineth in this place, shall go up unto the land of Zion.

6. Behold, it is said in my laws, or forbidden, to get in debt to thine
enemies; but, behold, it is not said at any time, that the Lord should not
take when he please, and pay as seemeth him good: wherefore, as ye are
agents, and ye are on the Lord's errand; and whatever ye do according
to the will of the Lord, is the Lord's business, and he hath set you to
provide for his saints in these last days, that they may obtain an inheritance in the land of Zion, and, behold, I, the Lord, declare unto you, and
my words are sure and shall not fail, that they shall obtain it; but all
things must come to pass in their time; wherefore be not weary in well-
doing, for ye are laying the foundation of a great work.   And out of
small things proceedeth that which is great.

7. Behold, the Lord requireth the heart and a willing mind; and the
willing and obedient shall eat the good of the land of Zion in these last
days; and the rebellious shall be cut off out of the land of Zion, and shall
be sent away, and shall not inherit the land; for, verily, I say that the
rebellious are not of the blood of Ephraim, wherefore they shall be
plucked out.   Behold, I, the Lord, have made my church in these last
days, like unto a judge sitting on a hill, or in a high place, to judge the
nations; for it shall come to pass, that the inhabitants of Zion shall judge
all things pertaining to Zion; and liars, and hypocrites shall be proved by
them, and they who are not apostles and prophets shall be known.

8. And even the bishop, who is a judge, and his counselors, if they are
not faithful in their stewardships, shall be condemned, and others shall

Jesus, which appears in the sixth chapter of St. John's gospel, he said: 'Verily, verily I say unto you, Ye seek me, not because ye saw the miracles, but because ye did eat of the loaves, and were filled.' So it was with Booth, and when he was disappointed by his own evil heart, he turned away, and as said before, became an apostate, and wrote a series of letters' which by their coloring, falsity, and vain calculations to overthrow the work of the Lord, exposed his weakness, wickedness, and folly, and left him a monument of his own shame for the world to wonder at.

"A conference was held, in which Brother W. W. Phelps was instructed to stop at Cincinnati on his way to Missouri Prepare to and purchase a press and type for the purpose establish a of establishing and publishing a monthly paper at press in Missouri. Independence, Jackson County, Missouri, to be called the *Evening and Morning Star*. The first Sunday in October, Orson Hyde, a clerk in Brothers Sidney Gilbert and Newel K. Whitney's store, in Kirtland, was baptized and became a member of the church. As he was soon after designated as one of the chosen men of the Lord, to bear his word to the nations, I feel a desire to notice him as he was and as he is. He was, in his own words, left in his infancy, an orphan with none to look upon him with a father's eye, and feel for him with a mother's heart. The hand that wiped his infant tears was still; the breast that gave him suck was cold, and slumbered in the arms of death. He was thrust abroad upon the cold and friendless bosom of an unfeeling world, so that for twenty long years he saw no one in whose veins flowed a drop of kindred blood, and consequently grew up as a wild and uncultivated plant of nature, and now had come into the new and everlasting covenant, to be renewed and receive grace for grace, and put himself under the fatherly care of Him whose yoke is easy, and whose burden is light; and who rewardeth his sons and daughters, who serve

be planted in their stead; for, behold, I say unto you that Zion shall flourish, and the glory of the Lord shall be upon her, and she shall be au ensign unto the people, and there shall come unto her out of every nation under heaven. And the day shall come, when the nations of the earth shall tremble because of her, and shall fear because of her terrible ones. The Lord hath spoken it. Amen.

him faithfully to the end, with eternal life."—*Times and Seasons*, vol. 5, p. 481.

Early in October a revelation was given.[10] Joseph continues as follows:—

"Soon after the above revelation was received I recommenced the translation of the Scriptures, in company with
Transla-
tion resumed. Elder Rigdon, who had removed to Hiram to act in his office of scribe to me. On the 11th of October a conference was held at Brother Johnson's, where I was living, at which the elders were instructed in the ancient manner of conducting meetings, of which knowledge most of them were ignorant. A committee of six were appointed to instruct the several branches of the church. Elders David Whitmer and Reynolds Cahoon were appointed as two of the said committee, with the further duty on their mission, of setting forth the condition of Bro. Joseph Smith, Jr., and Sidney Rigdon, that they might obtain means to continue the translation. This conference was adjourned till the 25th of October, to meet at the house of Serems Burnett, in Orange, Cuyahoga County. On the 21st I attended a special conference to settle a difficulty which had occurred in Kirtland, on account that William Cahoon and Peter Devolve had abused one of Brother Whitney's children. Myself and Elder Rigdon were appointed to go to Kirtland and settle the difficulty, which we did. At the conference, on the 25th, at Orange, twelve high priests, seventeen elders, four priests,

[10] 1. Hearken, and lo, a voice as of one from on high, who is mighty and powerful, whose going forth is unto the ends of the earth; yea, whose voice is unto men, Prepare ye the way of the Lord, make his paths straight. The keys of the kingdom of God are committed unto man on the earth, and from thence shall the gospel roll forth unto the ends of the earth, as the stone which is cut out of the mountain without hands shall roll forth, until it has filled the whole earth; yea, a voice crying, Prepare ye the way of the Lord, prepare ye the supper of the Lamb, make ready for the Bridegroom; pray unto the Lord; call upon his holy name; make known his wonderful works among the people, call upon the Lord, that his kingdom may go forth upon the earth; that the inhabitants thereof may receive it, and be prepared for the days to come, in the which the Son of Man shall come down in heaven, clothed in the brightness of his glory, to meet the kingdom of God which is set up on the earth; wherefore, may the kingdom of God go forth, that the kingdom of heaven may come, that thou, O God, may be glorified in heaven, so on earth, that thy enemies may be subdued; for thine is the honor, power, and glory, forever and ever. Amen.

three teachers, and four deacons, together with a large congregation attended. Much business was done, and the four remaining committee, authorized by the conference at Hiram, on the 11th, were appointed, and consisted of Simeon Carter, Orson Hyde, Hyrum Smith, and Emer Harris."— *Times and Seasons*, vol. 5, p. 482.

About this time a revelation was given to W. E. McLellin.[11]

A special conference was held, probably at Hiram, on Tuesday, November 1, on account of the proposed departure of Oliver Cowdery and John Whitmer for Missouri. At this conference further instruction was given and a preface to the Book of Commandments revealed.[12]

Preface to Book of Commandments.

[11] 1. Behold, thus saith the Lord, unto my servant, William E. McLellin, Blessed are you, inasmuch as you have turned away from your iniquities, and have received my truths, saith the Lord your Redeemer, the Savior of the world, even of as many as believe on my name. Verily I say unto you, Blessed are you for receiving mine everlasting covenant, even the fullness of my gospel, sent forth unto the children of men, that they might have life, and be made partakers of the glories, which are to be revealed in the last days, as it was written by the prophets and apostles in days of old.

2. Verily I say unto you, my servant William, that you are clean, but not all; repent therefore of those things which are not pleasing in my sight, saith the Lord, for the Lord will show them unto you. And now verily I, the Lord, will show unto you what I will concerning you, or what is my will concerning you; behold, verily I say unto you, that it is my will that you should proclaim my gospel from land to land, and from city to city; yea, in those regions round about where it has not been proclaimed.

3. Tarry not many days in this place; go not up unto the land of Zion, as yet; but inasmuch as you can send, send; otherwise think not of thy property. Go unto the eastern lands; bear testimony in every place, unto every people, and in their synagogues; reasoning with the people.

4. Let my servant Samuel H. Smith go with you, and forsake him not, and give him thine instructions; and he that is faithful shall be made strong in every place, and I, the Lord, will go with you.

5. Lay your hands upon the sick and they shall recover. Return not till I, the Lord, shall send you. Be patient in affliction. Ask and ye shall receive. Knock and it shall be opened unto you. Seek not to be cumbered. Forsake all unrighteousness. Commit not adultery, a temptation with which thou hast been troubled. Keep these sayings for they are true and faithful, and thou shalt magnify thine office, and push many people to Zion, with songs of everlasting joy upon their heads. Continue in these things, even unto the end, and you shall have a crown of eternal life at the right hand of my Father, who is full of grace and truth. Verily thus saith the Lord your God, your Redeemer, even Jesus Christ. Amen.

[12] 1. Hearken, O ye people of my church, saith the voice of him who dwells on high, and whose eyes are upon all men; yea, verily I say, Hearken ye people from afar, and ye that are upon the islands of the sea,

listen together; for verily the voice of the Lord is unto all men, and there is none to escape, and there is no eye that shall not see, neither ear that shall not hear, neither heart that shall not be penetrated; and the rebellious shall be pierced with much sorrow, for their iniquities shall be spoken upon the house tops, and their secret acts shall be revealed; and the voice of warning shall be unto all people, by the mouths of my disciples, whom I have chosen in these last days, and they shall go forth and none shall stay them, for I the Lord have commanded them.

2. Behold, this is mine authority, and the authority of my servants, and my preface unto the book of my commandments, which I have given them to publish unto you, O inhabitants of the earth: wherefore fear and tremble, O ye people, for what I the Lord have decreed, in them, shall be fulfilled. And verily, I say unto you, that they who go forth, bearing these tidings unto the inhabitants of the earth, to them is power given to seal, both on earth and in heaven, the unbelieving and rebellious; yea, verily, to seal them up unto the day when the wrath of God shall be poured out upon the wicked without measure; unto the day when the Lord shall come to recompense unto every man according to his work, and measure to every man according to the measure which he has measured to his fellow-man.

3. Wherefore the voice of the Lord is unto the ends of the earth, that all that will hear may hear: prepare ye, prepare ye for that which is to come, for the Lord is nigh; and the anger of the Lord is kindled, and his sword is bathed in heaven, and it shall fall upon the inhabitants of the earth; and the arm of the Lord shall be revealed; and the day cometh that they who will not hear the voice of the Lord, neither the voice of his servants, neither give heed to the words of the prophets and apostles, shall be cut off from among the people; for they have strayed from mine ordinances, and have broken mine everlasting covenant; they seek not the Lord to establish his righteousness, but every man walketh in his own way, and after the image of his own god, whose image is in the likeness of the world, that of an idol, which waxeth old and shall perish in Babylon, even Babylon the great, which shall fall.

4. Wherefore I the Lord, knowing the calamity which should come upon the inhabitants of the earth, called upon my servant Joseph Smith, Jr., and spake unto him from heaven, and gave him commandments, and also gave commandments to others, that they should proclaim these things unto the world; and all this that it might be fulfilled, which was written by the prophets: the weak things of the world shall come forth and break down the mighty and strong ones, that man should not counsel his fellow-man, neither trust in the arm of flesh, but that every man might speak in the name of God the Lord, even the Savior of the world; that faith also might increase in the earth; that mine everlasting covenant might be established; that the fullness of my gospel might be proclaimed by the weak and the simple, unto the ends of the world, and before kings and rulers.

5. Behold, I am God, and have spoken it; these commandments are of me, and were given unto my servants in their weakness, after the manner of their language, that they might come to understanding; and inasmuch as they erred it might be made known; and inasmuch as they sought wisdom they might be instructed; and inasmuch as they sinned they might be chastened, that they might repent; and inasmuch as they were humble, they might be made strong, and blessed from on high, and receive knowledge from time to time; and after having received the record of the Nephites, yea, even my servant Joseph Smith, Jr., might have power to translate, through the mercy of God, by the power of God, the Book of Mormon; and also those to whom these commandments were given might have power to lay the foundation of this church,

There was some murmuring among the elders about this
Some murmur concerning language in revelations. time regarding the language in which the revelations were couched, whereupon the following was given.[13]

and to bring it forth out of obscurity, and out of darkness, the only true and living church upon the face of the whole earth, with which I the Lord am well pleased, speaking unto the church collectively and not individually; for I the Lord cannot look upon sin with the least degree of allowance; nevertheless, he that repents and does the commandments of the Lord shall be forgiven; and he that repents not, from him shall be taken even the light which he has received, for my Spirit shall not always strive with man, saith the Lord of hosts.

6. And again, verily I say unto you, O inhabitants of the earth, I the Lord am willing to make these things known unto all flesh, for I am no respecter of persons, and willeth that all men shall know that the day speedily cometh, the hour is not yet, but is nigh at hand, when peace shall be taken from the earth, and the Devil shall have power over his own dominion; and also the Lord shall have power over his saints, and shall reign in their midst, and shall come down in judgment upon Idumea, or the world.

7. Search these commandments, for they are true and faithful, and the prophecies and promises which are in them shall all be fulfilled.

8. What I the Lord have spoken I have spoken, and I excuse not myself; and though the heavens and the earth pass away, my word shall not pass away, but shall all be fulfilled, whether by mine own voice, or by the voice of my servants, it is the same; for, behold, and lo, the Lord is God, and the Spirit beareth record, and the record is true, and the truth abideth forever and ever. Amen.

[13] 1. Behold, and hearken, O ye elders of my church, who have assembled yourselves together, whose prayers I have heard, and whose hearts I know, and whose desires have come up before me. Behold, and lo, mine eyes are upon you; and the heavens and the earth are in mine hands, and the riches of eternity are mine to give. Ye endeavored to believe that ye should receive the blessing which was offered unto you, but, behold, verily, I say unto you, There were fears in your hearts; and verily this is the reason that ye did not receive.

2. And now, I, the Lord, give unto you a testimony of the truth of these commandments which are lying before you; your eyes have been upon my servant Joseph Smith, Jr., and his language you have known; and his imperfections you have known; and you have sought in your hearts knowledge, that you might express beyond his language: this you also know: now seek ye out of the Book of Commandments, even the least that is among them, and appoint him that is the most wise among you; or if there be any among you, that shall make one like unto it, then ye are justified in saying that ye do not know that they are true; but if ye cannot make one like unto it, ye are under condemnation if ye do not bear record that they are true; for ye know that there is no unrighteousness in them; and that which is righteous cometh down from above, from the Father of lights.

3. And again, verily I say unto you, that it is your privilege, and a promise I give unto you that have been ordained unto this ministry, that inasmuch as you strip yourselves from jealousies and fears, and humble yourselves before me, for ye are not sufficiently humble, the veil shall be rent, and you shall see me and know that I am; not with the carnal, neither natural mind, but with the spiritual; for no man has seen God at

William E. McLellin made the effort to imitate one of the revelations, and failed. Joseph says of this effort: "The elders and all present that witnessed this vain attempt of a man to imitate the language of Jesus Christ, renewed their faith in the fullness of the gospel, and in the truth of the commandments and revelations which the Lord had given to the church through my instrumentality; and the elders signified a willingness to bear testimony of their truth to all the world."

Following this a revelation was given to Orson Hyde, Luke Johnson, Lyman Johnson, and William E. McLellin.[14]

any time in the flesh, except quickened by the Spirit of God; neither can any natural man abide the presence of God; neither after the carnal mind; ye are not able to abide the presence of God now, neither the ministering of angels; wherefore continue in patience until ye are perfected.

4. Let not your minds turn back, and when ye are worthy, in mine own due time, ye shall see and know that which was conferred upon you by the hands of my servant Joseph Smith, Jr. Amen.

[14] 1. My servant, Orson Hyde, was called, by his ordinance, to proclaim the everlasting gospel, by the Spirit of the living God, from people to people, and from land to land, in the congregations of the wicked, in their synagogues, reasoning with, and expounding all scriptures unto them. And, behold, and lo, this is an ensample unto all those who were ordained unto this priesthood, whose mission is appointed unto them to go forth; and this is the ensample unto them, that they shall speak as they are moved upon by the Holy Ghost; and whatsoever they shall speak when moved upon by the Holy Ghost, shall be scripture; shall be the will of the Lord; shall be the mind of the Lord; shall be the word of the Lord; shall be the voice of the Lord, and the power of God unto salvation: behold, this is the promise of the Lord unto you, O ye my servants: wherefore, be of good cheer, and do not fear, for I, the Lord, am with you, and will stand by you; and ye shall bear record of me, even Jesus Christ, that I am the Son of the living God, that I was, that I am, and that I am to come. This is the word of the Lord unto you my servant, Orson Hyde, and also unto my servant, Luke Johnson, and unto my servant, Lyman Johnson, and unto my servant, William E. McLellin; and unto all the faithful elders of my church. Go ye into all the world; preach the gospel to every creature, acting in the authority which I have given you, baptizing in the name of the Father, and of the Son, and of the Holy Ghost; and he that believeth, and is baptized, shall be saved, and he that believeth not shall be damned; and he that believeth shall be blessed with signs following, even as it is written; and unto you it shall be given to know the signs of the times, and the signs of the coming of the Son of Man; and of as many as the Father shall bear record, to you it shall be given power to seal them up unto eternal life. Amen.

2. And now concerning the items in addition to the covenants and commandments, they are these: There remaineth hereafter in the due time of the Lord, other bishops to be set apart unto the church to minister even according to the first; wherefore they shall be high priests

It was decided by the conference that Joseph Smith should arrange and get in readiness the revelations, and that Oliver Cowdery should carry them to Independence, Missouri, where W. W. Phelps had gone with a printing office, and have them published.

Revelations to be sent to Missouri.

who are worthy, and they shall be appointed by the first presidency of the Melchisedec priesthood, except they be literal descendants of Aaron, and if they be literal descendants of Aaron, they have a legal right to the bishopric, if they are the firstborn among the sons of Aaron; for the first-born holds the right of the presidency over this priesthood, and the keys or authority of the same. No man has a legal right to this office, to hold the keys of this priesthood, except he be a literal descendant and the firstborn of Aaron; but as a high priest of the Melchisedec priesthood has authority to officiate in all the lesser offices, he may officiate in the office of bishop when no literal descendant of Aaron can be found; provided, he is called and set apart, and ordained unto this power under the hands of the first presidency of the Melchisedec priesthood. And a literal descendant of Aaron, also, must be designated by this presidency, and found worthy, and anointed, and ordained under the hands of this presidency, otherwise they are not legally authorized to officiate in their priesthood; but by virtue of the decree concerning their right of the priesthood descending from father to son, they may claim their anointing, if at any time they can prove their lineage, or do ascertain it by revelation from the Lord under the hands of the above-named presidency.

3. And again, no bishop, or high priest, who shall be set apart for this ministry, shall be tried or condemned for any crime, save it be before the first presidency of the church; and inasmuch as he is found guilty before this presidency, by testimony that cannot be impeached, he shall be condemned, and if he repents he shall be forgiven, according to the covenants and commandments of the church.

4. And again, inasmuch as parents have children in Zion, or in any of her stakes which are organized, that teach them not to understand the doctrine of repentance; faith in Christ the Son of the living God; and of baptism and the gift of the Holy Ghost by the laying on of the hands when eight years old, the sin be upon the head of the parents; for this shall be a law unto the inhabitants of Zion, or in any of her stakes which are organized; and their children shall be baptized for the remission of their sins when eight years old, and receive the laying on of the hands: and they shall also teach their children to pray, and to walk uprightly before the Lord. And the inhabitants of Zion shall also observe the sabbath day to keep it holy. And the inhabitants of Zion, also, shall remember their labors, inasmuch as they are appointed to labor, in all faithfulness; for the idler shall be had in remembrance before the Lord. Now, I, the Lord, am not well pleased with the inhabitants of Zion, for there are idlers among them; and their children are also growing up in wickedness; they also seek not earnestly the riches of eternity, but their eyes are full of greediness. These things ought not to be, and must be done away from among them; wherefore let my servant Oliver Cowdery carry these sayings unto the land of Zion. And a commandment I give unto them, that he that observeth not his prayers before the Lord in the season thereof, let him be had in remembrance before the judge of my people. These sayings are true and faithful; wherefore transgress them not, neither take therefrom. Behold, I am Alpha and Omega, and I come quickly. Amen.

The elders desired more information concerning the

The appendix. preaching of the gospel and the gathering, and in answer to importunities, received on Thursday, November 3, what is known as the appendix to the Book of Doctrine and Covenants.[16]

[16] 1. Hearken, O ye people of my church, saith the Lord your God, and hear the word of the Lord concerning you; the Lord who shall suddenly come to his temple; the Lord who shall come down upon the world with a curse to judgment; yea, upon all the nations that forget God, and upon all the ungodly among you. For he shall make bare his holy arm in the eyes of all the nations, and all the ends of the earth shall see the salvation of their God.

2. Wherefore prepare ye, prepare ye, O my people; sanctify yourselves; gather ye together, O ye people of my church, upon the land of Zion, all you that have not been commanded to tarry. Go ye out from Babylon. Be ye clean that bear the vessels of the Lord. Call your solemn assemblies, and speak often one to another. And let every man call upon the name of the Lord; yea, verily I say unto you again, The time has come when the voice of the Lord is unto you, Go ye out of Babylon; gather ye out from among the nations, from the four winds, from one end of heaven to the other.

3. Send forth the elders of my church unto the nations which are afar off; unto the islands of the sea; send forth unto foreign lands; call upon all nations; firstly, upon the Gentiles, and then upon the Jews. And, behold, and lo, this shall be their cry, and the voice of the Lord unto all people: Go ye forth unto the land of Zion, that the borders of my people may be enlarged, and that her stakes may be strengthened, and that Zion may go forth unto the regions round about; yea, let the cry go forth among all people: Awake and arise and go forth to meet the Bridegroom. Behold, and lo, the Bridegroom cometh, go ye out to meet him. Prepare yourselves for the great day of the Lord.

4. Watch, therefore, for ye know neither the day nor the hour. Let them, therefore, who are among the Gentiles, flee unto Zion. And let them who be of Judah, flee unto Jerusalem, unto the mountains of the Lord's house. Go ye out from among the nations, even from Babylon, from the midst of wickedness, which is spiritual Babylon. But verily thus saith the Lord, Let not your flight be in haste, but let all things be prepared before you; and he that goeth, let him not look back, lest sudden destruction shall come upon him.

5. Hearken and hear O ye inhabitants of the earth. Listen ye elders of my church together, and hear the voice of the Lord, for he calleth upon all men and he commandeth all men everywhere to repent; for, behold, the Lord God hath sent forth the angel, crying through the midst of heaven, saying: Prepare ye the way of the Lord, and make his paths straight, for the hour of his coming is nigh, when the Lamb shall stand upon Mount Zion, and with him a hundred and forty-four thousand, having his Father's name written in their foreheads; wherefore, prepare ye for the coming of the Bridegroom; go ye, go ye out to meet him, for, behold, he shall stand upon the Mount of Olivet, and upon the mighty ocean, even the great deep, and upon the islands of the sea, and upon the land of Zion; and he shall utter his voice out of Zion, and he shall speak from Jerusalem, and his voice shall be heard among all people, and it shall be a voice as the voice of many waters, and as the voice of a great thunder, which shall break down the mountains, and the valleys shall not be found; he shall command the great deep and it shall be

driven back into the north countries, and the islands shall become one land, and the land of Jerusalem and the land of Zion shall be turned back into their own place, and the earth shall be like as it was in the days before it was divided. And the Lord even the Savior shall stand in the midst of his people, and shall reign over all flesh.

6. And they who are in the north countries shall come in remembrance before the Lord, and their prophets shall hear his voice, and shall no longer stay themselves, and they shall smite the rocks, and the ice shall flow down at their presence. And an highway shall be cast up in the midst of the great deep. Their enemies shall become a prey unto them, and in the barren deserts there shall come forth pools of living water; and the parched ground shall no longer be a thirsty land. And they shall bring forth their rich treasures unto the children of Ephraim my servants. And the boundaries of the everlasting hills shall tremble at their presence. And then shall they fall down and be crowned with glory, even in Zion, by the hands of the servants of the Lord, even the children of Ephraim; and they shall be filled with songs of everlasting joy. Behold, this is the blessing of the everlasting God upon the tribes of Israel, and the richer blessing upon the head of Ephraim and his fellows. And they also of the tribe of Judah, after their pain, shall be sanctified in holiness before the Lord to dwell in his presence day and night forever and ever.

7. And now verily saith the Lord, That these things might be known among you, O inhabitants of the earth, I have sent forth mine angel, flying through the midst of heaven, having the everlasting gospel, who hath appeared unto some, and hath committed it unto man, who shall appear unto many that dwell on the earth; and this gospel shall be preached unto every nation, and kindred, and tongue, and people, and the servants of God shall go forth, saying, with a loud voice: Fear God and give glory to him; for the hour of his judgment is come: and worship him that made heaven, and earth, and sea, and the fountains of waters, calling upon the name of the Lord day and night, saying: O that thou wouldst rend the heavens, that thou wouldst come down, that the mountains might flow down at thy presence. And it shall be answered upon their heads, for the presence of the Lord shall be as the melting fire that burneth, and as the fire which causeth the waters to boil.

8. O Lord, thou shalt come down to make thy name known to thine adversaries, and all nations shall tremble at thy presence. When thou doeth terrible things, things they look not for; yea, when thou comest down and the mountains flow down at thy presence, thou shalt meet him who rejoiceth and worketh righteousness, who remembereth thee in thy ways: for since the beginning of the world have not men heard nor perceived by the ear, neither hath any eye seen, O God, besides thee, how great things thou hast prepared for him that waiteth for thee.

9. And it shall be said, Who is this that cometh down from God in heaven with dyed garments; yea, from the regions which are not known, clothed in his glorious apparel, traveling in the greatness of his strength? And he shall say, I am he who spake in righteousness, mighty to save. And the Lord shall be red in his apparel, and his garments like him that treadeth in the wine vat, and so great shall be the glory of his presence, that the sun shall hide his face in shame; and the moon shall withhold its light; and the stars shall be hurled from their places; and his voice shall be heard, I have trodden the wine press alone, and have brought judgment upon all people; and none was with me; and I have trampled them in my fury, and I did tread upon them in mine anger, and their blood have I sprinkled upon my garments, and stained all my raiment; for this was the day of vengeance which was in my heart.

Joseph Smith in prayer dedicated "the Book of Commandments and Revelations" to the service of Almighty God,
after which he received a commandment concerning John

10. And now the year of my redeemed is come, and they shall mention
the loving kindness of their Lord, and all that he has bestowed upon
them, according to his goodness, and according to his loving kindness,
for ever and ever. In all their afflictions he was afflicted. And the angel of his presence saved them; and in his love, and in his pity, he
redeemed them, and bare them, and carried them all the days of old;
yea, and Enoch also, and they who were with him; the prophets who
were before him, and Noah also, and they who were before him, and
Moses also, and they who were before him, and from Moses to Elijah,
and from Elijah to John, who were with Christ in his resurrection, and
the holy apostles, with Abraham, Isaac, and Jacob, shall be in the presence of the Lamb. And the graves of the saints shall be opened, and
they shall come forth and stand on the right hand of the Lamb, when
he shall stand upon Mount Zion, and upon the holy city, the New Jerusalem, and they shall sing the song of the Lamb day and night forever
and ever.

11. And for this cause, that men might be made partakers of the glories
which were to be revealed, the Lord sent forth the fullness of his gospel,
his everlasting covenant, reasoning in plainness and simplicity, to prepare the weak for those things which are coming on the earth; and for
the Lord's errand in the day when the weak should confound the wise,
and the little one become a strong nation, and two should put their tens
of thousands to flight; and by the weak things of the earth, the Lord
should thresh the nations by the power of his Spirit. And for this cause
these commandments were given; they were commanded to be kept from
the world in the day that they were given, but now are to go forth unto
all flesh. And this according to the mind and will of the Lord, who ruleth over all flesh; and unto him that repenteth and sanctifieth himself before the Lord, shall be given eternal life. And upon them that
hearken not to the voice of the Lord, shall be fulfilled that which was
written by the Prophet Moses, that they should be cut off from among
the people.

12. And also that which was written by the Prophet Malachi: For,
behold, the day cometh that shall burn as an oven, and all the proud,
yea, and all that do wickedly, shall be stubble: and the day that cometh
shall burn them up, saith the Lord of hosts, that it shall leave them
neither root nor branch. Wherefore this shall be the answer of the Lord
unto them: In that day when I came unto my own, no man among you
received me, and you were driven out. When I called again, there was
none of you to answer, yet my arm was not shortened at all, that I could
not redeem, neither my power to deliver. Behold, at my rebuke I dry
up the sea. I make the rivers a wilderness; their fish stinketh, and dieth
for thirst. I clothe the heavens with blackness, and make sackcloth
their covering. And this shall ye have of my hand, ye shall lay down in
sorrow.

13. Behold, and lo, there are none to deliver you, for ye obeyed not my
voice when I called to you out of the heavens, ye believed not my servants; and when they were sent unto you ye received them not; wherefore, they sealed up the testimony and bound up the law, and ye were
delivered over unto darkness; these shall go away into outer darkness,
where there is weeping, and wailing, and gnashing of teeth. Behold, the
Lord your God hath spoken it. Amen.

Whitmer accompanying Oliver Cowdery to Independence.[16] This revelation also contained instruction concerning the duties of the Church Historian.

There has been some comment on this revelation by those who claim that it reflects on the honesty and trustworthiness of Oliver Cowdery; but when we reflect that his way lay hundreds of miles through a wild, half-civilized country, often beset with rogues and outlaws, we can see the wisdom of his having a trusted and true friend with him. Besides, there is no intimation in the revelation that the church was in danger of suffering loss because of Cowdery's unfaithfulness; but this precaution was for "Oliver Cowdery's sake"—for his protection and help.

Joseph continues:—

"My time was occupied closely in receiving the commandments and sitting in conference, for nearly two weeks; for we held from the first to the twelfth of November four special conferences. In the last, which was held at Brother Johnson's, in Hiram, after deliberate consideration, in consequence of the book of Revelations, now to be printed, being the foundation of the church in these last days and a benefit to the world, showing that the keys of the mysteries of the kingdom of our Savior are again intrusted to man; and the riches of eternity within the compass of those who are willing to live by every word that proceedeth out of the mouth of God, therefore the conference prized the revelations to be

---

[16] 1. Hearken unto me, saith the Lord your God, for my servant Oliver Cowdery's sake: it is not wisdom in me that he should be intrusted with the commandments and the moneys which he shall carry unto the land of Zion, except one go with him who will be true and faithful: wherefore I, the Lord, willeth that my servant John Whitmer should go with my servant Oliver Cowdery; and also that he shall continue in writing and making a history of all the important things which he shall observe and know concerning my church; and also that he receive counsel and assistance from my servant Oliver Cowdery, and others.

2. And also my servants who are abroad in the earth should send forth the accounts of their stewardships to the land of Zion, for the land of Zion shall be a seat and a place to receive and do all these things; nevertheless, let my servant John Whitmer travel many times from place to place, and from church to church, that he may the more easily obtain knowledge—preaching and expounding, writing, copying, selecting, and obtaining all things which shall be for the good of the church, and for the rising generations, that shall grow up on the land of Zion, to possess it from generation to generation, forever and ever. Amen.

worth to the church the riches of the whole earth, speaking
temporally. The great benefits to the world, which result
from the Book of Mormon and the revelations, which the
Lord has seen fit, in his infinite wisdom to grant unto us for
our salvation, and for the salvation of all that will believe,
were duly appreciated."—*Times and Seasons*, vol. 5, p. 512.

About this time Joseph received a revelation.[17]

Oliver Cowdery and John Whitmer, according to arrangement and commandment, left for Independence,
and Joseph continued the translation of the Scriptures, Sidney Rigdon acting as scribe. While thus engaged,

Cowdery and
Whitmer start.

---

[17] 1. Behold and hearken, O ye inhabitants of Zion, and all ye people
of my church, who are far off, and hear the word of the Lord, which I
give unto my servant Joseph Smith, Jr., and also unto my servant Martin
Harris, and also unto my servant Oliver Cowdery, and also unto my servant John Whitmer, and also unto my servant Sidney Rigdon, and also unto
my servant William W. Phelps, by the way of commandment unto them,
for I give unto them a commandment; wherefore hearken and hear, for
thus saith the Lord unto them, I, the Lord, have appointed them, and ordained them to be stewards over the revelations and commandments
which I have given unto them, and which I shall hereafter give unto
them; and an account of this stewardship will I require of them in the
day of judgment; wherefore I have appointed unto them, and this is
their business in the Church of God, to manage them and the concerns
thereof; yea, the benefits thereof.

2. Wherefore a commandment I give unto them, that they shall not
give these things unto the church, neither unto the world; nevertheless,
inasmuch as they receive more than is needful for their necessities, and
their wants, it shall be given into my storehouse, and the benefits shall be
consecrated unto the inhabitants of Zion, and unto their generations, inasmuch as they become heirs according to the laws of the kingdom.

3. Behold, this is what the Lord requires of every man in his stewardship, even as I, the Lord, have appointed, or shall hereafter appoint unto
any man. And, behold, none are exempt from this law who belong to
the church of the living God; yea, neither the bishop, neither the agent,
who keepeth the Lord's storehouse; neither he who is appointed in a
stewardship over temporal things; he who is appointed to administer
spiritual things, the same is worthy of his hire, even as those who are
appointed to a stewardship, to administer in temporal things; yea, even
more abundantly, which abundance is multiplied unto them through the
manifestations of the Spirit; nevertheless, in your temporal things you
shall be equal, and this not grudgingly, otherwise the abundance of the
manifestations of the Spirit shall be withheld.

4. Now this commandment I give unto my servants, for their benefit
while they remain, for a manifestation of my blessings upon their heads,
and for a reward of their diligence, and for their security for food and for
raiment, for an inheritance; for their houses and for lands, in whatsoever circumstances I, the Lord, shall place them; and whithersoever I,
the Lord, shall send them, for they have been faithful over many things,
and have done well inasmuch as they have not sinned. Behold, I, the
Lord, am merciful, and will bless them, and they shall enter into the joy
of these things. Even so. Amen.

they received a commandment to proclaim the gospel.[18]

In consequence of this revelation they postponed the work of translation for a time, and went to Kirtland, where on Sunday, December 4, 1831, the elders assembled together for counsel and instruction.

Council in Kirtland.

While yet assembled a revelation was given in which Newel K. Whitney was called to the office of bishop and appointed to be bishop of Kirtland.[19]

Bishop Whitney called.

[18] 1. Behold, thus saith the Lord unto you, my servants, Joseph Smith, Jr., and Sidney Rigdon, that the time has verily come that it is necessary and expedient in me that you should open your mouths in proclaiming my gospel, the things of the kingdom, expounding the mysteries thereof out of the scriptures, according to that portion of spirit and power, which shall be given unto you, even as I will.

2. Verily I say unto you, Proclaim unto the world in the regions round about, and in the church also, for the space of a season, even until it shall be made known unto you. Verily this is a mission for a season which I give unto you; wherefore labor ye in my vineyard. Call upon the inhabitants of the earth, and bear record, and prepare the way for the commandments and revelations which are to come. Now, behold, this is wisdom; whoso readeth let him understand and receive also; for unto him that receiveth it shall be given more abundantly, even power; wherefore, confound your enemies; call upon them to meet you, both in public and in private; and inasmuch as ye are faithful, their shame shall be made manifest. Wherefore let them bring forth their strong reasons against the Lord. Verily thus saith the Lord unto you, There is no weapon that is formed against you shall prosper; and if any man lift his voice against you, he shall be confounded in mine own due time; wherefore, keep my commandments: they are true and faithful. Even so. Amen.

[19] 1. Hearken, and listen to the voice of the Lord, O ye who have assembled yourselves together, who are the high priests of my church, to whom the kingdom and power has been given. For verily thus saith the Lord, It is expedient in me for a bishop to be appointed unto you, or of you unto the church, in this part of the Lord's vineyard; and verily in this thing ye have done wisely, for it is required of the Lord, at the hand of every steward, to render an account of his stewardship, both in time and in eternity. For he who is faithful and wise in time is accounted worthy to inherit the mansions prepared for them of my Father. Verily I say unto you, The elders of the church in this part of my vineyard shall render an account of their stewardship unto the bishop which shall be appointed of me, in this part of my vineyard. These things shall be had on record, to be handed over unto the bishop in Zion; and the duty of the bishop shall be made known by the commandments which have been given, and the voice of the conference.

2. And now, verily I say unto you, My servant Newel K. Whitney is the man who shall be appointed and ordained unto this power; this is the will of the Lord your God, your Redeemer. Even so. Amen.

3. The word of the Lord, in addition to the law which has been given, making known the duty of the bishop which has been ordained unto the church in this part of the vineyard, which is verily this: to keep the Lord's storehouse; to receive the funds of the church in this part of the vineyard; to take an account of the elders, as before has been com-

Joseph continues the history by stating:—

"From this time till the 8th or 10th of January, 1832, myself and Elder Rigdon continued to preach in Shalersville,

Missionary trip. Ravenna, and other places, setting forth the truth, vindicating the cause of our Redeemer; showing that the day of vengeance was coming upon this generation like a thief in the night: that prejudice, blindness, darkness, filled the minds of many, and caused them to persecute the true church, and reject the true light; by which means we did much towards allaying the excited feelings which were growing out of the scandalous letters then being published in the '*Ohio Star*,' at Ravenna, by the before-mentioned apostate, Ezra Booth."—*Times and Seasons*, vol. 5, p. 576.

manded; and to administer to their wants, who shall pay for that which they receive, inasmuch as they have wherewith to pay, that this also may be consecrated to the good of the church, to the poor and needy; and he who hath not wherewith to pay, an account shall be taken and handed over to the bishop of Zion, who shall pay the debt out of that which the Lord shall put into his hands; and the labors of the faithful who labor in spiritual things, in administering the gospel and the things of the kingdom unto the church, and unto the world, shall answer the debt unto the bishop in Zion; thus it cometh out of the church, for according to the law every man that cometh up to Zion must lay all things before the bishop in Zion.

4. And now, verily I say unto you, That as every elder in this part of the vineyard must give an account of his stewardship unto the bishop in this part of the vineyard, a certificate from the judge or bishop in this part of the vineyard, unto the bishop in Zion, rendereth every man acceptable, and answereth all things, for an inheritance, and to be received as a wise steward and as a faithful laborer; otherwise he shall not be accepted of the bishop in Zion. And now, verily I say unto you, Let every elder who shall give an account unto the bishop of the church, in this part of the vineyard, be recommended by the church, or churches, in which he labors, that he may render himself and his accounts approved in all things. And again, let my servants who are appointed as stewards over the literary concerns of my church have claim for assistance upon the bishop, or bishops, in all things, that the revelations may be published, and go forth unto the ends of the earth, that they also may obtain funds which shall benefit the church in all things, that they also may render themselves approved in all things, and be accounted as wise stewards. And now, behold, this shall be an ensample for all the extensive branches of my church, in whatsoever land they shall be established. And now I make an end of my sayings. Amen.

5. A few words in addition to the laws of the kingdom, respecting the members of the church; they that are appointed by the Holy Spirit to go up unto Zion, and they who are privileged to go up unto Zion. Let them carry up unto the bishop a certificate from three elders of the church, or a certificate from the bishop, otherwise he who shall go up unto the land of Zion shall not be accounted as a wise steward. This is also an ensample. Amen.

On Tuesday, January 10, 1832, a revelation was given com-
Translation resumed. manding them to resume the translation.[20]

Soon after another revelation was received.[21]

There was a conference held sometime in the month of
Conference at Amherst. January, at Amherst, in Lorain County, Ohio, of which Joseph says:—

"A few days before the conference was to commence in Amherst, Lorain County, I started in company with the elders that dwelt in my own vicinity, and arrived in due time.

"At this conference much harmony prevailed and considerable business was done to advance the kingdom and promulgate the gospel to the inhabitants of the surrounding country.

"The elders seemed anxious for me to inquire of the Lord that they might know his will, or learn what would

[20] 1. For verily thus saith the Lord, It is expedient in me that they should continue preaching the gospel, and in exhortation to the churches, in the regions round about, until conference; and then, behold, it shall be made known unto them, by the voice of the conference, their several missions.

2. Now, verily I say unto you, my servants Joseph Smith, Jr., and Sidney Rigdon, saith the Lord, It is expedient to translate again, and, inasmuch as it is practicable, to preach in the regions round about until conference, and after that it is expedient to continue the work of translation until it be finished. And let this be a pattern unto the elders until further knowledge, even as it is written. Now, I give no more unto you at this time. Gird up your loins and be sober. Even so. Amen.

[21] 1. For the unbelieving husband is sanctified by the wife, and the unbelieving wife is sanctified by the husband, else were your children unclean, but now are they holy.

2. For in the days of the apostles the law of circumcision was had among all the Jews who believed not the gospel of Jesus Christ. And it came to pass that there arose a great contention among the people concerning the law of circumcision, for the unbelieving husband was desirous that his children should be circumcised and become subject to the law of Moses, which law was fulfilled.

3. And it came to pass that the children being brought up in subjection to the law of Moses, and give heed to the traditions of their fathers, and believed not the gospel of Christ, wherein they become unholy; wherefore for this cause the apostle wrote unto the church, giving unto them a commandment, not of the Lord, but, of himself, that a believer should not be united to an unbeliever, except the law of Moses should be done away among them, that their children might remain without circumcision; and that the tradition might be done away, which saith that little children are unholy, for it was had among the Jews; but little children are holy, being sanctified through the atonement of Jesus Christ; and this is what the scriptures mean.

be most pleasing to him for them to do, in order to bring men to a sense of their condition; for, as it was written, all men have gone out of the way, so that none doth good; no not one."—*Times and Seasons*, vol. 5, p. 576.

In answer to this request a revelation was received.[11]

[11] 1. Verily, verily I say unto you, I who speak even by the voice of my Spirit; even Alpha and Omega, your Lord and your God; hearken, O ye who have given your names to go forth to proclaim my gospel, and to prune my vineyard. Behold, I say unto you, that it is my will that you should go forth and not tarry, neither be idle, but labor with your mights, lifting up your voices as with the sound of a trump, proclaiming the truth according to the revelations and commandments which I have given you, and thus if ye are faithful ye shall be laden with many sheaves, and crowned with honor, and glory, and immortality, and eternal life.

2. Therefore, verily I say unto my servant William E. McLellin, I revoke the commission which I gave unto him, to go unto the eastern countries, and I give unto him a new commission and a new commandment, in the which I, the Lord, chasteneth him for the murmurings of his heart; and he sinned, nevertheless I forgive him, and say unto him again, Go ye into the south countries; and let my servant Luke Johnson go with him and proclaim the things which I have commanded them, calling on the name of the Lord for the Comforter, which shall teach them all things that are expedient for them, praying always that they faint not; and inasmuch as they do this, I will be with them even unto the end. Behold, this is the will of the Lord your God concerning you. Even so. Amen.

3. And again, verily thus saith the Lord, Let my servant Orson Hyde and my servant Samuel H. Smith take their journey into the eastern countries, and proclaim the things which I have commanded them: and inasmuch as they are faithful, lo, I will be with them even unto the end. And again, verily I say unto my servant Lyman Johnson, and unto my servant Orson Pratt, They shall also take their journey into the eastern countries; and behold and lo, I am with them also even unto the end. And, again, I say unto my servant Asa Dodds and unto my servant Calves Wilson, that they also shall take their journey unto the western countries, and proclaim my gospel even as I have commanded them. And he who is faithful shall overcome all things, and shall be lifted up at the last day. And again, I say unto my servant Major N. Ashly and my servant Burr Riggs, Let them take their journey also unto the south country; yea, let all those take their journey as I have commanded them, going from house to house, and from village to village, and from city to city; and in whatsoever house ye enter, and they receive you, leave your blessings upon that house; and in whatsoever house ye enter, and they receive you not, ye shall depart speedily from that house, and shake off the dust of your feet as a testimony against them; and you shall be filled with joy and gladness and know this, that in the day of judgment you shall be judges of that house, and condemn them; and it shall be more tolerable for the heathen in the day of judgment, than for that house; therefore gird up your loins and be faithful and ye shall overcome all things and be lifted up at the last day. Even so. Amen.

4. And, again, thus saith the Lord unto you, O ye elders of my church, who have given your names that you might know his will concerning you: Behold, I say unto you, that it is the duty of the church to assist in supporting the families of those who are called and must needs be sent unto the world to proclaim the gospel unto the world; wherefore, I,

Upon his return from Amherst conference he resumed the translation of the Scriptures assisted by Sidney Rigdon as scribe.

It was while engaged in this work, on Thursday, February 16, 1832, that they saw the remarkable vision representing the different glories.[23]

Remarkable vision.

the Lord, give unto you this commandment, that ye obtain places for your families, inasmuch as your brethren are willing to open their hearts; and let all such as can, obtain places for their families, and support of the church for them, not fail to go into the world; whether to the east, or to the west, or to the north, or to the south, let them ask and they shall receive; knock and it shall be opened unto them, and made known from on high, even by the Comforter, whither they shall go.

5. And again, verily I say unto you, that every man who is obliged to provide for his own family, let him provide and he shall in no wise lose his crown; and let him labor in the church. Let every man be diligent in all things. And the idler shall not have place in the church, except he repents and mends his ways. Wherefore, let my servant Simeon Carter and my servant Emer Harris be united in the ministry. And also my servant Ezra Thayre and my servant Thomas B. Marsh. Also my servant Hyrum Smith and my servant Reynolds Cahoon; and also my servant Daniel Stanton and my servant Seymour Brunson; and also my servant Sylvester Smith and my servant Gideon Carter; and also my servant Ruggles Eames and my servant Stephen Burnett; and also my servant Micah B. Welton and also my servant Eden Smith. Even so. Amen.

[23] 1. Hear, O ye heavens, and give ear, O earth, and rejoice ye inhabitants thereof, for the Lord is God, and beside him there is no Savior; great is his wisdom; marvelous are his ways; and the extent of his doings, none can find out; his purposes fail not, neither are there any who can stay his hand; from eternity to eternity he is the same, and his years never fail.

2. For thus saith the Lord, I, the Lord, am merciful and gracious unto those who fear me, and delight to honor those who serve me in righteousness and in truth unto the end; great shall be their reward, and eternal shall be their glory; and to them will I reveal all mysteries; 'yea, all the hidden mysteries of my kingdom from days of old; and for ages to come will I make known unto them the good pleasure of my will concerning all things pertaining to my kingdom; yea, even the wonders of eternity shall they know, and things to come will I show them, even the things of many generations; their wisdom shall be great, and their understanding reach to heaven; and before them the wisdom of the wise shall perish, and the understanding of the prudent shall come to nought; for by my Spirit will I enlighten them, and by my power will I make known unto them the secrets of my will; yea, even those things which eye has not seen, nor ear heard, nor yet entered into the heart of man.

3. We, Joseph Smith, Jr., and Sidney Rigdon, being in the Spirit on the sixteenth of February, in the year of our Lord one thousand eight hundred and thirty-two, by the power of the Spirit our eyes were opened, and our understandings were enlightened, so as to see and understand the things of God; even those things which were from the beginning before the world was, which were ordained of the Father, through his only begotten Son, who was in the bosom of the Father, even from the beginning, of whom we bear record, and the record which we bear is the fullness of the gospel of Jesus Christ, who is the Son, whom we saw and with

The work of translation continued until sometime in February, when Joseph Smith and Sidney Rigdon were mobbed

Mobbed. and cruelly maltreated by a mob composed of jealous religionists and apostates. Whether it be admitted that the saints were right, in their doctrine and practice, or not, no better evidence need be required that their

whom we conversed in the heavenly vision; for while we were doing the work of translation, which the Lord had appointed unto us, we came to the twenty-ninth verse of the fifth chapter of John, which was given unto us as follows: speaking of the resurrection of the dead, concerning those who shall hear the voice of the Son of Man, and shall come forth: they who have done good in the resurrection of the just, and they who have done evil in the resurrection of the unjust. Now this caused us to marvel, for it was given unto us of the Spirit, and while we meditated upon these things, the Lord touched the eyes of our understandings, and they were opened, and the glory of the Lord shone round about; and we beheld the glory of the Son, on the right hand of the Father, and received of his fullness; and saw the holy angels, and they who are sanctified before his throne, worshiping God and the Lamb, who worship him forever and ever. And, now, after the many testimonies which have been given of him, this is the testimony, last of all, which we give of him, that he lives; for we saw him, even on the right hand of God; and we heard the voice bearing record that he is the Only Begotten of the Father; that by him, and through him, and of him, the worlds are and were created; and the inhabitants thereof are begotten sons and daughters unto God. And this we saw also, and bear record, that an angel of God, who was in authority in the presence of God, who rebelled against the only begotten Son; whom the Father loved, and who was in the bosom of the Father; and was thrust down from the presence of God and the Son, and was called Perdition; for the heavens wept over him; he was Lucifer, a son of the morning. And we beheld, and lo, he is fallen! is fallen! even a son of the morning. And while we were yet in the Spirit, the Lord commanded us that we should write the vision; for we beheld Satan, that old serpent, even the Devil, who rebelled against God, and sought to take the kingdom of our God and his Christ; wherefore he maketh war with the saints of God, and encompasses them round about. And we saw a vision of the sufferings of those with whom he made war and overcame, for thus came the voice of the Lord unto us.

4. Thus saith the Lord, concerning all those who know my power, and have been made partakers thereof, and suffered themselves, through the power of the Devil, to be overcome, and to deny the truth, and defy my power; they are they who are the sons of perdition, of whom I say it had been better for them never to have been born; for they are vessels of wrath, doomed to suffer the wrath of God, with the Devil and his angels, in eternity, concerning whom I have said there is no forgiveness in this world nor in the world to come; having denied the Holy Spirit, after having received it, and having denied the only begotten Son of the Father; having crucified him unto themselves, and put him to an open shame: these are they who shall go away into the lake of fire and brimstone, with the Devil and his angels, and the only ones on whom the second death shall have any power; yea, verily, the only ones who shall not be redeemed in the due time of the Lord, after the sufferings of his wrath; for all the rest shall be brought forth by the resurrection of the dead, through the triumph and the glory of the Lamb, who was slain,

enemies were wrong and possessed of a wicked and devilish spirit than the fact that they resorted to such foul, vile, and disreputable measures. We read with horror of such things transpiring in the Dark Ages, but when we think of like things being resorted to by professors of religion (even though intended to suppress supposed wrong) in this boasted age of

who was in the bosom of the Father before the worlds were made. And this is the gospel, the glad tidings which the voice out of the heavens bore record unto us, that he came into the world, even Jesus to be crucified for the world, and to bear the sins of the world, and to sanctify the world, and to cleanse it from all unrighteousness; that through him all might be saved, whom the Father had put into his power, and made by him; who glorifies the Father, and saves all the works of his hands, except those sons of perdition, who deny the Son after the Father hath revealed him; wherefore he saves all except them; they shall go away into everlasting punishment, which is endless punishment, which is eternal punishment, to reign with the Devil and his angels in eternity, where their worm dieth not and the fire is not quenched, which is their torment, and the end thereof, neither the place thereof, nor their torment, no man knows; neither was it revealed, neither is, neither will be revealed unto man, except to them who are made partakers thereof: nevertheless, I, the Lord, show it by vision unto many; but straightway shut it up again; wherefore the end, the width, the height, the depth, and the misery thereof, they understand not, neither any man except them who are ordained unto this condemnation. And we heard the voice saying, Write the vision, for lo, this is the end of the vision of the sufferings of the ungodly!

5. And again, we bear record for we saw and heard, and this is the testimony of the gospel of Christ, concerning them who come forth in the resurrection of the just: They are they who received the testimony of Jesus, and believed on his name, and were baptized after the manner of his burial, being buried in the water in his name, and this according to the commandment which he has given, that by keeping the commandments, they might be washed and cleansed from all their sins, and receive the Holy Spirit by the laying on of the hands of him who is ordained and sealed unto this power; and who overcome by faith, and are sealed by the Holy Spirit of promise, which the Father sheds forth upon all those who are just and true; they are they who are the church of the Firstborn; they are they into whose hands the Father has given all things: they are they who are priests and kings, who have received of his fullness, and of his glory, and are priests of the Most High after the order of Melchisedec, which was after the order of Enoch, which was after the order of the only begotten Son; wherefore, as it is written, they are gods, even the sons of God; wherefore all things are theirs, whether life or death, or things present, or things to come, all are theirs, and they are Christ's, and Christ is God's; and they shall overcome all things; wherefore let no man glory in man, but rather let him glory in God, who shall subdue all enemies under his feet; these shall dwell in the presence of God and his Christ forever and ever: these are they whom he shall bring with him, when he shall come in the clouds of heaven, to reign on the earth over his people; these are they who shall have part in the first resurrection; these are they who shall come forth in the resurrection of the just; these are they who are come unto Mount Zion, and unto the city of the living God, the heavenly place, the holiest of all; these

enlightenment, and under the flag of liberty and equal rights, we blush for humanity. It is a pity that the pages of history must be blotted by the record of such diabolical deeds.

We will allow Joseph to tell of this event and of his subsequent journey to Western Missouri:—

"According to previous calculations, we now began to

are they who have come to an innumerable company of angels; to the general assembly and the church of Enoch, and of the Firstborn; these are they whose names are written in heaven, where God and Christ are the judge of all; these are they who are just men made perfect through Jesus the mediator of the new covenant, who wrought out this perfect atonement through the shedding of his own blood; these are they whose bodies are celestial, whose glory is that of the sun, even the glory of God the highest of all; whose glory the sun of the firmament is written of as being typical.

6. And again, we saw the terrestrial world, and, behold, and lo; these are they who are of the terrestrial, whose glory differs from that of the church of the Firstborn, who have received the fullness of the Father, even as that of the moon differs from the sun of the firmament. Behold, these are they who died without law; and also they who are the spirits of men kept in prison, whom the Son visited, and preached the gospel unto them, that they might be judged according to men in the flesh, who received not the testimony of Jesus in the flesh, but afterwards received it; these are they who are honorable men of the earth, who are blinded by the craftiness of men; these are they who receive of his glory, but not of his fullness; these are they who receive of the presence of the Son, but not of the fullness of the Father; wherefore they are bodies terrestrial, and not bodies celestial, and differ in glory as the moon differs from the sun; these are they who are not valiant in the testimony of Jesus; wherefore they obtained not the crown over the kingdom of our God. And now this is the end of the vision which we saw of the terrestrial, that the Lord commanded us to write while we were yet in the Spirit.

7. And again, we saw the glory of the telestial, which glory is that of the lesser, even as the glory of the stars differs from that of the glory of the moon in the firmament; these are they who received not the gospel of Christ, neither the testimony of Jesus; these are they who deny not the Holy Spirit; these are they who are thrust down to hell; these are they who shall not be redeemed from the Devil, until the last resurrection, until the Lord, even Christ the Lamb, shall have finished his work; these are they who receive not of his fullness in the eternal world, but of the Holy Spirit through the ministration of the terrestrial; and the terrestrial through the ministration of the celestial: and also the telestial receive it of the administering of angels, who are appointed to minister for them, or who are appointed to be ministering spirits for them, for they shall be heirs of salvation. And thus we saw in the heavenly vision, the glory of the telestial which surpasses all understanding; and no man knows it except him to whom God has revealed it. And thus we saw the glory of the terrestrial, which excels in all things the glory of the telestial, even in glory, and in power, and in might, and in dominion. And thus we saw the glory of the celestial, which excels in all things; where God, even the Father, reigns upon his throne forever and ever, before whose throne all things bow in humble reverence and give him glory forever and ever. They who dwell in his presence are the church of the Firstborn; and they see as they are seen, and know as they are known,

make preparations to visit the brethren who had removed to the land of Missouri. Before going to Hiram to live with Father Johnson, my wife had taken two children (twins) of John Murdock, to bring up. She received them when only nine days old; they were now nearly eleven months. I would remark that nothing important had occurred since I came to reside in Father Johnson's house in Hiram; I had

having received of his fullness and of his grace; and he makes them equal in power, and in might, and in dominion. And the glory of the celestial is one, even as the glory of the sun is one. And the glory of the terrestrial is one, even as the glory of the moon is one. And the glory of the telestial is one, even as the glory of the stars is one, for as one star differs from another star in glory, even so differs one from another in glory in the telestial world; for these are they who are of Paul, and of Apollos, and of Cephas; these are they who say they are some of one and some of another, some of Christ, and some of John, and some of Moses, and some of Elias; and some of Esaias, and some of Isaiah, and some of Enoch, but received not the gospel, neither the testimony of Jesus, neither the prophets; neither the everlasting covenant; last of all, these all are they who will not be gathered with the saints, to be caught up unto the church of the Firstborn, and received into the cloud; these are they who are liars, and sorcerers, and adulterers, and whoremongers, and whosoever loves and makes a lie; these are they who suffer the wrath of God on the earth; these are they who suffer the vengeance of eternal fire; these are they who are cast down to hell and suffer the wrath of Almighty God until the fullness of times, when Christ shall have subdued all enemies under his feet, and shall have perfected his work, when he shall deliver up the kingdom and present it unto the Father spotless, saying: I have overcome and have trodden the wine press alone, even the wine press of the fierceness of the wrath of Almighty God; then shall he be crowned with the crown of his glory, to sit on the throne of his power to reign forever and ever. But, behold, and lo, we saw the glory and the inhabitants of the telestial world, that they were as innumerable as the stars in the firmament of heaven, or as the sand upon the seashore, and heard the voice of the Lord saying: These all shall bow the knee, and every tongue shall confess to him who sits upon the throne forever and ever; for they shall be judged according to their works; and every man shall receive according to his own works, and his own dominion, in the mansions which are prepared, and they shall be servants of the Most High, but where God and Christ dwell they cannot come, worlds without end. This is the end of the vision which we saw, which we were commanded to write while we were yet in the Spirit.

8. But great and marvelous are the works of the Lord and the mysteries of his kingdom which he showed unto us, which surpasses all understanding in glory, and in might, and in dominion, which he commanded us we should not write, while we were yet in the Spirit, and are not lawful for man to utter, neither is man capable to make them known, for they are only to be seen and understood by the power of the Holy Spirit, which God bestows on those who love him and purify themselves before him; to whom he grants this privilege of seeing and knowing for themselves; that through the power and manifestation of the Spirit, while in the flesh, they may be able to bear his presence in the world of glory. And to God and the Lamb be glory, and honor, and dominion forever and ever. Amen.

held meetings on the Sabbaths and evenings, and baptized a number.   Father Johnson's son, Olmsted Johnson, came home on a visit, during which I told him if he did not obey the gospel the spirit he was of would lead him to destruction; and then [when] he went away, he would never return or see his father again.   He went to the Southern States and Mexico; on his return took sick and died in Virginia.   In addition to the apostate Booth, Simonds Rider, Eli Johnson, Edward Johnson, and John Johnson, Jr., had apostatized.

"On the 25th of March, the twins before-mentioned, which had been sick of the measles for some time, caused us to be broke of our rest in taking care of them, especially my wife. In the evening I told her she had better retire to rest with one of the children, and I would watch with the sickest child. In the night she told me I had better lay down on the trundle-bed, and I did so, and was soon after awoke by her scream-ing 'Murder!' when I found myself going out of the door, in the hands of about a dozen men; some of whose hands were in my hair, and some hold of my shirt, drawers, and limbs. The foot of the trundle-bed was towards the door, leaving only room enough for the door to swing.   My wife heard a gentle tapping on the windows which she then took no particular notice of, (but which was unquestionably designed for ascer-taining whether we were all asleep,) and soon after the mob burst open the door and surrounded the bed in an instant, and, as I said. the first I knew I was going out of the door in the hands of an infuriated mob.   I made a desperate strug-gle, as I was forced out, to extricate myself, but only cleared one leg, with which I made a pass at one man, and he fell on the doorsteps.   I was immediately confined again; and they swore by God, they would kill me if I did not be still, which quieted me.   As they passed around the house with me, the fellow that I kicked came to me and thrust his hand into my face, all covered with blood, (for I hit him on the nose,) and with an exulting horse-laugh, muttered: 'Ge, gee, God damn ye, I'll fix ye.'

"They then seized me by the throat, and held on till I lost my breath.   After I came to, as they passed along with me, about thirty rods from the house, I saw Elder Rigdon stretched out on the ground, whither they had dragged him by the heels. I supposed he was dead.

"I began to plead with them, saying: 'You will have mercy and spare my life, I hope.' To which they replied: 'God damn ye, call on yer God for help, we'll show ye no mercy;' and the people began to show themselves in every direction: one coming from the orchard had a plank, and I expected they would kill me, and carry me off on the plank. They then turned to the right and went on about thirty rods further, about sixty rods from the house, and thirty from where I saw Elder Rigdon, into the meadow, where they stopped, and one said: 'Simonds, Simonds,' (meaning I supposed Simonds Rider.) 'pull up his drawers, pull up his drawers, he will take cold.' Another replied: 'A'nt ye going to kill 'im? A'nt ye going to kill 'im?' when a group of mobbers collected a little way off and said: 'Simonds, Simonds, come here;' and Simonds charged those who had hold of me to keep me from touching the ground (as they had done all the time) lest I should get a spring upon them. They went and held a council, and as I could occasionally overhear a word, I supposed it was to know whether it was best to kill me. They returned after awhile, when I learned that they had concluded not to kill me but pound and scratch me well, tear off my shirt and drawers, and leave me naked. One cried, 'Simonds, Simonds, where's the tar bucket?' 'I don't know,' answered one, 'where 'tis, Eli's left it.' They ran back and fetched the bucket of tar, when one exclaimed, 'God damn it, let us tar up his mouth;' and they tried to force the tar-paddle into my mouth; I twisted my head around, so that they could not; and they cried out: 'God damn ye, hold up yer head and let us give ye some tar.' They then tried to force a vial into my mouth, and broke it in my teeth. All my clothes were torn off me except my shirt collar; and one man fell on me and scratched my body with his nails like a mad cat, and then muttered out: 'God damn ye, that's the way the Holy Ghost falls on folks.'

"They then left me, and I attempted to rise, but fell again; I pulled the tar away from my lips, etc., so that I could breathe more freely, and after awhile I began to recover, and raised myself up, when I saw two lights. I made my way towards one of them, and found it was Father Johnson's. When I had come to the door, I was naked, and the tar made me look as though I had been covered with blood, and when my wife saw me she thought I was all mashed to pieces, and fainted. During the affray abroad the sisters of the neighborhood had collected at my room. I called for a blanket, they threw me one and shut the door; I wrapped it around me and went in.

"In the meantime, Brother John Poorman heard an outcry across the cornfield, and running that way met Father Johnson, who had been fastened in his house at the commencement of the assault, by having his door barred by the mob, but on calling to his wife to bring his gun, saying, he would blow a hole through the door, the mob fled, and Father Johnson seizing a club ran after the party that had Elder Rigdon, and knocked one man, and raised his club to level another, exclaiming: 'what are you doing here?' when they left Elder Rigdon and turned upon Father Johnson, who, turning to run towards his own house, met Brother Poorman coming out of the cornfield. Each supposing the other to be a mobber, an encounter ensued, and Poorman gave Johnson a severe blow on the left shoulder with a stick or stone, which brought him to the ground. Poorman ran immediately towards Father Johnson's, and arriving while I was waiting for the blanket, exclaimed: 'I'm afraid I've killed him.' Killed who? asked one; when Poorman hastily related the circumstances of the rencounter near the cornfield, and went into the shed and hid himself. Father Johnson soon recovered so as to come to the house, when the whole mystery was quickly solved concerning the difficulty between him and Poorman, who, on learning the facts, joyfully came from his hiding place.

"My friends spent the night in scraping and removing the tar, and washing and cleansing my body; so that by morning I was ready to be clothed again. This being Sabbath morning, the people assembled for meeting at the usual hour of worship, and among them came also the mobbers; viz.: Simonds Rider, a Campbellite preacher, and leader of the mob; one McClentic, son of a Campbellite minister; and Pelatiah Allen, Esq., who gave the mob a barrel of whiskey to raise their spirits; and many others. With my flesh all scarified and defaced, I preached to the congregation as usual, and in the afternoon of the same day baptized three individuals.

"The next morning I went to see Elder Rigdon, and found him crazy, and his head highly inflamed, for they had dragged him by his heels, and those too so high from the earth he could not raise his head from the rough frozen surface, which lacerated it exceedingly; and when he saw me he called to his wife to bring him his razor. She asked him what he wanted of it, and he replied to kill *me*. Sister Rigdon left the room, and he asked *me* to bring his razor. I asked him what he wanted of it, and he replied he wanted to kill his wife, and he continued delirious some days. The feathers which were used with the tar on this occasion, the mob took out of Elder Rigdon's house. After they had seized him and dragged him out, one of the banditti returned to get some pillows; when the women shut him in and kept him some time.

"During the mob, one of the twins received a severe cold, and continued to grow worse till Friday, and died. The mobbers were composed of various religious parties, but mostly Campbellites, Methodists, and Baptists, who continued to molest and menace Father Johnson's house for a long time. Elder Rigdon removed to Kirtland with his family, then sick with the measles, the following Wednesday, and on account of the mob, he went to Chardon on Saturday, April 1. Sunday, April 2, I started for Missouri, Journey to Missouri. in company with Newel K. Whitney, Peter Whitmer, and Jesse Gauze, to fulfill the revelation. Not wishing to go by Kirtland, as another mob existed in that neighborhood, (and indeed, the spirit of mobocracy was very prevalent through the region of country at the time,) Brother George Pitkin took us in his wagon, by the most expeditious route to Warren, where we arrived the same day, and were there joined by Elder Rigdon, who left Chardon in the morning; and proceeding onward, we arrived at

Wellsville the next day, and the day following at Steubenville, where we left the wagon; and on Wednesday, the fifth of April, we took passage on board a steam packet for Wheeling, Virginia, where we purchased a lot of paper for the press in Zion, then in care of W. W. Phelps. . .

"From Wheeling we took passage on board the steamer Trenton. While at the dock, during the night, the boat was twice on fire, burning the whole width of the boat through into the cabin, but with so little damage the boat went on in the morning; and when we arrived at Cincinnati, some of the mob which had followed us all the way round, left us, and we arrived at Louisville the same night; Captain Brittle offered us protection on board of his boat, and gave us supper and breakfast gratuitously. At Louisville we were joined by Elder Titus Billings, who was journeying with a company of saints from Kirtland to Zion, and we took passage on the steamer Charleston for St. Louis, where we parted with Brother Billings and company, and by stage arrived at Independence, Missouri, on the twenty-fourth of April, a distance of about three hundred miles from St. Louis. We found the brethren generally enjoying health and faith, and extremely glad to welcome us among them.

"On the 26th I called a general council of the church, and was acknowledged as the president of the high priesthood, according to a previous ordination at a conference Council called. of high priests, elders, and members, held at Amherst, Ohio, on the twenty-fifth of January, 1832. The right hand of fellowship was given to me by the bishop, Edward Partridge, in behalf of the church. The scene was solemn, impressive, and delightful. During the intermission, a difficulty or hardness which had existed between Bishop Partridge and Elder Rigdon was amicably settled, and when we came together in the afternoon, all hearts seemed to rejoice."— *Times and Seasons*, vol. 5, pp. 611, 612, 624.

During the month of March four revelations were given.[24]

---

[24] 1. The Lord spake unto Enoch, saying, Hearken unto me saith the Lord your God, who are ordained unto the high priesthood of my church, who have assembled yourselves together, and listen to the counsel of him who has ordained you, from on high, who shall speak in your ears the

An incidental mention is made in the above historical statement of the ordination of Joseph as "president of the high priesthood," at Amherst, Ohio, on January 25, 1832. This seems to be a very meager mention of so important an event, but we see that provision had been made for such an office, even before the church was organized; which the reader may see by referring to Doctrine and Covenants 17:17, where the person to hold such office is

Acknowledged president of the high priesthood.

words of wisdom, that salvation may be unto you in that thing which you have presented before me, saith the Lord God; for verily I say unto you, The time has come, and is now at hand; and, behold, and lo, it must needs be that there be an organization of my people, in regulating and establishing the affairs of the storehouse for the poor of my people, both in this place and in the land of Zion, or in other words, the city of Enoch, for a permanent and everlasting establishment and order unto my church, to advance the cause which ye have espoused, to the salvation of man, and to the glory of your Father who is in heaven, that you may be equal in the bands of heavenly things; yea, and earthly things also, for the obtaining of heavenly things; for if ye are not equal in earthly things, ye cannot be equal in obtaining heavenly things; for if you will that I give unto you a place in the celestial world, you must prepare yourselves by doing the things which I have commanded you and required of you.

2. And now, verily thus saith the Lord, It is expedient that all things be done unto my glory, that ye should, who are joined together in this order; or in other words, let my servant Ahashdah, and my servant Gazelam, or Enoch, and my servant Pelagoram, sit in council with the saints which are in Zion; otherwise Satan seeketh to turn their hearts away from the truth, that they become blinded, and understand not the things which are prepared for them; wherefore a commandment I give unto you, to prepare and organize yourselves by a bond or everlasting covenant that cannot be broken.

3. And he who breaketh it shall lose his office and standing in the church, and shall be delivered over to the buffetings of Satan until the day of redemption. Behold, this is the preparation wherewith I prepare you, and the foundation, and the ensample, which I give unto you, whereby you may accomplish the commandments which are given you, that through my providence, notwithstanding the tribulation which shall descend upon you, that the church may stand independent above all other creatures beneath the celestial world, that you may come up unto the crown prepared for you, and be made rulers over many kingdoms, saith the Lord God, the Holy One of Zion, who hath established the foundations of Adam-ondi-Ahman; who hath appointed Michael, your prince, and established his feet, and set him upon high; and given unto him the keys of salvation under the counsel and direction of the Holy One, who is without beginning of days or end of life.

4. Verily, verily I say unto you, Ye are little children, and ye have not as yet understood how great blessings the Father has in his own hands, and prepared for you; and ye cannot bear all things now; nevertheless be of good cheer, for I will lead you along; the kingdom is yours and the blessings thereof are yours; and the riches of eternity are yours; and he who receiveth all things, with thankfulness, shall be made glorious, and the things of this earth shall be added unto him, even an hundredfold, yea, more; wherefore do the things which I have commanded you, saith

called "president of the high priesthood (or presiding elder)."
This parenthetical clause explains and makes clear the clause
in paragraph 1 of the same section, where it is said Joseph
was called "to be the *first* elder of this church," etc.   Thus
the two are connected and the person to hold such position
pointed out.   Hence the ordination referred to is in harmony
with provision made, and done also in harmony with the
provision; viz., by direction of a General Conference, or it
was as nearly a General Conference as circumstances would

your Redeemer, even the Son Ahman, who prepareth all things before he
taketh you; for ye are the church of the Firstborn, and he will take you
up in the cloud, and appoint every man his portion. And he that is a
faithful and wise steward shall inherit all things. Amen.

1. Verily I say unto you, that it is my will that my servant Jared Carter should go again into the eastern countries, from place to place, and
from city to city, in the power of the ordination wherewith he has been
ordained, proclaiming glad tidings of great joy, even the everlasting gospel, and I will send upon him the Comforter which shall teach him the
truth and the way whither he shall go; and inasmuch as he is faithful I will crown him again with sheaves; wherefore let your heart be
glad, my servant Jared Carter, and fear not saith your Lord, even Jesus
Christ. Amen.

1. Verily, thus saith the Lord, unto you, my servant Stephen Burnett,
Go ye, go ye into the world, and preach the gospel to every creature that
cometh under the sound of your voice, and inasmuch as you desire a
companion I will give unto you my servant Eden Smith; wherefore go
ye and preach my gospel, whether to the north, or to the south; to the
east, or to the west, it mattereth not, for ye cannot go amiss; therefore
declare the things which ye have heard and verily believe, and know to
be true. Behold, this is the will of him who hath called you, your Redeemer, even Jesus Christ. Amen.

1. Verily, verily I say unto you, my servant, Frederick G. Williams,
Listen to the voice of him who speaketh, to the word of the Lord your
God, and hearken to the calling wherewith you are called, even to be a
high priest in my church, and a counselor unto my servant, Joseph
Smith, Jr., unto whom I have given the keys of the kingdom, which belongeth always unto the presidency of the high priesthood; therefore,
verily I acknowledge him and will bless him, and also thee, inasmuch as
thou art faithful in council, in the office which I have appointed unto
you, in prayer always vocally, and in thy heart, in public and in private;
also in thy ministry in proclaiming the gospel in the land of the living,
and among thy brethren; and in doing these things thou wilt do the
greatest good unto thy fellow-beings, and will promote the glory of him
who is your Lord; wherefore, be faithful, stand in the office which I
have appointed unto you, succor the weak, lift up the hands which hang
down, and strengthen the feeble knees· and if thou art faithful unto the
end thou shalt have a crown of immortality and eternal life in the
mansions which I have prepared in the house of my Father. Behold,
and lo, these are the words of Alpha and Omega, even Jesus Christ.
Amen.

allow. A part of the church was far away in Missouri with no adequate means of transportation, but to make good this deficiency (if deficiency it was) he was, on Thursday, April 26, 1832, presented to the church in Missouri at a "general council of the church," and the action of the church at Amherst ratified.

In the last revelation referred to; viz., section 80, provision is also made for further perfecting the quorum of three presidents, which was afterwards consummated by the calling of F. G. Williams to be "a counselor unto my servant, Joseph Smith, Jr., unto whom I have given the keys of the kingdom, which belongeth always unto the presidency of the high priesthood," etc.

There is one point in the ordination at Amherst that may trouble some; viz., that this council of high priests ordained Ordination Joseph to a higher office than was held by themconsidered. selves. But this is in harmony with the event mentioned before, where the office of elder in the Melchisedec priesthood was bestowed upon Oliver Cowdery under the hands of Joseph Smith, prior to Joseph's ordination; and also in harmony with the action of elders ordaining high priests at the June conference of 1831. These examples make it clear that those in whom the rights of priesthood exist may officiate in any ordination, where emergency demands and a command of God directs; though where the church is perfectly organized the general rule is for the greater to ordain the lesser.

At this council more instruction was received concerning the poor, and the enlargement of Zion.[2]

---

[2] 1. Verily I say unto you, my servants, that inasmuch as you have forgiven one another your trespasses, even so I, the Lord, forgive you; nevertheless there are those among you who have sinned exceedingly; yea, even all of you have sinned, but verily I say unto you, Beware from henceforth and refrain from sin lest sore judgments fall upon your heads; for unto whom much is given much is required; and he who sins against the greater light shall receive the greater condemnation. Ye call upon my name for revelations, and I give them unto you; and inasmuch as ye keep not my sayings which I give unto you, ye become transgressors, and justice and judgment is the penalty which is affixed unto my law; therefore, what I say unto one I say unto all, Watch, for the adversary spreadeth his dominions and darkness reigneth; and the anger of God kindleth against the inhabitants of the earth; and none doeth good, for all have gone out of the way.

The council continued the next day, of which Joseph says:—

"On the 27th we transacted considerable business for the salvation of the saints, who were settling among a ferocious set of mobbers, like lambs among wolves. It was my endeavor to so organize the church that the brethren might eventually be independent of every incumbrance beneath the celestial kingdom, by bonds and covenants of mutual friendship and mutual love.

"On the 28th and 29th I visited the brethren above Big

2. And now, verily I say unto you, I, the Lord, will not lay any sin to your charge; go your ways and sin no 'more; but unto that soul who sinneth shall the former sins return, saith the Lord your God.

3. And again, I say unto you, I give unto you a new commandment, that you may understand my will concerning you, or, in other words, I give unto you directions how you may act before me, that it may turn to you for your salvation. I, the Lord, am bound when ye do what I say, but when ye do not what I say, ye have no promise.

4. Therefore, verily I say unto you, that it is expedient for my servant Alam and Ahashdah, Mahalaleel and Pelagoram, and my servant Gazelam, and Horah, and Olihah, and Shalemanasseh, and Mehemson, be bound together by a bond and covenant that cannot be broken by transgression except judgment shall immediately follow, in your several stewardships, to manage the affairs of the poor, and all things pertaining to the bishopric both in the land of Zion, and in the land of Shinehah, for I have consecrated the land of Shinehah in mine own due time for the benefit of the saints of the Most High, and for a stake to Zion; for Zion must increase in beauty, and in holiness; her borders must be enlarged; her stakes must be strengthened; yea, verily I say unto you, Zion must arise and put on her beautiful garments; therefore, I give unto you this commandment, that ye bind yourselves by this covenant, and it shall be done according to the laws of the Lord. Behold, here is wisdom, also, in me, for your good. And you are to be equal, or in other words, you are to have equal claims on the properties, for the benefit of managing the concerns of your stewardships, every man according to his wants and his needs, inasmuch as his wants are just; and all this for the benefit of the church of the living God, that every man may improve upon his talent, that every man may gain other talents; yea, even an hundredfold, to be cast into the Lord's storehouse, to become the common property of the whole church, every man seeking the interest of his neighbor, and doing all things with an eye single to the glory of God.

5. This order I have appointed to be an everlasting order unto you and unto your successors, inasmuch as you sin not; and the soul that sins against this covenant, and hardeneth his heart against it, shall be dealt with according to the laws of my church, and shall be delivered over to the buffetings of Satan until the day of redemption.

6. And now, verily I say unto you, and this is wisdom, Make unto yourselves friends with the mammon of unrighteousness, and they will not destroy you. Leave judgment alone with me, for it is mine and I will repay. Peace be with you; my blessings continue with you, for even yet the kingdom is yours, and shall be forever if you fall not from your steadfastness. Even so. Amen.

Blue River, in Kaw Township, twelve miles west of Independence, and received a welcome only known by brethren and sisters united as one in the same faith, and by the same baptism, and supported by the same Lord. The Colesville branch, in particular, rejoiced as the ancient saints did with Paul. It is good to rejoice with the people of God. On the 30th I returned to Independence, and again sat in council with the brethren."—*Times and Seasons*, vol. 5, p. 625.

At this second council held on Monday, the 30th, a further communication was received.[26]

Joseph continues:—

"Our council was continued on the first of May, when it was ordered that three thousand copies of the Book of Commandments be printed the first edition; that William W. Phelps, Oliver Cowdery, and John Whitmer be appointed to review and prepare such revelations as shall be deemed proper for publication, for the press, and print them as soon as possible, at Independence, Missouri; 'published by W. W. Phelps & Co.' It was also ordered that W. W. Phelps correct and print the hymns which had been selected by Emma Smith, in fulfillment of the revelation.

Book of Commandments and Hymn Book.

"Arrangements were also made for supplying the saints with stores in Missouri and Ohio, which with a few exceptions, was hailed with joy by the brethren. Before we left Independence, Elder Rigdon preached two most powerful discourses, which, so far as outward appearance is concerned, gave great satisfaction to the people.

"On the sixth of May I gave the parting hand to the breth-

[26] 1. Verily thus saith the Lord, in addition to the laws of the church concerning women and children, those who belong to the church, who have lost their husbands or fathers: Women have claim on their husbands for their maintenance until their husbands are taken; and if they are not found transgressors they shall have fellowship in the church; and if they are not faithful, they shall not have fellowship in the church; yet they may remain upon their inheritances according to the laws of the land.

2. All children have claim upon their parents for their maintenance until they are of age; and after that, they have claim upon the church; or, in other words, upon the Lord's storehouse, if their parents have not wherewith to give them inheritances. And the storehouse shall be kept by the consecrations of the church, that widows and orphans shall be provided for. as also the poor. Amen.

ren in Independence, and in company with Brothers Rigdon
Journey to Kirtland. and Whitney commenced a return to Kirtland, by
stage to St. Louis, from thence to Vincennes, In-
diana; and from thence to New Albany, near the falls of the
Ohio River. Before we arrived at the latter place the horses
Inc'dents by the way. became frightened, and while going at full speed
Bishop Whitney attempted to jump out of the
coach, but having his coat fast, caught his foot in the wheel
and had his leg and foot broken in several places; at the
same time I jumped out unhurt, and we put up at Mr. Porter's public house, in Greenville, for four weeks, while
Elder Rigdon went directly forward to Kirtland. During all
this time Brother Whitney lost not a meal of victuals or a
night's sleep, and Doctor Porter, our landlord's brother, who
attended him, said it was a d——d pity we had not got some
Mormon there, they can set broken bones or do anything
else. I tarried with Brother Whitney and administered to
him till he was able to be moved. While at this place I frequently walked out in the woods, where I saw several fresh
graves; and one day when I rose from the dinner table I
walked directly to the door and commenced vomiting most
profusely. I raised large quantities of blood and poisonous
matter, and so great were the muscular contortions of my system that my jaw was dislocated in a few moments. This I
succeeded in replacing with my own hands, and made my
way to Brother Whitney (who was on the bed) as speedily
as possible; he laid his hands on me and administered in the
name of the Lord, and I was healed in an instant, although
the effect of the poison had been so powerful as to cause
much of the hair to become loosened from my head. Thanks
be to my heavenly Father for his interference in my behalf
at this critical moment, in the name of Jesus Christ, Amen.

"Brother Whitney had not had his foot moved from the
bed for near four weeks, when I went into his room, after a
walk in the grove, and told him if he would agree to start
for home in the morning, we would take a wagon to the
river, about four miles, and there would be a ferryboat in
waiting which would take us quickly across, where we would
find a hack which would take us directly to the landing,

where we should find a boat in waiting, and we will be going up the river before ten o'clock, and have a prosperous journey home. He took courage and told me he would go. We started next morning, and found everything as I had told him, for we were passing rapidly up the river before ten o'clock, and landing at Wellsville, took stage coach to Chardon, from thence in a wagon to Kirtland, where we arrived sometime in June."—*Times and Seasons*, vol. 5, pp. 625, 626.

As soon after as affairs could be arranged the work of translating the Scriptures was resumed.

In June, the first number of the *Evening and Morning Star*, published at Independence, Missouri, by W. W. Phelps and Company, was issued. Of its first appearance in Kirtland, Ohio, Joseph writes:—

"In July we received the first number of the '*Evening and Morning Star*,' which was a joyous treat to the saints. Delightful, indeed, was it to contemplate that the little band of brethren had become so large and grown so strong in so short a space as to be able to issue a paper of their own, which contained not only some of the revelations, but other information also, which would gratify and enlighten the humble inquirer after truth.

Evening and Morning Star.

"So embittered was the public mind against the truth that the press universally had been arrayed against us; and although many newspapers published the prospectus of our new paper, yet it appeared to have been done more to calumniate the editor than give publicity to the sheet. Editors thought to do us harm, while the saints rejoiced that they could do nothing against the truth, but for it."—*Times and Seasons*, vol. 5, p. 626.

As so much has been said regarding this publication by enemies of the church, it may be well here to produce an extract from the prospectus which had preceded this issue. The reader may see that the purpose in establishing a paper was to promulgate religious and moral principles; and not, as has been asserted, to interfere with political conditions or agitate political issues:—

"The *Evening and the Morning Star*, besides the secret of the Lord, which is now with them that fear him, and the ever-

lasting gospel, which must go to all nations, before the Holy
One shall stand upon the Mount of Olivet, and upon the
mighty ocean, even the great deep, and upon the islands of
the sea, and upon the land of Zion, to destroy the wicked
with the brightness of his coming,—will also contain whatever of truth or information that can benefit the saints of
God temporally as well as spiritually, in these last days,
whether in prose or poetry, without interfering with politics,
broils, or the gainsayings of the world. While some may
say this paper is opposed to all combinations under whatever plausible character, others will know that it is for an
eternal union whose maker and supporter is God; thus all
must be as they are, inasmuch as they that plow iniquity and
sow wickedness reap the same; but wisdom is justified of her
children."—*Times and Seasons*, vol. 5, pp. 610, 611.

The position taken by this the first publication issued by
Common
school-.
the church on "common schools" might be of interest to many:—

"The disciples should lose no time in preparing schools
for their children, that they may be taught as is pleasing
unto the Lord, and brought up in the way of holiness.
Those appointed to select and prepare books for the use of
schools, will attend to that subject, as soon as more weighty
matters are finished. But the parents and guardians in the
Church of Christ need not wait—it is all-important that children, to become good should be taught so. Moses, while
delivering the words of the Lord to the congregation of
Israel, the parents, says, 'And these words which I command
thee this day, shall be in thy heart: And thou shalt teach
them diligently unto thy children, and shalt talk of them
when thou sittest in thy house, and when thou walkest by the
way, and when thou liest down, and when thou risest up.
And thou shalt bind them for a sign upon thy hand, and they
shall be as frontlets between thine eyes.' If it were necessary then to teach their children diligently, how much more
necessary is it now, when the Church of Christ is to be an
ensign, yea, even a sample to the world, for good? A word
to the wise ought to be sufficient, for children soon become
men and women. Yes, they are they that must follow us,

and perform the duties which not only appertain to this world, but to the second coming of the Savior, even preparing for the Sabbath of creation, and for eternity."—*Evening and Morning Star*, vol. 1, pp. 7, 8.

In August and September the elders came to Kirtland from their several missions, and on Saturday and Sunday, September 22 and 23, 1832, to them was given the interesting revelation "On Priesthood."[27] This is

Revelation on priesthood.

---

[27] 1. A revelation of Jesus Christ unto his servant Joseph Smith, Jr., and six elders, as they united their hearts and lifted their voices on high; yea, the word of the Lord concerning his church, established in the last days for the restoration of his people, as he has spoken by the mouth of his prophets, and for the gathering of his saints to stand upon Mount Zion, which shall be the city New Jerusalem; which city shall be built, beginning at the Temple Lot, which is appointed by the finger of the Lord, in the western boundaries of the State of Missouri, and dedicated by the hand of Joseph Smith, Jr., and others, with whom the Lord was well pleased.

2. Verily, this is the word of the Lord, that the city New Jerusalem shall be built by the gathering of the saints, beginning at this place, even the place of the temple, which temple shall be reared in this generation; for verily, this generation shall not all pass away until an house shall be built unto the Lord, and a cloud shall rest upon it, which cloud shall be even the glory of the Lord, which shall fill the house. And the sons of Moses, according to the holy priesthood, which he received under the hand of his father-in-law, Jethro; and Jethro received it under the hand of Caleb; and Caleb received it under the hand of Elihu; and Elihu under the hand of Jeremy; and Jeremy under the hand of Gad; and Gad under the hand of Esaias; and Esaias received it under the hand of God; Esaias also lived in the days of Abraham and was blessed of him, which Abraham received the priesthood from Melchisedec; who received it through the lineage of his fathers, even till Noah; and from Noah till Enoch, through the lineage of their fathers; and from Enoch to Abel, who was slain by the conspiracy of his brother; who received the priesthood by the commandments of God, by the hand of his father Adam, who was the first man; which priesthood continueth in the church of God in all generations, and is without beginning of days or end of years.

3. And the Lord confirmed a priesthood also upon Aaron and his seed throughout all their generations, which priesthood also continueth and abideth forever, with the priesthood which is after the holiest order of God. And this greater priesthood administereth the gospel and holdeth the key of the mysteries of the kingdom, even the key of the knowledge of God. Therefore, in the ordinances thereof the power of godliness is manifest; and without the ordinances thereof, and the authority of the priesthood, the power of godliness is not manifest unto men in the flesh; for without this, no man can see the face of God, even the Father, and live.

4. Now, this Moses plainly taught to the children of Israel in the wilderness, and sought diligently to sanctify his people that they might behold the face of God; but they hardened their hearts, and could not endure his presence, therefore, the Lord, in his wrath (for his anger was kindled against them), swore that they should not enter into his rest, while in the wilderness, which rest is the fullness of his glory. Therefore, he took Moses out of their midst and the holy priesthood also; and

an important revelation, containing much instruction and many glorious promises, and is a cheering recognition of

the lesser priesthood continued, which priesthood holdeth the key of the ministering of angels and the preparatory gospel, which gospel is the gospel of repentance and of baptism, and the remission of sins, and the law of carnal commandments, which the Lord, in his wrath, caused to continue with the house of Aaron, among the children of Israel until John, whom God raised up, being filled with the Holy Ghost from his mother's womb: for he was baptized while he was yet in his childhood, and was ordained by the angel of God at the time he was eight days old unto this power: to overthrow the kingdom of the Jews, and to make straight the way of the Lord before the face of his people; to prepare them for the coming of the Lord, in whose hand is given all power.

5. And again, the office of elder and bishop are necessary appendages belonging unto the high priesthood. And again, the offices of teachers and deacons are necessary appendages belonging to the lesser priesthood, which priesthood was confirmed upon Aaron and his sons.

6. Therefore, as I said concerning the sons of Moses—for the sons of Moses and also the sons of Aaron shall offer an acceptable offering and sacrifice in the house of the Lord, which house shall be built unto the Lord in this generation upon the consecrated spot, as I have appointed; and the sons of Moses and of Aaron shall be filled with the glory of the Lord upon Mount Zion in the Lord's house, whose sons are ye; and also many whom I have called and sent forth to build up my church; for whoso is faithful unto the obtaining these two priesthoods of which I have spoken, and the magnifying their calling, are sanctified by the Spirit unto the renewing of their bodies: they become the sons of Moses and of Aaron, and the seed of Abraham, and the church and kingdom and the elect of God; and also all they who receive this priesthood receiveth me, saith the Lord, for he that receiveth my servants receiveth me, and he that receiveth me receiveth my Father, and he that receiveth my Father receiveth my Father's kingdom. Therefore, all that my Father hath shall be given unto him; and this is according to the oath and covenant which belongeth to the priesthood. Therefore, all those who receive the priesthood receive this oath and covenant of my Father, which he cannot break, neither can it be removed; but whoso breaketh this covenant, after he hath received it, and altogether turneth therefrom, shall not have forgiveness of sins in this world nor in the world to come. And all those who come not unto this priesthood, which ye have received, which I now confirm upon you who are present, this day, by mine own voice out of the heavens, and even I have given the heavenly hosts and mine angels charge concerning you.

7. And now I give unto you a commandment to beware concerning yourselves, to give diligent heed to the words of eternal life; for you shall live by every word that proceedeth forth from the mouth of God. For the word of the Lord is truth, and whatsoever is truth is light, and whatsoever is light is Spirit, even the Spirit of Jesus Christ; and the Spirit giveth light to every man that cometh into the world; and the Spirit enlighteneth every man through the world, that hearkeneth to the voice of the Spirit; and every one that hearkeneth to the voice of the Spirit, cometh unto God, even the Father; and the Father teacheth him of the covenant which he has renewed and confirmed upon you, which is confirmed upon you for your sakes, and not for your sakes only, but for the sake of the whole world: and the whole world lieth in sin, and groaneth under darkness and under the bondage of sin: and by this you may know they are under the bondage of sin, because they come not

their arduous labors, which they had performed by much sacrifice and under adverse circumstances.

unto me; for whoso cometh not unto me is under the bondage of sin; and whoso receiveth not my voice is not acquainted with my voice, and is not of me; and by this you may know the righteous from the wicked, and that the whole world groaneth under sin and darkness even now.

8. And your minds in times past have been darkened because of unbelief, and because you have treated lightly the things you have received, which vanity and unbelief hath brought the whole church under condemnation. And this condemnation resteth upon the children of Zion, even all; and they shall remain under this condemnation until they repent and remember the new covenant, even the Book of Mormon and the former commandments which I have given them, not only to say, but to do according to that which I have written, that they may bring forth fruit meet for their Father's kingdom, otherwise there remaineth a scourge and a judgment to be poured out upon the children of Zion; for, shall the children of the kingdom pollute my holy land? Verily, I say unto you, Nay.

9. Verily, verily I say unto you, who now have my words, which is my voice, Blessed are ye inasmuch as you receive these things: for I will forgive you of your sins with this commandment, that you remain steadfast in your minds in solemnity, and the spirit of prayer, in bearing testimony to all the world of those things which are communicated unto you.

10. Therefore, go ye into all the world, and whatsoever place ye cannot go into, ye shall send, that the testimony may go from you into all the world, unto every creature. And as I said unto mine apostles, even so I say unto you; for you are mine apostles, even God's high priests: ye are they whom my Father hath given me; ye are my friends; therefore, as I said unto mine apostles, I say unto you again, that every soul who believeth on your words, and is baptized by water for the remission of sins, shall receive the Holy Ghost; and these signs shall follow them that believe:

11. In my name they shall do many wonderful works; in my name they shall cast out devils: in my name they shall heal the sick: in my name they shall open the eyes of the blind, and unstop the ears of the deaf: and the tongue of the dumb shall speak: and if any man shall administer poison unto them, it shall not hurt them: and the poison of a serpent shall not have power to harm them. But a commandment I give unto them, that they shall not boast themselves of these things, neither speak them before the world: for these things are given unto you for your profit and for salvation.

12. Verily, verily, I say unto you, They who believe not on your words, and are not baptized in water, in my name, for the remission of their sins, that they may receive the Holy Ghost, shall be damned, and shall not come into my Father's kingdom, where my Father and I am. And this revelation unto you, and commandment, is in force from this very hour upon all the world, and the gospel is unto all who have not received it. But verily I say unto all those to whom the kingdom has been given, From you it must be preached unto them that they shall repent of their former evil works: for they are to be upbraided for their evil hearts of unbelief: and your brethren in Zion for their rebellion against you at the time I sent you.

13. And again I say unto you my friends (for from henceforth I shall call you friends), It is expedient that I give unto you this commandment, that ye become even as my friends in days when I was with them traveling to preach this gospel in my power; for I suffered them not to have

purse or scrip, neither two coats; behold, I send you out to prove the world, and the laborer is worthy of his hire. And any man that shall go and preach this gospel of the kingdom, and fail not to continue faithful in all things, shall not be weary in mind, neither darkened, neither in body, limb or joint; and an hair of his head shall not fall to the ground unnoticed. And they shall not go hungry, neither athirst.

14. Therefore, take no thought for the morrow, for what ye shall eat, or what ye shall drink, or wherewithal ye shall be clothed; for consider the lilies of the field, how they grow, they toil not, neither do they spin; and the kingdoms of the world, in all their glory, are not arrayed like one of these; for your Father who art in heaven, knoweth that you have need of all these things. Therefore, let the morrow take thought for the things of itself. Neither take ye thought beforehand what ye shall say, but treasure up in your minds continually the words of life, and it shall be given you in the very hour that portion that shall be meted unto every man.

15. Therefore, let no man among you (for this commandment is unto all the faithful who are called of God in the church, unto the ministry), from this hour, take purse or scrip, that goeth forth to proclaim this gospel of the kingdom. Behold, I send you out to reprove the world of all their unrighteous deeds, and to teach them of a judgment which is to come. And whoso receiveth you, there will I be also; for I will go before your face: I will be on your right hand and on your left, and my Spirit shall be in your hearts, and my angels round about you, to bear you up.

16. Whoso receiveth you receiveth me, and the same will feed you, and clothe you, and give you money. And he who feeds you, or clothes you, or gives you money, shall in no wise lose his reward: and he that doeth not these things is not my disciple: by this you may know my disciples. He that receiveth you not, go away from him alone by yourselves, and cleanse your feet, even with water, pure water, whether in heat or in cold, and bear testimony of it unto your Father which is in heaven, and return not again unto that man. And into whatsoever village or city ye enter, do likewise. Nevertheless, search diligently and spare not; and woe unto that house, or that village, or city, that rejecteth you, or your words, or testimony concerning me. Woe, I say again, unto that house, or that village, or city, that rejecteth you, or your words, or your testimony of me; for I, the Almighty, have laid my hands upon the nations to scourge them for their wickedness; and plagues shall go forth, and they shall not be taken from the earth until I have completed my work, which shall be cut short in righteousness; until all shall know me, who remain, even from the least unto the greatest, and shall be filled with the knowledge of the Lord, and shall see eye to eye, and shall lift up their voice, and with the voice together sing this new song, saying:—

17. The Lord hath brought again Zion:
The Lord hath redeemed his people, Israel,
According to the election of grace,
Which was brought to pass by the faith
And covenant of their fathers.
The Lord hath redeemed his people,
And Satan is bound, and time is no longer:
The Lord hath gathered all things in one:
The Lord hath brought down Zion from above:
The Lord hath brought up Zion from beneath;
The earth hath travailed and brought forth her strength;
And truth is established in her bowels;
And the heavens have smiled upon her;
And she is clothed with the glory of her God:
For he stands in the midst of his people:

Glory, and honor, and power, and might,
Be ascribed to our God, for he is full of mercy,
Justice, grace and truth, and peace,
Forever and ever, Amen.

18. And again, verily, verily I say unto you, It is expedient, that every man who goes forth to proclaim mine everlasting gospel, that inasmuch as they have families, and receive moneys by gift, that they should send it unto them, or make use of it for their benefit, as the Lord shall direct them, for thus it seemeth me good. And let all those who have not families, who receive moneys, send it up unto the bishop in Zion, or unto the bishop in Ohio, that it may be consecrated for the bringing forth of the revelations and the printing thereof, and for establishing Zion.

19. And if any man shall give unto any of you a coat, or a suit, take the old and cast it unto the poor, and go your way rejoicing. And if any man among you be strong in the Spirit, let him take with him he that is weak, that he may be edified in all meekness, that he may become strong also.

20. Therefore, take with you those who are ordained unto the lesser priesthood, and send them before you to make appointments, and to prepare the way, and to fill appointments that you yourselves are not able to fill. Behold, this is the way that mine apostles, in ancient days, built up my church unto me.

21. Therefore, let every man stand in his own office, and labor in his own calling; and let not the head say unto the feet it hath no need of the feet, for without the feet how shall the body be able to stand? Also, the body hath need of every member, that all may be edified together, that the system may be kept perfect.

22. And, behold, the high priests should travel, and also the elders, and also the lesser priests; but the deacons and teachers should be appointed to watch over the church, to be standing ministers unto the church.

23. And the bishop, Newel K. Whitney, also, should travel round about and among all the churches, searching after the poor, to administer to their wants by humbling the rich and the proud; he should also employ an agent to take charge and to do his secular business, as he shall direct: nevertheless, let the bishop go unto the city of New York, and also to the city of Albany, and also to the city of Boston, and warn the people of those cities with the sound of the gospel, with a loud voice, of the desolation and utter abolishment which awaits them if they do reject these things; for if they do reject these things, the hour of their judgment is nigh, and their house shall be left unto them desolate. Let him trust in me, and he shall not be confounded, and an hair of his head shall not fall to the ground unnoticed.

24. And verily I say unto you, the rest of my servants, Go ye forth as your circumstances shall permit, in your several callings, unto the great and notable cities and villages, reproving the world, in righteousness, of all their unrighteous and ungodly deeds, setting forth clearly and understandingly the desolation of abomination in the last days; for with you, saith the Lord Almighty, I will rend their kingdoms; I will not only shake the earth, but the starry heavens shall tremble; for I, the Lord, have put forth my hand to exert the powers of heaven; ye cannot see it now, yet a little while and ye shall see it, and know that I am, and that I will come and reign with my people. I am Alpha and Omega, the beginning and the end. Amen.

CHAPTER 11.

1832–1833.

DURING the latter part of the summer and autumn of 1832
Joseph spent the time in translating, and in ministering to the churches in Ohio, with the exception

Translating.

of a hurried journey to Albany, New York, and Boston,
Massachusetts, in company with Bishop Whitney.

Trip East.

One letter written to his wife while on this journey,
and dated New York, October 13, 1832, has been preserved,

*Joseph writes
to his wife.*

and is now in the hands of President Joseph
Smith, of Lamoni, Iowa, who was born on the 6th
day of November following the date of this letter, which circumstance will serve to explain the extract that we shall here
produce. We gladly quote from this letter, for it gives us
a partial insight into the inner life of the man and his feelings and solicitude for loved ones. Sometimes we can only
get at the true character of a man by some such incident,
where we are enabled to read that which was not intended
for the public.

The letter throughout is expressive of the tenderest love
and sympathy, of which the following is a specimen:—

"I returned to my room to meditate and calm my mind,
and behold, the thoughts of home, of Emma and Julia, rush
upon my mind like a flood; and I could wish for a moment to
be with them. My breast is filled with all the feelings and
tenderness of a parent and a husband, and could I be with

you I would tell you many things. . . I hope you will excuse me for writing this letter so soon after writing, for I feel as if I wanted to say something to you, to comfort you in your peculiar trial and present affliction. I hope God will give you strength that you may not faint. I pray God to soften the hearts of those around you to be kind to you and take the burden off your shoulders as much as possible, and not afflict you. I feel for you, for I know your state and that others do not; but you must comfort yourself knowing that God is your friend in heaven, and that you have one true and living friend on earth, your husband,

"JOSEPH SMITH."

In this letter, not intended for the public eye or ear, hence which could not have been written with any thought of deception, we recognize not only the sentiments of a tender and affectionate husband and father, but also of a man who could with supreme confidence in God trust these loved ones, even in the darkest trial, to his loving-kindness and tender care.

As soon as his obligations would permit he hurried home, Birth of his son Joseph. if possible to be with his wife in her approaching trial. He reached Kirtland on Tuesday, November 6, immediately after his son Joseph was born.

This was their fourth child; one son was born to them at Harmony, Pennsylvania, in July, 1828, who died at birth. Other children. Early in 1831 they lost a pair of twins at Kirtland, who also died at birth. In place of these they adopted the motherless twins of Elder Murdock, one of whom died as before-related; the other is the Julia spoken of in the letter from New York.

On Tuesday, November 27, Joseph wrote W. W. Phelps as follows:—

"It is contrary to the will and commandment of God that those who receive not their inheritance by consecration, Letter to Phelps. agreeably to his law, which he has given that he may tithe his people to prepare them against the day of vengeance and burning, should have their names enrolled with the people of God; neither is their genealogy to be kept, or to be had where it may be found on any of the records or history of the church; their names shall not be found, neither the names of the fathers, the names of the children written in the book of the law of God, saith the Lord of Hosts; yea, thus saith the still small voice, which whispereth through and pierceth all things, and oftentimes it maketh my bones to quake while it maketh manifest, saying: 'And it shall come to pass that I the Lord God will send one mighty and strong, holding the sceptre of power in his hand, clothed with light for a covering, whose mouth shall utter words, eternal words, while his bowels shall be a fountain of truth, to set in order the house of God, and to arrange by lot the inheritances of the saints whose names are found, and the names of their fathers, and of their children, enrolled in the book of the law of God; while that man, who was called of God and appointed, that putteth forth his hand to steady the ark of God, shall fall by the shaft of death, like as a tree that is smitten by the vivid shaft of lightning; and all they who are not found written in the book of remembrance, shall find none inheritance in that day, but they shall be cut asunder and their portion shall be appointed them among unbelievers, where is wailing and gnashing of teeth.   These things I say not of myself, therefore as the Lord speaketh he will also fulfill.' "— *Times and Seasons*, vol. 5, pp. 673, 674.

On Thursday, December 6, 1832, a revelation was received explaining the parable of the wheat and tares.[1]

[1] 1. Verily thus saith the Lord unto you, my servants, concerning the parable of the wheat and of the tares: Behold, verily I say that the field was the world, and the apostles were the sowers of the seed; and after they have fallen asleep, the great persecutor of the church, the apostate, the whore, even Babylon, that maketh all nations to drink of her cup, in whose hearts the enemy, even Satan, sitteth to reign; behold, he soweth the tares, wherefore the tares choke the wheat and drive the church into the wilderness.

2. But, behold, in the last days, even now, while the Lord is beginning to bring forth the word, and the blade is springing up and is yet tender, behold, verily I say unto you, The angels are crying unto the Lord day and night, who are ready and waiting to be sent forth to reap down the fields; but the Lord saith unto them, Pluck not up the tares while the blade is yet tender (for verily your faith is weak), lest you destroy the wheat also; therefore let the wheat and the tares grow together until the harvest is fully ripe; then ye shall first gather out the wheat from among the tares, and after the gathering of the wheat, behold, and lo, the tares are bound in bundles, and the field remaineth to be burned.

On Tuesday, December 25, 1832, the revelation on the Rebellion was given, foretelling accurately, as the reader will Revelation see, many of the leading events of the late war. on Rebellion. South Carolina had, the November before, in convention assembled, passed the famous Nullification Act. Histor- This was met by the prompt and decisive action of ical events. President Jackson, in declaring that he would treat nullification as treason, and for a time war was threatened. The government made preparations to invade South Carolina, and the State prepared to defend. This difficulty was finally settled by Henry Clay's Compromise Tariff Act of 1833, and all preparations for hostilities ceased.

To those who supposed that it was based upon the then existing South Carolina trouble, it began to look as though the revelation had failed. Probably some who had looked for its fulfillment may have grown doubtful, for surely that would have been the tendency of the natural mind.

Joseph, however, still remained confident that a great and bloody conflict would be forced upon our country, for on Letter to Friday, January 4, 1833, he wrote Mr. N. E. Seaton, Seaton. editor of a paper published at Rochester, New York, from which letter we make the following extract:—

"And now I am prepared to say by the authority of Jesus Christ, that not many years shall pass away before the United States shall present such a scene of *bloodshed* as has not a parallel in the history of our nation; pestilence, hail, famine, and earthquakes will sweep the wicked of this generation from off the face of the land, to open and prepare the way for the return of the lost tribes of Israel from the north country. The people of the Lord, those who have complied with the requisitions of the new covenant, have already

---

3. Therefore, thus saith the Lord unto you, with whom the priesthood hath continued through the lineage of your fathers, for ye are lawful heirs, according to the flesh, and have been hid from the world with Christ in God: therefore your life and the priesthood hath remained, and must needs remain, through you and your lineage, until the restoration of all things spoken by the mouths of all the holy prophets since the world began.

4. Therefore, blessed are ye if ye continue in my goodness, a light unto the Gentiles, and through this priesthood, a savor unto my people Israel. The Lord hath said it. Amen.

commenced gathering together to Zion, which is in the State of Missouri; therefore I declare unto you the warning which the Lord has commanded me to declare unto this generation, remembering that the eyes of my Maker are upon me, and that to him I am accountable for every word I say, wishing nothing worse to my fellow men than their eternal salvation; therefore, 'fear God and give glory to him, for the hour of his judgment is come.' Repent ye, repent ye, and embrace the everlasting covenant, and flee to Zion before the over-flowing scourge overtake you, for there are those now living upon the earth whose eyes shall not be closed in death until they see all these things, which I have spoken, fulfilled. *Remember* these things; call upon the Lord while he is near, and seek him while he may be found, is the exhortation of your unworthy servant,   JOSEPH SMITH, JR."

— *Times and Seasons*, vol. 5, p. 707.

Others also retained confidence in the revelation, and Elder F. D. Richards published the full text of it in a work entitled "The Pearl of Great Price," published at Liverpool, England, in 1851. Here is the revelation as it appears on page 35 of that work:—

Published by Richards.

"A REVELATION AND PROPHECY BY THE PROPHET, SEER, AND REVELATOR, JOSEPH SMITH.

'*Given December 25, 1832.*

"Verily thus saith the Lord, concerning the wars that will shortly come to pass, beginning at the rebellion of South Carolina, which will eventually terminate in the death and misery of many souls. The days will come that war will be poured out upon all nations, beginning at that place; for be-hold, the Southern States shall be divided against the Northern States, and the Southern States will call on other nations, even the nation of Great Britain, as it is called, and they shall also call upon other nations, in order to defend themselves against other nations; and thus war shall be poured out upon all nations. And it shall come to pass, after many days, slaves shall rise up against their Masters, who shall be marshalled and disciplined for war: And it shall come to pass also, that the remnants who are left of the land will marshal themselves, and shall become exceeding angry, and shall vex the Gentiles with a sore vexation; and thus, with the sword, and by bloodshed, the inhabitants of the earth shall mourn; and with famine, and plague, and earthquakes, and the thunder of heaven, and the fierce and vivid lightning also, shall the inhabitants of the earth be made to feel the wrath, and indignation and chastening hand of an Almighty God, until the consumption decreed, hath made a full end of all nations; that the cry of the saints, and of the blood of the saints, shall cease to come up into the ears of the Lord of Sabbaoth, from the earth, to be avenged of their enemies. Wherefore, stand ye in holy places, and be not moved, until the day of the Lord come; for behold it cometh quickly, saith the Lord. Amen."

We need not occupy space to point out how literally some of the events of the late conflict are foretold. It is so accurate that often it has been asserted that "the Mormons have gotten this up since the war." This assertion however is proved false by "The Pearl of Great Price," bearing date of 1851, which is now lying before us. Elder John Hyde, Jun.,

John Hyde. published a work in 1857, three years before the secession of South Carolina, in which he cites a statement of Joseph Smith made on April 6, 1843, concerning this matter, showing that Joseph declared publicly the place where it would begin and the cause.

"I prophesy in the name of the Lord God, that the commencement of the difficulties which will cause much bloodshed, previous to the coming of the Son of Man, will be in South Carolina (it probably may arise through the slave question); this a voice declared to me, while I was praying earnestly on the subject, December 25, 1832."—Mormonism by Elder Hyde, p. 174.

On Thursday, December 27, 1832, a lengthy and important revelation was received.[a]

---

[a] 1. Verily, thus saith the Lord unto you, who have assembled yourselves together to receive his will concerning you. Behold, this is pleasing unto your Lord, and the angels rejoice over you; the alms of your prayers have come up into the ears of the Lord of Sabbaoth, and are recorded in the book of the names of the sanctified, even them of the celestial world. Wherefore I now send upon you another Comforter,

About this time troubles arose in Missouri, which occasioned the authorities at Kirtland much anxious concern. Joseph

Trouble in
Missouri.

wrote them warning them that the judgments of God awaited them if they repented not. A council of twelve high priests also took the matter under advisement and appointed Orson Hyde and Hyrum Smith to write them,

even upon you, my friends, that it may abide in your hearts, even the Holy Spirit of promise, which other Comforter is the same that I promised unto my disciples, as is recorded in the testimony of John.

2. This Comforter is the promise which I give unto you of eternal life, even the glory of the celestial kingdom; which glory is that of the church of the Firstborn, even of God, the holiest of all, through Jesus Christ, his Son; he that ascended up on high, as also he descended below all things, in that he comprehended all things, that he might be in all and through all things, the light of truth, which truth shineth. This is the light of Christ. As also he is in the sun, and the light of the sun, and the power thereof by which it was made. As also he is in the moon, and is the light of the moon, and the power thereof by which it was made. As also the light of the stars, and the power thereof by which they were made. And the earth also, and the power thereof, even the earth upon which you stand.

3. And the light which now shineth, which giveth you light, is through him who enlighteneth your eyes, which is the same light that quickeneth your understandings; which light proceedeth forth from the presence of God, to fill the immensity of space. The light which is in all things; which giveth life to all things; which is the law by which all things are governed; even the power of God who sitteth upon his throne, who is in the bosom of eternity, who is in the midst of all things.

4. Now, verily I say unto you, that through the redemption which is made for you, is brought to pass the resurrection from the dead. And the spirit and the body is the soul of man. And the resurrection from the dead is the redemption of the soul; and the redemption of the soul is through him who quickeneth all things, in whose bosom it is decreed, that the poor and the meek of the earth shall inherit it. Therefore, it must needs be sanctified from all unrighteousness, that it may be prepared for the celestial glory; for after it hath filled the measure of its creation, it shall be crowned with glory, even with the presence of God the Father; that bodies who are of the celestial kingdom may possess it forever and ever; for, for this intent was it made and created; and for this intent are they sanctified.

5. And they who are not sanctified through the law which I have given unto you, even the law of Christ, must inherit another kingdom, even that of a terrestrial kingdom, or that of a telestial kingdom. For he who is not able to abide the law of a celestial kingdom, cannot abide a celestial glory; and he who cannot abide the law of a terrestrial kingdom, cannot abide a terrestrial glory; he who cannot abide the law of a telestial kingdom, cannot abide a telestial glory: therefore, he is not meet for a kingdom of glory. Therefore, he must abide a kingdom which is not a kingdom of glory.

6. And again, verily I say unto you, The earth abideth the law of a celestial kingdom, for it filleth the measure of its creation, and transgresseth not the law. Wherefore, it shall be sanctified; yea, notwithstanding it shall die, it shall be quickened again, and shall abide the power by which it is quickened, and the righteous shall inherit it: for,

and each of these epistles breathed an excellent spirit. But we here record them that our readers may judge for themselves.

"KIRTLAND, January 11, 1833.

"*Brother William W. Phelps:*—I send you the olive leaf which we have plucked from the tree of paradise, the Lord's mes-

notwithstanding they die, they also shall rise again a spiritual body: they who are of a celestial spirit shall receive the same body, which was a natural body: even ye shall receive your bodies, and your glory shall be that glory by which your bodies are quickened. Ye who are quickened by a portion of the celestial glory, shall then receive of the same, even a fullness; and they who are quickened by a portion of the terrestrial glory, shall then receive of the same, even a fullness: and also they who are quickened by a portion of the telestial glory, shall then receive of the same, even a fullness: and they who remain shall also be quickened; nevertheless, they shall return again to their own place, to enjoy that which they are willing to receive, because they were not willing to enjoy that which they might have received.

7. For what doth it profit a man if a gift is bestowed upon him, and he receive not the gift? Behold, he rejoices not in that which is given unto him, neither rejoices in him who is the giver of the gift.

8. And again, verily I say unto you, That which is governed by law, is also preserved by law, and perfected and sanctified by the same. That which breaketh a law, and abideth not by law, but seeketh to become a law unto itself, and willeth to abide in sin, and altogether abideth in sin, cannot be sanctified by law, neither by mercy, justice, or judgment; therefore, they must remain filthy still.

9. All kingdoms have a law given: and there are many kingdoms; for there is no space in the which there is no kingdom; and there is no kingdom in which there is no space, either a greater or lesser kingdom. And unto every kingdom is given a law; and unto every law there are certain bounds also, and conditions.

10. All beings who abide not in those conditions, are not justified; for intelligence cleaveth unto intelligence; wisdom receiveth wisdom; truth embraceth truth; virtue loveth virtue; light cleaveth unto light: mercy hath compassion on mercy, and claimeth her own; justice continueth its course, and claimeth its own; judgment goeth before the face of him who sitteth upon the throne, and governeth and executeth all things: he comprehendeth all things, and all things are before him, and all things are round about him; and he is above all things, and in all things, and is through all things, and is round about all things: and all things are by him, and of him; even God, forever and ever.

11. And again, verily I say unto you, He hath given a law unto all things by which they move in their times, and their seasons; and their courses are fixed; even the courses of the heavens, and the earth; which comprehend the earth and all the planets; and they give light to each other in their times, and in their seasons, in their minutes, in their hours, in their days, in their weeks, in their months, in their years: all these are one year with God, but not with man.

12. The earth rolls upon her wings; and the sun giveth his light by day, and the moon giveth her light by night; and the stars also giveth their light, as they roll upon their wings, in their glory, in the midst of the power of God. Unto what shall I liken these kingdoms, that ye may understand? Behold, all these are kingdoms, and any man who hath

sage of peace to us; for though our brethren in Zion indulge in feelings towards us which are not according to the requirements of the new covenant, yet we have the satisfaction of knowing that the Lord approves of us, and has accepted

seen any or the least of these, hath seen God moving in his majesty and power. I say unto you, He hath seen him: nevertheless, he who came unto his own was not comprehended. The light shineth in darkness, and the darkness comprehendeth it not; nevertheless, the day shall come when you shall comprehend even God; being quickened in him, and by him. Then shall ye know that ye have seen me, that I am, and that I am the true light that is in you, and that you are in me, otherwise ye could not abound.

13. Behold, I will liken these kingdoms unto a man having a field, and he sent forth his servants into the field, to dig in the field; and he said unto the first, Go ye and labor in the field, and in the first hour I will come unto you, and ye shall behold the joy of my countenance: and he said unto the second, Go ye also into the field, and in the second hour I will visit you with the joy of my countenance; and also unto the third, saying, I will visit you; and unto the fourth, and so on unto the twelfth.

14. And the lord of the field went unto the first in the first hour, and tarried with him all that hour, and he was made glad with the light of the countenance of his lord; and then he withdrew from the first that he might visit the second also, and the third, and the fourth, and so on unto the twelfth; and thus they all received the light of the countenance of their lord: every man in his hour, and in his time, and in his season; beginning at the first, and so on unto the last, and from the last unto the first, and from the first unto the last; every man in his own order, until his hour was finished, even according as his lord had commanded him, that his lord might be glorified in him, and he in him, that they all might be glorified.

15. Therefore, unto this parable will I liken all these kingdoms, and the inhabitants thereof; every kingdom in its hour, and in its time, and in its season; even according to the decree which God hath made.

16. And again, verily I say unto you, my friends, I leave these sayings with you, to ponder in your hearts with this commandment which I give unto you, that ye shall call upon me while I am near; draw near unto me, and I will draw near unto you; seek me diligently and ye shall find me; ask and ye shall receive; knock and it shall be opened unto you; whatsoever ye ask the Father in my name it shall be given unto you, that is expedient for you; and if ye ask anything that is not expedient for you, it shall turn unto your condemnation.

17. Behold, that which you hear is as the voice of one crying in the wilderness; in the wilderness, because you cannot see him: my voice, because my voice is Spirit; my Spirit is truth: truth abideth and hath no end; and if it be in you it shall abound.

18. And if your eye be single to my glory, your whole bodies shall be filled with light, and there shall be no darkness in you, and that body which is filled with light comprehendeth all things. Therefore, sanctify yourselves that your minds become single to God, and the days will come that you shall see him: for he will unveil his face unto you, and it shall be in his own time, and in his own way, and according to his own will.

19. Remember the great and last promise which I have made unto you: cast away your idle thoughts and your excess of laughter far from you; tarry ye, tarry ye in this place, and call a solemn assembly, even of those who are the first laborers in this last kingdom; and let those whom they

us, and established his name in Kirtland for the salvation of the nations; for the Lord will have a place from whence his word will go forth in these last days, in purity; for if Zion will not purify herself so as to be approved of in all things

have warned in their traveling, call on the Lord, and ponder the warning in their hearts which they have received, for a little season. Behold, and lo, I will take care of your flocks and will raise up elders and send unto them.

20. Behold, I will hasten my work in its time; and I give unto you who are the first laborers in this last kingdom, a commandment, that you assemble yourselves together, and organize yourselves, and prepare yourselves; and sanctify yourselves; yea, purify your hearts, and cleanse your hands and your feet before me, that I may make you clean; that I may testify unto your Father, and your God, and my God, that you are clean from the blood of this wicked generation, that I may fulfill this promise, this great and last promise which I have made unto you, when I will.

21. Also, I give unto you a commandment, that ye shall continue in prayer and fasting from this time forth. And I give unto you a commandment, that you shall teach one another the doctrine of the kingdom; teach ye diligently and my grace shall attend you, that you may be instructed more perfectly in theory, in principle, in doctrine, in the law of the gospel, in all things that pertain unto the kingdom of God, that is expedient for you to understand; of things both in heaven, and in earth, and under the earth; things which have been; things which are; things which must shortly come to pass; things which are at home; things which are abroad; the wars and the perplexities of the nations; and the judgments which are on the land; and a knowledge also of countries, and of kingdoms, that ye may be prepared in all things when I shall send you again, to magnify the calling whereunto I have called you, and the mission with which I have commissioned you.

22. Behold, I sent you out to testify and warn the people, and it becometh every man who hath been warned, to warn his neighbor; therefore, they are left without excuse, and their sins are upon their own heads. He that seeketh me early shall find me, and shall not be forsaken.

23. Therefore, tarry ye, and labor diligently, that you may be perfected in your ministry, to go forth among the Gentiles for the last time, as many as the mouth of the Lord shall name, to bind up the law, and seal up the testimony, and to prepare the saints for the hour of judgment, which is to come; that their souls may escape the wrath of God, the desolation of abomination, which await the wicked, both in this world, and in the world to come. Verily, I say unto you, Let those who are not the first elders, continue in the vineyard, until the mouth of the Lord shall call them, for their time is not yet come; their garments are not clean from the blood of this generation.

24. Abide ye in the liberty wherewith ye are made free; entangle not yourselves in sin, but let your hands be clean, until the Lord come, for not many days hence and the earth shall tremble, and reel to and fro as a drunken man, and the sun shall hide his face, and shall refuse to give light, and the moon shall be bathed in blood, and the stars shall become exceeding angry, and shall cast themselves down as a fig that falleth from off a fig tree.

25. And after your testimony, cometh wrath and indignation upon the people; for after your testimony cometh the testimony of earthquakes, that shall cause groanings in the midst of her, and men shall fall upon the ground, and shall not be able to stand. And also cometh the testimony

in his sight, he will seek another people: for his work will go on until Israel is gathered, and they who will not hear his voice, must expect to feel his wrath.   Let me say unto you, Seek to purify yourselves, and also all the inhabitants

of the voice of thunderings, and the voice of lightnings, and the voice of tempests, and the voice of the waves of the sea, heaving themselves beyond their bounds.   And all things shall be in commotion; and surely men's hearts shall fail them; for fear shall come upon all people; and angels shall fly through the midst of heaven, crying with a loud voice, sounding the trump of God, saying, Prepare ye, prepare ye, O inhabitants of the earth, for the judgment of our God is come: behold, and lo, the Bridegroom cometh, go ye out to meet him.

26. And immediately there shall appear a great sign in heaven, and all people shall see it together.   And another angel shall sound his trump, saying, That great church, the mother of abominations, that made all nations drink of the wine of the wrath of her fornication, that persecuteth the saints of God, that shed their blood: she who sitteth upon many waters, and upon the islands of the sea; behold, she is the tares of the earth, she is bound in bundles, her bands are made strong, no man can loose them; therefore, she is ready to be burned.   And he shall sound his trump both long and loud, and all nations shall hear it.

27. And there shall be silence in heaven for the space of half an hour, and immediately after shall the curtain of heaven be unfolded, as a scroll is unfolded after it is rolled up, and the face of the Lord shall be unveiled; and the saints that are upon the earth, who are alive, shall be quickened, and be caught up to meet him.   And they who have slept in their graves, shall come forth; for their graves shall be opened, and they also shall be caught up to meet him in the midst of the pillar of heaven: they are Christ's, the first fruits: they who shall descend with him first, and they who are on the earth and in their graves, who are first caught up to meet him; and all this by the voice of the sounding of the trump of the angel of God.

28. And after this, another angel shall sound, which is the second trump; and then cometh the redemption of those who are Christ's at his coming; who have received their part in that prison which is prepared for them, that they might receive the gospel, and be judged according to men in the flesh.

29. And again, another trump shall sound, which is the third trump: and then cometh the spirits of men who are to be judged, and are found under condemnation: and these are the rest of the dead, and they live not again until the thousand years are ended, neither again, until the end of the earth.

30. And another trump shall sound, which is the fourth trump, saying, These are found among those who are to remain until that great and last day, even the end, who shall remain filthy still.

31. And another trump shall sound, which is the fifth trump, which is the fifth angel who committeth the everlasting gospel, flying through the midst of heaven, unto all nations, kindreds, tongues, and people; and this shall be the sound of his trump, saying to all people, both in heaven and in earth, and that are under the earth; for every ear shall hear it, and every knee shall bow, and every tongue shall confess, while they hear the sound of the trump, saying, Fear God, and give glory to him who sitteth upon the throne, forever and ever: for the hour of his judgment is come.

32. And again, another angel shall sound his trump, which is the sixth

of Zion, lest the Lord's anger be kindled to fierceness. Repent, repent is the voice of God to Zion; and yet, strange as it may appear yet, it is true, mankind will persist in self-justification until all their iniquity is exposed, and their

angel, saying, She is fallen, who made all nations drink of the wine of the wrath of her fornication: she is fallen! is fallen!

33. And again, another angel shall sound his trump, which is the seventh angel, saying: It is finished! it is finished! the Lamb of God hath overcome, and trodden the wine press alone; even the wine press of the fierceness of the wrath of Almighty God; and then shall the angels be crowned with the glory of his might, and the saints shall be filled with his glory, and receive their inheritance and be made equal with him.

34. And then shall the first angel again sound his trump in the ears of all living, and reveal the secret acts of men, and the mighty works of God in the first thousandth year.

35. And then shall the second angel sound his trump, and reveal the secret acts of men, and the thoughts and intents of their hearts, and the mighty works of God in the second thousandth year: and so on, until the seventh angel shall sound his trump; and he shall stand forth upon the land and upon the sea, and swear in the name of him who sitteth upon the throne, that there shall be time no longer, and Satan shall be bound, that old serpent, who is called the Devil, and shall not be loosed for the space of a thousand years. And then he shall be loosed for a little season, that he may gather together his armies; and Michael, the seventh angel, even the archangel, shall gather together his armies, even the hosts of heaven. And the Devil shall gather together his armies, even the hosts of hell, and shall come up to battle against Michael and his armies: and then cometh the battle of the great God! And the Devil and his armies shall be cast away into their own place, that they shall not have power over the saints any more at all; for Michael shall fight their battles, and shall overcome him who seeketh the throne of him who sitteth upon the throne, even the Lamb. This is the glory of God and the sanctified; and they shall not any more see death.

36. Therefore, verily I say unto you, my friends, Call your solemn assembly, as I have commanded you; and as all have not faith, seek ye diligently and teach one another words of wisdom; yea, seek ye out of the best books words of wisdom; seek learning even by study, and also by faith. Organize yourselves; prepare every needful thing, and establish a house, even a house of prayer, a house of fasting, a house of faith, a house of learning, a house of glory, a house of order, a house of God; that your incomings may be in the name of the Lord; that your outgoings may be in the name of the Lord; that all your salutations may be in the name of the Lord, with uplifted hands unto the Most High.

37. Therefore cease from all your light speeches; from all laughter, from all your lustful desires, from all your pride and light-mindedness, and from all your wicked doings. Appoint among yourselves a teacher, and let not all be spokesmen at once, but let one speak at a time, and let all listen unto his sayings, that when all have spoken, that all may be edified of all, and that every man may have an equal privilege.

38. See that ye love one another; cease to be covetous; learn to impart one to another as the gospel requires; cease to be idle; cease to be unclean; cease to find fault one with another; cease to sleep longer than is needful; retire to thy bed early, that ye may not be weary; arise early, that your bodies and your minds may be invigorated; and above all things, clothe

character past being redeemed, and that which is treasured up in their hearts be exposed to the gaze of mankind. I say to you, (and what I say to you, I say to all,) Hear the warning voice of God, lest Zion fall, and the Lord swear in his wrath 'The inhabitants of Zion shall not enter into my rest.'

"The brethren in Kirtland pray for you unceasingly, for,

yourselves with the bonds of charity, as with a mantle, which is the bond of perfectness and peace; pray always, that you may not faint until I come; behold, and lo, I will come quickly, and receive you unto myself. Amen.

39. And again, the order of the house prepared for the presidency of the school of the prophets, established for their instruction in all things that are expedient for them, even for all the officers of the church, or, in other words, those who are called to the ministry in the church, beginning at the high priests, even down to the deacons; and this shall be the order of the house of the presidency of the school: He that is appointed to be president, or teacher, shall be found standing in his place, in the house, which shall be prepared for him; therefore he shall be first in the house of God, in a place that the congregation in the house may hear his words carefully and distinctly, not with loud speech. And when he cometh into the house of God (for he should be first in the house; behold, this is beautiful, that he may be an example)

40. Let him offer himself in prayer upon his knees before God, in token or remembrance of the everlasting covenant; and when any shall come in after him, let the teacher arise, and, with uplifted hands to heaven, yea, even directly, salute his brother or brethren with these words:

41. Art thou a brother or brethren, I salute you in the name of the Lord Jesus Christ, in token or remembrance of the everlasting covenant, in which covenant I receive you to fellowship, in a determination that is fixed, immovable, and unchangeable, to be your friend and brother, through the grace of God, in the bonds of love, to walk in all the commandments of God blameless, in thanksgiving, forever and ever. Amen.

42. And he that is found unworthy of this salutation shall not have place among you; for ye shall not suffer that mine house shall be polluted by them.

43. And he that cometh in and is faithful before me, and is a brother, or if they be brethren, they shall salute the president or teacher, with uplifted hands to heaven, with this same prayer and covenant, or by saying Amen, in token of the same.

44. Behold, verily I say unto you, This is a sample unto you for a salutation to one another in the house of God, in the school of the prophets. And ye are called to do this by prayer and thanksgiving, as the Spirit shall give utterance, in all your doings in the house of the Lord, in the school of the prophets, that it may become a sanctuary, a tabernacle, of the Holy Spirit to your edification.

45. And ye shall not receive any among you into this school, save he is clean from the blood of this generation; and he shall be received by the ordinance of the washing of feet, for unto this end was the ordinance of the washing of feet instituted.

46. And again, the ordinance of washing feet is to be administered by the president, or presiding elder of the church. It is to be commenced with prayer; and after partaking of bread and wine, he is to gird himself, according to the pattern given in the thirteenth chapter of John's testimony concerning me. Amen.

knowing the terrors of the Lord, they greatly fear for you: you will see that the Lord commanded us, in Kirtland, to build an house of God, and establish a school for the prophets. This is the word of the Lord to us, and we must, yea, the Lord helping us, we will obey: as on conditions of our obedience he has promised us great things; yea, even a visit from the heavens to honor us with his own presence. We greatly fear before the Lord lest we should fail of this great honor, which our Master proposes to confer on us; we are seeking for humility and great faith lest we be ashamed in his presence. Our hearts are greatly grieved at the spirit which is breathed, both in your letter, and that of Brother G————'s; the very spirit which is wasting the strength of Zion like a pestilence; and if it is not detected and driven from you, it will ripen Zion for the threatened judgments of God. Remember God sees the secret springs of human action, and knows the hearts of all living.

"Brother, suffer us to speak plainly, for God has respect to the feelings of his saints, and he will not suffer them to be tantalized with impunity. Tell Brother G————t that low insinuations, God hates; but he rejoices in an honest heart, and knows better who is guilty than he does. We send him this warning voice, and let him fear greatly for himself, lest a worse thing overtake him; all we can say by way of conclusion, is, if the fountain of our tears are not dried up, we will still weep for Zion. This from your brother who trembles for Zion, and for the wrath of heaven, which awaits her if she repent not.

"P. S. I am not in the habit of crying peace, when there is no peace, and knowing the threatened judgments of God; I say, Woe unto them who are at ease in Zion; fearfulness will speedily lay hold of the hypocrite. I did not expect that you had lost the commandments, but thought from your letters you had neglected to read them, otherwise you would not have written as you did.

"It is in vain to try to hide a bad spirit from the eyes of them who are spiritual, for it will shew itself in speaking and in writing, as well as all our other conduct. It is also needless to make great pretensions when the heart is not

right; the Lord will expose it to the view of his faithful saints. We wish you to render the *Star* as interesting as possible, by setting forth the rise, progress, and faith of the church, as well as the doctrine; for if you do not render it more interesting, than at present, it will fall, and the church suffer a great loss thereby.

"JOSEPH SMITH, JR.

"Kirtland Mills, Geauga Co., Ohio,

"January 14, 1833."

"From a conference of twelve high priests, to the bishop, his council, and the inhabitants of Zion.

"Orson Hyde and Hyrum Smith being appointed by the said conference, to write this epistle in obedience to the commandment, given the twenty-second and twenty-third of September last, which says, 'But verily I say unto all those to whom the kingdom has been given, from you it must be preached unto them, that they shall repent of their former evil works, for they are to be upbraided for their evil hearts of unbelief; and your brethren in Zion, for their rebellion against you at the time I sent you.'

"Brother Joseph, and certain others, have written to you on this all-important subject, but you have never been apprised of these things, by the united voice of a conference of those high priests that were present at the time this commandment was given.

"We therefore, Orson and Hyrum, the committee appointed by said conference to write this epistle, having received the prayers of said conference that we might be enabled to write the mind and will of God upon this subject, now take up our pen to address you in the name of the conference, relying upon the arm of the great head of the church.

"In the commandment above alluded to, the children of Zion were all, yea, even every one, under condemnation, and were to remain in that state until they repented and remembered the new covenant, even the Book of Mormon, and the former commandments, which the Lord had given them, not only to say but to do them, and bring forth fruit meet for the Father's kingdom; otherwise there remaineth a scourge and a judgment to be poured out upon the children of Zion:

for shall the children of the kingdom pollute the holy land? I say unto you nay!

"The answers received from those letters, which have been sent to you upon this subject, have failed to bring to us that satisfactory confession and acknowledgment, which the Spirit of our Master requires. We, therefore, feeling a deep interest for Zion, and knowing the judgments of God that will come upon her except she repent, resort to these last and most effectual means in our power to bring her to a sense of her standing before the Most High.

"At the time Joseph, Sidney, and Newel left Zion, all matters of hardness and misunderstanding were settled and buried (as they supposed) and you gave them the hand of fellowship; but, afterwards, you brought up all these things again, in a censorious spirit, accusing Brother Joseph in rather an indirect way of seeking after monarchial power and authority. This came to us in Brother Carroll's letter of June 2. We are sensible that this is not the thing Brother Joseph is seeking after, but to magnify the high office and calling whereunto he has been called and appointed by the command of God and the united voice of this church. It might not be amiss for you to call to mind the circumstances of the Nephites, and the children of Israel rising up against their prophets, and accusing them of seeking after kingly power, etc., and see what befell them, and take warning before it is too late.

"Brother Gilbert's letter of December 10, has been received and read attentively, and the low, dark, and blind insinuations which were in it were not received by us as from the fountain of light. though his claims and pretensions to holiness were great. We are not unwilling to be chastened or rebuked for our faults, but we want to receive it in language that we can understand, as Nathan said to David, 'Thou art the man.' We are aware that Brother G. is doing much, and a multitude of business on hand; but let him purge out all the old leaven, and do his business in the Spirit of the Lord, and then the Lord will bless him, otherwise the frown of the Lord will remain upon him. There is manifestly an uneasiness in Brother Gilbert, and a fearfulness that God will not provide for his saints in these last days, and these fears lead him on to covetousness. This ought not so to be; but let him do just as the Lord has commanded him, and then the Lord will open his coffers, and his wants will be liberally supplied. But if this uneasy, covetous disposition be cherished by him, the Lord will bring him to poverty, shame, and disgrace.

"Brother Phelps' letter is also received of December 15, and carefully read, and it betrays a lightness of spirit that ill becomes a man placed in the important and responsible station that he is placed in. If you have fat beef and potatoes, eat them in singleness of heart, and boast not yourselves in these things. Think not, brethren, that we make a man an offender for a word; this is not the case; but we want to see a spirit in Zion by which the Lord will build it up; that is the plain, solemn, and pure spirit in Christ. Brother Phelps requested in his last letter that Brother Joseph should come to Zion; but we say that Brother Joseph will not settle in Zion until she repent and purify herself, and abide by the new covenant, and remember the commandments that have been given her, to do them as well as say them.

"You may think it strange that we manifest no cheerfulness of heart upon the reception of your letter; you may think that our minds are prejudiced so much that we can see no good that comes from you; but rest assured, brethren, that this is not the case.

"We have the best of feelings, and feelings of the greatest anxiety for the welfare of Zion: we feel more like weeping over Zion than we do like rejoicing over her, for we know the judgments of God hang over her, and will fall upon her except she repent and purify herself before the Lord, and put away from her every foul spirit. We now say to Zion, this once, in the name of the Lord, Repent! Repent! Awake! Awake! Put on thy beautiful garments, before you are made to feel the chastening rod of him whose anger is kindled against you! Let not Satan tempt you to think we want to make you bow to us to domineer over you, for God knows this is not the case: our eyes are watered with tears, and our hearts are poured out to God in prayer for you, that he will spare you, and turn away his anger from you.

"There are many things in the last letters from Brothers G. and P. that are good, and we esteem them much. The idea of having 'certain ones appointed to regulate Zion, and traveling elders have nothing to do with this part of the matter,' is something we highly approbate, and you will doubtless know before this reaches you why William E. McLellin opposed you in this move. We fear there was something in Brother Gilbert, when he returned to this place from New York, last fall, in relation to his Brother William, that was not right; for Bro. Gilbert was asked two or three times about his Brother William, but gave evasive answers, and at the same time he knew that William was in Cleveland: but the Lord has taken him. We merely mention this, that all may take warning to work in the light, for God will bring every secret thing to light.

"We now close our epistle by saying unto you, The Lord has commanded us to purify ourselves, to wash our hands and our feet, that he may testify to his Father, and our Father, to his God and our God, that we are clean from the blood of this generation, and before we could wash our hands and our feet, we were constrained to write this letter. Therefore, with the feelings of inexpressible anxiety for your welfare we say again, Repent, repent, or Zion must suffer, for the scourge and judgment must come upon her!

"Let the bishop read this to the elders, that they may warn the members of the scourge that is coming, except they repent. Tell them to read the Book of Mormon and obey it: read the commandments that are printed, and obey them: yea, humble yourselves under the mighty hand of God, that peradventure he may turn away his anger from you. Tell them that they have not come up to Zion to sit down in idleness, neglecting the things of God, but they are to be diligent and faithful in obeying the new covenant.

"There is one clause in Brother Joseph's letter which you may not understand; that is this: 'If the people of Zion did not repent, the Lord would seek another place, and another people!' Zion is the place where the temple will be built, and the people gathered, but all people upon that holy land being under condemnation the Lord will cut off, if they repent not, and bring another race upon it, that will serve him. The Lord will seek another place to bring forth and prepare his word to go forth to the nations, and as we said before so say we again, Brother Joseph will not settle in Zion except she repent, and serve God, and obey the new covenant. With this explanation, the conference sanctions Brother Joseph's letter.

"Brethren, the conference meets again this evening to hear this letter read, and if it meets their minds, we have all agreed to kneel down before the Lord and cry unto him with all our hearts that this epistle, and Brother Joseph's and the revelations also, may have their desired effect, and accomplish the thing, whereunto they are sent, and that they may stimulate you to cleanse Zion, that she mourn not. Therefore when you get this know ye that a conference of twelve high priests have cried unto the Lord for you, and are still crying, saying, Spare thy people, O Lord, and give not thy heritage to reproach. We now feel that our garments are clean from you, and all men, when we have vashed our feet and hands according to the commandment

"We have written plainly this time, but we believe not harshly. Plainness is what the Lord requires, and we should not feel ourselves clear unless we had done so; and if the things we have told you be not attended to, you will not long have occasion to say, or to think rather, that we may be wrong in what we have stated. Your unworthy brethren are determined to pray unto the Lord for Zion, as long as we can shed the sympathetic tear, or feel any spirit to supplicate a throne of grace in her behalf.

"The school of the prophets will commence, if the Lord will, in two or three days. It is a general time of health with us. The cause of God seems to be rapidly advancing in the eastern country; the gifts are beginning to break forth so as to astonish the world, and even believers marvel at the power and goodness of God. Thanks be rendered to his holy name for what he is doing. We are your unworthy brethren in the Lord, and may the Lord help us all to do his will that we may at last be saved in his kingdom.

"ORSON HYDE.

"HYRUM SMITH.

"N. B.—We stated that Brother Gilbert knew that William was in Cleveland last fall, when he was in Kirtland. We wrote this upon the strength of hearsay; but William being left at St. Louis, strengthened our suppositions that such was the fact. We stated further, respecting this matter, or this item, than the testimony will warrant us. With this exception the conference sanction this letter."—*Times and Seasons*, vol. 5, pp. 720-723.

These premonitions of the authorities at Kirtland and their solemn warning to the saints in Zion, taken in connection with the trouble that came upon them very soon after, are suggestive, and lead one to ask, Could they not have remained and builded Zion if they had thoroughly repented and been sufficiently humble? However, it is not 'the province of the historian to speculate on what might have been, but it is his duty simply to relate what was, and leave the reader to form conclusions.

Resuming the thread of history we quote from Joseph Smith as follows:—

"This winter was spent in translating the Scriptures, in the school of the prophets, and sitting in conferences. I had many glorious seasons of refreshings. The gifts which follow them that believe and obey the gospel, as tokens that the Lord is ever the same in his dealings with the humble lovers and followers of truth, began to be poured out among us, as in ancient days; for as we, viz., Joseph Smith, Jr., Sidney Rigdon, Frederick G. Williams, Newel K. Whitney, Hyrum Smith, Zebedee Coltrin, Joseph Smith, Sen., Samuel H. Smith, John Murdock, Lyman Johnson, Orson Hyde, Ezra Thayer, high priests; and Levi Hancock, and William Smith, elders, were assembled in conference, on the twenty-second day of January, I spoke to the conference in another tongue, and was followed in the same gift by Brother Zebedee Coltrin, and he by Brother William Smith, after which the Lord poured out his Spirit in a miraculous manner until all the elders spoke in tongues,

Gift of tongues.

and several members, both male and female. Great and glorious were the divine manifestations of the Holy Spirit. Praises were sung to God and the Lamb; speaking and praying, all in tongues, occupied the conference, until a late hour at night, so rejoiced were we at the return of these long absent blessings.

"On the twenty-third, we again assembled in conference; when, after much speaking, singing, praying and praising God, all in tongues, we proceeded to the washing of feet, (according to the practice recorded in the thirteenth chapter of John's Gospel,) as commanded of the Lord. Each elder washed his own feet first, after which I girded myself with a towel, and washed the feet of them all, wiping them with the towel with which I was girded. Among the number my father presented himself, but before I washed his feet I asked of him a father's blessing, which he granted by laying his hands upon my head, in the name of Jesus Christ, and declaring that I should continue in the priest's office until Christ comes, etc. At the close of the scene Brother Frederick G. Williams, being moved upon by the Holy Ghost, washed my feet in token of his fixed determination to be with me in suffering or in journeying, in life or in death, and to be continually on my right hand; in which I accepted him in the name of the Lord.

Washing of feet.

"I then said to the elders, 'As I have done, so do ye. Wash ye, therefore, one another's feet;' and by the power of the Holy Ghost I pronounced them all clean from the blood of this generation; but if any of them should sin willfully after they were thus cleansed and sealed up unto life eternal, they should be given over unto the buffetings of Satan until the day of redemption. Having continued all day in fasting, and prayer, and ordinances, we closed by partaking of the Lord's supper. I blessed the bread and wine in the name of the Lord, when we all ate and drank and were filled; then sung a hymn and went out.

"I completed the translation and receiving of the New Testament, on the second of February, 1833, and sealed it up, no more to be opened till it arrived in Zion."—*Times and Seasons*, vol. 5, p. 723.

Translation of New Testament finished.

On Wednesday, February 27, 1833, the revelation
Word of familiarly known as the "Word of Wisdom" was
Wisdom. , given.[3] This is a peculiar and unique document,
but we think it will bear the closest investigation; and
though it is now over sixty-three years old, and the subjects
treated of have been investigated and discussed by men of
learning, it will be found to be in harmony with or in advance of the best minds of the age.

On Friday, March 8, a revelation was given assuring
Keys of the Joseph that the keys of the kingdom would never
kingdom. be taken from him, though the oracles should be
given to the church.[4]

[3] 1. Behold, verily thus saith the Lord unto you, In consequence of
evils and designs which do and will exist in the hearts of conspiring men
in the last days, I have warned you, and forewarn you, by giving unto
you this word of wisdom by revelation, that inasmuch as any man drink-
eth wine or strong drink among you, behold, it is not good, neither meet
in the sight of your Father, only in assembling yourselves together, to
offer up your sacraments before him. And, behold, this should be wine;
yea, pure wine of the grape of the vine, of your own make. And again,
strong drinks are not for the belly, but for the washing of your bodies.
And again, tobacco is not for the body, neither for the belly, and is not
good for man, but is an herb for bruises, and all sick cattle, to be used with
judgment and skill. And again, hot drinks are not for the body or belly.
2. And again, verily I say unto you, All wholesome herbs God hath
ordained for the constitution, nature, and use of man, every herb in the
season thereof, and every fruit in the season thereof. All these to be
used with prudence and thanksgiving. Yea, flesh also, of beasts and of
the fowls of the air, I, the Lord, hath ordained for the use of man, with
thanksgiving. Nevertheless, they are to be used sparingly; and it is
pleasing unto me that they should not be used only in times of winter,
or of cold, or famine. All grain is ordained for the use of man and of
beasts, to be the staff of life, not only for man, but for the beasts of the
field, and the fowls of heaven, and all wild animals that run or creep on
the earth; and these hath God made for the use of man only in times of
famine and excess of hunger.
3. All grain is good for the food of man, as also the fruit of the vine,
that which yieldeth fruit, whether in the ground or above the ground.
Nevertheless, wheat for man, and corn for the ox, and oats for the horse,
and rye for the fowls, and for swine, and for all beasts of the field, and
barley for all useful animals, and for mild drinks, as also other grain.
And all saints who remember to keep and do these sayings, walking in
obedience to the commandments, shall receive health in their navel, and
marrow to their bones, and shall find wisdom and great treasures of
knowledge, even hidden treasures; and shall run and not be weary, and
shall walk and not faint; and I, the Lord, give unto them a promise that
the destroying angel shall pass by them, as the children of Israel, and not
slay them. Amen.

[4] 1. Thus saith the Lord, Verily, verily I say unto you, my son, Thy
sins are forgiven thee, according to thy petition, for thy prayers and the
prayers of thy brethren have come up into my ears; therefore thou art

In this revelation further provision is also made for the Presidency of the church. F. G. Williams had been named First Presidency. before; now the name of Sidney Rigdon is mentioned, and they are to be accounted as equal with Joseph in holding the keys.

Did ever an impostor do a work like this, to place in the hands of two men power to overrule him?

There is one clause in the above-mentioned revelation that

blessed from henceforth that bear the keys of the kingdom given unto you; which kingdom is coming forth for the last time.

2. Verily I say unto you, The keys of this kingdom shall never be taken from you, while thou art in the world, neither in the world to come; nevertheless, through you shall the oracles be given to another; yea, even unto the church. And all they who receive the oracles of God, let them beware how they hold them, lest they are accounted as a light thing, and are brought under condemnation thereby; and stumble and fall, when the storms descend, and the winds blow, and the rains descend, and beat upon their house.

3. And again, verily I say unto thy brethren Sidney Rigdon and Frederick G. Williams, Their sins are forgiven them also, and they are accounted as equal with thee in holding the keys of this last kingdom; as also through your administration the keys of the school of the prophets, which I have commanded to be organized, that thereby they may be perfected in their ministry for the salvation of Zion, and of the nations of Israel, and of the Gentiles, as many as will believe, that through your administration, they may receive the word, and through their administration, the word may go forth unto the ends of the earth, unto the Gentiles first, and then, ·behold, and lo, they shall turn unto the Jews; and then cometh the day when the arm of the Lord shall be revealed in power in convincing the nations, the heathen nations, the house of Joseph, of the gospel of their salvation.

4. For it shall come to pass in that day, that every man shall hear the fullness of the gospel in his own tongue, and in his own language, through those who are ordained unto this power, by the administration of the Comforter, shed forth upon them, for the revelation of Jesus Christ.

5. And now, verily I say unto you, I give unto you a commandment, that you continue in the ministry and presidency, and when you have finished the translation of the prophets, you shall from henceforth preside over the affairs of the church and the school; and from time to time, as shall be manifest by the Comforter, receive revelations to unfold the mysteries of the kingdom, and set in order the churches, and study and learn, and become acquainted with all good books, and with languages, tongues, and people. And this shall be your business and mission in all your lives to preside in council and set in order all the affairs of this church and kingdom. Be not ashamed, neither confounded; but be admonished in all your highmindedness and pride, for it bringeth a snare upon your souls. Set in order your houses; keep slothfulness and uncleanliness far from you.

6. Now, verily I say unto you, Let there be a place provided as soon as possible, for the family of thy counselor and scribe, even Frederick G. Williams; and let mine aged servant Joseph Smith, Sr., continue with his family upon the place where he now lives, and let it not be sold until

may be misunderstood; viz., that in which they were instructed to finish the translation of the prophets, for the reason that the history has spoken of the New Testament being finished on February 2, 1833. It is evident, however, that the New Testament was first finished, the prophets remaining incomplete at the time this revelation was given. It appears from this revelation that the primary right of presiding over the church, and of regulating and setting in order all the affairs of the same, is resident in the First Presidency; and that the true philosophy of the organization is, that if others should be appointed to those duties, these rights and prerogatives inhere in them in a secondary sense, to be exercised under the direction and counsel of the First Presidency. At the time of the giving of this revelation, and for some time after, the incomplete organization

the mouth of the Lord shall name. And let thy counselor, even Sidney Rigdon, remain where he now resides, until the mouth of the Lord shall name. And let the bishop search diligently, to obtain an agent; and let it be a man who has got riches in store; a man of God and of strong faith; that thereby he may be enabled to discharge every debt; that the storehouse of the Lord may not be brought into disrepute before the eyes of the people. Search diligently, pray always, and be believing, and all things shall work together for your good, if ye walk uprightly, and remember the covenant wherewith ye have covenanted one with another. Let your families be small, especially mine aged servant Joseph Smith, Sr., as pertaining to those who do not belong to your families; that those things that are provided for you, to bring to pass my work, are not taken from you and given to those that are not worthy, and thereby you are hindered in accomplishing those things which I have commanded you.

7. And again, verily I say unto you, It is my will that my handmaid, Vienna Jaques, should receive money to bear her expenses, and go up unto the land of Zion; and the residue of the money may be consecrated unto me, and she be rewarded in mine own due time. Verily I say unto you, that it is meet in mine eyes, that she should go up unto the land of Zion, and receive an inheritance from the hand of the bishop, that she may settle down in peace inasmuch as she is faithful, and not be idle in her days from thenceforth.

8. And, behold, verily I say unto you, that ye shall write this commandment, and say unto your brethren in Zion, in love greeting, that I have called you also to preside over Zion in mine own due time; therefore let them cease wearying me concerning this matter. Behold, I say unto you, that your brethren in Zion begin to repent, and the angels rejoice over them; nevertheless, I am not well pleased with many things; and I am not well pleased with my servant William E. McLellin, neither with my servant Sidney Gilbert; and the bishop also; and others have many things to repent of; but verily I say unto you, that I, the Lord, will contend with Zion and plead with her strong ones, and chasten her, until she overcomes and is clean before me; for she shall not be removed out of her place. I, the Lord, have spoken it. Amen.

rendered it also necessary for them to give these matters much direct and personal attention. In this sense is the revelation of 1837 to be understood which says: "For on them have I laid [past tense] the burden of all the churches for a little season." In our opinion this cannot, for manifest reasons, mean that after that little season all their primary rights and prerogatives in this connection were to be transferred to others, but to us it is evident that the import of this language is that as the little season had now passed, they were to be measurably relieved of the burden of the churches by those who had been appointed to assist in this work under their watchcare and direction. The reader will excuse us for this explanation, for in our opinion if the true philosophy of the organization receives no notice, the history of the church will be of little practical benefit.

When in translating Joseph came to that part of the
Old Testament called the Apocrypha, he received
Apocrypha. instruction concerning it. [6]

On the fifteenth a revelation was given. [6]

On Monday, March 18, the school of the prophets was or-
Presidency ganized, in which the counselors to the President
organized. of the High Priesthood were ordained.

On Saturday, the 23d, a council was held to consider the purchasing of lands.

Of these two events Joseph writes:—

"On the eighteenth of March the high priests assembled in the schoolroom of the prophets and were organized accord-

---

[6] 1. Verily, thus saith the Lord unto you, concerning the Apocrypha, There are many things contained therein that are true, and it is mostly translated correctly; there are many things contained therein that are not true, which are interpolations by the hands of men. Verily I say unto you, that it is not needful that the Apocrypha should be translated. Therefore, whoso readeth it let him understand, for the Spirit manifesteth truth; and whoso is enlightened by the Spirit shall obtain benefit therefrom; and whoso receiveth not by the Spirit, cannot be benefited; therefore, it is not needful that it should be translated. Amen.

[6] 1. Verily, thus saith the Lord, I give unto the united order, organized agreeable to the commandment previously given, a revelation and commandment concerning my servant Shederlaomach, that ye shall receive him into the order. What I say unto one I say unto all.

2. And again, I say unto you, my servant Shederlaomach, You shall be a lively member in this order; and inasmuch as you are faithful in keeping all former commandments, you shall be blessed forever. Amen.

ing to revelation, in prayer, by S. Rigdon. Doctor Hurlbut was ordained an elder; after which Elder Rigdon expressed a desire that himself and Brother F. G. Williams should be ordained to the office, to which they had been called; viz., that of presidents of the high priesthood, and to be equal in holding the keys of the kingdom with Brother Joseph Smith, Junior, according to the revelation given on the eighth of March, 1833.

"Accordingly I laid my hands on Brother Sidney and Frederick and ordained them to take part with me in holding the keys of this last kingdom, and to assist in the presidency of the high priesthood, as my counselors; after which I exhorted the brethren to faithfulness, and diligence in keeping the commandments of God, and gave much instruction for the benefit of the saints, with a promise that the pure in heart would see a heavenly vision; and after remaining a short time in secret prayer, the promise was verified; for many present had the eyes of their understandings opened by the Spirit of God so as to behold many things.

"I then blessed the bread and wine, and distributed a portion to each, after which many of the brethren saw a heavenly vision of the Savior, and concourses of angels, and many other things, of which each one has a record of what they saw, etc.

"March 23. A council was called for the purpose of appointing a committee to purchase land in Kirtland upon which the saints might build a stake of Zion. Brothers Joseph Coe and Moses Daily were appointed to ascertain the terms of sale of certain farms; and that Brother Ezra Thayer ascertain the price of Peter French's farm; and the brethren agreed to continue in prayer and fasting for the ultimate success of their mission.

"After an absence of about three hours, Brothers Coe and Daily returned and reported that Elijah Smith's farm could be obtained for four thousand dollars, and Mr. Morley's for twenty-one hundred, and Brother Thayer reported that Peter French would sell his farm for five thousand dollars. The council decided to purchase the farms, and appointed Ezra Thayre and Joseph Coe to superintend the purchase, and they were ordained under the hands of Sidney Rigdon, and set apart as general agents of the church for that purpose."—*Times and Seasons*, vol. 5, p. 738.

On Tuesday, March 26, 1833, a council of high priests met at Independence, Jackson County, Missouri.

Of this council Joseph writes:—

"On the twenty-sixth of March a council of high priests, twenty-one in number, convened for the general welfare of the church, in what was then called Zion, in Jackson County, Missouri, on account of a revelation, my letter, and an epistle from the church in Kirtland; a solemn assembly had been called, and a sincere and humble repentance manifested, insomuch, that on the twenty-sixth of February, one month previous, a general epistle had been written in conference, which was satisfactory to the Presidency and church at Kirtland.

Affairs in Zion.

"At the sitting of the council of the 26th of March, according to the plan taught at the solemn assembly, which was, that the seven high priests who were sent from Kirtland to build up Zion; viz., Oliver Cowdery, W. W. Phelps, John Whitmer, Sidney Gilbert, Bishop Partridge, and his two counselors, should stand at the head of affairs, relating to the church, in that section of the Lord's vineyard; and these seven men, with the common consent of the branches, comprising the church, were to appoint presiding elders, to take the watchcare of the several branches, as they were appointed. Now, therefore, as many of the high priests and elders went up to Zion and commenced regulating and setting the branches in order, allowing themselves as much power by the authority of their priesthood and gift of the Holy Ghost as those set apart and appointed to preside over the branches, it became necessary to call the council now spoken of, to set in order the elders of Israel; when, after a long discussion, it was decided from the revelations that the order taught in the solemn assembly was correct; and that the elders, when they arrived at Zion, were bound by the authorities set in the church, to be submissive to the powers that be; their labors and callings being more particularly to push the people together from the ends of the earth to the places the Lord appointed. This decision in council gave general satisfaction, and the elders soon saw the beauty of every man in his place."—*Times and Seasons*, vol. 5, pp. 788, 739.

Joseph also writes of affairs both in Kirtland and Zion as follows:—

"April 2. F. G. Williams was appointed, by a council of high priests, an agent, to superintend and employ men to labor in the brickyard, on the French farm, also to rent the farm. The French farm was purchased on account of the stone quarry thereon, and the facilities for making brick, each essential to the building up of the city. The council also instructed Bro. E. Thayre to purchase the Tannery of Arnold Mason, in Kirtland.

"On the 6th of April, in the land of Zion, which was within the western boundaries of the State of Missouri, about eighty official, together with some unofficial members of the church, met for instruction, and the service of God at the ferry on Big Blue River, near the western limits of Jackson County, which is the confines of the State and the United States. It was an early spring, and the leaves and blossoms, like a glimpse at paradise, enlivened and gratified the soul of man.

"The day was spent in a very agreeable manner, in giving and receiving knowledge which appertained to this last kingdom. It being just eighteen hundred years since the Savior laid down his life that men might have everlasting life, and only three years since the church had come out of the wilderness, preparatory for the last dispensation. They had great reason to rejoice: they thought upon the time when this world came into existence and the morning stars sang together and all the sons of God shouted for joy: when Israel ate the 'passover' as wailing came up for the loss of the firstborn of Egypt, and they felt like the shepherds who watched their flocks by night, when the angelic choir sweetly sung that electrifying strain, '*Peace on earth and good will to man*,' and the solemnities of eternity rested upon them. This was the first attempt made by the church to celebrate her birthday, and those who professed not our faith talked about it as a strange thing."—*Times and Seasons*, vol. 5, p. 752.

On Thursday, March 21, Joseph wrote the following letter to Zion which speaks for itself:—

"KIRTLAND, March 21, 1833.

"*Dear Brethren in Zion:*—Agreeable to a notice we gave you, in Brother Whitney's last letter to you with respect to answering your letters, we now commence, after giving thanks to our heavenly Father for every expression of his goodness in preserving our unprofitable lives to the present time, and the health and other blessings which we now enjoy through his mercies.

Letter to Zion.

"With joy we received your general epistle, written the twenty-sixth of February, which contained the confession of our brethren concerned, all of which was to our entire satisfaction. It was read by the brethren in Kirtland with feelings of the deepest interest, knowing as we did that the anger of the Lord was kindled against you, and nothing but repentance, of the greatest humility, would turn it away; and I will assure you that expressions of joy burned [beamed] on every countenance when they saw that our epistle and the revelation were received by our brethren in Zion, and it had had its desired effect. . . .

"With respect to Brother Gilbert's letter of the tenth of December, I would say to him; firstly, we believe he wrote it in all sincerity of his heart, and we were pleased in the style, and composition; but, upon mature reflection, and inquiry at the hand of the Lord, we find some things that are unreconcilable, especially to some: I mean with respect to hints given, that are not clearly explained. As every letter that comes from Zion must go the rounds of the brethren for inspection, it is necessary that there should be no disguise in them, but that every subject written from brethren should be plain to the understanding of all, that no jealousy may be raised and when we rebuke, do it in all meekness. The letter written the twenty-fourth of February was not written in that contrition of heart which it should have been, for it appears to have been written in too much of a spirit of justification; but the letter to Brother Whitney of the twentieth of March, was written to our entire satisfaction.

"Now I would say to Brother Gilbert that I do not write this by way of chastisement, but to show him the absolute necessity of having all his communications written plainly, and understandingly. We are well aware of the great care upon his mind, in consequence of much business; but he must put his trust in God, and he may rest assured that he has our prayers day and night, that he may have strength to overcome every difficulty. We have learned of the Lord that it is his duty to assist all the poor brethren that are pure in heart, and that he has done wrong in withholding credit from them, as they must have assistance; and the Lord established him in Zion for that express purpose.

"It is not the will of the Lord to print any of the New Translation in the *Star;* but when it is published, it will all go to the world together; in a volume by itself; and the New Testament and the Book of Mormon will be printed together.

"With respect to Brother Oliver's private letter to me on the subject of giving deeds, and receiving contributions from brethren, etc., I have nothing further to say on the subject, but to make yourselves acquainted with the commandments of the Lord, and the laws of the State, and govern yourselves accordingly. Brother Elliot was here yesterday and showed me a letter from Brother Phelps, and we were well pleased with the spirit in which it was written. The probability is that he will not go to Zion at present, as he has bought in Chagrin.

"We rejoice to hear that the Seminary lands are reduced in price, and are coming into market: and be assured that we shall use our influence to send brethren to Zion who are able to help you in the purchase of lands, etc., etc.

"We have just received a letter from Brother Sidney; he has built up a church of eight members, in Medina County, Ohio, and prospects of more. With respect to the deaths in Zion, we feel to mourn with those that mourn, but remember that the God of all the earth will do right. And now, my beloved brethren, I commend you to God and his grace, praying him to keep and preserve you blameless, to the coming of our Lord Jesus Christ: Amen.

"JOSEPH SMITH, JR.

"P. S. – Say to Brother Corrill that his confession gave me great satisfaction, and all things are now settled on my part.   J. S."

CHAPTER 12.

1833.

IN April, 1833, there commenced a series of persecutions
and outrages which has no parallel in the history of our
country. We heartily wish we could pass these

Persecution in Zion.

things unnoticed; but alas! they are a part of the
history, and must be recorded. We are not willing to say
that the Latter Day Saints always acted wisely, or that they
were in every particular right. Joseph Smith

Saints err.

acknowledged that, at the time, and doubtless
many others have acknowledged the same. He wrote:—

"But to return to my subject: After having ascertained
the very spot, and having the happiness of seeing quite a
number of the families of my brethren comfortably situated
upon the land, I took leave of them and journeyed back to
Ohio, and used every influence and argument that lay in my
power to get those who believe in the everlasting covenant,
whose circumstances would admit and whose families were
willing to remove to the place which I now designate to be
the land of Zion. And thus the sound of the gathering,
and of the doctrine, went abroad into the world; and many,
we have reason to fear, having a zeal not according to knowledge, not understanding the pure principles of the doctrine
of the church, have no doubt, in the heat of enthusiasm,
taught and said many things which are derogatory to the

genuine character and principles of the church, and for these things we are heartily sorry, and would apologize if an apology would do any good."—*Messenger and Advocate*, vol. 1, p. 180.

However, we say, and without hesitation or fear of contradiction, that there was nothing in the actions of the saints, No excuse for enemies. that gave the least color of excuse for the outrages they suffered at the hands of lawless mobs, or for the treatment they often received at the hands of officers of the law. To us it seems strange, but no less strange than commendable, that they bore their persecution with as much fortitude and patience as they did. It seems evident that some influence such as mortals are not usually controlled by held them in check; and that Joseph Smith also used his influence to restrain the people from excesses.

Joseph mentions this first hostile demonstration together with events happening at Kirtland as follows:—

"In the month of April the first regular mob rushed together, in Independence (Zion), to consult upon a plan for the removal or immediate destruction of the church in Jackson County. The number of the mob was about three hundred. A few of the first elders met in secret, and prayed to Him who said to the winds, 'Be still,' to frustrate them in their wicked design. They, therefore, after spending the day in a fruitless endeavor to unite upon a general scheme for 'moving the Mormons out of their diggings' (as they asserted), and becoming a little the worse for liquor, broke up in a regular Missouri 'row,' showing a determined resolution that every man would 'carry his own head.'

"April 30 a conference of high priests assembled at the schoolroom, in Kirtland, and appointed Brother Albert Brown a committee to circulate a subscription to procure money to pay for the use of the house where meetings had been held the past season; and John P. Green was instructed to go and take charge of the branch of the church in Parkman, carrying with him an epistle to the brethren, and as soon as convenient remove his family to that place.

"On the fourth of May, 1833, a conference of high priests assembled in Kirtland, to take into consideration the necessity of building a schoolhouse, for the accommodation of the elders, who should come together to receive instruction preparatory for their missions, and ministry, according to a revelation on that subject, given March 8, 1833, and by unanimous voice of the conference, Hyrum Smith, Jared Carter, and Reynolds Cahoon were appointed a committee to obtain subscriptions, for the purpose of erecting such a building."— *Times and Seasons*, vol. 5, pp. 754, 755.

On Tuesday, May 6, 1833, two more revelations were given.[1]

[1] 1. Verily, thus saith the Lord, It shall come to pass that every soul who forsaketh their sins and cometh unto me, and calleth on my name, and obeyeth my voice, and keepeth my commandments, shall see my face, and know that I am, and that I am the true light that lighteth every man that cometh into the world; and that I am in the Father and the Father in me, and the Father and I are one; the Father because he gave me of his fullness; and the Son because I was in the world and made flesh my tabernacle, and dwelt among the sons of men. I was in the world and received of my Father, and the works of him were plainly manifest; and John saw and bore record of the fullness of my glory; and the fullness of John's record is hereafter to be revealed. And he bore record saying, I saw his glory that he was in the beginning before the world was; therefore, in the beginning the Word was; for he was the Word, even the messenger of salvation, the light and the Redeemer of the world; the Spirit of truth, who came into the world because the world was made by him; and in him was the life of men and the light of men. The worlds were made by him. Men were made by him. All things were made by him, and through him, and of him. And I, John, bare record that I beheld his glory, as the glory of the Only Begotten of the Father, full of grace and truth; even the Spirit of truth which came and dwelt in the flesh, and dwelt among us.

2. And I, John, saw that he received not of the fullness at the first, but received grace for grace; and he received not of the fullness at first, but continued from grace to grace, until he received a fullness; and thus he was called the Son of God, because he received not of the fullness at the first. And I, John, bare record, and lo, the heavens were opened and the Holy Ghost descended upon him in the form of a dove, and sat upon him, and there came a voice out of heaven saying, This is my beloved Son. And I, John, bare record that he received a fullness of the glory of the Father; and he received all power, both in heaven and on earth; and the glory of the Father was with him, for he dwelt in him.

3. And it shall come to pass, that if you are faithful, you shall receive the fullness of the record of John. I give unto you these sayings that you may understand and know how to worship, and know what you worship, that you may come unto the Father in my name, and in due time receive of his fullness, for if you keep my commandments you shall receive of his fullness and be glorified in me as I am in the Father: therefore, I say unto you, You shall receive grace for grace.

4. And now, verily I say unto you, I was in the beginning with the Father, and am the Firstborn; and all those who are begotten through me, are partakers of the glory of the same, and are the church of the Firstborn. Ye were also in the beginning with the Father; that which is Spirit, even the Spirit of truth; and truth is knowledge of things as

they are, and as they were, and as they are to come; and whatsoever is
more or less than this, is the spirit of that wicked one, who was a liar
from the beginning.   The Spirit of truth is of God.   I am the Spirit of
truth.   And John bore record of me, saying, He received a fullness of
truth; yea, even of all truth, and no man receiveth a fullness unless he
keepeth his commandments.   He that keepeth his commandments, receiveth truth and light, until he is glorified in truth, and knoweth all
things.

5. Man was also in the beginning with God.   Intelligence, or the light
of truth, was not created or made, neither indeed can be.   All truth is
independent in that sphere in which God has placed it, to act for itself,
as all intelligence also, otherwise there is no existence.   Behold, here is
the agency of man, and here is the condemnation of man, because that
which was from the beginning is plainly manifest unto them, and they
receive not the light.   And every man whose spirit receiveth not the
light is under condemnation, for man is spirit.   The elements are eternal,
and spirit and element, inseparably connected, receiveth a fullness of joy;
and when separated, man cannot receive a fullness of joy.   The elements
are the tabernacle of God; yea, man is the tabernacle of God, even temples; and whatsoever temple is defiled, God shall destroy that temple.

6. The glory of God is intelligence, or, in other words, light and truth;
light and truth forsaketh that evil one.   Every spirit of man was innocent in the beginning, and God having redeemed man from the fall, men
became again in their infant state, innocent before God.   And that
wicked one cometh and taketh away light and truth, through disobedience, from the children of men, and because of the tradition of their
fathers.   But I have commanded you to bring up your children in light
and truth; but verily I say unto you, my servant Frederick G. Williams,
You have continued under this condemnation; you have not taught your
children light and truth, according to the commandments, and that
wicked one hath power, as yet, over you, and this is the cause of your
affliction.   And now a commandment I give unto you, if you will be
delivered: you shall set in order your own house, for there are many
things that are not right in your house.

7. Verily I say unto my servant Sidney Rigdon, that in some things he
hath not kept the commandments, concerning his children; therefore,
firstly set in order thy house.

8. Verily I say unto my servant Joseph Smith, Jr., or, in other words,
I will call you friends, for you are my friends, and ye shall have an inheritance with me.   I called you servants for the world's sake, and ye
are their servants for my sake; and now verily I say unto Joseph
Smith, Jr., you have not kept the commandments, and must needs stand
rebuked before the Lord.   Your family must needs repent and forsake
some things, and give more earnest heed unto your sayings, or be removed
out of their place.   What I say unto one I say unto all: Pray always, lest
that wicked one have power in you, and remove you out of your place.

9. My servant Newel K. Whitney, also a bishop of my church, hath
need to be chastened, and set in order his family, and see that they are
more diligent and concerned at home, and pray always, or they shall be
removed out of their place.

10. Now I say unto you, my friends, Let my servant Sidney Rigdon go
his journey, and make haste, and also proclaim the acceptable year of
the Lord, and the gospel of salvation, as I shall give him utterance, and
by your prayer of faith with one consent, I will uphold him.

11. And let my servant Joseph Smith, Jr., and Frederick G. Williams,
make haste also, and it shall be given them even according to the prayer
of faith; and inasmuch as you keep my sayings, you shall not be confounded in this world, nor in the world to come.

In June, 1833, another revelation was received. *

12. And verily I say unto you, that it is my will that you should hasten to translate my scriptures, and to obtain a knowledge of history, and of countries, and of kingdoms, of laws of God and man, and all this for the salvation of Zion. Amen.

1. And again, verily I say unto you, my friends, A commandment I give unto you, that ye shall commence a work of laying out and preparing a beginning and foundation of the city of the stake of Zion, here in the land of Kirtland, beginning at my house: and, behold, it must be done according to the pattern which I have given unto you. And let the first lot on the south be consecrated unto me for the building of an house for the presidency, for the work of the presidency, in obtaining revelations, and for the work of the ministry of the presidency, in all things pertaining to the church and kingdom.

2. Verily I say unto you, that it shall be built fifty-five by sixty-five feet in the width thereof, and in the length thereof, in the inner court; and there shall be a lower court, and an higher court, according to the pattern which shall be given unto you hereafter; and it shall be dedicated unto the Lord from the foundation thereof, according to the order of the priesthood, according to the pattern which shall be given unto you hereafter; and it shall be wholly dedicated unto the Lord for the work of the presidency. And ye shall not suffer any unclean thing to come in unto it; and my glory shall be there, and my presence shall be there; but if there shall come into it any unclean thing, my glory shall not be there, and my presence shall not come into it.

3. And again, verily I say unto you, The second lot on the south shall be dedicated unto me, for the building of an house unto me, for the work of the printing of the translation of my scriptures, and all things whatsoever I shall command you; and it shall be fifty-five by sixty-five feet in the width thereof, and the length thereof, in the inner court; and there shall be a lower and a higher court; and this house shall be wholly dedicated unto the Lord, from the foundation thereof, for the work of the printing, in all things whatsoever I shall command you, to be holy, undefiled, according to the pattern, in all things, as it shall be given unto you.

4. And on the third lot shall my servant Hyrum Smith receive his inheritance. And on the first and second lots, on the north, shall my servants Reynolds Cahoon and Jared Carter receive their inheritance, that they may do the work which I have appointed unto them, to be a committee to build mine houses, according to the commandment which I, the Lord God, have given unto you. These two houses are not to be built until I give unto you a commandment concerning them.

5. And now I give unto you no more at this time. Amen.

* 1. Verily, thus saith the Lord unto you, whom I love, and whom I love I also chasten, that their sins may be forgiven, for with the chastisement I prepare a way for their deliverance, in all things, out of temptation; and I have loved you:- Wherefore, ye must needs be chastened, and stand rebuked before my face, for ye have sinned against me a very grievous sin, in that ye have not considered the great commandment in all things, that I have given unto you, concerning the building of mine house, for the preparation wherewith I design to prepare mine apostles to prune my vineyard for the last time, that I may bring to pass my strange act, that I may pour out my Spirit upon all flesh. But, behold, verily I say unto you, There are many who have been ordained among you, whom I have called, but few of them are chosen: they who are not

On Monday, June 3, a council met in the translating room in Kirtland, of which Joseph writes:—

"A conference of high priests convened in the translating room in Kirtland on the third of June, and the first case pre- sented was that of Dr. P. Hurlbut, who was accused of unchristian conduct with the women, while on a mission to the East. On investigation it was decided that his commission be taken from him, and that he be no longer a member of the Church of Christ.

Conference of high priests.

Hurlbut's trial.

"The next case before the conference was to ascertain what should be the dimensions or size of the house that is to be built for a house of worship and the school of the prophets, and received a revelation on the size of the house. The word of the Lord was, that it shall be fifty-five feet wide, and sixty-five feet long, in the inner court; and the conference appointed Joseph Smith, Jr., Sidney Rigdon, and Frederick G. Williams to obtain a draft or construction of the inner court of the house.

Dimensions of temple.

chosen have sinned a very grievous sin, in that they are walking in dark- ness at noonday; and for this cause, I gave unto you a commandment, that you should call your solemn assembly; that your fastings and your mourning might come up into the ears of the Lord of Sabaoth, which is, by interpretation, The Creator of the first day; the beginning and the end.

2. Yea, verily I say unto you, I gave unto you a commandment, that you should build an house, in the which house I design to endow those whom I have chosen with power from on high, for this is the promise of the Father unto you; therefore, I commanded you to tarry, even as mine apostles at Jerusalem; nevertheless my servants sinned a very grievous sin; and contentions arose in the school of the prophets, which was very grievous unto me, saith your Lord; therefore I sent them forth to be chastened.

3. Verily I say unto you, It is my will that you should build an house; if you keep my commandments, you shall have power to build it; if you keep not my commandments the love of the Father shall not continue with you; therefore you shall walk in darkness. Now here is wisdom and the mind of the Lord: let the house be built, not after the manner of the world, for I give not unto you, that ye shall live after the manner of the world; therefore let it be built after the manner which I shall show unto three of you, whom ye shall appoint and ordain unto this power. And the size thereof shall be fifty and five feet in width, and let it be sixty-five feet in length, in the inner court thereof; and let the lower part of the inner court be dedicated unto me for your sacrament offering, and for your preaching; and your fasting, and your praying, and the offering up your most holy desires unto me, saith your Lord. And let the higher part of the inner court, be dedicated unto me for the school of mine apostles, saith Son Ahman; or, in other words, Alphus; or, in other words, Omegus; even Jesus Christ your Lord. Amen.

"On the fourth a similar conference assembled at the same place and took into consideration how the French farm could be disposed of. The conference could not agree who should take charge of it, but all agreed to inquire of the Lord."— *Times and Seasons*, vol. 6, p. 784.

It will be seen by the above that Dr. Hurlbut, who afterwards played so conspicuous a part in ferreting out the Spalding Romance and in striving to connect Sidney Rigdon with it, was expelled from the church for immorality.

In answer to the inquiry mentioned above, a revelation was received.[s]

On Thursday, June 6, a conference was held at Kirtland. at which two very important items of business were transacted to which we wish to invite special attention; viz., the preparation for beginning the erection of a temple; and the hearing of Dr. Hurlbut's case, on appeal, and his confession of guilt. Joseph's account of it is as follows:—

"June 6. A conference of high priests assembled and chose Orson Hyde a clerk to the Presidency of the High Priesthood. This conference was more especially called to counsel the committee. who had been appointed to take the oversight of the building of the house

Erection of temple.

---

[s] 1. Behold, I say unto you, Here is wisdom whereby ye may know how to act concerning this matter, for it is expedient in me that this stake that I have set for the strength of Zion, should be made strong; therefore, let my servant Ahashdah take charge of the place which is named among you, upon which I design to build mine holy house; and again let it be divided into lots, according to wisdom, for the benefit of those who seek inheritances, as it shall be determined in council among you. Therefore, take heed that ye see to this matter, and that portion that is necessary to benefit mine order, for the purpose of bringing forth my word to the children of men, for, behold, verily I say unto you, This is the most expedient in me, that my word should go forth unto the children of men, for the purpose of subduing the hearts of the children of men, for your good. Even so. Amen.

2. And again, verily I say unto you, It is wisdom, and expedient in me, that my servant Zombre, whose offering I have accepted, and whose prayers I have heard, unto whom I give a promise of eternal life, inasmuch as he keepeth my commandments from henceforth; for he is a descendant of Seth, and a partaker of the blessings of the promise made unto his fathers. Verily I say unto you, It is expedient in me that he should become a member of the order, that he may assist in bringing forth my word unto the children of men; therefore ye shall ordain him unto this blessing; and he shall seek diligently to take away incumbrances, that are upon the house named among you, that he may dwell therein. Even so. Amen.

of the Lord. The conference voted that the committee (Reynolds Cahoon, Jared Carter, and Hyrum Smith) proceed immediately to commence building the house; or, to obtaining materials, stone, brick, lumber, etc., for the same.

"Doctor Hurlbut being dissatisfied with the decision of the council on his case, presented the following appeal:—

"'I, Doctor P. Hurlbut, having been tried before the bishop's council of high priests on a charge of unchristianlike con- Hurlbut duct with the female sex, and myself being absent on appeal. at the time, and considering that strict justice was not done me, I do, by these presents, most solemnly enter my appeal unto the President's council of high priests, for a rehearing, according to the privilege guaranteed to me in the laws of the church, which council is now assembled in the schoolroom, in Kirtland, this twenty-first day of June, 1833.'

"It was voted by the council present, when this was received, that Brother Hurlbut be granted a rehearing; and after prayer (which was customary at the opening of all councils of the church), the council proceeded to ordain two high priests to make out the number (twelve) that the council or church court might be organized. Brothers John and William Smith were ordained under the hands of Elder Rigdon, by the choice of the council.

"Brother Hurlbut's case was then laid before the court, and the testimony against him given in by Orson Hyde and Hyrum Smith, and duly investigated. The decision of the court was that Brother Hurlbut should be forgiven because of the liberal confession which he made. This court also decided that the bishop's council decided correctly on the case, and that Bro. Hurlbut's crime was sufficient to cut him off from the church; but on his confession he was restored. . . .

"June 23. Brother Doctor P. Hurlbut was called in question, by a general council; and Brother Gee, of Thompson, testified that Brother Hurlbut said that he deceived Joseph Smith's God, or the spirit by which he was actuated, etc. There was also corroborating testimony brought against him, by Brother Hodges, and the council cut him off from the church."—*Times and Seasons*, vol. 6, p. 785.

Monday, June 24, there was a conference of the elders held at Westfield, when the following plat of the city of Zion was adopted and ordered sent to the brethren in Zion:—

"This plat contains one mile square, all the squares of the plat contain ten acres each, being forty rods square. You will observe that the lots are laid off alternately in the squares; in one square running from the south and north to the line through the center of the square; and in the next, the lots run from the east and west to the center line. Each lot is four perches in front, and twenty back, making one half of an acre in each lot, so that no one street will be built on, entirely through the street; but one square the houses will stand on one street, and on the next one another, except the middle range of squares, which runs north and south, in which range are the painted squares.

"The lots are laid off in these squares north and south, all of them; because these squares are forty perches by sixty, being twenty perches longer than the other, their greatest length being east and west, and by running all these squares, north and south, it makes all the lots in the city of one size.

"The painted squares in the middle are for public buildings. The one without any figures is for storehouses for the bishop, and to be devoted to his use. Figure first is for temples for the use of the Presidency; the circles inside of the square are the places for the temples. You will see it contains twelve figures, two are for the temples of the lesser priesthood. It is also to contain twelve temples. The whole plat is supposed to contain from fifteen to twenty thousand people: you will therefore see that it will require twenty-four buildings to supply them with houses of worship, schools, etc.; and none of these temples are to be smaller than the one of which we send you a draft. This temple is to be built in the square marked figure first; and to be built where the circle is, which has a cross on it; on the north and south of the plat where the line is drawn, is to be laid off for barns, stables, etc., for the use of the city; so that no barns or stables will be in the city among the houses; the ground to be occupied by these must be laid off according to wisdom.

"On the north and south are to be laid off the farms for the agriculturist, and sufficient quantity of land to supply the whole plat; and if it cannot be laid off without going too great a distance from the city, there must also be some laid off on the east and west.

"When this square is thus laid off and supplied, lay off another in the same way, and so fill up the world in these last days; and let every man live in the city, for this is the city of Zion. All the streets are of one width, being eight perches wide. Also the space round the outer edge of the painted squares is to be eight perches between the temple and the street, on every side.

"No one lot, in this city, is to contain more than one house, and that to be built twenty-five feet back from the street, leaving a small yard in front, to be planted in a grove, according to the taste of the builder; the rest of the lot for gardens, etc.; all the houses to be built of brick and stone." —*Times and Seasons*, vol. 6, p. 786.

On June 25 the Presidency wrote a letter to W. W. Letter to Phelps and others in Zion, which contains some valuable instruction, and so we insert it:—

"*Brethren:*—We have received your last, containing a number of questions which you desire us to answer. This we do the more readily, as we desire with all our hearts the prosperity of Zion and the peace of her inhabitants; for we have as great an interest in the welfare of Zion as you can have:

"First, as respects getting the Book of Commandments bound, we think that it is not necessary. They will be sold well without binding, and there is no bookbinder to be had as we know of, nor are there materials to be had for binding without keeping the book too long from circulation. With regard to the Books of Mormon, which are in the hands of Brother Burket, we say to you, Get them from Brother Burket, give him a receipt for them in the name of the literary firm. Let Brother Gilbert pay Brother Chapin his money.

"We have not found the Book of Jasher, nor any of the other lost books mentioned in the Bible as yet; nor will we obtain them at present. Respecting the Apocrypha, the Lord said to us that there are many things in it which were true, and there were many things in it that were not true, and to those who desire it, it should be given by the Spirit to know the true from the false. We have received some revelations, within a short time back, which you will obtain in due time; as soon as we can get time we will review the manuscripts of the Book of Mormon, after which they will be forwarded to you.

"We commend the plan highly of your choosing a teacher to instruct the high priests, that they may be able to silence gainsayers. Concerning bishops, we recommend the following: Let Brother Isaac Morley be ordained second bishop in Zion, and let Brother John Corrill be ordained third. Let Brother Edward Partridge choose as counselors in their place, Brother Parley P. Pratt, and Brother Titus Billings, ordaining Brother Billings to the high priesthood. Let Brother Morley choose for his counselors, Brother Christian Whitmer, whom ordain to the high priesthood, and Bro. Newel Knight. Let Brother Corrill choose Brother Daniel Stanton and Brother Hezekiah Peck for his counselors; let Brother Hezekiah also be ordained to the high priesthood. . . .

"The truth triumphs gloriously in the East; multitudes are embracing it. I, Sidney, who write this letter, in behalf of the Presidency, had the privilege of seeing my aged mother baptized into the faith of the gospel, a few weeks since, at the advanced age of seventy-five. She now resides with me.

"We send by this mail, a draft of the city of Zion, with explanations, and a draft of the house to be built immediately, in Zion, for the Presidency, as well as all purposes of religion and instruction.

"Kirtland, the stake of Zion, is strengthening continually. When the enemies look at her they wag their heads and march along. We anticipate the day when the enemies will have fled away and be far from us. You will remember that the power of agency must be signed by the wives as well as the husbands, and the wives must be examined separate and apart from the husbands, the same as signing a deed, and a specification to that effect inserted at the bottom, by the justice before whom such acknowledgment is made, otherwise the power will be of none effect. . . .

"The following errors we have found in the commandments, as printed: Fortieth chapter, tenth verse, third line, instead of corruptible, put corrupted. Fourteenth verse of the same chapter, fifth line, instead of respecter to persons, put respecter of persons. Twenty-first verse, second line of the same chapter, instead of respecter to, put respecter of. Forty-fourth chapter, twelfth verse, last line, instead of hands, put heads.

"Brother Edward Partridge; Sir:—I proceed to answer your questions, concerning the consecration of property: First, it is not right to condescend to very great particulars in taking inventories. The fact is this: a man is bound by the law of the church to consecrate to the bishop before he can be considered a legal heir to the kingdom of Zion; and this, too, without constraint; and unless he does this he cannot be acknowledged before the Lord, on the church book: therefore, to condescend to particulars, I will tell you that every man must be his own judge how much he should receive, and how much he should suffer to remain in the hands of the bishop. I speak of those who consecrate more than they need for the support of themselves and their families.

"The matter of consecration must be done by the mutual consent of both parties; for, to give the bishop power to say how much every man shall have, and he be obliged to comply with the bishop's judgment, is giving to the bishop more power than a king has; and, upon the other hand, to let every man say how much he needs, and the bishop be obliged to comply with his judgment, is to throw Zion into confusion, and make a slave of the bishops. The fact is, there must be a balance or equilibrium of power between the bishop and the people; and thus harmony and good will, be preserved among you.

"Therefore, those persons consecrating property to the bishop in Zion, and then receiving an inheritance back, must show reasonably to the bishop that he wants as much as he claims. But in case the two parties cannot come to a mutual agreement, the bishop is to have nothing to do about receiving their consecrations; and the case must be laid before a council of twelve high priests; the bishop not being one of the council, but he is to lay the case before them. . . .

"We are not a little surprised to hear that some of our letters of a public nature, which we sent for the good of Zion, have been kept back from the bishop. This is conduct which we highly disapprobate.

"Answers to queries in Brother Phelps' letter of June 4: First, in relation to the poor. When the bishops are appointed according to our recommendation, it will devolve upon them to see to the poor, according to the laws of the church. In regard to the printing of the New Translation; it cannot be done until we can attend to it ourselves, and this we will do as soon as the Lord permits. . . .

"Say to the brethren, Hulets, and to all others that the Lord never authorized them to say that the Devil, nor his angels, nor the son of perdition should ever be restored, for their state of destiny was not revealed to man, is not revealed, nor ever shall be revealed, save to those who are made partakers thereof: consequently those who teach this doctrine have not received it of the Spirit of the Lord. Truly Brother Oliver declared it to be the doctrine of devils. We, therefore, command that this doctrine be taught no more in Zion. We sanction the decision of the bishop and his council, in relation to this doctrine's being a bar of communion.

"The number of disciples in Kirtland is about one hundred and fifty. We have commenced building the house of the Lord, in this place, and it goes on rapidly. Good news from the East and South of the success of the laborers is often saluting our ears. A general time of health among us; families all well: and day and night we pray for the salvation of Zion. . . .

"We conclude our letter by the usual salutation, in token of the new and everlasting covenant. We hasten to close because the mail is just going.

"JOSEPH SMITH, JR.
"SIDNEY RIGDON.
"F. G. WILLIAMS.

"P. S.—We feel gratified with the way which Brother

William W. Phelps is conducting the *Star* at present; we hope he will render it more and more interesting. In relation to the size of the bishopric: when Zion is once properly regulated there will be a bishop to each square of the size of the one we send you with this; but at present it must be done according to wisdom. It is needful, brethren, that you should be all of one heart and of one mind, in doing the will of the Lord. There should exist the greatest freedom and familiarity among the rulers in Zion. We were exceeding sorry to hear the complaint that was made in Brother Edward's letter, that the letters attending the olive leaf had been kept from him, as it is meet that he should know all things in relation to Zion, as the Lord has appointed him to be a judge in Zion. We hope, dear brethren, that the like circumstance will not take place again. When we direct letters to Zion, to any of the high priests, which pertains to the regulation thereof, we always design that they should be laid before the bishop, so as to enable him to perform his duty. We say so much hoping it will be received in kindness; and our brethren will be careful of each others feelings, and walk in love, honoring one another more than themselves, as is required of the Lord.

"Yours as ever."
—*Times and Seasons*, vol. 6, pp. 800-802.

We also insert a letter written to Zion by the Presidency, July 2, 1833:—

"KIRTLAND, July 2, 1833.

"*To the Brethren in Zion:*—We received your letters of June 7; one from Brothers William and Oliver, one from Brother

Letter
to Zion.

David Whitmer, and one from Brother S. Gilbert, for which we are thankful to our heavenly Father to hear of your welfare, as well as the prosperity of Zion. Having received your letters in the mail of to-day, we hasten to answer to go with to-morrow's mail.

"We are exceedingly fatigued owing to a great press of business. We this day finished the translating of the scriptures, for which we returned gratitude to our heavenly Father, and sat immediately down to answer your letters. . . .

"As to the gift of tongues, all we can say is, that in this place we have received it as the ancients did. We wish you, however, to be careful, lest in this you be deceived. Guard against evils which may arise from any accounts given of women, or otherwise; be careful in all things lest any root of bitterness spring up among you and thereby many be defiled. Satan will no doubt trouble you about the gift of tongues, unless you are careful; you cannot watch him too closely, nor pray too much. May the Lord give you wisdom in all things. In a letter mailed last week, you will doubtless, before you receive this, have obtained information about the New Translation. Consign the box of the Books of Commandments, to N. K. Whitney & Co., Kirtland, Geauga County, Ohio; care of Kelly & Walworth, Cleveland, Cuyahoga County, Ohio.

"I Sidney write this in great haste, in answer to yours to Brother Joseph, as I am going off immediately, in company with Brother Frederick, to proclaim the gospel; we think of starting to-morrow. Having finished the translation of the Bible, a few hours since, and needing some recreation, we know of no way we can spend our time more to divine acceptance, than endeavoring to build up his Zion, in these last days, as we are not willing to idle any time away, which can be spent to useful purposes. Doors are open continually for proclaiming; the spirit of bitterness among the people is fast subsiding, and a spirit of inquiry is taking its place. I proclaimed last Sunday at Chardon, our county seat. I had the courthouse. There was a general turnout, good attention, and a pressing invitation for more meetings, which will be granted if the Lord will, when we return from this tour.

"Brother Joseph is going to take a tour with Brother George James, of Brownhelm, as soon as Brother George comes to this place. We hope, our brethren, that the greatest freedom and frankness will exist between you and the bishop, not withholding from each other, any information from us, but communicate with the greatest freedom, lest you should produce evils of a serious character, and the Lord become offended: for know assuredly, if we, by our wickedness, bring evil on our own heads, the Lord will let us bear it till we get weary and hate iniquity.

"We conclude by giving our heartiest approbation to every measure calculated for the spread of the truth, in these last days; and our strongest desires, and sincerest prayers for the prosperity of Zion. Say to all the brethren and sisters in Zion, that they have our hearts, our best wishes, and the strongest desires of our spirits, for their welfare, temporal, spiritual, and eternal. And we salute you in the name of the Lord Jesus. Amen.

"SIDNEY RIGDON.
"JOSEPH SMITH, JR.
"F. G. WILLIAMS."

—*Times and Seasons*, vol. 6, pp. 802, 803

Early in July the mob in Missouri again renewed their hostilities, of which Joseph Smith writes:—

"July, which once dawned upon the virtue and independence of the United States, *now* dawned upon the savage barbarity and mobocracy of Missouri. Most of the clergy, acting as missionaries to the Indians, or to the frontier inhabitants, were among the most prominent characters that rose up and rushed on to destroy the rights of the church, as well as the lives of her members. One Pixley, who had been sent by the Missionary Society, to civilize and christianize the heathen of the West, was a black rod in the hand of Satan, as well as a poisoned shaft in the power of our foes, to spread lies and falsehoods.

Hostilities in Missouri.

"He followed writing horrible accounts to the religious papers in the East, to sour the public mind from time to time, besides using his influence among Indians and whites to overthrow the church. On the first of July he wrote a slanderous article entitled, 'Beware of false Prophets,' which he actually carried from house to house to incense the inhabitants against the church to mob them and drive them away.

"The July number of the *Evening and Morning Star* pursued a mild and pacific course, the first article therein, entitled 'Beware of false Prophets,' was calculated to disabuse the honest public mind from Pixley's falsehoods; and the caution against 'Free people of color' settling in Missouri, was sufficient to silence the fears of every sober mind, yet it was all in vain; the hour of trial must come: and, notwithstanding the Constitution of Missouri, as published in the same paper, says:—

"'Article 4. That all men have a natural and indefeasible right to worship Almighty God according to the dictates of their own consciences; and that no man can be compelled to erect, support, or attend any place of worship, or to maintain any minister of the gospel or teacher of religion; that no human authority can control or interfere with the rights of conscience; that no person can ever be hurt, molested, or restrained in his religious professions or sentiments, if he do not disturb others in their religious worship.

"'5. That no person, on account of his religious opinions, can be rendered ineligible to any office of trust or profit under this State; that no preference can ever be given by law to any sect or mode of worship,' yet, because the saints believed and taught differently from their neighbors, and according to the laws of heaven, in spiritual things, Satan said, 'Let there be a mob,' and a mob there was, and they drew up and published a manifesto, which will appear in its place."—*Times and Seasons*, vol. 6, p. 816.

The reader may understand the attitude of the church in Missouri regarding morals and religion, policy and politics, Letter of elders in Zion. by referring to an epistle published in the July number of the *Evening and Morning Star*, entitled, "The elders stationed in Zion to the churches abroad, in love; greeting."⁴ By this it will be seen that while they

---

⁴ *Dear Brethren:*—One year having passed since we addressed the churches abroad on the situation of Zion and the state of the gathering, it seems to be our duty to again address the saints on the same subjects. Although you frequently learn through the medium of the *Star* our situation and progress, yet we indulge a hope that a circular from us, particularly setting these things forth at this time, will be received by you in fellowship.

We have abundant reason to thank the Lord for his goodness and mercy manifested unto us since we were planted in this land.

With the exception of the winter season, the gathering has continued slowly. At present we have not the exact number of the disciples, but suppose that there are near seven hundred. Include these, with their

admit the wrongdoing of some, they teach that all should be industrious; that all should pay just debts; that the laws of

children, and those who belong to families, and the number will probably amount to more than twelve hundred souls.

Many have been planted upon their inheritances, where, blessed with a fruitful soil and a healthy climate, they are beginning to enjoy some of the comforts of life, in connection with peace and satisfaction of pure and undefiled religion, which is to visit the widow and the fatherless in their afflictions and to keep ourselves unspotted from the world. This brings down the blessings of peace and love from our Father, and confirms our faith in the promise that we shall see him in the flesh, when he comes to be glorified in his saints and to be admired in all them that believe in that day.

Here let us remark that our duty urges us to notice a few letters which have been sent from this place by persons seeking the loaves and fishes, or by such as have lost their standing among men of character in the world. In the letters alluded to are some facts, but the most of them are false.

It is said that women go out to work. This is a fact, and not only women, but men too; for in the Church of Christ all that are able have to work to fulfill the commandments of the Lord; and the situation in which many have come up here has brought them under the necessity of seeking employment from those who do not belong to the church; yet we can say as far as our knowledge extends, that they have been honorably compensated. And we are willing that the decree concerning mankind, thou shalt eat thy bread by the sweat of thy brow, should be fulfilled. Members of the church have, or will have, "deeds" in their own name.

One Bates from New London, Ohio, who subscribed fifty dollars for the purpose of purchasing lands and the necessaries for the saints, after his arrival here sued Edward Partridge and obtained a judgment for the same. Bates shortly after denied the faith and ran away on Sunday, leaving debts unpaid. We do not mention this to cast reflections, but to give a sample of his work manifested since he came to this land.

No man that has consecrated property to the Lord, for the benefit of the poor and the needy, by a deed of gift according to the laws of the land, has thought of suing for it, any more than the men of the world, who give or donate to build meetinghouses, or colleges, or to send missionaries to India or the Cape of Good Hope.

Every saint that has come to this land to escape the desolations which await the wicked, and prepare for the coming of the Lord, is well satisfied with the country and the order of the kingdom of our God; and we are happy to say that the inhabitants of Zion are growing in grace and in the knowledge of those things which lead to peace and eternal glory. And our hearts are filled with thanksgiving for the privilege of bearing this testimony concerning our brethren on this land.

One object in writing this epistle is to give some instructions to those who come up to the land of Zion. Through a mistaken idea many of the brethren abroad that had property have given some away, and sacrificed some, they hardly know how. This is not right, nor according to the commandments.

We would advise in the first place that every disciple, if in his power, pay his just debts, so as to owe no man, and then if he has any property left, let him be careful of it; and he can help the poor by consecrating some for their inheritances; for as yet there has not been enough consecrated to plant the poor in inheritances according to the regulation of the church and the desire of the faithful.

the land should be observed; that great care should be used
lest too many of the poor should be brought into the country

This might have been done had such as had property been prudent.
It seems as though a notion was prevalent in Babylon that the Church of
Christ was a common stock concern. This ought not so to be, for it is
not the case. When a disciple comes to Zion for an inheritance it is his
duty, if he has anything to consecrate to the Lord, for the benefit of the
poor and the needy, or to purchase lands, to consecrate it according to the law of the Lord, and also according to the law of the
land; and the Lord has said that in keeping his law we have no
need to break the laws of the land. And we have abundant reason
to be thankful that we are permitted to establish ourselves under the
protection of a government that knows no exceptions to sect or society,
but gives all its citizens a privilege of worshiping God according to their
own desire.

Again, while in the world, it is not the duty of a disciple to exhaust all
his means in bringing the poor to Zion; and this because, if all should do
so, there would be nothing to put in the storehouse in Zion, for the purpose which the Lord has commanded.

Do not think brethren by this that we would advise or direct that the
poor be neglected in the least; this is not the desire of our hearts; for we
are mindful of the word of our Father, which informs us that in his
bosom it is decreed that the poor and meek of the earth shall possess it.

The welfare of the poor has always a place in our hearts; yet we are
confident that our experience, even had we nothing else to prompt us to
advise on this point, and that wholly for the good of the cause in which
we labor, would be sufficient in the minds of our brethren abroad to excuse a plainness on this important part of our subject.

To see numbers of disciples come to this land destitute of means to
procure an inheritance, and much less the necessaries of life, awakens a
sympathy in our bosoms of no ordinary feeling; and we should do injustice to the saints were we to remain silent, when, perhaps, a few words
by way of advice may be the means of instructing them that hereafter
great difficulties may be avoided.

For the disciples to suppose that they can come to this land without
aught to eat, or to drink, or to wear, or anything to purchase these necessaries with, is a vain thought. For them to suppose that their clothes
and shoes will not wear out upon the journey, when the whole of it lies
through a country where there are thousands of sheep from which wool
in abundance can be procured to make them garments, and cattle upon
a thousand hills to afford leather for shoes, is just as vain.

The circumstances of the saints in gathering to the land of Zion in
these last days are very different from those of the children of Israel,
after they despised the promised rest of the Lord, after they were brought
out of the land of Egypt. Previous to that the Lord promised them, if
they would obey his voice and keep his commandments, that he would
send the hornet before them and drive out those nations which then inhabited the promised land, so that they might have peaceable possession
of the same, without the shedding of blood. But in consequence of their
unbelief and rebellion they were compelled to obtain it by the sword,
with the sacrifice of many lives.

But to suppose that we can come up here and take possession of this
land by the shedding of blood, would be setting at nought the law of the
glorious gospel, and also the word of our great Redeemer; and to suppose
that we can take possession of this country, without making regular pur-
chases of the same according to the laws of our nation, would be

at one time, and that the taking of the land by force is condemned; also that prudence and economy in all things is taught.

We here present to our readers the appeal of the saints to

reproaching this great republic, in which the most of us were born, and under whose auspices we all have protection.

We feel as though enough was said on this point, knowing that a word to the wise is sufficient, and that all our brethren are aware of the fact that all the tithes cannot be gathered into the storehouse of the Lord, that the windows of heaven may be opened and a blessing poured out that there is not room enough to contain it, if all the means of the saints are exhausted before they reach the place where they can have a privilege of so doing.

Do not conclude from these remarks brethren that we doubt in the least that the Lord will fail to provide for his saints in these last days, or that we would extend our hands to steady his ark; for this is not the case. We know that the saints have the unchangeable word of God that they shall be provided for; yet we know if any are imprudent, or lavish, or negligent, or indolent in taking that proper care and making that proper use of what the Lord has made them stewards over, which is their duty to, they are not counted wise; for a strict account of every one's stewardship is required, not only in time, but will be in eternity.

Neither do we apprehend that we shall be considered as putting out our hands to steady the ark of God by giving advice to our brethren upon important points relative to their coming to Zion, when the experience of almost two years' gathering has taught us to revere that sacred word from heaven, "Let not your flight be in haste, but let all things be prepared before you."

Then brethren we would advise that where there are many poor in a church, that the elders counsel together and make preparations to send a part at one time and a part at another. And let the poor rejoice in that they are exalted, but the rich in that they are made low, for there is no respect of persons in the sight of the Lord.

The disciples of Christ, blessed with immediate revelations from him, should be wise and not take the way of the world nor build air castles, but consider that when they have been gathered to Zion, means will be needed to purchase their inheritances, and means will be needed to purchase food and raiment for at least one year; or, at any rate, food; and where disciples or churches are blessed with means to do as much as this, they would be better off in Zion than in the world, troubled as it is, and will shortly be, with plagues, famines, pestilences, and utter destructions upon the ungodly.

On the subject of false reports which are put in circulation by evil-minded men, to ridicule the idea of the gathering of Israel in these last days, we would say to our brethren abroad, believe them not: *The Evening and the Morning Star* was established expressly to publish the truth and the word of the Lord, that the saints might not be deceived by such as make broad the borders of their garments and love the uppermost rooms at feasts; yea, by such as bind heavy burdens which are grievous to be borne, and lay them upon men's shoulders, but will not move them with their fingers. Yea, we give this caution that the disciples may not give heed to the gainsaying of those who seek the honor of this world and the glory of the same, rather than seek the honor of God and his glory; nor those who have turned away from the Church of Christ and denied the faith delivered to his saints in these last days.

Governor Dunklin, in which is incorporated the resolutions passed by the citizens of Jackson County; also the reply of Governor Dunklin. Each of these documents speaks for itself, hence a lengthy comment would be superfluous:—

Appeal to the Governor.

"*To His Excellency, Daniel Dunklin, Governor of the State of Missouri.*

"We, the undersigned, citizens of the republic of the

Brethren, the Lord has begun to gather his children, even Israel, that they may prepare to enter into and enjoy his rest when he comes in his glory, and he will do it. No matter what our ideas and notions may be upon the subject; no matter what foolish report the wicked may circulate to gratify an evil disposition, the Lord will continue to gather the righteous, and destroy the wicked, till the sound goes forth, "It is finished."

It ought to be known abroad that much improvement is needed in the cattle, sheep, and hogs, in this part of the country. For the sake of comfort and convenience, as cows here are worth from ten to fifteen dollars, our brethren would do well, and we would advise them, to purchase before they arrive in this region.

In fact, if they journey according to the commandments of the Lord, pitching their tents by the way, like Israel in days of old, it would be no more than right to drive cows enough to supply every family, or company, with milk on the way.

They would then have them when they arrived here; and if they selected of the best breeds, they would lay a foundation for improvement, a thing of which all our brethren who are acquainted with raising stock will at once see the propriety.

The sheep of this State are large, but as their wool is coarse, the breed would soon be improved if our brethren would drive with them some Merinos or Saxony. As soon as wool and flax are had among the brethren, sufficient for the purpose, they will manufacture cloth for their own use in the church.

The swine in this country are not good, being the old-fashioned shack breed, and much inferior to the large white grass breed of the Eastern States. If any could introduce this breed into the church in Zion, what little pork might be wanted in the winter would be much better, and easier raised.

It is a matter of some surprise to us that our brethren should come up to the land of Zion, as many do, without bringing garden seeds, and even seeds of all kinds. The Jaredites and Nephites took with them of all kinds; and the Jaredites all kinds of animals. And although the Lord has said that it was his business to provide for his saints, yet he has not said that he would do it unless they kept his commandments.

And notwithstanding the fullness of the earth is for the saints, they can never expect it unless they use the means put into their hands to obtain the same in the manner provided by our Lord. When you flee to Zion we enjoin the word, Prepare all things that you may be ready to labor for a living, for the Lord has promised to take the curse off the land of Zion in his own due time, and the willing and the obedient will eat the good of the same; not the idle, for they are to be had in remembrance before the Lord.

One very important requisition for the saints that come up to the land

United States of America, inhabitants of the State of Missouri, and residents of Jackson County, members of the Church of Christ (vulgarly called Mormons;, believing in

of Zion is. that before they start they procure a certificate from three elders of the church, or from the bishop in Ohio, according to the commandments; and when they arrive to present it to the bishop in Zion, otherwise they are not considered wise stewards, and cannot be received into fellowship with the church till they prove themselves by their own goodness.

Some of our brethren may at the first instant think, perhaps, that this is useless and formal; but a few reflections will be sufficient for them to see the propriety of it, and more especially when they learn that it is a commandment given us of our Lord.

Our brethren will find an extract of the law of this State relative to free people of color, on another page of this paper. Great care should be taken on this point. The saints must shun every appearance of evil. As to slaves, we have nothing to say. In connection with the wonderful events of this age much is doing towards abolishing slavery and colonizing the blacks in Africa.

The foregoing remarks have been addressed to our brethren abroad, considered as one general body, and have been designed as general information to all. We cannot close this epistle compatible with our duty without particularly addressing ourselves to our brethren, the elders, to whom is intrusted the preaching the everlasting gospel, the glad tidings of salvation to Israel, and to all the Gentiles, if they will listen to the invitation.

Brethren, we are aware of your many afflictions, or at least in part, some of us having been eyewitnesses to the things of God, and having been called to bear testimony of the same from the first since this gospel has been proclaimed in these last days. The desire of our hearts for your prosperity we can truly say is inexpressible, for when you are prospered we are, and when you are blessed we are blessed also. The afflictions which you are necessarily called to undergo in these days of tribulation and vengeance upon the wicked call forth from our hearts unceasing prayers to our common Parent in your behalf. that you may be enabled to deliver his message in the demonstration of his Spirit. and call together his elect from the ends of the earth to the place of the name of the Lord of hosts, even to Mount Zion.

By those few expressions you will see, brethren, how important we view your callings. We do not consider that it is our duty to direct you in your missions, but we will give you in few words what we have reason to expect relative to the gathering of the saints, according to the revelations of the Lord.

By the authority of your callings and ordinances you no doubt will admit that it will be expected that you will know your duty, and at all times and in all places teach the disciples theirs; but we are sorry to say that in some instances some of our brethren have failed to do so.

We would remind our brethren of a clause in the Covenants which informs us that all who are ordained in this church are to be ordained according to the gifts and callings of God unto them, by the power of the Holy Ghost which is in the one who ordains them. We would also remind them of one valuable caution recorded in Paul's first letter to Timothy, which says, "Lay hands suddenly on no man, neither be partaker of other men's sins."

Those cautions, however, are particularly addressed to our young brethren in the ministry. We know that many of our brethren are wise

God, and worshiping him according to his revealed will contained in the Holy Bible, and the fullness of the gospel contained in the Book of Mormon, and the revelations and

in these important parts of their labors, and have rid their garments of the blood of this generation, and are approved before the Lord.

We will proceed further brethren to notice some particular items immediately connected with your duties and what, as we said before, we have reason to expect from you, according to the revelations. In one given December 4, 1831, we learn that it is the duty of the elders of the church in the East, to render an account of their stewardship unto the bishop appointed unto the church in that part of the Lord's vineyard.

The Lord says: "And now, verily I say unto you, that as every elder in this part of the vineyard [the East], must give an account of his stewardship unto the bishop in this part of the vineyard, a certificate from the judge or bishop in this part of the vineyard, unto the bishop in Zion, rendereth every man acceptable, and answereth all things for an inheritance, and to be received as a wise steward, and as a faithful laborer; otherwise he shall not be accepted of the bishop in Zion.

"And now, verily I say unto you, let every elder who shall give an account unto the bishop of the church, in this part of the vineyard [the East], be recommended by the church or churches, in which he labors, that he may render himself and his accounts approved in all things."

We hope brethren that you will be particular to teach the disciples abroad prudence and economy in all things. Teach them in plainness, that without regular recommends they cannot be received in fellowship with the church in Zion until after they have proven themselves worthy by their godly walk. And those who are recommended by you, we expect, will be such as are personally known to you to be disciples indeed, and worthy the confidence of all saints.

Viewing the quotation relative to your obtaining a certificate from the bishop in the East concerning your worthiness, you cannot blame us, brethren, if we are strict on this point. It may be understood therefore, by our brethren, the elders, who come from the East, and do not bring a regular certificate showing that their labors have been accepted there, that they cannot be accepted in Zion. We do not set ourselves up as judges in this; we have only a desire to see the order of our Redeemer's kingdom observed in all things; for his commandments are precious with us: we have them in our hands, and they are sacred to our hearts.

Our brethren who labor in the churches a distance to the west of the residence of the bishop in the East, who do not render their accounts to him, should be particular to bring recommends from the churches in which they do labor, and present them, with the accounts of their labors to the bishop immediately after their arrival here. And those elders who labor continually in preaching the gospel to the world, should also be particular to render their accounts of the same, that they may show themselves approved in all things, and be known to be worthy of the high office in which they stand in the Church of Christ.

Having said considerable concerning those particular points which are necessary to be observed by our brethren who journey to this land, and also a few words to the elders, we deem it a privilege before we conclude to say something more to the church at large. In the previous remarks, however, we presume our brethren may make many improvements; and, perhaps discover some errors; if so, we can say, that the best of motives have prompted us to write to our brethren; and if some small errors are to be found, we are certain that the general ideas are correct, and will

commandments of God through Jesus Christ, respectfully
show:—

"That we your petitioners, having purchased lands of the
United States, and of the State of Missouri, and of the inhabitants of said State, for the purpose of im,roving the
same and peaceably enjoying our rights, privileges, immunities, and religion, according to the Constitution and laws of the
State and National Governments, have suffered unjustly and
unlawfully in property, in person, and in reputation, as follows: First. In the spring of 1832, some persons, in the
deadly hours of the night, commenced stoning or brickbatting some of our houses and breaking in our windows, disturbing ourselves. our wives, and our children; and also,
some few days after, they called a county meeting to consult
measures to remove us, but after some confusion among
themselves, they dispersed with doing no more than threatening, on that day. In the fall of the same year, they or
some one, burned a large quantity of hay in the stack; and
soon after commenced shooting into some of our houses, and
at many times insulting with abusive language.

"Secondly. About the middle of July last, yea, in fact,
previous, they commenced brickbatting our houses again,
and breaking in our windows. At this time, July 18, the following document was in circulation:—

" 'We, the undersigned, citizens of Jackson County, believing that an important crisis is at hand as regards our civil
society, in consequence of a pretended religious sect of people that have settled and are still settling in our county,
styling themselves Mormons, and intending as we do to rid
our society "peaceably if we can, forcibly if we must," and
believing as we do that the arm of the civil law does not
afford us a guarantee, or at least a sufficient one against the

be a means of doing good, if those who are immediately interested in the
same, give heed to them.

Dear brethren in the new covenant, accept this as a token for a salutation in the name of the Lord Jesus Christ, from your brethren in Zion.
While we are permitted to witness the great things which are continually taking place in fulfillment of the prophecies concerning the last
days, as the children of God are gathered home to prepare themselves
for the supper of the Lamb, our language, that is, the English tongue,
fails to express our joy.—*Evening and Morning Star*, pp. 219-222.

evils which are now inflicted upon us, and seem to be increasing by the said religious sect, deem it expedient, and of the highest importance, to form ourselves into a company for the better and easier accomplishment of our purpose, a purpose which we deem it almost superfluous to say, is justified as well by the law of nature, as by the law of self-preservation.

" 'It is more than two years since the first of these fanatics or knaves (for one or the other they undoubtedly are) made their first appearance amongst us, and pretending as they did and now do to hold personal communication and converse face to face with the most high God; to receive communications and revelations direct from heaven; to heal the sick by laying on hands; and, in short, to perform all the wonder-working miracles wrought by the inspired apostles and prophets of old.

" 'We believed them deluded fanatics or weak and designing knaves, and that they and their pretensions would soon pass away; but in this we were deceived. The arts of a few designing leaders amongst them have thus far succeeded in holding them together as a society, and since the arrival of the first of them they have been daily increasing in numbers, and if they had been respectable citizens in society, and thus deluded they would have been entitled to our pity rather than to our contempt and hatred; but from their appearance, from their manners, and from their conduct, since their coming among us, we have every reason to fear that with but very few exceptions, they were of the very dregs of that society from which they came; lazy, idle, and vicious. This we conceive is not idle assertion, but a fact susceptible of proof, for with these few exceptions above-named, they brought into our county little or no property with them, and left less behind them, and we infer that those only yoked themselves to the Mormon car who had nothing earthly or heavenly to lose by the change; and we fear that if some of the leaders amongst them had paid the forfeit due to crime, instead of being chosen embassadors of the Most High, they would have been inmates of solitary cells. But their conduct here stamps their characters in their true colors. More than a year since it was ascertained that they had been tampering with our slaves and endeavoring to sow dissensions and ra'se seditions amongst them. Of this their Mormon leaders were informed, and they said they would deal with any of their members who should again in like case offend. But how specious are appearances. In a late number of the *Star*, published in Independence by the leaders of the sect, there is an article inviting free negroes and mulattoes from other States to become Mormons and remove and settle among us. This exhibits them in still more odious colors. It manifests a desire on the part of their society to inflict on our society an injury that they know would be to us entirely insupportable, and one of the surest means of driving us from the county; for it would require none of the supernatural gifts that they pretend to, to see that the introduction of such a caste amongst us would corrupt our blacks and instigate them to bloodshed.

" 'They openly blaspheme the most high God and cast contempt on his holy religion by pretending to receive revelations direct from heaven, by pretending to speak unknown tongues by direct inspiration, and by diverse pretenses derogatory of God and religion, and to the utter subversion of human reason.

" 'They declare openly that their God hath given them this county of land, and that sooner or later they must and will have the possession of our lands for an inheritance, and in fine they have conducted themselves on many other occasions in such a manner that we believe it a duty we owe ourselves, to our wives and children, to the cause of public morals, to remove them from among us, as we are not prepared to give up our pleasant places and goodly possessions to them, or to receive into the bosom of our families as fit companions for our wives and daughters the degraded and corrupted free negroes and mulattoes that are now invited to settle among us.

" 'Under such a state of things even our beautiful county would cease to be a desirable residence, and our situation intolerable! We, therefore, agree, that after timely warning, and receiving an adequate compensation for what little property they cannot take with them, they refuse to leave us in peace, as they found us, we agree to use such means as may be sufficient to remove them, and to that end we each pledge to each other our bodily powers, our lives, fortunes, and sacred honors.

"'We will meet at the courthouse at the town of Independence, on Saturday next, 20th inst., to consult ulterior movements.'

"Among the hundreds of names attached to the above document were: Lewis Franklin, Jailer; Samuel C. Owens, County Clerk; Russel Hicks, Deputy Clerk; R. W. Cummins. Indian Agent; Jones H. Flournoy, Post Master; S. D. Lucas, Colonel and Judge of the Court; Henry Childs, Attorney at Law; N. K. Olmstead, M. D.; John Smith, J. P.; Samuel Weston, J. P.; William Brown, Constable; Abner F. Staples, Captain; Thomas Pitcher, Deputy Constable; Moses G. Wilson, Thomas Wilson, Merchants.

"On Saturday, the 20th July last, according to the foregoing document, there assembled suddenly in the town of Independence at the courthouse between four and five hundred persons who sent Robert Johnson, James Campbell, Moses Wilson, Joel F. Childs, Richard Bristoe, Abner F. Staples, Gan Johnson, Lewis Franklin, Russell Hicks, S. D. Lucas, Thomas Wilson, James M. Hunter, and Richard Simpson, to some of your petitioners; namely, Edward Partridge, A. S. Gilbert, John Corrill, Isaac Morley, John Whitmer, and W. W. Phelps, and demanded that we should immediately stop the publication of the *Evening and Morning Star*, and close printing in Jackson County, and that we as elders of said church should agree to remove out of the county forthwith. We asked for three months, for consideration. They would not grant it. We asked for ten days. They would not grant it but said fifteen minutes was the longest, and refused to hear any reasons. Of course the conversation broke up.

"The four or five hundred persons, as a mob, then proceeded to demolish or raze to the ground the printing office and dwelling house of W. W. Phelps & Co. Mrs. Phelps, with a sick infant child and the rest of her children, together with the furniture in the house, were thrown out doors, the press was broken, the type pied, the book work, furniture, apparatus, property, etc., of the office were principally destroyed and the office thrown down, whereby seven hands were thrown out of employment and three families left destitute of the means of subsistence.

"The loss of the whole office, including the stoppage of the *Evening and Morning Star*, a monthly paper, and the *Upper Missouri Advertiser*, a weekly paper, was about six thousand dollars, without the damages, which must result in consequence of their suspension.

"The mob then proceeded to demolish the storehouse and destroy the goods of Gilbert, Whitney & Co., but Mr. Gilbert assuring them that the goods should be packed by the 23d inst., they then stopped the destruction of property and proceeded to do personal violence. They took Edward Partridge, the Bishop of the Church, from his dwelling house by force, and a Mr. Allen, and stripping them of their coats, vests, and hats, or caused them to do it themselves, tarred and feathered them in the presence of the mob before the courthouse. They caught other members of the church to serve them in like manner, but they made their escape. With horrid yells and the most blasphemous epithets, they sought for other leading elders, but found them not. It being late, they adjourned until the 23d inst.

"On the 23d inst., early in the day, the mob again assembled to the number of about five hundred, many of them armed with rifles, dirks, pistols, clubs, and whips; one or two companies riding into town bearing the red flag, raising again the *horrid yell*. They proceeded to take some of the leading elders by force, declaring it to be their intention to whip them from fifty to five hundred lashes apiece, to demolish their dwelling houses, and let their negroes loose to go through our plantations and lay open our fields for the destruction of our crops; whereupon John Corrill, John Whitmer, W. W. Phelps, A. S. Gilbert, Edward Partridge, and Isaac Morley, made no resistance, but offered themselves a ransom for the church, willing to be scourged or die, if that would appease their anger toward the church; but being assured by the mob that every man, woman, and child would be whipped or scourged until they were driven out of the county, as the mob declared that they or the Mormons must leave the county, or they or the Mormons must die.

"The mob then chose a new committee, consisting of Samuel C. Owens, Leonidas Oldham, G. W. Simpson, M. L Irwin, John Harris, Henry Childs, Harvey H. Younger, Hugh H. Brazeale, N. K. Olmstead, James C. Sadler, William Bowers, Benjamin Majors, Zachariah Waller, Harman Gregg, Aaron Overton, and Samuel Weston, who with Edward Partridge, Isaac Morley, John Corrill, W. W. Phelps, A. S. Gilbert, and John Whitmer, entered into the following stipulation:—

" 'Memorandum of agreement between the undersigned of the Mormon society, in Jackson County, Missouri, and a committee appointed by a public meeting of the citizens of said county, made the 23d day of July, 1833.

" 'It is understood that the undersigned members of the society do give their solemn pledge each for himself, as follows; to wit:—

" 'That Oliver Cowdery, W. W. Phelps, William E. McLellin, Edward Partridge, Lyman Wight, Simeon Carter, Peter and John Whitmer, and Harvey Whitlock, shall remove with their families out of this county on or before the first day of January next, and that they, as well as the two hereinafter named, use all their influence to induce all the brethren now here to remove as soon as possible—one half, say, by the first of January next, and all by the first day of April next; to advise and try all means in their power to stop any more of their sect from moving to this country; and as to those now on the road, they will use their influence to prevent their settling permanently in the county, but that they shall only make arrangements for temporary shelter, till a new location is agreed on for the society. John Corrill and A. S. Gilbert are allowed to remain as general agents to wind up the business of the society, so long as necessity shall require; and said Gilbert may sell out his merchandise now on hand, but is to make no new importations.

" 'The *Star* is not again to be published, nor a press set up by any of the society in this county.

" 'If the said Edward Partridge and W. W. Phelps move their families by the first day of January as aforesaid, that they themselves will be allowed to go and come in order to transact and wind up their business.

" 'The committee pledge themselves to use all their influence to prevent any violence being used so long as a compliance with the foregoing terms is observed by the parties concerned.' To which agreement is subscribed the names of the above-named committee, as also those of the Mormon brethren named in the report as having been present.

"The damages, which your petitioners have sustained in consequence of this outrage and stipulation are at present incalculable. A great number of industrious inhabitants who were dependent on their labors for support have been thrown out of employment and are kept so by the threatenings of those who composed the mob. [See their resolutions as published in the *Western Monitor*, numbers 1, 2, 3, 4, and 5.] In estimating the damages which have resulted from the beginning to this time from those illegal and inhuman proceedings against your poor and persecuted petitioners, were they to name many thousands of dollars, it would be short of a remuneration. Most of the mechanics' shops have been closed, two pair of blacksmith's bellows have been cut in pieces. Our merchant, as you will see by the foregoing stipulation, has been forbidden to import or bring into the country any more goods, by which his business has been ruined. Soon after the above stipulation was made, some of your petitioners proceeded to make a new location in Van Buren County on the south, but the settlers in that county drew up an agreement among themselves to drive us from that county after we had commenced laboring there; they threatened to shoot our cattle and destroy our labor, and in fact, 'The foxes have holes and the birds of the air have nests, but we have not where to lay our heads'—We were obliged to return.

"Since the stipulation was entered into some of our houses have been broken open and the inmates threatened to be

hot if they stirred, and also, some of our houses have been
stoned or brickbatted.

"Also, that since some publications have appeared in the
Western Monitor and other papers, censuring the conduct of
the mob, the *leaders have begun to threaten life*, declaring that
f any of the Mormons attempted to seek redress by law or
otherwise, for character, person, or property, they would
lie!

"Now therefore, for ourselves, as members of the church
we declare, with the exception of poverty, which has
not yet become a crime, by the laws of the land, that the
crimes charged against us (so far as we are acquainted) contained in the documents above written, and those in the proceedings of the mob, as published in the *Western Monitor* of
August 2, *are not true.* In relation to inviting free people
of color to emigrate to this section of country, and other matters relative to our society, see the 109th, 10th, and 11th
pages of the *Evening and Morning Star*, and the *Extra* accompanying the same, dated July 16, which are annexed to this
petition. Our situation is a critical one; we are located upon
the western limits of the State, and of the United States—
where desperadoes can commit outrages, and even murder,
and escape, in a few minutes, beyond the reach of process;
where the most abandoned of all classes from almost every
State may too often pass to the Mexican states, or to the
more remote regions of the Rocky Mountains to escape the
grasp of justice; where numerous tribes of Indians, located
by the general government amid the corrupting influence of
midday mobs; might massacre our defenseless women and
children with impunity.

"Influenced by the precepts of our beloved Savior, when
we have been smitten on the one cheek we have turned the
other also; when we have been sued at the law and our coat
been taken, we have given them our cloak also; when they
have compelled us to go with them a mile we have gone with
them twain. We have borne the above outrages without
murmuring. but we cannot patiently bear them any longer;
according to the laws of God and man we have borne enough.
Believing, with all honorable men. that whenever that fatal

hour shall arrive that the poorest citizen's person, property, or rights and privileges, shall be trampled upon by a lawless mob with impunity, that moment a dagger is plunged into the heart of the Constitution, and the Union must tremble! Assuring ourselves that no republican will suffer the liberty of the press, the freedom of speech, and the liberty of conscience, to be silenced by a mob, without raising a helping hand, to save his country from disgrace, we solicit assistance to obtain our rights, holding ourselves amenable to the laws of our country whenever we transgress them.

"Knowing as we do that the threats of this mob, in most cases have been put into execution; and knowing also, that every officer, civil and military, with a very few exceptions, has pledged his life and honor to force us from the county, dead or alive; and believing that civil process cannot be served without the aid of the Executive; and not wishing to have the blood of our defenseless women and children to stain the *land* which has once been stained by the blood of our fathers to purchase our liberty;—we appeal to the Governor for aid; asking him by express proclamation or otherwise to raise a sufficient number of troops, who, with us, may be empowered to defend our rights, that we may sue for damages in the loss of property—for abuse, for defamation, as to ourselves, and if advisable try for treason against the government; that the law of the land may not be defied nor nullified, but peace restored to our country. And we will ever pray."

"CITY OF JEFFERSON, Executive Department,
"October 19, 1833.

"To Edward Partridge, W. W. Phelps, Isaac Morley, John Corrill, A. S. Gilbert, John Whitmer and others:—

"Your memorial soliciting my interposition against violence threatened you, and redresses for injuries received by a portion of the citizens of Jackson County, has been received, and its contents duly considered. His reply. I should think myself unworthy the confidence with which I have been honored by my fellow-citizens, did I not promptly employ all the means which the Constitution and laws have placed at my disposal to avert the calamities with which you are threatened.

"Ours is a Government of laws. To them we owe all obedience, and their faithful administration is the best guarantee for the enjoyment of our rights.

"No citizen, nor number of citizens, have a right to take the redress of their grievances, whether real or *imaginary*, into their own hands. Such conduct strikes at the very existence of society, and subverts the foundation on which it is based. Not being willing to persuade myself that any portion of the citizens of the State of Missouri are so lost to a sense of these truths as to require the exercise of *force*, in order to insure a respect for them.

"After advising with the Attorney General, and exercising my best judgment, I would advise you to make a trial of the efficacy of the laws. The judge of your circuit is a conservator of the peace. If an affidavit is made before him by any of you that your lives are threatened and you believe them in danger, it would be his duty to have the offenders apprehended and bind them to keep the peace. Justices of the Peace in their respective counties have the same authority, and it is made their duty to exercise it. Take, then, this course, obtain a warrant, let it be placed in the hands of the proper officer, and the experiment will be tested whether the laws can be peaceably executed or not. In the event they cannot be, and that fact is officially notified to me, my duty will require me to take such steps as will enforce a favorable execution of them.

"With regard to the injuries you have sustained by destruction of property, etc., the law is open to redresses, I cannot permit myself to doubt that the courts will be open to you, nor that you will find difficulty in procuring legal advocates to sue for damages therein.

"Respectfully, Your obedient servant.

"DANIEL DUNKLIN.

"W. W. Phelps, Esq., Independence, Mo."

—*Evening and Morning Star*, pp. 226-231.

As the resolutions above-quoted refer to an article in the *Evening and Morning Star*, we here present this article enti-

tled, "Free People of Color," found on pages 218 and 219
of volume 2 of the *Evening and Morning Star*. By
carefully perusing this, all may see just how
much truth, if any, there is in the statement that it invited
"free negroes and mulattoes from other States to become
Mormons and remove and settle among us":—

Free Peo-
ple of Color.

"To prevent any misunderstanding among the churches
abroad, respecting free people of color, who may think of
coming to the western boundaries of Missouri, as members
of the church, we quote the following clauses from the laws
of Missouri:—

" 'Section 4. Be it further enacted, that hereafter no free
negro or mulatto, other than a citizen of some one of
the United States, shall come into or settle in this State
under any pretext whatever; and upon complaint made to
any justice of the peace, that such person is in his county,
contrary to the provisions of this section, if it shall appear
that such person is a free negro or mulatto, and that he hath
come into this State after the passage of this act, and such
person shall not produce a certificate, attested by the seal
of some court of record in some one of the United States,
evidencing that he is a citizen of such State, the justice
shall command him forthwith to depart from this State; and
in case such negro or mulatto shall not depart from the
State within thirty days after being commanded so to do as
aforesaid, any justice of the peace, upon complaint thereof
to him made, may cause such person to be brought before
him and may commit him to the common gaol of the county
in which he may be found, until the next term of the Circuit
Court to be held in such county. And the said court shall
cause such person to be brought before them and examine
into the cause of commitment; and if it shall appear that
such person came into the State contrary to the provisions
of this act, and continued therein after being commanded to
depart as aforesaid, such court may sentence such person to
receive ten lashes on his or her bare back, and order him to
depart the State; and if he or she shall not depart, the same
proceedings shall be had and punishment inflicted, as often as
may be necessary, until such person shall depart the State

" 'Section 5. Be it further enacted, that if any person shall, after the taking effect of this act, bring into this State any free negro or mulatto, not having in his possession a certificate of citizenship as required by this act [he or she] shall forfeit and pay, for every person so brought, the sum of five hundred dollars, to be recovered by action of debt in the name of the State, to the use of the University, in any court having competent jurisdiction; in which action the defendant may be held to bail, of right and without affidavit; and it shall be the duty of Attorney General or Circuit Attorney of the district in which any person so offending may be found, immediately upon information given of such offenses, to commence and prosecute an action as aforesaid.'

"Slaves are real estate in this and other States, and wisdom would dictate great care among the branches of the Church of Christ, on this subject. So long as we have no special rule in the church, as to people of color, let prudence guide; and while they, as well as we, are in the hands of a merciful God, we say, Shun every appearance of evil.

"While on the subject of law, it may not be amiss to quote some of the Constitution of Missouri. It shows a liberality of opinion of the great men of the West, and will vie with that of any other State. It is good; it is just, and it is the citizens' right.

" '4. That all men have a natural and indefeasible right to worship Almighty God according to the dictates of their own consciences; that no man can be compelled to erect, support, or attend any place of worship, or to maintain any minister of the gospel or teacher of religion; that no human authority can control or interfere with the rights of conscience; that no person can ever be hurt, molested, or restrained in his religious professions or sentiments, if he do not disturb others in their religious worship.

" '5. That no person, on account of his religious opinions can be rendered ineligible to any office of trust or profit under this State; that no preference can ever be given by law to any sect or mode of worship; and that no religious corporation can ever be established in this State.' "

It is true that the saints in general were unalterably opposed to human bondage or slavery in any form, but we have seen no evidence that they ever interfered with existing legal conditions in Missouri or elsewhere. It is possible that individual members of the church spoke hastily or unwisely regarding existing evils. It would have been strange indeed if they did not. If so, however, such unwise interference was never approved by the church or her authorities.

Slavery.

To tell of all the outrages committed and the sufferings entailed upon the saints during that summer and autumn would be impossible, but we will here quote a few testimonies in connection with the indignities mentioned in the foregoing appeal to Governor Dunklin. Though an agreement was entered into, as appears in the petition quoted above, providing that certain parties should leave by January 1, 1834, and the remainder by April 1, 1834; and that the mob in said agreement had pledged "themselves to use all their influence to prevent any violence being used so long as a compliance with the foregoing terms is observed by the parties concerned," yet without waiting for the time to expire, the mob began hostilities in October; and the very men whose names were signed to the agreement participated in the outrages.

Mob violate their agreement.

Here we will allow Parley P. Pratt, an eyewitness and a victim of these unhallowed persecutions, to tell the tale. The following is from "Persecution of the Saints," pages 31-52:—

P. P. Pratt's account.

"It was believed by many of the Mormons that the leaders of the mob would not suffer so barefaced a violation of the agreement before the time therein set forth; but Thursday night, the 31st of October, gave them abundant proof that no pledge, verbal or written, was longer to be regarded, for on that night between forty and fifty, many of whom were armed with guns, proceeded against a branch of the church, about eight miles west of town, and unroofed and partly demolished ten dwelling houses; and in the midst of the shrieks and screams of women and children, whipped and beat, in a savage manner, several of the men; and with their

orrid threats frightened women and children into the wil-
rness. Such of the men as could escape fled for their
ves; for very few of them had arms, neither were they
nbodied; and they were threatened with death if they
ade any resistance. Such therefore as could not escape
y flight received a pelting by rocks and a beating by guns
id whips.

"On Friday, the first of November, women and children
illied forth from their gloomy retreats to contemplate with
eart-rending anguish the ravages of a ruthless mob, in the
iangled bodies of their husbands and in the destruction of
ieir houses and furniture. Houseless, and unprotected by
ie arm of civil law in Jackson County, the dreary month of
ovember staring them in the face and loudly proclaiming a
iore inclement season at hand, the continual threats of the
iob that they would drive every Mormon from the county,
id the inability of many to remove because of their pov-
rty, caused an anguish of heart indescribable.

"These outrages were committed about two miles from my
isidence; news reached me before daylight the same morn-
ig, and I immediately repaired to the place, and was filled
ith anguish at the awful sights of houses in ruins, and
irniture destroyed and strewed about the streets; women
i different directions were weeping and mourning, while
ime of the men were covered with blood from the blows
iey had received from the enemy; others were endeavoring
i collect the fragments of their scattered furniture, beds,
tc.

"I endeavored to collect together as many men as possi-
le, and after consultation we concluded to embody for
efense. Accordingly we collected some sixty men, armed
urselves as well as we could, and took shelter next evening
i a log house. We set a guard, and sent out spies through
ie different parts of the settlement to watch the movements
f the mob; but sometime in the night two of the enemy
dvanced to our guard, being armed with guns and pistols,
nd while they were conversing I walked near them, and
ne of them struck me over the head, with all his might,
ith his gun. I staggered back, the blood streaming down

my face, but I did not fall. As I had command of our party, I ordered our men to disarm the two ruffians and secure them, which was done; and this probably prevented a general attack of the mob that night. The next morning they were let go in peace.

"The same night (Friday) a party in Independence commenced stoning houses, breaking down doors and windows, destroying furniture, etc. This night the brick part of a dwelling house belonging to A. S. Gilbert was partly demolished, and the windows of his dwelling broken in while a gentleman lay sick in his house.

"The same night the doors of the house of Messrs. Gilbert and Whitney were split open and the goods strewed in the street, to which fact upwards of twenty witnesses can attest.

"After midnight a party of our men marched for the store, etc., and when the mob saw them approach they fled. But one of their number, a Richard McCarty, was caught in the act of throwing rocks in at the door, while the goods lay strung around him in the street. He was immediately taken before Samuel Weston, Esq., and a warrant requested, that said McCarty might be secured; but his justiceship refused to do anything in the case, and McCarty was then liberated.

"The same night many of their houses had poles and rails thrust through the shutters and sash, into the rooms of defenseless women and children, from whence their husbands and fathers had been driven by the attacks of the mob which were made by ten or twenty men upon one house at a time. On Saturday, the 2d November, all the families of these people who lived in Independence, moved out of town about one half mile west, and embodied for the preservation of themselves and property. Saturday night a party of the mob made an attack upon a settlement about six miles west of the town. Here they tore the roof from a dwelling, broke open another house, found the owner, Mr. David Bennett, sick in bed, whom they beat inhumanly, and swore they would blow his brains out, and discharging a pistol, the ball cut a deep gash across the top of his head. In this skirmish one of their men was shot in the thigh.

"On Sunday evening about sunset myself and a Mr. Marsh set out on horseback to visit the Circuit Judge at Lexington, a distance of some forty miles. We were under the necessity of going the most private paths across the country, in order to avoid our enemies; but we had a most faithful pilot, who knew every crook and turn of the country. We had rode but a few miles, when it became so extremely dark that we could not see each other. Our pilot dismounted several times and felt his way; but at length we came to a halt, and lay down upon the ground until it broke away and became some lighter, and then we were enabled to go on; but the rain began to fall in torrents, and continued all the latter part of the night; we soon became completely drenched, and every thread about us perfectly wet; but still we dare not stop for any refreshment or shelter until day dawned, when we found ourselves forty miles from home and at the door of a friend, where we breakfasted and refreshed ourselves.

"We then repaired to Lexington and made oath, before Judge Riland, of the outrages committed upon us, but were refused a warrant; the Judge advising us to fight and kill the mob whenever they came upon us. We then returned to the place where we breakfasted; and, night coming on, we retired to bed. Having been without sleep for the three previous nights, and much of the time drenched in rain, together with the severe wound I had received, I was well-nigh exhausted. No sooner had sleep enfolded me in her kind embrace, than a vision opened before me:—

"I found myself in Jackson County, heard the roar of firearms, and saw the killed and wounded lying in their blood. At this I awoke from my slumber; and awaking Brother Marsh and the family with whom we tarried, I told them what I had seen and heard in my dream, and observed to them that I was sure that a battle had just ensued. Next morning we arose and pursued our journey homeward, with feelings of anxiety and amazement which cannot be described.

"Every officer of the peace had abandoned us to our fate, and it seemed as if there was no way but for men, women, and children to be exterminated. But as we rode on, ruminating upon these things, a man met us from Independence, who told us that there was a battle raging when he left, and how it was terminated he knew not.

"This only heightened our feelings of anxiety and suspense. We were every moment drawing nearer to where a moment would decide whether we were to find our friends alive and victorious, or whether they were slain, and we in the hands of a worse than savage enemy.

"On coming within four miles of Independence we ventured to inquire the distance, at a certain house. This we did in order to pass as strangers, and also in hopes to learn some news.

"The man seemed frightened, and inquired where we were from. We replied, 'From Lexington.' Said he, 'Have you heard what has happened?'

"We replied that we had understood there was some difficulty respecting the Mormons, but of all the particulars we had not been informed. 'Why,' said he, 'The Mormons have riz and have killed six men!' At this we seemed much surprised, and inquired if the government would not put down such an insurrection. We then passed on, and as soon as we were out of sight we left the road and rode into the woods. Taking a circuitous route through thickets of hazel, interwoven with grapevine, etc., and after some difficulty and entanglement we came in sight of Independence and advanced toward it, wishing to pass through, in order to get to a camp of our men near half a mile west of town. But seeing parties of armed men advancing towards us, we wheeled about and retreated a distance, and turned again to the woods, and struck round on the side of the town, through the wilderness, towards the tents of our brethren, rushing our horses with the greatest speed; thus we avoided being taken, and arrived safe. But what was our astonishment when we found our brethren without arms, having surrendered them to their enemies. The truth of the matter was this: on Monday eve, while I lay sleeping at our friend's, near Lexington, the same evening that I dreamed of the battle, the mob again advanced upon the settlement where they had first destroyed the ten houses, and commenced an attack upon houses and property, and threatening women and children with immediate destruction. While some sixty of the mob were thus engaged, about thirty of our men marched near them, and a battle ensued, in which the mob were entirely routed, leaving two of their number dead on the field, together with a number of horses. Several were severely wounded on both sides, and one young man of the church died the next day; his name was Barber.

"One of the enemy who fell was an attorney by the name of Brazeale. He had been heard a short time before to say that he would wade to his knees in blood or drive the Mormons from the county.

"The same night runners were dispatched in every direction, under pretense of calling out the militia; spreading, as they went, every rumor calculated to excite the unwary; such as, that the Mormons had taken Independence, and the Indians had surrounded it, being allied together, etc. The same evening, November 4, the said McCarty, who had been detected in breaking open the store of Gilbert & Co., was suffered to take out a warrant and arrest the said Gilbert and others of the church for a pretended assault and false imprisonment of said McCarty.

"Late in the evening while the court were proceeding with the trial in the courthouse a gentleman unconnected with the court, perceiving the prisoners to be without counsel and in imminent danger, advised said Gilbert and his brethren to move for jail as the only alternative to save life; for the north door was already barred, and a mob thronged the house with a determination to beat and kill; accordingly Gilbert and four others were committed to jail, the dungeons of which must have been a palace compared to the court room where dignity and mercy were strangers, and naught but the wrath of man in horrid threats stifled the ears of the prisoners. The same night, Gilbert, Morley, and Corrill were liberated from jail, that they might have an interview with their brethren, and try to persuade them to leave the county: and on their return to jail, about two o'clock on Tuesday morning, in custody of the sheriff, an armed force of six or seven men stood near the jail and hailed; they were answered by the sheriff. who gave his name and the names of his prisoners, crying, 'Don't fire, don't fire, the prisoners are in my charge,' etc.   They, however, fired one or two guns, when Morley and Corrill retreated; Gilbert stood, with several guns pointed at him. Two, more desperate than the rest, attempted to shoot, but one of the guns flashed, and the other missed fire. Gilbert was then knocked down by Thomas Wilson. About this time a few of the inhabitants arrived, and Gilbert again entered jail; from which he and three others were liberated about sunrise, without further prosecution of the trial.   The same morning, November 5, the town began to be crowded with armed men from every quarter, and it was said that the militia had been called out, under the sanction of Lieutenant Governor Boggs, and that one Colonel Pitcher had the command.   Among this militia (so-called), were the most conspicuous characters of the mob.   Very early on the same morning several branches of the church on hearing of the outrages in Independence, volunteered, and united their forces, and marched towards town to defend their brethren. When within one mile of town they halted and were soon informed that the militia were called out for their protection.   But in this they placed little confidence; for the body congregated had every appearance of a country mob, which subsequent events verified.   On application to Colonel Pitcher it was found that there was no alternative but for the church to leave the country forthwith, and to deliver up certain men to be tried for murder said to have been committed by them in the battle the previous evening.   The arms of this people were also demanded by the Colonel, and among the committee appointed to receive their arms were several of the most unrelenting of the old mob committee of July, who had directed in the demolishing of the printing office, etc.; viz.: Henry Chiles, Abner Staples, and Lewis Franklin.

"Rather than have submitted to these outrageous requirements. the saints would willingly have shed their blood; but they knew that if they resisted this mob the lies of the designing and the prejudice of the ignorant would construe their resistance into a violation of law, and thus bring certain destruction upon them: therefore they surrendered their arms to the number of fifty, and agreed to leave the county forthwith. The men who were demanded as prisoners were also surrendered and imprisoned, but were dismissed in a day or two without trial. A few hours after the surrender we arrived at the camp of our brethren near Independence, on our return from Lexington, as stated in the foregoing, and when we found that the struggle was over, and our liberties completely trampled under foot, I retired into the woods and kneeled down, and wept before the Lord.

"The sun was then setting, and twelve miles separated me from my family, but I determined to reach home that night. My horse being weary, I started on foot, and walked through the wilderness in the midst of darkness, avoiding the road, lest I should fall into the hands of the enemy. I arrived home about the middle of the night, spent a few hours with my family, and arose again before day and fled to the wilderness, as the mob were driving our people and hunting them in every direction. After walking a few miles I found a brother by the name of Lowry, who was moving from the county in a covered wagon, he having a permit from the mob to pass in safety.

"This man concealed me in his wagon, and thus we passed in safety, although frequently meeting armed men who were pursuing our brethren. When night again overtook us we were on the bank of the Missouri River which divided between Jackson and Clay Counties. Here we encamped for the night, as we could not cross the ferry till morning. I left the camp and ascended the tall bluff, and finding a cavity of a rock I slept therein. But before morning I was joined by Mr. Morley and several others, who fled for their lives and brought news that the mob were driving and probably butchering men, women, and children. On hearing this news we tried to pray, but we could say but little. Next morning we crossed over the river and found ourselves once more in a land of peace. While I thus made my escape, companies of ruffians were ranging the county in every direction, bursting into houses without fear, knowing that the arms were secured, frightening women and children, and threatening to kill them if they didn't flee immediately. At the head of one of these companies appeared the Rev. Mr. McCoy (a noted Missionary to the Indians) with a gun upon his shoulder, ordering the Mormons to leave immediately and surrender everything in the shape of arms. Other pretended preachers of the gospel took part in the persecution, calling the Mormons the common enemy of mankind, and exulting in their afflictions. On Tuesday and Wednesday nights, the 5th and 6th of November, women and children fled in every direction, before a merciless mob. One party of about a hundred and fifty women and children fled to the prairie, where they wandered for several days, mostly without food, and nothing but the open firmament for their shelter. Other parties fled towards the Missouri. During this dispersion of women and children, parties of the mob were hunting men, firing upon some, tying up and whipping others; and some they pursued upon horses for several miles.

"Thursday, November 7, the shore began to be lined on both sides of the ferry, with men, women, and children, goods, wagons, boxes, chests, provisions, etc., while the ferrymen were very busily employed in crossing them over; and when night again closed upon us the wilderness had much the appearance of a camp meeting. Hundreds of people were seen in every direction. Some in tents and some in the open air, around their fires, while the rain descended in torrents. Husbands were inquiring for wives, and women for their husbands, parents for children, and children for parents. Some had the good fortune to escape with their family, household goods, and some provisions; while others knew not the fate of their friends, and had lost all their goods. The scene was indescribable, and I am sure would have melted the hearts of any people upon earth, except our blind oppressors and a prejudiced and ignorant community. Next day, our company still increased, and we were chiefly engaged in felling small cottonwood trees, and erecting them into temporary cabins, so when night again came on we had the appearance of a village of wigwams, and the night being clear, we began to enjoy some degree of comfort.

'"About two o'clock the next morning we were aroused from our slumbers by the cry of 'Arise, and behold the signs in the heavens.' We arose, and to our great astonishment all heaven seemed enwrapped in a splendid fireworks, as if every star in the broad expanse had been suddenly hurled from its course and sent lawless through the wilds of ether. I can give the reader no better idea of this scene than by allusion to the shooting of a bright meteor with a long train of light following its course such as most of us have seen in a bright starlight night. Now suppose that thousands of such meteors with their fiery trains were to run lawless through the heavens for hours together, this would be a scene such as our eyes beheld on that memorable morning; and the scene only closed by giving place to the superior light and splendor of the king of day. No sooner was this scene beheld by some of our camp than the news reached every tent and aroused every one from their slumbers; every eye was lifted towards the heavens, and every heart was filled with joy at this majestic display of signs and wonders showing the near approach of the coming of the Son of God.

"In fact we looked up and lifted up our heads rejoicing, knowing that our redemption drew near. It is a singular coincidence that this wonder should happen at the very time of our dispersion. And let others think as they may, I take it as a special manifestation to fulfill the Scriptures, and to rouse our drooping spirits, by a fresh memorial, reminding us of a coming Messiah for the redemption of those who look for him; and to the destruction of their oppressors.

"After a few days I sent a lad with a horse for my wife, who escaped in safety by riding fifteen miles on horseback; leaving all our goods, which, however, I afterwards obtained at the risk of my life. But all my provisions for the winter were destroyed or plundered; and my grain left growing on the ground for our enemies to harvest. My house was after-

wards burned, and my apple trees, rails, and improvements
destroyed or plundered. In short, every member of the
society was driven from the county, and fields of corn were
plundered and destroyed. Stacks of wheat were burned,
household goods plundered, and improvements and every
kind of property lost; and at length no less than TWO HUN-
DRED AND THREE HOUSES BURNED, according to the esti-
mate of their own people in Jackson.

"The saints who fled took refuge in the neighboring
counties – mostly in Clay County, which received them with
some degree of kindness. Those who fled to the county of
Van Buren were again driven, and compelled to flee; and
those who fled to Lafayette County were soon expelled, or
the most part of them, and had to move wherever they could
find protection.

"When the news of these outrages reached the Governor of the State, courts of inquiry, both civil and military,
were ordered by him; but nothing effectual was ever done
to restore our rights, or to protect us in the least. It is
true the Attorney General, with a military escort and our
witnesses, went to Jackson County and demanded indict-
ments, but the court and jurors refused to do anything in
the case, and the military and witnesses were mobbed out of
the county, and thus that matter ended. The Governor also
ordered them to restore our arms which they had taken from
us, but they never were restored; and even our lands in that
county were robbed of their timber, and either occupied by
our enemies for years, or left desolate."

Lyman Wight, one of the men especially mentioned in the
agreement, who was to leave by January 1, records the following in his private journal: —

L. Wight's
experience.

"The mob continued to commit depredations and outrages
upon us until the 13th of November, 1833, such as tearing
down a printing office, destroying books, unroofing houses,
and thrusting rails into the windows, and whipping many
of our friends in a horrible manner, and shooting others; on
which day they finished the work of driving every Mormon,
numbering about twelve hundred persons, from the country.
Our crops became free booty to their horses, hogs, and

cattle. They also burned two hundred and three houses.

"I was chased by about sixty of these ruffians five miles. I fled to the south and my wife was driven north to Clay County, and for three weeks I knew not whether my family were dead or alive, neither did they know what was my fate. At one time I was three days without food. When I found my family I found them on the banks of the Missouri River under a rag carpet tent, short of food and raiment. In this deplorable situation, on the 27th of December, my wife bore me a son."

The reader will note that this happened in November and December, and that this man was named in the agreement as one of those to go unmolested, providing he went by January 1. We doubt not but the saints sometimes did wrong, and sometimes resisted when forbearance would have been better policy. For instance, this man Wight is said to have been one of the fighting characters; especially so in the later trials of 1838; but is it any wonder, when looking at it from a natural standpoint, that he would fight when confronted by such men as S. D. Lucas and Moses Wilson, the very men who were instrumental in heaping such hardships and indignities upon his family, while his wife was in such a critical and delicate condition, and he absent from home, fleeing for his life?

Elder Hiram Rathbun, of Lansing, Michigan, who was an Rathbun's eyewitness to some of these scenes, testified untestimony. der oath in the famous Temple Lot suit as follows:—

"Members of the church were living here from 1831 to 1833. They left here in the month of November, 1833. The occasion of their leaving was that they had to leave. They were driven out of the country by the citizens of Independence and the vicinity. They were driven out by the people around about here.

"The cause of their being driven out, the people here became dissatisfied and displeased with the citizens here known as the Church of Jesus Christ of Latter Day Saints; that is, the citizens who did not belong to that church became dissatisfied with the citizens who did belong to it.

The church members had some peculiar sentiments that were antislavery, while those here were proslavery; and then their religious sentiments were different from those of other people here, and that excited some friction. There was a difference between the religious and political sentiments of the class of citizens that belonged to the Church of Jesus Christ of Latter Day Saints and the citizens that did not belong to that organization, and that difference eventually led to friction, and finally the citizens who objected to the people that belonged to the church became so dissatisfied that they rose up in what we called mobs, and met together and held some meetings, and passed resolutions, and proceeded to such extremities, that finally they drove them out. They met, finally, and did a good deal of damage and mischief to the people. There were several instances of mob violence, and on one instance they stoned houses here; the houses of the people who belonged to the Latter Day Saints Church. They stoned them at night, after dark. I know that, for amongst the others that were stoned was the house of my father, and they did that, although at the time my father was away with some of the others in council. I do not know why, but our house was stoned, and the door was broken open. One stone as large as my fist struck my mother, and she screamed 'Murder,' and then they ran away at her screaming. The next morning, very early, I went through the village, and I found Mr. Phillips' house torn down, and the printing office, which was in the upper room of, I think, a brick house, with a stairway on the outside that went up to the printing office, and the printing press was broken, the type and all the furniture of the office was thrown down into what we might call a jamb, piled together, and the printing press was broken, and the little boys came around and carried off the type and other things as they saw proper; and Mr. Gilbert's store was broken into, and his goods taken out on the street, and the bolts of factory and calicoes, and cloth, etc., were unrolled. It had the appearance of having been taken by the end and running off with it until they unwound them. The streets were almost covered with these pieces of cloth that were unrolled in that manner, and other goods scattered around. My father's shop was broken into, and his tools thrown out on the street. That was the condition of things the morning after this demonstration or outbreak. Things were in a state of great confusion, for everyone was greatly excited at the time; but things ran along for a couple of days, and then they caught some of the elders of the church here, and among them my father, and brought them up here to the square to tar and feather them. My father made his escape, but he was the only one that did escape, and the others were tarred and feathered. I know that, for I stood but a short distance away, and could see it done. If my memory serves me right there were three tarred and feathered; there was Bishop Partridge, a man by the name of Allen, the other name I do not remember. I remember very particularly in regard to Bishop Partridge and the manner in which he went away.

"Well, finally the women and household goods of the members of the church were taken to the Temple Lot, and piled up there on the Temple Plot in the woods; and we were there, I think it was three days. I would not be positive, but I think it was about three days we were there in the woods, and they were yelling and hollering and swearing and shooting around there night and day. We could not go to sleep, and our condition was about as bad as bad could be, from almost any point of view. Finally the time came when we were to move and cross the river. We crossed the river down here about three miles,—got over on the other side. These are about the outlines of the particulars regarding the expulsion of the people, as I remember them. The people left Independence, and crossed the river through fear of violence, and to save our lives."—Plaintiff's Abstract, pp. 216, 217.

Mr. Jacob Gregg, who was Sheriff of Jackson County at the time, testified in the same suit as follows:—

"Jacob Gregg, of lawful age, being produced. sworn, and examined on the part of the Plaintiff, testified as follows:—

"My name is Jacob Gregg; I reside at Grain Valley, in Jackson County, Missouri. I have resided in this county sixty-seven years; I resided in the State of Missouri nearly

eighty years.   My age is ninety or a little past.   I was
ninety years old the ninth day of last month.

"I have held a good many offices first and last in Jackson
County.   The first office was before this county was organized as a county.   I was one of its executive offi-
Sheriff
Gregg on   cers, commonly called a constable.   That was the
the situation.   first office I held; that was in 1826.   I held the
office of sheriff in this county in 1833.   The term was two
years; I was elected for two terms, and held the office four
years altogether.

"During my term of office is when the Mormons were
driven from Jackson County, Missouri.   I was not in that
affair in any way; the first movement that was made, was
when they tore down the printing office of the Mormon people.   When I came in town one morning I saw a crowd of
men standing by the courthouse; saw that one of them had
a rope in his hand.   When I got up about half way to them,
two men came up to meet me; said they had some business
back at the tavern.   They took me back in a room there,
and one of them went out and locked the door after him, and
left me with the other one, and I know nothing about what
was going on outside until I got out of there.

"They had torn down the printing office, and dispersed
before I got out to see what was being done.   After I was
let out of the house all was quiet; everything had quieted
down, and was civil enough after I got out.   I cannot say
what had been done by the mob or the citizens while I was
in that room.   I learned afterwards that they had demolished
the printing office, for they seemed to think that was the
seat of trouble, and they had demolished it."—Plaintiff's
Abstract, pp. 287, 288.

John Corrill, also one of the expelled citizens of Jackson
County, wrote a letter in December, 1833, concern-
John Corrill.   ing the trouble, which is published in the *Evening
and Morning Star*, pages 246-250.

"LIBERTY, Clay County, Missouri,
"December, 1833.

"*Brother O. Cowdery:* Inasmuch as many reports have
gone abroad respecting the affairs of the church in these

parts, and not knowing whether any person has given you the particulars, I will give you a brief, correct, and impartial account as nearly as I can; but to give all the particulars would require a volume, yet I will give you as much, and that in order, as will enable you to have a general and correct understanding of the whole transaction.

"The raising and spreading many slanderous and false reports against us as a society; the coming out against us in *night mobs!* stoning our houses; breaking our windows, burning our hay; their meeting together and binding themselves, even in writing, to each other, in which they pledged their lives, their property, and their *sacred* honors, forcibly to drive us from the county, if we would not go without; the demolishing the printing office on the 20th July, tarring and feathering the bishop of the church and another member, and their meeting on the 23d to go on with the work of destruction, are facts so well known that I need not name their particulars at this time.

"It is also well known, that we, seeing that there was no other alternative for us, to save the destruction of lives and property, at that time we agreed, six of us, to leave the county, and to use our influence with the church to persuade them to leave also, one half by the first of January, and the other half by the first of April next; supposing, that before the time arrived the mob would see their error and stop their violence; or that some means might be employed so that we could stay in peace and enjoy our privileges as guaranteed in the Constitution and laws of our country. But after waiting some weeks, and seeing that their wrath did not abate, but their threatenings continually increased upon us, and losing all hopes of their withdrawing their wicked purposes, and also despairing of having the laws executed in Jackson County without assistance, we therefore thought it would be wisdom to appeal to the Governor for aid.

"We accordingly drew up a petition and circulated it in as prudent a manner as possible; for the mob threatened, that if we petitioned or prosecuted, they would *massacre* us *in toto*. But on presenting the petition to the Governor, he manifested a willingness to assist us, but said he could not, until we had tried to enforce the law; and then if we could not he would enable us to do it.

"We therefore saw plainly that we were under the necessity of making a trial in our weak situation, in opposition to the wrath and violence of the enemy. And notwithstanding we should in so doing become exposed to death and destruction from the hands of the mob, yet we determined to magnify the laws of the land, and honor the advice of the Governor, by entering a prosecution against them. Accordingly we employed counsel for that purpose, and when the mob had learned this fact, their wrath seemed for a few days to abate; but they soon began to rage again, and to threaten to do their mischief in the night.

"Until this time we had been in a defenseless situation, perfectly so, not even pretending to use any weapons, or even standing in our own defense. But on seeing that the wrath of the mob, was great, and that our lives, as well as our property, was in danger; knowing also that we had suffered as much as the law of man or of God required of us, and even more without resisting; and also being advised by good counsel, we concluded on the whole to prepare ourselves for self-defense.

"But in this we found ourselves somewhat lame; for many of us had not weapons to defend ourselves with. And again, a question arose in our minds to what extent we might go in defending ourselves; but on inquiry we found that a man was justified in defending his own person, his family, and his house. But again, another difficulty arose, which was this: one man in his house alone could not defend it against many. We again asked counsel, and found that inasmuch as the mob gathered together to destroy us, we were justified in gathering together to defend ourselves.

"We then came to the conclusion, that inasmuch as they should embody and come against us, we would embody to defend ourselves; although we knew that in this we should labor under great disadvantages; yet we supposed that if we prepared ourselves as well as we could for self-defense, that this would have a tendency to stop the enemy from coming on us; but in this we were disappointed.

"They proceeded to stone our houses in Independence in the night time, and to threaten the lives of individuals; but did no great damage until Tuesday night, October 31, when about forty or fifty in number, many of whom were armed with guns, proceeded against the branch above, or west of the Blue, sometimes called the Whitmer settlement, and unroofed and partly demolished ten houses; and also whipped and pounded several persons in a shocking manner, and diligently sought for others who fled for safety.

"Now, the brethren at that time, were not collected together for defense, supposing that they had not a perfect right to assemble until the mob had; they therefore neglected this until the mob was upon them; and then they had no time. And although some of them had guns, yet being alone, and seeing the mob also had guns and threatened their lives, if they resisted, found it of no use to undertake to defend themselves. However, they dispersed after committing such depredations as they thought proper at that time, (without being resisted,) after having threatened to come again in a more violent manner than ever.

"This news was soon spread abroad, and none but the sufferers themselves can imagine the feelings that it produced. To have their houses pulled down over their heads; their women and children exposed to the storms and blasts of a cold and dreary winter; and after laboring hard to lay up provisions for the winter, then to be driven from it and have it destroyed, and no means of obtaining more; and in addition to this, to be hunted and beaten in an unmerciful manner, was asking more of us than we felt willing to submit to. But the question was, What shall be done? We were in a scattered situation, and could not embody immediately; and if we gathered the brethren to defend one part, the mob would fall upon another. Our neighbors who felt to pity us, though very few in number, dare not lift a finger in our behalf for fear of sharing the same fate. We could see no relief from any quarter; our only strength was within our own body, trusting in God: but something must be done; night was approaching in which we expected more or less of us to suffer.

"We concluded at all hazards to try for a peace warrant against certain head ones of the mob. We accordingly went to a magistrate and applied for one, but to no purpose; he refused to grant one on our oath. We then read to him the Governor's letter, which directed us to proceed in that way, but he disregarded it, and said he cared nothing about it.

"Having no time to lose we concluded to advise each branch of the church to gather into bodies the best way they could for their own preservation. Threatenings were heard from the mob in different quarters. Night came on, and a party of their men proceeded to the branch on the prairie, sometimes called the Colesville branch. Two of their num-ber were sent out as spies, well armed with two guns and three pistols: they were discovered by some of our brethren, with whom they held some conversation; and after one of them had struck one of our men over the head with the breech of his gun, they were taken by our brethren, their guns and pistols taken from them, and they kept till morn-ing; their guns and pistols were then given to them and they let go without injury. It being dark, and the rest of the mob not showing themselves, were only heard by some of the brethren in the adjoining woods to inquire why their spies did not return.

"The same night (Friday, November 1) another party commenced stoning our houses in Independence, breaking down our doors and windows, and destroying furniture, etc. A number of us were gathered together about a half a mile west of Independence from whence we could distinctly hear them; but we concluded that unless they did something more than stone and brickbat our houses, we would not meddle with them. But on sending some to discover what they were about, we learned that they had commenced pulling down the dwelling house of Brother A. S. Gilbert.

"We then thought it best, and accordingly proceeded in order into town, and as we drew near the store of Brother Gilbert, we saw a number of men sending stones and brick-bats against the same; but as soon as they saw us they fled. However, we were successful in taking one of them in the act, who appeared to be much frightened. And we found that they had broken down the store doors, and scattered some of the goods in the streets. Then Brother G. on seeing this, took the man whom we had taken in spoiling the store, and in company with two or three others went with him to the magistrate, and entered a complaint against him in order to get a warrant and have him secured; but the magistrate refused to do anything about it, and therefore, we were obliged to let him go again. We then went home and there was no more done that night as I know of.

"The next day (Saturday, November 2) we knew not what to do for our safety; we talked some of the propriety of bringing our families and effects into one place; and this we knew would be attended with great inconvenience: for we had no houses nor shelters for our families, nor fodder for our cattle; and as the mob was upon us night after night, we had no time to do it; therefore we must do the best we could. However, all the families in town removed as much together as they could, about half a mile west of town, and we concluded to send men to the circuit judge, who lived about forty miles off, to get a peace warrant.

"A party of the mob gathered that night and went against the branch at the Blue; and after tearing the roof from one house and doing some injury to the furniture, they divided their company, and one party went to pulling the roof from one dwelling house, while the other party went to another; they broke open the house, and found the owner in bed, whom they took and beat unmercifully. But here they were met by a party of the brethren who had been wise enough to prepare for them; a firing of guns commenced, they say, by our men, but our men say, by them upon us; but as near as I can learn from those who were there, it can be easily proven that it commenced by them.

"However, while they were in the act of pounding the brother whom they found in bed, one of them drew a pistol and swore he would blow out his brains: but as the Lord would have it, the ball, instead of going through his head only cut a gash on the top of it. All was confusion: our women and children crying and screaming with terror, were mixed in the crowd; and in the skirmish, a young man of the mob was shot through the thigh, and this stopped the affray that night.

"The next day (Sunday, November 3) we dispatched four men to the circuit judge, to obtain a peace warrant. At the same time our enemies were busily engaged in gathering all the force they could to come against us, and we saw that they were terribly enraged: we were told that they were going to get a six pounder and come against us openly the next day; and we were also told by those who professed to be our friends, that we would certainly all be massacred. We saw that they were increasing their numbers, and we had nothing to expect but a terrible work of destruction to commence the next day, and we warned our brethren to be prepared for it as well as they could; therefore, two or three branches west of the Blue gathered together as well as they could, leaving their houses and property to the ravages of the mob.

"Next day came on (Monday, November 4), and a large party of the mob gathered above the Blue, took the ferry-boat, and threatened some lives, etc., and for some cause they abandoned their purpose at that time, and returned to Wilson's about a mile west of the Blue. However, word had gone to our brethren, who had assembled themselves together at the Colesville branch west of the Blue, that the mob were doing damage on the east side of the Blue, and that the brethren there wanted help.

"Accordingly nineteen of our men volunteered and started to go to their assistance, but when they had proceeded a part of the way they learned that the mob were not doing mischief at that time, but were at Wilson's store, so they turned about to go home, when the mob by some means found out that a party of our men were on the road west of them, and a party of them, thirty or forty, started on horseback with guns to fall upon our men; and after riding two or two and a half miles they overtook them; and as soon as the brethren saw them, they dispersed and fled; and some ran immediately to the main body of our brethren to let them know that the mob were upon them.

"But the mob not being willing to give up the brethren

without injuring them, pursued after, and hunted in order to find them. They searched in the cornfield of Christian Whitmer, and fed their horses freely upon his corn. They also took him and pointed their guns at him, threatening to kill him if he did not tell them where the brethren were. They also got upon the top of his house, and threatened some women and children.

"Thus they were employed in hunting and threatening the brethren until one of our men returned with assistance from the main body, which was about three miles off. And when the mob saw our men they fired upon them, and our men immediately fired in return. The mob immediately fled, and the brethren followed them a few rods and let them go. Two of the mob and some of their horses were killed on the ground, and others badly wounded. Several of our brethren were wounded, one mortally, who died the next day. The others are likely to recover. Brother Dibble was shot in the bowels, and he says, by the first gun that was fired.

"The same day at Independence, Brother A. S. Gilbert, Wm. E. McLellin, I. Morley, myself, and three or four others were taken for an *assault and battery*, and *false imprisonment*, by the man whom we had taken the Friday night previous in the act of stoning the store. Although we could not obtain a warrant against him for breaking open the store, yet he had gotten one for us, for catching him at it. We were prisoners in the courthouse when news came to town of the battle last mentioned. But instead of coming correctly, it was stated, 'that the Mormons had gone into the house of Wilson and shot his son.' This greatly enraged the people; and the courthouse being filled, a rush was made upon us by some to kill us; but the court esteeming it too dishonorable to have us killed while in their hands, on our request shut us up in the jail to save our lives.

"The people had become desperate, and were busily employed in getting guns and ammunition, and preparing themselves for a general massacre of our people the next day. And we were frequently told that night, while in the jail, and that too by men of note, that without any doubt many lives would be lost the next day; for now, not only the mob, but the whole county were engaged and greatly enraged against us, and that nothing would stop them short of our leaving the county forthwith; and they thought that they were so enraged that even this would not stop them from taking our lives.

"We accordingly sent word that night to our brethren that they might not expect anything the next day but a general slaughter of our people, and that they must take care of themselves the best way they could. However, we at the same time came to the conclusion, on seeing the rage of the people, that it would be wisdom for us to leave the county immediately, rather than to have so many lives lost as probably would be. The sheriff and two others took us out of the jail and went with us to see our brethren upon this subject. Our brethren agreed to it; and as we were returning to the jail about one o'clock at night, we were hailed by a party of men with guns, who intended no doubt to kill us. I wheeled and left them, they fired a rifle at me; Brother Morley also left them; but Bro. Gilbert stood his ground. They came up to him; presented two guns in order to kill him, but as Providence would, one snapped and the other flashed in the pan. He was then knocked down by one of them, but his life was preserved and he not materially hurt.

"Our agreement to leave the county not being known to only a few, the people in their wrath collected together in the morning, well armed for war, and Col. Pitcher called out the militia, as he said, to quell the mob: but it would have been difficult for one to have distinguished between the militia and the mob, for all the most conspicuous characters engaged in the riot were found in his ranks. Our proposals to leave the county, however, were laid before the people, and we were told that it was with much difficulty that they were constrained to let us go, but seemed determined on taking our lives.

"At the same time our brethren west of Independence, not knowing that we had agreed to leave the county, and supposing that nothing but death awaited them, gathered together and marched towards town, and arrived within one mile of the place by eight or nine o'clock in the morning (Tuesday, November 5), with a determination to make a stand about half a mile west of town, at the spot where the brethren at Independence branch had collected together, and there maintain the ground or die upon it, if the mob fell upon them. But on being told that we had agreed to leave the county, and also that the militia had been called out to make peace, they turned aside into the woods, and concluded to disperse and go home. But some persons on seeing them in the morning marching toward town, had carried news that our people were on the march toward the place, no doubt, 'they supposed, with an intention to do mischief.'

"On hearing this the militia became enraged, and Col. Pitcher would not give us peace only on the conditions that we should deliver up those men who were engaged in the battle the day before, to have them tried for murder; and also, that we must deliver up our arms, and then, he said, we should be safely protected out of the county.

"This being the only alternative for us, we accordingly agreed to it, and delivered up our arms, there being forty-nine guns and one pistol. We also delivered up the prisoners who had been demanded by them, and began to prepare to leave the county. They kept the prisoners whom we delivered up to be tried for murder, a day and a night, and after threatening them much, and bringing them to a trial, let them go for an old watch.

"We plainly saw that the militia of the county with Col. Pitcher at their head, had taken from us our arms when we were using them only for self-defense against an outrageous mob. And instead of quelling the mob, he left them in full power to come upon us when they pleased, and promised us no protection against them, only while we were fleeing from our houses and homes with our women and children, to seek a shelter in the open air the best way we could.

"Thus we were obliged, not only by the mob, but also by the militia, to leave the county of Jackson. And on reflection the next morning, we concluded to go south into Van Buren County and there make another settlement about forty or fifty miles off. But the people, on hearing this, although it was agreed to by some half a dozen of the leading men in Jackson County, rose up against it, and said we should not go, if we did, they would follow us.

"The same day (Wednesday, November 6) a part of the mob, between fifty and eighty in number, supposing that Col. Pitcher had not done his duty as faithfully as he ought, mounted their horses with their guns on their shoulders, went to visit the brethren and frighten the members of the church: some they fired at, others they whipped, and some they chased upon horses for several miles; others they sought for diligently, as they said to kill them; and they burst open doors in an abrupt manner, and searched houses for guns and other weapons of war. As they passed through the branch at the Blue, they swore that if the people were not off by the time they returned at night, they would massacre the whole of them.

"Accordingly, some started for Clay County, and about one hundred and thirty women and children, with six men, started without goods or furniture, and the most of them on foot, and wandered several days on the prairie, not knowing where to go, supposing that it was not their privilege to return and take their goods. Some have since returned and taken some of their things, and others I have not heard from particularly. But the more part of the church waited to take some or the principal part of their goods.

"When we found that we could not go south peaceably, we came across the Missouri River into Clay County, where we found the inhabitants as accommodating as we could reasonably expect. Many of us have obtained houses and shelters for our families, and others have built huts in the woods, while some who have lately come over are yet in tents, or in the open air.

"Some few of the brethren thought that they could remain after the others had come away, but on Saturday, November 23, the mob held another meeting and appointed a committee to warn off those families that remained. Accordingly, on Sunday and Monday following, the brethren that remained were ordered off with many threatenings if they did not go immediately. They have, since that time, been getting away as fast as possible. Some few families, I learn, have gone south to Grand River, and some others have gone east. Great sacrifices have been made: some being destitute of money, have sold their cattle and other effects at a very low rate.

"Much property that was left behind has been destroyed, and other property that yet remains probably will be before it can be taken care of. Some families are as it were entirely destitute, and must unavoidably suffer unless God interposes in their behalf. This is the present condition of the church.

"And now, the question is, What can be done? The Governor has manifested a willingness to restore us back, and will if we request it; but this will be of little use unless he could leave a force there to help protect us, for the mob say, that three months shall not pass before they will drive us again. And he cannot leave a force without calling a special legislature for that purpose, unless the President should see fit to place a company of rangers here with power to assist us in time of need.

"To enter a criminal prosecution against them would be of little or no use; for I am satisfied that a grand jury cannot be had in Jackson County at present that would indict them for their crimes; and the law, I am informed, requires that criminals shall be tried in their own county. And if the heads of the mob should be taken and put into jail, it undoubtedly would be torn down and they liberated.

"If we could be placed back, and become organized into independent companies, and armed with power and liberty to stand in our own defense, it would be much better for us. But then, as their numbers are double ours, this would be paving the way or laying the foundation for another scene of murder and bloodshed.

"What can or will be done I know not; but I think that the State of Missouri is brought to the test, whether it can and will protect the persons and rights of its own citizens or not; or whether it will suffer its government and laws to be trodden down and trampled under the feet of a lawless banditti, without bringing them to justice.

"As it respects the charges and crimes which they accuse us of being guilty, I think that they are not worthy of notice; for the law is open and they hold the execution of it in their own hands; and if we were guilty of crimes they certainly would have brought us to an account for them. But their not doing this, is clearly an evidence that we are innocent.

"And again, in their declaration or memorial, published after they tore down the printing office, they, as nearly as I can recollect, say, that the thing or crime for which they proceeded against us, was that that could not have been foreseen by any legislature: therefore no law has been enacted against it. This is plainly acknowledging that we are guilty of no crime for which the law could take any hold of us.   Yours, etc.,

"JOHN CORRILL."

Bishop Partridge's testimony concerning the mobbing of himself at the beginning of these difficulties may be of inter-

Bishop Partridge.

est here. This testimony was published immediately after the occurrence, in July (1833) extra of *Evening and Morning Star*, when, if ever, he would have been embittered, and filled with the spirit of resentment and revenge; hence it is valuable as showing the spirit of Christlike meekness exhibited by church leaders in this trying hour.

This testimony will be found in the history of Joseph Smith as stated in *Times and Seasons*, volume 6, pages 818 and 819, continued on pages 832, 881, 882, 896–898.

"On the 20th the mob collected, and demanded the discontinuance of the printing in Jackson County, a closing of the store, and a cessation of all mechanical labors. The brethren refused compliance, and the consequence was that the house of W. W. Phelps, which contained the printing establishment, was thrown down, the materials taken possession of by the mob, many papers destroyed, and the family and furniture thrown out doors.

"The mob then proceeded to violence towards Edward Partridge, the Bishop of the Church, as he relates in his autobiography: 'I was taken from my house by the mob,

George Simpson being their leader, who escorted me about half a mile, on to the courthouse, the public square in Independence; and then and there, a few rods from said courthouse, surrounded by hundreds of the mob, I was stripped of my hat, coat, and vest, and daubed with tar from head to foot, and then had a quantity of feathers put upon me; and all this because I would not agree to leave the county, my home where I had lived two years.

" 'Before tarring and feathering me, I was permitted to speak. I told them that the saints had had to suffer persecution in all ages of the world, that I had done nothing which ought to offend anyone. That if they abused me, they would abuse an innocent person. That I was willing to suffer for the sake of Christ; but, to leave the country I was not then willing to consent to it. By this time the multitude made so much noise that I could not be heard: some were cursing and swearing, saying, "Call upon your Jesus," etc.; others were equally noisy in trying to still the rest, that they might be enabled to hear what I was saying.

" 'Until after I had spoken, I knew not what they intended to do with me, whether to kill me, to whip me, or what else I knew not. I bore my abuse with so much resignation and meekness that it appeared to astound the multitude, who permitted me to retire in silence, many looking very solemn, their sympathies having been touched as I thought; and, as to myself, I was so filled with the Spirit and love of God, that I had no hatred towards my persecutors, or anyone else.'

"Charles Allen was next stripped and tarred and feathered, because he would not agree to leave the county, or deny the Book of Mormon.

"Others were brought up to be served likewise or whipped, but from some cause the mob ceased operations and adjourned until Tuesday the 23d. Elder Gilbert, the keeper of the store, agreed to close that; and that may have been one reason why the work of destruction was suddenly stopped for two days.

"In the course of this day's wicked outrageous and unlawful proceedings, many solemn realities of human degrada-

tion, as well as thrilling incidents, were presented to the
saints. An armed and well-organized mob in a government
professing to be governed by law, with the Lieutenant Governor, (Lilburn W. Boggs,) the second officer in the State,
calmly looking on, and secretly aiding every movement, saying to the saints, 'You now know what our Jackson boys
can do, and you must leave the country,' and all the justices,
judges, constables, sheriffs, and military officers, headed by
such western missionaries and clergymen as the Reverends
McCoy, Kavanaugh, Hunter, Fitzhugh, Pixley, Likens,
Lovelady, and Bogard, consisting of Methodists, Baptists,
Presbyterians, and all the different sects of religionists that
inhabited that country; with that great moral reformer, and
Register of the Land Office at Lexington, forty miles east,
known as the head and father of the Cumberland Presbyterians, even the Reverend Finis Ewing, publicly publishing
that the 'Mormons were the common enemies of mankind,
and ought to be destroyed;' all these solemn realities were
enough to melt the heart of a savage; while there was not a
solitary offense on record, or proof that a saint had broken
the law of the land.

"And when B'shop Partridge, who was without guile,
and Elder Charles Allen, walked off, amid the horrid yells of
an infuriated mob, coated like some unnamed, unknown
biped, and one of the sisters cried aloud; 'while you, who
have done this wicked deed, must suffer the vengeance of
God; they, having endured persecution, *can rejoice*, for
henceforth, for them, is laid up a crown, eternal in the heavens;' surely there was a time of awful reflection, that man,
unrestrained, like the brute beast, may torment the body;
but God, in return, will punish the soul.

"After the mob had ceased yelling, and retired; and while
evening was spreading her dark mantle over the unblushing
scenery, as if to hide it from the gaze of day; men, women,
and children, who had been driven or frightened from their
homes by yells and threats, began to return from their hiding places, in thickets, cornfields, woods, and groves, and
view with heavy hearts the scenery of desolation and woe;
and while they mourned over fallen man, they rejoiced with

joy unspeakable that they were accounted worthy to suffer in the glorious cause of their divine Master.

"There lay the printing office a heap of ruins; Elder Phelp's furniture strewed over the garden as common plunder; the revelations, bookwork, papers, and press in the hands of the mob as the booty of highway robbers; there was Bishop Partridge in the midst of his family, with a few friends, endeavoring to scrape off the 'tar,' which, from eating his flesh, seemed to have been prepared with lime, pearlash, acid, or some flesh-eating commodity, to destroy him; and there was Charles Allen in the same awful condition. As the heart sickens at the recital, how much more at the picture! More than once, those people, in this boasted land of liberty, were brought into jeopardy, and threatened with expulsion or death because they wished to worship God according to the revelations of heaven, the Constitution of their country, and the dictates of their own consciences. Oh liberty, how art thou fallen! Alas! clergymen! where is thy charity? In the smoke that ascendeth up forever and ever.

"Early in the morning of the 23d of July, the mob again assembled, armed with weapons of war, and bearing a red flag. Whereupon the elders, led by the Spirit of God, and in order to save time, and stop the effusion of blood, entered into a treaty with the mobbers to leave the county within a certain time, which treaty, with accompanying documents, will appear in its proper place. The execution of this treaty presented an opportunity for the brethren in Zion to confer with the presidency in Kirtland concerning their situation, which they improved by dispatching Elder O. Cowdery, a special messenger, after a delay of two or three days.

"Thursday night, the 31st of October, gave the saints in Zion abundant proof that no pledge, written or-verbal, was longer to be regarded; for on that night, between forty and fifty in number, many of whom were armed with guns, proceeded against a branch of the church west of Big Blue, and unroofed and partly demolished *ten dwelling houses*, and in the midst of the shrieks and screams of women and children whipped and beat in a savage and brutal manner several of the men, and with their horrid threats frightened women and children into the wilderness. Such of the men as could escape fled for their lives, for very few of them had arms, neither were they embodied, and they were threatened with death if they made any resistance. Such therefore as could not escape by flight received a pelting by rocks and a beating with guns, sticks, etc.

"On Friday, the 1st of November, women and children sallied forth from their gloomy retreats to contemplate with heartrending anguish the ravages of a ruthless mob, in the mangled bodies of their husbands and in the destruction of their houses and some of their furniture. Houseless and unprotected by the arm of the civil law in Jackson County, the dreary month of November staring them in the face and loudly proclaiming an inclement season at hand, the continual threats of the mob that they would drive out every Mormon from the county, and the inability of many to remove, because of their poverty, caused an anguish of heart indescribable.

"On Friday night, the 1st of November, a party of the mob proceeded to attack a branch of the church at the prairie, about twelve or fourteen miles from the village. Two of their number were sent in advance as spies; viz., Robert Johnson and one Harris, armed with two guns and three pistols. They were discovered by some of the saints, and without the least injury being done to them, said (mob) Johnson struck Parley P. Pratt with the breech of his gun over the head, after which they were taken and detained till morning, which, it was believed, prevented a general attack of the mob that night. In the morning they were liberated without receiving the least injury.

"The same night (Friday) another party in Independence commenced stoning houses, breaking down doors and windows, destroying furniture, etc. This night the brick part attached to the dwelling house of A. S. Gilbert was partly pulled down and the windows of his dwelling broken in with brickbats and rocks, while a gentleman stranger lay sick with a fever in his house.

"The same night three doors of the store of Messrs. Gilbert and Whitney were split open, and after midnight the goods lay scattered in the streets, such as calicoes, handkerchiefs, shawls, cambrics, etc. An express came from the village after midnight to a party of their men who had embodied about half a mile from the village for the safety of their lives, stating that the mob were tearing down houses and scattering the goods of the store in the streets. The main body of the mob fled at the approach of this company. One Richard McCarty was caught in the act of throwing rocks and brickbats into the doors, while the goods lay strung around him in the streets, and was immediately taken before Samuel Weston, Esq., and a complaint was then made to said Weston and a warrant requested that said McCarty might be secured; but said Weston refused to do anything in the case at that time. Said McCarty was then liberated.

"The same night some of their houses in the village had long poles thrust through the shutters and sash into the rooms of defenseless women and children, from whence their husbands and fathers had been driven by the dastardly attacks of the mob which were made by ten, fifteen, or twenty men upon a house at a time.

"Saturday, the 2d of November, all the families of the saints in the village moved about half a mile out, with most of their goods, and embodied to the number of thirty for the preservation of life and personal effects. This night a party from the village met a party from the west of the Blue and made an attack upon a branch of the church located at the Blue, about six miles from the village. Here they tore the roof from one dwelling, and broke open another house, found the owner David Bennett sick in bed, whom they beat most inhumanly, swearing they would blow out his brains, and discharged a pistol the ball of which cut a deep gash across the top of his head. In this skirmish a young man of the mob was shot in the thigh, but by which party remains yet to be determined.

"The next day, Sunday, November 3, four of the church; viz., Joshua Lewis, Hiram Page, and two others were dispatched for Lexington to see the circuit judge and obtain a peace warrant. Two called on Esquire Silvers, who refused to issue one, on account, as he has declared, of his fears of the mob. This day many of the citizens, professing friendship, advised the saints to clear from the county as speedily as possible, for the Saturday night affray had enraged the whole county and they were determined to come out on Monday and massacre indiscriminately. And, in short, it was proverbial among the mob that 'Monday would be a bloody day.'

"Monday came, and a large party of the mob gathered at the Blue, took the ferry boat belonging to the church, threatened lives, etc. But they soon abandoned the ferry and went to Wilson's store about one mile west of the Blue. Word had previously gone to a branch of the church several miles west of the Blue, that the mob were destroying property on the east side of the Blue and the sufferers there wanted help to preserve their lives and property. Nineteen men volunteered and started for their assistance; but discovering that fifty or sixty of the mob had gathered at said Wilson's, they turned back.

"At this time two small boys passed on their way to Wilson's, who gave information to the mob that the Mormons were on the road west of them. Between forty and fifty of the mob immediately started with guns in pursuit. After riding about two or two and a half miles they discovered them, when the said company of nineteen immediately dispersed and fled in different directions. The mob hunted them, turning their horses into a cornfield belonging to the saints, searching their cornfields and houses, threatening women and children that they would pull down their houses and kill them if they did not tell where the men had fled.

"Thus they were employed hunting the men and threatening the women, until a company of thirty of the saints from the prairie, armed with seventeen guns, made their appearance.

"The former company of nineteen had dispersed and fled and but one or two of them had returned to take part in the subsequent battle. On the approach of the latter company of thirty men, some of the mob cried, 'fire, God damn ye, fire.' Two or three guns were then fired by the mob, which were returned by the other party without loss of time. This company is the same that is represented by the mob as having gone forth in the evening of the battle bearing the olive branch of peace. The mob retreated early after the first fire, leaving some of their horses in Whitmer's cornfield, and two of their number, Hugh L. Brazeale and Thomas Linvill, dead on the ground. Thus fell H. L. Brazeale, one who had been heard to say, 'with ten fellows, I will wade to my knees in blood, but that I will drive the Mormons from Jackson County.' The next morning the corpse of said Brazeale was discovered on the battle ground with a gun by his side. Several were wounded on both sides, but none mortally except one Barber, on the part of the saints, who expired the next day. This battle was fought about sunset, Monday, November 4; and the same night runners were dispatched in every direction under pretense of calling out the militia; spreading as they went every rumor calculated to alarm and excite the unwary, such as that the Mormons had taken Independence, and the Indians had surrounded it, being colleagued together, etc.

"The same evening, November 4, not being satisfied with breaking open the store of Gilbert and Whitney, and demolishing a part of the dwelling house of said Gilbert, the Friday night previous, they permitted the said McCarty, who was detected on Friday night as one of the breakers of the store doors, to take out a warrant and arrest the said Gilbert and others of the church for a pretended assault and false imprisonment of the said McCarty. Late in the evening, while the court was proceeding with their trial in the courthouse, a gentleman unconnected with the court, as was believed, perceiving the prisoners to be without counsel and in imminent danger, advised said Gilbert and his brethren to go to jail as the only alternative to save life, for the north door was already barred, and an infuriated mob thronged the house with a determination to beat and kill; but through the interposition of this gentleman (Samuel C. Owens, Clerk of the County Court, whose name will appear more fully hereafter), said Gilbert and four of his brethren were committed to the county jail of Jackson County, the dungeon of

which must have been a palace, compared to a court room
where dignity and mercy were strangers, and naught but
the wrath of man in horrid threats stifled the ears of the
prisoners.

"The same night the prisoners, Gilbert, Morley, and Corrill were liberated from jail that they might have an interview with their brethren, and try to negotiate some measures
for peace, and on their return to jail about two o'clock Tuesday morning, in custody of the deputy sheriff, an armed
force of six or seven men stood near the jail and hailed them.
They were answered by the Sheriff, who gave his name, and
the names of his prisoners, crying, 'Don't fire, don't fire, the
prisoners are in my charge, etc.' They however fired one
or two guns, when Morley and Corrill retreated; but Gilbert stood with several guns presented at him, firmly
held by the sheriff. Two, more desperate than the rest,
attempted to shoot; but one of their guns flashed, and the
other missed fire. Gilbert was then knocked down by
Thomas Wilson, a grocer in the village. About this time a
few of the inhabitants arrived, and Gilbert again entered
jail, from which he, with three of his brethren, were liberated about sunrise without further prosecution of the trial.
William E. McLellin was one of the prisoners.

"On the morning of the 5th of November the village began to be crowded with individuals from different parts of
the county, with guns, etc., and report said the militia had
been called out under the sanction or instigation of Lieutenant Governor Boggs, and that one Colonel Pitcher had the
command. Among this militia (so-called) were embodied the
most conspicuous characters of the mob, and it may truly be
said that the appearance of the ranks of this body was well
calculated to excite suspicions of their horrible designs.
Very early on the same morning several branches of the
church received intelligence that a number of their brethren
were in prison, and the determination of the mob was to
kill them; and that the branch of the church near the village
of Independence was in imminent danger, as the main body
of the mob were gathered at that place.

"In this critical situation, about one hundred of the saints from different branches volunteered for the protection of their brethren near Independence, and proceeded on the road towards Independence and halted about one mile west of the village, where they awaited further information concerning the movements of the mob. They soon learned that the prisoners were not massacred, and that the mob had not fallen upon the branch of the church near Independence, as was expected. They were also informed that the militia had been called out for their protection; but in this they placed but little confidence, for the body congregated had every appearance of a county mob, which subsequent events fully verified in a majority of said body.

"On application to Colonel Pitcher it was found that there was no alternative but for the church to leave the county forthwith and deliver into his hands certain men, to be tried for murder said to have been committed by them in the battle the evening before. The arms of the saints were also demanded by Colonel Pitcher. Among the committee appointed to receive the arms of the church were several of the most unrelenting of the old July mob committee who had directed in the demolishing of the printing office and the personal injuries of that day; viz., Henry Chiles, Abner Staples, and Lewis Franklin, who have not ceased to pursue the saints from the first to the last with feelings of the most hostile kind. These unexpected requisitions of the Colonel made him appear like one standing at the head of civil and military law, taking a stretch beyond the constitutional limits of our republic.

"Rather than have submitted to these unreasonable requirements, the saints would have cheerfully shed their blood in defense of their rights, the liberties of their country, and of their wives and children; but the fear of violating law in resisting this pretended militia, and the flattering assurances of protection and honorable usage promised by Lieut. Governor Boggs, in whom they had reposed confidence up to this period, induced them to submit, believing that he did not tolerate so gross a violation of all law as has been practiced in Jackson County. But the great change that may appear to some, in the views, designs, and craft of this man to rob an innocent people of their arms by stratagem and leave more than one thousand defenseless men, women, and children to be driven from their homes, among strangers in a strange land of. to appearances, barbarians, to seek a shelter from the stormy blast of winter's cold embrace, is so glaringly exposed in the sequel that all earth and hell cannot deny that a baser knave, a greater traitor, and a more wholesale butcher or murderer of mankind never went untried, unpunished, and unhung; as hanging is the popular method of execution among the Gentiles, in all countries professing Christianity, instead of blood for blood according to the law of heaven.

"The conduct of Colonels Lucas and Pitcher, had long proven them to be open and avowed enemies. Both of these men had their names attached to the mob circular as early as July last, the object of which was to drive the saints from Jackson County. With assurances from the Lieutenant Governor and others that the object was to disarm the combatants on both sides, and that peace would be the result, the brethren surrendered their arms to the number of fifty or upwards; and the men present, who were accused of being in the battle the evening before, gave themselves up for trial. After detaining them one day and a night on a pretended trial for murder, in which time they were threatened, brickbatted, etc., Colonel Pitcher, after receiving a watch of one of the prisoners to satisfy costs, etc., took them into a cornfield and said to them, 'Clear.'

"After the surrender of their arms, which were used only in self-defense, the neighboring tribes of Indians in time of war let loose upon the women and children could not have appeared more hideous and terrific than did the companies of ruffians who went in various directions well armed, on foot and on horseback, bursting into houses without fear, knowing the arms were secured, frightening distracted women with what they would do to their husbands if they could catch them, warning women and children to flee immediately or they would tear their houses down over their heads and massacre them before night. At the head of one of these companies appeared the Reverend Isaac McCoy, with a gun

upon his shoulder, ordering the saints to leave the county
forthwith and surrender what arms they had.   Other pretended preachers of the gospel took a conspicuous part in
the persecution, calling the 'Mormons' the 'common enemy
of mankind,' and exulting in their afflictions.

"On Tuesday and Wednesday nights, the 5th and 6th of
November, women and children fled in every direction before
the merciless mob.   One party of about one hundred and
fifty women and children fled to the prairie, where they
wandered for several days, under the broad canopy of
heaven, with about six men to protect them.   Other parties
fled to the Missouri River and took lodgings for the night
where they could find it.   One Mr. Bennett opened his
house for a night's shelter to a wandering company of distressed women and children who were fleeing to the river.
During this dispersion of the women and children parties of
the mob were hunting the men, firing upon some, tying up
and whipping others, and some they pursued upon horses
for several miles.

"On the 5th, Elders Phelps, Gilbert, and McLellin went
to Clay County and made an affidavit similar to the foregoing
sketch, and forwarded the same to the Governor by express;
and the Governor immediately upon the reception thereof
ordered a court of inquiry to be held in Clay County for the
purpose of investigating the whole affair and meting out
justice to all; but alas! corruption, wickedness, and power
have

"Left the wretches unwhipt of justice,
And innocence mourns in tears unwiped.

"Thursday, November 7.   The shore began to be lined on
both sides of the ferry with men, women, and children, goods,
wagons, boxes, chests, provisions, etc., while the ferrymen
were busily employed in crossing them over; and when
night again closed upon the saints the wilderness had much
the appearance of a camp meeting.   Hundreds of people
were seen in every direction, some in tents, and some in the
open air around their fires, while the rain descended in torrents.   Husbands were inquiring for their wives, and women
for their husbands; parents for children, and children for

parents. Some had the good fortune to escape with their
family, household goods, and some provisions; while others
knew not the fate of their friends and had lost all their
goods.   The scene was indescribable, and would have melted
the hearts of any people upon earth except the blind oppres-
sor and prejudiced and ignorant bigot. Next day the company increased, and they were chiefly engaged in felling
small cottonwood trees and erecting them into temporary
cabins, so that when night came on they had the appearance
of a village of wigwams, and the night being clear, the
occupants began to enjoy some degree of comfort.

"Lieutenant Governor Boggs presented a curious external appearance; yet he was evidently the head and front of
the mob; for, as may easily be seen by what follows, no important move was made without his sanction. He certainly was
the *secret spring* of the [proceedings of the]20th and 23 l of July,
and, as will appear in the sequel, by his authority the mob was
molded into militia, to effect by stratagem what he knew, as
well as his hellish host, could not be done by legal force. As
Lieutenant Governor he had only to wink, and the mob went
from maltreatment to murder.   The horrid calculations of
this second Nero were often developed in a way that could
not be mistaken. Early on the morning of the 5th, say at
one o'clock a. m., he came to Phelps, Gilbert, and Partridge,
and told them to flee for their lives. Now, unless he had
given the order so to do, no one would have attempted to
murder, after the church had agreed to go away.   His conscience vacillated on its rocky moorings and gave the secret
alarm to these men.

"The saints who fled took refuge in the neighboring counties, mostly in Clay County, which received them with some
degree of kindness. Those who fled to the county of Van
Buren were again driven and compelled to flee, and those
who fled to Lafayette County were soon expelled, or the
most of them, and had to move wherever they could find
protection.

"November 18. About four o'clock a. m. I was awakened
by Brother Davis knocking at my door, and calling on me to
arise and behold the signs in the heavens. I arose, and to

my great joy, beheld the stars fall from heaven like a shower of hailstones; a literal fulfillment of the word of God as recorded in the Holy Scriptures as a sure sign that the coming of Christ is close at hand. In the midst of this shower of fire I was led to exclaim, How marvelous are thy works O Lord! I thank thee for thy mercy unto thy servant, save me in thy kingdom for Christ's sake: Amen!

"The appearance of these signs varied in different sections of the country; in Zion, all heaven seemed enwrapped in splendid fireworks, as if every star in the broad expanse had been suddenly hurled from its course and sent lawless through the wilds of ether. Some at times appeared like bright shooting meteors with long trains of light following in their course, and in numbers resembled large drops of rain in sunshine. Some of the long trains of light following the meteoric stars were visible for some seconds; those streaks would cut and twist up like serpents writhing. The appearance was beautiful, grand, and sublime beyond description, as though all the artillery and fireworks of eternity were set in motion to enchant and entertain the saints, and terrify and awe the sinners on the earth. Beautiful and terrific as was the scenery, which might be compared to the falling figs or fruit when the tree is shaken by a mighty wind, yet it will not fully compare with the time when the sun shall become black like sackcloth of hair, the moon like blood (Rev. 6:12); and the stars fall to the earth, as these appeared to vanish when they fell behind the trees, or came near the ground."

We might fill a volume with such testimonies concerning these difficulties, but the foregoing are doubtless sufficient to make the reader acquainted with the history of this trouble and its causes.

We will, in conclusion, simply quote letters from Attorney General Wells, Judge Ryland, and A. S. Gilbert, and the indorsement by Attorney Amos Reese, as found on pages 912, 913, volume 6, *Times and Seasons*.

"CITY OF JEFFERSON, Nov. 21, 1833.

"*Gentlemen:*—From conversation I have had with the Governor, I believe I am warranted in saying to you, and through you

to the Mormons, that if they desire to be replaced in their
Attorney property, that is, their houses in Jackson County,
General Wells. an adequate force will be sent forthwith to effect
that object. Perhaps a direct application had better be
made to him for that purpose, if they wish thus to be repossessed. The militia have been ordered to hold themselves
in readiness.

"If the Mormons will organize themselves into regular
companies, or a regular company of militia, either volunteers or otherwise, they will, I have no doubt, be supplied
with public arms. This must be upon application, therefore, as a volunteer company must be accepted by the
Colonel, and that is a matter in *his* discretion. Perhaps the
best way would be to organize and elect officers as is done in
ordinary cases—*not* volunteers; you could give them the
necessary directions on these points. If the Colonel should
refuse to order an election of company officers, after they
have reported themselves to him for that purpose, he would
I presume, be court martialled therefor, on a representation
to the Governor of the facts. As only a certain quantity
of public arms can be distributed in each county, those who
first apply will be most likely to receive them. The less,
therefore, that is said upon the subject, the better.

"I am with great respect your obedient servant,
"(Signed)   R. W. WELLS."

"LEXINGTON, Nov. 24, 1833.
"*Dear Sir:—*I have been requested by the Governor to inform him about the outrageous acts of unparalleled violence
that have lately happened in Jackson County, and
Judge Ryland. have also been requested to examine into these
outrages and take steps to punish the guilty and screen
the innocent.

"I cannot proceed unless some person shall be willing to
make the proper information before me. I now request you
to inform me whether the Mormons are willing to take legal
steps against the citizens of Jackson County; whether they
wish to return there or not; and let me know all the matters connected with this unhappy affair. It will be necessary for you to see the persons injured, and be informed

of their desires and intentions. The military force will repair to Jackson County, to aid the execution of any order I make on this subject. Be particular in your information to me. I am willing to go any time to Jackson County, for the purpose of holding a court of inquiry and binding over to keep the peace such persons as I shall think ought to be restrained.

"It is a disgrace to the State for such acts to happen within its limits, and the disgrace will attach to our official characters if we neglect to take proper means to insure the punishment due such offenders.

"I wish to know whether Joshua Lewis and Hiram Page handed the writ to the sheriff of Jackson County that I made and issued on their affidavit against some of the ringleaders of the mob in Jackson County, dated the sixth of this month.

"I will know why he refused to execute the writ, if it ever came to his hands. Inquire into this subject and let me know. I should be glad to see you and agree upon what course to take. After you have sufficiently informed yourself, come down and see me; as you live near the scene of these outrages you are better able to receive all information necessary and prepare for future action than I am.

"Write me as soon as you are properly informed, and state when you can come down and see me on this business. Keep copies of all the letters you write on this subject.

"Your friend,

"(Signed)   JOHN F. RYLAND.

"(*Confidential.*)   LIBERTY, Clay County, November 29, 1833.

"*Dear Sir:*—Yesterday I saw Mr. Doniphan, an attorney of this place, who informed me that he saw the Attorney General. Mr. Wells, in Saline County, last Satur-

A. S. Gilbert.

day week, and that Mr. Wells had acquainted him with your intention of ordering a court of inquiry to be held in Jackson County, in relation to the late riotous proceedings in that county. Mr. Doniphan is of opinion from the conversation he had with Mr. Wells that said order will be suspended till a communication is received from our people, or their counsel. This is therefore to acquaint your excellency that most of the heads of our church had an interview yesterday on the subject of an *immediate* court of inquiry to be held in Jackson County, and by their request to me I hasten to lay before your excellency serious difficulties attending our people on an *immediate* court of inquiry being called.

"Our church is at this time scattered in every direction; some in the new county of Van Buren, a part in this county, and a part in Lafayette, Ray, etc. Some of our principal witnesses would be women and children, and while the rage of the mob continues it would be impossible to gather them in safety at Independence. And that your excellency may know of the unabating fury with which the last remnant of our people remaining in that county are pursued at this time, I here state that a few families, perhaps fifteen to twenty, who settled themselves more than two years ago on the prairie about fifteen miles from the county seat of Jackson County, had hoped from the obscurity of their location that they might escape the vengeance of the enemy through the winter; consequently they remained on their plantations, receiving occasionally a few individual threats, till last Sunday, when a mob made their appearance among them, some with pistols cocked and presented to their breasts, commanding them to leave the county in three days or they would tear their houses down over their heads, etc., etc.

"Two expresses arrived here from said neighborhood last Monday morning for advice, and the council advised their speedy removal for the preservation of life and their personal effects. I suppose these families will be out of the county of Jackson this week. In this distressed situation, in behalf of my brethren I pray your excellency to await a further communication, which will soon follow this, setting forth among other things the importance of our people being restored to their possessions, that they may have an equal chance with their enemies in producing important testimony before the court, which the enemy are now determined to deprive them of. Trusting that your excellency will perceive the agitation and consternation that must necessarily prevail among most of our people at this day from the unparalleled usage they have received, and many of them wandering at this time destitute of shelter, that an *immediate* court of inquiry called while our people are thus situated would give our enemies a decided advantage in point of testimony, while they are in possession of their *own* homes, and *ours* also, with no enemy in the county to molest or make them afraid.

"Very respectfully, your obedient servant,

"A. S. GILBERT.

"To His Excellency *Daniel Dunklin*, Jefferson City, Missouri:—

"I have seen and read the above letter, and on reflection, I concur entirely in the opinion therein expressed. I also think that at the next regular term of the court, an examination of the criminal matter cannot be gone into, without a guard for the court and witnesses.

"(Signed) AMOS REESE."

CHAPTER 13.

1833.

WHILE the foregoing scenes were being enacted in Zion
the church in Kirtland and the East was actively pushing
Active mis-
sionary work. the missionary work, organizing and solidifying
their forces. Their active sympathies and prayers
were also exercised in behalf of the church in the West, and
as close communication with them as the times and means of
transportation would permit, was kept up. It is worthy of
mention that on the 23d of July, 1833, the very day when
the brethren were maltreated in Zion, the corner stones of
the temple were laid at Kirtland.

Two revelations were given in Kirtland through Joseph
Smith; one on August 2, and the other on August 6, which,
Revela-
tions on Zion. when we consider that they were given before tidings could reach him of the troubles then being
enacted in Missouri, are quite significant.[1]

[1] 1. Verily I say unto you my friends, I speak unto you with my voice,
even the voice of my Spirit, that I may show unto you my will concerning your brethren in the land of Zion, many of whom are truly humble,
and are seeking diligently to learn wisdom and to find truth; verily,
verily I say unto you, Blessed are all such for they shall obtain, for I, the
Lord, showeth mercy unto all the meek, and upon all whomsoever I will,
that I may be justified, when I shall bring them into judgment.

2. Behold, I say unto you, concerning the school in Zion, I, the Lord,
am well pleased that there should be a school in Zion; and also with my
servant Parley P. Pratt, for he abideth in me; and inasmuch as he continueth to abide in me, he shall continue to preside over the school, in
the land of Zion, until I shall give unto him other commandments; and
I will bless him with a multiplicity of blessings, in expounding all
scriptures and mysteries to the edification of the school, and of the
church in Zion, and to the residue of the school, I, the Lord, am willing
to show mercy, nevertheless there are those that must needs be chas-

Joseph relates several items of business pertaining to church affairs which are best told in his own language,

tened, and their works shall be made known. The ax is laid at the root of the trees, and every tree that bringeth not forth good fruit, shall be hewn down and cast into the fire; I, the Lord, have spoken it. Verily I say unto you, All among them who know their hearts are honest, and are broken, and their spirits contrite, and are willing to observe their covenants by sacrifice; yea, every sacrifice which I, the Lord, shall command, they are all accepted of me, for I, the Lord, will cause them to bring forth as a very fruitful tree which is planted in a goodly land, by a pure stream, that yieldeth much precious fruit.

3. Verily I say unto you, that it is my will that an house should be built unto me in the land of Zion, like unto the pattern which I have given you; yea, let it be built speedily by the tithing of my people: behold, this is the tithing and the sacrifice which I, the Lord, require at their hands, that there may be an house built unto me for the salvation of Zion; for a place of thanksgiving, for all saints, and for a place of instruction for all those who are called to the work of the ministry, in all their several callings, and offices; that they may be perfected in the understanding of their ministry; in theory; in principle and in doctrine; in all things pertaining to the kingdom of God on the earth, the keys of which kingdom have been conferred upon you.

4. And inasmuch as my people build an house unto me, in the name of the Lord, and do not suffer any unclean thing to come into it, that it be not defiled, my glory shall rest upon it; yea, and my presence shall be there, for I will come into it, and all the pure in heart that shall come into it, shall see God: but if it be defiled I will not come into it, and my glory shall not be there, for I will not come into unholy temples.

5. And now, behold, if Zion do these things, she shall prosper and spread herself and become very glorious, very great, and very terrible; and the nations of the earth shall honor her, and shall say, Surely Zion is the city of our God; and surely Zion cannot fall, neither be moved out of her place, for God is there, and the hand of the Lord is there, and he hath sworn by the power of his might to be her salvation, and her high tower; therefore verily thus saith the Lord, Let Zion rejoice, for this is Zion, THE PURE IN HEART; therefore let Zion rejoice, while all the wicked shall mourn; for, behold, and lo, vengeance cometh speedily upon the ungodly, as the whirlwind, and who shall escape it; the Lord's scourge shall pass over by night and by day; and the report thereof shall vex all people; yet, it shall not be staid until the Lord come; for the indignation of the Lord is kindled against their abominations, and all their wicked works; nevertheless Zion shall escape if she observe to do all things whatsoever I have commanded her, but if she observe not to do whatsoever I have commanded her, I will visit her according to all her works, with sore affliction, with pestilence, with plague, with sword, with vengeance, with devouring fire; nevertheless, let it be read this once in their ears, that I, the Lord, have accepted of their offering: and if she sin no more, none of these things shall come upon her, and I will bless her with blessings, and multiply a multiplicity of blessings upon her, and upon her generations, forever and ever, saith the Lord your God. Amen.

1. Verily I say unto you, my friends, Fear not, let your hearts be comforted, yea, rejoice evermore, and in everything give thanks, waiting patiently on the Lord; for your prayers have entered into the ears of the Lord of Sabaoth, and are recorded with this seal and testament: the Lord hath sworn and decreed that they shall be granted; therefore, he giveth

which is found on page 850 of volume 6, *Times and Seasons:*—

"August 21.   At a council of high priests in Zion, Elder

this promise unto you, with an immutable covenant, that they shall be fulfilled, and all things wherewith you have been afflicted, shall work together for your good, and to my name's glory saith the Lord.

2. And now, verily I say unto you, concerning the laws of the land, It is my will that my people should observe to do all things whatsoever I command them, and that law of the land, which is constitutional, supporting that principle of freedom, in maintaining rights and privileges belongs to all mankind and is justifiable before me; therefore, I, the Lord, justifieth you, and your brethren of my church, in befriending that law which is the constitutional law of the land; and as pertaining to law of man, whatsoever is more or less than these, cometh of evil.   I, the Lord God, maketh you free; therefore, ye are free indeed: and the law also maketh you free; nevertheless when the wicked rule the people mourn; wherefore honest men and wise men should be sought for, diligently, and good men and wise men, ye should observe to uphold; otherwise whatsoever is less than these, cometh of evil.

3. And I give unto you a commandment, that ye shall forsake all evil and cleave unto all good, that ye shall live by every word which proceedeth forth out of the mouth of God; for he will give unto the faithful, line upon line, precept upon precept; and I will try you, and prove you herewith; and whoso layeth down his life in my cause, for my name's sake, shall find it again; even life eternal; therefore, be not afraid of your enemies; for I have decreed in my heart, saith the Lord, that I will prove you in all things, whether you will abide in my covenant, even unto death, that you may be found worthy; for if ye will not abide in my covenant, ye are not worthy of me; therefore, renounce war and proclaim peace, and seek diligently to turn the hearts of their children to their fathers, and the hearts of the fathers to the children.   And again, the hearts of the Jews unto the prophets; and the prophets unto the Jews, lest I come and smite the whole earth with a curse, and all flesh be consumed before me.   Let not your hearts be troubled, for in my Father's house are many mansions, and I have prepared a place for you, and where my Father and I am, there ye shall be also.

4. Behold, I, the Lord, am not well pleased with many who are in the church at Kirtland, for they do not forsake their sins, and their wicked ways, the pride of their hearts, and their covetousness, and all their detestable things, and observe the words of wisdom and eternal life which I have given unto them.   Verily I say unto you, that I, the Lord, will chasten them and will do whatsoever I list, if they do not repent and observe all things whatsoever I have said unto them.   And again, I say unto you, If ye observe to do whatsoever I command you, I, the Lord, will turn away all wrath and indignation from you, and the gates of hell shall not prevail against you.

5. Now, I speak unto you, concerning your families; if men will smite you, or your families, once, and ye bear it patiently and revile not against them, neither seek revenge, ye shall be rewarded; but if ye bear it not patiently, it shall be accounted unto you as being meted out a just measure unto you.   And again, if your enemy shall smite you the second time, and you revile not against your enemy, and bear it patiently, your reward shall be an hundredfold.   And again, if he shall smite you the third time, and ye bear it patiently, your reward shall be doubled unto you fourfold; and these three testimonies shall stand against your enemy, if he repent not, and shall not be blotted out.   And now, verily I say unto you, If that enemy shall escape my vengeance that he be not brought

Christian Whitmer was ordained to the high priesthood; and on the 28th, the council resolved, that no high priest, elder, or priest, shall ordain any priest, elder, or high priest in the

into judgment before me; then ye shall see to it, that ye warn him in my name that he come no more upon you, neither upon your family, even your children's children unto the third and fourth generation; and then if he shall come upon you, or your children, or your children's children unto the third and fourth generation, I have delivered thine enemy into thine hands, and then if thou wilt spare him thou shalt be rewarded for thy righteousness; and also thy children and thy children's children unto the third and fourth generation; nevertheless thine enemy is in thine hands, and if thou reward him according to his works, thou art justified, if he has sought thy life, and thy life is endangered by him; thine enemy is in thine hands, and thou art justified.

6. Behold, this is the law I gave unto my servant, Nephi; and thy father Joseph, and Jacob, and Isaac, and Abraham, and all mine ancient prophets and apostles. And again, this is the law that I gave unto mine ancients, that they should not go out unto battle against any nation, kindred, tongue, or people, save I, the Lord, commanded them. And if any nation, tongue, or people should proclaim war against them, they should first lift a standard of peace unto that people, nation, or tongue, and if that people did not accept the offering of peace, neither the second nor the third time, they should bring these testimonies before the Lord; then, I, the Lord, would give unto them a commandment, and justify them in going out to battle against that nation, tongue, or people, and I, the Lord, would fight their battles, and their children's battles and their children's children until they had avenged themselves on all their enemies, to the third and fourth generation; behold, this is an ensample unto all people, saith the Lord, your God, for justification before me.

7. And again, verily I say unto you, If, after thine enemy has come upon thee the first time, he repent and come unto thee praying thy forgiveness thou shalt forgive him, and shall hold it no more as a testimony against thine enemy, and so on unto the second and the third time; and as oft as thine enemy repenteth of the trespass wherewith he has trespassed against thee, thou shalt forgive him, until seventy times seven; and if he trespass against thee and repent not the first time, nevertheless thou shalt forgive him; and if he trespass against thee the second time, and repent not, nevertheless thou shalt forgive him; and if he trespass against thee the third time and repent not, thou shalt also forgive him; but if he trespass against thee the fourth time, thou shalt not forgive him but shall bring these testimonies before the Lord, and they shall not be blotted out until he repent and reward thee fourfold in all things wherewith he has trespassed against you; and if he do this thou shalt forgive him with all thine heart, and if he do not this, I, the Lord, will avenge thee of thine enemy an hundredfold; and upon his children, and upon his children's children, of all them that hate me, unto the third and fourth generation; but if the children shall repent, or the children's children and turn unto the Lord their God with all their hearts, and with all their might, mind, and strength, and restore fourfold for all their trespasses, wherewith they have trespassed, or wherewith their fathers have trespassed or their father's fathers, then thine indignation shall be turned away and vengeance shall no more come upon them, saith the Lord your God, and their trespasses shall never be brought any more as a testimony before the Lord against them. Amen.

land of Zion, without the consent of a conference of high priests.

"Soon after the arrival of Oliver Cowdery at Kirtland arrangements were made to dispatch Elders Orson Hyde and John Gould to Jackson County, Missouri, with advice to the saints in their unfortunate situation through the late outrage of the mob.

Oliver Cowdery arrives in Kirtland.

"On the 11th of September, the following members, residing in Kirtland; viz., F. G. Williams, Sidney Rigdon, N. K. Whitney, with myself, and Oliver Cowdery, delegate to represent the residue of the members in Independence, Missouri, met in council to consider the expediency of establishing a printing press in Kirtland, when it was resolved, unanimously, that a press be established, and conducted under the firm of F. G. Williams & Co.

Action on publication.

"Resolved, that the above firm publish a paper, as soon as arrangements can be made, entitled the *Latter Day Saints' Messenger and Advocate.*

"Resolved, also, that the *Star*, formerly published in Jackson County, Missouri, by the firm of W. W. Phelps & Co., be printed in this place by the firm of F. G. Williams & Co.; and to be conducted by Oliver Cowdery, one of the members of the firm, until it is transferred to its former location.

"The same day Bishop Partridge was acknowledged by the council in Zion, to be the head of the church, of Zion, at that time; and, by virtue of his office, was acknowledged the moderator or president of the council or conferences.

"Ten high priests were appoined to watch over the ten branches of the church in Zion.

"A hymn, concerning the travels, toils, troubles, and tribulations of the Nephites, was sung in tongues by Elder W. W. Phelps; interpreted by Elder Lyman Wight.

"September 26. The council again assembled in Zion, and ordained Jesse Hitchcock, Elias Higbee, and Isaac Higbee, high priests.

"Brother John Tanner sent his two sons to Kirtland to learn the will of the Lord, whether he should remove to Zion or Kirtland, and it was decided by the unanimous voice of the council on the 28th of September that it was the will of the Lord for all who were able and willing, to build up and strengthen the stake in Kirtland; and Brother Tanner was counselled accordingly.

"About this time Elders Hyde and Gould arrived at Zion, and the church having made the necessary preparations, Elders W. W. Phelps and Orson Hyde were dispatched to the Governor of Missouri, residing at Jefferson City, with the following petition."

Hyde and Gould arrive in Zion.

The petition referred to has already been quoted in chapter 12.

On the 5th of October, 1833, Joseph Smith, Sidney Rigdon, and Freeman Nickerson started from Kirtland on a mission to Canada, which mission was very successful, as will be seen hereafter.

Mission to Canada.

On October 10, Elder F. G. Williams, of the First Presidency, wrote a letter to the brethren in Zion, which we here present to the reader, because of its historical importance, as well as for the sound advice it gives concerning the manner of seeking redress, selling inheritances, the gift of tongues, and other matters. The epistle is found on pages 864 and 865 of *Times and Seasons*, vol. 6, and reads as follows:—

Letter of F. G. Williams.

"*Dear Brethren:*—It is a long time since we have received any intelligence from you, save a letter received by Brother Elliott from Elder John Whitmer, which informed us that he had written four letters since Elder Oliver Cowdery left; but we have not received any of them, nor from any other one in Zion, except one from Bishop Partridge of August 13, and have had no information concerning the riot, and the situation of the brethren in Zion, to be depended upon; and considering that the enemy have commenced intercepting our letters, I direct this to Mrs. Billings, thinking by so doing, that you may get it.

"The brethren here are all engaged in the work of the Lord, and are using every exertion in their power for the welfare of Zion, and for the promotion of the great cause of our Redeemer. Immediately after the arrival of Oliver we sat in council to know what should be done. The decision of the council was, that measures should be immediately taken to seek redress by the laws of your country, for your grievances; accordingly two messengers were dispatched for that purpose. (Let this suffice, for this may fall into the hands of the enemy.) We have received no revelation for a long time, and none concerning the present situation of Zion, which has been written; but it has been manifested to Joseph, and communicated to me by him, that the brethren in Zion should not sell any of their inheritances, nor move out of the county, save those who signed the agreement to go, and if it becomes necessary for those to move, for their personal safety, let them be directed by wisdom, and seek for homes where the Lord shall open the way.

"If Elder Phelps is obliged to move from that place, let him take his family and Elder Cowdery's wife, and come to Kirtland, but not to bring anything with him, except his bedding and clothing; and let Elder Gilbert furnish him with the means to bear his expenses; but it would not be expedient for Elder Phelps to come, provided the prospect is favorable for a reconciliation, so that the saints are not obliged to leave the county. We can do no more for you than we are doing, but we have this great consolation that God will deliver Zion, and establish you upon the land of your everlasting inheritance. Remember that this is only for the trial of your faith, and he that overcomes and endures to the end, will be rewarded a hundredfold in this world, and in the world to come eternal life; so brethren you have great reason to rejoice, for your redemption draweth nigh.

"President Joseph and Sidney are absent on a mission, and we do not expect their return till sometime in November. They have gone down the lake to Niagara, from thence they expect to go into Upper Canada as far as Long Point, and preach in all the most noted places on their way.

"We held a council this morning on the subject of building, etc. It was decided by the council that we should discontinue the building of the temple during the winter for want of materials; and to prepare and get all things in readiness to recommence it early in the spring. It was also agreed to set the hands immediately to erect a house for the printing office, which is to be thirty by thirty-eight feet on

the ground, the first story to be occupied for the school of
the prophets this winter, and the upper story for the printing press.

"Oliver started for New York the first instant, for the
printing establishment, with eight hundred dollars. There
will be as many hands employed upon the house as can work,
and every exertion made to get the printing into operation,
and publish the *Star*, commencing from the last number
printed; and to be conducted by Oliver, (until an opportunity
offers to transfer it again to Zion, to be conducted by W. W.
Phelps & Co., as usual,) and under the firm of F. G. Williams & Co., entitled *The Latter Day Saint's Messenger and
Advocate*. The probability is that the *Star* will be forwarded to subscribers by the first of December. Oliver has
written to you for the names and residence of the subscribers for the *Star*, and if you have not sent them, we wish you
to send them immediately, that there may be no delay in the
papers going to subscribers as soon as they can be printed.

"Bishop Whitney also started for New York at the same
time, to replenish his store in Kirtland, with money enough
to pay all the debts of both establishments, and expects to
bring a larger supply of goods than at any former time.
Thus you see the goodness and mercy of God in providing
for his saints. Not one week before Bishop Whitney
started, the way seemed hedged up and ten or twelve hundred dollars was the most that he had, and knew not where
to obtain the amount he wanted; but by a remarkable interposition of Divine Providence, he was furnished with all he
wanted, for which let us all raise our hearts in gratitude to
God and praise his holy name that he is a present help in
every time of need.

"We have seen a letter written to Sr. Whitney, in Nelson,
that has a great deal to say about the gift of tongues, and
the interpretation which was given by way of prophecy;
namely: 'that Zion would be delivered by judgments,' and
that certain ones named would go to such and such places
among the Lamanites, and 'great things would be done by
them;' and also, that two Lamanites were at a meeting, and
the following prophecy was delivered to them, 'that they

were our friends, and that the Lord had sent them there, and the time would soon come when they should embrace the gospel,' and also, 'that if we will not fight for ourselves, the Indians will fight for us.' Though all this may be true, yet, it is not needful that it should be spoken, for it is of no service to the saints, and has a tendency to stir up the people to anger.

"No prophecy spoken in tongues should be made public, for this reason: many who pretend to have the gift of interpretation are liable to be mistaken, and do not give the true interpretation of what is spoken; therefore, great care should be had, as respects this thing; but, if any speak in tongues, a word of exhortation, or doctrine, or the principles of the gospel, etc., let it be interpreted for the edification of the church.

"When you receive this letter I wish you to write immediately, and direct your letters to David Elliott, Chagrin, Cuyahoga County, Ohio, and put this mark X on the back of it, if you do not wish it broken open, and he will forward it to us; and you will please to name in your letter, where and to whom we shall direct, and thus we may evade interception.

"Yours in the bonds of love,

"F. G. WILLIAMS."

Of this period Joseph wrote:—

"At this time the evil and designing circulated a report that *Zion* was to be *extended* as far *east* as *Ohio*, which in some degree tended to distract the minds of the saints, and produced a momentary indecision about removing thither according to the commandments; but the report was soon corrected, and the brethren continued to remove to Zion and Kirtland."—*Times and Seasons*, vol. 6, p. 865.

While at Perrysburgh, New York, enroute to Canada Joseph received a revelation concerning their families, their mission, Zion, and other interests.[2]

---

[2] 1. Verily, thus saith the Lord unto you my friends, Sidney, and Joseph, your families are well; they are in mine hands, and I will do with them as seemeth me good; for in me there is all power; therefore, follow me, and listen to the counsel which I shall give unto you. Behold, and lo, I have much people in this place, in the regions round

An extract from the journal of Joseph Smith concerning the mission in Canada will prove to be of general interest. The following is found on page 866, *Times and Seasons*, volume 6:—

"On the day following,[a] Elder Rigdon preached to a large congregation, at Freeman Nickerson's, and I bore record while the Lord gave us his Spirit in a remarkable manner.

"Monday, 14th. Continued our journey towards Canada, and arrived at Lodi, where we had an appointment, and preached in the evening to a small assembly, and made an appointment for Tuesday, the 13th, at ten o'clock a. m , to be in the Presbyterian meetinghouse. When the hour arrived the keeper of the house refused to open the doors, and the meeting was then prevented. We came immediately away, leaving the people in great confusion, and continued our journey till Friday, the 17th, when we arrived at the house of Freeman A. Nickerson in Upper Canada; having

about, and an effectual door shall be opened in the regions round about in this eastern land; therefore, I, the Lord, have suffered you to come unto this place; for thus it was expedient in me for the salvation of souls; therefore, verily I say unto you, Lift up your voices unto this people; speak the thoughts that I shall put into your hearts, and ye shall not be confounded before men; for it shall be given you in the very hour, yea, in the very moment, what ye shall say.

2. But a commandment I give unto you, that ye shall declare whatsoever things ye declare in my name, in solemnity of heart, in the spirit of meekness, in all things. And I give unto you this promise, that inasmuch as ye do this, the Holy Ghost shall be shed forth in bearing record unto all things whatsoever ye shall say.

3. And it is expedient in me that you, my servant Sidney, should be a spokesman unto this people; yea, verily, I will ordain you unto this calling, even to be a spokesman unto my servant Joseph; and I will give unto him power to be mighty in testimony; and I will give unto thee power to be mighty in expounding all scriptures, that thou mayest be a spokesman unto him, and he shall be a revelator unto thee, that thou mayest know the certainty of all things pertaining to the things of my kingdom on the earth. Therefore, continue your journey and let your hearts rejoice; for, behold, and lo, I am with you even unto the end.

4. And now I give unto you a word concerning Zion: Zion shall be redeemed, although she is chastened for a little season. Thy brethren, my servants, Orson Hyde and John Gould, are in my hands, and inasmuch as they keep my commandments they shall be saved. Therefore, let your hearts be comforted, for all things shall work together for good to them that walk uprightly, and to the sanctification of the church; for I will raise up unto myself a pure people, that will serve me in righteousness; and all that call on the name of the Lord and keep his commandments, shall be saved. Even so. Amen.

[a] The giving of the revelation.

passed through a fine and well-cultivated country after entering the Province; and having had many peculiar feelings in relation to both the country and people. We were kindly received at Freeman A. Nickerson's.

"Sunday morning, the 19th, at ten o'clock, we met an attentive congregation at Brantford and the same evening a large assembly at Mount Pleasant, at Mr. Nickerson's. The people gave good heed to the things spoken.

"Tuesday, 21st. We went to the village of Colburn, and although it snowed severely, we held a meeting by candle light on Wednesday evening and were publicly opposed by a Wesleyan Methodist. He was very tumultuous, but exhibited a great lack of reason, knowledge, and wisdom; and gave us no opportunity to reply. Twenty-third, at the house of Mr. Beman in Colburn, where we left on the 24th for Waterford, where we spoke to a small congregation, occasioned by the rain; thence to Mount Pleasant, and preached to a large congregation the same evening, when Freeman Nickerson and his wife declared their belief in the work and offered themselves for baptism. Great excitement prevailed in every place we visited. Twenty-fifth, preached at Mount Pleasant; the people were very tender and inquiring.

"Sunday, 26th. Preached to a large congregation at Mount Pleasant, after which I baptized twelve; and others were deeply impressed and desired another meeting, which I appointed for the day following. Twenty-seventh, in the evening, we broke bread, and laid on hands for the gift of the Holy Ghost and for confirmation, having baptized two more. The Spirit was given in great power to some, and peace to others. Twenty-eighth; after preaching at ten o'clock a. m., I baptized two and confirmed them at the water's side. Last evening we ordained E. F. Nickerson an elder, and one of the sisters received the gift of tongues, which made the saints rejoice exceedingly."

On Monday, November 4, Joseph and Sidney Rigdon returned to Kirtland, and Joseph says:—

"Found my family well according to the promise of the Lord in the revelation of October 12, for which I felt to thank my heavenly Father."—*Times and Seasons,* vol. **6,** p. 881.

On November 19, Joseph expressed his opinion of and pronounced blessing upon Sidney Rigdon and F. G. Williams. (*Times and Seasons,* vol. 6, p. 899.)

About December 1, 1833, Elder Oliver Cowdery and Bishop Whitney arrived at Kirtland, Ohio, with a new press and *New press and type.* type, and on the 4th they began to distribute type preparatory to issuing from Kirtland the *Evening and Morning Star* which had been suppressed at Independence, Missouri.

On the 5th Joseph wrote thus to Bishop Partridge:—

"We are now distributing the type and calculate to commence setting to-day, and issue a paper the last of this week, or beginning of next."

On the 6th he says:—

"Being prepared to commence our labors in the printing business, I ask God, in the name of Jesus, to establish it forever, and cause that his name may speedily go forth to the nations of the earth to the accomplishment of his great work, in bringing about the restoration of the house of Israel."—Ibid., p. 915.

On December 10 Joseph wrote to Edward Partridge and others, and we give place to the letter here because it gives *Counsel to exiled saints.* a fair idea of the counsel given to the exiled members of the church; and, as in every other such case, an appeal to the law is recommended as the proper way to gain redress for wrongs.[*]

[*]KIRTLAND MILLS, Ohio, Dec. 10, 1833.

Beloved Brethren:—E. Partridge, W. W. Phelps, J. Whitmer, A. S. Gilbert, J. Corrill, I. Morley, and all the saints whom it may concern: -

This morning's mail brought Bishop Partridge's and Elders Corrill's and Phelps' letters, all mailed at Liberty, November 19, which gave us the melancholy intelligence of your flight from the land of your inheritance, having been driven before the face of your enemies in that place.

From previous letters we learned that a number of our brethren had been slain, but we could not learn from those referred to above, as there had been but one, and that was Brother Barber, and Brother Dibble was wounded in the bowels. We were thankful to learn that no more had been slain, and our daily prayers are that the Lord will not suffer his saints, who have gone up to his land to keep his commandments, to stain his holy mountain with their blood.

I cannot learn from any communication by the Spirit to me that Zion has forfeited her claim to a celestial crown, notwithstanding the Lord has caused her to be thus afflicted, except it may be some individuals who have walked in disobedience and forsaken the new covenant; all such will be made manifest by their works in due time. I have always expected that Zion would suffer some affliction, from what I could learn from the commandments which have been given. But I would remind you of a certain clause in one which says that, "after *much* tribulation cometh the *blessing*." By this, and also others, and also one received of late, I know that Zion, in the own due time of the Lord, will be redeemed; but how many will be the days of her purification, tribulation, and affliction, the Lord has kept hid from my eyes; and when I inquire concerning this subject, the voice of the Lord is, "Be still, and know that I am God! all those who suffer for my name shall reign with me, and he that layeth down his life for my sake shall find it again." Now there are two things of which I am ignorant, and the Lord will not shew them unto me, perhaps for a wise purpose in himself—I mean in some respects—and they are these: why God has suffered so great a calamity to come upon Zion; and what the great moving cause of this great affliction is; and again, by what means he will return her back to her inheritance with songs of everlasting joy upon her head. These two things, brethren, are in part kept back that they are not plainly manifest, in consequence of those who have incurred the displeasure of the Almighty.

When I contemplate upon all things that have been manifested, I am sensible that I ought not to murmur and do not murmur only in this, that those who are innocent are compelled to suffer for the iniquities of the guilty; and I cannot account for this only on this wise, that the saying of the Savior has not been strictly observed: "If thy right eye offend thee, pluck it out and cast it from thee; or if thy right arm offend thee, cut it off and cast it from thee." Now the fact is, if any of the members of our body are disordered, the rest of our body will be affected with them, and then all is brought into bondage together: and yet, notwithstanding all this, it is with difficulty that I can restrain my feelings when I know that you, my brethren, with whom I have had so many happy hours, sitting, as it were, in heavenly places in Christ Jesus: and also, having the witness which I feel and ever have felt of the purity of your motives, are cast out and are as strangers and pilgrims on the earth, exposed to hunger, cold, nakedness, peril, sword, etc;—I say when I contemplate this, it is with difficulty that I can keep from complaining and murmuring against this dispensation. But I am sensible that this is not right, and may God grant that notwithstanding your great afflictions and sufferings there may not anything separate us from the love of Christ.

Brethren, when we learn your sufferings it awakens every sympathy of our hearts; it weighs us down; we cannot refrain from tears, yet we are not able to realize, only in part, your sufferings. And I often hear the brethren saying they wish they were with you that they might bear a part of your sufferings. And I myself should have been with you had not God prevented it in the order of his providence, that the yoke of affliction might be less grievous upon you, God having forewarned me, concerning these things, for your sakes. And also, Elder Cowdery could not have lightened your afflictions by tarrying longer with you, for his presence would have so much the more enraged your enemies; therefore God hath dealt mercifully with us.

O brethren, let us be thankful that it is as well with us as it is and we are yet alive, that peradventure God hath laid up in store great good for us in this generation and grant that we may yet glorify his name.

I feel thankful that there have no more denied the faith. I pray God in the name of Jesus that you all may be kept in the faith unto the end. Let your sufferings be what they may, it is better in the eyes of God that you should die than that you should give up the land of Zion, the inheritances which you have purchased with your moneys; for every man that giveth not up his inheritance, though he should die, yet when the Lord shall come he shall stand upon it, and with Job in his flesh he shall see God. Therefore, this is my counsel, that you retain your lands, even unto the uttermost, and seek every lawful means to seek redress of your enemies, etc., etc.; and pray to God, day and night, to return you in peace and in safety to the lands of your inheritance. And when the judge fails you, appeal unto the Executive; and when the Executive fails you, appeal unto the President; and when the President fails you, and all laws fail you, and the humanity of the people fails you, and all things else fail you but God alone, and you continue to weary him with your importunings, as the poor woman did the unjust judge, he will not fail to execute judgment upon your enemies, and to avenge his own elect that cry unto him day and night.

Behold, he will not fail you! He will come with ten thousand of his saints, and all his adversaries shall be destroyed with the breath of his lips! All those who keep their inheritances, notwithstanding they should be beaten and driven, shall be likened unto the wise virgins who took oil in their lamps. But all those who are unbelieving and fearful, will be likened unto the foolish virgins, who took no oil in their lamps; and when they shall return and say unto the saints, "Give us of your lands," behold, there will be no room found for them. As respects giving deeds; I would advise you to give deeds as far as the brethren have legal and just claims for them, and then let every man answer to God for the disposal of them.

I would suggest some ideas to Elder Phelps, not knowing as they will be of any real benefit, but suggest them for consideration. I would be glad that he were here, but dare not advise, were it possible for him to come, not knowing what shall befall us, as we are under very heavy and serious threatenings from a great many people in this place.

But perhaps the people in Liberty may feel willing, God having power to soften the hearts of all men, to have a press established there; and if not, in some other place; any place where it can be the most convenient, and it is possible to get to it; God will be willing to have it in any place where it can be established in safety. We must be wise as serpents and harmless as doves. Again, I desire that Elder Phelps would collect all the information, and give us a true history of the beginning and rise of Zion, her calamities, etc.

Now hear the prayer of your unworthy brother in the new and everlasting covenant: O my God! thou who hast called and chosen a few, through thy weak instrument, by commandment, and sent them to Missouri, a place which thou didst call Zion, and commanded thy servants to consecrate it unto thyself for a place of refuge and safety for the gathering of thy saints, to be built up a holy city unto thyself; and as thou hast said that no other place should be appointed like unto this; therefore, I ask thee, in the name of Jesus Christ, to return thy people unto their houses and their inheritances, to enjoy the fruit of their labors; that all the waste places may be built up; that all the enemies of thy people, who will not repent and turn unto thee, be destroyed from off the face of the land; and let a house be built and established unto thy name; and let all the losses that thy people have sustained be rewarded unto them, even more than fourfold; that the borders of Zion be enlarged forever, and let her be established no more to be thrown down; and let all thy saints when they are scattered like sheep and are persecuted, flee unto Zion, and be established in the midst of her, and let

On the 16th a revelation was received explaining why the
Reasons for trouble was permitted to come upon the inhabit-
Zion's trouble. ants of Zion, but promising a return of favors on
conditions of faithfulness. [5]

her be organized according to thy law, and let this prayer ever be
recorded before thy face. Give thy Holy Spirit unto my brethren,
unto whom I write; send thine angels to guard them, and deliver them
from all evil; and when they turn their faces towards Zion and bow
down before thee and pray, may their sins never come up before
thy face, neither have place in the book of thy remembrance, and
may they depart from all their iniquities. Provide food for them as
thou doest for the ravens; provide clothing to cover their nakedness, and
houses that they may dwell therein; give unto them friends in abundance,
and let their names be recorded in the Lamb's book of life, eternally before thy face. Amen.

Finally, brethren, the grace of our Lord Jesus Christ be with you all
until his coming and kingdom. Amen.

JOSEPH SMITH, JR.
—*Times and Seasons*, vol. 6, pp. 928, 929.

[5] 1. Verily, I say unto you, concerning your brethren who have been
afflicted, and persecuted, and cast out from the land of their inheritance,
I, the Lord, have suffered the affliction to come upon them, wherewith
they have been afflicted in consequence of their transgressions; yet, I will
own them, and they shall be mine in that day when I shall come to
make up my jewels.

2. Therefore, they must needs be chastened, and tried, even as Abraham, who was commanded to offer up his only son; for all those who will
not endure chastening, but deny me, cannot be sanctified.

3. Behold, I say unto you, there were jarrings, and contentions, and
envyings, and strifes, and lustful and covetous desires among them;
therefore by these things they polluted their inheritances. They were
slow to hearken unto the voice of the Lord their God; therefore, the
Lord their God is slow to hearken unto their prayers, to answer them in
the day of their trouble. In the day of their peace they esteemed lightly
my counsel; but in the day of their trouble, of necessity they feel after
me.

4. Verily, I say unto you, Notwithstanding their sins, my bowels are
filled with compassion toward them; I will not utterly cast them off; and
in the day of wrath I will remember mercy. I have sworn, and the decree hath gone forth by a former commandment which I have given
unto you, that I would let fall the sword of mine indignation in the
behalf of my people; and even as I have said, it shall come to pass.
Mine indignation is soon to be poured out without measure upon all
nations, and this will I do when the cup of their iniquity is full. And
in that day, all who are found upon the watchtower, or in other words, all
mine Israel shall be saved. And they that have been scattered shall be gathered; and all they who have mourned shall be comforted; and all they who
have given their lives for my name shall be crowned. Therefore, let your
hearts be comforted concerning Zion, for all flesh is in mine hands: be
still, and know that I am God. Zion shall not be moved out of her place,
notwithstanding her children are scattered, they that remain and are pure
in heart shall return and come to their inheritances; they and their children, with songs of everlasting joy; to build up the waste places of Zion.
And all these things, that the prophets might be fulfilled. And, behold,

On December 18, 1833, the elders of Kirtland assembled
a the printing office and dedicated the press and appurte-

here is none other place appointed than that which I have appointed,
either shall there be any other place appointed than that which I have
ppointed for the work of the gathering of my saints, until the day com-
th when there is found no more room for them; and then I have other
laces which I will appoint unto them, and they shall be called stakes,
or the curtains, or the strength of Zion.

5. Behold, it is my will, that all they who call on my name, and wor-
hip me according to mine everlasting gospel, should gather together
nd stand in holy places, and prepare for the revelation which is to
ome when the veil of the covering of my temple, in my tabernacle,
'hich hideth the earth, shall be taken off, and all flesh shall see me
ogether. And every corruptible thing, both of man, or of the beasts of
he field, or of the fowls of heaven, or of the fish of the sea, that dwell
pon all the face of the earth, shall be consumed; and also, that of ele-
ient shall melt with fervent heat; and all things shall become new, that
y knowledge and glory may dwell upon all the earth. And in that day
he enmity of man, and the enmity of beasts; yea, the enmity of all flesh
hall cease from before my face. And in that day whatsoever any man
hall ask it shall be given unto him. And in that day Satan shall not
ave power to tempt any man. And there shall be no sorrow because
here is no death. In that day an infant shall not die until he is old,
nd his life shall be as the age of a tree, and when he dies he shall not
leep (that is to say in the earth), but shall be changed in the twinkling
f an eye, and shall be caught up, and his rest shall be glorious. Yea,
erily I say unto you, In that day when the Lord shall come he shall
eveal all things; things which have passed, and hidden things which
o man knew; things of the earth by which it was made, and the pur-
ose and the end thereof; things most precious; things that are above,
nd things that are beneath; things that are in the earth, and upon the
arth, and in heaven. And all they who suffer persecution for my name,
nd endure in faith, though they are called to lay down their lives for
y sake, yet shall they partake of all this glory. Wherefore, fear not
ven unto death; for in this world your joy is not full, but in me your
oy is full. Therefore, care not for the body, neither the life of the
ody; but care for the soul, and for the life of the soul, and seek the face
f the Lord always, that in patience ye may possess your souls, and ye
hall have eternal life. When men are called unto mine everlasting
ospel, and covenant with an everlasting covenant, they are accounted
the salt of the earth, and the savor of men. They are called to be the
ivor of men. Therefore, if that salt of the earth lose its savor, behold,
is thenceforth good for nothing, only to be cast out and trodden under
e feet of men. Behold, here is wisdom concerning the children of
ion; even many, but not all; they were found transgressors, therefore,
ey must needs be chastened. He that exalteth himself shall be abased,
nd he that abaseth himself shall be exalted.

6. And now, I will show unto you a parable that you may know my
ill concerning the redemption of Zion. A certain nobleman had a spot
f land, very choice; and he said unto his servants, Go ye into my vine-
ard, even upon this very choice piece of land, and plant twelve olive
ees; and set watchmen round about them and build a tower, that one
ay overlook the land round about, to be a watchman upon the tower;
iat mine olive trees may not be broken down, when the enemy shall
ome to spoil and take unto themselves the fruit of my vineyard. Now
e servants of the nobleman went and did as their lord commanded

nances to the work of the Lord; then took the proof sheets
of the first number of the *Evening and Morning Star*

Printing office dedicated.

issued from Kirtland and edited by Oliver Cowdery.   This is a continuation of the paper published at Independence, and is number 15 of volume 2.

them; and planted the olive trees, and built a hedge round about, and
set watchmen, and began to build a tower.   And while they were yet
laying the foundation thereof, they began to say among themselves, And
what need hath my lord of this tower? and consulted for a long time,
saying among themselves, What need hath my lord of this tower, seeing
this is a time of peace? Might not this money be given to the exchang-
ers? for there is no need of these things!   And while they were at variance one with another they became very slothful, and they hearkened
not unto the commandments of their lord, and the enemy came by night
and broke down the hedge, and the servants of the nobleman arose, and
were affrighted, and fled; and the enemy destroyed their works and
broke down the olive trees.

7. Now, behold, the nobleman, the lord of the vineyard, called upon
his servants, and said unto them, Why! what is the cause of this great
evil? ought ye not to have done even as I commanded you? and after ye
had planted the vineyard, and built the hedge round about, and set
watchmen upon the walls thereof, built the tower also, and set a watchman
upon the tower, and watched for my vineyard, and not have fallen
asleep, lest the enemy should come upon you? and, behold, the watchman upon the tower would have seen the enemy while he was yet afar
off, and then you could have made ready and kept the enemy from
breaking down the hedge thereof, and saved my vineyard from the
hands of the destroyer. And the lord of the vineyard said unto one of
his servants, Go and gather together the residue of my servants; and
take all the strength of mine house, which are my warriors, my young
men, and they that are of middle age also, among all my servants, who
are the strength of mine house, save those only whom I have appointed
to tarry; and go ye straightway unto the land of my vineyard, and redeem my vineyard, for it is mine, I have bought it with money.   Therefore, get ye straightway unto my land; break down the walls of mine
enemies, throw down their tower, and scatter their watchmen; and inasmuch as they gather together against you, avenge me of mine enemies;
that by and by I may come with the residue of mine house and possess the land.

8. And the servant said unto his lord, When shall these things be?
And he said unto his servant, When I will: go ye straightway: and do
all things whatsoever I have commanded you; and this shall be my seal
and blessing upon you; a faithful and wise steward in the midst of mine
house; a ruler in my kingdom. And his servant went straightway, and
did all things whatsoever his lord commanded him, and after many
days all things were fulfil ed.

9. Again, verily I say unto you, I will show unto you wisdom in me
concerning all the churches, inasmuch as they are willing to be guided
in a right and proper way for their salvation, that the work of the gathering together of my saints may continue, that I may build them up unto
my name upon holy places; for the time of harvest is come, and my
word must needs be fulfilled. Therefore, I must gather together my
people according to the parable of the wheat and the tares, that the
wheat may be secured in the garners to possess eternal life, and be

About this time Joseph pronounced some blessings upon Oliver Cowdery; also upon his own father's house, espe-

crowned with celestial glory when I shall come in the kingdom of my Father, to reward every man according as his work shall be; while the tares shall be bound in bundles, and their bands made strong, that they may be burned with unquenchable fire. Therefore, a commandment I give unto all the churches, that they shall continue to gather together unto the places which I have appointed; nevertheless, as I have said unto you in a former commandment, let not your gathering be in haste, nor by flight; but let all things be prepared before you; and in order that all things be prepared before you, observe the commandments which I have given concerning these things, which saith, or teacheth, to purchase all the lands by money, which can be purchased for money, in the region round about the land which I have appointed to be the land of Zion, for the beginning of the gathering of my saints; all the land which can be purchased in Jackson County, and the counties round about, and leave the residue in mine hand.

10. Now, verily I say unto you, Let all the churches gather together all their moneys; let these things be done in their time, be not in haste; and observe to have all things prepared before you. And let honorable men be appointed, even wise men, and send them to purchase these lands; and every church in the eastern countries when they are built up, if they will hearken unto this counsel, they may buy lands and gather together upon them, and in this way they may establish Zion. There is even now already in store a sufficient, yea, even abundance to redeem Zion, and establish her waste places, no more to be thrown down, were the churches, who call themselves after my name, willing to hearken to my voice. And again I say unto you, Those who have been scattered by their enemies, it is my will that they should continue to importune for redress, and redemption, by the hands of those who are placed as rulers, and are in authority over you, according to the laws and Constitution of the people which I have suffered to be established, and should be maintained for the rights and protection of all flesh, according to just and holy principles, that every man may act in doctrine, and principle pertaining to futurity, according to the moral agency which I have given unto them, that every man may be accountable for his own sins in the day of judgment. Therefore, it is not right that any man should be in bondage one to another. And for this purpose have I established the Constitution of this land, by the hands of wise men whom I raised up unto this very purpose, and redeemed the land by the shedding of blood.

11. Now, unto what shall I liken the children of Zion? I will liken them unto the parable of the woman and the unjust judge (for men ought always to pray and not faint), which saith, There was in a city a judge which feared not God, neither regarded man. And there was a widow in that city, and she came unto him, saying, Avenge me of mine adversary. And he would not for awhile, but afterward he said within himself, Though I fear not God, nor regard man, yet because this widow troubleth me I will avenge her, lest by her continual coming, she weary me. Thus will I liken the children of Zion.

12. Let them importune at the feet of the judge; and if he heed them not, let them importune at the feet of the governor; and if the governor heed them not, let them importune at the feet of the President; and if the President heed them not, then will the Lord arise and come forth out of his hiding place, and in his fury vex the nation, and in his hot displeasure, and in his fierce anger, in his time, will cut off these wicked, unfaithful, and unjust stewards, and appoint them their portion among

cially his father and mother, and his brothers Hyrum, Samuel, and Will m; which the reader may be pleased to peruse. They a found on page 947, volume 6, *Times and Seasons.*

On December 1 , 1833, William Pratt and David W. Pat-
Dispatches to Zion. ten star ed from Kirtland for Zion, bearing dis-patches or the brethren in Zion.

In the December number of the *Evening and Morning Star,*
Epistle to breth-ren abroad. the first · published in Kirtland, the elders in Kirt-land published an epistle to their brethren abroad, to which we give place, believing it will be of general interest. This may be found on page 239, volume 2, and reads as follows:—

"*The Elders in Kirtland, to their brethren abroad.*

"Dear brethren in Christ, and companions in tribulation:— It seemeth good unto us to drop a few lines to you, giving you some instruction relative to conducting the affairs of the kingdom of God, which has been committed unto us in these latter times, by the will and testament of our Mediator. whose intercessions in our behalf are lodged in the bosom of the eternal Father, and ere long will burst with blessings upon the heads of all the faithful:

"We have all been children, and are too much so at the

hypocrites and unbelievers; even in outer darkness, where there is weep-ing, and wailing, and gnashing of teeth. Pray ye, therefore, that their ears may be opened unto your cries, that I may be merciful unto them, that these things may not come upon them. What I have said unto you, must needs be, that all men may be left without excuse; that wise men and rulers may hear and know that which they have never considered; that I may proceed to bring to pass my act, my strange act, and perform my work, my strange work. That men may discern between the right-eous and the wicked, saith your God.

18. And again, I say unto you, It is contrary to my commandment, and my will, that my servant Sidney Gilbert should sell my storehouse. which I have appointed unto my people, into the hands of mine enemies. Let not that which I have appointed, be polluted by mine enemies, by the consent of those who call themselves after my name; for this is a very sore and grievous sin against me, and against my people, in conse-quence of those things which I have decreed, and are soon to befall the nations. Therefore, it is my will that my people should claim, and hold claim, upon that which I have appointed unto them, though they should not be permitted to dwell thereon; nevertheless, I do not say they shall not dwell thereon; for inasmuch as they bring forth fruit and works meet for my kingdom, they shall dwell thereon; they shall build, and another shall not inherit it; they shall plant vineyards, and they shall eat the fruit thereof. Even so. Amen.

present time; but we hope in the Lord that we may grow in grace and be prepared for all things which the bosom of futurity may disclose unto us. Time is rapidly rolling on, and the prophecies must be fulfilled. The days of tribulation are fast approaching, and the time to test the fidelity of the saints has come. Rumor with her ten thousand tongues is diffusing her uncertain sounds in almost every ear; but in these times of sore trial let the saints be patient and see the salvation of God. Those who cannot endure persecution and stand in the day of affliction, cannot stand in the day when the Son of God shall burst the veil and appear in all the glory of his Father with all the holy angels.

"On the subject of ordination, a few words are necessary: In many instances there has been too much haste in this thing, and the admonition of Paul has been too slightingly passed over, which says: *'Lay hands suddenly upon no man.'* Some have been ordained to the ministry, and have never acted in that capacity, or magnified their calling at all. Such may expect to lose their calling, except they awake and magnify their office. Let the elders abroad be exceedingly careful upon this subject, and when they ordain a man to the holy ministry, let it be a *faithful man,* who is able to teach others also; that the cause of Christ suffer not. It is not the multitude of preachers that is to bring about the glorious millennium, but it is those who are *'called, and chosen, and faithful.'*

"Let the elders be exceedingly careful about *unnecessarily* disturbing and harrowing up the feelings of the people. Remember that your business is to preach the gospel in all humility and meekness, and warn sinners to repent and come to Christ. Avoid contentions and vain disputes with men of corrupt minds, who do not desire to know the truth. Remember that *'it is a day of warning, and not a day of many words.'* If they receive not your testimony in one place, flee to another, remembering to cast no reflections, nor throw out any bitter sayings. If you do your duty it will be just as well with you as though all men embraced the gospel.

"Be careful about sending boys to preach the gospel to the world; if they go, let them be accompanied by some one who is able to guide them in the proper channel, lest they become puffed up, and fall under condemnation and into the snare of the Devil. Finally, in these critical times, be careful, call on the Lord day and night. Beware of pride; beware of *false brethren*, who will creep in among you to spy out your liberties. etc. Awake to righteousness and sin not; let your light shine, and show yourselves workmen that need not be ashamed, rightly dividing the word of truth. Apply yourselves diligently to study, that your minds may be stored with all necessary information.

"We remain your brethren in Christ, anxiously praying for the day of redemption to come, when iniquity shall be swept from the earth; and everlasting righteousness brought in. Farewell."

Thus the year closed in comparative peace for the church in Kirtland, and the church growing and extending in the Eastern States and in Canada. A printing press was established and prospects were bright, though much sorrow was felt for their suffering brethren in Zion.

Some murmurings and threats were heard around Kirtland, but no open violence was offered, though they knew not how soon they would be called upon to suffer banishment or death as their brethren had.

Threats around Kirtland.

CHAPTER 14.

1833.

DEPREDATIONS OF THE MOB—SAINTS ENGAGE COUNSEL—THEIR
CREDIT GOOD—APPEAL TO GOVERNOR—PERSECUTION IN VAN
BUREN COUNTY—LETTER FROM PHELPS—AGED FAMILIES ABUSED
—BURR JOYCE ON THE EXODUS—A CONTRAST—PRAYERS FOR ZION.

RETURNING to Zion we find the mob hunting down and
abusing all scattered families who chanced for any cause to
Depredations of the mob. remain behind their brethren, destroying their
property, and in some instances their lives; while
the saints were using every means in their power to gain
redress, and to be restored to their rights by appeal to legal
tribunals.

They engaged Messrs. Wood, Reese, Doniphan, and Atchison as attorneys to bring all suits they might wish brought
Saints engage counsel. against the mob, for which they were to pay one
thousand dollars, and for which W. W. Phelps and
Edward Partridge gave their joint note. These gentlemen
were among the leading members of the bar in that country.

This incident has a striking significance. Phelps and
Partridge, with their business destroyed, their homes
Their credit good. broken up, their property laid waste, and themselves exiled and charged by their former neighbors with being fanatics and disturbers of the public peace,
are considered by leading lawyers, to whom all the facts are
known, to be good for one thousand dollars. Does it not
appear that these attorneys had confidence in the honor of
these men, and hence knew that charges against, and rumors
concerning them were untrue?

On Friday, December 6, 1833, six of the brethren petitioned
Appeal to Governor. the Governor for help to be reinstated to their possessions in Jackson County. But their petition as
recorded in *Times and Seasons*, vol. 6, page 915, speaks for
itself. It is as follows:—

"*To his Excellency, Daniel Dunklin, Governor of the State of Missouri:*—We, the undersigned, leading members of the Church of Christ, vulgarly called Mormons, would respectfully represent to your Excellency, in addition to the petition presented to you by Messrs. Phelps and Hyde and the affidavit of Messrs. Phelps, Gilbert, and McLellin, after having read the letters of the Attorney General and District Judge of this circuit to Mr. Reese; that whereas, our society, men, women, and children, after having been in some cases wounded, scourged, and threatened with death, have been driven by *force of arms* from their lands, houses, and much of their property in Jackson County, (most of which lands, houses, and property have been possessed by the mob of Jackson County, or others,) and are now unlawfully detained from the use and possession of our people; and that, whereas, our people have been driven and scattered into the counties of Clay, Ray, Van Buren, Lafayette, and others, where in many cases they are destitute of the common necessaries of life in this, even this winter season; and that whereas, the guns which were taken from our people, as set forth in the affidavit, are kept from them; Therefore, in behalf of our society, which is so scattered and suffering, we, your petitioners, ask aid and assistance of your Excellency, that we may be *restored* to our lands, houses, and property, and protected in them by the militia of the State, if legal, or by a detachment of the United States Rangers, which might be located at Independence, instead of Cantonment Leavenworth, till peace is restored.   [This could be done probably, by conferring with the President, or perhaps Colonel Dodge.] Also, we ask that our men may be organized into companies of Jackson Guards, and be furnished with arms by the State, to assist in maintaining their rights against the unhallowed power of the mob of Jackson County.

"And then, when arrangements are made to protect us in our persons and property (which cannot be done without an armed force, nor would it be prudent to risk our lives there without guards, till we receive strength from our friends to protect ourselves), we wish a court of inquiry instituted to

nvestigate the whole matter of the mob against the Mor-
nons; and we will ever pray.

"W. W. PHELPS.
"JOHN WHITMER.
"JOHN CORRILL.
"ISAAC MORLEY.
"EDWARD PARTRIDGE.
"A. S. GILBERT.

"The following letter accompanied the foregoing petition:—

"LIBERTY, December 6, 1833.

"*Dear Sir:*—Your Excellency will perceive by the petition
earing date with this letter, that we intend to return to
ackson County as soon as arrangements can be made to
rotect us, after we are again placed into our possessions.

"We do not wish to go till we know that our lives are not
n danger of a lawless mob. Your Excellency will under-
tand that, at this inclement season, it will require time to
estore us, and troops to *protect* us, after we are there, for
he threats of the mob have not ceased.

"Your obedient servant,

"W. W. PHELPS.

"To Daniel Dunklin, Governor of Missouri."

On Thursday, December 12, a messenger arrived at
iberty, Missouri, bearing the intelligence that the saints
who had removed from Jackson County to Van
Buren County were about to be driven from there.
In the history of Joseph Smith as published in
imes and Seasons, volume 6, pages 929, 930, it is thus
tated:—

erseoution
Van
uren County.

"December 12. An express arrived at Liberty, from Van
uren County, with information, that those families which
ad fled from Jackson County and located there are about to
e driven from that county, after building their houses and
arting their winter's store of provision, grain, etc., forty or
fty miles. Several families are already fleeing from thence.
'he contaminating influence of the Jackson County mob is
redominant in this new county of Van Buren, the whole
opulation of which is estimated at about thirty or forty
milies. The destruction of crops, household furniture, and
lothing is very great, and much of their stock is lost. The
nain body of the church is now in Clay County, where the
eople are as kind and accommodating as could reasonably be

expected. The continued threats of death to individuals of the church, if they make their appearance in Jackson County, prevent the most of them, even at this day, from returning to that county to secure personal property which they were obliged to leave in their flight."

On Sunday, December 15, W. W. Phelps wrote from Clay County, Missouri, to the brethren in Kirtland a letter which gives an index to the situation. [1]

Letter from Phelps.

[1] *Dear Brethren:*—It has been some time since I have dropped you a line, and in the midst of solitude I write. I need not give you new details of our persecutions, for, as all true Christians that have gone before us, from Abel down to the beginners of reëstablishing Zion *now*, have invariably suffered all manner of affliction, from common scourging even unto death. It would not alter the decrees of God, nor lessen the necessary chastisement of them that are chosen from the foundation of the world, but who have to be tried as gold seven times purified before they are found faithful and true for that kingdom, *where the sons of God only* are made equal with Jesus Christ, *having overcome*, by righteousness.

The situation of the saints, as scattered, is dubious, and affords a gloomy prospect. No regular order can be enforced; nor any usual discipline kept up—among the world; yea, the most wicked part of it, some commit one sin, and some another. (I speak of the rebellious, for there are saints that are as immovable as the everlasting hills.) And what can be done? We are in Clay, Ray, Lafayette, Jackson, Van Buren, etc., and cannot hear from each other oftener than we do from you. I know it was right that we should be driven out of the land of Zion, that the rebellious might be sent away. But brethren, if the Lord will, I should like to know what the honest in heart shall do? Our clothes are worn out—we want the necessaries of life, and shall we lease, buy, or otherwise obtain land where we are, to till that we may raise enough to eat? Such is the common language of the honest, for they want to do the will of God. I am sensible that we shall not be able to live again in Zion, till God or the President rules out the mob.

The Governor is willing to restore us, but as the Constitution gives him no power to guard us, when back, we are not willing to go. The mob swear if we come we shall die! If, from what has been done in Zion, we, or the most of us, have got to be persecuted from city to city, and from synagogue to synagogue, we want to know it; for there are those among us that would rather earn eternal life on such conditions, than lose it. But we hope for better things; and shall wait patiently for the word of the Lord.

I do not write this letter to entertain you with news, or for to wake you up to our dreadful condition, but that you may timely give us some advice what is best to do in our tarry till Zion is redeemed. Sometimes I think I will go right to work upon a small piece of land and obtain what I want for my growing family; then again I feel like writing the horrid history of the mob against the "Mormons"—preambling it with the martyrs that have been nailed to the cross, burned alive, thrown to wild beasts and devoured, fried in pans, broiled in gridirons, or beheaded for the sake of their religion and faith in Jesus Christ. "Blessed are the poor in spirit, for theirs is the kingdom of heaven," etc. If this world embraced much of eternity, I should soon be sick of it; but for all our sorrow we shall have joy!

On the night of December 24, 1833, the mob fell upon me aged families near Independence, destroying their
sd famil-
i abused. property and endangering their lives. We insert this item, together with other historical items, in e language of Joseph Smith, as found in volume 6 of *Times d Seasons*, pages 960, 961:—

"On the night of the 24th of December, four aged milies living near the village of Independence, whose nury and infirmities incident to old age forbade a speedy moval, were driven from their houses by a party of the ob, who tore down their chimneys, broke in their doors id windows, and hurled large rocks into their houses, by hich the life of old Mr. Miller, in particular, was greatly idangered. Mr. Miller is aged sixty-five years, being the ungest man in the four families. Some of these men have iled and bled in the defense of their country; and old Mr. nes, one of the sufferers, served as lifeguard to General eorge Washington, in the Revolution. Well may the soler of Seventy-Six contemplate with horror the scenes hich surround him at this day in Jackson County, where berty, law, and equal rights are trodden under foot. It is w apparent that no man embracing the faith of this peo- e, whatever be his age or former standing in society, may pe to escape the wrath of the Jackson County mob, when- er it is in their power to inflict abuse.

"A court of inquiry was held at Liberty, Clay County, issouri, the latter part of this month, to inquire into the nduct of Colonel Pitcher for driving the saints or Mormons om Jackson County, which resulted in his arrest for fur- ier trial by a court martial. . . .

"The mob sold the materials, or rather gave Davis & elley leave to take the *Evening and Morning Star* establish- ent to Liberty, Clay County, where they commenced the

---

Our people fare very well, and when they are discreet, little or no per- cution is felt. The militia in the upper counties is in readiness at a oment's warning, having been ordered out by the Governor to guard a urt martial, and court of inquiry, etc., but we cannot attend a court of quiry, on account of the expense, till we are restored and protected. Till the Lord delivers, or brings us together, I am,

W. W. PHELPS.

publication of *The Missouri Enquirer*, a weekly paper. They also paid our lawyers, employed as counsel against the mob, three hundred dollars on the one thousand dollar note, on agreement: a small amount towards an establishment which, with the book work and furniture, had cost some three or four thousand dollars.

"From the very features of the celebrated mob circular, previously inserted, it will be seen that they meditated a most daring infraction of the Constitution of our country, that they might gratify a spirit of persecution against an innocent people. To whom shall blame be attached in this tragedy, when they in July last boldly made known their determination to drive the Mormons from Jackson County, 'peaceably if they could, forcibly if they must,' openly declaring that 'the arm of the civil law did not afford them a sufficient guarantee against the increasing evils of this religious sect.' And in their circular they further say, 'We deem it expedient, and of the highest importance, to form ourselves into a company for the better and easier accomplishment of our purposes,' and conclude with these high-toned words: 'We therefore agree, that after timely warning, and upon receiving an adequate compensation for what little property they cannot take with them, they refuse to leave us in peace as they found us, we agree to use such means as may be sufficient to remove them; and to this end we each pledge to each other our lives, our bodily powers, fortunes, and sacred honors.'

"In answer to their bold and daring resolves to guard against anticipated evils, I give the following extract from the Governor's letter in relation to this affair, dated October 19, 1833: 'No citizen, or number of citizens, has a right to take the redress of their grievances, whether real or imaginary, into their own hands. Such conduct strikes at the very existence of society, and subverts the foundation on which it is based.'

"I ask again, To whom shall blame be attached in this tragedy, when the mob previously and publicly declared their intentions; and the principles involved were understood by the Executive, as appears by the foregoing; and also by the judiciary, according to Judge Ryland's letter; and the Constitution of the land guarantees equal rights and privileges to all; to whom should blame be attached, but Jackson County mobbers and Missouri?"

Of some matters mentioned above more will be said on succeeding pages.

We present an account of the exodus from Jackson County from the pen of "Burr Joyce," in the St. Louis *Globe-Democrat*, of November 24, 1887, and copied in *Saints' Herald*, volume 34, pages 805, 806:—

"But October 30 the Jackson County Gentiles were again in arms and raiding the 'saints.' Ten houses of the Mormons, on the Big Blue, were demolished, and the inmates driven away. The following day a number of houses at Independence and in other parts of the county were plundered, and much Mormon property was forcibly taken and appropriated. Some of the scenes enacted are said to have been altogether disgraceful, rivaling, if not surpassing, the worst excesses of the Kansas jayhawkers and Missouri bushwhackers during the civil war.

"In some instances the Mormons resisted. November 2 in a skirmish at Linwood, two miles southeast of Kansas City, in what was known as the Whitmer settlement, two Gentiles were killed and several wounded. At last, the State militia, under Lieutenant-Governor Boggs, was called out to 'preserve the peace.' The militia, however, were anti-Mormon to a man, and the unhappy saints, knowing this, realized that they were at the mercy of their enemies, and saw that they had no alternative but to flee. It was absolutely perilous for a solitary Mormon to show himself in a town or village.

"Affrighted and terror-stricken, the Mormons crossed the river and sought safety in Clay County. November 7 the crossing began. The weather was cold and rainy, and there was great discomfort and misery among the fugitives; the plundered, half-clad women and children, especially, suffered severely. But the people of Clay received the newcomers kindly. They allowed them to remain, rented them houses, furnished them provisions, and gave them employment. For

(marginal note: Burr Joyce on the exodus.*)*

this the Clay County people were long intensely hated by their neighbors in Jackson.   Some of the Mormons fled to Cass County (then Van Buren), but were again compelled to flee. In after years, during the civil war, when the counties of Cass and Jackson were among those depopulated and dev- astated by General Ewing's 'order No. 11,' the Mormons declared it a divine judgment on those counties for their persecution of the 'saints' thirty years before.

"The public authorities of the State, or some of them at least, were indignant at these lawless proceedings and sym- pathized with the efforts of the Mormons to obtain redress. The Attorney-General, Hon. Robert W. Wells, wrote to them that if they desired to be reëstablished in their possessions in Jackson County an adequate public force would be sent for their protection.   He also advised them to remain in the State and organize themselves into a regular company of militia, promising them a supply of the public arms if they should do so.

"But the Mormons were averse to fighting or to taking any steps that should lead to further trouble with the citi- zens of Missouri, whose good will they seemed anxious to secure in order that they might be allowed to remain in the State in peace.   The Territory of Kansas then belonged to the Indians and was not open to white settlement; so they began to seek for new homes on the north side of the Mis- souri.   In June, 1834, Joe Smith visited them in Clay County and counseled them to make no violent attempt to recover the 'New Jerusalem,' to which, he assured them, his church should be restored 'in God's own time.'

"As the Jackson County people had seized upon and occu- pied the houses and lands of the Mormons, and expected to retain them, it was but natural that they should desire some legal title to them.   They sent a proposition to the Mor- mons in Clay to buy their lands, offering them per acre the Government price, $1.25, allowing nothing for improve- ments.   The Mormons refused the proposition, and it was finally agreed that the matter should be submitted to certain prominent citizens of Clay for arbitration.   The arbiters met at Liberty, and Jackson sent over thirteen commissioners.

The Mormons were properly represented. The Jackson men, seeing that their case was a poor one, and that the decision would in all probability be against them, withdrew after a few hours session of the council, and, accusing the Clay County men of sympathy with the Mormons, left Liberty in great indignation, after a fight had been prevented only by persistent effort."

Thus ended the eventful year of 1833.

At the beginning of the year there was a peaceful, happy people gathered from almost every clime unto the fruitful land of this western Zion. Rejoicing in their new-found faith, and happy in their new prospectively prosperous homes, they flattered themselves that they had come to plant their permanent abode in this beautiful and peaceful land.

A contrast.

When the genial sun had warmed the icebound streams and set their dancing waters towards the sea, and the warm south wind had kissed the folded buds, causing them to burst forth into flower and leaf, these hardy sons of toil might have been seen turning the virgin soil upon the hillside and plain, planting and sowing the seed with glad hearts; while upon the Sabbath the music of their songs and the pathos of their prayers rang out upon the air from the native groves that crowned Zion's hill. As the summer advanced their fields of grain gave promise of a bountiful harvest, and many of their humble homes were adorned by the vine and flower, trained by the gentle hand of the housewife as she, from a full heart of praise, sang the beautiful songs of Zion.

Blessed with peace and prospective plenty they little thought that ere the sear and yellow leaf of autumn should appear their sacred homes would be in ashes, their fruitful fields trodden under the feet of the ruthless beast, themselves exiled wanderers hunted by a cruel and relentless foe, while some laid low by the assassin's hand would sleep the sleep of death upon the green hillside. Yet such was the case.

When the year closed this once happy and prosperous people were scattered over several counties, plundered, robbed, and distressed; in poverty, want, and suffering; exposed in temporary and insufficient shelters to the inclemency of the winter's storm. Yet their faith in God was strong. They believed in the Christ, and in his truth. Ah, yes! they believed that Zion would yet arise and put on her beautiful attire, and that the faithful would return with songs of everlasting joy. From those flaming camp fires and humble huts arose a fervent prayer which echoed down the years and succeeding generations have prayed, as one of our poets has expressed it:—

Prayers for Zion.

> "Remember bleeding Zion,
>   Our tears for her shall flow;
> While time's unerring dial
>   Points to one hour of woe."

Shall not God hear their prayer though he bear long with them?

The church in the East was in much more favorable surroundings though anxious for Zion and her children.

CHAPTER 15.

1834.

THE year 1834 opened with gloomy surroundings for Zion, yet a hopeful and determined people met the situation with courage born of conviction that right would triumph.

On January 1, 1834, a conference was held at the house of Elder Parley P. Pratt, in Clay County, Missouri, Bishop Edward Partridge presiding. In addition to other business, Lyman Wight and P. P. Pratt were sent as special messengers to Kirtland, Ohio, to repre- sent the situation in Zion to the Presidency and ask advice. For the account of this journey and the circumstances and preparation preceding it we refer you to the Autobiography of P. P. Pratt, pages 114-116:—

Messengers sent to Kirtland.

"After making our escape into the county of Clay, being reduced to the lowest poverty, I made a living by day labor, jobbing, building, or wood cutting, till sometime in the win- ter of 1834, when a General Conference was held at my house, in which it was decided that two of the elders should be sent to Ohio, in order to counsel with President Smith and the church at Kirtland, and take some measures for the relief or restoration of the people thus plundered and driven from their homes. The question was put to the conference: 'Who would volunteer to perform so great a journey?'

"The poverty of all and the inclement season of the year made all hesitate. At length Lyman Wight and myself offered our services, which were readily accepted. I was at this time entirely destitute of proper clothing for the journey; and I had neither horse, saddle, bridle, money, nor provisions to take with me; or to leave with my wife, who lay sick and helpless most of the time.

"Under these circumstances I knew not what to do. Nearly all had been robbed and plundered, and all were poor. As we had to start without delay, I almost trembled at the undertaking; it seemed to be all but an impossibility; but 'to him that believeth all things are possible.' I started out of my house to do something towards making preparation; I hardly knew which way to go, but I found myself in the house of Brother John Lowry, and was intending to ask him for money; but as I entered his miserable cottage in the swamp, amid the low, timbered bottoms of the Missouri River, I found him sick in bed with a heavy fever, and two or three others of his family down with the same complaint, on different beds in the same room. He was vomiting severely, and was hardly sensible of my presence. I thought to myself, 'Well, this is a poor place to come for money, and yet I must have it; I know of no one else that has got it; what shall I do?' I sat a little while confounded and amazed. At length another elder happened in.

"We laid hands on them and rebuked the disease; Brother Lowry rose up well; I did my errand, and readily obtained all I asked. This provided in part for my family's sustenance while I should leave them. I went a little further into the woods of the Missouri bottoms, and came to a camp of some brethren, by the name of Higbee, who owned some horses; they saw me coming, and, moved by the Spirit, one of them said to the other, 'There comes Brother Parley; he's in want of a horse for his journey—I must let him have old Dick;' this being the name of the best horse he had. 'Yes,' said I, 'brother, you have guessed right; but what will I do for a saddle?' 'Well,' says the other, 'I believe I'll have to let you have mine.' I blessed them and went on my way rejoicing.

"I next called on Sidney A. Gilbert, a merchant, then sojourning in the village of Liberty—his store in Jackson County having been broken up, and his goods plundered and destroyed by the mob. 'Well,' says he, 'Brother Parley, you certainly look too shabby to start a journey; you must have a new suit; I have got some remnants left that will make you a coat,' etc. A neighboring tailoress and two or three other sisters happened to be present on a visit, and hearing the conversation, exclaimed, 'Yes, Brother Gilbert, you find the stuff and we'll make it up for him.' This arranged, I now lacked only a cloak; this was also furnished by Brother Gilbert.

"Brother Wight was also prospered in a similar manner in his preparations. Thus faith and the blessings of God had cleared up our way to accomplish what seemed impossible. We were soon ready, and on the first of February we mounted our horses, and started in good cheer to ride one thousand or fifteen hundred miles through a wilderness country. We had not one cent of money in our pockets on starting.

"We traveled every day, whether through storm or sunshine, mud, rain, or snow; except when our public duties called us to tarry. We arrived in Kirtland early in the spring, all safe and sound; we had lacked for nothing on the road, and now had plenty of funds in hand. President Joseph Smith and the church in Kirtland received us with a hospitality and joy unknown except among the saints; and much interest was felt there, as well as elsewhere, on the subject of our persecution. The President inquired of the Lord concerning the matter, and a further mission was appointed us."[1]

Lyman Wight in his private journal differs from Elder Pratt on the date of starting; in all other particulars their accounts agree. He writes:—

Difference in date.

"[The] 12th of January, 1834: I again left my family, my wife with a babe two weeks old, and started to Kirtland, Ohio, and to Geneseo, New York, a distance of one thousand three hundred miles, from which date I have kept a daily journal."

[1] See revelation, Doctrine and Covenants, section 100. This revelation was given February 24, 1834. The time is too short for them to have ridden on horseback from February 1, so we think the dates given by Elder Wight in his account are correct.

According to this journal they arrived at Kirtland February 22, and he with Sidney Rigdon started for the East on the 28th. Think of this, reader; would men without abiding confidence in the truth of their cause make such exertion and sacrifice as this? Leaving their families sick and destitute, they started on this long and perilous journey without a cent, relying on Him who had promised to provide.

Arrive at Kirland.

On January 9, Elder Gilbert wrote the following letter to Governor Dunklin supplementary to the petition of December 6, signed by himself and others. This is found in volume 6, pages 962 and 963, *Times and Seasons.* We recommend a careful reading not only because of its historic value, but because, to the careful investigator, its pacific spirit will be significant:—

Gilbert writes the Governor.

"LIBERTY, Clay County, January 9, 1834.

"*Dear Sir:—*Since my communication of the 29th of November, and a petition dated the 6th of December last, to which my name was attached, I am induced to trespass again upon your patience with further particulars in relation to the unfortunate faction in Jackson County, on which subject I should be silent were it not that I entertain a hope of suggesting some ideas that may ultimately prove useful in ameliorating the present suffering condition of my brethren, and in some degree restoring peace to both parties.

"Being particularly acquainted with the situation of both parties at this day, my desire is to write impartially; notwithstanding I feel very sensibly the deep wound that has been inflicted upon the church of which I am a member, by the citizens of Jackson County. The petition to your Excellency, dated the 6th of December last, was drawn up hastily by Mr. Phelps and signed by several of us just before the closing of the mail; and there is one item in particular in said petition that needs some explanation: the request that 'our men may be organized into companies of Jackson Guards, and furnished with arms by the State' was made at the instance of disinterested advisers and also a communication from the Attorney General to Messrs. Doniphan and Atchison, dated the 21st of November last, giving his views as to the propriety of organizing into regular companies, etc. The necessity of being compelled to resort to arms, to regain our possessions in Jackson County, is by no means agreeable to the feelings of the church, and would never be thought of but from pure necessity.

"In relation to the court of inquiry, serious difficulties continue to exist well calculated to preclude the most important testimony of our church, and there appears to be no evil which man is capable of inflicting upon his fellow creature man but what our people are threatened with at this day by the citizens of Jackson County. This intimidates a great many, particularly females and children, and no military guard would diminish their fears so far as to induce them to attend the court in that county. This with other serious difficulties will give a decided advantage to the offenders, in a court of inquiry, while they triumph in power, numbers, etc.

"The citizens of Jackson County are well aware that they have this advantage, and the leaders of the faction, if they must submit to such a court, would gladly hasten it. The church are anxious for a thorough investigation into the whole affair, if their testimony can be taken without so great peril as they have reason to fear. It is my opinion, from present appearances, that not one fourth of the witnesses of our people can be prevailed upon to go into Jackson County to testify. The influence of the party that compose that faction is considerable, and this influence operates in some degree upon the drafted militia, so far as to lessen confidence in the loyalty of that body. And I am satisfied that the influence of the Jackson County faction will not be entirely put down while they have advocates among certain religious sects.

"Knowing that your Excellency must be aware of the unequal contest in which we are engaged, and that the little handful that compose our church are not the only sufferers that feel the oppressive hand of priestly power, with these difficulties, and many others not enumerated, it would be my wish to adopt such measures as are best calculated to allay the rage of Jackson County, and restore the injured to their rightful possessions. And to this end, I would suggest the propriety of purchasing the possessions of the most violent leaders of the faction, and if they assent to this proposition, about twenty of the most influential in that county, (which would embrace the very leaders of the faction,) could be obtained, I think the majority would cease in their persecutions, at least, when a due exercise of executive counsel and authority was manifested. I suggest this measure because it is of a pacific nature, well knowing that no legal steps are calculated to subdue their obduracy, only when pushed with energy by the highest authorities of the State.

"In this proposal I believe that I should have the concurrence of my brethren. I therefore give this early intimation of our intention, on the part of some of the leading men in the church, to purchase out some of the principal leaders of the faction, if funds sufficient can be raised; hoping thereby to regain peaceful possession of their homes; and in making a trial of this measure at a future day, we may deem it important, and of great utility, if we could avail ourselves of counsel and directions from your Excellency, believing there will be a day in negotiations for peace, in which an executive interposition would produce a salutary effect to both parties.

"In this communication, with honesty of heart I have endeavored *briefly* to touch upon a few interesting points in plain truth, believing that I have given no wrong bias on either side, and with earnest prayers to our great Benefactor that the chief ruler of this State may come to a full knowledge of the grand outrage in Jackson County. I subscribe myself, Your obedient servant,

"ALGERNON S. GILBERT.

"To his Excellency, Daniel Dunklin, Jefferson City, Missouri."

Governor Dunklin replied to the petition of the saints, which reply we here present as published in *Times and Seasons*, pages 977, 978:—

"CITY OF JEFFERSON, February 4, 1834.

"*Gentlemen:*—Your communication of the 6th of December was regularly received, and duly considered; and had I not

expected to have received the evidence brought out on the
inquiry ordered into the military conduct of
Colonel Pitcher, in a short time after I received
your petition, I should have replied to it long since.

"Last evening I was informed that the further inquiry of
the court was postponed until the 20th instant. Then, before
I could hear anything from this court, the court of civil
jurisdiction will hold its session in Jackson County, consequently I cannot receive anything from one preparatory to
arrangements for the other.

"I am very sensible indeed of the injuries your people
complain of, and should consider myself very remiss in the
discharge of my duties were I not to do everything in my
power consistent with the legal exercise of them to afford
your society the redress to which they seem entitled. One
of your requests needs no evidence to support the right to
have it granted; it is that your people be put in possession
of their homes from which they have been expelled. But
what may be the duty of the Executive after that, will depend upon contingencies.

"If upon inquiry it is found that your people were wrongfully dispossessed of their arms, by Colonel Pitcher, then an
order will be issued to have them returned; and should your
men organize according to law, which they have a right to
do, (indeed it is their duty to do so, unless exempted by religious scruples,) and apply for public arms, the Executive
could not distinguish between their right to have them, and
the right of every other description of people similarly situated.

"As to the request for keeping up a military force to protect your people and prevent the commission of crimes and
injuries, were I to comply, it would transcend the power
with which the Executive of this State is clothed. The
Federal Constitution has given to Congress the power to
provide for calling forth the militia to execute the laws of
the Union, suppress insurrection, or repel invasion; and for
these purposes the President of the United States is authorized to make the call upon the executives of the respective
States; and the laws of this State empower the 'commander

in chief in case of actual or threatened invasion, insurrection, or war, or public danger, or other emergency, to call forth into actual service such portion of the militia as he may deem expedient.' These, together with the general provision in our State Constitution that 'the Governor shall take care that the laws are faithfully executed,' are all this branch of Executive powers. None of these, as I consider, embrace the part of your request. The words, 'or other emergency' in our militia law seem quite broad, but the emergency, to come within the object of that provision, shall be of a public nature.

"Your case is certainly a very emergent one, and the consequences as important to *your society*, as if the war had been waged against the whole State; yet, the *public* has no other interest in it, than that the laws be faithfully executed; thus far, I presume the whole community feel a deep interest; for that which is the case of the *Mormons* to-day, may be the case of the *Catholics* to-morrow, and after them any other sect that may become obnoxious to a majority of the people of any section of the State. So far as a faithful execution of the laws is concerned, the Executive is disposed to do everything consistent with the means furnished him by the legislature; and I think I may safely say the same of the judiciary.

"As now advised, I am of the opinion that a military guard will be necessary to protect the State witnesses and officers of the court, and to assist in the execution of its orders, while sitting in Jackson County. By this mail I write to Mr. Reese, inclosing him an order on the captain of the 'Liberty Blues,' requiring the captain to comply with the requisition of the circuit attorney in protecting the court and officers and executing their precepts and orders during the progress of these trials. Under the protection of this guard your people can, if they think proper, return to their homes in Jackson County, and be protected in them during the progress of the trial in question, by which time facts will be developed upon which I can act more definitely. The Attorney General will be required to assist the circuit attorney, if the latter deems it necessary.

"On the subject of civil injuries, I must refer you to the court; such questions rest with them exclusively. The laws are sufficient to afford a remedy for every injury of this kind, and, whenever you make out a case, entitling you to damages, there can be no doubt entertained of their ample award. Justice is sometimes slow in its progress, but is not less sure on that account.

"Very respectfully, your obedient servant,

"(Signed) DANIEL DUNKLIN.

"To Messrs. W. W. Phelps, Isaac Morley, John Whitmer, Edward Partridge, John Corrill, and A. S. Gilbert."

This letter, and in fact all the acts of Governor Dunklin in this difficulty, show him to have been a fair, liberal-minded man, disposed to deal justly and honorably with all.

On February 24 court convened in Independence, and some of the leading men of the church were present as witnesses in the case of "The State of Missouri vs. Colonel Thomas Pitcher." They were protected by military guard under command of Captain Atchison. The mob again collected and so intimidated the court that no trial was had. In regard to this incident we present the account given by W. W. Phelps in a letter written from Clay County, Missouri, February 27, 1834, and published in *Evening and Morning Star*, pages 276, 277.

Col. Pitcher on trial.

"Clay County, February 27, 1834.

"*Dear Brethren:*—The times are so big with events, and the anxiety of everybody so great to watch them, that I feel somewhat impressed to write oftener than I have done, in order to give you more of the 'strange acts' of this region. I have just returned from Independence, the seat of war in the West. About a dozen of our brethren, among whom were Brn. Partridge, Corrill, and myself, were subpoenaed in behalf of the State, and on the 23d (February) about twelve o'clock we were on the bank, opposite Everit's ferry, where we found Captain Atchison's company of 'Liberty Blues,' near fifty rank and file, ready to guard us into Jackson County. The soldiers were well armed with United States muskets, bayonets fixed, etc., and to me the scene was one 'passing strange,' and long to be remembered. The

martial law in force to guard the civil! About twenty-five
men crossed over to effect a landing in safety, and when
they came near the warehouse, they fired six or eight guns,
though the enemy had not gathered to witness the landing.

"After we were all across, and waiting for the baggage
wagon, it was thought not advisable to encamp in the
woods, and the witnesses with half the company, marched
nearly a mile towards Independence, to build night fires, as
we were without tents, and the weather cold enough to snow
a little. While on the way the Quartermaster, and others,
that had gone on ahead to prepare quarters in town, sent an
express back, which was not the most, pacific appearance
that could be. Captain Atchison continued the express to
Colonel Allen for the two hundred drafted militia; and also
to Liberty for more ammunition; and the night passed off in
warlike style, with the sentinels marching silently at a
proper distance from the watch fires.

"Early in the morning we marched strongly guarded by
the troops, to the seat of war, and quartered in the block-
house, formerly the tavern stand of S. Flournoy. After
breakfast, we were visited by the District Attorney, Mr.
Rees, and the Attorney General, Mr. Wells. From them we
learned that all hopes of *criminal prosecution* were at an end.
Mr. Wells had been sent by the Governor to investigate, as
far as possible, the Jackson outrage, but the bold front of
the mob, bound even unto death (as I have heard), was not
to be penetrated by civil law, or awed by Executive influence. Shortly after Captain A. informed me that he had
just received an order from the Judge, that his company's
service was no longer wanted in Jackson County, and we
were marched out of town to the tune of Yankee Doodle in
quick time, and soon returned to our camp ground without
the loss of any lives. In fact much credit is due to Captain
Atchison for his gallantry and hospitality, and I think I
can say of the officers and company that their conduct as
soldiers and men is highly reputable; so much so, knowing
as I do, the fatal result, had the militia come, or not come, I
can add that the Captain's safe return, refreshed my mind,
with Zenophon's retreat of the ten thousand. Thus ends all

hopes of 'redress,' even with a guard ordered by the Governor, for the protection of the court and witnesses.

"Before a crop is harvested, it becomes ripe of itself. The dreadful deeds now done in Jackson County, with impunity, must bring matters to a focus shortly. Within two or three weeks past, some of the most savage acts ever witnessed, have been committed by these bitter branches. Old Father Linsey, whose locks have been whitened by the blasts of nearly seventy winters, had his house thrown down, after he was driven from it; his goods, corn, etc., piled together, and fire put to it; but fortunately, after the mob retired, his son extinguished it.

"The mob has quit whipping, and now beat with clubs. Lyman Leonard, one of the number that returned from Van Buren, had two chairs broke to splinters about him, and was then dragged out of doors and beaten with clubs till he was supposed to be dead—but he is yet alive. Josiah Sumner and Barnet Cole were severely beaten at the same time. The mob have commenced burning houses, stacks, etc., and we shall not think it out of their power, by any means, to proceed to murder any of our people that shall try to live in that county, or perhaps, only go there.

"Such scenes as are transpiring around us, are calculated to arouse feelings and passions in all, and to strengthen the faith and fortify the hearts of the saints for great things. Our Savior laid down his life for our sakes, and shall we, who profess to live by every word that proceeds out of the mouth of God, shall we, the servants of the Lord of the vineyard, who are called and chosen to prune it for the last time, shall we, yea, verily, we, who are enlightened by the wisdom of heaven, shall we fear to do as much for Jesus as he did for us? No; we will obey the voice of the Spirit, that good may overcome the world.

"I am a servant, etc.,

' W. W. PHELPS."

In confirmation of the account given by Elder Phelps of the mobbing of Lyman Leonard, Abigail Leonard his wife made affidavit.[2]

[2] I, Abigail Leonard, depose and say that on the night of the 20th of

Convinced now that recourse to the courts of Jackson County would be unavailing their next step was to appeal to

Appeal to
President
Jackson. the President of the United States for protection, in their homes, after they should be reinstated by the Governor. On April 10 the following petition was forwarded to President Jackson:—

"LIBERTY, Clay County, Missouri, April 10, 1834.

"*To the President of the United States of America:*—We, the undersigned, your petitioners, citizens of the United States of America, and residents of the county of Clay, in the State of Missouri, being members of the Church of Christ, reproachfully called Mormons, beg leave to refer the President to our former petition, dated in October last, and also to lay before him the accompanying handbill, dated December 12, 1833, with assurances that the said handbill exhibits but a faint sketch of the sufferings of your petitioners and their brethren up to the period of its publication.

"The said handbill shows that at the time of dispersion, a number of our families fled into the new and unsettled county of Van Buren, but being unable to procure provis-

---

February, 1834, in the county of Jackson, and State of Missouri, a company of men, armed with whips and guns, about fifty or sixty in number, came to the house of my husband; among them was John Youngs, Mr. Yocum, Mr. Cantrell, Mr. Patterson, and Mr. Noland. Five of the number entered the house, among them was John Youngs. They ordered my husband to leave the house, threatening to shoot him if he did not. He not complying with their desires, one of the five took a chair and struck him upon the head, knocking him down, and then dragging him out of the house, I in the meantime begging of them to spare his life, when one of the number called to the others telling them to take me into the house, for I would "*overpower every devil of them.*" Three of the company then approached me, and presenting their guns, declared with an oath, if I did not go in they would blow me through. While this was transpiring, Mr. Patterson jumped upon my husband with his heels; my husband then got up, they stripped his clothes all from him excepting his pantaloons, then five or six attacked him with whips and gunsticks, and whipped him till he could not stand but fell to the ground. I then went to them, and took their whips from them. I then called for Mrs. Bruce, who lived in the same house with us, to come out and help me to carry my husband into the house. When carried in he was very much lacerated and bruised, and unable to lie upon a bed, and was also unable to work for a number of months. Also, at the same time and place, Mr. Josiah Sumner was taken from the house, and came in very bloody and bruised from whipping.

(Signed)   ABIGAIL LEONARD.
—*Times and Seasons*, vol. 6, p. 1023.

ions in that county through the winter, many of them were compelled to return to their homes in Jackson County or perish with hunger. But they had no sooner set foot upon the soil, which a few months before we had purchased of the United States, than they were again met by the citizens of Jackson County, and a renewal of savage barbarities inflicted upon these families by beating with clubs and sticks, presenting knives and firearms, and threatening with death if they did not flee from the county. These inhuman assaults upon a number of these families were repeated at two or three different times through the past winter, till they were compelled at last to abandon their possessions in Jackson County and flee with their mangled bodies into this county, here to mingle their tears and unite their supplications, with hundreds of their brethren, to our heavenly Father, and to the chief ruler of our nation.

"Between one and two thousand of the people called Mormons have been driven by force of arms from Jackson County, in this State, since the first of November last, being compelled to leave their highly cultivated fields, the greater part of which had been bought of the United States, and all this on account of our belief in direct revelation from God to the children of men, according to the Holy Scriptures. We know that such illegal violence has not been inflicted upon any sect or community of people by the citizens of the United States since the Declaration of Independence.

"That this is a religious persecution, is notorious throughout our county; for while the officers of the county, both civil and military, were accomplices in these unparalleled outrages, engaged in the destruction of the printing office, dwelling houses, etc., yet the records of the judicial tribunals of that county are not stained with a crime against our people. Our numbers being greatly inferior to the enemy, we were unable to stand up in self-defense; and our lives, at this day, are continually threatened by that infuriated people, so that our personal safety forbids one of our number going into that county on business.

"We beg leave to state that no impartial investigation into this criminal matter can be made, because the offenders must be tried in the county where the offense was committed, and the inhabitants of the county, both magistrates and people, were combined, wi;h the exception of a few; justice cannot be expected. At tnis day your petitioners do not know of a solitary family belonging to our church but what have been violently expelled from Jackson County by the inhabitants thereof.

"Your petitioners have not gone into detail with an account of their individual sufferings from death and bruised bodies and the universal distress which prevails at this day, in a greater or less degree, throughout our whole body. Not only because those sacred rights guaranteed to every religious sect have been publicly invaded, in open hostility to the spirit and genius of free government, but such of their houses as have not been burnt, their lands and most of the products of the labor of their hands for the last year have been wrested from them by a band of outlaws, congregated in Jackson County on the western frontiers of the United States, within about thirty miles of the United States' military post at Fort Leavenworth, on the Missouri River.

"Your petitioners say that they do not enter a minute detail of the sufferings in this petition, lest they should weary the patience of the venerable chief whose arduous duties they know are great, and daily accumulating. We only hope to show him that [in] this unprecedented emergency in the history of our country—that the magistracy thereof is set at defiance, and justice checked in open violation of its laws, and that we, your petitioners, who are almost wholly native born citizens of these United States, of whom they purchased their lands in Jackson County, Missouri, with intent to cultivate the same as peaceable citizens, are now forced from them, and dwelling in the counties of Clay, Ray, and Lafayette in the State of Missouri, without permanent homes, and suffering all the privations which must necessarily result from such inhuman treatment. Under these sufferings your petitioners petitioned the Governor of this State, in December last, in answer to which, we received the following letter."

[Here follows the Governor's letter of February 4.]

"By the foregoing letter from the Governor, the President will perceive a disposition manifested by him to enforce the laws as far as means have been furnished him by the legislature of this State. But the powers vested in the Executive of this State appear to be inadequate for relieving the distresses of your petitioners in their present emergency. He is willing to send a guide to conduct our families back to their possessions, but is not authorized to direct a military force to be stationed any length of time for the protection of your petitioners. This step would be laying the foundation for a more fatal tragedy than the first, as our numbers at present are too small to contend single handed with the mob of said county; and as 'the Federal Constitution has given to Congress the power to provide for calling forth the militia to execute the laws of the Union, suppress insurrections, or repel invasions, and for these purposes the President of the United States is authorized to make the call upon the Executives of the respective States.' Therefore, we your petitioners, in behalf of our society, which is so scattered and suffering, most humbly pray that we may be restored to our lands, houses, and property in Jackson County, and protected in them by an armed force, till peace can be restored, and as in duty bound, will ever pray.

"Here followed one hundred and fourteen signatures; viz.: 'Edward Partridge, John Corrill, John Whitmer, Isaac Morley, A. S. Gilbert, W. W. Phelps,' etc., etc.

"The following letter accompanied the foregoing petition:—

"'LIBERTY, Clay County, Mo., April 10, 1834.

" '*To the President of the United States:*—We the undersigned, whose names are subscribed to the accompanying petition, some of the leading members of the Church of Christ, beg leave to refer the President to the petition and handbill herewith. (See *Times and Seasons,* volume 6, page 881.) We are not insensible of the multiplicity of business and numerous petitions, by which the cares and perplexities of our chief ruler are daily increased; and it is with diffidence we venture to lay before the Execu-

tive at this emergent period, these two documents, wherein
is briefly portrayed the most unparalleled persecution,
and flagrant outrage of law that has disgraced the country, since the Declaration of Independence; but knowing
the independent fortitude, and vigorous energy for preserving the rights of the citizens of this republic, which has
hitherto marked the course of our chief magistrate, we are
encouraged to hope that this communication will not pass
unnoticed, but that the President will consider our location
on the extreme western frontier of the United States, exposed to many ignorant and lawless ruffians, who are already
congregated, and determined to nullify all law that will secure to your petitioners the peaceable possession of their
lands in Jackson County.   We again repeat, that our society
are wandering in adjoining counties at this day, bereft of
their houses and lands, and threatened with death by the
aforesaid outlaws of Jackson County.

" 'And lest the President should have been deceived in regard to our true situation, by the misrepresentations of certain individuals, who are disposed to cover the gross
outrages of the mob, from *religious, political*, and *speculative*
motives, we beg leave to refer him to the Governor of this
State, at the same time informing that the number of men
composing the mob of Jackson County may be estimated at
from three to five hundred, most of them prepared with firearms.

" 'After noting the statements here made, if it should be
the disposition of the President to grant aid, we most humbly entreat that *early* relief may be extended to suffering
families, who are now expelled from their possessions by
force of arms.   Our lands in Jackson County are about
thirty miles distant from Fort Leavenworth, on the Missouri
River.   With due respect, we are Sir,

" 'Your obedient servants,

" 'A. S. GILBERT.
" 'W. W. PHELPS.
" 'EDWARD PARTRIDGE.

" 'P. S.—In February last a number of our people were
marched under guard furnished by the Governor of the State,

into Jackson County, for the purpose of prosecuting the mob criminally; but the Attorney General of the State, and the District Attorney, knowing the force and power of the mob, advised us to relinquish all hope of criminal prosecution to effect anything against the band of outlaws, and we returned under guard, without the least prospect of ever obtaining our rights and possessions in Jackson County, with any other means than a few companies of the United States' regular troops to guard and assist us till we are safely settled.' "—*Times and Seasons,* vol. 6, pp. 1041, 1042, 1057.

On the same date the following letter was forwarded to Governor Dunklin asking his coöperation:—

"LIBERTY, Clay County, Mo., April 10, 1834.

"*To His Excellency, Daniel Dunklin, Governor of Missouri; Dear Sir:*—Notwithstanding you may have become somewhat tired of receiving communications from us, yet we beg of your Excellency to pardon us for this, as we have this day forwarded a petition to the President of the United States, setting forth our distressed condition, together with your Excellency's views of it, as well as the limited powers with which you are clothed, to afford that protection, which we need to enjoy our rights and lands in Jackson County. A few lines from the Governor of the State, in connection with our humble entreaties for our possessions and privileges, we think would be of considerable consequence towards bringing about the desired effect, and would be gratefully acknowledged by us and our society, and we may add, by all honorable men.

Letter to Dunklin.

"We therefore, as humble petitioners, ask the favor of your Excellency to write to the President of the United States, that he may assist us, or our society, in obtaining our rights in Jackson County, and help protect us when there, till we are safe, as in duty bound, we will ever pray.

"(Signed)   "W. W. PHELPS.
"JOHN WHITMER.
"A. S. GILBERT.
"E. PARTRIDGE.
"JOHN CORRILL."

—*Times and Seasons,* vol. 6, p. 1058.

To this letter he wisely replied as follows:—

LIBRARY
OF THE
UNIVERSITY

"City of Jefferson, April 20, 1834.

"*To Messrs. W. W. Phelps, E. Partridge, John Corrill, John Whitmer, and A. S. Gilbert; Gentlemen:* — Yours of the 10th inst. was received yesterday, in which you re-

His reply.

quest me, as Executive of this State, to join in an appeal to the President of the United States for protection in the enjoyment of your rights in Jackson County. It will readily occur to you, no doubt, the possibility of your having asked of the President protection in a way that he, no more than the Executive of this State, can render. If you have [asked] for that which I may be of opinion he has power to grant, I should have no objection to join in urging it upon him. But I could no more ask the President, however willing I am to see your society restored and protected in their rights, to do that which I may believe he has no power to do, than I could do such an act myself. If you will send me a copy of your petition to the President, I will judge of his rights to grant it, and if of opinion he possesses the power, I will write in favor of its exercise.

"I am now in correspondence with the Federal Government, on the subject of deposits of munitions of war on our northern and western borders, and have no doubt but shall succeed in procuring one, which will be located, if left to me, (and the Secretary at War seems willing to be governed by the opinion of the Executive of this State,) somewhere near the State line, either in Jackson or Clay County. The establishment will be an 'arsenal' and will probably be placed under the command of a lieutenant of the army. This will afford you the best means of military protection the nature of your case will admit. Although I can see no direct impropriety in making the subject of this paragraph public, yet I should prefer it not to be so considered for the present, as the erection of an arsenal is only in expectancy.

"Permit me to suggest to you that as you now have greatly the advantage of your adversaries in public estimation, that there is a great propriety in retaining that advantage, which you can easily do by keeping your adversaries in the wrong. The laws, both civil and military, seem deficient in affording your society proper protection; nevertheless public sentiment is a powerful corrector of error, and you should make it your policy to continue to deserve it.

"With much respect, and great regard,

"I am your obedient servant,

"DANIEL DUNKLIN."

—*Times and Seasons*, vol. 6, p. 1059.

In answer to the petition to President Jackson the following was received:—

"WAR DEPARTMENT, May 2, 1834.

"*Gentlemen:*—The President has referred to this depart-

Lewis Cass replies for the President. ment the memorial and letter addressed to him by yourselves and other citizens of Missouri, requesting his interposition in order to protect your persons and property.

"In answer, I am instructed to inform you that the offenses of which you complain are violations of the laws of the State of Missouri, and not of the laws of the United States. The powers of the President under the Constitution and laws, to direct the employment of a military force in cases where the ordinary civil authorities are found insufficient, extend only to proceedings under the laws of the United States.

"Where an insurrection in any State exists against the government thereof, the president is required on the application of such State, or of the Executive, (when the Legislature cannot be convened,) to call forth such a number of the militia as he may judge sufficient to suppress such insurrection.

"But this State of things does not exist in Missouri, or if it does, the fact is not shown in the mode pointed out by law. The President cannot call out a military force to aid in the execution of the State laws, until the proper requisition is made upon him by the constituted authorities.

"Very respectfully, your obedient servant,

"(Signed)   LEWIS CASS. [Secretary of War.]

"To Messrs. A. S. Gilbert, W. W. Phelps, E. Partridge, and others, Liberty, Clay County, Missouri."

—*Times and Seasons*, vol. 6, p. 1073.

It is evident that the then unsettled doctrine of States'

States' rights. rights, which was differently understood by different officials, prevented the execution of justice.

On April 24 the elders in Clay County again wrote the Governor as follows:—

"LIBERTY, Clay County, Missouri, April 24, 1834.

"Dear Sir:—In our last communication of the 10th inst., we omitted to make inquiry concerning the evidence brought
Letter to
Governor. up before the court of inquiry in the case of Colonel Pitcher. The court met pursuant to adjournment on the 20th February last, and, for some reasons unknown to us, we have not been able to obtain information concerning the opinion or decision of that court. We had hoped that the testimony would have been transmitted to your Excellency before this, that an order might be issued for the return of our arms, of which we have been wrongfully dispossessed, as we believe will clearly appear to the commander in chief when the evidence is laid before him.

"As suggested in your communication of the 4th of February, we have concluded to organize according to law and apply for public arms, but we feared that such a step, which must be attended with public ceremonies, might produce some excitement, and we have thus far delayed any movement of that nature, hoping to regain our arms from Jackson that we might independently equip ourselves and be prepared to assist in the maintenance of our constitutional rights and liberties as guaranteed to us by our country, and also to defend our persons and property from a lawless mob when it shall please the Executive, at some future day, to put us in possession of our homes, from which we have been most wickedly expelled. We are happy to make an expression of our thanks for the willingness manifested by the Executive to enforce the laws, as he can consistently 'with the means furnished him by the legislature,' and we are firmly persuaded that a future day will verify to him whatever aid we may receive from the Executive has not been lavished upon a band of traitors, but upon a people whose respect and veneration for the laws of our country, and its pure republican principles, are as great as that of any other society in the United States.

"As our Jackson foes and their correspondents are busy in circulating slanderous and wicked reports concerning our people, their views, etc., we have deemed it expedient to inform your Excellency that we have received communications from our friends in the East, informing us that a number of our brethren, perhaps two or three hundred, would remove to Jackson County in the course of the ensuing summer, and we are satisfied that when the Jackson mob get the intelligence that a large number of our people are about to remove into that county, they will raise a great hue and cry, and circulate many bugbears through the medium of their favorite press. But we think your Excellency is well aware that our object is purely to defend ourselves and possessions against another unparalleled attack from the mob, inasmuch as the Executive of this State cannot keep up a military force 'to protect our people in that country without transcending his power.' We want, therefore, the privilege of defending ourselves and the Constitution of our country, while God is willing we should have a being on his footstool.

"We do not know at what time our friends will arrive, but expect more certain intelligence in a few weeks. Whenever they do arrive, it would be the wish of our people in this county to return to our homes in company with our friends under guard, and when once in legal possession of our homes in Jackson County, we shall endeavor to take care of them without further wearying the patience of our worthy Chief Magistrate. We will write hereafter, or send an express. During the intermediate time we would be glad to hear of the prospect of recovering our arms.

"With due respect, we are, sir,

"Your obedient servants,

"(Signed)   "A. S. GILBERT.
                                        "EDWARD PARTRIDGE.
                                        "JOHN WHITMER.
                                        "W. W. PHELPS.
                                        "JOHN CORRILL.

"P. S. — Many of our brethren who are expected on, had made arrangements to emigrate to this State before the outrages of the mob last fall. We hope the painful emergency of our case will plead an excuse for our frequent communications."— *Times and Seasons*, vol. 6, p. 1072.

To this Governor Dunklin replied as follows:—

"CITY OF JEFFERSON, May 2, 1834.

"*To Messrs. W. W. Phelps and others; Gentlemen:*—Yours of the 24th ult., is before me, in reply to which I can inform
His reply. you that becoming impatient at the delay of the court of inquiry in making their report in the case of Lieutenant Colonel Pitcher; on the 11th ult. I wrote to General Thompson for the reasons of such delay; last night I received his reply, and with it the report of the court of inquiry, from the tenor of which I find no difficulty in deciding that the arms your people were required to surrender on the 5th of last November should be returned; and have issued his order to Colonel Lucas to deliver them to you or your order, which order is here inclosed.

"Respectfully, your obedient servant,

"(Signed)   DANIEL DUNKLIN."

—*Times and Seasons*, vol. 6, p. 1073.

By the following it will be seen that a competent court decided unanimously that the calling out of the troops by
Col. Pitcher condemn'd. Col. Pitcher, in November, 1833, was illegal, and the demanding of the arms of the Mormons was unnecessary. Thus were the brethren vindicated by the court.

This order for the return of their arms was issued by Governor Dunklin, as commander in chief, and is as follows:—

"CITY OF JEFFERSON, May 2, 1834.

"*To Samuel D. Lucas, Colonel Thirty-third Regiment; Sir:*—The court ordered to inquire into the conduct of Lieutenant
Return of arms ordered. Colonel Pitcher, in the movement he made on the 5th November last, report it as their unanimous opinion that there was no insurrection on that day, and that Colonel Pitcher was not authorized to call out his troops on the 5th November, 1833. It was then unnecessary to require the Mormons to give up their arms. Therefore, you will deliver to W. W. Phelps, E. Partridge, John Corrill, John Whitmer, and A. S. Gilbert, or their order, the fifty-two guns, and one pistol reported by Lieutenant Colonel Pitcher to you on the 3d December last, as having been received by

him from the Mormons on the 5th of the preceding November.   Respectfully,

"DANIEL DUNKLIN, Commander in Chief."

—*Times and Seasons*, vol. 6, pp. 1073, 1074.

On May 7 the brethren again wrote the Governor as follows:—

"LIBERTY, Clay County, May 7, 1834.

"*Dear Sir:*—Your favor of the 20th ult. came to hand the 1st inst., which gives us a gleam of hope that the time will come when we may experience a partial mitigation of our sufferings. The salutary advice at the conclusion of your letter is received with great deference.

"Since our last of the 24th ult., the mob of Jackson County have burned our dwellings. As near as we can ascertain, between one hundred and one hundred and fifty were consumed by fire in about one week; our arms were also taken from the depository (the jail) about ten days since and distributed among the mob. Great efforts are now making by said mob to stir up the citizens of this county and Lafayette to similar outrages against us, but we think they will fail of accomplishing their wicked designs in this county. We here annex a copy of the petition to the President, signed by about one hundred and twenty.

"With great respect, etc.,

"(Signed)   "A. S. GILBERT.
                                                            "W. W. PHELPS.

"Daniel Dunklin, Governor of Missouri."

—*Times and Seasons*, vol. 6, p. 1074.

On May 15 they wrote Colonel Lucas, inclosing the order of the commander in chief for the arms. The following is a copy of their letter:—

"LIBERTY, Clay County, May 15, 1834.

"*Col. S. D. Lucas; Sir:*—We have this day received a communication from the Governor of this State, covering the order herewith, and we hasten to forward the said order to you, by the bearer, Mr. Richardson, who is instructed to receive your reply. We would further remark that, under existing circumstances, we hope to receive our arms on this side the river, and we would name a place near one of the ferries for your convenience. As the arms are few in number, we request that they may be delivered with as little delay as possible.

"Respectfully, yours,

"(Signed)   "A. S. GILBERT.
                                  "JOHN CORRILL.
                                  "W. W. PHELPS.
                                  "EDWARD PARTRIDGE.
                                  "JOHN WHITMER.

"P. S.—We will thank you for a written communication, in answer to this letter, and the accompanying order."— *Times and Seasons*, vol. 6, p. 1075.

They waited on Colonel Lucas until the 29th, when upon receiving no reply from him, they wrote again to the Executive, as follows:—

"LIBERTY, Missouri, May 29, 1834.

"*Sir:*—Your communication to us of May 2 containing or inclosing an order on Colonel S. D. Lucas for the arms which were forcibly taken from us last November, was received the 15th inst., and the order forwarded to Colonel Lucas, at Independence, on the 17th, giving him the privilege of returning our arms at either of the several ferries in this county. His reply to the order was, that he would write what he would do the next mail (May 22). But as he has removed to Lexington without writing, we are at a loss to know whether he means to delay returning them for a season, or entirely refuse to restore them.

"At any rate, the excitement, or rather spite of the mob, runs so high against our people, that we think best to request your Excellency to have said arms returned through the agency of Colonel Allen or Captain Atchison. Report says the arms will not be returned, and much exertion is making by the mob to prevent our return to our possessions in Jackson County. We also understand that the mob is employing certain influential gentlemen to write to your Excellency, to persuade us to compromise our matters in difference with the Jackson mob, and probably divide Jackson County. We ask for our rights and no more.

"Respectfully, your Excellency's servants,

"(Signed)   "W. W. PHELPS.
                                  "JOHN CORRILL.
                                  "A. S. GILBERT.
                                  "EDWARD PARTRIDGE."

—*Times and Seasons*, vol. 6, pp. 1075, 1076.

Again on June 5 they wrote:—

"LIBERTY, June 5, 1834.

"*Dear Sir:*—We think the time is just at hand when our society will be glad to avail themselves of the protection of a military guard, that they may return to Jackson County. We do not know the precise day, but Mr. Reese gives his opinion that there would be no impropriety in petitioning your Excellency for an order on the commanding officer to be sent by return of mail that we might have it in our hands to present when our people are ready to start. If this should meet your approbation and the order sent by return of mail, we think it would be of *great convenience* to our society.

"We would also be obliged to your Excellency for information concerning the necessary expenses of ferriage, etc. Are our people bound to pay the ferriage on their return? As they have already sustained heavy losses, and many of them lost their all, a mitigation of expenses on their return at this time, where they could legally be reduced, would afford great relief; not only ferriage across the Missouri River, but other items of expense that could lawfully be reduced.

"We remain your Excellency's most obedient servants,

"A. S. GILBERT.
"W. W. PHELPS.
"EDWARD PARTRIDGE."

—*Times and Seasons*, vol. 6, pp. 1076, 1077.

Notwithstanding the order to General Lucas to deliver up arms, he never did so, nor were they ever recovered.

While affairs were in this condition some of the citizens
Compromise negotiated. of Clay County offered their services to negotiate a compromise.

CHAPTER 16.

1834.

THE year 1834 opened with activity upon the part of the church in Kirtland. The leading officers humbled them-
Special prayers. selves in special and earnest prayer for certain purposes. Of this and other items of history the writings of Joseph Smith are the best authority. He states:—

"On the evening of the eleventh of January, Joseph Smith, Jr., Frederick G. Williams, Newel K. Whitney, John Johnson, Oliver Cowdery, and Orson Hyde united in prayer, and asked the Lord to grant the following petitions:—

"That the Lord would grant that our lives might be precious in his sight, that he would watch over our persons, and give his angels charge concerning us and our families. that no evil nor unseen hand might be permitted to harm us. . . .

"That the Lord would grant that Brother Joseph might prevail over his enemy, even Doctor Hurlbut, who has threatened his life, whom Joseph has caused to be taken with a precept; that the Lord would fill the heart of tho court with a spirit to do justice, and cause that the law of the land may be magnified in bringing him to justice.

"That the Lord would provide in the order of his providence the bishop of this church with means sufficient to discharge every debt that the order owes, in due season, that the church may not be brought into disrepute and the saints be afflicted by the hands of their enemies.

"That the Lord would protect our printing press from the

hands of evil men, and give us means to send forth his record, even his gospel, that the ears of all may hear it, and also that we may print his Scriptures; and also that he would give those who were appointed to conduct the press wisdom sufficient that the cause may not be hindered, but that men's eyes may thereby be opened to see the truth.

"That the Lord would deliver Zion, and gather in his scattered people to possess it in peace; and also, while in their dispersion, that he would provide for them that they perish not by hunger or cold; and finally, that God, in the name of Jesus, would gather his elect speedily, and unveil his face, that his saints might behold his glory, and dwell with him. Amen. . . .

"On the 22d, the Presidency of the High Priesthood wrote from Kirtland to the brethren in Christ Jesus, scattered from Zion, scattered abroad from the land of their inheritance; *Greeting:*—We your companions in tribulation embrace the present opportunity of sending you this token of our love and good will, assuring you that our bowels are filled with compassion, and that our prayers are daily ascending to God in the name of Jesus Christ in your behalf.

"We have just received intelligence from you through the medium of Brother Elliott, of Chagrin, making inquiries concerning the course which you are to pursue. In addition to the knowledge contained in the above on this subject, we say if it is not the duty of the Governor to call out and keep a standing force in Jackson County to protect you on your lands, (which it appears, must be done, as we understand the mob are determined to massacre you if the Governor takes you back upon your lands and leaves you unpro-tected,) it will become your duty to petition the Governor to petition the President to send a force there to protect you when you are reinstated.

"The Governor proposes to take you back to your lands whenever you are ready to go, (if we understand correctly,) but cannot keep up any army to guard you; and while the hostile feelings of the people of Jackson County remain unabated, probably you dare not go back to be left un-guarded. Therefore, in your petition to the Governor, set all these things forth in their proper light, and pray him to notify the President of your situation, and also petition the President yourselves, according to the direction of the Lord. We have petitioned Governor Dunklin in your behalf, and inclosed it in a printed revelation, the same as this, which we now send to you. The petition was signed by something like sixty brethren, and mailed for Jefferson City, one week ago, and he will probably receive it two weeks before you receive this.

"We also calculate to send a petition and this revelation to the President forthwith, in your behalf, and then we will act the part of the poor widow to perfection, if possible, and let our rulers read their destiny if they do not lend a helping hand. We exhort you to prosecute and try every lawful means to bring the mob to *justice*, as fast as circumstances will permit. With regard to your tarrying in Clay County, we cannot say; you must be governed by circumstances; perhaps you will have to hire out, and take farms to cultivate, to obtain bread until the Lord delivers.

"We sent you a fifty dollar United States note some time ago. If you have received it, please acknowledge the receipt of it, to us, that we may be satisfied you received it. We shall do all that is in our power to assist you in every way we can. We know your situation is a trying one, but be patient and not murmur against the Lord, and you shall see that all these things shall turn to your greatest good.

"Inquire of Elder Marsh and find out the entire secret of mixing and compounding lead and antimony, so as to make type metal, and write us concerning it. Joseph has sent you another fifty dollar note, making in all one hundred dollars; write us concerning it. There is a prospect of the eastern churches doing something pretty handsome towards the deliverance of Zion, in the course of a year, if Zion is not delivered otherwise.

"Though the Lord said this affliction came upon you because of your sins, polluting your inheritances, etc., yet there is an exception of some; namely, the heads of Zion, for the Lord said your brethren in Zion begin to repent, and the angels rejoice over them, etc. You will also see an exception at the top of the second column of this revelation: therefore this affliction came upon the church to chasten those in transgression, and prepare the hearts of those who had repented, for an endowment from the Lord.

"We shall not be able to send you any more money at present, unless the Lord puts it into our hands unexpectedly. There is not quite so much danger of a mob upon us as there has been. The hand of the Lord has thus far been stretched out to protect us. Doctor P. Hurlbut, an apostate elder from this church, has been to the State of New York, and gathered up all the ridiculous stories that could be invented, and some affidavits respecting the character of Joseph, and the Smith family, and exhibited them to numerous congregations in Chagrin, Kirtland, Mentor, and Painesville, and fired the minds of the people with much indignation against Joseph and the church.

"Hurlbut also made many harsh threats, etc., that he would take the life of Joseph, if he could not destroy Mormonism without. Bro. Joseph took him with a peace warrant and after three days trial, and investigating the merits of our religion, in the town of Painesville, by able attorneys on both sides, he was bound over to the county court. Thus his influence was pretty much destroyed, and since the trial the spirit of hostility seems to be broken down in a good degree, but how long it will continue so we cannot say.

"You purchased your inheritances with money; therefore, behold, you are blessed; you have not purchased your lands by the shedding of blood, consequently you do not come under the censure of this commandment, which says, 'If by blood, lo your enemies are upon you, and ye shall be driven from city to city.' Give yourselves no uneasiness on this account.

"Farewell in the bonds of the new covenant, and partakers in tribulation.

"(Signed) ORSON HYDE,
"Clerk of the Presidency of the Church."
—*Times and Seasons*, vol. 6, pp. 963, 976, 977.

A council of high priests was held at the house of President Joseph Smith, in Kirtland, Ohio, on February 12, 1834, of which Joseph states:—

"At a council of the high priests and elders, at my house, in Kirtland, on the evening of the 12th of February, I re-
Council of high priests.
marked that I should endeavor to set before the council the dignity of the office' which had been conferred on me by the ministering of the angel of God, by his own voice, and by the voice of this church; that I had never set before any council in all the order of it, which it ought to be conducted, which, perhaps, has deprived the councils of some, or many blessings.

"And I continued and said, No man is capable of judging a matter, in council, unless his own heart is pure; and that we frequently are so filled with prejudice, or have a beam in our own eye, that we are not capable of passing right decisions, etc.

"But to return to the subject of order: In ancient days councils were conducted with such strict propriety that no one was allowed to whisper, be weary, leave the room, or get uneasy in the least; until the voice of the Lord, by revelation, or by the voice of the council by the Spirit, was obtained; which has not been observed in this church to the present. It was understood in ancient days, that if one man could stay in council, another could; and if the President could spend his time, the members could also; but in our councils, generally, one will be uneasy, another asleep; one praying, another not; one's mind on the business of the council, and another thinking on something else, etc.

"Our acts are rendered, and at a future day they will be laid before us, and if we should fail to judge right and injure our fellow beings, they maybe there, perhaps, condemn us; there they are of great consequence, and to me the consequence appears to be of force, beyond anything which I am able to express, etc. Ask yourselves, brethren, how much you have exercised yourselves in prayer since you heard of this council; and if you are now prepared to sit in council upon the soul of your brother?

"I then gave a relation of my situation at the time I obtained the record, the persecutions I met with, etc., and prophesied that I would stand and shine like the sun in the firmament, when my enemies and the gainsayers of my testimony shall be put down and cut off, and their names blotted out from among men."—*Times and Seasons*, vol. 6, p. 992.

On February 17, 1834, the standing High Council of the church was organized at the house of President

Organiza-
tion of High
Council.

Joseph Smith, in Kirtland, Ohio. For an account of this organization and other matters connected with it, we cite the history of Joseph Smith:—

"Minutes of the organization of the High Council of the Church of Christ of Latter Day Saints, Kirtland, February 17, 1834.

"This day a general council of twenty four high priests assembled at the house of Joseph Smith, Jr., by revelation, and proceeded to organize the high council of the Church of Christ, which was to consist of twelve high priests, and one or three presidents, as the case might require. This high council was appointed by revelation for the purpose of settling important difficulties, which might arise in the church, which could not be settled by the church, or the bishop's council, to the satisfaction of the parties.

"Joseph Smith, Jr., Sidney Rigdon, and Frederick G. Williams, were acknowledged presidents by the voice of the council; and Joseph Smith, Sr., John Smith, Joseph Coe, John Johnson, Martin Harris, John S. Carter, Jared Carter, Oliver Cowdery, Samuel H. Smith, Orson Hyde, Sylvester Smith, and Luke Johnson, high priests, were chosen to be a standing council for the church, by the unanimous voice of the council. The above-named councilors were then asked whether they accepted their appointments, and whether they would act in that office according to the law of heaven; to which they all answered, that they accepted their appointments, and would fill their offices according to the grace of God bestowed upon them.

"The number composing the council, who voted in the name and for the church in appointing the above-named councilors, were forty-three, as follows: nine high priests, seventeen elders, four priests, and thirteen members.

"Voted: that the high council cannot have power to act without seven of the above-named councilors, or their regularly appointed successors, are present. These seven shall have power to appoint other high priests, whom they may consider worthy and capable, to act in the place of absent councilors.

"Voted: that whenever any vacancy shall occur by the death, removal from office for transgression, or removal from the bounds of this church government, of any one of the above-named councilors, it shall be filled by the nomination of the president or presidents, and sanctioned by the voice of the general council of high priests, convened for that purpose, to act in the name of the church.

"The president of the church, who is also the president of the council, is appointed by revelation, and acknowledged, in his administration, by the voice of the church; and it is according to the dignity of his office, that he should preside over the high council of the church; and it is his privilege to be assisted by two other presidents, appointed after the same manner that he himself was appointed; and in case of the absence of one or both of those who are appointed to assist him, he has power to preside over the council without an assistant; and in case that he himself is absent, the other presidents have power to preside in his stead, both or either of them.

"Whenever a high council of the Church of Christ is regularly organized, according to the foregoing pattern, it shall be the duty of the twelve councilors to cast lots by numbers, and thereby ascertain who, of the twelve, shall speak first, commencing with number 1; and so in succession to number 12.

"Whenever this council convenes to act upon any case, the twelve councilors shall consider whether it is a difficult one or not; if it is not, two only of the councilors shall speak upon it, according to the form above written. But if it is thought to be difficult, four shall be appointed; and if more difficult, six: but in no case shall more than six be appointed to speak. The accused, in all cases, has a right to one half of the council, to prevent insult or injustice; and the councilors appointed to speak before the council, are to present the case, after the evidence is examined, in its true light, before the council; and every man is to speak according to equity and justice. Those councilors who draw even numbers, that is, 2, 4, 6, 8, 10, and 12, are the individuals who are to stand up in the behalf of the accused, and prevent insult or injustice.

"In all cases the accuser and the accused shall have a privilege of speaking for themselves, before the council, after the evidences are heard, and the councilors who are appointed to speak on the case, have finished their remarks. After the evidences are heard, the councilors, accuser, and accused have spoken, the president shall give a decision according to the understanding which he shall have of the case, and call upon the twelve councilors to sanction the same by their vote. But should the remaining councilors, who have not spoken, or any one of them, after hearing the evidences and pleadings impartially, discover an error in the decision of the president, they can manifest it, and the case shall have a rehearing; and if, after a careful rehearing, any additional light is shown upon the case, the decision shall be altered accordingly; but in case no additional light is given, the first decision shall stand, the majority of the council having power to determine the same.

"In cases of difficulty respecting doctrine, or principle (if there is not a sufficiency written to make the case clear to the minds of the council), the president may inquire and obtain the mind of the Lord by revelation.

"The high priests, when abroad, have power to call and organize a council after the manner of the foregoing, to settle difficulties when the parties, or either of them, shall request it; and the said council of high priests shall have power to appoint one of their own number, to preside over such council for the time being. It shall be the duty of said council to transmit, immediately, a copy of their proceedings, with a full statement of the testimony accompanying their decision, to the high council of the seat of the first presidency of the church. Should the parties, or either of them, be dissatisfied with the decision of said council, they may appeal to the high council of the seat of the first presidency of the church, and have a rehearing, which case shall there be conducted, according to the former pattern written, as though no such decision had been made.

"This council of high priests abroad, is only to be called on the most difficult cases of church matters; and no common or ordinary case is to be sufficient to call such council.   The traveling or located high priests abroad, have power to say whether it is necessary to call such a council or not.

"There is a distinction between the high council of traveling high priests abroad, and the traveling high council composed of the twelve apostles, in their decisions: from the decision of the former there can be an appeal, but from the decision of the latter there cannot.   The latter can only be called in question by the general authorities of the church in case of transgression.

"Resolved, that the president, or presidents of the seat of the first presidency of the church, shall have power to determine whether any such case, as may be appealed, is justly entitled to a rehearing, after examining the appeal and the evidences and statements accompanying it.

"The twelve councilors then proceeded to cast lots, or ballot, to ascertain who should speak first, and the following was the result, namely:—

OLIVER COWDERY,	No. 1	JOHN JOHNSON,	No. 7
JOSEPH COE,	" 2	ORSON HYDE,	" 8
SAMUEL H. SMITH,	" 3	JARED CARTER,	" 9
LUKE JOHNSON,	" 4	JOSEPH SMITH, Sr.,	" 10
JOHN S. CARTER,	" 5	JOHN SMITH,	" 11
SYLVESTER SMITH,	" 6	MARTIN HARRIS,	" 12

After prayer the conference adjourned.

OLIVER COWDERY, } Clerks.
ORSON HYDE,

"On the 18th I reviewed and corrected the minutes of the organization of the high council; and on the 19th of February the council assembled, according to adjournment from the 17th, when the revised minutes were presented and read to the council.   I urged the necessity of prayer, that the Spirit might be given, that the things of the Spirit might be judged thereby, because the carnal mind cannot discern the things of God, etc.   The minutes were read three times, and unanimously adopted and received for a form and constitution of the high council of the Church of Christ hereafter; with this provision, that if the president should hereafter discover any lack in the same he should be privileged to fill it up.

"The number present, who received the above named documents was twenty-six high priests, eighteen elders, three priests, one teacher, and fourteen private members, making in all sixty-two.

"After giving such instruction as the Spirit dictated, I laid my hands severally upon the heads of the two assistant presidents and blessed them, that they might have wisdom to magnify their offices, and power over all the power of the adversary.

"I also laid my hands upon the twelve councilors, and commanded a blessing to rest upon them, that they might have wisdom and power to counsel in righteousness upon all subjects that might be laid before them. I also prayed that they might be delivered from those evils to which they were most exposed, and that their lives might be prolonged on the earth.

"My father Joseph then laid his hands upon my head and said, 'Joseph, I lay my hands upon thy head and pronounce the blessings of thy progenitors upon thee, that thou mayest hold the keys of the mysteries of the kingdom of heaven, until the coming of the Lord; Amen.'

"He also laid hands upon the head of his son Samuel and said, 'Samuel, I lay my hands upon thy head, and pronounce the blessing of thy progenitors upon thee, that thou mayest remain a priest of the Most High God, and like Samuel of old, hear his voice, saying, "Samuel, Samuel;" Amen.'

"John Johnson, also, laid his hand upon the head of his son Luke and said, 'My Father in heaven. I ask thee to bless this my son, according to the blessings of his forefathers, that he may be strengthened in his ministry, according to his holy calling; Amen.'

"I then gave the assistant presidents a solemn charge, to do their duty in righteousness, and in the fear of God; I also charged the twelve councilors in a similar manner, all in the name of Jesus Christ.

"We all raised our hands to heaven in token of the everlasting covenant, and the Lord blessed us with his Spirit. I then declared the council organized according to the ancient order, and also according to the mind of the Lord."—*Times and Seasons*, vol. 6, pp. 993-995.

A conference met at Kirtland on February 19, and on the next day—the 20th—the High Council was called to decide a Word of Wisdom. question concerning the worthiness of a man to officiate who disregarded the "Word of Wisdom." But we will quote the words of Joseph Smith on this meeting and decision:—

"KIRTLAND, February 20, 1834.

"The high council met this evening to determine concerning the elders going out to preach, etc. The president opened the council by prayer.

"At a church meeting held in Pennsylvania, Erie County, and Springfield Township, by Orson Pratt and Lyman Johnson, high priests, some of the members of that church refused to partake of the sacrament, because the elder administering it did not observe the Words of Wisdom to obey them. Elder Johnson argued that they were justified in so doing, because the elder was in transgression. Elder Pratt argued that the church was bound to receive the supper under the administration of an elder, so long as he retained his office or license. Voted that six councilors should speak upon the subject.

"The council then proceeded to try the question, whether disobedience to the Word of Wisdom was a transgression sufficient to deprive an official member from holding an office in the church, after having it sufficiently taught him.

"Councilors Samuel H. Smith, Luke Johnson, John S. Carter, Sylvester Smith, John Johnson, and Orson Hyde, were called to speak upon the case then before the council. After the councilors had spoken, the president proceeded to give a decision:—

"That no official member in this church is worthy to hold an office, after having the Words of Wisdom properly taught to him, and he the official member neglecting to comply with or obey them; which decision the council confirmed by vote.

"The president then asked if there were any elders present who would go to Canada and preach the gospel to that people; for they have written a number of letters for help. And the whole council felt as though the Spirit required the elders to go there.   It was therefore decided by the council that Lyman Johnson and Milton Holmes should travel together into Canada.   And also that Zebedee Coltrin and Henry Harriman travel together into Canada.   It was also decided that Jared Carter and Phineas Young travel together, if they can arrange their affairs at home so as to be liberated.

"It was also decided that Elder Oliver Granger should travel eastward as soon as his circumstances will permit, and that he should travel alone on account of his age; it was also decided that Elder Martin Harris should travel alone whenever he travels; that Elder John S. Carter and Jesse Smith travel east together as soon as they can.   The council also decided that Elder Brigham Young should travel alone it being his own choice, decided also that James Durfee and Edward Marvin should travel together eastward; also that Sidney Rigdon and John P. Green go to Strongsville; also that Orson Pratt and Harrison Sagers travel together for the time being; and that there should be a general conference held in Saco, in the State of Maine, on the 13th day of June, 1834.

"It was furthermore voted that Elder Orson Hyde, accompanied by Elder Orson Pratt, go east to obtain donations for Zion, and means to redeem the farm on which the house of the Lord stands.

"The church and council then prayed with uplifted hands that they might be prospered in their mission.

"Orson Hyde.

"Oliver Cowdery, Clerks."

—Times and Seasons, vol. 6, pp. 1022, 1023.

On February 22 Parley P. Pratt and Lyman Wight, messengers from Missouri, arrived in Kirtland, and on Sunday, the 23d, they addressed the people at the Methodist church.

Messengers from Zion arrive.

On the 24th a revelation concerning Zion was received.[1]

---

[1] 1. Verily I say unto you, my friends, Behold, I will give unto you a revelation and commandment, that you may know how to act in the discharge of your duties concerning the salvation and redemption of your brethren, who have been scattered on the land of Zion, being driven and smitten by the hands of mine enemies; on whom I will pour out my

In the February number of the *Evening and Morning Star*
are letters from M. C. Nickerson, from Canada, and John

wrath without measure in mine own time; for I have suffered them thus
far, that they might fill up the measure of their iniquities, that their
cup might be full, and that those who call themselves after my name
might be chastened for a little season, with a sore and grievous chastisement, because they did not hearken altogether unto the precepts and
commandments which I gave unto them.

2. But verily I say unto you, that I have decreed a decree which my
people shall realize, inasmuch as they hearken from this very hour, unto
the counsel which I, the Lord, their God, shall give unto them. Behold,
they shall, for I have decreed it, begin to prevail against mine enemies
from this very hour, and by hearkening to observe all the words which I,
the Lord their God, shall speak unto them, they shall never cease to prevail until the kingdoms of the world are subdued under my feet; and the
earth is given unto the saints, to possess it forever and ever. But inasmuch as they keep not my commandments, and hearken not to observe
all my words, the kingdoms of the world shall prevail against them, for
they were set to be a light unto the world, and to be the saviors of men;
and inasmuch as they are not the saviors of men, they are as salt that has
lost its savor, and is thenceforth good for nothing but to be cast out and
trodden under foot of men.

3. But verily I say unto you, I have decreed that your brethren, which
have been scattered, shall return to the land of their inheritances and
build up the waste places of Zion; for after much tribulation, as I have
said unto you in a former commandment, cometh the blessing. Behold,
this is the blessing which I have promised after your tribulations, and
the tribulations of your brethren; your redemption, and the redemption
of your brethren; even their restoration to the land of Zion, to be established, no more to be thrown down; nevertheless, if they pollute their
inheritances, they shall be thrown down; for I will not spare them if
they pollute their inheritances. Behold, I say unto you, The redemption
of Zion must needs come by power; therefore I will raise up unto my
people a man, who shall lead them like as Moses led the children of
Israel, for ye are the children of Israel, and of the seed of Abraham; and
ye must needs be led out of bondage by power, and with a stretched out
arm; and as your fathers were led at the first, even so shall the redemption of Zion be. Therefore, let not your hearts faint, for I say not unto
you as I said unto your fathers, Mine angel shall go up before you, but
not my presence; but I say unto you, Mine angels shall go before you,
and also my presence, and in time ye shall possess the goodly land.

4. Verily, verily I say unto you, that my servant Baurak Ale is the
man to whom I likened the servant to whom the Lord of the vineyard
spoke in the parable which I have given unto you.

5. Therefore, let my servant Baurak Ale say unto the strength of my
house, my young men and the middle aged, Gather yourselves together
unto the land of Zion, upon the land which I have bought with moneys
that have been consecrated unto me; and let all the churches send up
wise men, with their moneys, and purchase lands even as I have commanded them; and inasmuch as mine enemies come against you to drive
you from my goodly land, which I have consecrated to be the land of
Zion; even from your own lands after these testimonies, which ye have
brought before me, against them, ye shall curse them; and whomsoever
ye curse, I will curse; and ye shall avenge me of mine enemies; and my
presence shall be with you, even in avenging me of mine enemies, unto
the third and fourth generation of them that hate me.

Boynton, dated at Saco, Maine, from which we make ex·
tracts to show the progress of the work in these places:—

"WENDHAM, December 20, 1833.

"*Dear Brother:*—I have long been expecting to receive a letter from you, but as yet have received none. I received one
^{Work in} from Brother Joseph, a short time since, which in-
^{Canada.} formed me that you had returned safe to your
friends and families, which I was happy to hear. Your
labors while in Canada have been the beginning of a good .
work: there are thirty-four members attached to the church
at Mount Pleasant, all of whom appear to live up to their
profession, five of whom have spoken in tongues, and three
sing in tongues: and we live at the top of the mountain! For
my part, I feel that I cannot be thankful enough for what I
have received: the Scriptures have been opened to my view
beyond account, and the Revelation of John is become quite

6. Let no man be afraid to lay down his life for my sake; for whoso
layeth down his life for my sake, shall find it again. And whoso is not
willing to lay down his life for my sake, is not my disciple. It is my will
that my servant Sidney Rigdon shall lift up his voice in the congregations, in the eastern countries, in preparing the churches in keeping the
commandments which I have given unto them, concerning the restoration and redemption of Zion. It is my will that my servant Parley P.
Pratt, and my servant Lyman Wight should not return to the
land of their brethren, until they have obtained companies to go up
unto the land of Zion, by tens, or by twenties, or by fifties, or by an
hundred, until they have obtained to the number of five hundred of
the strength of my house. Behold, this is my will; ask and you shall
receive, but men do not always do my will; therefore, if you cannot
obtain five hundred, seek diligently that peradventure you may
obtain three hundred; and if ye cannot obtain three hundred,
seek diligently that peradventure ye may obtain one hundred. But
verily I say unto you, A commandment I give unto you, that ye
shall not go up unto the land of Zion, until you have obtained one
hundred of the strength of my house, to go up with you unto the
land of Zion. Therefore, as I said unto you, Ask and ye shall receive;
pray earnestly that peradventure my servant Baurak Ale may go with
you and preside in the midst of my people, and organize my kingdom
upon the consecrated land; and establish the children of Zion, upon the
laws and commandments which have been, and which shall be given,
unto you.

7. All victory and glory is brought to pass unto you through your diligence, faithfulness, and prayers of faith. Let my servant Parley P.
Pratt, journey with my servant Joseph Smith, Jr. Let my servant
Lyman Wight, journey with my servant Sidney Rigdon. Let my servant Hyrum Smith, journey with my servant Frederick G. Williams. Let
my servant Orson Hyde, journey with my servant Orson Pratt; whithersoever my servant Joseph Smith, Jr., shall counsel them in obtaining the
fulfillment of these commandments, which I have given unto you, and
leave the residue in my hands. Even so. Amen.

plain; I discover the monster there described in his true colors and by his right name.

"Your friends in Canada often speak of you and brother Joseph. Mr. and Mrs. Beamer are seriously inquiring after the truth: they often speak of Brothers Sidney and Joseph; and all the people with whom I am acquainted, or have talked with upon the subject of religion, appear to be much engaged, some for, and the remainder against; but I find those blessed promises to be verified, that God's grace shall be sufficient for our day and time of need. I find that those places where I thought the cross was going to be the hardest, is often the lightest, and then I often obtain the greatest blessings.

"If you can send a couple of preachers out here, as soon as you receive this, you would do us a kindness; for Brother Freeman is often called from home, and it is necessary that some one should be there. Send those that you have confidence in or none; the work requires competent workmen, for the harvest is truly great. I feel thankful that I have been spared to see this time. I shall be up to see you in the spring, if the Lord will.

"From your brother in the bonds of the gospel,

"M. C. NICKERSON."

"SACO, Maine, January 20, 1834.

"*Brethren in the Lord:*—I improve a few moments to inform you that I am well, that the Lord is present with me; his Spirit warms my heart, gives life to my soul, is my friend among enemies, my joy among friends, my comforter when alone, my companion in trouble; brings a hope like an anchor, makes the crown look near, and insures us the victory by an endurance of faith unto the end.

In Maine.

"The fifteenth number of the *Star* arrived here a few days since, which was gladly received; but it caused some painful emotions to read of the dreadful persecution at the West; yet there is a secret joy, for we can lift up our heads and rejoice, knowing that our redemption draweth nigh; for Jesus said, 'In the world ye shall have tribulation, but in me ye shall have peace.'

"Agreeably to your request I would inform you that I

have been laboring in this part of the vineyard for some time to lay before the people the new and everlasting covenant, and the glorious things of the kingdom that God has been pleased to reveal in these last days.

"I have baptized about forty in this section, and there are more convinced of the truth, but are still lingering on the threshold of the church, and I think the Lord will gather some of them into his kingdom.

"Brother E. M. Green labored with me from the 16th of January, 1833, till the October following. While we were together we baptized about one hundred and thirty, then at a council at Rowley, Massachusetts, it was decided that he should travel with Brother H. Cowen to Kirtland. Accordingly they started on their mission, and I went to Boston and visited the church in that place and baptized one. I then returned to this place and organized this branch of the church. I am yours in Christ,

"JOHN F. BOYNTON."
—Evening and Morning Star, pp. 269, 270.

In compliance with the revelation given on the 24th Joseph Smith and P. P. Pratt started east on February 26, and Sidney Rigdon and Lyman Wight, on the 28th. We are not in possession of the dates when others started, but it was soon after the command was given, showing prompt and decisive action when a duty was enjoined.

Mission East.

We give Joseph's account of this mission and the work done by himself and companion, which will indicate the nature of the work done by all for the redemption of Zion and the restoration of their brethren to their inheritance. We think it necessary to give this as fully as possible, because the doings and intentions of "Zion's Camp," which soon after went to Missouri, under arms, has been the subject of much comment and adverse criticism.

Purpose of Zion's camp.

A careful examination of what is written on the subject will convince the investigator that they had no thought of aggressive war on Missouri, but that they were armed for defense, while they carried clothing and other supplies to their destitute brethren, and were prepared to defend their homes when reinstated by the Governor, as was then contemplated.

To arm themselves was declared by the Governor to be not only their right but their duty, and in so doing they were acting under advice from officers of State.

Joseph states:—

"Wednesday, February 26, I started from home to obtain volunteers for Zion, in compliance with the foregoing revelation, and the 27th staid at Brother Roundy's."

He continues:—

"We continued our journey and on the 28th February staid at a stranger's, who entertained us very kindly; and on the first of March arrived at Brother Lewis'; and on the 2d which was the Sabbath, Brother Parley preached, and I preached in the evening; we had a good meeting. There is a small church in this place, which seems strong in the faith. O may God keep them in the faith, and save them and lead them to Zion.

"March 3 we intended to start on our journey east, but concluded to tarry another day. O may God bless us with the gift of utterance to accomplish the journey and the errand on which we are sent, and return safe to the land of Kirtland, and find my family all well. O Lord bless my little children with health and long life, to do good in their generation for Christ's sake, Amen.

"After leaving Kirtland we had passed through Thompson, Springfield, Elk Creek, Erie, Westfield, Livonia, Silver Creek, Perrysburg, Collins, China, Warsaw, Geneseo, Centerville, Catlin, and Spafford, before we arrived at Westfield. On the 4th inst. we continued our journey from Westfield, accompanied by Elder Gould, and after a ride of thirty-three miles at Villanova and tarried all night with a Brother McBride. The next morning, March 5, we went to Brother Nickerson's, and found him and his household full of faith and of the Holy Spirit.

"We called the church together, and related unto them what had happened to our brethren in Zion, and opened to them the prophecies and revelations concerning the order of the gathering to Zion, and the means of her redemption; and I prophesied to them, and the Spirit of the Lord came mightily upon them, and with all readiness the young and middle aged volunteered for Zion. The same evening we held two meetings, three or four miles distant from each other.

"March 6. We held another meeting at Bro. Nickerson's. The few unbelievers that attended were outrageous, and the meeting ended in complete confusion.

"March 7. We proceeded on our journey accompanied by Bro. Nickerson, leaving Brothers Gould and Matthews to prepare and gather up the companies, in the churches in that region, and meet us in Ohio, ready for Zion on the first of May. We arrived after dark, at Elliotville, the county seat of Cattaraugus, and tried for lodgings at every tavern in the place. It being court time we found no room, but were obliged to ride on in the dark, through mud and rain, and found shelter, after traveling about one mile, for which we paid more than tavern fare.

"On the 8th we arrived at Palmersville, at the house of Elder McGown's, where we were invited to go to Esquire Walker's to spend the evening. We found them very friendly and somewhat believing, and tarried all night.

"Sunday 9th, we preached in a schoolhouse, and had great attention. We found a few disciples who were firm in the faith; and. after meeting, found many believing and could hardly get away from them, and appointed a meeting in Freedom for Monday, the 10th, and staid at Mr. Cowdery's, where we were blessed with a fullness of temporal and spiritual blessings, even all we needed or were worthy to receive.

"Monday. Met our appointment, and preached to a great congregation; and at evening, preached again to a crowded assembly, an overflowing house. After meeting I proposed if any wished to obey, and would make it manifest, we would stay and administer at another meeting. the next day.

"Tuesday 11th. Fulfilled our appointment, and baptized Heman Hyde, after which we rode nine miles and put up at Stuart's tavern.

"Wednesday 12th. We arrived at Father Bosley's, after a ride of thirty-six miles.

"Thursday 13th. I preached.

"Friday 14th. At Father Beman's.

"March 15th. While at Father Beman's, Elders Rigdon

and Wight arrived, much to the joy of their souls, and the saints in Livonia.

"Sunday 16th. Elder Rigdon preached to a very large congregation in Geneseo. Elder Pratt preached in the afternoon of Monday the 17th.

"There was also the same day, March 17, a conference of elders, at Avon, Livingston County, New York, at the house of Alvah Beman, which I attended. There were present also Sidney Rigdon, Parley Pratt, Lyman Wight, John Murdock, Orson Pratt, and Orson Hyde, high priests, and six elders. I stated that the object of the conference was to obtain young men and middle aged to go and assist in the redemption of Zion, according to the commandment; and for the church to gather up their riches, and send them to purchase lands according to the commandment of the Lord; also to devise means, or obtain money for the relief of the brethren in Kirtland, say two thousand dollars, which sum would deliver the church in Kirtland from debt; and also determine the course which the several companies shall pursue, or the manner they shall journey when they shall leave this place.

"It was voted by the council that Fathers Bosley and Nickerson, Elder McWithey, and Bro. R. Orton, should exert themselves to obtain two thousand dollars, for the present relief in Kirtland. They all agreed to do what they could to obtain it, firmly believing it could be accomplished by the first of April. It was also decided that Elder Orson Hyde should tarry and preach in the regions round about, till the money should be obtained and carry it with him to Kirtland. It was also voted that I should return to Kirtland accompanied by Elders Rigdon and Wight. Elders John Murdock and Orson Pratt were appointed to journey to Kirtland, preaching by the way; and Elders Parley P. Pratt and Henry Brown to visit the churches in Black River country, and obtain all the means they could to help Zion.

"Tuesday, March 18. Tarried at Father Bosley's through the day.

"On the 19th commenced my journey for Kirtland, and staid this night at Bro. Withey's tavern.

"20th; continued our journey, dined at Bro. Joseph Holbrook's, and at night tried three times to procure lodgings in the name of disciples, but could not succeed. After night had commenced we found a man, in China, named Reuben Wilson, who would keep us for money; thus we learn there is more places for money than for the disciples of Jesus. . .

"March 21. We came to a man named Starks, six miles east of Springville, and on the 22d arrived at Bro. Vinson Knight's, in Perrysburgh, Cattaraugus County. On the 23d we arrived at Father Nickerson's, in Perrysburgh, where we held a meeting, etc. On the 24th I was not able to start, but felt determined to go the next morning. Twenty-fifth; journeyed from Father Nickerson's to Father Lewis' in Westfield, accompanied by Father Nickerson. On the 26th continued our journey to Elk Creek, and staid with Elder Hunt. The 27th I came to Springfield, where I found Elder Rigdon, who had come on by a different route, and we arrived that night within sixteen miles of Painesville, and arrived home at Kirtland, on the 28th of March, finding my family all well, and the Lord be praised for this blessing. The 29th, remained at home and had great joy with my family. Sunday the 30th, was at home, except going to hear Elder Rigdon preach."—*Times and Seasons*, vol. 6, pp. 1026, 1027.

In connection with the above an item from the journal of Elder Wight will serve to show the spirit of the times and the purpose of this special mission. Under date of April 13 he writes:—

"Preached to a large congregation (in Kirtland) upon the subject of having been driven from Jackson County, of our extreme sufferings, and of the great necessity of being obedient to the commandments; and also the necessity of those of like faith sympathizing with their brothers and sisters. This discourse appeared to have a good effect; about seventy volunteered to fly to their relief even if death should be the consequence thereof. Many donated largely of their substance to supply the wants of the needy. I spent the night with Bro. Joseph. and had much conversation with him concerning our peculiar circumstances."

Joseph gives the following account of the trial of Dr. Hurl-

but, which shows that Joseph was vindicated by courts of
civil law as well as by church courts, and that Hurlbut was
condemned by both. He states:—

"Monday, March 31. I went to Chardon to attend the
court, in the case against Dr. P. Hurlbut."

He continues the account as follows:—

"April 1, 1834. This day at Brother Rider's, in Chardon.
The court has not brought forward Hurlbut's trial yet, and
we were engaged in issuing subpœnas for witnesses. My
soul delighteth in the law of the Lord, for he forgiveth my
sins, and will confound mine enemies.

"Wednesday the 2d and Thursday the 3d, attended the
Hurlbut   court. Hurlbut was on trial for threatening my
on trial.   life. Friday morning I returned home.

"Saturday, March 5. I went to Chardon, as a witness for
Father Johnson, and returned in the evening. Mr. Russell,
the State's Attorney, for Portage County, called on me. He
appeared in a gentlemanly manner, and treated me with
great respect.

"April 7. Bishop Whitney, Elders Frederick G. Williams,
Oliver Cowdery, Heber C. Kimball, and myself met in the
council room, and bowed down before the Lord, and prayed
that he would furnish the means to deliver the Firm from debt,
that they might be set at liberty; also that I might prevail
against the wicked man, Hurlbut, and that he might be put
to shame.

"April 9. After an impartial trial the court decided that
Doctor P. Hurlbut be bound over under two hundred dollar
bonds, to keep the peace for six months, and pay the cost,
which amounted to near three hundred dollars, all of which
was in answer to our prayers, for which I thank my heavenly
Father."—*Times and Seasons*, vol. 6, pp. 1040, 1041.

The court record of the case agrees with this.[2]

_____

[2]Pleas before the Court of Common Pleas within and for the County
of Geauga in the State of Ohio at a term of said Court begun and held at
Chardon in said County on the thirty-first day of March in the year of
our Lord one thousand eight hundred and thirty-four.
    Be it remembered that now at this term of the Court came Reuben
Hitchcock Esquire on behalf of the State of Ohio and placed on file a
transcript from the docket of William Holbrook Esquire, in the words

On April 14, 1834, it was agreed that Hyrum Smith and Lyman Wight should go west by the way of Michigan and H Smith the northern part of Illinois, visiting the churches and Wight go and ascertaining what they would do for the breth-via Michigan. ren in Missouri, while Joseph, with the main company, was to take a more southerly route.

and figures following, that is to say: The State of Ohio Geauga County ss.

The State of Ohio ⎱ Complaint to compel the defendant to give bond to
v ⎰ keep the peace. On complaint of Joseph Smith
Doctor P. Hurlbut. ⎰ Junr. against the defendant against J. C. Dowen a Justice of the Peace for Kirtland Township in said County made on the 21st day of Dec. 1833 a warrant was issued by said J. C. Dowen, Justice aforesaid which was returned before me William Holbrook a Justice of the Peace for Painesville township in the County aforesaid on the 4th day of January A D 1834 by Stephen Sherman a Constable of Kirtland township with defendant in Court. And not being ready for the examination said Constable is directed to keep the defendant in custody and return him again before the Court on the 6th day of January A. D. 1834 at 9 O'clock A. M. at his office in Painesville; at which time the defendant again appeared and not being yet ready for the examination on the part of the State this cause is again postponed to the 13th of January 1834 at 9 O'clock A. M. and the defendant required to be kept in custody by A Ritch Const. of Painesville township, at which time the defendant was again brought before the Court by A Ritch Constable. And all parties being ready for trial the Court commenced the examination and the following witnesses were examined on the part of the State, Amos Hodges C. Hodges, Sarah Wait [Waite], Burr Priggs [Riggs] Mary Copley Joseph Allen M. Hodges D. Elliot J. Smith Jr. L. Copley C. Holmes S. I. Whitney S. Slayton Mr. Wakefield, I. Wait and E. Goodman and the same were examined by the defendant. The examination commenced Monday the 13th January 1834 and ended January 13, 1834. After hearing the testimony it is the opinion of the Court that the complainant had reason to fear that Doctor P. Hurlbut would beat wound or kill him or injure his property as set forth in his complaint, and it is the consideration of the Court that the defendant enter into a recognizance to keep the peace generally and especially towards the complainant and also to appear before the Court of Common Pleas on the first day of the term thereof next to be holden in and for said County and not depart without leave, or stand committed till the Judgment of the Court be complied with.

The defendant forthwith complied with the judgment of the Court & entered into a recognizance as provided by the Statute.

The State of Ohio ⎱ I certify the foregoing to be substantially a true
Geauga County ss ⎰ copy of my docket entry in the above entitled examination.

William Holbrook Justice of the Peace.

And thereupon came the Prosecuting Attorney for the County and also the said defendant, and the Court having heard the said complaint and also all the testimony adduced by the said complainant, and also by the said defendant and having duly considered the same are of opinion that the said complainant had ground to fear that the said Doctor P. Hurlbut would wound, beat or kill him or destroy his property as set forth in said complaint. Wherefore it is ordered and adjudged by the Court that the said Doctor P. Hurlbut enter into a new recognizance with good

On the 21st Elders Smith and Wight started on their mission, traveling by team.

Of current events Joseph wrote as follows:—

"Friday, April 11. I attended meeting, and Father Tyler was restored to the fellowship of the church.

"On the 12th I went to the lake and spent the day in fishing and visiting the brethren in that place.

"Sunday the 13th; was sick and unable to attend meeting.

"On Monday 14th I purchased some hay and oats and got them home.

"Tuesday 15th; drew a load of hay, and on Wednesday ploughed and sowed oats for Brother Frederick.

"Thursday, the 17th of April, I attended a meeting agreeably to appointment, at which time the important subject of the deliverance of Zion and the building of the Lord's house in Kirtland, was discussed by Elder Rigdon. After the lecture I requested the brethren and sisters to contribute all the money they could for the deliverance of Zion, and received twenty-nine dollars and sixty-eight cents.

and sufficient security in the sum of two hundred dollars hereafter to keep the peace and be of good behavior to the citizens of the State of Ohio generally and to the said Joseph Smith Junior in particular for the period of of six months, and it is further ordered that the said Doctor P. Hurlbut pay the costs of this prosecution taxed at the sum of one hundred and twelve dollars and fifty-nine cents. And thereupon came the said Doctor P. Hurlbut with Charles A. Holmes and Elijah Smith as his sureties in open Court, entered into a recognizance in the penal sum of two hundred dollars each, conditioned that the said Doctor P. Hurlbut shall for the period of six months from and after this day keep the peace and be of good behavior to all the citizens of the State of Ohio generally and to the said Joseph Smith Jun. in particular.

M. BIRCHARD P. J.

Certificate to Common Pleas Record.

The State of Ohio,)
Geauga County, ss.)

I, B. D. Ames Clerk of the Court of Common Pleas, within and for said County,

And in whose custody the Files, Pleadings, Journals, Records, Execution Dockets, and Seal of said Court, are required by the Laws of the State of Ohio to be kept, hereby certify that the foregoing copy of Record is taken and copied from the Records of the proceedings of the Court of Common Pleas within and for said Geauga County, and that said foregoing copy has been compared by me with the original Record and that the same is a correct transcript therefrom.

In Testimony Whereof, I do hereunto subscribe my name officially, and affix the Seal of said Court, at the Court House in Chardon in said County, this 16th day of July, A. D. 1896.

(Seal)   B. D. AMES Clerk.

"April 18. I left Kirtland in company with E'ders Sidney Rigdon, Oliver Cowdery, and Zebedee Coltrin, for New Portage, to attend a conference. Dined at W. W. Williams', in Newburgh, and continuing our journey, after dark we were hailed by a man who desired to ride. We were checked by the Spirit, and refused. He professed to be sick, but in a few minutes was joined by two others, who followed us hard, cursing and swearing, but we were successful in escaping their hands, through the providence of the Lord, and staid that night at a tavern, where we were treated with civility.

"On the 19th continuing our journey, dined at Brother Joseph Bosworth's, in Copley, Medina County. Brother Bosworth was strong in the faith, and if faithful may do much good. We arrived the same day at Brother Jonathan Taylor's, in Norton, where we were received with kindness. We soon retired to the wilderness, where we united in prayer and supplication for the blessings of the Lord to be given unto his church. We called upon the Father in the name of Jesus to go with the brethren who were going to the land of Zion, and that I might have strength and wisdom and understanding sufficient to lead the people of the Lord, and to gather back and establish the saints upon the land of their inheritances, and organize them according to the will of heaven, that they be no more cast down forever. We then united in the laying on of hands.

"Elders Rigdon, Cowdery, and Coltrin laid their hands on my head and conferred upon me all the blessings necessary to qualify me to stand before the Lord, in my calling, and be returned again in peace, and triumph, to enjoy the society of my brethren.

"Those present then laid their hands upon Elder Rigdon, and confirmed upon him the blessings of wisdom and knowl-

Preparations for starting to Zion.

edge to preside over the church in my absence; to have the Spirit to assist Elder Cowdery in conducting the *Star*, and arrange the covenants, and the blessings of old age and peace till Zion is built up and Kirtland established, till all his enemies are under his feet, and a crown of eternal life in the kingdom of God with us.

"Previous to blessing Elder Rigdon we laid hands on

Elder Cowdery and confirmed upon him the blessings of wisdom and understanding sufficient for his station, that he be qualified to assist Elder Rigdon in arranging the church covenants, which are soon to be published; and have intelligence in all things to do the work of printing.

"After blessing Elder Rigdon we laid our hands upon Brother Zebedee, and confirmed the blessings of wisdom to preach the gospel even till it spreads to the islands of the seas, and to be spared to see threescore years and ten, and see Zion built up and Kirtland established forever, and even at last to receive a crown of life. Our hearts rejoiced and we were comforted with the Holy Spirit.

"Sunday, April 20. Elder Rigdon entertained a large congregation of saints with an interesting discourse upon the dispensation of the fullness of times, etc.

"On the 21st I attended conference, and had a glorious time. Some volunteered to go to Zion, and others donated sixty-six dollars and thirty-seven cents, for the benefit of the scattered brethren in Zion. The following are extracts from the minutes of the conference:—

"This day a conference of elders assembled at the dwelling house of Brother Carpenter, President Joseph Smith, Jun., read the second chapter of Joel's prophecy, prayed, and addressed the conference as follows:—

"It is very difficult for us to communicate to the churches all that God has revealed to us, in consequence of tradition; for we are differently situated from any other people that ever existed upon this earth, consequently those former revelations cannot be suited to our conditions; they were given to other people, who were before us; but in the last days, God was to call a remnant, in which was to be deliverance, as well as in Jerusalem and Zion. Now if God should give no more revelations, where will we find Zion and this remnant? The time is near when desolation is to cover the earth, and then God will have a place of deliverance in his remnant, and in Zion, etc.

"The President then gave a relation of obtaining and translating the Book of Mormon, the revelation of the priesthood of Aaron, the organization of the church in 1830, the revelation of the high priesthood, and the gift of the Holy Spirit poured out upon the church. . .

"Elder Rigdon adverted to the former covenants to Abraham, Isaac, and Jacob, and others of the ancients which were to be realized in the last days, etc., and spoke at some length upon the deliverance of Zion; the endowment of the elders with power from on high, according to the former promises, and the spreading of the word of the Lord to the four winds. He first referred to the situation of the brethren in Missouri, and urged the importance of those who could, giving heed to the revelations by going up to their assistance; and those who could not go to help those who are going, to means for their expenses. etc.

"Elder Cowdery gave a brief relation of the mobbing in Missouri, etc., and called for a contribution. Elders Ambrose Palmer and Salmon Warner followed on the same subject. Brother Joseph Bosworth spoke on the deliverance of Zion; and said he had no property, but if necessary for her deliverance he would sell his clothes at auction, if he might have left him as good a garment as the Savior had in the manger. Others spoke on the same subject.

"Elder Rigdon in speaking on the second item gave an account of the endowment of the ancient apostles, and laid before the conference the dimensions of the House to be built in Kirtland, and rehearsed the promise to the elders in the last days, which they were to realize after the house of the Lord was built. Brother Bosworth then related a few items of a vision, which he gave as a testimony of those things contained in the revelations read by Elder Rigdon, and his remarks thereon. President Smith explained the revelation concerning the building of the Lord's house.

"President Smith then laid hands on certain children and blessed them in the name of the Lord. Elder Rigdon administered the sacrament. There were present seven high priests and thirteen elders. Adjourned to the Monday preceding the second Sunday in September. Closed by singing 'Now my remnant of days,' etc.   OLIVER COWDERY,
"(Signed)   Clerk of the Conference."
          —*Times and Seasons*, vol. 6, pp. 1058–1061.

On the 22d Joseph returned to Kirtland and on the 23d received the revelation to Enoch.[a]

[a] 1. Verily I say unto you, my friends, I give unto you counsel and a commandment, concerning all the properties which belong to the order, which I commanded to be organized and established, to be an united order, and an everlasting order for the benefit of my church, and for the salvation of men until I come, with promise immutable and unchangeable, that inasmuch as those whom I commanded were faithful, they should be blessed with a multiplicity of blessings; but inasmuch as they were not faithful, they were nigh unto cursing. Therefore, inasmuch as some of my servants have not kept the commandment, but have broken the covenant, by covetousness and with feigned words, I have cursed them with a very sore and grievous curse; for I, the Lord, have decreed in my heart, that inasmuch as any man, belonging to the order, shall be found a transgressor; or in other words, shall break the covenant with which ye are bound, he shall be cursed in his life, and shall be trodden down by whom I will, for I, the Lord, am not to be mocked in these things; and all this that the innocent among you, may not be condemned with the unjust; and that the guilty among you may not escape, because I, the Lord, have promised unto you a crown of glory at my right hand. Therefore, inasmuch as you are found transgressors, ye cannot escape my wrath in your lives; inasmuch as ye are cut off by transgression, ye cannot escape the buffetings of Satan until the day of redemption.

2. And I now give unto you power from this very hour, that if any man among you, of the order, is found a transgressor, and repenteth not of the evil, that ye shall deliver him over unto the buffetings of Satan; and he shall not have power to bring evil upon you. It is wisdom in me; therefore, a commandment I give unto you, that ye shall organize yourselves, and appoint every man his stewardship, that every man may give an account unto me of the stewardship which is appointed unto him; for it is expedient that I, the Lord, should make every man accountable, as stewards over earthly blessings, which I have made and prepared for my creatures. I, the Lord, stretched out the heavens, and builded the earth as a very handy work; and all things therein are mine; and it is my purpose to provide for my saints, for all things are mine; but it must needs be done in mine own way; and, behold, this is the way, that I, the Lord, have decreed to provide for my saints: that the poor shall be exalted, in that the rich are made low; for the earth is full, and there is enough and to spare; yea, I prepared all things, and have given unto the children of men to be agents unto themselves. Therefore, if any man shall take of the abundance which I have made, and impart not his portion, according to the law of my gospel, unto the poor and the needy, he shall, with the wicked, lift up his eyes in hell, being in torment.

3. And now, verily I say unto you, concerning the properties of the order: Let my servant Pelagoram have appointed unto him the place where he now resides, and the lot of Tahhanes, for his stewardship, for his support while he is laboring in my vineyard, even as I will when I shall command him; and let all things be done according to counsel of the order, and united consent, or voice of the order, which dwell in the land of Shinehah. And this stewardship and blessing, I, the Lord, confer upon my servant Pelagoram, for a blessing upon him, and his seed after him; and I will multiply blessings upon him, inasmuch as he shall be humble before me.

4. And again, let my servant Mahemson have appointed unto him, for his stewardship, the lot of land which my servant Zombre obtained in exchange for his former inheritance, for him and his seed after him; and inasmuch as he is faithful, I will multiply blessings upon him and his

May 1. Over twenty of those who had volunteered to go to Zion started from Kirtland, with four baggage wagons.

seed after him. And let my servant Mahemson devote his moneys for the proclaiming of my words, according as my servant Gazelam shall direct.

5. And again, let my servant Shederlaomach have the place upon which he now dwells. And let my servant Olihah have the lot which is set off joining the house which is to be for the Lane-shine-house, which is lot number one; and also the lot upon which his father resides. And let my servant Shederlaomach and Olihah have the Lane-shine-house and all things that pertain unto it; and this shall be their stewardship which shall be appointed unto them; and inasmuch as they are faithful, behold, I will bless, and multiply blessings upon them; and this is the beginning of the stewardship which I have appointed them, for them and their seed after them; and inasmuch as they are faithful, I will multiply blessings upon them and their seed after them; even a multiplicity of blessings.

6. And again, let my servant Zombre have the house in which he lives, and the inheritance, all save the ground which has been reserved for the building of my houses, which pertains to that inheritance; and those lots which have been named for my servant Olihah. And inasmuch as he is faithful, I will multiply blessings upon him. And it is my will that he should sell the lots that are laid off for the building up of the city of my saints, inasmuch as it shall be made known to him by the voice of the Spirit, and according to the counsel of the order; and by the voice of the order. And this is the beginning of the stewardship which I have appointed unto him, for a blessing unto him, and his seed after him; and inasmuch as he is faithful, I will multiply a multiplicity of blessings upon him.

7. And again, let my servant Ahashdah have appointed unto him, the houses and lot where he now resides, and the lot and building on which the Ozondah stands; and also the lot which is on the corner south of the Ozondah; and also the lot on which the Shule is situated; and all this I have appointed unto my servant Ahashdah, for his stewardship, for a blessing upon him and his seed after him, for the benefit of the Ozondah of my order, which I have established for my stake in the land of Shinehah; yea, verily this is the stewardship which I have appointed unto my servant Ahashdah; even this whole Ozondah establishment, him and his agent, and his seed after him; and inasmuch as he is faithful in keeping my commandments, which I have given unto him, I will multiply blessings upon him, and his seed after him, even a multiplicity of blessings.

8. And again, let my servant Gazelam have appointed unto him, the lot which is laid off for the building of my house, which is forty rods long, and twelve wide, and also the inheritance upon which his father now resides; and this is the beginning of the stewardship which I have appointed unto him, for a blessing upon him, and upon his father; for, behold, I have reserved an inheritance for his father, for his support; therefore he shall be reckoned in the house of my servant Gazelam; and I will multiply blessings upon the house of my servant Gazelam, inasmuch as he is faithful, even a multiplicity of blessings.

9. And now a commandment I give unto you concerning Zion, that you shall no longer be bound as an united order to your brethren of Zion, only on this wise: after you are organized, you shall be called the united order of the stake of Zion, the city of Shinehah. And your brethren, after they are organized, shall be called the united order of the city of Zion; and they shall be organized in their own names, and in their own

They traveled as far as New Portage and tarried there, waiting for the rest of the company from Kirtland to arrive.

name; and they shall do their business in their own name, and in their own names; and you shall do your business in your own name, and in your own names. And this I have commanded to be done for your salvation, and also for their salvation in consequence of their being driven out, and that which is to come. The covenants being broken through transgression, by covetousness and feigned words; therefore, you are dissolved as a united order with your brethren, that you are not bound only up to this hour, unto them, only on this wise, as I said, by loan, as shall be agreed by this order, in council, as your circumstances will admit, and the voice of the council direct.

10. And again, a commandment I give unto you concerning your stewardship which I have appointed unto you; behold, all these properties are mine, or else your faith is vain, and ye are found hypocrites, and the covenants which ye have made unto me are broken; and if the properties are mine then ye are stewards, otherwise ye are no stewards. But verily I say unto you, I have appointed unto you to be stewards over mine house, even stewards indeed; and for this purpose I have commanded you to organize yourselves, even to Shinelah my words, the fullness of my scriptures, the revelations which I have given unto you, and which I shall hereafter, from time to time, give unto you, for the purpose of building up my church and kingdom on the earth, and to prepare my people for the time when I shall dwell with them, which is nigh at hand.

11. And ye shall prepare for yourselves a place for a treasury, and consecrate it unto my name; and ye shall appoint one among you to keep the treasury, and he shall be ordained unto this blessing; and there shall be a seal upon the treasury, and all the sacred things shall be delivered into the treasury, and no man among you shall call it his own, or any part of it, for it shall belong to you all with one accord; and I give it unto you from this very hour; and now see to it, that ye go to and make use of the stewardship which I have appointed unto you, exclusive of the sacred things, for the purpose of Shinelane these sacred things, as I have said; and the avails of the sacred things shall be had in the treasury, and a seal shall be upon it, and it shall not be used or taken out of the treasury by anyone, neither shall the seal be loosed which shall be placed upon it, only by the voice of the order, or by commandment. And thus shall ye preserve the avails of the sacred things in the treasury, for sacred and holy purposes; and this shall be called the sacred treasury of the Lord; and a seal shall be kept upon it, that it may be holy and consecrated unto the Lord.

12. And again, there shall be another treasury prepared and a treasurer appointed to keep the treasury, and a seal shall be placed upon it; and all moneys that you receive in your stewardships, by improving upon the properties which I have appointed unto you, in houses or in lands, or in cattle, or in all things save it be the holy and sacred writings, which I have reserved unto myself for holy and sacred purposes, shall be cast into the treasury as fast as you receive moneys, by hundreds or by fifties, or by twenties, or by tens, or by fives, or in other words, if any man among you obtain five talents let him cast them into the treasury; or if he obtain ten, or twenty, or fifty, or an hundred, let him do likewise; and let not any man among you say that it is his own, for it shall not be called his, nor any part of it; and there shall not any part of it be used, or taken out of the treasury, only by the voice and common consent of the order. And this shall be the voice and common consent of the order: that any man among you, say unto the treasurer, I have

On May 3 a conference was held at Kirtland, at which time action was taken on the name of the church. Previous Name of to this no official action had been taken, and no the Church. uniformity of practice had obtained, hence to insure uniformity in records it was necessary to have some official action. The church had been called the "Church of Christ," "The Church of Jesus Christ," "Church of God," "Church of the Firstborn," or whatever appellation suited the write or speaker best. The minutes of this conference are as follows:—

"KIRTLAND, Ohio, May 3, 1834.

"Minutes of a conference of the elders of the Church of Christ, which church was organized in the township of Fayette, Seneca County, New York, on the 6th of April, A. D. 1830.

"The conference come to order, and Joseph Smith, Jr.,

need of this to help me in my stewardship; if it be five talents, or if it be ten talents, or twenty, or fifty, or an hundred, the treasurer shall give unto him the sum which he requires, to help him in his stewardship, until he be found a transgressor, and it is manifest before the council of the order plainly, that he is an unfaithful and an unwise steward; but so long as he is in full fellowship, and is faithful, and wise in his stewardship, this shall be his token unto the treasurer that the treasurer shall not withhold. But in case of transgression the treasurer shall be subject unto the council and voice of the order. And in case the treasurer is found an unfaithful, and an unwise steward, he shall be subject to the counsel and voice of the order, and shall be removed out of his place, and another shall be appointed in his stead.

13. And again, verily I say unto you, concerning your debts, Behold, it is my will that you should pay all your debts; and it is my will that you should humble yourselves before me, and obtain this blessing by your diligence and humility, and the prayer of faith; and inasmuch as you are diligent and humble, and exercise the prayer of faith, behold, I will soften the hearts of those to whom you are in debt, until I shall send means unto you for your deliverance. Therefore write speedily unto Cainhannoch, and write according to that which shall be dictated by my Spirit, and I will soften the hearts of those to whom you are in debt, that it shall be taken away out of their minds to bring affliction upon you. And inasmuch as ye are humble and faithful and call on my name, behold, I will give you the victory. I give unto you a promise, that you shall be delivered this once, out of your bondage; inasmuch as you obtain a chance to loan money by hundreds, or thousands, even until you shall loan enough to deliver yourselves from bondage, it is your privilege, and pledge the properties which I have put into your hands, this once, by giving your names, by common consent, or otherwise, as it shall seem good unto you. I give unto you this privilege, this once, and, behold, if you proceed to do the things which I have laid before you, according to my commandments, all these things are mine, and ye are my stewards, and the master will not suffer his house to be broken up. Even so. Amen.

was chosen moderator, and Frederick G. Williams and Oliver Cowdery were appointed clerks.

"After prayer the conference proceeded to discuss the subject of names and appellations, when a motion was made by Sidney Rigdon, and seconded by Newel K. Whitney, that this church be known hereafter by the name of 'The Church of the Latter Day Saints.' Appropriate remarks were delivered by some of the members, after which the motion was put by the moderator, and passed by unanimous voice.

"Resolved that this conference recommend to the conferences and churches abroad, that in making out and transmitting minutes of their proceedings, such minutes and proceedings be made out under the above title.

"Resolved that these minutes be signed by the moderator and clerks, and published in the *Evening and Morning Star.*

"JOSEPH SMITH, Jr., Moderator.

"FREDERICK G. WILLIAMS, ⎱ Clerks."
"OLIVER COWDERY,   ⎰

—*Evening and Morning Star*, vol. 2, p. 352.

It has been stated that in this action the name of Christ was entirely disregarded, but it will be observed that it is called in the beginning of the minutes, "the Church of Christ;" so we conclude that the appellation given in this resolution was intended to be additional.

"An appeal," published in the *Evening and Morning Star* (vol. 2, page 361) for the following August, signed W. W. Phelps, David Whitmer, John Whitmer, Edward Partridge, John Corrill, Isaac Morley, Parley P. Pratt, Lyman Wight, Newel Knight, Thomas B. Marsh, Simeon Carter, and Calvin Beebe, contains the following sentence: "The Church of Christ recently styled the Church of the Latter Day Saints."

Joseph continues:—

"May 5. Having gathered and prepared clothing and other necessaries to carry to our brethren and sisters who

Start for Zion.

had been robbed and plundered of nearly all their effects; and having provided for ourselves horses and wagons, and firearms, and all sorts of munitions of war of the most portable kind for self-defense, as our enemies were thick on every hand, I started with the remainder of the company, from Kirtland, for Missouri, and on the 6th we arrived, and joined our brethren who had gone before, at New Portage, about fifty miles distance.

"My company from Kirtland consisted of about one hundred, mostly young men, and nearly all elders, priests, teachers, or deacons, and as our wagons were nearly filled with baggage we had mostly to travel on foot.

"On the 7th we made preparations for traveling, gathered all the moneys of every individual of the company, and appointed F. G. Williams Paymaster of the company from the funds thus collected. The whole company now consisted of more than one hundred and fifty men, accompanied by twenty baggage wagons, and we were more than sixty miles on our journey, having left but few men in Kirtland; viz.: Elder Sidney Rigdon and Oliver Cowdery and a few working on the Temple, except the aged. Zerubbabel Snow was appointed Commissary General at the time Williams was appointed Paymaster.

"Through the remainder of this day and a part of the 8th, I continued to organize the company, appoint such other general officers as the case required, and gave such instructions as were necessary for the discipline, order, comfort, and safety of all concerned. I also divided the whole band into companies of twelve, each company electing their own captain, who severally assigned each man, in their respective companies, his part and duty, which was generally in the following order: Two cooks, two firemen, two tentmakers, two watermen, one runner, two wagoners and horsemen, and one commissary. We purchased flour, baked our own bread, and cooked our own provisions, generally, which was good though sometimes scanty; and sometimes we had johnny cake, or corn dodger, instead of flour bread. Every night before retiring to rest, at the sound of the trumpet, we bowed before the Lord in the several tents, and presented our thank offerings with prayer and supplication; and at the sound of the morning trumpet every man was again on his knees before the Lord, imploring his blessing for the day." —*Times and Seasons*, vol. 6, pp. 1074, 1075.

In harmony with the testimony of Joseph concerning the
Kimball on   purpose of this expedition is the statement of H.
the expedition. C. Kimball, as published in *Times and Seasons*, volume 6, page 771:—

"At this time also our brethren were suffering great persecution in Jackson County, Missouri; about twelve hundred
were driven, plundered, and robbed; and their houses burned
and some were killed. The whole country seemed to be in
arms against us, ready to destroy us. Brother Joseph received a lengthy revelation concerning the redemption of
Zion, which remains to be fulfilled in a great measure. But
he thought it best to gather together as many of the brethren
as he conveniently could, with what means they could spare,
and go up to Zion to render all the assistance that we could
to our afflicted brethren. We gathered clothing and other
necessaries to carry up to our brethren and sisters who had
been stripped; and putting our horses to the wagons, and
taking our firelocks and ammunition, we started on our journey; leaving only Oliver Cowdery, Sidney Rigdon, and the
workmen who were engaged at the Temple; so that there
were very few men left in Kirtland. Our wagons were about
full with baggage, etc., consequently we had to travel on
foot. We started on the 5th of May, and truly this was a
solemn morning to me. I took leave of my wife and children and friends, not expecting ever to see them again, as
myself and brethren were threatened both in that country
and in Missouri by the enemies, that they would destroy us
and exterminate us from the land."

Parley P. Pratt, on this point writes as follows:—

"It was now the first of May, 1834, and our mission had
resulted in the assembling of about two hundred men at
Pratt on the   Kirtland, with teams, baggage, provisions, arms,
expedition.   etc., for a march of one thousand miles, for the
purpose of carrying some supplies to the afflicted and persecuted saints in Missouri, and to reinforce and strengthen
them; and, if possible, to influence the Governor of the State
to call out sufficient additional force to coöperate in restoring them to their rights. This little army was led by President Joseph Smith in person. It commenced its march

about the first of May. Passing through Ohio, Indiana, and Illinois, it entered Missouri sometime in June."—Autobiography of Parley P. Pratt, p. 122.

These witnesses all agree, and show that the object of the expedition was honorable and charitable.

Thursday, May 8, found them ready to start from New Portage, Ohio, on this long and perilous journey.

CHAPTER 17.

1834.

JOSEPH gives an account of the journey, which will be of interest to the reader. He writes:—

"After completing the organization of the companies on the 8th, we recommenced our march towards Zion,
The march.
and pitched our tents in a beautiful grove, at Chippeway, twelve miles from New Portage, for the night.
Incidents by the way.
On the 9th we proceeded onward, and on Saturday, the 10th, passing through Mansfield, encamped for the Sabbath in Richfield.

"Sunday 11th. Elder Sylvester Smith preached, and the company received the sacrament of bread and wine.

"Monday the 12th: We left Richfield for the Miami River, where we arrived, after daily marches, on the 16th.

"We forded the Miami River with our baggage wagons, and the men waded through the waters. On the 17th of May we crossed the State line of Ohio, and encamped for the Sabbath just within the limits of Indiana, having traveled forty miles that day. Our feet were very sore and blistered, our stockings wet with blood, the weather being very warm. This night one of our enemies' spies attempted to get into our camp, but was prevented by our guards. We had our sentinels every night on account of spies, who were continually striving to harass us.

"About this time the saints in Clay County, Missouri, established an armory, where they commenced manufacturing swords, dirks, pistols, stocking rifles, and repairing arms in general for their own defense against mob violence. Many arms were purchased, for the leading men in Clay County rendered every facility in their power, in order, as they said 'to help the Mormons settle their own difficulties, and pay the Jackson mob in their own way.'

"Sunday 18th. We had preaching as usual, and the administration of the sacrament.[1] Monday 19th. Although threatened by our enemies that we should not, we passed through Vandalia quietly, and unmolested; all the inhabitants were silent and appeared as though possessed with fear. At night we encamped on an eminence, where we lost one horse.

"Wednesday 21st. We forded White River. Sunday 25th. Arrived at the State line of Illinois. We had no meeting but attended to washing, baking, and preparing to resume our journey, which we did on Monday the 26th, and at night were aroused by the continual threats of our enemies. Notwithstanding our enemies were continually breathing threats of violence, we did not fear, neither did we hesitate to prosecute our journey, for God was with us and his angels went before us, and the faith of our little band was unwavering. We know that angels were our companions, for we saw them.

---

[1] This day Joseph wrote to his wife as follows:—

CAMP OF ISRAEL in Indiana State, Town of Richmond, 18th May.

My Dear Wife:—Meeting being over, I sit down in my tent to write a few lines to you, to let you know that you are on my mind, and that I am sensible of the duties of a husband and father, and that I am well, and I pray God to let his blessings rest upon you and the children, and all that are around you, until I return to your society. The few lines you wrote and sent by the hand of Bro. Lyman, gave me satisfaction and comfort, and I hope you will continue to communicate to me by your own hand, for this is a consolation to me to converse with you in this way in my lonely moments which is not easily described. I will endeavor to write every Sunday, if I can, and let you know how I am, and Bro. Frederick will write to Oliver and give him the names of the places we pass through and a history of our journey, from time to time, so that it will not be necessary for me to endeavor to write it. But I feel a satisfaction to write a few lines with my own hand. In this way I can have the privilege to communicate some of my feelings that I should not dare to reveal, as you know that my situation is a very critical one. Bro. Jenkins, and William, Jesse, and George are all well, and are humble, are determined to be faithful; and finally all the Kirtland brethren are well and cannot fail. I must close, for I cannot write on my knees sitting on the ground, to edification. O, may the blessings of God rest upon you, is the prayer of your husband until death.

Emma Smith. JOSEPH SMITH.

"On Tuesday, the 27th, we arrived at the deep river Kaskaskia, where we found two skiffs, which we lashed together, and on which we ferried our baggage across the stream. We then swam our horses and wagons, and when they arrived at the opposite shore the brethren attached ropes to them and helped them out of the water and up the steep bank. Some of the brethren felled trees across the river, on which they passed over. Thus we all safely passed the river, and the day following arrived at Decatur, where another horse died.

"Saturday evening, May 31. We encamped one mile from Jacksonville, and made preparations for the Sabbath.

"Sunday, June 1, 1834. We had preaching, and many of the inhabitants of the town came to hear. Elder John Carter, who had formerly been a Baptist preacher, spoke in the morning, and was followed by four other elders in the course of the day, all of whom had formerly been preachers for different denominations. When the inhabitants heard these elders they appeared much interested, and were very desirous to know who we were, and we told them one had been a Baptist preacher, and one a Campbellite; one a Reformed Methodist, and another a Restorationer, etc. During the day many questions were asked but no one could learn our names, profession, business, or destination, and, although they suspected we were Mormons, they were very civil. Our enemies had threatened that we should not cross the Illinois River, but on Monday the 2d we were ferried over without any difficulty. The ferryman counted and declared there were five hundred of us, yet our true number was only about one hundred and fifty. Our company had been increased since our departure from Kirtland, by volunteers from different branches of the church through which we had passed. We encamped on the bank of the river until Tuesday the 3d. During our travels we visited several of the mounds which had been thrown up by the ancient inhabitants of this county, Nephites, Lamanites, etc., and this morning I went up on a high mound, near the river, accompanied by the brethren. From this mound we could overlook the tops of the trees and view the prairie on each side of the river as far as our vision could extend, and the scenery was truly delightful.

"On the top of the mound were stones which presented the appearance of three altars having been erected one above the other, according to ancient order; and human bones were strewn over the surface of the ground. The brethren procured a shovel and hoe, and removing the earth to the depth of about one foot discovered [a] skeleton of a man, almost entire, and between his ribs was a Lamanitish arrow, which evidently produced his death. Elder Brigham Young retained the arrow and the brethren carried some pieces of the skeleton to Clay County.

"Continuing our journey on the 4th we encamped on the banks of the Mississippi River. At this place we were somewhat afflicted, and our enemies strongly threatened that we should not cross over into Missouri. The river being nearly one mile and a half wide and having but one ferry boat, it took two days for us to pass over. While some were ferrying others were engaged in hunting, fishing, etc.; as we arrived we encamped on the bank, within the limits of Missouri. While at this place Sylvester Smith rebelled against the order of the company, and gave vent to his feelings against myself in particular. This was the first outbreak of importance which had occurred to mar our peace since we commenced the journey.

"The same day, June 6, we resumed our journey, and at evening of the 7th encamped in a piece of woods, near a spring of water, at Salt River, where was a branch of the church. Sunday, the 8th, we had preaching, and in the course of the day were joined by my brother Hyrum Smith, and Lyman Wight, with a company of volunteers which they had gathered in Michigan, etc. The whole company now consisted of two hundred and five men, and twenty-five baggage wagons with two or three horses each. We remained at Salt River until the 12th, refreshing and reorganizing, which was done by electing Lyman Wight general of the camp. I chose twenty men for my life guards, of whom my brother Hyrum was chosen captain, and George A. Smith was my armor-bearer. The remainder of the company was organized according to the pattern at New Portage. While at Salt River General Wight marched the camp on the prairie, inspected our firelocks, ordered a discharge of the same at target by platoons, drilled us about half a day, and returned to the bank of the river."—*Times and Seasons*, vol. 6, pp. 1075, 1076, 1088.

Lyman Wight gives a detailed account of the travels of Hyrum Smith and himself from Kirtland to this place; from Travels of the which we learn that they visited branches of the other company. church at Florence, Ohio; Pontiac, Michigan; Huron County, Michigan; and a branch called the "Ritchey branch," in Illinois (locality not given); as well as various neighborhoods where were scattered members; obtaining some means and several volunteers for the expedition; among whom we find the names of Charles Rich, Samuel Bent, Elijah Fordham, Osmon Houghton, Lyman Curtis, Mecham Curtis, Waldo Littlefield, Josiah Littlefield, Lyman Littlefield, David Dort, James Dunn, George Fordham. By union of these two companies there were over two hundred in the Camp.

The list of the names of the company as published by Andrew Jenson in his "Historical Record," volume 8, Names of Zion's Camp. page 940, is here given:—

MEMBERS OF ZION'S CAMP.

Aldrich, Hazen	Bent, Samuel	Cherry, William
Allen, Joseph	Blackman, Hiram	Chidester, John M.
Allred, Isaac	Booth, Lorenzo	Childs, Alden
Allred, James, Captain	Brooks, George W.	Childs, Nathaniel
Allred, Martin, Captain	Brown, Albert	Childs, Stephen
Andrus, Milo	Brown, Harry	Colborn, Thomas
Angell, Solomon	Brown, Samuel	Colby, Alanson
Avery, Allen A.	Brownell, John	Cole, Zera S.
Babbitt, Almon W.	Buchanan, Peter	Coltrin, Zebedee
Badlam, Alexander	Burdick, Alden	Coon, Libeus T.
Baker, Samuel	Burgess, Harrison	Cowan, Horace
Baldwin, Nathan B.	Byur, David	Curtis, Lyman
Barber, Elam	Cahoon, William F.	Curtis, Mecham
Barlow, Israel	Carpenter, John	Denton, Solomon W.
Barnes, Lorenzo D.	Carter, John S.	Doff, Peter
Barney, Edson	Cathcart, Daniel	Dort, David D.
Barney, Royal	Champlin, Alonzo	Duncan, John
Benner, Henry	Chapman, Jacob	Dunn, James

Duzette, Philemon
Elleman, Philip
Elliott, Bradford W.
Elliott, David
Evans, David
Field, Asa
Fisher, Edmund
Fisk, Alfred
Fisk, Hezekiah
Fordham, Elijah
Fordham, George
Forney, Fredrick
Fossett, John
Foster, James
Foster, Solon
Gates, Jacob
Gifford, Benjamin
Gifford, Levi
Gilbert, Sherman
Glidden, True
Gould, Dean C.
Grant, Jedediah M.
Green, Addison
Griffith, Michael
Griswold, Everett
Groves, Elisha
Hancock, Joseph
Hancock, Levi W.
Harmon, Joseph
Herriman, Henry
Harris, Martin
Hartshorn, Joseph
Hayes, Thomas
Higgins, Nelson
Hitchcock, Seth
Hogers, Amos
Holbrook, Chandler
Holbrook, Joseph
Holmes, Milton
Houghton, Osmon
Hubbard, Marshal
Humphrey, Solomon
Huntsman, Joseph
Hustin, John
Hutchins, Elias
Hyde, Heman T.

Hyde, Orson
Ingalls, Warren S.
Ivie, Edward
Ivie, James R.
Ivie, John A.
Ivie, William S.
Jessop, William
Johnson, Luke S.
Johnson, Lyman E.
Johnson, Noah
Johnson, Seth
Jones, Isaac
Jones, Levi
Kelley, Charles
Kimball, Heber C.
Kingsley, Samuel
Lake, Dennis
Lawson, Jesse B.
Lewis, L. S.
Littlefield, Josiah
Littlefield, Lyman O.
Littlefield, Waldo
Lyman, Amasa M.
Martin, Moses
Marvin, Edward W.
McBride, Reuben
McCord, Robert
Miller, Eleazer
Miller, John
Morse, Justin [Justus]
Murdock, John
Nickerson, Freeman
Nickerson, Levi S.
Nickerson, Uriah C.
Nicholas, Joseph
Noble, Joseph B.
North, Ur.
Orton, Roger
Parker, John D.
Parrish, Warren
Patten, David W.
Pratt, Orson
Pratt, Parley P.
Pratt, William D.
Rich, Charles C.
Rich, Leonard

Richardson, Darwin
Riggs, Burr
Riggs, Harpin
Riggs, Nathaniel
Riley, Milcher
Ripley, Alanson
Robbins, Lewis
Rudd, Erastus
Sagers, William Henry
Salisbury, Jenkins
Sherman, Henry
Sherman, Lyman
Shibley, Henry
Smalling, Cyrus
Smith, Avery
Smith, George A.
Smith, Hyrum
Smith, Jackson
Smith, Jazariah B.
Smith, Jesse B.
Smith, Joseph
Smith, Lyman
Smith, Sylvester
Smith, William
Snow, Willard
Snow, Zerubbabel
Stanley, Harvey
Stephens, Daniel
Stratton, Hyrum
Strong, Elial
Tanner, John
Tanner, Nathan
Thayer, Ezra
Thompson, James L.
Thompson, Samuel
Tippetts, William P.
Thomas, Tinney
Tubbs, Nelson
Waughn, Joel
Warner, Salmon
Weden, William
Wells, Elias
Whitesides, Alexander
Whitlock, Andrew
Wight, Lyman
Wilcox, Eber

Wilkinson, Sylvester B. Winchester, S., Captain Wissmiller, Henry
Williams, Frederick G. Winegar, Alvin   Woodruff, Wilford
Winchester, Alanzo   Winegars, Samuel   Young, Brigham
Winchester, Benjamin Winter, Hiram   Young, Joseph
——— ——— (unknown)

WOMEN WHO WENT UP IN ZION'S CAMP.

Alvord, Charlotte, from Michigan.

Chidester, Mrs., wife of John M. Chidester.

Curtis, Sophronia.

Drake, Diana.

Gates, Mary Snow, wife of Jacob Gates.

Holbrook, Eunice, wife of Chandler Holbrook.

Holbrook, Nancy L., wife of Joseph Holbrook.

Houghton, Mrs., wife of Osmon Houghton.

Parrish, Betsey, wife of Warren Parrish.

Ripley, Mrs., wife of Alanson Ripley.

There were also a few children in the Camp, among whom were Diana, daughter of Chandler Holbrook; Sarah Lucretia and Charlotte, daughters of Joseph Holbrook; and a daughter of Alvin Winegar.

Joseph continues:—

"June 12. We left Salt River and traveled about fourteen miles, encamping that night on the prairie. The inhabitants of Salt River manifested a great respect for us, and many of them accompanied us some distance on our journey. We continued our march daily until the 18th, when we pitched our tents one mile from Richmond, Ray County. . . .

"Thursday 19. We passed through the town as soon as it was light and before the inhabitants were arisen from their slumbers, meeting with no opposition, but we had not proceeded many miles before one wagon broke down, and by the time that was repaired wheels run off from others, and such like incidents continued through the day to impede our progress. When we started in the morning we intended to arrive in Clay County that day, but in vain. At a seasonable hour we encamped on an elevated piece of ground between two branches of Fishing River, having traveled about fifteen miles. Fishing River, at this point, was composed of seven small streams, and those betwixt which we encamped were two of them.

"As we halted and were making preparations for the night, five men armed with guns rode into our camp and told us we should see hell before morning, and their accompanying oaths partook of all the malice of demons. They told us that sixty men were coming from Richmond, Ray County, and seventy more from Clay County, sworn to our utter destruction. The weather was pleasant at this time.

"During this day the Jackson County mob, to the number of about two hundred, made arrangements to cross the Missouri River, about the mouth of Fishing River, at William's Ferry, into Clay County, and be ready to meet the Richmond mob near Fishing River Ford, for our utter destruction. But after the first scow load of about forty had been set over the river, the scow in returning was met by a squall, and had great difficulty in reaching the Jackson side by dark.

"Soon after the five men left the camp swearing vengeance, we discovered a small black cloud rising in the west, and in twenty minutes, or thereabouts, it began to rain and hail, and this was the squall that troubled the Jackson boat.

The storm.

"The storm was tremendous; wind and rain, hail and thunder met them in great wrath, and soon softened their direful courage, and frustrated all their designs to 'kill Joe Smith and his army.' Instead of continuing a cannonading, which they commenced the sun about one hour high, they crawled under wagons, into hollow trees, filled one old shanty, etc., till the storm was over, when their ammunition was soaked, and the forty in Clay County were extremely anxious in the morning to return to Jackson, having experienced the pitiless peltings of the storm all night, and as soon as arrangements could be made, this 'forlorn hope' took the 'back track' for Independence, to join the main body of the mob. . . .

An attack prevented.

"Very little hail fell in our camp, but from half to a mile around, the stones or lumps of ice cut down the crops of corn and vegetation generally, even cutting limbs from trees, themselves were twisted into withes by the wind. The lightning flashed incessantly, which caused it to be so light in our camp through the night that we could discern the most minute object, and the roaring of the thunder was tremendous. The earth trembled and quaked; the rain fell in torrents, and, united, it seemed as if the mandate of vengeance had gone forth from the God of battles to protect his servants from the destruction of their enemies; for the hail fell on them, and not on us, and we suffered no harm except the blowing down of some of our tents and getting some wet, while our enemies had holes made in their hats and otherwise received damage, even the breaking of their rifle stocks, and the fleeing of their horses through fear and pain.

"Many of my little band sheltered in an old meetinghouse through this night, and in the morning the water in Big Fishing River was about forty feet deep, where the previous evening it was no more than to our ankles, and our enemies swore that the water rose thirty feet in thirty minutes in the Little Fishing River.

"Friday the 20th. We went five miles on the prairie to procure food for ourselves and horses, and establish ourselves for the moment in some secure place where we could defend ourselves from the rage of our enemies; and while in this situation, on Saturday the 21st, Colonel Sconce, with two other leading men from Ray County, came to see us, desiring to know what our intentions were; for, said he, 'I see that there is an almighty power that protects this people, for I started from Richmond, Ray County, with a company of armed men, having a full determination to destroy you, but was kept back by the storm, and was not able to reach you.' When he entered our camp he was seized with such a trembling that he was obliged to sit down to compose himself; and when he had made known his object of their visit, I arose, and addressing them, gave a relation of the sufferings of the saints in Jackson County, and also of our persecution generally, and what we had suffered by our enemies for our religion, and that we had come one thousand miles to assist our brethren, to bring them clothing, etc., and to reinstate them upon their own lands; and that we had no intention to molest or injure any people, but only to administer to the wants of our afflicted friends; and that the evil reports circulated about us were false, and gotten up by our enemies to procure our destruction. When I had closed a lengthy speech, the spirit of which melted them into compassion, they arose and offered me their hands, and said they would use their influence to allay the excitement which everywhere prevailed against us, and they wept when they heard of our afflictions and persecutions, and that our intentions were good. Accordingly they went forth and rode among the people and made unwearied exertions to allay the excitement."—*Times and Seasons*, vol. 6, pp. 1088, 1091, 1092.

H. C. Kimball in his journal writes of this journey a little more fully, and gives a similar account of the storm:—

"On the 12th we again resumed our march. Many of the inhabitants went with us several miles; they seemed to have much respect for us. We traveled about fourteen miles, and camped on a large prairie.

"Friday the 13th. My horses got loose and went back ten miles, with others. I pursued after them and returned back to the camp in about two hours. We tarried in the middle of this prairie, which is about twenty-eight miles across, on account of a rupture which took place in camp. Here F. G. Williams and Roger Orton received a very serious chastisement from Brother Joseph for not obeying orders previously given. The chastisement given to Roger Orton was given more particularly for suffering me to go back after the horses, as I was one of Joseph's life guard, and it belonged to Roger to attend to the team; but, as the team was my own and I had had the care of it all through, he still throwed the care on me, which was contrary to orders, inasmuch as the responsibility rested upon him to see to the team. In this place further regulations were made in regard to the organization of the camp.

"A day or two after this Bishop Partridge met us, direct from Clay County, as we were camping on the bank of the Wacondah [Wakenda] River in the woods. We received much information from Brother Partridge concerning the hostile feelings and prejudices that existed against us in Missouri in all quarters. It gave us great satisfaction to receive intelligence from him, as we were in perils, and threatened all the while. I will here mention one circumstance that transpired during our stay at this place, which was, that of Brother Lyman Wight baptizing Dean Gould, as he was not previously a member of the church, yet had accompanied us all the way from Kirtland.

"We pursued our journey and followed the bank of the river for several miles. As we left the river and came into a very beautiful prairie Brother William Smith . . . killed a very large deer, which made us some very nourishing soup, and added to our comfort considerably.

"On Wednesday, the 18th, at night, we camped one mile from the town of Richmond, Ray County. On Thursday the 19th, we arose as soon as it was light and passed through the town before the inhabitants were up. As Luke Johnson and others, were passing through before the teams came along, Brother Luke observed a black woman in a gentleman's garden near the road. She beckoned to him and said, 'Come here massa.' She was evidently much agitated in her feelings. He went up to the fence and she said to him, 'There is a company of men laying in wait here who are calculating to kill you this morning as you pass through.' This was nothing new to us, as we had been threatened continually through the whole journey, and death and destruction seemed to await us daily. This day we only traveled about fifteen miles. One wagon broke down, and the wheels ran off from others, and there seemed to be many things to hinder our progress, although we strove with all diligence to speed our way forward. Our intentions were when we started to go through to Clay County that day, but all in vain. This night we camped on an elevated piece of land between the two branches of the Fishing River, the main branch of which was formed by seven small streams or branches, these being two of them. Just as we halted and were making preparations for the night, five men rode into the camp and told us we should see hell before morning, and such horrible oaths as came from their lips I never heard before. They told us that sixty men were coming from Richmond, Ray County, who had sworn to destroy us; also that seventy more were coming from Clay County to assist in our destruction. These men were armed with guns, and the whole country was in a rage against us, and nothing but the power of God could save us. All this time the weather was fine and pleasant. Soon after these men left us we discovered a small black cloud rising in the west, and not more than twenty minutes passed away before it began to rain and hail, but we had very little of the hail in our camp. All around us the hail was heavy; some of the hailstones, or rather lumps of ice, were as large as hen's eggs. The thunders rolled with awful majesty, and the red lightnings flashed through the horizon, making it so light that I could see to pick up a pin almost any time through the night; the earth quaked and trembled, and there being no cessation, it seemed as though the Almighty had issued forth his mandate of vengeance. The wind was so terrible that many of our tents were blown over and we were not able to hold them; but there being an old meetinghouse close at hand, many of us fled there to secure ourselves from the storm. Many trees were blown down, and others twisted and wrung like a withe. The mob came to the river, two miles from us, and the river had risen to that height that they were obliged to stop without crossing over. The hail fell so heavily upon them that it beat holes in their hats, and in some instances even broke the stocks off their guns. Their horses being frightened fled, leaving the riders on the ground, their powder was wet, and it was evident the Almighty fought in our defense. This night the river raised forty feet.

"In the morning I went to the river in company with Brother Joseph Smith, Hyrum Smith, Brigham Young, and others, as we had it in contemplation to proceed that morning to Liberty, Clay County; but we could not continue our journey, as there was no way to cross the river. It was then overflowing its banks, and we have seen the river since and proved that it was full forty feet from the top of the banks to the bottom of the river. Previous to this rain falling, it was no more than ankle deep. Such a time never was known by us before; still, we felt calm all night and the Lord was with us. The water was ankle deep to us all night, so we could not sleep.

"At this place, W. W. Phelps, S. W. Denton, John Corrill, with many others from Liberty, joined us, from whom we received much information concerning the situation of the brethren who had been driven from Jackson County, and the fixed determination of our enemies to drive or exterminate them from that county.

"The next day when we moved into the country we saw that the hail had destroyed the crops and we saw that it had come in some directions within a mile, and in other directions within half a mile, of our camp. After passing a short distance the ground was literally covered with branches of trees which had been cut off by the hail. We went a distance of five miles on a prairie to get food for our horses, and also to get provisions for ourselves; and to get into some secure place, where we could defend ourselves from the rage of the enemy. We stayed here three or four days until the rage of the people was allayed.

"On the 21st Colonel Searcy and two other leading men from Ray County came to see us, desiring to know what our intentions were; for said he, 'I see that there is an Almighty power that protects this people, for I started from Richmond, Ray County, with a company of armed men, having a fixed determination to destroy you, but was kept back by the storm and was not able to reach you.' When he came into the camp he was seized with such a trembling, that he was obliged to sit down in order to compose himself. When he desired to know what our intentions were, Brother Joseph arose and began to speak, and the power of God rested upon him. He gave a relation of the sufferings of our people in Jackson County, and also of all our persecutions and what we had suffered by our enemies for our religion; and that we had come one thousand miles to assist our brethren, to bring them clothing, and to reinstate them upon their own lands; that we had no intentions to molest or injure any people, but only to administer to the wants of our afflicted brethren; and that the evil reports, which were circulated about us, were false, and were circulated by our enemies to get us destroyed.

"After he had gotten through and had spoke quite lengthily, the power of which melted them into compassion. they arose and offered him their hands, and said they would use their influence to allay the excitement which everywhere prevailed against us."—*Times and Seasons*, vol. 6, pp. 789, 790, 803, 804.

Lyman Wight, under date of June 19, 1834, writes:—

"This day passed through Richmond. . . . Four miles farther, between the two branches of Fishing River, encamped near a Baptist meetinghouse. About the setting of the sun the clouds commenced rising with a frightful appearance. Heavier thunder or sharper lightning probably never was heard or seen. The rain commenced falling in torrents, and continued nearly through the night. Those two rivers had increased from a low ebb to from sixteen to twenty feet of water, overflowing the bottom for several miles. This proved, however, to be a beneficial circumstance to us, as a mob had collected on both sides of the road, and were rapidly increasing in numbers, with a determination to fall upon us this night. Thirty or forty of this mob crowded themselves into an old cabin, and in endeavoring to hold their horses by their bridles, many of them were severely injured by the falling of the hail. About three miles from where we encamped the hailstones fell from the size of a rifle ball to that of turkey's eggs. We spent a doleful night."

Soon after crossing the Mississippi River they delegated Orson Hyde and P. P. Pratt to visit Governor Dunklin, to present before him the nature of their mission and ask his protection and aid. P. P. Pratt in his Autobiography writes of this interview as follows:—

Hyde and Pratt visit Gov. Dunklin.

"Arriving in the Allred settlement, near Salt River, Missouri, where there was a large branch of the church, the camp rested a little, and dispatched Elder Orson Hyde and myself to Jefferson City, to request of His Excellency, Governor Daniel Dunklin, a sufficient military force, with orders to reinstate the exiles, and protect them in the possession of their homes in Jackson County.

"We had an interview with the Governor, who readily acknowledged the justice of the demand, but frankly told us he dare not attempt the execution of the laws in that respect, for fear of deluging the whole country in civil war and bloodshed. He advised us to relinquish our rights, for the sake of peace, and to sell our lands from which we had been driven. To this we replied with firmness, that we would hold no terms with land pirates and murderers. If we could not be permitted to live on lands which we had purchased of the United States, and be protected in our persons and rights, our lands would, at least, make a good burying ground, on which to lay our bones; and, like Abraham's possession in Canaan, we should hold on to our possessions in the county of Jackson, for this purpose, at least. He replied that he did not blame us in the least, but trembled for the country, and dare not carry out the plain, acknowledged, and imperative duties of his office. We retired, saying to ourselves: 'That poor coward ought, in duty, to resign; he owes this, morally at least, in justice to his oath of office.'

"We returned to the camp, which was then on the march, somewhere below the county of Ray. President Joseph Smith, his brother Hyrum, L. Wight, and others, repaired with us into a solitary grove, apart, to learn the result of our mission.

"After hearing our report, the President called on the God of our fathers to witness the justice of our cause and the sincerity of our vows, which we engaged to fulfill, whether in this life or in the life to come. For, as God lives, truth, justice, and innocence shall triumph, and iniquity shall not reign."—Pp. 123, 124.

This sounds strangely out of harmony with Governor Dunklin's character as indicated in his actions in this trouble both before and after this time. If this account of Mr. Pratt is true, he must have weakened in his intention to restore and protect the saints, being intimidated by the lawless element. But in justice to Mr. Dunklin it is but fair to say that Lyman Wight, who was the commanding officer of the "camp," states in his daily journal under date of June 13, 1834, when Messrs. Hyde and Pratt returned and reported, as follows:—

"Traveled five miles and met Parley P. Pratt and Orson Hyde, who had been sent to the Governor to seek redress for the saints who had been driven from Jackson County.

They brought the intelligence that the Governor would execute the law, whatever it might be."

Not being able to reconcile this difference, we give both statements and leave them with the reader without further comment.

Joseph continues the narrative as follows:—

"June 22. Cornelius Gillium, the sheriff of Clay County, came to the camp to hold consultation with us. I marched my company into a grove near by and formed in a circle, with Gillium in the center. Gillium commenced by saying that he had heard that Joseph was in the camp and if so he would like to see him. I arose and replied, 'I am the man.' This was the first time that I had been discovered or made known to my enemies since I left Kirtland. Gillium then gave us some instruction concerning the manners, customs, and dispositions of the people, etc., and what course we ought to [pursue to] secure their favor and protection, making certain inquiries, to which we replied, which were afterwards published and will appear under date of publication."—*Times and Seasons*, vol. 6, p. 1104.

Sheriff Gillium visits the camp.

The accounts of H. C. Kimball, Lyman Wight, and P. P. Pratt agree substantially with the above. The questions of the sheriff and the answers by the company, referred to in the above, are not, so far as we know, available; but this interview evidently brought out the following statement from the sheriff:—

Statement of sheriff.

"Being a citizen of Clay County, and knowing that there is considerable excitement amongst the people thereof; and also knowing that different reports are arriving almost hourly; and being requested by the Hon. J. F. Ryland, to meet the Mormons under arms, and obtain from the leaders thereof the correctness of the various reports in circulation—the true intent and meaning of their present movements, and their views generally regarding the difficulties existing between them and Jackson County—I did, in company with other gentlemen, call upon the said leaders of the Mormons, at their camp, in Clay County; and now give to the people

of Clay County their written statement, containing the substance of what passed between us.

"(Signed)   CORNELIUS GILLIUM.

"PROPOSITIONS, ETC., OF THE 'MORMONS.'

"Being called upon by the above-named gentlemen, at our
camp, in Clay County, to ascertain from the leaders of our
men, our intentions, views, and designs, in approaching this
county in the manner that we have; we therefore, the more
cheerfully comply with their request, because we are called
upon by gentlemen of good feelings, and who are disposed
for peace and an amicable adjustment of the difficulties existing between us and the people of Jackson County.   The reports of our intentions are various, and have gone abroad in
a light calculated to arouse the feelings of almost every man.
For instance; one report is that we intend to demolish the
printing office in Liberty; another report is, that we intend
crossing the Missouri River on Sunday next, and falling
upon women and children, and slaying them; another is that
our men were employed to perform this expedition, being
taken from manufacturing establishments in the East that
had closed business; also that we carried a flag, bearing
'peace' on one side and 'war or blood' on the other; and various others too numerous to mention;—all of which, a plain
declaration of our intentions, from under our own hands,
will show are not correct.   In the first place, it is not our
intention to commit hostilities against any man or set of men.
It is not our intention to injure any man's person or property,
except in defending ourselves.   Our flag has been exhibited
to the above gentlemen, who will be able to describe it.   Our
men were not taken from any manufacturing establishment.
It is our intention to go back upon our lands in Jackson
County, by order of the Executive of the State, if possible.
We have brought our arms with us for the purpose of self-
defense, as it is well known to almost every man of the
State that we have every reason to put ourselves in an attitude of defense, considering the abuse we have suffered in
Jackson County.   We are anxious for a settlement of the difficulties existing between us, upon honorable and constitu-
tional principles.   We are willing for twelve disinterested

men, six to be chosen by each party, and these men shall say what the possessions of those men are worth who cannot live with us in the county; and they shall have their money in one year; and none of the Mormons shall enter that county to reside until the money is paid. The damages that we have sustained in consequence of being driven away shall also be left to the above twelve men. Or they may all live in the county, if they choose, and we will never molest them if they will let us alone and permit us to enjoy our rights. We want to live in peace with all men, and equal rights is all we ask. We wish to become permanent citizens of this State, and wish to bear our proportion in support of the Government, and to be protected by its laws. If the above proposals are complied with, we are willing to give security on our part; and we shall want the same of the people of Jackson County for the performance of this agreement. We do not wish to settle down in a body, except where we can purchase the lands with money; for to take possession by conquest or the shedding of blood, is entirely foreign to our feelings. The shedding of blood we shall not be guilty of, until all just and honorable means among men prove insufficient to restore peace.

"JOSEPH SMITH, JUN.

"F. G. WILLIAMS.

"LYMAN WIGHT.

"ROGER ORTON.

"ORSON HYDE.

"J. S. CARTER."

—*Evening and Morning Star*, vol. 2, p. 351.

While in this camp, which was on land belonging to a Fishing River revelation. member of the church by the name of John Cooper, the revelation known as the Fishing River revelation was given. [a]

[a] 1. Verily I say unto you, who have assembled yourselves together that you may learn my will concerning the redemption of mine afflicted people:—

2. Behold, I say unto you, Were it not for the transgressions of my people, speaking concerning the church and not individuals, they might have been redeemed even now; but, behold, they have not learned to be obedient to the things which I require at their hands, but are full of all manner of evil, and do not impart of their substance, as becometh saints, to the poor and afflicted among them, and are not united according to the union required by the law of the celestial kingdom; and Zion cannot

Joseph resumes the history as follows:—

"About this time Brothers Thayre and Hayes were attacked with the cholera, and Brother Hancock was taken

Cholera.   during the storm. I called the camp together and
                told them that in consequence of the disobedience
of some who had been unwilling to listen to my words, but

be built up unless it is by the principles of the law of the celestial kingdom, otherwise I cannot receive her unto myself; and my people must
needs be chastened until they learn obedience, if it must needs be, by
the things which they suffer.

3. I speak not concerning those who are appointed to lead my people,
who are the first elders of my church, for they are not all under this condemnation; but I speak concerning my churches abroad; there are many
who will say, Where is their God? Behold, he will deliver in time of
trouble; otherwise we will not go up unto Zion, and will keep our moneys.
Therefore, in consequence of the transgression of my people, it is expedient in me that mine elders should wait for a little season for the redemption of Zion, that they themselves may be prepared, and that my
people may be taught more perfectly, and have experience, and know
more perfectly, concerning their duty, and the things which I require
at their hands; and this cannot be brought to pass until mine elders are
endowed with power from on high; for, behold, I have prepared a great
endowment and blessing to be poured out upon them, inasmuch as they
are faithful, and continue in humility before me; therefore, it is expedient in me that mine elders should wait for a little season, for the redemption of Zion; for, behold, I do not require at their hands to fight the
battles of Zion; for, as I said in a former commandment, even so will I
fulfill, I will fight your battles.

4. Behold, the destroyer I have sent forth to destroy and lay waste
mine enemies; and not many years hence, they shall not be left to pollute mine heritage, and to blaspheme my name upon the lands which I
have consecrated for the gathering together of my saints.

5. Behold, I have commanded my servant Baurak Ale, to say unto the
strength of my house, even my warriors, my young men and middle-aged, to
gather together for the redemption of my people, and throw down the towers
of mine enemies, and scatter their watchmen; but the strength of mine
house have not hearkened unto my words; but inasmuch as there are
those who have hearkened unto my words, I have prepared a blessing
and an endowment for them, if they continue faithful. I have heard
their prayers, and will accept their offering; and it is expedient in me,
that they should be brought thus far, for a trial of their faith.

6. And now, verily I say unto you, A commandment I give unto you,
that as many as have come up hither, that can stay in the region round
about, let them stay; and those that cannot stay, who have families in
the east, let them tarry for a little season, inasmuch as my servant Joseph shall appoint unto them, for I will counsel him concerning this
matter; and all things whatsoever he shall appoint unto them shall be
fulfilled.

7. And let all my people who dwell in the regions round about, be very
faithful, and prayerful, and humble before me, and reveal not the things
which I have revealed unto them, until it is wisdom in me that they
should be revealed. Talk not judgment, neither boast of faith, nor of
mighty works; but carefully gather together, as much in one region as
can be consistently with the feelings of the people; and, behold, I will

had rebelled, God had decreed that sickness should come upon them, and that they should die like sheep with the rot, that I was sorry, but could not help it. Previous to this, while on our journey, I had predicted and warned them of the danger of such chastisement; but there were some who would not give heed to my words.

"On the 23d resumed our march for Liberty, Clay County, taking a circuitous course round the heads of Fishing River, to avoid the deep water. When within five or six miles of

give unto you favor and grace in their eyes, that you may rest in peace and safety, while you are saying unto the people, Execute judgment and justice for us according to law, and redress us of our wrongs.

8. Now, behold, I say unto you, my friends, In this way you may find favor in the eyes of the people, until the army of Israel becomes very great; and I will soften the hearts of the people, as I did the heart of Pharaoh, from time to time, until my servant Baurak Ale, and Baneemy, whom I have appointed, shall have time to gather up the strength of my house, and to have sent wise men, to fulfill that which I have commanded concerning the purchasing of all the lands in Jackson County, that can be purchased, and in the adjoining counties round about; for it is my will that these lands should be purchased, and after they are purchased that my saints should possess them according to the laws of consecration which I have given; and after these lands are purchased, I will hold the armies of Israel guiltless in taking possession of their own lands, which they have previously purchased with their moneys, and of throwing down the towers of mine enemies, that may be upon them, and scattering their watchmen, and avenging me of mine enemies, unto the third and fourth generation of them that hate me.

9. But firstly, let my army become very great, and let it be sanctified before me, that it may become fair as the sun, and clear as the moon, and that her banners may be terrible unto all nations; that the kingdoms of this world may be constrained to acknowledge that the kingdom of Zion is in very deed the kingdom of our God and his Christ; therefore, let us become subject unto her laws.

10. Verily I say unto you, It is expedient in me that the first elders of my church should receive their endowment from on high, in my house, which I have commanded to be built unto my name in the land of Kirtland; and let those commandments which I have given concerning Zion and her law, be executed and fulfilled, after her redemption. There has been a day of calling, but the time has come for a day of choosing; and let those be chosen that are worthy; and it shall be manifest unto my servant, by the voice of the Spirit, those that are chosen, and they shall be sanctified; and inasmuch as they follow the counsel which they receive, they shall have power after many days to accomplish all things pertaining to Zion.

11. And again, I say unto you, Sue for peace, not only the people that have smitten you, but also to all people; and lift up an ensign of peace, and make a proclamation for peace unto the ends of the earth; and make proposals for peace, unto those who have smitten you, according to the voice of the Spirit which is in you, and all things shall work together for your good; therefore, be faithful, and, behold, and lo, I am with you even unto the end. Even so. Amen

Liberty we were met by General Atchison and other gentlemen, who desired us not to go to Liberty, as the feelings of
the people were so much enraged against us.   At their communication we wheeled to the left, and crossing the prairie
and woodland came to Sidney Gilbert's residence, and encamped on the bank of Rush Creek, in Bro. Burket's field.
During this a council of High Priests assembled in fulfillment of the revelation given the day previous, and the following individuals were called and chosen as they were
made manifest unto me by the voice of the Spirit, and revelation, to receive their endowment:—

"Edward Partridge was called and chosen to go to Kirtland and receive his endowment with power from
on high, and also to stand in his office of Bishop
to purchase lands in the State of Missouri.

Some called to
go to Kirtland.

"William W. Phelps was called and chosen, and it was appointed unto him for to receive his endowment with power
from on high and help to carry on the printing establishment in Kirtland until Zion is redeemed.

"Isaac Morley and John Corrill were called and chosen,
and it was appointed unto them to receive their endowment
with power from on high in Kirtland and assist in gathering
up the strength of the Lord's house and preach the gospel.

"John Whitmer and David Whitmer were called and
chosen, and appointed to receive their endowments in Kirtland and continue in their offices.

"Algernon S. Gilbert was called and chosen, and appointed
to receive his endowment in Kirtland, and to assist in gathering up the strength of the Lord's house, and to proclaim
the everlasting gospel until Zion is redeemed.   But he said
he 'could not do it.'

"Peter Whitmer, Jr., Simeon Carter, Newel Knight, Parley P. Pratt, Christian Whitmer, and Solomon Hancock were
called and chosen, and it was appointed unto them to receive
their endowment in Kirtland with power from on high; to
assist in gathering up the strength of the Lord's house; and
to preach the everlasting gospel.

"Thomas B. Marsh was called and chosen; and it was appointed unto him to receive his endowment in Kirtland, his office to be made known hereafter.

"Lyman Wight was called and chosen; and it was appointed unto him to receive his endowment in Kirtland with power from on high; and to return to Zion and have his office appointed unto him hereafter."—*Times and Seasons*, vol. 6, pp. 1105, 1106.

This selection of men to go to Kirtland and receive endowments was in accordance with the late revelation.

In relation to the cholera and other items Joseph writes as follows:—

"June 24. This night the cholera burst forth among us, and about midnight it was manifest in its most terrible form. Our ears were saluted with cries and moanings and lamentations on every hand; even those on guard fell to the earth with their guns in their hands, so sudden and powerful was the attack of this terrible disease. At the commencement I attempted to lay on hands for their recovery, but I quickly learned by painful experience that when the great Jehovah decrees destruction upon any people, makes known his determination, man must not attempt to stay his hand. The moment I attempted to rebuke the disease, that moment I was attacked; and had I not desisted, I must have saved the life of my brother by the sacrifice of my own, for when I rebuked the disease it left him and seized me.

"Early on the morning of the 25th the camp was separated into small bands, and dispersed among the brethren living in the vicinity, and I wrote and sent by express, to 'Messrs. Thornton, Doniphan, and Atchison,' as follows:—

" 'Rush Creek, Clay County, June 25, 1834.

" '*Gentlemen:*— Our company of men advanced yesterday from their encampment beyond Fishing River to Rush Creek, where their tents are again pitched. But feeling disposed to adopt every pacific measure that can be done, without jeopardizing our lives, to quiet the prejudices and fears of some part of the citizens of this county, we have concluded that our company shall be immediately dispersed and continue so till every effort for an adjustment of differences between us and the people of Jackson has been made on our

part that would in anywise be required of us by disinterested
men of republican principles.

    " 'I am respectfully, your obédient servant,

                            " 'JOSEPH SMITH, JR.

    " 'N. B.—You are now corresponding with the Governor
(as I am informed). Will you do us the favor to acquaint
him of our efforts for a compromise? This information we
want conveyed to the Governor, inasmuch as his ears are
stifled with reports from Jackson of our hostile intentions,
etc.'

"I left Rush Creek the same day, in company with David
Whitmer and two other brethren, for the western part of
Clay County. While traveling we called at a house for a
drink of water. The women of the house shouted from the
door that they had 'no water for Mormons, that they were
afraid of the cholera,' etc. We turned and departed, according to the commandment, and before a week had passed
the cholera entered that house, and that woman and three
others of the family were dead.

"When the cholera made its appearance Elder John S.
Carter was the first man who stepped forward to rebuke it,
and upon this was inⁿtantly seized and became the first victim in the camp. He died about six o'clock afternoon; and
Seth Hitchcock died in about thirty minutes after. As it
was impossible to obtain coffins, the brethren rolled them in
blankets, carried them on a horse sled about half a mile,
buried them in the bank of a small stream which empties
into Rush Creek, all of which was accomplished by dark.
When they had returned from the burial, the brethren
united, covenanted and prayed, hoping the disease would be
staid; but in vain, for while thus covenanting, Eber Wilcox
died; and while some were digging the grave others stood
sentry with their firearms, watching their enemies. . . .

"The cholera continued its ravages about four days, when
an effectual remedy for their purging, vomiting, and cramping was discovered; viz., dipping the persons afflicted in cold
water, or pouring it upon them. About sixty eight of the
saints suffered from this disease, of which number thirteen
died; viz., John S. Carter, Eber Wilcox, Seth Hitchcock,

Erastus Rudd, Algernon Sidney Gilbert, Alfred Frisk, Edward Ives, Noah Johnson, Jesse B. Lawson, Robert McCord, Elial Strong, Jesse Smith, and Betsey Parrish.

"The last days of June I spent with my old Jackson County friends in the western part of Clay County.

"On the first of July I crossed the Missouri River, in company with a few friends, into Jackson County, to set my feet once more on the 'goodly land,' and on the 2d I went down near Liberty and visited the brethren."—*Times and Seasons,* vol. 6, pp. 1106–1108.

Of these events Elder H. C. Kimball in his journal writes:—

"Here Brother Thayre was taken sick with the cholera, and also Brother Hayes. We left them there, and also Brother Hancock who had been taken with the cholera during the storm. Bro. Joseph called the camp together, and told us that in consequence of the disobedience of some who had not been willing to listen to his words, but had been rebellious, God had decreed that sickness should come upon us, and we should die like sheep with the rot; and said he, 'I am sorry, but I cannot help it.' When he spake these things it pierced me like a dart, having a testimony that so it would be. In the afternoon of this day we began to receive the revelation known as the 'Fishing River revelation.'

"On Monday we held a council as follows:—

"Clay County, Mo., June 23, 1834.

"A council of high priests met according to a revelation received the previous day, to choose some of the first elders to receive their endowment; being appointed by the voice of the Spirit, through Joseph Smith, Jr., president of the church.

"They proceeded: Edward Partridge is called and chosen, and is to go to Kirtland and receive his endowment with power from on high, and also stand in his office as bishop to purchase land in Missouri.

"W. W. Phelps is called and chosen, and it is appointed unto him to receive his endowment with power from on high; and help carry on the printing establishment till Zion is redeemed.

"Isaac Morley is called and chosen, and it is appointed

unto him to receive his endowment with power from on high in Kirtland; and assist in gathering up the strength of the Lord's house, and preach the gospel. John Corrill the same as Isaac Morley.

"John Whitmer is called and chosen, and it is appointed unto him to receive his endowment in Kirtland, with power from on high; and continue in his office.

"David Whitmer is called and chosen, and it is appointed unto him to receive his endowment in Kirtland, with power from on high; and stand in the office appointed unto him.

"A. S. Gilbert is called and chosen, and it is appointed unto him to receive his endowment from on high in Kirtland; and to assist in gathering up the strength of the Lord's house; and to proclaim the everlasting gospel till Zion is redeemed. He said in his heart he could not do it, and died in about three days.

"Peter Whitmer is called and chosen, and it is appointed unto him to receive his endowment in Kirtland, with power from on high; and assist in gathering up the strength of the Lord's house; and proclaim the gospel.

"Simeon Carter is called and chosen, and it is appointed unto him to receive his endowment in Kirtland, with power from on high; and assist in gathering up the strength of the Lord's house; and proclaim the everlasting gospel.

"Newel Knight is called and chosen, and it is appointed unto him to receive his endowment in Kirtland with power from on high; and assist in gathering up the strength of the Lord's house; and preach the gospel.

"Thomas B. Marsh is called and chosen, and it is appointed unto him to receive his endowment in Kirtland with power from on high; and his office will be made known hereafter.

"Lyman Wight is called and chosen, and it is appointed unto him to receive his endowment in Kirtland with power from on high; to return to Zion, and his office shall be appointed to him hereafter.

"Parley P. Pratt is called and chosen, and it is appointed unto him to receive his endowment in Kirtland with power from on high; and assist in gathering up the strength of the Lord's house; and proclaim the gospel.

"Christian Whitmer is called and chosen, and it is appointed unto him to receive his endowment in Kirtland with power from on high; and assist in gathering up the strength of the Lord's house; and proclaim the gospel.

"Solomon Hancock is called and chosen, and it is appointed unto him to receive his endowment in Kirtland with power from on high; and assist in gathering up the strength of the Lord's house; and proclaim the everlasting gospel.

"F. G. WILLIAMS, Clerk.

"On the morning of the 24th we started for Liberty, Clay County, where our brethren were residing, who had been driven from Jackson County, taking our course round the head of Fishing River, in consequence of high water. When we got within five or six miles of Liberty, General Atchison and several other gentlemen met us, desiring that we would not go to Liberty, as the feelings of the people of that place was much enraged against us. Changing our course and bearing to the left we pursued our way across a prairie; then passing through a wood until we came to Brother Sidney Gilbert's, where we camped on the bottom of Rush Creek, in a field belonging to brother Burket, on the 25th.

"This night the cholera came upon us, as we had been warned by the servant of God. About twelve o'clock at night we began to hear the cries of those who were seized with the cholera, and they fell before the destroyer. Even those on guard fell, with their guns in their hands, to the ground, and we had to exert ourselves considerably to attend to the sick; for they fell on every hand. Thus it continued till morning, when the camp was separated into several small bands and were dispersed among the brethren.

"I was left at the camp in company with three or four of my brethren in care of those who were sick. We staid with and prayed for them, hoping they would recover; but all hope was lost, for about six o'clock p. m. John S. Carter expired, he being the first that died in the camp.

"When the cholera first broke out in the camp Brother John S. Carter was the first who went forward to rebuke it, but himself was immediately seized by it, and as before stated, was the first who was slain. In about thirty minutes after his death Seth Hitchcock followed him; and it appeared as though we must sink under the destroyer with them.

"We were not able to obtain boards to make them coffins, but were under the necessity of rolling them up in their blankets and burying them in that manner. So we placed them on a sled, which was drawn by a horse about half a mile, where we buried them in a little bluff by the side of a small stream that emptied into Rush Creek. This we accomplished by dark, and returned back.

"Our hopes were that no more would die, but while we were uniting in a covenant to pray once more with uplifted hands to God, we looked at our beloved brother, Elder Wilcox, and he was gasping his last. At this scene my feelings were beyond expression. Those only who witnessed it can realize anything of the nature of our sufferings, and I felt to weep and pray to the Lord that he would spare my life that I might behold my dear family again. I felt to covenant with my brethren, and I felt in my heart never to commit another sin while I lived. We felt to sit and weep over our brethren, and so great was our sorrow that we could have washed them with our tears, to realize that they had traveled one thousand miles through so much fatigue to lay down their lives for our brethren. And who hath greater love than he who is willing to lay down his life for his brethren? This increased our love to them. About twelve o'clock at night we placed him on a small sled, which we drew to the place of interment, with one hand hold of the rope, and in the other we bore our firelocks for our defense. While one or two were digging the grave, the rest stood with their arms to defend them.

"This was our situation, the enemies around us, and the destroyer in our midst. Soon after we returned back another brother was taken away from our little band; thus it continued until five out of ten were taken away.

"It was truly affecting to see the love manifested among the brethren for each other, during this affliction; even Brother Joseph, seeing the sufferings of his brethren, stepped forward to rebuke the destroyer, but was immediately seized with the disease himself; and I assisted him a short distance from the place when it was with difficulty he could walk. All that kept our enemies from us was the fear of the destroyer which the Lord so sent among us.

"After burying these five brethren, or about this time, I was seized by the hand of the destroyer, as I had gone in the woods to pray. I was instantly struck blind, and saw no way whereby I could free myself from the disease, only to exert myself by jumping and thrashing myself about, until my sight returned to me, and my blood began to circulate in my veins. I started and ran some distance, and by this means, through the help of God, I was enabled to extricate myself from the grasp of death. This circumstance transpired in a piece of woods just behind Brother Sidney Gilbert's house.

"On the 26th, Algernon Sidney Gilbert, keeper of the Lord's storehouse, signed a letter to the Governor, in connection with others, which was his last public act; for he had been called to preach, and he said he would rather die than go forth and preach the gospel to the Gentiles. The Lord took him at his word; he was attacked with the cholera and died about the 29th.

"Two other brethren died at Brother Gilbert's house about this same time. One of these was a cousin to brother Joseph Smith, the Prophet. The names of those brethren who were with me to assist in taking care of the sick are as follows: Joseph B. Noble, John D. Parker, and Luke Johnson; also Brother Ingleson, who died soon after we left. . . .

"I went to Liberty, to the house of Brother Peter Whitmer, which place I reached with difficulty, being much. afflicted myself with the disease that was among us. I stayed there until I started for home. I received great kindness from them, and also from Sister Vienna Jaques, who administered to my wants and also to my brethren. May the Lord reward them for their kindness.

"While I was here a council was called at Brother Lyman Wight's, which I attended with the rest of the brethren. The church was organized; a presidency and high council chosen and organized and many were chosen from them to go to Kirtland to be endowed.

"From that time the destroyer ceased, having afflicted us about four days. Sixty-eight were taken with the disease, of which number fourteen died, the remainder recovered, as we found out an effectual remedy for this disease, which was, by dipping the person afflicted into cold water, or pouring it on him, which had the desired effect of stopping the purging, vomiting, and cramping. Some of the brethren, when they were seized with the disease and began to cramp and purge, the fever raging upon them, desired to be put into cold water, and some stripped and plunged themselves into the stream and obtained immediate relief. This led us to try the experiment on others, and in every case it proved highly beneficial and effectual, where it was taken in season.

"On the 23d of June Brother Joseph received a revelation, as before stated, saying that the Lord had accepted our offering, even as he accepted that of Abraham, therefore he had a great blessing laid up in store for us, and an endowment for all, and those who had families might return home, and those who had no families should tarry until the Lord said they should go.

"I received an honorable discharge, in writing, from the hand of our general, Lyman Wight, to the effect that I had discharged my duty in my office and that I was at liberty to return home. Before we separated the money which had been put into the hands of our paymaster and had not been used was equally divided amongst the company, making one dollar and sixteen cents each. Some of these brethren had no money when we started from Kirtland, but they received an equal share with the rest."—*Times and Seasons*, vol. 6, pp. 804, 805, 838-840.

Of the cholera plague Lyman Wight states:—

"June 23, 1834: In the course of this night some slight symptoms of sickness were discovered in the camp.

"24th. This morning, horrible to relate, the astounding news that the cholera had made its appearance in our midst was announced. I immediately, in company with four other elders, passed from tent to tent, and truly we found many who fell, apparently from a state of perfect health, upon their couches, in the most excruciating pain conceivable. We used due diligence through the day, both physical and spiritual, to relieve them from this distressing disease; but despite all our efforts four of them fell victims to death, and were buried in the course of the night. We continued with the camp all night, doing all that lay in our power to relieve their distresses.

"25th. We continued our labors through this day, but despite all our efforts five more fell victims to its ravages in the course of the day.

"To-day we disbanded the company and as many as were able scattered abroad among the brethren in the country. Many flew to our relief and gave us rest."

Camp disbanded.

Thus ended the expedition of "Zion's Camp," and the camp passed into history.

What was accomplished by all this sacrifice? Impossible to tell. Such questions mortals cannot decide. Could we know what would have been the result upon the church, and their brethren in Zion, had they failed to go, we might by comparison form some conclusion; but that is impossible. It at least served to show the courage and determination of these early adherents of the faith under the most adverse circumstances and most appalling perils. It did more—it emphasized this important truth: That Zion must be redeemed by purchase and not by blood. All honor to the brave men who suffered or died in the heroic struggle to relieve their brethren in distress.

Deductions.

CHAPTER 18.

1834.

COMPROMISE SOUGHT—SECOND ORDER FOR ARMS—JUDGE RYLAND'S
LETTER—THE REPLY—A PUBLIC MEETING—LETTER TO JACK-
SON COUNTY — A PROPOSITION—COMMUNICATION TO THE GOV-
ERNOR—LETTER FROM THE MOB—LAWLESS ACTS—HIGH COUN-
CIL ORGANIZED—AN APPEAL—INSTRUCTION GIVEN—JOSEPH
RETURNS TO KIRTLAND — LETTER TO OWENS — ARRIVAL AT
KIRTLAND.

As MENTIONED in a former chapter, efforts were made in
the early part of the year 1834 to compromise the differences

Compro-
mise sought. which existed between the Jackson County people
and the saints. Col. J. Thornton wrote a letter to
Governor Dunklin with a view to accomplishing this, which
was indorsed by Messrs. Reese, Atchison, and Doniphan,
attorneys for the saints; to which the Governor replied as
follows:—

"From the *Missouri Enquirer* of June 25.

"Copy of a letter from Daniel Dunklin, Governor of the
State of Missouri, to Colonel J. Thornton, dated

" 'CITY OF JEFFERSON, June 6, 1834.

" '*Dear Sir:*—I was pleased at the receipt of your letter,
concurred in by Messrs. Reese, Atchison, and Doniphan, on
the subject of the Mormon difficulties. I should be gratified
indeed, if the parties could compromise on the terms you
suggest, or, indeed, upon any other terms satisfactory to
themselves. But I should travel out of the line of my strict
duty, as chief Executive officer of the Government, were I to
take upon myself the task of effecting a compromise between
the parties. Had I not supposed it possible, yes, probable,
that I should, as Executive of the State, have to act, I should
before now have interfered individually, in the way you suggest, or in some other way, in order if possible to effect a
compromise. Uncommitted, as I am, to either party, I shall
feel no embarrassment in doing my duty; though it may be
done with the most extreme regret. My duty in the relation

in which I now stand to the parties is plain and straightfor-
ward. By an official interposition, I might embarrass my
course, and urge a measure for the purpose of effecting a
compromise, and it should fail, and in the end, should I find
it my duty to act contrary to the advice I had given, it might
be said that I either advised wrong, or that I was partial to
one side or the other, in giving advice that I would not, as
an officer, follow. A more clear and indisputable right does
not exist, that the Mormon people, who were expelled from
their homes in Jackson County, to return and live on their
lands, and if they cannot be persuaded as a matter of policy
to give up that right, or to qualify it, my course, as the chief
Executive officer of the State, is a plain one. The Constitution of the United States declares, "That the citizens of
each State be entitled to all privileges and immunities of citizens in the several States." Then we cannot interdict any
people who have a political franchise in the United States
from emigrating to this State, nor from choosing what part
of the State they will settle in, provided they do not trespass
on the property or rights of others. Our State Constitution
declares that the people's "right to bear arms, *in defense of
themselves*, and of State, cannot be questioned." Then it is
their constitutional right to arm themselves. Indeed, our
militia law makes it the duty of every man, not exempted by
law, between the ages of eighteen and forty-five, to arm
himself with a musket, rifle, or some firelock, with a certain
quantity of ammunition, etc. And again, our constitution
says, "that all men have a natural and indefeasible right to
worship Almighty God according to the dictates of their
own consciences." I am fully persuaded that the eccen-
tricity of the religious opinions and practices of the Mormons, is at the bottom of the outrages committed against
them.

" 'They have the right constitutionally guaranteed to
them, and it is indefeasible, to believe and worship Jo Smith
as a *man*, an *angel*, or even as the only true and living God,
and to call their habitation Zion, the Holy Land, or even
heaven itself. Indeed there is nothing so absurd or ridiculous, that they have not a right to adopt their religion, so

that in its exercise, they do not interfere with the rights of others.

" 'It is not long since an impostor assumed the character of Jesus Christ, and attempted to minister as such; but I never heard of any combination to deprive him of his rights.

" 'I consider it the duty of every good citizen of Jackson and the adjoining counties to exert themselves to effect a compromise of these difficulties, and were I assured that I would not have to act in my official capacity in the affair, I would visit the parties in person and exert myself to the utmost to settle it. My first advice would be to the Mormons, to sell out their lands in Jackson County and to settle somewhere else, where they could live in peace, if they could get a fair price for them, and reasonable damages for injuries received. If this failed I would try the citizens and advise them to meet and rescind their illegal resolves of last summer; and agree to conform to the laws in every particular, in respect to the Mormons. If both these failed, I would then advise the plan you have suggested, for each party to take separate territory and confine their members within their respective limits, with the exception of the public right of egress and regress upon the highway. If all these failed, then the simple question of legal right would have to settle it. It is this last that I am afraid I shall have to conform my action to in the end; and hence the necessity of keeping myself in the best situation to do my duty impartially.

" 'Rumor says that each party are preparing themselves with cannon. That would be illegal. It is not necessary to self-defense, as guaranteed by the Constitution. And as there are no artillery companies organized in this State, nor field pieces provided by the public, any preparation of that kind will be considered as without right; and, in the present state of things, would be understood to be with a criminal intent. I am told that the people of Jackson County expect assistance from the adjoining counties, to oppose the Mormons in taking or keeping possession of their lands. I should regret it extremely if any should be so imprudent as to do so; it would give a different aspect to the affair.

" 'The citizens of Jackson County have a right to arm

themselves and parade for military duty in their own county, independent of the commander in chief; but if citizens march there in arms from other counties, without order from the commander in chief, or some one authorized by him, it would produce a very different state of things. Indeed the Mormons have no right to march to Jackson County in arms, unless by the order or permission of the commander in chief. Men must not "levy war" in taking possession of their rights, any more than others should in opposing them in taking possession.

" 'As you have manifested a deep interest in a peaceable compromise of this important affair, I presume you will not be unwilling to be placed in a situation, in which perhaps, you can be more serviceable to these parties. I have therefore taken the liberty of appointing you an aid to the commander in chief, and hope it will be agreeable to you to accept. In this situation you can give your propositions all the influence they would have, were they to emanate from the Executive without committing yourself or the commander in chief in the event of a failure.

" 'I should be glad if you or some of the other gentlemen who joined you in your communication, would keep a close correspondence with these parties, and by each mail write to me.

" 'The character of the State has been injured in consequence of this unfortunate affair; and I sincerely hope it may not be disgraced by it in the end.

" 'With high respect, your obedient servant,
" '(Signed) DANIEL DUNKLIN.' "
—*Evening and Morning Star*, pp. 349, 350.

About the same time Governor Dunklin issued a second order (addressed to W. W. Phelps and others) for the restoration of the arms of the saints, by which it appears that Colonel Lucas resigned his commission to avoid delivering the same. The letter accompanying, and the order, read as follows:—

Second order for arms.

"CITY OF JEFFERSON, June 9, 1834.

"Herewith you have a second order for the delivery of your arms now in the possession of the militia of Jackson

County. Colonel Lucas has resigned his command, he informs me. If Lieutenant Colonel Pitcher shall be arrested before you receive this, you will please hold up the order until I am informed who may be appointed to the command of the regiment.   Respectfully,

"(Signed)   ·   DANIEL DUNKLIN.

"Thomas Pitcher, Lieutenant Colonel Commandant of the 33d Regiment; Sir: – On the 2d day of last May I issued an order to Colonel Lucas to deliver the fifty-two guns and one pistol which you received from the Mormons on the fifth day of November last, and reported to him on the third day of the succeeding December to W. W. Phelps, E. Partridge, John Corrill, John Whitmer, and A. S. Gilbert, or their order. On the 24th ult. Colonel Lucas wrote and informed me that he had resigned his commission and left the county of Jackson. You as commandant of said regiment are therefore commanded to collect the said arms, if they are not already in your possession, and deliver them to the aforesaid gentlemen or their order.   Respectfully,

"DANIEL DUNKLIN,   ·
"Commander in Chief."

—*Times and Seasons*, vol. 6, p. 1088.

Judge Ryland also wrote to the saints as follows:—

"RICHMOND, June 10, 1834.

"Mr. A. S. Gilbert; Sir:— Deeply impressed with a desire to do all in my power to settle or allay the disturbances between the 'Mormons' and the citizens of Jackson County, I have concluded that it might have some tendency to effectuate this object by having the Mormons called together at Liberty next Monday, and there explaining to them my notions and views of their present situation, and the circumstances attendant. I therefore request you, Sir, to use all your influence with your brethren, to get them to meet me next Monday in Liberty. I much fear and dread the consequences that are yet to ensue, unless I should succeed in my wishes to restore peace. It is the duty of all good men to use all proper and laudable means to restore peace. I expect a deputation of some of the most respectable citizens of Jackson County will meet me on Monday

Judge Ryland's letter.

next at Liberty. I call upon you in the name of humanity, therefore, to leave no efforts untried to collect your brethren at Liberty as requested. Should my efforts to make peace fail of success, there can at least be no wrong, Sir, in the attempt, and I shall enjoy the consolation of having done my duty as a man, as well as a Christian.

"I hope, Sir, you will duly appreciate the motive which prompts me to address this letter to you, and will aid me with all your influence with your brethren, in the prosecution of an object so much to be desired by all good men and citizens.　　　　　　Yours very respectfully,

"JOHN F. RYLAND."
—*Times and Seasons*, vol. 6, p. 1088.

A meeting was called, and the following reply was agreed to and sent to their attorneys for indorsement, and for presentation to the Judge:—

"Near LIBERTY, June 14, 1834.

"*Hon. J. F. Ryland; Dear Sir:*—Your communication of the 9th inst. from Richmond was duly received, and at a public meeting of our society this day its contents made known. Our brethren unanimously tender their thanks for the laudable disposition manifested on your part to effect peace between our society and the inhabitants of Jackson County, and as many as conveniently can will be present on Monday next. Entertaining some fears that your honor in his zeal for peace might unwarily recommend a sale of our lands in Jackson County, we have thought it expedient to give seasonable notice that no such proposition could possibly be acceded to by our society.

The reply.

"We have not heard that it was the intention of your honor to urge any such measure, but our enemies in Jackson County have long been trying to effect this object. In a letter from the Governor to us, he says, 'I have been requested to advise the Mormons to sell out and move away, but believing that it could have no good effect I have withheld my advice.' We give this quotation from the Governor's letter to disprove the statement made in the *Upper Missouri Enquirer* of last Wednesday, and conclude by adding that 'home is home,' and that we want possession of our homes, from which we have been wickedly expelled, and those rights which belong to us as native freeborn citizens of the United States.   We are respectfully,

"Your friends and servants,

"JOHN CORRILL, Chairman.

"A. S. GILBERT, Secretary.

"*Gentlemen:*—Will you be so good as to read the inclosed, then seal and hand to the Judge. We have given him an early hint, fearing that he might be induced by the solicitations of our enemies to propose a sale of our lands, which you well know would be like selling our children into slavery, and the urging of such a measure would avail nothing, unless to produce an excitement against us in this county. As requested last Thursday, we hope you will be present on Monday.   Your friends and servants,

"JOHN CORRILL.

"A. S. GILBERT.

"To Messrs. Doniphan and Atchison."

—*Times and Seasons*, vol. 6, p. 1089.

On Monday, June 16, 1834, the meeting referred to was

Public meeting. held at the courthouse in Liberty, of which Joseph Smith in his history gives the following account:—

"Monday, June 16. The citizens of Clay County (to the number of eight hundred or a thousand, among whom were the brethren,) assembled at the courthouse in Liberty, agreeably to the request of Judge Ryland, and a deputation from Jackson who presented the following:—

" 'PROPOSITIONS OF THE PEOPLE OF JACKSON COUNTY
TO THE MORMONS.

" 'The undersigned committee, being fully authorized by the people of Jackson County, hereby propose to the Mormons, that they will buy all the land that the said Mormons own in the county of Jackson; and also all the improvements which the said Mormons had on any of the public lands in said county of Jackson, as they existed before the first disturbance between the people of Jackson and the Mormons, and for such as they have made since. They further propose that the valuation of said land and improvements shall be ascertained by three disinterested arbitrators to be chosen and agreed to by both parties. They further propose, that should the parties disagree in the choice of arbitrators, then —————— —————— is to choose them. They further propose, that twelve of the Mormons shall be permitted to go along with the arbitrators to show them their land and improvements while valuing the same, and such other of the Mormons as the arbitrators shall wish to do so, to give them information; and the people of Jackson hereby guarantee their entire safety while doing so. They further propose, that when the arbitrators report the value of the land and improvements, as aforesaid, the people of Jackson will pay the valuation, *with one hundred per cent added thereon*, to the Mormons, within thirty days thereafter. They further propose, that the Mormons are not to make any effort, ever after, to settle, either collectively or individually, within the limits of Jackson County. The Mormons are to enter into bonds to insure the conveyance of their land in Jackson County, according to the above terms, when the payment shall be made; and the committee will enter into a like bond, with such security as may be deemed sufficient, for the payment of the money, according to the above proposition. While the arbitrators are investigating and deciding upon the matters referred to them, the Mormons are not to attempt to enter into Jackson County, or to settle there, except such as are by the foregoing propositions permitted to go there. They further propose, that the people of Jackson will sell all their lands, and improvements on public lands, in Jackson County, to the Mormons,—the valuation to be obtained in the same manner,—the same per cent, in addition to be paid, and the time the money is to be paid is the same, as the above set forth in our propositions to buy, the Mormons to give good security for the payment of the money, and the undersigned will give security that the land will be conveyed to the Mormons. They further propose, that all parties are to remain as they are till the payment is made, at which time the people of Jackson will give possession.

" '(Signed) " 'SAMUEL C. OWENS.

" 'RICHARD FRISTOE.

" 'THOS. HAYTON, SR.

" 'Thos. Campbell.
" 'John Davis.
" 'Thos. Jeffreys.
" 'Smallwood Noland.
" 'Robert Rickman.
" 'Abraham M. Clellan.
" 'S. K. Noland.'

"On presentation of the foregoing, Samuel C. Owens made a flaming war speech, and General Doniphan replied on the side of peace. The Rev. M. Riley, a Baptist priest, made a hot speech against the Mormons, and said, 'The Mormons have lived long enough in Clay County; and they must either clear out, or be cleared out.' Turnham, the moderator of the meeting, answered in a masterly manner, saying, 'Let us be republicans; let us honor our country, and not disgrace it like Jackson County. For God's sake don't disfranchise or drive away the Mormons. They are better citizens than many of the old inhabitants.'

"General Doniphan exclaimed, 'That's a fact, and as the Mormons have armed themselves, if they don't fight they are cowards. I love to hear that they have brethren coming to their assistance. Greater love can no man show than he who lays down his life for his brethren.'

"At this critical instant the cocking of pistols and jingle of implements of death denoted desperation. One motioned to 'adjourn;' another said, 'Go on,' and in the midst of this awful crisis a person bawled into the door, 'A man stabbed.' The mass instantly rushed out to the spot, in hopes, as some said, that 'one damn'd Mormon had got killed.' But as good luck would have it, only one Missourian had dirked another. (One Calbert, a blacksmith, had stabbed one Wales, who had previously whipped one Mormon nearly to death, and boasted of having whipped many more.) The wound was dangerous, and as if the Lord was there, it seemed as though the occurrence was necessary to break up the meeting without further bloodshed, and give the saints a chance to consult what would be most advisable in such a critical instant, and they immediately penned the following answer to the propositions from Jackson County, presented by Owens, etc.:—

" 'Gentlemen:—Your propositions for an adjustment of the difficulties between the citizens of Jackson County and the Mormons is before us; and, as explained to you in the court-house this day, we are not authorized to say to you that our brethren will submit to your proposals; but we agree to spread general notice, and call a meeting of our people in all, the present week, and lay before you an answer as soon as Saturday or Monday next. We can say for ourselves, and in behalf of our brethren, that peace is what we desire and what we are disposed to cultivate with all men; and to effect peace we feel disposed to use all our influence, as far as would be required at our hands, as freeborn citizens of these United States. And as fears have been expressed that we designed hostilities against the inhabitants of Jackson County, we hereby pledge ourselves to them, and to the hospitable citizens of Clay County, that we will not, and neither have designed, as a people, to commence hostilities against the aforesaid citizens of Jackson County or any other people.

" 'Our answer shall be handed to Judge Turnham, the chairman of the meeting, even earlier than the time before stated, if possible.

   '(Signed)
                                " 'W. W. PHELPS.
                                " 'WM. E. McLELLIN.
                                " 'A. S. GILBERT.
                                " 'JOHN CORRILL.
                                " 'ISAAC MORLEY.

" 'N. B.—As we are informed that a large number of our people are on their way to Jackson County, we agree to use our influence immediately to prevent said company from entering into Jackson County, until you shall receive an answer to the propositions aforenamed.'

"It may be thought, at first view, that the mob committee made a fair proposition to the saints, in offering to buy their lands at one hundred per cent, in thirty days, and offering theirs on the same terms. But when it is understood that the mob held possession of a much larger quantity of land than the saints, and that they only offered thirty days for the payment, having previously robbed them of nearly everything, it will be readily seen that they were only making a sham to cover their previous unlawful conduct. But the tempest of an immediate conflict seemed to be checked, and the Jackson mob to the number of about fifteen, with Samuel C. Owens and James Campbell at their head, started for Independence, Jackson County, to raise an army sufficient to meet me, before I could get into Clay County. Campbell swore, as he adjusted his pistols in his holsters, 'The eagles and turkey buzzards shall eat my flesh if I do not fix Joe Smith and his army so that their skins will not hold shucks, before two days are passed.'

"They went to the ferry and undertook to cross the Missouri River, after dusk, and the angel of God saw fit to sink the boat, about the middle of the river, and seven out of twelve that attempted to cross were drowned. Thus suddenly, and justly, went they to their own place by water. Campbell was among the missing. He floated down the river some four or five miles, and lodged upon a pile of driftwood, where the eagles, buzzards, ravens, crows, and wild animals ate his flesh from his bones, to fulfill his own words, and left him a horrible looking skeleton of God's vengeance; which was discovered about three weeks after, by one Mr. Purtle.

"Owens saved his life only, after floating four miles down the stream, where he lodged upon an island, 'swam off naked about daylight, borrowed a mantle to hide his shame, and slipped home rather shy of the vengeance of God.' "—*Times and Seasons*, vol. 6, pp. 1089-1091.

On Saturday, June 21, in accordance with agreement, a letter was written to the Jackson County Committee, as follows:—

"Clay County, 21st June, 1834.

"*Gentlemen:*—Your propositions of Monday last have been generally made known to our people, and we are instructed to inform you that they cannot be acceded to.

"Honorable propositions to you are now making on our part, and we think we shall be enabled to deliver the same
Letter to Jackson County. to you the early part of next week. We are happy to have it in our power to give you assurances that our brethren here, together with those who have arrived from the East, are unanimously disposed to make

every sacrifice for an honorable adjustment of our differences that could be required of free citizens of the United States.

"Negotiations at the camp are now going on between some gentlemen of this county and our brethren, which are calculated to allay the great excitement in your county. We are informed that the citizens of Jackson entertain fears that our people intend to invade their territory in a hostile manner. We assure you that their fears are groundless; such is not and never was our intention.

"(Signed)   "W. W. PHELPS.

"A. S. GILBERT.

"W. E. McLELLIN.

"JOHN CORRILL.

"ISAAC MORLEY.

"To S. C. Owens, and others of the Jackson committee."— *Times and Seasons*, vol. 6, p. 1092.

On June 23, a proposition was made to the Jackson County committee as follows:—

"We the undersigned committee, having full power and authority to settle and adjust all matters and differences existing between our people or society and the in-
A proposition. habitants of Jackson County, upon honorable and constitutional principles; therefore, if the said inhabitants of Jackson County will not let us return to our lands in peace, we are willing to propose, firstly; that twelve disinterested men, six to be chosen by our people, and six by the inhabitants of Jackson County; and these twelve men shall say what the lands of those men are worth in that county who cannot consent to live with us, and they shall receive their money for the same in one year from the time the treaty is made, and none of our people shall enter the county to reside till the money is paid. The said twelve men shall have power also to say what the damages shall be for the injuries we have sustained in the destruction of property and in being driven from our possessions, which amount of damages shall be deducted from the amount for their lands. Our object is peace, and an early answer will be expected.

"(Signed)   "W. W. PHELPS.

"EDWARD PARTRIDGE.

"ISAAC MORLEY.

"JOHN CORRILL.

"JOHN WHITMER.

"A. S. GILBERT."

— *Times and Seasons*, vol. 6, p. 1106.

On June 26, 1834, the following communication was sent to the Governor:—

"*Sir:*—A company of our people, exceeding two hundred men, arrived in this county the 19th inst. and encamped about twelve miles from Liberty, where they were met by several gentlemen from this and Ray County, who went by request of the people, to ascertain the motives and designs of our people in approaching this county; and as the deputation was composed of gentlemen who appeared to possess humane and republican feelings, our people were rejoiced at the opportunity of an interchange of feelings and an open and frank avowal of all their views and intentions in emigrating to this country with their arms. A full explanation having been given in a public address by our Brother Joseph Smith, Jun., which produced great satisfaction, the same in substance was afterwards reduced in writing and handed to the aforesaid gentlemen that it might be made public, as the shedding of blood is, and ever has been, foreign and revolting to our feelings. For this reason we have patiently endured the greatest indignities that free men of this republic have ever been called to suffer, and we still continue to bear with heartrending feelings a deprivation of our rights, having commenced negotiations with the inhabitants of Jackson for a compromise wherein proposals, on our part, have been made, which have been acknowledged by every disinterested man to be highly honorable and liberal. An answer to our propositions has not yet been received from Jackson.

"If we fail in this attempt, we intend to make another effort, and go all lengths that would be required by human or divine law. As our proposals and correspondence with the inhabitants of Jackson will doubtless hereafter be published, we think it unnecessary to detail the same in this communication. Our right to our soil in Jackson County we shall forever claim, and to obtain peaceful possession we are willing to make great sacrifices. To allay excitement in the

LIBRARY
OF THE
UNIVERSITY
OF CALIFORNIA

county, the aforesaid company of emigrants have dispersed, to await the final end of all negotiations that can be made with the said county of Jackson.

"Within the last week one of our men, being near the ferry, was seized by some Jackson citizens, while in this county, threatened with death if he made resistance, and carried over the river prisoner to Independence, where he was put under guard one day, and after hearing many threats, was liberated. The houses of several of our brethren in this county have been forcibly entered by some of the inhabitants of Jackson, and a number of guns and small arms taken therefrom. Where the men were absent from their houses, loaded guns were presented to the females and their lives threatened if they made resistance, as we have been informed, and have no doubt of the fact.

"Your second order for the restoration of our arms was received last mail. We have not yet done anything with it. Hoping that the influence of the inhabitants of Jackson County will materially lessen in the surrounding counties, and the people become more tranquil, we think it wisdom to defer petitioning for a guard while there exists a hope of a compromise, etc.

"We believe that the President would render us assistance in obtaining possession of our lands, if aided by the Executive of this State in a petition, and thereby put an end to serious evils that are growing out of the Jackson outrage. In a letter from Your Excellency, of April 20, we had a word on the subject of petitioning. We should be pleased to hear further, and would here observe that no communication from the Executive, giving his opinion or advice, will be made public, if requested not to do so.

"We are respectfully, and with great regard,
"Your obedient servants,
"A S. GILBERT.
"W. W. PHELPS.
"JOHN CORRILL."
—*Times and Seasons*, vol. 6, p. 1107.

This was the last public act of A. S. Gilbert. [1]

[1] The drafting and signing of the above was the last public act of the keeper of the Lord's storehouse, Algernon S. Gilbert; for he was at-

On the same day the chairman of the Jackson County mob wrote Mr. Reese, attorney for the saints, as follows:—

Letter
from mob.

"INDEPENDENCE, Missouri, June 26, 1834.

"*Mr. Amos Reese; Dear Sir:*—Since my return from Liberty I have been busily engaged in conversing with the most influential men of our county, endeavoring to find out, if possible, what kind of a compromise will suit with the Mormons on their part. The people here, en masse, I find out, will do nothing like according to their last proposition. We will have a meeting, if possible, on Monday next, at which time the proposals of the Mormons will be answered. In the meantime I would be glad that they, the Mormons, would cast an eye back of Clinton and see if that is not a country calculated for them.

"Yours respectfully,

"S. C. OWENS."

—*Times and Seasons*, vol. 6, p. 1108.

From the foregoing records it will appear that the saints had but two propositions open to them, the compliance with which would bring peace; namely: To sell their possessions in Jackson County, or to buy the whole county at double its value. The first they were religiously opposed to doing, and the second they were financially unable to do. While they were suing for peace and making every possible effort to obtain justice, always declaring allegiance to law and order, the mob were continuing their lawless deeds whenever and wherever opportunity offered. As already mentioned in the letter to the Governor, the mob crossed over into Clay County, intimidating defenseless women, and otherwise maltreating members of the church. One instance is related by Joseph Smith, that transpired on March 31, that can scarcely be too severely condemned.[2]

Lawless acts.

---

tacked with the cholera the same day and died in a few hours, according to his own words that he "would rather die than go forth to preach the gospel to the gentiles."—*Times and Seasons*, vol. 6, p. 1107.

[2]This day, also, Ira I. Willis, a young man who had been in the church for some time, and who was driven from Jackson County into Clay, returned thither to look for a stray cow; and while at the house of Esquire Manship's, a Justice of the Peace, (where he had called with Bro. John

On July 3, 1834, the High Council of Zion was organized,
High Coun- of which and other items connected with it, Jo-
cil organized. seph wrote:—

"On the third of July the high priests of Zion assembled
in Clay County, and I proceeded to organize a High Council,
agreeably to revelation given at Kirtland, for the purpose of
settling important business that might come before them,
which could not be settled by the bishop and his council.
David Whitmer was elected president, and W. W. Phelps
and John Whitmer assistant presidents. The following
high priests; viz., Christian Whitmer, Newel Knight,
Lyman Wight, Calvin Beebe, William E. McLellin, Solomon
Hancock, Thomas B. Marsh, Simeon Carter, Parley P.
Pratt, Orson Pratt, John Murdock, Levi Jackman, were appointed councilors, and the council adjourned to Monday.

"Frederick G. Williams was clerk of the meeting.

"From this time I continued to give instruction to the
members of the High Council, elders, those who had traveled in the camp with me, and such others as desired information, until the 7th, when the council assembled according
to adjournment at the house of Elder Lyman Wight; present,
fifteen high priests, eight elders, four priests, eight teachers, three deacons, and members.

"After singing and prayer I gave the council such instructions in relation to their high calling as would enable them
to proceed to minister in their office agreeably to the pattern
heretofore given; read the revelation on the subject, and
told them that if I should now be taken away, I had accomplished the great work the Lord had laid before me, and
that which I had desired of the Lord; and that I had done
my duty in organizing the High Council, through which
council the will of the Lord might be known on all important occasions in the building up of Zion and establishing truth in the earth.

Follet, to prove his title to the cow,) was caught by that unhung land-
pirate and inhuman monster, Moses Wilson, and whipped in a most cruel
and savage manner, while surrounded by some half dozen of the
old mobbers. This was an unpardonable act; all that know Mr. Willis
can bear testimony that he is a young man, honest, peaceable, and unof-
fending, working righteousness and molesting no one. May God reward
Moses Wilson according to his works.—*Times and Seasons*, vol. 6, p. 1028.

"It was voted that those who were appointed on the third should be confirmed in their appointments. I then ordained David Whitmer, president, and W. W. Phelps and John Whitmer assistants, and their twelve councilors. The twelve councilors then proceeded to cast lots, to know who should speak first, and the order of speaking, which resulted as follows; viz.:—

Simeon Carter	1,	Parley P. Pratt	2,
Wm. E. McLellin	3,	Calvin Beebe	4,
Levi Jackman	5,	Solomon Hancock	6,
Christian Whitmer	7,	Newel Knight	8,
Orson Pratt	9,	Lyman Wight	10,
Thomas B. Marsh	11,	John Murdock	12.

"Father Whitmer came forward and blessed his three sons, David, John, and Christian Whitmer, in the name of the Lord. Also Father Knight blessed his son, Newel. Bishop Partridge stated to the council that a greater responsibility rested upon him than before their organization, as it was not his privilege to counsel with any of them except the president, and his own councilors, and desired their prayers that he might be enabled to act in righteousness.

"I next presented the case of W. W. Phelps to the council, to have their decision whether he should take his family to Kirtland, and if so, when he shall start, as it had been deemed necessary for him to assist in the printing establishment. It was motioned and carried that four of the councilors speak on the subject, two on each side; viz., Simeon Carter and Wm. E. McLellin for the plaintiff; and Parley P. Pratt and Calvin Beebe for the church. After hearing the pleas the president decided that it was the duty of W. W. Phelps to go to Kirtland to assist in printing, and that his family remain in the region where they were, and that he have an honorable discharge from his station in Zion for a season (as soon as he can accomplish his business). Signed by the president and clerk.

"It was then proposed by W. W. Phelps that David Whitmer, the president of the church in Zion, should go to Kirtland and assist in promoting the cause of Christ, as being one of the three witnesses. This case was argued by Levi Jackman and Christian Whitmer on behalf of the plaintiffs, and Solomon Hancock and Newel Knight for the church; after which it was decided, as before, that Bro. David Whitmer go to the East and assist in the great work of the gathering and be his own judge as to leaving his family or taking them with him. It was also decided that John Whitmer and Wm. E. McLellin go east, as soon as convenient.

"The high priests, elders, priests, teachers, deacons, and members present then covenanted with hands uplifted to heaven that you [they] would uphold Bro. David Whitmer, as president in Zion, in my absence, and John Whitmer and W. W. Phelps as assistant presidents or councilors, and myself as first president of the church, and one another by faith and prayer.

"Previous to entering into this covenant, and in pursuance of the revelation to the saints to sue for and proclaim peace to the ends of the earth, the following appeal was written, and sanctioned by the High Council and First Presidency of the church, at the foregoing sitting.

"President Whitmer closed the council by prayer.

"F. G. WILLIAMS, Clerk."

—*Times and Seasons*, vol. 6, pp. 1109, 1110.

The "Appeal" here referred to as being indorsed by the High Council of Zion is quite lengthy, but we bespeak for it An appeal. a careful reading, and we recommend its lofty and sublime sentiment, its patriotic devotion to law and country, its pacific attitude towards the enemy, and its adherence to principles of truth. It is as follows:—

"AN APPEAL.

"Whereas the Church of Christ, recently styled the Church of the Latter Day Saints, contumeliously called Mormons or Mormonites, has suffered many privations, afflictions, persecutions, and losses on account of the religious belief and faith of its members, which belief and faith are founded in the revealed word of God, as recorded in the Holy Bible, or the Book of Mormon, the revelations and commandments of our Savior, Jesus Christ; and whereas the said church, by revelation, commenced removing to the western boundaries of the State of Missouri, where lands were purchased of the

Government, and where it was calculated to purchase of those who were unwilling to reside with the church as a society, all lands that could be bought, for the purpose of building up a holy city unto God, a New Jerusalem, a place which we were desirous to call Zion, as we believe a place of refuge from the scourges and plagues which are so often mentioned in the Bible by the prophets and apostles, that should be poured out upon the earth in the last days; and whereas the inhabitants of Jackson County, Missouri, have leagued and combined against said church, and have driven the saints from their lands, and taken their arms from them, and burned down many of their houses, without any provocation; and whereas we have petitioned the Governor of this State, and the President of the United States, for redress of wrongs (the law being put to defiance in Jackson County), and for redemption of rights, that we might be legally repossessed of our lands and property; and whereas the said inhabitants of Jackson County have not only bound themselves to keep us out of that county, but have armed themselves, *cap-a-pie*, and even with cannon for war; and whereas our people, residing in the Upper Missouri, have recently armed themselves for military duty and self-defense, seeing their arms taken from them by the inhabitants of Jackson County, were purposely kept from them; and whereas a number of the members of the church in the East have emigrated to this region of country to settle and join their brethren, with arms to answer the military law, which has created some excitement among the inhabitants of the upper counties of this State; whereupon, to show that our object was only the peaceable possession of our rights and property, and to purchase more land in the regions round about, we met a committee from Jackson County for compromise; and our emigrating brethren met some gentlemen from Clay and other counties to satisfy them that their motives were good, and their object peace, which they did; and whereas the propositions of the Jackson committee could not be accepted on our part, because they proposed to 'buy or sell,' and to sell our land would amount to a denial of our faith, as that land is the place where the Zion of God shall stand, according to our faith and belief in the revelations of God, and upon which Israel shall be gathered according to the prophets; and secondly, the propositions were unfair, notwithstanding they offered double price for our lands, in thirty days, or sell theirs at the same rate, for this plain reason, that the whole large county of Jackson would be as thirty to one, or nearly so, in comparison with the matter in question, and, in supposition, for one thousand dollars, two thousand dollars to our people, was asking for three hundred thousand dollars the exorbitant sum of six hundred thousand dollars, taking the land rich and poor, in thirty days! with the reproachable, vicious, un-American, and unconstitutional proviso that the committee on our part bind themselves 'that no Mormon should ever settle in Jackson County;' and whereas our committee proposed to the said Jackson committee, (if they would not grant us our rights otherwise,) that our people would buy the land of those that were unwilling to live among our people, in that county, and pay them in one year, they allowing the damage we have sustained in the loss of a printing office, apparatus and book work, houses, property, etc., to come out of the purchase money, but no answer returned; and whereas, to show our honest intentions, and awaken the friends of virtue, humanity, and equal rights, it becomes our duty to lay our case before the world, to be weighed in the balances of public opinion:—

"Now therefore, as citizens of the United States, and leading elders in the Church of the Latter Day Saints, residing in the State of Missouri, in behalf of the church, we, the undersigned, do make this solemn APPEAL to the people and constituted authorities of this nation, and to the ends of the earth, for PEACE: that we may have the privilege of enjoying our religious rights and immunities and worship God according to the dictates of our own consciences, as guaranteed to every citizen by the constitutions of the National and State Governments. That, although the laws have been broken, and are defied in Jackson County, we may be enabled to regain and enjoy our rights and property, agreeable to law in this boasted land of liberty.

"Since the disgraceful combination of the inhabitants of

Jackson County has set the law at defiance, and put all hopes of criminal prosecution, against them, in that vicinage, beyond the reach of judge and jury, and left us but a distant expectation of civil remuneration for the great amount of damage we have sustained, necessity compels us to complain to the world. And if our case and calamity are not sufficient to excite the commiseration of the humane, and open the hearts of the generous, and fire the spirits of the patriotic, then has sympathy lost herself in the wilderness, and justice fled from power; then has the dignity of the ermine shrunk at the gigantic front of a mob, and the sacred mantle of freedom been caught up to heaven where the weary are at rest and the wicked cannot come.

"To be obedient to the commandments of our Lord and Savior, some of the heads of the church commenced purchasing lands in the western boundaries of the State of Missouri, according to the revelation of God, for the city of Zion; in doing which no law was evaded, no rights infringed, nor no principle of religion neglected, but the laudable foundation of a glorious work begun, for the salvation of mankind, in the last days, agreeable to our faith, and according to the promises in the sacred Scriptures of God,

"We verily believed, knowing that the National and State Constitutions, and the statute laws of the land, and the commandments of the Lord, allowed all men to worship as they pleased, that we should be protected, not only by all the law of a free republic, but by every republican throughout the realms of freedom.

"The holy prophets had declared, 'that it should come to pass in the last days, that the mountain of the Lord's house should be established in the top of the mountains, and should be exalted above the hills, and all nations should flow unto it. And many people should go and say, Come ye, and let us go up to the mountain of the Lord, to the house of the God of Jacob: and he will teach us of his ways, and we will walk in his paths: for out of Zion shall go forth the law, and the word of the Lord from Jerusalem.' And again it was said by Joel, seemingly to strengthen the faith of the Latter Day Saints in the above, 'that whosoever should call on the

name of the Lord should be delivered, for in mount Zion and
in Jerusalem, shall be deliverance, as the Lord hath said,
and in the remnant whom the Lord shall call.' The Book of
Mormon, which we hold equally sacred with the Bible, says,
'that a New Jerusalem should be built up on this land, unto
the remnant of the seed of Joseph, for the which things
there has been a type.' In fact all the prophets from Moses
to John the revelator have spoken concerning these things,
and in all good faith, by direct revelation from the Lord, as
in days of old, we commenced the glorious work, that a holy
city, a New Jerusalem, even Zion, might be built up, and a
temple reared in this generation, whereunto, as saith the
Lord, all nations should be invited. Firstly the rich and the
learned, the wise and the noble; and after that cometh the
day of his power; but the inhabitants of Jackson County
arrayed themselves against us, because of our faith and
belief, and destroyed our printing establishment, to prevent
the spread of the work, and drove men, women, and children
from their lands, houses and homes, to perish in the
approaching winter; while every blast carried the wailing of
women and the shrieks of children across the widespread
prairies, sufficiently horrible to draw tears from the savage,
or melt a heart of stone!

"Now, that the world may know that our faith in the work
and word of the Lord is firm and unshaken, and to show all
nations, kindreds, tongues, and people that our object is
good, for the good of all, we come before the great family of
mankind for peace, and ask their hospitality and assistance
for our comfort, and the preservation of our persons and
property, and solicit their charity for the great cause of God.
We are well aware that many slanderous reports and ridiculous stories are in circulation against our religion and society; but as wise men will hear both sides and then judge,
we sincerely hope and trust that the still small voice of truth
will be heard, and our great revelations read and candidly
compared with the prophecies of the Bible, that the great
cause of our Redeemer may be supported by a liberal share
of public opinion, as well as the unseen power of God.

"It will be seen by a reference to the Book of Command-

ments, page 135, that the Lord has said to the church, and
we mean to live by his words, 'Let no man break the laws of
the land, for he that keepeth the laws of God hath no need
to break the laws of the land' [Doctrine and Covenants 58: 5];
therefore, as the people of God, we come before the world
and claim protection, by law, from the common officers of
justice, in every neighborhood where our people may be: we
claim the same at the hands of the Governors of the several
States, and of the President of the United States, and of the
friends of humanity and justice, in every clime and country
on the globe.

"By the desperate acts of the inhabitants of Jackson
County, many hundreds of American citizens are deprived of
their lands and rights: and it is reported that we mean to
regain our possessions, and even Jackson County, 'by the
shedding of blood.' But if any man will take the pains to
read the one hundred and fifty-third page of the Book of
Commandments, he will find it there said, 'Wherefore the
land of Zion shall not be obtained but by purchase, or by
blood, otherwise there is none inheritance for you. And if
by purchase, behold you are blessed: and if by blood,
as *you are forbidden to shed blood*, lo, your enemies are upon
you, and you shall be scourged from city to city and from
synagogue to synagogue, and but few shall stand to
receive an inheritance' [Doctrine and Covenants 63: 8].
So we declare that we have ever meant and now mean,
to purchase the land of our inheritance, like all other
honest men, of the Government, and of those who would
rather sell their farms than live in our society. And, as
thousands have done before us, we solicit the aid of the children of men, and of government, to help us obtain our rights
in Jackson County, and the land whereon the Zion of God,
according to our faith, shall stand in the last days, for the
salvation and gathering of Israel.

"Let no man be alarmed because our society has commenced gathering to build a city and a house for the Lord,
as a refuge from present evils and coming calamities. Our
forefathers came to the goodly land of America, to shun persecution and enjoy their religious opinions and rights, as

they thought proper; and the Lord, after much tribulation, blessed them, and has said that we should continue to importune for redress and redemption by the hands of those who are placed as rulers, and are in authority over us, according to the laws and Constitution of the people, which he has suffered to be established and should be maintained for the rights and protection of all flesh, according to just and holy principles; that every man may act in doctrine and in principle, pertaining to futurity, according to the moral agency which he has given unto them; that every man may be accountable for his own sins in the day of judgment. And for this purpose he has established the Constitution of this land by the hands of wise men whom he raised up unto this very purpose, and redeemed the land by the shedding of blood.

"Now we seek peace, and ask our rights, even redress and redemption, at the hands of the rulers of this nation: not only our lands and property in Jackson County, but for free trade with all men, and unmolested emigration to any part of the Union, and for our inherent right to worship God as we please. We ask the restoration of these rights because they have been taken from us, or abridged by the violence and usurpation of the inhabitants of Jackson County. As a people we hold ourselves amenable to the laws of the land, and while the government remains as it is, the right to emigrate from State to State, from territory to territory, from county to county, and from vicinity to vicinity, is open to all men of whatever trade or creed, without hindrance or molestation; and as long as we are justifiable and honest in the eyes of the law, we claim it, whether we remove by single families, or in bodies of hundreds, with that of carrying the necessary arms and accouterments for military duty. And we believe that all honest men, who love their country and their country's glory, and have a wish to see the law magnified and made honorable, will not only help perpetuate the great legacy of freedom, that came unimpaired from the hands of our venerable fathers, to us, but they will also protect us from insult and injury, and aid the work of God, that they may reap a reward in the regions of bliss, when all men receive according to their works.

"In relation to our distress, from the want of our lands in Jackson County, and for the want of the property destroyed by fire and waste, rather than do any act contrary to law, we solemnly appeal to the people with whom we tarry, for protection from insult and harm, and for the comforts of life by labor or otherwise, while we seek peace and satisfaction of our enemies through every possible and honorable means which humanity can dictate, or philanthropy urge, or religion require. We are citizens of this republic, and we ask our rights as republicans, not merely in our restoration to our lands and property in Jackson County, Missouri; but in being considered honest in our faith, honest in our deal, and honest before God, till, by due course of law we may be proved otherwise; reserving the right of every man's being held amenable to the proper authority for his own crimes and sins.

"'Crowns won by blood, by blood must be maintained,' and to avoid blood and strife, and more fully satisfy the world that our object is peace and good will to all mankind, we hereby APPEAL for peace to the ends of the earth, and ask the protection of all people, while we use every fair means in our power to obtain our rights and immunities without force: setting an example for all true believers, that we will not yield our faith and principles for any earthly consideration, whereby a precedent might be established, that a majority may crush any religious sect with impunity; knowing that if we give up our rights in Jackson County, farewell to society! farewell to religion! farewell to right! farewell to property! farewell to life! The fate of our church now, might become the fate of the Methodists next week; the Catholics next month, and the overthrow of all societies next year; leaving nation after nation a wide waste where reason and friendship once were!

"Another and the great object which we mean to help accomplish, is the salvation of the souls of men. And to bring to pass such a glorious work, like many other religious denominations, in all ages, we shall license elders to preach the everlasting gospel to all nations, according to the great commandment of our Lord and Savior Jesus Christ, as recorded in St. Matthew: 'Go ye, therefore, and teach all nations, baptizing them in the name of the Father, and of the Son, and of the Holy Ghost: teaching them to observe all things whatsoever I have commanded you: and, lo, I am with you alway, even unto the end of the world.'

"Thus we shall send laborers into the Lord's vineyard to gather the wheat, and prepare the earth against the day when desolations shall be poured out without measure; and as it now is, and ever has been considered one of the most honorable and glorious employments of men, to carry good tidings to the nations, so we shall expect the clemency of all men, while we go forth, for the last time, to gather Israel for the glory of God, that he may suddenly come to his temple; that all nations may come and worship in his presence, when there shall be none to molest or make afraid, but the earth shall be filled with his knowledge and glory.

"We live in an age of fearful imagination. With all the sincerity that common men are endowed with, the saints have labored, without pay, to instruct the people of the United States, that the gathering had commenced in the western boundaries of Missouri, to build a holy city. . . .

"The faith and religion of the Latter Day Saints are founded upon the old Scriptures, the Book of Mormon, and direct revelation from God; and while every event that transpires around us is evidence of the truth of them, and an index that the great and terrible day of the Lord is near, we entreat the philanthropist, the moralist, and the honorable men of all creeds and sects to read our publications, to examine the Bible, the Book of Mormon, and the Commandments, and listen to the fullness of the gospel, and judge whether we are entitled to the credit of the world, for honest motives and pure principles.

"A cloud of bad omen seems to hang over this generation. Men start up at the impulse of the moment and defy and outstrip all law, while the destroyer is also abroad in the earth wasting flesh without measure, and none can stay his course. In the midst of such portentous times, we feel an anxious desire to prepare, and help others prepare, for coming events; and we candidly believe that no honest man will

put forth his hand to stop the work of the Lord or persecute
the saints.   In the name of Jesus we entreat the people of
this nation to pause before they reject the words of the
Lord, or his servants: These, like all flesh, may be imper-
fect; *but God is pure, hear ye him!*

"While we ask peace and protection for the saints, wherever they may be, we also solicit the charity and benevolence
of all the worthy on earth, to purchase the righteous a holy
home, a place of rest, and a land of peace, believing that no
man who knows he has a soul will keep back his mite, but
cast it in for the benefit of Zion; thus, when time is no
longer, he, with all the ransomed of the Lord, may stand, in
the fullness of joy, and view the grand pillar of heaven,
which was built by the faith and charity of the saints, beginning at Adam, with this motto in the base: '*Repent and live;*'
surrounded with a beautiful circle sign, supported by a
cross, about midway up its lofty column, staring the world
in letters of blood: 'The kingdom of heaven is at hand,' and
finished with a plain top, towering up in the midst of the
celestial world, around which is written, by the finger of
Jehovah: 'Eternal life is the greatest gift of God.'

"Although we may fail to show all men the truth of the
fullness of the gospel, yet we hope to be able to convince
some that we are neither deluded nor fanatics, but, like other
men, have a claim on the world for land, and for a living, as
good and as great as our venerable fathers had for Independence and liberty: That though the world has been made to
believe, by false reports and vague stories, that the saints
(called Mormons) were meaner than the savages, still God
has been our help in time of trouble, and has provided for us
in due season; and to use the language of Pope, he has let
the work 'spread undivided,' and 'operate unspent.'

"For the honor of our beloved country and the continuation of its free Government, we appeal for peace; for an
example of forbearance, and the diffusion of the everlasting
gospel, we appeal to the humanity of all nations; and for the
glory of God, before whom we must all answer for the deeds
done in life, and for the hope of holiness hereafter, we mean
to remain faithful to the end, continuing to pray to the Lord

to spare us, and the people, from whatever is evil, and not calculated to humble us, and prepare us for his presence and glory: at the same time beseeching him, in the name of Jesus, to extend his blessings to whom he will, and his mercy to all, till, by righteousness, the kingdoms of this world become fair as the sun and clear as the moon.

"W. W. PHELPS.
"DAVID WHITMER.
"JOHN WHITMER.
"EDWARD PARTRIDGE.
"JOHN CORRILL.
"ISAAC MORLEY.
"PARLEY P. PRATT.
"LYMAN WIGHT.
"NEWEL KNIGHT.
"THOMAS B. MARSH.
"SIMEON CARTER.
"CALVIN BEEBE.

"Missouri, (United States,) July, 1834."
—*Evening and Morning Star*, vol. 2, pp. 361-366.

Lyman Wight writes of this organization and the remarks of President Smith, as follows:—

"Our next business was to organize a council for the benefit of the church; and accordingly, David Whitmer, John Whitmer, and W. W. Phelps were set apart and ordained to preside over the council, and the following named persons were chosen as councilors: Parley P. Pratt, Orson Pratt, Christian Whitmer, Newel Knight, Simeon Carter, John Murdock, Thomas B. Marsh, Solomon Hancock, Calvin Beebe, Levi Jackman, William E. McLellin, and myself. We then organized and ordained several according to our calling. Brother Joseph Smith then arose and addressed us at some length upon the all-important obligations which we were under to execute justice to our brethren according to the law of God, saying that he had lived to see the Church of Jesus Christ established on earth according to the order of heaven; and should he now be taken from this body of people, the work of the Lord would roll on, and the gathering of the house of Israel take place in spite of earth and hell. And he further said that he was now willing to return home, that he was fully satisfied that he had done the

Instruction given.

will of God, and that the Lord had accepted our sacrifice
and offering, even as he had Abraham's when he offered his
son Isaac; and in his benediction asked the heavenly Father
to bless us with eternal life and salvation. The day passed
off with gratitude to our heavenly Father who so kindly bestows his Holy Spirit upon all who seek him with an honest
heart."

On Sunday, June 8, 1834, Joseph went to the eastern part
of Clay County and held a meeting at night.

On Monday the 9th he started for Kirtland by wagon in
Joseph returns company with Hyrum Smith, F. G. Williams, W.
to Kirtland. E. McLellin, and others.

On the 12th Elder John Corrill wrote Samuel C. Owens,
Letter inclosing a letter to Colonel Pitcher. The letters
to Owens. were as follows:—

"*Sir:*—The last time I saw you in Liberty you said that an
answer to our proposals you thought would be forwarded
soon. But it has not been done. We are anxiously waiting
to have a compromise effected if possible. Respecting our
wheat in Jackson County, can it be secured so that we can
receive the avails of it or not, seeing we are at present pro-
hibited the privilege?

"JOHN CORRILL.

"P. S.—Please hand the following to Colonel Pitcher."

"LIBERTY, July 10, 1834.

"*Colonel Thomas Pitcher; Sir:*—The following is a true copy
of an order from the Governor for our arms. Have the
goodness to return an answer as soon as possible, that we
may know whether we can have the arms upon said order
or not, also when. Send where we can receive them, and
we will appoint an agent to receive and receipt the same.
Be assured we do not wish to obtain them from any hostile
intentions, but merely because the right of property is ours.
If I remember right there is one gun and a sword more than
the order calls for.

"JOHN CORRILL."

—*Times and Seasons*, vol. 6, p. 1123.

Joseph arrived at Kirtland about August 1, 1834, having
been absent three months. He writes:—

"About this time I arrived at Kirtland, after a tedious journey, from the midst of enemies, mobs, cholera, and ex- cessively hot weather, having parted from those whom I started with on the 9th ult., at different points of the journey."

Arrival at Kirtland.

CHAPTER 19.

1834.

IN the absence of Joseph Smith, Sidney Rigdon presided
over the church at Kirtland and took the general oversight
of the affairs of the church. The principal work
to which attention was given was the erection of
the Temple, on which all worked under most adverse circumstances and at great sacrifice.

Rigdon presides at Kirtland.

Heber C. Kimball records in his journal that he returned
from Missouri to Kirtland on July 26, 1834. He then
states:—

"At this time the brethren were laboring night and day
building the house of the Lord. Our women were engaged
in spinning and knitting in order to clothe those who were
laboring at the building, and the Lord only knows the
scenes of poverty, tribulation, and distress which we passed
through in order to accomplish this thing. My wife toiled
all summer in lending her aid towards its accomplishment.
She had a hundred pounds of wool, which, with the assistance of a girl, she spun in order to furnish clothing for
those engaged in the building of the Temple; and although
she had the privilege of keeping half the quantity of wool
for herself, as a recompense for her labor, she did not reserve even so much as would make her a pair of stockings, but
gave it for those who were laboring at the house of the
Lord. She spun and wove, and got the cloth dressed and
cut and made up into garments, and gave them to those men
who labored on the Temple. Almost all the sisters in Kirt-

land labored in knitting, sewing, spinning, etc., for the purpose of forwarding the work of the Lord, while we went up to Missouri to endeavor to reinstate our brethren on their lands, from which they had been driven. Elder Rigdon when addressing the brethren upon the importance of building this house, spake to this effect: that we should use every effort to accomplish this building by the time appointed; and if we did, the Lord would accept it at our hands; and on it depends the salvation of the church and also of the world. Looking at the sufferings and poverty of the church, he frequently used to go upon the walls of the building both by night and day and frequently wetting the walls with his tears, crying aloud to the Almighty to send means whereby we might accomplish the building. After we returned from our journey to the West, the whole church united in this undertaking, and every man lent a helping hand. Those who had ı teams went to work in the stone quarry and prepared the b nes for drawing to the house. President Joseph Smith Jr., being our foreman in the quarry; the Presidency, high priests, and elders all alike assisting. Those who had teams assisted in drawing the stone to the house. These all laboring one day in the week, brought as many stones to the house as supplied the masons through the whole week. We continued in this manner until the walls of the house were reared. The committee who were appointed by revelation to superintend the building of the house were, Hyrum Smith, Reynolds Cahoon, and Jared Carter. These men used every exertion in their power to forward the work."—*Times and Seasons*, vol. 6, pp. 867, 868.

During the summer the *Evening and Morning Star* was Evening and published monthly at Kirtland, by Oliver Cowdery. Morning Star. From the May number we learn of the establishment of branches in the following places: Sugar Creek, Shelby County, Indiana, with nineteen members; Drury Creek, Campbell County, Kentucky, eight members; five or Progress of six small branches in New York; a branch at the church. Freedom, twenty-six members; of seven being baptized at Salisbury, Connecticut. The June number contains notices of conferences to be held at Andover, Vermont,

July 19 and 20; at Benson, Vermont, July 26; and at Bolton, New York, August 2, 1834.

During the summer an attack was made on the faith by Alexander Campbell, through *The Millennial Harbinger,* which was answered by Oliver Cowdery through the *Evening and Morning Star.*

Alexander Campbell.

On August 11, 1834, the High Council of Kirtland met to investigate charges preferred against President Joseph Smith, by Sylvester Smith, a member of the High Council, charging him with "criminal conduct during his journey to and from Missouri." After a lengthy examination, during which several of those who went with him were examined, the council vindicated and exonerated Joseph.

Charges against Joseph Smith.

Notwithstanding this Sylvester Smith continued to assert his complaints, and Sidney Rigdon preferred charges against him before the High Council as follows:—

"*To Newel K. Whitney, Bishop of the Church of Latter Day Saints in Kirtland; Sir:*—I prefer the following charges against Sylvester Smith, a high priest of said church:—

"1st. He has refused to submit to the decision of a council of the high priests and elders of this church, held in this place on the 11th of this month, given in a case of difficulty between said Sylvester Smith and Joseph Smith, Jun.

"2d. He continues to charge said Joseph Smith, contrary to the decision of the before-mentioned council, with improper conduct in his proceedings as President of the Church of the Latter Day Saints, during his journey the past season to the State of Missouri. As these things are exceedingly grievous to many of the saints in Kirtland, and very prejudicial to the cause of truth in general, I therefore require that you summon the High Council of this church, to investigate this case, that a final decision may be had upon the same. I say the High Council, because it is a case affecting the Presidency of said church.

"SIDNEY RIGDON.

"KIRTLAND, Ohio, August 23, 1834."

—Millennial Star, vol. 15, p. 170.

The council met on August 28, 1834, and after a thorough examination rendered a verdict that fully vindicated Pres.-

dent Smith and required his accuser to make public confession of his wrong.

The August number of the *Evening and Morning Star* contains a notice of a conference to be held in Norton, Ohio, and the minutes of a conference held at Saco, Maine. The minutes are as follows:—

Conferences.

"Saco, June 15, 1834.

"*Bro. O. Cowdery:*—I take this opportunity to forward to you the minutes of the conference held in this place on the 13th day of the present month. It was an interesting scene, and no doubt will prove beneficial, and much good proceed from it. The public meeting commenced at half-past ten o'clock; those that stood in defense of the cause of God were blessed with the Spirit, and the people gave good attention. At four o'clock p. m. the elders' conference commenced — the conference came to order, and Jared Carter was chosen moderator. After prayer the conference made choice of Sylvester B. Stoddard, for clerk. It was then moved that the elders present proceed to give an account of themselves and the several churches to which they belonged. They then proceeded, and seventeen branches of the church were represented, and said to be in good standing. Two of the branches represented are located in Pennsylvania, three in the State of New York, and the remaining twelve east of the State of New York. We have also heard of twenty-three branches in York State, and other places east of Ohio, which are not represented in this conference.

"There were many interesting narratives of the travels of the brethren related, which were edifying. Bro. John F. Boynton then addressed the conference. Much instruction was given, and his address very appropriate. The conference then adjourned to seven o'clock a. m. on the next day, when we again met, and after prayer Bro. Jared Carter made known his mission concerning the building of the house of the Lord in Kirtland. By the voice of the conference it was agreed that there should be a contribution. The conference then adjourned till five o'clock p. m., in order to attend public meeting. After the meeting the conference again met, and after prayer proceeded to business. It was then motioned and seconded that the elders, priests, teachers, and deacons in this conference abide by the Word of Wisdom, and passed by a unanimous vote. The subject of ordination then came before the conference, and six were ordained— three to the lesser priesthood, one to the office of a teacher, and two to the office of deacon, which was done in the name of the Lord. The conference then voted to appoint a conference in St. Johnsbury, Vermont, on the 28th day of the present month, and then closed by prayer. On the following day, being the first day of the week, we again repaired to the meetinghouse, where a numerous concourse had assembled to hear the word of the Lord, and God manifested himself to his servants and they were enabled to lay before them the great work of the Lord, and the glory of his kingdom which has been revealed in these last days. The people listened in a very becoming manner, and many were heard to say, 'We have heard the truth to-day;' and according to the appearance much good may proceed from the interview that we have had with the people in this section. There have been several baptized since the commencement of this conference, and some from a distance, who came to investigate the work, have united themselves with the people of God, and have returned with an olive leaf. The Lord has been pleased to manifest himself by accompanying the administration of laying on hands for reception of the Holy Ghost, in a manner convincing to all around, even to those that were not disciples! And as there were many from different parts, it will be likely to make room for the spread of the glorious gospel of Christ, and the upbuilding of his kingdom that he has established in these last days; which may God grant for the Redeemer's sake.

> "I remain yours, etc.,
> "SYLVESTER B. STODDARD,
> "Clerk of Conference."

—Evening and Morning Star, vol. 2, pp. 360, 361.

Joseph writes:—

"The excitement of the people began to repose, and the saints, both in Missouri and Ohio, began to enjoy a little peace. The elders began to go forth, two and two, preaching the word to all that would hear, and many were added to the church monthly.

"September 1, 1834. I continued to preside over the church in Kirtland, and in forwarding the building of the

Work on Temple. house of the Lord. I acted as foreman in the Temple stone quarry, and when other duties would permit, labored with my own hands."—*Millennial Star*, vol. 15, p. 181.

A conference was held September 8, 1834, at New Portage, Ohio, over which Joseph Smith presided and Oliver Cowdery acted as clerk; the business of which, though of local importance, is of little historical value.

The High Council, of Kirtland, convened September 24, 1834, a conference being in session at the same time. At this council Sylvester Smith was dropped from membership

Sylvester Smith. in the High Council, but was permitted to retain his office as a high priest. The President nominated Hyrum Smith to succeed him. This nomination was confirmed both by the council and the conference. Elders John P. Green and Brigham Young were chosen to act as members of the council, pro tem. in the places of Jared Carter and Martin Harris, who were absent.

In this council Elders Joseph Smith, Jr., Oliver Cowdery, Sidney Rigdon, and F. G. Williams were appointed a com-

Committee on doctrine. mittee "to arrange the items of the doctrine of Jesus Christ," for the government of the church; with the provision that, "These items are to be taken from the Bible, Book of Mormon, and the revelations which have been given unto the church, up to this date, or shall be until such arrangements are made." To this committee was intrusted the duty of arranging and publishing the "Book of Covenants."

A resolution was passed providing: "that high priests be

High priest's license ordained hereafter, in the High Council at Kirtland, and receive license, signed by the clerk of the council."

Of the busy events of those times Joseph writes:—

"Great exertions were made to expedite the work of the Lord's house; and notwithstanding it was commenced, as it were, with nothing, as to means, yet the way opened as we proceeded, and the saints rejoiced.

"October.   The former part of October was spent in arranging matters respecting the Lord's house and the printing office; for it had previously been published that the *Evening and Morning Star* would be discontinued, and a new paper, entitled *The Latter Day Saints' Messenger and Advocate*, issued in its place.

Publications.

"Having accomplished all that could be done at present, on the 16th of the month, I, in company with my brother, Hyrum Smith, and Elders David Whitmer, F. G. Williams, Oliver Cowdery, and Roger Orton, left Kirtland for the purpose of visiting some saints in the State of Michigan, where, after a tolerably pleasant journey, we arrived at Pontiac on the 20th.

Visit to Michigan.

"While on our way up the lake, on board the steamer Monroe, Elder Cowdery had a short discourse with a man calling his name Elmer. He said he was 'personally acquainted with Joe Smith;' had 'heard him preach his lies,' and *now 'since he was dead,' 'he was glad!'* He had heard Joe Smith preach in *Bainbridge*, Chenango County, New York, five years since; he knew it to be *him*, that 'he was a *dark complexioned man*,' etc. He appeared to exult the most in that *Joe was dead*, and made his observations in my presence. I concluded he had learned it from the popular priests of the day, who, through fear that their *craft* will be injured, if their systems are compared with the truth, seek to ridicule those that teach it; and thus am I suffering under the tongue of slander, for Christ's sake, unceasingly. God have mercy on such, if they will quit their lying. I need not state my complexion to those that have seen me; and those who have read my history thus far, will recollect that five years ago, I was not a preacher, as Elmer represented; neither was I ever in Bainbridge.

"After preaching, and teaching the saints, as long as our time would allow, we returned to Kirtland, greatly refreshed from our journey, and much pleased with our friends in that section of the Lord's vineyard.

"It now being the last of the month, and the elders beginning to come in, it was necessary to make preparations for

the school for the elders, wherein they might be more
School of
the elders. perfectly instructed in the great things of God, during the coming winter. A building for a printing
office was nearly finished, and the lower story of this building was set apart for that purpose (the school) when it was
completed. So the Lord opened the way according to our
faith and works, and blessed be his name.

"No month ever found me more busily engaged than
November; but as my life consisted of activity and unyield-
ing exertions, I made this my rule: *When the Lord commands,
do it.*"—*Millennial Star*, vol. 15, pp. 183. 184.

The last number of the *Evening and Morning Star* was
Messenger
and Advocate. issued in September, 1834. and it was succeeded
by the *Messenger and Advocate*, the first number
appearing in October, 1834.

Oliver Cowdery, who had been editor of the *Star* since its
removal to Kirtland, was also editor of the *Messenger and Advocate*. In his opening "address" he lays down clearly the
platform upon which he and the people he represents propose to stand, and invites criticism from "men of character
and respectability."[1]

---

[1] That our principles may be fully known we here state them briefly:—
We believe in God, and his Son Jesus Christ. We believe that God,
from the beginning, revealed himself to man; and that whenever he has
had a people on earth, he always has revealed himself to them by the
Holy Ghost, the ministering of angels, or his own voice. We do not believe that he ever had a church on earth without revealing himself to
that church: consequently, there were apostles, prophets, evangelists,
pastors, and teachers, in the same. We believe that God is the same in
all ages; and that it requires the same holiness, purity, and religion, to
save a man *now*, as it did anciently; and that, as he is no respecter of
persons, always has, and always will reveal himself to men when they
call upon him.
We believe that God has revealed himself to men in this age, and con-
menced to raise up a church preparatory to his second advent, when he
will come in the clouds of heaven with power and great glory.
We believe that the popular religious theories of the day are incorrect;
that they are without parallel in the revelations of God, as sanctioned by
him; and that however faithfully they may be adhered to, or however
zealously and warmly they may be defended, they will never stand the
strict scrutiny of the word of life.
We believe that all men are born free and equal; 'that no man, combination of men, or government of men, have power or authority to
compel or force others to embrace any system of religion, or religious
creed, or to use force or violence to prevent others from enjoying their
own opinions, or practicing the same, so long as they do not molest or
disturb others in theirs, in a manner to deprive them of their privileges

In the first number of the *Messenger and Advocate* is a
Sylvester   letter from Sylvester Smith confessing his wrong
Smith's letter. in his difficulty with President Joseph Smith and
fully exonerating President Smith.[2]

as free citizens, or of worshiping God as they choose; and that any attempt to the contrary is an assumption unwarrantable in the revelations
of heaven, and strikes at the root of civil liberty, and is a subversion of
all equitable principles between man and man.

We believe that God has set his hand the second time to recover the
remnant of his people Israel, and that the time is near when he will
bring them from the four winds, with songs of everlasting joy, and reinstate them upon their own lands which he gave their fathers by covenant.

And further: We believe in embracing good wherever it may be found;
of proving all things, and holding fast that which is righteous.

This, in short, is our belief, and we stand ready to defend it upon its
own foundation whenever it is assailed by men of character and respectability. And while we act upon these broad principles, we trust in God
that we shall never be confounded!

Neither shall we wait for opposition; but with a firm reliance upon the
justice of such a course, and the propriety of disseminating a knowledge
of the same, we shall endeavor to persuade men to turn from error and
vain speculation; investigate the plan which heaven has devised for our
salvation; prepare for the year of recompense, and the day of vengeance
which are near, and thereby be ready to meet the Bridegroom!

OLIVER COWDERY.

KIRTLAND, Ohio, October, 1834.

—Messenger and Advocate, vol. 1, p. 2.

[2] *Dear Brother:*—Having heard that certain reports are circulating
abroad, prejudicial to the character of Bro. Joseph Smith, Jr., and that
said reports purport to have come from me, I have thought proper to
give the public a plain statement of the fact concerning this matter. It
is true that some difficulties arose between Bro. J. Smith, Jr., and myself, in our travels the past summer to Missouri; and that on our return
to this place I laid my grievances before a general council, where they
were investigated in full, in an examination which lasted several days;
and the result showed to the satisfaction of all present, I believe, but especially to myself, that in all things Bro. J. S., Jr., had conducted
worthily, and adorned his profession as a man of God, while journeying
to and from Missouri. And it is no more than just that I should confess
my faults by saying unto all people, so far as your valuable and instruct-
ive paper has circulation, that the things that I accused Bro. S. of were
without foundation; as was most clearly proven by the evidence which
was called, to my satisfaction. And in fact, I have not at any time withdrawn my confidence and fellowship from Bro. J. S., Jr., but thought
that he had inadvertently erred, being but flesh and blood, like the rest
of Adam's family. But I am now perfectly satisfied that the errors of
which I accused him, before the council, did not exist, and were never
committed by him; and my contrition has been and still continues to be
deep, because I admitted thoughts into my heart which were not right
concerning him, and because that I have been the means of giving rise
to reports which have gone abroad, censuring the conduct of Bro. J. S.,
Jr., which reports are without foundation. And I hope that this dis-
closure of the truth, written by my own hand, and sent abroad into the
world, through the medium of the *Messenger and Advocate*, will put a

On November 25, 1834, a revelation was given to W. A. Cowdery.[3]

There is, in the December number of the *Messenger and Advocate*, a letter from Joseph Smith which is valuable for two points, at least; namely: It explains what is meant, in the early part of his history, by his reference to many vices and follies of which he was guilty; and second, that he had not claimed to be more than a man subject to error and dependent upon the grace of God.[4]

Joseph Smith's letter.

final end to all evil reports and censurings, which have sprung out of anything that I have said or done.

I wish still further to state, for the better relief of my own feelings, which, you must be sensible, are deeply wounded, in consequence of what has happened, that I know for myself, because I have received testimony from the heavens, that the work of the Lord, brought forth by means of the Book of Mormon, in our day, through the instrumentality of Bro. Joseph Smith, Jr., is eternal truth, and must stand, though the heavens and the earth pass away.

Please give publicity to the above, and oblige a lover of righteousness and truth.

Yours in the testimony of Jesus,

SYLVESTER SMITH.

To O. Cowdery, Kirtland, October 28, 1834.

—*Messenger and Advocate*, vol. 1, pp. 10, 11.

[3] 1. It is my will that my servant, Warren A. Cowdery, should be appointed and ordained a presiding high priest over my church in the land of Freedom, and the regions round about, and should preach my everlasting gospel, and lift up his voice and warn the people, not only in his own place, but in the adjoining countries, and devote his whole time in this high and holy calling which I now give unto him, seeking diligently the kingdom of heaven and its righteousness, and all things necessary shall be added thereunto; for the laborer is worthy of his hire.

2. And again, verily I say unto you, The coming of the Lord draweth nigh, and it overtaketh the world as a thief in the night; therefore, gird up your loins that you may be the children of the light, and that day shall not overtake you as a thief.

3. And again, verily I say unto you, There was joy in heaven when my servant, Warren, bowed to my scepter, and separated himself from the crafts of men; therefore, blessed is my servant, Warren, for I will have mercy on him, and notwithstanding the vanity of his heart, I will lift him up inasmuch as he will humble himself before me; and I will give him grace and assurance wherewith he may stand; and if he continues to be a faithful witness and a light unto the church, I have prepared a crown for him in the mansions of my Father. Even so. Amen.

[4] *Brother O. Cowdery:*—Having learned from the first number of the *Messenger and Advocate* that you were, not only about to "give a history of the rise and progress of the Church of the Latter Day Saints;" but, that said "history would necessarily embrace my life and character." I have been induced to give you the time and place of my birth; as I have learned that many of the opposers of those principles which I have held

This number also contains intelligence from Elders D. W. Patten and W. Parrish that they had opened the work in
<small>Elders' reports</small> Tennessee, were preaching to large congregations, and had baptized seven at Paris. Letters from James Blakeslee, Woodville, New York; D. Nelson and M. Wilbur, Providence, Rhode Island; B. F. Bird, Southport, New York; John Lawson, Kortright, New York; W. A. Cowdery, Freedom, New York; Zerubbabel Snow, Mount Pleasant, Canada; Zebedee Coltrin and N. West, Liberty, Indiana; Abel Allton, Jay, Vermont; and J. H. Hitchcock and S. Chase, Franklin County, Missouri, give encouraging accounts of the spread of the work at that period.

forth to the world profess a personal acquaintance with me, though when in my presence, represent me to be another person in age, education, and stature, from what I am.

I was born, (according to the record of the same, kept by my parents,) in the town of Sharon, Windsor County, Vermont, on the 23d of December, 1805.

At the age of ten my father's family removed to Palmyra, New York, where, and in the vicinity of which, I lived, or made it my place of residence, until I was twenty-one—the latter part, in the town of Manchester.

During this time, as is common to most or all youths, I fell into many vices and follies; but as my accusers are, and have been forward to accuse me of being guilty of gross and outrageous violations of the peace and good order of the community, I take the occasion to remark that, though, as I have said above, "as is common to most, or all youths, I fell into many vices and follies," I have not, neither can it be sustained, in truth, been guilty of wronging or injuring any man or society of men; and those imperfections to which I allude, and for which I have often had occasion to lament, were a light, and too often, vain mind, exhibiting a foolish and trifling conversation.

This being all, and the worst, that my accusers can substantiate against my moral character, I wish to add, that it is not without a deep feeling of regret that I am thus called upon in answer to my own conscience, to fulfill a duty I owe to myself, as well as to the cause of truth, in making this public confession of my former uncircumspect walk, and unchaste conversation: and more particularly, as I often acted in violation of those holy precepts which I knew came from God. But as the "Articles and Covenants" of this church are plain upon this particular point, I do not deem it important to proceed further. I only add that I do not, nor never have, pretended to be any other than a man "subject to passion," and liable, without the assisting grace of the Savior, to deviate from that perfect path in which *all* men are commanded to walk!

By giving the above a place in your valuable paper, you will confer a lasting favor upon myself, as an individual, and, as I humbly hope, subserve the cause of righteousness.

I am, with feelings of esteem, your fellow laborer in the gospel of our Lord,   JOSEPH SMITH, JR.

—Messenger and Advocate, vol. 1, p. 40.

On the 29th of November, 1834, Joseph Smith and Oliver Cowdery made covenant, which will be seen to be quite in A covenant. harmony with the general law of tithing. A few items from the pen of Joseph Smith will be of interest here:—

"On the evening of the 29th of November, I united in prayer with Brother Oliver, for the continuance of blessings. After giving thanks for the relief which the Lord had lately sent us by opening the hearts of the brethren from the east, to loan us four hundred and thirty dollars; after commencing and rejoicing before the Lord on this occasion, we agreed to enter into the following covenant with the Lord; viz.:—

"'That if the Lord will prosper us in our business, and open the way before us, that we may obtain means to pay our debts, that we be not troubled nor brought into disrepute before the world, nor his people; after that, of all that he shall give us, we will give a tenth, to be bestowed upon the poor in his church, or as he shall command; and that we will be faithful over that which he has intrusted to our care, that we may obtain much; and that our children after us, shall remember to observe this sacred and holy covenant; and that our children, and our children's children. may know of the same, we have subscribed our names with our own hands.

" 'JOSEPH SMITH, JR.
" 'OLIVER COWDERY.

"'And now, O Father, as thou didst prosper our father Jacob, and bless him with protection and prosperity wherever he went, from the time he made a like covenant before and with thee; as thou didst, even the same night, open the heavens unto him, and manifest great mercy and power, and give him promises, so wilt thou do with us his sons; and as his blessings prevailed above his progenitors unto the utmost bounds of the everlasting hills, even so may our blessings prevail like his; and may thy servants be preserved from the power and influence of wicked and unrighteous men; may every weapon formed against us fall upon the head of him who shall form it; may we be blessed with a name and a place among thy saints here, and thy sanctified when they shall rest. Amen.'

"While reflecting upon the goodness and mercy of God this evening (November 30) a prophecy was put into our hearts, that in a short time the Lord would arrange his providences in a merciful manner, and send us assistance to deliver us from debt and bondage.

"December 1. Our school for the elders was now well attended, and with the lectures on theology, which were regularly delivered, absorbed for the time being everything else of a temporal nature. The classes being mostly elders, gave the most studious attention to the all-important object of qualifying themselves, as messengers of Jesus Christ, to be ready to do his will in carrying glad tidings to all that would open their eyes, ears, and hearts."—*Millennial Star*, vol. 15, pp. 203, 204.

Thus ended the year 1834 in Kirtland; the Temple building in progress and a special effort being made to complete it; the elders striving to qualify themselves for greater usefulness; while cheering news was reaching them from many places.

CHAPTER 20.

1834.

AFTER the departure of Joseph from Clay County, Missouri, on June 9, 1834, the church in Missouri continued its exertions to obtain a recognition of its rights.

On July 12, 1834, and also on the 31st, the High Council in Zion held meetings. [1]

---

[1] On the 12th, the High Council of Zion assembled in Clay County, and appointed Edward Partridge, Orson Pratt, Isaac Morley, and Zebedee Coltrin to visit the scattered and afflicted brethren in that region, and teach them the ways of truth and holiness, and set them in order according as the Lord should direct; but, that it was not wisdom for the elders generally to hold public meetings in that region. It was decided that Amasa Lyman assist Lyman Wight in his mission, of gathering the strength of the Lord's house, as I had appointed him.

July 31. The High Council of Zion assembled, and heard the report of Edward Partridge, Orson Pratt, Zebedee Coltrin, and Isaac Morley, concerning the mission appointed them at the previous council. President David Whitmer gave the council some good instructions; that it was their duty to transact all business in order, and when any case is brought forward for investigation, every member should be attentive and patient to what is passing, in all cases, and avoid confusion and contention, which is offensive in the sight of the Lord. He also addressed the elders, and said it was not pleasing in the sight of the Lord for any man to go forth to preach the gospel of peace unless he is qualified to set forth its principles in plainness to those he endeavors to instruct; and also the rules and regulations of the Church of Latter Day Saints; for just as a man is, and as he teaches and acts, so will his followers be, let them be ever so full of notions and whims. He also addressed the congregation, and told them that it was not wisdom for the brethren to vote at the approaching election, and the council acquiesced in the instructions of the President.

William W. Phelps proposed to the council to appoint a certain number of elders to hold public meetings in that section of country, as often as should be deemed necessary, to teach the disciples how to escape the indignation of their enemies, and keep in favor with those who were friendly disposed; and Simeon Carter, John Corrill, Parley P. Pratt, and Orson Pratt were appointed by the unanimous voice of the council and congregation to fill the mission.

The council gave the following letter to the elders appointed to visit the churches in Clay County, etc.:—

"To the Latter Day Saints who have been driven from the land of

By these minutes it appears that the church was desirous for peace, and to preserve it they were willing even to sacrifice for the time rights sacred and dear to every American citizen. The council advised refraining from holding public meetings, and counseled members of the church not to vote at the approaching election. What more could have been required of them? Could this have been required of them in any degree of propriety? Reader, if disposed to censure, ask yourself, "Would I have yielded this right for the sake of peace?"

On August 6, 1834, the High Council met to investigate the case of strange spiritual manifestations in the Hulet
Spiritual   branch. This was a case that caused much local
man festations agitation, but it is of no historical consequence.
It was satisfactorily adjusted by the council.

Thus matters passed along without much friction between the opposing elements for a few months.

During the time W. W. Phelps wrote a series of letters
Phelps' letter.   from Missouri to Kirtland. By reference to an
              extract from one of them the reader may obtain

their inheritance, and also those who are gathering in the regions round about, in the western boundaries of Missouri: The High Council established according to the pattern given by our blessed Savior Jesus Christ, sends greeting:—

"*Dear Brethren:*—We have appointed our beloved brother and companion in tribulation, John Corrill, to meet you in the name of the Lord Jesus. He, in connection with others duly appointed also, will visit you alternately, for the purpose of instructing you in the necessary qualifications of the Latter Day Saints; that they may be perfected, that the officers and members of the body of Christ may become very prayerful and very faithful, strictly keeping the commandments and walking in holiness before the Lord continually; that those that mean to have the 'destroyer pass over them, as the children of Israel, and not slay them,' may live according to the 'Word of Wisdom;' that the saints by industry, diligence, faithfulness, and the prayer of faith, may become purified, and enter upon their inheritance to build up Zion according to the word of the Lord.

"We are sure, if the saints are very humble, very watchful, and very prayerful, that few will be deceived by those who have not authority to teach, or who have not the spirit to teach according to the power of the Holy Ghost, in the Scriptures. Lest any man's blood be required at your hands, we beseech you, as you value the salvation of souls, and are within, to set an example worthy to be followed by those without the kingdom of our God and his Christ, that peace by grace, and blessings by righteousness, may attend you, till you are sanctified and redeemed. "Dated, Clay County, Aug. 1, 1834."

—*Times and Seasons*, vol. 6, pp. 1123, 1124.

an idea of the condition of the country and the situation of the people in Missouri.[2]

[2] But lest I become irksome on too many things at once, let me turn to some of the advantages and disadvantages which are natural to the land as it is. It is a great advantage to have land already cleared to your hands, as the prairies are; and there is no small disadvantage to lack timber for fencing, fuel, and buildings. Notwithstanding there are many good springs of water, yet there is a want upon the prairies in some places; and, generally, water privileges for grist and saw mills, and carding machines and clothiers' works are scarce. That patriotism, which results in good roads and bridges, labor-saving machines, and excellent mills, is yet dormant. I do not know of a clothier's works in the upper or lower country. It costs one fourth or one fifth of our grain to grind it. Run-round horse mills, or those on the inclined plane order, for horses and oxen, are all the dependence at present. There is a small steam saw and grist mill, of about ten horse power engine, in Clay; a steam saw mill at Lexington, and a flouring mill nearly finished, on the Little Blue, in Jackson. It may be supposed, in those States where negroes do the work, that they can saw boards with a whip saw, and drive team to grind in an animal power mill.

Let it be remembered that the most of the land is free from stones, even too much so, for, excepting limestone, in some places, there are very few if any for use. But suffice it to be that with all the lacks and inconveniences now extant, grain is raised so easy that a man may live as well on three days' work in a week here as on six in some other distant places. It is not uncommon for wheat, when ripe, to be let to cut and thresh at the half. Corn at twenty cents per bushel, and wheat at forty, are, however, the lowest selling prices latterly; and I conclude that from the great quantity of corn and wheat, or flour, necessary to supply the garrison, it will never be lower. So much on things as they naturally are.

Now with all the country has, and all it has not, without witty inventions, let us reflect that God has made and prepared it for the use of his people, like all the rest of the world, with good and bad to try them. Here are wanting many things to expedite ease and opulence. Here sickness comes, and where does it not? The ague and fever: the chill fever, a kind of cold plague, and other diseases, prey upon emigrants till they are thoroughly seasoned to the climate. Here death puts an end to life, and so it does all over the globe. Here the poor have to labor to procure a living, and so they do anywhere else. Here the saints suffer trials and tribulations, while the wicked enjoy the world and rejoice, and so it has been since Cain built a city for the ungodly to revel in.

But it is all right, and I thank God that it is so. The wicked enjoy this world and the saints the next. They exercise their agency, and the saints theirs, are left to choose for themselves; and blessed be God that it is so, for it saves heaven from torment and righteousness from blemishes.

The lacks that seem most prominent will soon sink with the fading glories of perishable things; and then the banks of long continuance will be thrown down, and the rough places made smooth; yea, the glory of Lebanon will come upon the land of the Lord, the fir tree, the pine tree, and the box together to beautify the place of his sanctuary, and make the place of his feet glorious. Then there will be a river of pure water to gladden the soul of the saint. Then every man will speak in the name of God. Then the righteous will feed themselves on the finest of wheat. Then the enmity of man and the enmity of beasts will cease. Then the vail spread over all nations, will be taken off and the pure in heart see

November 25, 1834, Hon. J. T. V. Thompson, a Missouri State Senator, wrote W. W. Phelps as follows:—

"JEFFERSON CITY.

"*Dear Sir:*—I will say to you, that your case with the Jackson people has been mentioned to the highest officer of Thompson's the State, the Governor. He speaks of it in his letter. message and so much of his message will be referred to a committee. I am not able to s iy what will be their report, but I will write you again.

"I have the honor, etc.

"J. T. V. THOMPSON."

—*Millennial Star*, vol. 15, p. 185.

The extract from Governor Dunklin's message referred to in the above letter is as follows:—

"In July, 1833, a large portion of the citizens of Jackson County organized themselves and entered into resolutions to Dunklin's expel from that county a religious sect called Mor-message. mons, who had become obnoxious to them. In November following they effected their object, not however without the loss of several lives. In the judicial inquiry into these outrages, the civil authorities who had cognizance of them deemed it proper to have a military guard for the

God in his glory. Then for brass the Lord will bring gold, and for iron silver, and for wood brass. Then the saints' officers will be peace, and their exactors righteousness: and then the land will be worth possessing and the world fit to live in.

With all these glories ahead, who would fail to seek them? Who would idle or revel away a few years of fleshly gratification, and lose a thousand years' happiness, and an eternity of glory? Who would serve the Devil to be a demon in darkness, when by pleasing the Savior and keeping his commandments he may be a son of God in the celestial world, where praise, and glory, and power, and dominion have an eternal now for space and duration, and the best from worlds to expand and beautify their sublimity? O that the whole empire of God might shout, None! But it will not be so, for Satan spreads himself and copes with thousands that must welter in woe unutterable, where their worm dieth not and the fire is not quenched. Alas, alas, alas, for their fate! Who knows it?

Men of God, from this let us learn to take oil in our lamps from the great Spirit-fountain above, and light them in the blaze of that noble fire, where a Hancock, a Jefferson, and a Washington lit their tapers, that while there is a hope in heaven, or a gleam on earth, we may not covet this world, nor fear death, but, as Peter, as Paul, as James, die for the sake of righteousness, having fought the good fight, and overcome through grace: Amen.   As ever,

W. W. PHELPS.

To Oliver Cowdery, Esq.

purpose of giving protection during the progress of the trials. This was ordered, and the Attorney General was requested to give his attention during the investigation, both of which were performed, but all to no purpose. As yet none have been punished for these outrages, and it is believed that under our present laws conviction for any violence committed upon a Mormon cannot be had in Jackson County. These unfortunate people are now forbidden to take possession of their homes; and the principal part of them, I am informed, are at this time living in an adjoining county, in a great measure, upon the charity of its citizens. It is for you to determine what amendments the laws may require so as to guard against such acts of violence for the future."— *Messenger and Advocate*, vol. 1, p. 41.

On December 11, W. W. Phelps wrote Hon. J. T. V. Thompson in answer to his of November 25, and received answer from Messrs. Thompson and Atchison. Of this and the closing scenes of the year Joseph writes:—

Phelps to Thompson.

"On the 11th Elder Phelps wrote from Liberty, Clay County, to J. T. V. Thompson, Jefferson City—in reply to his letter of the 25th November—expressive of thankfulness to His Excellency for introducing the sufferings of the saints in his message; also asking counsel 'whether it would avail anything for the society to petition his honorable body (the Legislature) for an act to reinstate them in their rights,' etc.; and requesting him to confer with his friends and His Excellency on the subject, and give an early answer.

"About the middle of the month the message of Governor Dunklin, of Missouri, to the Legislature, arrived at Kirtland, was read with great interest, and revived the hopes of the church for the scattered brethren of Jackson County.

"Elder Phelps wrote again to Esquire Thompson, on the 18th, as follows:—

"'*Dear Sir:*—By this mail I have forwarded to Captain Atchison, of the Lower House, a petition and documents, on the subject of our rights in Jackson County. He will hand them to you for the Senate, when through in the House. I shall be greatly obliged if you will lay them before your

honorable body; and any information you may require, or
even personal attendance, write, and you shall have it if in
my power.   As a people, all we ask, is our rights.

" 'With esteem, etc.,

" 'W. W. Phelps.'

'On the 20th Messrs. Thompson and Atchison wrote Elder
Phelp3 from the 'Senate Chamber,' acknowledging the
Thompson's   receipt of his letter, stating that the committee on
reply.   the Governor's message had not reported, and
recommending the saints to get up a petition to the legislature, with as many signatures as possible, promising their
assistance and influence to obtain redress of grievance.   A
petition was accordingly forwarded; but, without bringing
anything to pass for the relief of the saints in Missouri, the
year closed."—*Millennial Star*, vol. 15, p. 204.

CHAPTER 21.

1835.

In the early part of the year 1835 some very important
events transpired in the church at Kirtland. The organization of the Quorum of Twelve Apostles, and of the
Quorum of Seventy as auxiliaries to them in their
work, is of very great importance in the history of the church.
The events of the first two or three months of 1835 are given
quite fully in the history of Joseph Smith as published in
the *Millennial Star*, volume 15. We will give our readers
the benefit of this account copied from that journal.

We think, however, that it is our duty to record the fact
that the *Messenger and Advocate*, published monthly during
the same period of time, at Kirtland, Ohio, by F. G. Williams
and Company, and edited by Oliver Cowdery, makes no mention of these events. It is strange that a church periodical
published at the same place, and edited by one of the principal actors, should not have mentioned events of so much
importance.

There is no question but that such quorums were organized about that time, and from corroborative testimony we
think they were organized at the *place* and *dates* given in this
account; though as it was not published until nearly nine
years after the death of Joseph Smith, we think it possible
that the details were enlarged upon; nor can we vouch for
the absolute correctness of all the teachings here recorded,
though in the main we think them correct.

It will be seen that the following testimony by H. C.
Kimball correspond with the history as published. Kimball in his journal writes:—

"Most of us continued about six weeks, when a meeting
was called for the camp of Zion to be assembled, to receive
what was called a Zion's blessing. After being assembled,
the Presidency having duly organized the meeting, told us
there were twelve men to be chosen, to be called the Twelve
Apostles or Traveling High Council. . . .

"It was far from my expectation of being one of the number,
as heretofore I had known nothing about it, not having had
the privilege of seeing the revelations, as they were not
printed. I will now mention their names as they were first
chosen: Lyman Johnson, Brigham Young, Heber C. Kimball, David W. Patten, Luke Johnson, William E. McLellin,
Orson Hyde, William Smith, John F. Boynton, Orson Pratt,
Thomas B. Marsh, and Parley P. Pratt. After having expressed our feelings on this occasion, we were severally
called into the stand, and there received our ordinations,
under the hands of Oliver Cowdery, David Whitmer, and
Martin Harris. These brethren ordained us to the apostleship, and predicted many things which should come to pass,
that we should have power to heal the sick, cast out devils,
raise the dead, give sight to the blind, have power to remove
mountains, and all things should be subject to us through
the name of Jesus Christ, and angels should minister unto
us, and many more things too numerous to mention. After
we had been thus ordained by these brethren, the First
Presidency laid their hands on us, and confirmed these blessings and ordination, and likewise predicted many things
which should come to pass.

"After being chosen there being but nine of us present,
we assembled from time to time as opportunity would permit, and received such instruction as the Lord would bestow
upon us, and truly he blessed us with his Spirit, and inspired his prophet to speak for our edification. One evening when we were assembled to receive instruction, the
revelation contained in the third section of the Book of Doctrine and Covenants, on Priesthood, was given to Brother

Joseph as he was instructing us, and we praised the Lord."
— *Times and Seasons*, vol. 6, pp. 868, 869.

The March number of the *Messenger and Advocate* contains
the minutes of "a council;" and though it is not stated to be
_{Corroborative evidence.} a council of the Twelve, it is signed by Orson
Hyde and William E. McLellin, who, according to
the account, were chosen clerks by the council.[1]

There is also a communication in the May number, from
Westfield, signed by Elders Hyde and McLellin, and dated
May 12, in which occurs the statement: "Elder Marsh, our
presiding elder." And this also: "The conference continued
until about two o'clock p. m. and then adjourned until three
o'clock, when public preaching commenced by Elder B.
Young, and followed by the farewell exhortation of the
Twelve." (*Messenger and Advocate*, vol. 1, pp. 115, 116.)

From the above corroborative statements we feel safe in
presenting the following from the *Star* as the history of the
events of the times:—

"During the month of January, I was engaged in the
school of the elders, and in preparing the Lectures on the-
_{Lectures.} ology for publication in the Book of Doctrine and
Covenants, which the committee appointed last
September were now compiling.

"Certain brethren from Bolton, New York, came for coun-

---

[1] KIRTLAND, March 8, 1835.

Bro. O. Cowdery:—A council being called this evening to take into
consideration the many pressing requests from the eastern churches for
conferences to be held among them during the present year, it was
unanimously resolved that conferences should be held in the following
places to be attended by the traveling elders from Kirtland; viz.: In
Westfield, Chautauqua County, New York, May 9, 1835; in Freedom,
Cattaraugus County, New York, May 22; in Lyonstown, Wayne County,
New York, June 5; at Pillow Point, Jefferson County, New York, June
19; in West Loborough, near Kingston, Upper Canada, June 29; in Johnsbury, Vermont, July 17; in Bradford, Massachusetts, August 7; in Dover,
New Hampshire, September 4; in Saco, Maine, September 18; and in
Farmington, Maine, October 2, 1835, etc., etc.

The brethren in various churches and places mentioned above may
expect public preaching on the two days following each conference, and
they are requested to see that the appointments are made at the most
convenient houses. This we leave for them to do for their own convenience. All the elders within reasonable bounds of these conferences are
requested to attend them, and it will be their duty so to do.

ORSON HYDE,   }
W. E. McLELLIN, } Clerks.

—*Messenger and Advocate*, vol. 1, p. 90.

sel, relative to their proceeding to the West; and the High

Advice to
Tanner.
Council assembled on the 18th. After a long investigation, I decided that Elder Tanner assist with his might to build up the cause by tarrying in Kirtland; which decision received the unanimous vote of the Council.

"The school still continued, and arrangements were also made, according to the revelation of June, 1829, for choosing 'the Twelve' to be especial messengers to bear the gospel among all nations.

"On the Sabbath previous to the 14th of February, Brothers Joseph and Brigham Young came to my house after meeting, and sung for me; the Spirit of the Lord was poured out upon us, and I told them I wanted to see those brethren together, who went up to Zion in the camp, the previous summer, for I had a blessing for them; and a meeting was notified, of which the following are the minutes:—

" 'Kirtland, February 14, 1835. This day, a meeting was called of those who journeyed to Zion for the purpose of lay-

Camp
of Zion.
ing the foundation of its redemption, last season, together with as many others of the brethren and sisters as were disposed to attend.

" 'President Joseph Smith, Jun., presiding, read the fifteenth chapter of John, and said: "Let us endeavor to solemnize our minds that we may receive a blessing, by calling on the Lord." After an appropriate and affecting prayer the brethren who went to Zion were requested to take their seats together in a part of the house by themselves.

" 'President Smith then stated that the meeting had been called, because God had commanded it; and it was made known to him by vision and by the Holy Spirit. . . .

" 'The President also said many things; such as the weak things, even the smallest and weakest among us, shall be powerful and mighty, and great things shall be accomplished by you from this hour; and you shall begin to feel the whisperings of the Spirit of God; and the work of God shall begin to break forth from this time; and you shall be endowed with power from on high.

" 'President Smith then called upon all those who went to Zion, if they were agreed with him in the statement which

he had made, to arise; and they all arose and stood upon their feet.

" 'He then called upon the remainder of the congregation, to know if they also sanctioned the movements, and they all raised the right hand. . . .

" 'President Joseph Smith, Jr., after making many remarks on the subject of choosing the Twelve, wanted an expression from the brethren, if they would be satisfied to have the Spirit of the Lord dictate in the choice of the elders to be apostles; whereupon all the elders present expressed their anxious desire to have it so.

" 'A hymn was then sung, "Hark, listen to the trumpeters," etc. President Hyrum Smith prayed, and meeting was dismissed for one hour.

" 'Assembled pursuant to adjournment, and commenced with prayer.

" 'President Joseph Smith, Jr., said that the first business Choosing of the meeting was, for the three witnesses of the the Twelve. Book of Mormon, to pray, each one, and then proceed to choose twelve men from the church, as apostles, to go to all nations, kindreds, tongues, and people.

" 'The three witnesses; viz., Oliver Cowdery, David Whitmer, and Martin Harris, united in prayer.

" 'These three witnesses were then blessed by the laying on of the hands of the Presidency.

" 'The witnesses then, according to a former commandment, proceeded to make choice of the Twelve. Their names are as follows:—

1. Lyman E. Johnson.	7. William E. McLellin.
2. Brigham Young.	8. John F. Boynton.
3. Heber C. Kimball.	9. Orson Pratt.
4. Orson Hyde.	10. William Smith.
5. David W. Patten.	11. Thomas B. Marsh.
6. Luke Johnson.	12. Parley P. Pratt.

" 'Lyman E. Johnson, Brigham Young, and Heber C. Kimball came forward; and the three witnesses laid their hands upon each one's head and prayed, separately. . . .

" 'A hymn was then sung, "Glorious things of thee are spoken," etc.; and the congregation dismissed by President Joseph Smith, Jr.

" 'Sunday, February 15, the congregation again assembled.

" 'President Cowdery made some observations upon the nature of the meetings, calling upon the Lord for his assistance. . . .

" 'President Cowdery then called forward Orson Hyde, David W. Patten, and Luke Johnson, and proceeded to their ordinations and blessings. [Also those of McLellin, Boynton, and William Smith.] . . .

" 'Kirtland, February 21, 1835. Pursuant to adjournment a meeting of the church was held; and, after prayer by President David Whitmer, and a short address by President Oliver Cowdery to the congregation, Elder Parley P. Pratt was called to the stand, and ordained one of the Twelve, by President Joseph Smith, Jr., David Whitmer, and Oliver Cowdery. . . .

" 'Thomas B. Marsh and Orson Pratt were absent on a mission.

" 'Elder Marsh returned to Kirtland on the 25th of April, and Elder Pratt on the 26th, and received their ordinations and blessing. . . .

" 'The following charge was given to the Twelve by President O. Cowdery: Dear brethren, previous to delivering the charge, I shall read a part of a revelation. It is known to you that previous to the organizing of this church in 1830 the Lord gave revelations, or the church could not have been organized. The people of this church were weak in faith compared with the ancients. Those who embarked in this cause were desirous to know how the work was to be conducted. They read many things in the Book of Mormon, concerning their duty, and the way the great work ought to be done; but the minds of men are so constructed that they will not believe without a testimony of seeing or hearing. The Lord gave us a revelation that in process of time, there should be twelve men chosen to preach his gospel to Jew and Gentile. Our minds have been on a constant stretch, to find who these twelve were: when the time should come we could not tell; but we sought the Lord by fasting and prayer, to have our lives prolonged to see this

Charge to the Twelve.

day, to see you, and to take a retrospect of the difficulties through which we have passed; but, having seen the day, it becomes my duty to deliver to you a charge; and first, a few remarks respecting your ministry. You have many revelations put into your hands; revelations to make you acquainted with the nature of your mission: you will have difficulties by reason of your visiting all the nations of the world. You will need wisdom in a tenfold proportion to what you have ever had; you will have to combat all the prejudices of all nations.

"'He then read the revelation, and said: Have you desired this ministry with all your hearts? If you have desired it you are called of God, not of man, to go into all the world.

"'He then read again, from the revelation, what the Lord said to the Twelve. Brethren, you have your duty presented in this revelation. You have been ordained to the holy priesthood, you have received it from those who have their power and authority from an angel; you are to preach the gospel to every nation. Should you in the least degree come short of your duty, great will be your condemnation; for the greater the calling the greater the transgression. I there-fore warn you to cultivate great humility; for I know the pride of the human heart. Beware lest 'the flatterers of the world lift you up; beware lest your affections are captivated by worldly objects. Let your ministry be first. Remember, the souls of men are committed to your charge; and if you mind your calling, you shall always prosper.

"'You have been indebted to other men, in the first in-stance, for evidence; on that you have acted; but it is neces-sary that you receive a testimony from heaven for yourselves; so that you can bear testimony to the truth of the Book of Mormon, and that you have seen the face of God. That is more than the testimony of an angel. When the proper time arrives you shall be able to bear this testimony to the world. When you bear testimony that you have seen God, this testimony God will never suffer to fall, but will bear you out; although many will not give heed, yet others will. You will therefore see the necessity of getting this testimony from heaven.

" 'Never cease striving till you have seen God, face to face. Strengthen your faith; cast off your doubts, your sins, and all your unbelief; and nothing can prevent you from coming to God. Your ordination is not full and complete till God has laid his hands upon you. We require as much to qualify us as did those who have gone before us; God is the same. If the Savior in former days laid his hands on his disciples, why not in latter days?

" 'With regard to superiority I must make a few remarks. The ancient apostles sought to be great; but lest the seeds of discord be sown in this matter, understand particularly the voice of the Spirit on this occasion. God does not love you better or more than others. You are to contend for the faith once delivered to the saints. Jacob, you know, wrestled till he obtained. It was by fervent prayer and diligent search that you have obtained the testimony you are now able to bear. You are as one; you are equal in bearing the keys of the kingdom to all nations. You are called to preach the gospel of the Son of God to the nations of the earth; it is the will of your heavenly Father, that you proclaim his gospel to the ends of the earth, and the islands of the sea.

" 'Be zealous to save souls. The soul of one man is as precious as the soul of another. You are to bear this message to those who consider themselves wise: and such may persecute you; they may seek your life. The adversary has always sought the life of the servants of God; you are therefore to be prepared at all times to make a sacrifice of your lives, should God require them in the advancement and building up of his cause. Murmur not at God. Be always prayerful; be always watchful. You will bear with me while I relieve the feelings of my heart. We shall not see another day like this; the time has fully come, the voice of the Spirit has come, to set these men apart.

" 'You will see the time when you will desire to see such a day as this, and you will not see it. Every heart wishes you peace and prosperity, but the scene with you will inevitably change. Let no man take your bishopric; and beware that you lose not your crowns. It will require your whole souls, it will require courage like Enoch's.

" 'The time is near when you will be in the midst of congregations who will gnash their teeth upon you. This gospel must roll, and will roll until it fills the whole earth. Did I say congregations would gnash upon you? Yea, I say nations will gnash upon you; you will be considered the worst of men. Be not discouraged at this. When God pours out his Spirit, the enemy will rage; but God, remember, is on your right hand and on your left. A man, though he be considered the worst, has joy, who is conscious that he pleases God. The lives of those who proclaim the true gospel will be in danger; this has been the case ever since the days of righteous Abel. The same opposition has been manifest whenever men came forward to publish the gospel. The time is coming when you will be considered the worst, by many, and by some the best of men. The time is coming when you will be perfectly familiar with the things of God. This testimony will make those who do not believe your testimony seek your lives; but there are whole nations who will receive your testimony. They will call you good men. Be not lifted up when you are called good men. Remember you are young men, and you shall be spared. I include the other three. Bear them in mind in your prayers; carry their cases to a throne of grace; although they are not present, yet you and they are equal. This appointment is calculated to create an affection in you for each other, stronger than death. You will travel to other nations; bear each other in mind. If one, or more, is cast into prisons, let the others pray for him, and deliver him by their prayers; your lives shall be in great jeopardy; but the promise of God is that you shall be delivered.

" 'Remember you are not to go to other nations till you receive your endowment. Tarry at Kirtland until you are endowed with power from on high. You need a fountain of wisdom, knowledge, and intelligence, such as you never had. Relative to the endowment, I make a remark or two, that there be no mistake. The world cannot receive the things of God. He can endow you without worldly pomp or great parade. He can give you that wisdom, that intelligence, and that power, which characterized the ancient saints, and now characterizes the inhabitants of the upper world. The greatness of your commission consists in this: you are to hold the keys of this ministry; you are to go to the nations afar off, nations that sit in darkness. The day is coming when the work of God must be done. Israel shall be gathered. The seed of Jacob shall be gathered from their long dispersion. There will be a feast to Israel the elect of God. It is a sorrowful tale, but the gospel must be preached, and God's ministers be rejected; but where can Israel be found and receive your testimony, and not rejoice? Nowhere! The prophecies are full of great things that are to take place in the last days. After the elect are gathered out, destructions shall come on the inhabitants of the earth; all nations shall feel the wrath of God, after they have been warned by the saints of the Most High. If you will not warn them, others will, and you will lose your crowns.

"'You must prepare your minds to bid a long farewell to Kirtland, even till the great day come. You will see what you never expected to see; you will need the mind of Enoch or Elijah, and the faith of the brother of Jared; you must be prepared to walk by faith, however appalling the prospect to human view; you and each of you should feel the force of the imperious mandate, Son, go labor in my vineyard, and cheerfully receive what comes; but in the end you will stand while others will fall. You have read in the revelation concerning ordination: Beware how you ordain, for all nations are not like this nation; they will willingly receive the ordinances at your hands to put you out of the way. There will be times when nothing but the angels of God can deliver you out of their hands.

"'We appeal to your intelligence, we appeal to your understanding, that we have so far discharged our duty to you. We consider it one of the greatest condescensions of our heavenly Father, in pointing you out to us; you will be stewards over this ministry; you have a work to do that no other men can do; you must proclaim the gospel in its simplicity and purity: and we commend you to God and the word of his grace. You have our best wishes; you have our most fervent prayers, that you may be able to bear this testimony, that you have seen the face of God. Therefore, call upon him in faith and mighty prayer till you prevail; for it is your duty and your privilege to bear such testimony for yourselves. We now exhort you to be faithful to fulfill your calling; there must be no lack here; you must fulfill in all things: and permit us to repeat, all nations have a claim on you; you are bound together as the three witnesses were; you, notwithstanding, can part and meet, and meet and part again, till your heads are silvered over with age.

" 'He then took them separately by the hand, and said, Do you with full purpose of heart take part in this ministry, to proclaim the gospel with all diligence, with these your brethren, according to the tenor and intent of the charge you have received? Each of whom answered in the affirmative.

" 'KIRTLAND, February 27.

" 'This evening, nine of the Twelve; viz., Lyman Johnson, Brigham Young, Heber C. Kimball, Orson Hyde, David W. Patten, Luke Johnson, William E. McLellin, John F. Boynton, and William Smith, assembled at the house of President Joseph Smith, Jr., who was present, with Frederick G. Williams, Sidney Rigdon, Bishop Whitney, and three elders. Parley P. Pratt had gone to New Portage, and Orson Pratt and Thomas B. Marsh had not yet arrived to receive their ordination.

A council.

" 'After prayer by President Joseph Smith, Jr., he said if he were heard patiently he could lay before the council an item which would be of importance. He had for himself learned a fact, by experience, which, on reflection, always gave him deep sorrow. It is a fact, if I now had in my possession, every decision which has been had upon important items of doctrine and duties, since the commencement of this work, I would not part with them for any sum of money; but we have neglected to take minutes of such things, thinking, perhaps, that they would never benefit us afterwards; which, had we now, would decide almost every point of doctrine which might be agitated. But this has been neglected, and now we cannot bear record to the church and to the world of the great and glorious manifestations which have been made to us, with that degree of power and authority we otherwise could if we now had these things to publish abroad.

" 'Since the Twelve are now chosen, I wish to tell them a course which they may pursue, and be benefited hereafter, in a point of light of which they are not now aware. If they will, on every time they assemble, appoint a person to preside over them during the meeting, and one or more to keep a record of their proceedings, and on the decision of every question or item, be it what it may, let such decision be written; and such decision will forever remain upon record, and appear an item of covenant or doctrine. An item thus decided may appear, at the time, of little or no worth; but, should it be published, and one of you lay hands on it after, you will find it of infinite worth, not only to your brethren, but it will be a feast to your own souls.

" 'Here is another important item. If you assemble from time to time, and proceed to discuss important questions, and pass decisions upon the same, and fail to note them down, by and by you will be driven to straits from which you will not be able to extricate yourselves, because you may be in a situation not to bring your faith to bear with sufficient perfection or power to obtain the desired information; or, perhaps, for neglecting to write these things when God revealed them, not esteeming them of sufficient worth, the Spirit may withdraw, and God may be angry; and here is, or was, a vast knowledge of infinite importance which is now lost. What was the cause of this? It came in consequence of slothfulness, or a neglect to appoint a man to occupy a few moments in writing all these decisions. Here let me prophesy. The time will come when, if you neglect to do this thing, you will fall by the hands of unrighteous men. Were you to be brought before the authorities, and be accused of any crime or misdemeanor, and be as innocent as the angels of God, unless you can prove yourselves to have been somewhere else, your enemies will prevail over you; but, if you can bring twelve men to testify that you were in a certain place, at that time, you will escape their hands. Now, if you will be careful to keep minutes of these things, as I have said, it will be one of the most important records ever seen, for every such decision will ever after remain as items of doctrine and covenants.

" 'The council then expressed their approbation concerning the foregoing remarks of President Smith, and appointed Orson Hyde and William E. McLellin clerks for the meeting.

" 'President Smith proposed the following question: What importance is there attached to the calling of these Twelve Apostles, different from the other callings or officers of the church?

" 'After the question was discussed by Counselors Patten, Young, Smith, and McLellin, President Joseph Smith, Jr., gave the following decision:—

" 'They are the Twelve Apostles, who are called to the office of Traveling High Council, who are to preside over all the churches of the saints, among the Gentiles, where there is a Presidency established; and they are to travel and preach among the Gentiles, until the Lord shall command them to go to the Jews. They are to hold the keys of this ministry, to unlock the door of the kingdom of heaven unto all nations, and to preach the gospel to every creature. This is the power, authority, and virtue of their apostleships. " 'Oliver Cowdery, Clerk.'

"On the 28th, the church in council assembled, commenced selecting certain individuals from the number of those who went up to Zion with me, in the camp; and the following are the names of those who were ordained and blessed at that time, to begin the organization of the First Quorum of the Seventies, according to the visions and revelations which I have received; the Seventies to constitute Traveling Quorums, to go into all the earth, whithersoever the Twelve Apostles should call them:—

Choosing the seventy.

Hiram Winters,	Lorenzo Booth,	John D. Parker,
Elias Hutchins,	Zera S. Cole,	Daniel Stearns,
Henry Shibley,	Leonard Rich,	Hiram Stratton,
Roger Orton,	Harrison Burgess,	Sylvester Smith,
J. B. Smith,	Alden Burdick,	William Pratt,
Harvey Stanley,	William F. Cahoon,	Ezra Thayre,
Jedediah M. Grant,	Harper Riggs,	Levi W. Hancock,
Lyman Sherman,	Bradford Elliot,	Solomon Warner,

Joseph Hancock,	Burr Riggs,	Israel Barlow,
Lyman Smith,	Lewis Robbins,	Willard Snow,
Peter Buchanan,	Darwin Richardson,	Hazen Aldrich,
David Elliot,	Joseph Young,	Charles Kelley,
Almon W. Babbitt,	Alexander Badlam,	Jenkins Salisbury,
Levi Gifford,	Zebedee Coltrin,	George A. Smith,
Joseph B. Nobles,	Solomon Angel,	Nathan B. Baldwin,

"The Council adjourned to the day following, March 1; when, after attending the funeral of Seth Johnson, several who had recently been baptized were confirmed, and the sacrament was administered to the church.

The sacrament.

Previous to the administration I spoke of the propriety of this institution in the church, and urged the importance of doing it with acceptance before the Lord, and asked, How long do you suppose a man may partake of this ordinance, unworthily, and the Lord not withdraw his Spirit from him? How long will he thus trifle with sacred things and the Lord not give him over to the buffetings of Satan until the day of redemption? The church should know if they are unworthy from time to time to partake, lest the servants of God be forbidden to administer it. Therefore our hearts ought to humble themselves, and we to repent of our sins, and put away evil from among us.

"After sacrament the council continued the ordination and blessing of those previously called; also John Murdock and S. W. Denton were ordained and blessed; Benjamin Winchester, Hyrum Smith, and Frederick G. Williams were blessed; and Joseph Young and Sylvester Smith were ordained Presidents of the Seventies.

"'Kirtland, March 7, 1835. This day a meeting of the Church of Latter Day Saints was called for the purpose of blessing, in the name of the Lord, those who have heretofore assisted in building (by their labor and other means) the house of the Lord in this place.

"'The morning was occupied by President Joseph Smith, Jun., in teaching the church the propriety and necessity of purifying itself. In the afternoon the names of those who had assisted to build the house were taken, and further instructions received from President Smith. He said that those who had distinguished themselves thus far by consecrating to the upbuilding of the House of the Lord, as well as laboring thereon, were to be remembered; that those who build it should own it and have the control of it.

" 'After further remarks, those who performed the labor on the building voted unanimously that they would continue to labor thereon till the house should be completed.

" 'President Sidney Rigdon was appointed to lay on hands and bestow blessings in the name of the Lord.

" 'The Presidents were blessed; and Reynolds Cahoon, Hyrum Smith, and Jared Carter, the building committee (the last two) though not present, yet their rights in the house were preserved.

" 'The following are names of those who were blessed in consequence of their labor on the House of the Lord in Kirtland, and those who consecrated to its upbuilding:—

" 'Sunday afternoon, March 8.

Sidney Rigdon,	Aaron E. Lyon,	Henry Baker,
Joseph Smith, Jr.,	Thomas Burdick,	William Fisk,
F. G. Williams,	Truman Wait,	Henry Wilcox,
Joseph Smith, Sen.,	Edmund Bosley,	George Gee,
Oliver Cowdery,	William Bosley,	Lorenzo Young,
N. K. Whitney,	William Perry,	David Clough,
Reynolds Cahoon,	Don Carlos Smith,	James Durfee,
Hyrum Smith,	Shadrack Roundy,	Joseph Coe,
Jared Carter,	Joel Johnson,	Thomas Gates,
Jacob Bump.	Oliver Higley,	Loren Babbit,
Artemas Millet,	Evan M. Green,	Blake Baldwin,
Alpheus Cutler,	Levi Osgood,	Joseph B. Bosworth,
Asa Lyman,	Alpheus Harmon,	Gad Yale,
Josiah Butterfield,	Joseph C. Kingsbury,	John Johnson,
Noah Packard,	Ira Bond,	John Tanner,
James Putnam,	Z. H. Brewster,	Henry G. Sherwood,
Isaac Hill,	Samuel Thomson,	Sidney Tanner,
Edmund Durfee. Sen.,	John Ormsby,	Joseph Tippits,
Edmund Durfee, Jun.,	Luman Carter,	Robert Quigley,
Gideon Ormsby,	John Smith,	Erastus Babbit,
Albert Miner,	Samuel H. Smith,	Samuel Canfield,
Ira Ames,	Thomas Fisher,	Phineas H. Young,
Salmon Gee,	Starry Fisk,	Samuel Rolfe,
Peter Shirts,	Amos R. Orton,	Calvin W. Stoddard,
Isaac Hubbard,	Almon Sherman,	Josiah Fuller,
Horace Burgess,	Warren Smith,	Erastus Rudd,
Dexter Stillman,	Moses Bailey,	Isaac G. Bishop,

Amos F. Herrick,
Mayhew Hillman,
William Carter,
William Burgess,
Giles Cook,
Malcum C. Davis,
Jaman Aldrich,
John Young, Sen.,
Ezra Strong,
Joel McWithy,
Matthew Foy,
James Randall,
John P. Green,

Sebe Ives,
Andrew H. Aldrich,
Ebenezer Jennings,
Oliver Granger,
Orson Johnson,
James Lake,
William Redfield,
Cyrus Lake,
Harvey Smith,
Isaac Cleveland,
William Barker,
Samuel S. Brannan,
John Wheeler,

Roswell Murray,
Benjamin Wells,
Nehemiah Harman,
Oliver Wetherby,
Thomas Hancock,
Joshua Grant,
William Draper,
Ransom V. Beuren,
Tunis Rappellee,
John Reed,
Samuel Wilcox,
Benjamin Johnson.

" 'Kirtland, March 12, 1835. This evening the Twelve assembled, and the Council was opened by President Joseph Smith, Jr., and he proposed we take our first mis- sion through the Eastern States, to the Atlantic Ocean, and hold conferences in the vicinity of the several branches of the Church for the purpose of regulating all things necessary for their welfare.

Conferences of the twelve.

" 'It was proposed that the Twelve leave Kirtland on the 4th day of May, which was unanimously agreed to.

" 'It was then proposed that during their present mission Elder Brigham Young should open the door to the remnants of Joseph, who dwell among the Gentiles, which was carried.

" 'It was motioned and voted that the Twelve should hold their first conference in Kirtland, May 2; in Westfield, New York, May 9; in Freedom, New York, May 22; in Lyons-town, New York, June 5; on Pillow Point, June 19; in West Loboro', Upper Canada, June 29; in Johnsbury, Vermont, July 17; in Bradford, Massachusetts, August 7; in Dover, New Hampshire, September 4; in Saco, Maine, September 18; Farmington, Maine, October 2.

" 'Orson Hyde,
" 'Wm. McLellin, } Clerks.

" 'Kirtland, March 28.

" 'This afternoon the Twelve met in council and had a time of general confession. On reviewing our past course we are satisfied, and feel to confess also, that we have not realized the importance of our calling to that degree that we ought; we have been lightminded and vain, and in many things done wrong, *wrong*. For all these things we have asked the forgiveness of our heavenly Father; and wherein we have grieved or wounded the feelings of the Presidency, we ask their forgiveness. The time when we are about to separate is near; and when we shall meet again, God only knows; we therefore feel to ask of him whom we have acknowledged to be our Prophet and Seer, that he inquire of God for us, and obtain a revelation, (if consistent,) that we may look upon it when we are separated, that our hearts may be comforted. Our worthiness has not inspired us to make this request, but our unworthiness. We have unitedly asked God our heavenly Father to grant unto us through his Seer, a revelation of his mind and will concerning our duty the coming season, even a great revelation, that will enlarge our hearts, comfort us in adversity, and brighten our hopes amidst the power of darkness.

"'ORSON HYDE,
" 'WM. E. MCLELLIN, } Clerks.

" 'To President Joseph Smith, Jr., Kirtland, Ohio.'

"In compliance with the above request, I inquired of the Lord, and received answer.[*]

"The school closed, the last week in March. to give the elders an opportunity to go forth and proclaim the gospel preparatory to the endowment.

---

[*] 1. There are, in the church, two priesthoods; namely: the Melchisedec, and the Aaronic, including the Levitical priesthood. Why the first is called the Melchisedec priesthood, is because Melchisedec was such a great high priest: before his day it was called *the holy priesthood, after the order of the Son of God;* but out of respect or reverence to the name of the Supreme Being, to avoid the too frequent repetition of his name, they, the church, in ancient days, called that priesthood after Melchisedec, or the Melchisedec priesthood.

2. All other authorities, or offices in the church are appendages to this priesthood; but there are two divisions, or grand heads—one is the Melchisedec priesthood, and the other is the Aaronic, or Levitical priesthood.

3. The office of an elder comes under the priesthood of Melchisedec. The Melchisedec priesthood holds the right of presidency, and has power and authority over all the offices in the church, in all ages of the world, to administer in spiritual things.

4. The presidency of the high priesthood, after the order of Melchisedec, have a right to officiate in all the offices in the church.

5. High priests, after the order of the Melchisedec priesthood, have a right to officiate in their own standing, under the direction of the presidency, in administering spiritual things, and also in the office of an elder, priest (of the Levitical order), teacher, deacon, and member.

"Sunday, March 29. I preached about three hours, at Huntsburgh—where William E. McLellin had been holding

6. An elder has a right to officiate in his stead when the high priest is not present.

7. The high priest and elder are to administer in spiritual things, agreeably to the covenants and commandments of the church; and they have a right to officiate in all these offices of the church when there are no higher authorities present.

8. The second priesthood is called the priesthood of Aaron, because it was conferred upon Aaron and his seed, throughout all their generations. Why it is called the lesser priesthood is, because it is an appendage to the greater, or the Melchisedec priesthood, and has power in administering outward ordinances. The bishopric is the presidency of this priesthood, and holds the keys or authority of the same. No man has a legal right to this office, to hold the keys of this priesthood, except he be a literal descendant of Aaron. But as a high priest of the Melchisedec priesthood has authority to officiate in all the lesser offices, he may officiate in the office of bishop when no literal descendant of Aaron can be found, provided he is called and set apart and ordained unto this power by the hands of the presidency of the Melchisedec priesthood.

9. The power and authority of the higher, or Melchisedec, priesthood, is to hold the keys of all the spiritual blessings of the church; to have the privilege of receiving the mysteries of the kingdom of heaven; to have the heavens opened unto them; to commune with the general assembly and church of the Firstborn; and to enjoy the communion and presence of God the Father, and Jesus the Mediator of the new covenant.

10. The power and authority of the lesser, or Aaronic, priesthood is, to hold the keys of the ministering of angels, and to administer in outward ordinances—the letter of the gospel—the baptism of repentance for the remission of sins, agreeably to the covenants and commandments.

11. Of necessity, there are presidents, or presiding offices, growing out of, or appointed of, or from among those who are ordained to the several offices in these two priesthoods. Of the Melchisedec priesthood, three presiding high priests, chosen by the body, appointed and ordained to that office, and upheld by the confidence, faith, and prayer of the church, form a quorum of the presidency of the church. The twelve traveling counselors are called to be the twelve apostles, or special witnesses of the name of Christ, in all the world; thus differing from other officers in the church in the duties of their calling. And they form a quorum equal in authority and power to the three presidents previously mentioned. The seventy are also called to preach the gospel, and to be especial witnesses unto the Gentiles and in all the world—thus differing from other officers in the church in the duties of their calling; and they form a quorum equal in authority to that of the twelve especial witnesses, or apostles, just named. And every decision made by either of these quorums must be by the unanimous voice of the same; that is, every member in each quorum must be agreed to its decisions, in order to make their decisions of the same power or validity one with the other. (A majority may form a quorum, when circumstances render it impossible to be otherwise.) Unless this is the case, their decisions are not entitled to the same blessings which the decisions of a quorum of three presidents were anciently, who were ordained after the order of Melchisedec, and were righteous and holy men. The decisions of these quorums, or either of them, are to be made in all righteousness, in holiness and lowliness of heart, meekness and long-suffering, and in faith and virtue and knowledge; temperance, patience, godliness, brotherly kind-

a public discussion, on a challenge from J. M. Tracy, a Campbellite preacher, the two days previous, on the divinity of the Book of Mormon, at the close of which two were bap-

ness, and charity, because the promise is, if these things abound in them, they shall not be unfruitful in the knowledge of the Lord. And in case that any decision of these quorums is made in unrighteousness, it may be brought before a general assembly of the several quorums which constitute the spiritual authorities of the church, otherwise there can be no appeal from their decision.

12. The twelve are a traveling, presiding high council, to officiate in the name of the Lord, under the direction of the presidency of the church, agreeably to the institution of heaven, to build up the church and regulate all the affairs of the same, in all nations; first unto the Gentiles, and secondly unto the Jews.

13. The seventy are to act in the name of the Lord, under the direction of the twelve, or the traveling high council, in building up the church, and regulating all the affairs of the same, in all nations; first unto the Gentiles, and then to the Jews; the twelve being sent out, holding the keys to open the door by the proclamation of the gospel of Jesus Christ; and first unto the Gentiles, and then unto the Jews.

14. The standing high councils, at the stakes of Zion, form a quorum equal in authority, in the affairs of the church, in all their decisions, to the quorum of the presidency or to the traveling high council.

15. The high council in Zion forms a quorum equal in authority, in the affairs of the church, in all their decisions, to the councils of the twelve at the stakes of Zion.

16. It is the duty of the traveling high council to call upon the seventy, when they need assistance, to fill the several calls for preaching and administering the gospel, instead of any others.

17. It is the duty of the twelve, in all large branches of the church, to ordain evangelical ministers, as they shall be designated unto them by revelation.

18. The order of this priesthood was confirmed to be handed down from father to son, and rightly belongs to the literal descendants of the chosen seed, to whom the promises were made. This order was instituted in the days of Adam, and came down by lineage in the following manner:—

19. From Adam to Seth, who was ordained by Adam at the age of 69 years, and was blessed by him three years previous to his (Adam's) death, and received the promise of God by his father, that his posterity should be the chosen of the Lord, and that they should be preserved unto the end of the earth, because he (Seth) was a perfect man, and his likeness was the express likeness of his father, insomuch that he seemed to be like unto his father in all things; and could be distinguished from him only by his age.

20. Enos was ordained at the age of 134 years, and four months, by the hand of Adam.

21. God called upon Cainan in the wilderness, in the fortieth year of his age, and he met Adam in journeying to the place Shedolamak: he was eighty-seven years old when he received his ordination.

22. Mahalaleel was 496 years and seven days old when he was ordained by the hand of Adam, who also blessed him.

23. Jared was 200 years old when he was ordained under the hand of Adam, who also blessed him.

24. Enoch was 25 years old when he was ordained under the hand of Adam, and he was 65 and Adam blessed him—and he saw the Lord: and

tized; and on Monday four more came forward for baptism.

"[The following is the copy of a letter from certain members of the Irvingite church (so-called) in England, pre-

he walked with him, and was before his face continually: and he walked with God 365 years: making him 430 years old when he was translated.

25. Methuselah was 100 years old when he was ordained under the hand of Adam.

26. Lamech was 32 years old when he was ordained under the hand of Seth.

27. Noah was 10 years old when he was ordained under the hand of Methuselah.

28. Three years previous to the death of Adam, he called Seth, Enos, Cainan, Mahalaleel, Jared, Enoch, and Methuselah, who were all high priests, with the residue of his posterity, who were righteous, into the valley of Adam-ondi-ahman, and there bestowed upon them his last blessing. And the Lord appeared unto them, and they rose up and blessed Adam, and called him Michael, the Prince, the Archangel. And the Lord administered comfort unto Adam, and said unto him, I have set thee to be at the head: a multitude of nations shall come of thee; and thou art a prince over them forever.

29. And Adam stood up in the midst of the congregation, and notwithstanding he was bowed down with age, being full of the Holy Ghost, predicted whatsoever should befall his posterity unto the latest generation. These things were all written in the Book of Enoch, and are to be testified of in due time.

30. It is the duty of the twelve, also, to ordain and set in order all the other officers of the church, agreeably to the revelation which says:—

31. To the Church of Christ in the land of Zion, in addition to the church laws, respecting church business: Verily, I say unto you, says the Lord of hosts, There must needs be presiding elders, to preside over those who are of the office of an elder; and also priests, to preside over those who are of the office of a priest; and also teachers to preside over those who are of the office of a teacher, in like manner; and also the deacons: wherefore, from deacon to teacher, and from teacher to priest, and from priest to elder, severally as they are appointed, according to the covenants and commandments of the church; then comes the high priesthood, which is the greatest of all; wherefore, it must needs be that one be appointed, of the high priesthood, to preside over the priesthood; and he shall be called president of the high priesthood of the church, or. in other words, the presiding high priest over the high priesthood of the church. From the same comes the administering of ordinances and blessings upon the church, by the laying on of the hands.

32. Wherefore the office of a bishop is not equal unto it; for the office of a bishop is in administering all temporal things: nevertheless, a bishop must be chosen from the high priesthood, unless he is a literal descendant of Aaron: for unless he is a literal descendant of Aaron he cannot hold the keys of that priesthood. Nevertheless, a high priest, that is after the order of Melchisedec, may be set apart unto the ministering of temporal things, having a knowledge of them by the Spirit of truth, and also to be a judge in Israel, to do the business of the church, to sit in judgment upon transgressors, upon testimony, as it shall be laid before him, according to the laws, by the assistance of his counselors, whom he has chosen, or will choose among the elders of the church. This is the duty of a bishop who is not a literal descendant of Aaron, but has been ordained to the high priesthood after the order of Melchisedec.

33. Thus shall he be a judge, even a common judge among the inhab-

sented to certain elders of the Church of Latter Day Saints, in the evening of the 10th of June, 1835, by a gentleman named in the same, at the time calling himself a communi-cant and preacher of that church.]

" 'To the Saints of the Most High.

itants of Zion, or in a stake of Zion, or in any branch ·of the church where he shall be set apart unto this ministry, until the borders of Zion are enlarged, and it becomes necessary to have other bishops, or judges in Zion, or elsewhere: and inasmuch as there are other bishops appointed they shall act in the same office.

34. But a literal descendant of Aaron has a legal right to the presi-dency of this priesthood, to the keys of this ministry, to act in the office of bishop independently, without counselors, except in a case where a presi-dent of the high priesthood, after the order of Melchisedec, is tried; to sit as a judge in Israel. And the decision of either of these councils, agreeably to the commandment which says:—

35. Again, verily I say unto you: The most important business of the church, and the most difficult cases of the church, inasmuch as there is not satisfaction upon the decision of the bishop, or judges, it shall be handed over and carried up unto the council of the church, before the presidency of the high priesthood; and the presidency of the council of the high priesthood shall have power to call other high priests, even twelve, to assist as counselors; and thus the presidency of the high priesthood, and its counselors shall have power to decide upon testimony according to the laws of the church. And after this decision it shall be had in remembrance no more before the Lord; for this is the highest council of the Church of God, and a final decision upon controversies, in spiritual matters.

36. There is not any person belonging to the church, who is exempt from this council of the church.

37. And inasmuch as a president of the high priesthood shall trans-gress, he shall be had in remembrance before the common council of the church, who shall be assisted by twelve councilors of the high priest-hood; and their decision upon his head shall be an end of controversy concerning him. Thus, none shall be exempted from the justice and the laws of God; that all things may be done in order and solemnity, before him, according to truth and righteousness.

38. And again, verily I say unto you, The duty of a president over the office of a deacon, is to preside over twelve deacons, to sit in council with them, and to teach them their duty—edifying one another, as it is given according to the covenants.

39. And also the duty of the president over the office of the teachers, is to preside over twenty-four of the teachers, and to sit in council with them—teaching them the duties of their office, as given in the covenants.

40. Also the duty of the president over the priesthood of Aaron, is to preside over forty-eight priests, and sit in council with them, to teach them the duties of their office, as is given in the covenants. This presi-dent is to be a bishop; for this is one of the duties of this priesthood.

41. Again, the duty of the president over the office of elders is to pre-side over ninety-six elders, and to sit in council with them, and to teach them according to the covenants. This presidency is a distinct one from that of the seventy, and is designed for those who do not travel into all the world.

42. And again, the duty of the president of the office of the high priest-hood is to preside over the whole church, and to be like unto Moses.

" '*Dear Brethren in the Lord:*—At a council of the pastors
of our church, held March 28, 1835, upon the propriety of
the Rev. John Hewitt visiting you, it was resolved
Irvingites. and approved that as he had an anxious desire to
go to America to see the things that are spoken of in one of
your papers brought here by a merchant from New York,
he should have, as he desired, the sanction of the council,
and if it pleased the Lord, his approval. The Lord hath
seen our joy and gladness to hear that he was raising up a
people for himself in that part of the New World, as well as
here. O, may our faith increase that he may have evangelists, apostles, and prophets, filled with the power of the
Spirit, and performing his will in destroying the works of
darkness.

" 'The Rev. Mr. Hewitt was Professor of Mathematics in
Rotherham Independent Seminary, and four years pastor of
Barnsley Independent Church. He commenced preaching
the doctrines we taught about two years since, and was
excommunicated. Many of his flock followed him, so that
he was eventually installed in the same church, and the
Lord's work prospered. As he is a living epistle, you will
have, if all be well, a full explanation. Many will follow,
should he approve of the country, etc., who will help the
cause, because the Lord hath favored them with this world's
goods. We had an utterance during our meeting, which

Behold, here is wisdom, yea, to be a seer, a revelator, a translator, and
a prophet: having all the gifts of God which he bestows upon the head
of the church.

43. And it is according to the vision, showing the order of the seventy,
that they should have seven presidents to preside over them, chosen out
of the number of the seventy, and the seventh president of these presidents is to preside over the six; and these seven presidents are to choose
other seventy besides the first seventy, to whom they belong, and are to
preside over them; and also other seventy until seven times seventy, if
the labor in the vineyard of necessity requires it. And these seventy are
to be traveling ministers unto the Gentiles, first, and also unto the Jews,
whereas other officers of the church, who belong not unto the twelve
neither to the seventy, are not under the responsibility to travel among
all nations, but are to travel as their circumstances shall allow, notwithstanding they may hold as high and responsible offices in the church.

44. Wherefore, now let every man learn his duty, and to act in the
office in which he is appointed, in all diligence. He that is slothful
shall not be counted worthy to stand, and he that learns not his duty and
shows himself not approved, shall not be counted worthy to stand. Even
so. Amen.

caused us to sing for joy. The Lord was pleased with our brother's holy determination to see you; and we understand that persecution had been great among you, or would be, but we were commanded not to fear, for he would be with us. Praise the Lord.

" 'The time is at hand when distance shall be no barrier between us; but when, on the wings of love, Jehovah's messages shall be communicated by his saints. The Lord bless our brother, and may he prove a blessing to you. Be not afraid of our enemies; they shall, unless they repent, be cast down by the Lord of Hosts. The workers of iniquity have been used by the Prince of Darkness to play the counterfeit; but discernment has been given to us, that they were immediately put to shame, by being detected, so that the flock never suffered as yet by them.

" 'Grace, mercy, and peace be unto you from God our Father, and from the Spirit, Jesus Christ our Lord. Amen.

" 'I am, dear sir, your brother in the gospel,

" 'THOMAS SHAW.

" 'BARNSLEY, April 21, 1835.

" '[One object, and only one, has induced us to lay the foregoing letter from England before our readers; and that is, the good of the cause of God. It might have remained in our possession, perhaps for years, in silence, had it not been for circumstances, which we will briefly mention hereafter.]

" 'On the 26th of April, the Twelve Apostles, and the Seventy who had been chosen, assembled in the Temple (although unfinished) with a numerous concourse of people, to receive their charge and instructions from President Joseph Smith, Jr., relative to their mission and duties. The congregation being assembled, Elder Orson Pratt arrived from the south part of the State, making our numbers complete, Elder Thomas B. Marsh having arrived the day previous.

Public meeting.

" '28th. The Twelve met this afternoon at the School-room, for the purpose of prayer and consultation. Elder David W. Patten opened the meeting by prayer.

" 'Motioned and carried, that when any member of the council wishes to speak, he shall arise and stand upon his feet.

" 'Elder McLellin read the commandment given concerning the choosing of the Twelve; when it was voted that we each forgive one another every wrong that has existed among us, and that from henceforth each one of the Twelve love his brother as himself, in temporal 'as well as in spiritual things, always inquiring into each other's welfare.

" 'Decided that the Twelve be ready and start on their mission from Elder Johnson's tavern, on Monday at two o'clock a. m., May 4.

" 'Elder B. Young then closed by prayer.

" 'Orson Hyde,
" 'W. E. McLellin, } Clerks.'

" 'May 2. A grand Council was held in Kirtland, composed of the following officers of the church; viz.: Presidents Joseph Smith, Jr., David Whitmer, Oliver Cowdery, Sidney Rigdon, Frederick G. Williams, Joseph Smith, Sen., and Hyrum Smith, with the Council of the Twelve Apostles, Bishop Partridge and Council, Bishop Whitney and Council, and some of the Seventy, with their Presidents; viz., Sylvester Smith, Leonard Rich, Lyman Sherman, Hazen Aldrich, Joseph Young, and Levi Hancock; and many elders from different parts; President Joseph Smith, Jr., presiding.

A Grand Council.

" 'After the conference was opened, and the Twelve had taken their seats, President Joseph Smith, Jr., said that it would be the duty of the Twelve, when in council, to take their seats together according to age, the oldest to be seated at the head, and preside in the first council, the next oldest in the second, and so on until the youngest had presided; and then begin at the oldest again, etc.

" 'The Twelve then took their seats according to age, as follows: Thomas B. Marsh, David W. Patten, Brigham Young, Heber C. Kimball, Orson Hyde, William E. McLelln, Parley P. Pratt, Luke Johnson, William Smith, Orson Pratt, John F. Boynton, and Lyman E. Johnson.

" 'President Joseph Smith then stated that the Twelve will have no right to go into Zion, or any of its stakes, and there undertake to regulate the affairs thereof, where there is a standing high council; but it is their duty to go abroad and regulate all matters relative to the different branches of the church. When the Twelve are together, or a quorum of them, in any church, they will have authority to act independently, and make decisions, and those decisions will be valid. But where there is not a quorum, they will have to do business by the voice of the church. No standing high council has authority to go into the churches abroad, and regulate the matters thereof, for this belongs to the Twelve. No standing high council will ever be established only in Zion or one of its stakes. When the Twelve pass a decision, it is in the name of the church, therefore it is valid.

" 'No official member of the church has authority to go into any branch thereof, and ordain any minister for that church, unless it is by the voice of that branch. No elder has authority to go into any branch of the church, and appoint meetings, or attempt to regulate the affairs of the church, without the advice and consent of the presiding elder of that branch. If the first Seventy are all employed, and there is a call for more laborers, it will be the duty of the Seven presidents of the first Seventy to call and ordain other seventy and send them forth to labor in the vineyard, until, if needs be, they set apart seven times seventy, and even until there are one hundred and forty and four thousand thus set apart for the ministry. The Seventy are not to attend the conferences of the Twelve, unless they are called upon or requested so to do by the Twelve. The Twelve and the Seventy have particularly to depend upon their ministry for their support, and that of their families; and they have a right, by virtue of their offices, to call upon the churches to assist them.

" 'Elder Henry Herriman was ordained one of the Seventy.

" 'The circumstances of the Presidents of the Seventy were severally considered, relative to their traveling in the vineyard; and it was unanimously agreed that they should hold themselves in readiness, to go at the call of the Twelve, when the Lord opens the way. Twenty-seven of the Seventy were also considered, and it was decided they should hold themselves in readiness to travel in the ministry, at the call of the President of the Seventy, as the Lord opens the way.

" 'After an adjournment of one hour, the council reassembled. . . .

" 'Lorenzo Barnes was ordained one of the Seventy; also Henry Benner, Michael Griffiths, Royal Barney, and Lebbeus T. Coon, who, together with twenty others, were called upon to hold themselves in readiness to travel when circumstances permit.

" 'The Elders of Kirtland and its vicinity were then called upon, or their circumstances considered; and their names being enrolled, President Joseph Smith, Jr., arose with the lists in his hand, and made some very appropriate remarks, relative to the deliverance of Zion; and, so much of the authority of the church being present, moved that we never give up the struggle for Zion, even until death, or until Zion is redeemed.

" 'The vote was unanimous, and with deep feeling.

" 'Voted, that all the elders of the church are bound to travel in the world to preach the gospel, with all their might, mind, and strength, when their circumstances will admit of it; and that the door is now opened.

" 'Voted, that Elders Brigham Young, John P. Green, and Amos Orton be appointed to go and preach the gospel to the remnants of Joseph, the door to be opened by Elder Brigham Young; and this will open the door to the whole house of Joseph.

" 'Voted, that when another Seventy is required, the Presidency of the first Seventy shall choose, ordain, and set them apart from among the most experienced of the elders of the church.

" 'Voted, that whenever the labor of other Seventy is required, they are to be set apart and ordained to that office; those who are residing at Kirtland and the regions round about, who can come to Kirtland, and be set apart and ordained by the direction of the Presidency of the church in Kirtland.

" 'William E. McLellin, Clerk.'

" 'The Twelve left Kirtland this morning, and embarked on board the steamer Sandusky, at Fairport, and landed at Dunkirk, New York, five o'clock p. m.; and after preaching in those regions a few days, met in Conference at Westfield, May 9, according to previous appointment; the church being present, and Thomas B. Marsh, the oldest of the quorum, presiding.

The Twelve depart.

" 'The following items were suggested for the consideration of the council.

" '1. Resolved: That the limits of this conference extend south and west to the line of Pennsylvania, north as far as Lake Erie, and east as far as Lodi, embracing the branches of Westfield, Silver Creek, Perrysburg, and Lavona, to be called the "Westfield conference."

" '2. Inquire into the standing of all the elders within the bounds of this conference.

" '3. Inquire into the manner of their teaching, doctrines, etc.

" '4. Inquire into the teaching, conduct, and faithfulness of all traveling elders who have recently labored within the bounds of this conference.

" '5. Hear a representation of the several branches of the church.

" 'On investigation, the standing and teaching of the elders present met the approbation of the council, except the teaching of Elder Joseph Rose, which was that "the Jewish Church was the sun, and the Gentile Church was the moon, etc.; when the Jewish Church was scattered, the sun was darkened; and when the Gentile Church is cut off, the moon will be turned to blood;" also some things relative to the apocalyptic beast with seven heads and ten horns, etc.

" 'He was shown his error, and willingly made a humble confession.

" 'The faithfulness of all the traveling elders was found to be good. . . .

" 'After further instructions on general principles, the conference adjourned until eight o'clock a. m., Monday evening, May 11.

" 'Sunday, 10. Elders Marsh and Patten preached to an attentive congregation of about five hundred; after sacrament, five persons desired baptism, which was attended to by Elder McLellin.

" 'May 11. Conference met pursuant to adjournment.

" 'Resolved unanimously: That this conference go to, immediately, and appoint their "wise men," and gather up their riches, and send them to Zion to purchase land according to previous commandment, that all things be prepared before them in order to their gathering.

" 'Much was said to the conference upon these important things; and they covenanted before the Lord that they would be strict to attend to our teaching.

" 'After preaching by Elder Young at three o'clock p. m., and the farewell exhortation of the Twelve, seven individuals were baptized by Elder Hyde, who were confirmed in the evening.   And after laying hands on many sick, who obtained relief, adjourned to the 22d instant, to meet in Freedom, New York.

" 'Orson Hyde, Clerk.'

"About the middle of May, W. W. Phelps and John Whitmer, Presidents of the Church in Missouri, arrived at Kirtland, and John Whitmer was appointed to take the place of President Oliver Cowdery, in conducting the *Messenger and Advocate*.

Literary concerns.

"Frederick G. Williams was appointed to edit the *Northern Times*, a weekly newspaper, which we had commenced in February last, in favor of Democracy; and W. W. Phelps (with his son Waterman) made his home with my family, and assisted the committee in compiling the Book of Doctrine and Covenants.

" 'May 22. The Twelve met in conference with .the church in Freedom, New York, when, after an agreeable salutation and rejoicing in each other's prosperity, Elder D. W. Patten being chairman, conference was opened by singing, and prayer by the President.

Work of the Twelve.

" '[Here let it be remarked that it was the universal custom of the Twelve and the Presidency of the Church, to open and close all conferences and councils by prayer, and generally singing, so that this need not be named in this history hereafter.]

" 'Resolved: That the limits of this conference extend from Lodi in the west, so far east as to include Avon, south

to Pennsylvania, and north to Lake Ontario, called the
"Freedom conference," including the branches of Freedom,
Rushford, Portage, Grove, Burns, Genesee, Avon, Java,
Holland, Aurora, Greenwood, and Niagara.

" 'The report concerning the labors and teachings of the
elders in the conference, and those who had recently
traveled through, was good.

" 'The branch in Freedom numbered sixty-five; Rushford,
twenty-eight; Burns, thirty; Holland, fifteen; represented
by P. P. Pratt, as having suffered much from false teachings by hypocrites and knaves; Aurora, four; Niagara, four;
the numbers of the remaining branches not ascertained, but
generally reported in good standing.

" 'The council gave instruction concerning the "Word of
Wisdom," the gift of tongues, prophesying, etc.; and
adjourned till to-morrow morning.

" '23d. Conference met to take into consideration the
redemption of Zion.

" 'After addresses from five of the council, the church
expressed their determination to put into practice the teachings we had given, when the conference adjourned.

" 'May 25. The Twelve met in council, to pray for one
another until they should meet again; and, resolved: That
we recommend and counsel Elders John Murdock, and
Lloyd Lewis, to go to the churches at Chenango Point, New
York; and Springville, Pennsylvania (among whom we
understand there is some difficulty), and set in order the
things that are wanting in those branches.

" 'Resolved: That Elder Brigham Young go immediately
from this place to an adjacent tribe of the remnants of
Joseph, and open the door of salvation to that long dejected
and afflicted people. The council, according to his request,
laid their hands upon him, that he might have their faith and
prayers, to fill (with humility and power) that very important mission.

" 'They also laid hands on Elders John P. Green and Amos
Orton, for the same purpose, as they expected to accompany
him.

" 'Orson Hyde, Clerk.'

" 'On the 5th of June, nine of the Twelve met in council at Rose, or Lyons town, New York. There being so few of the brethren in that region, it was resolved: That it was not necessary to establish a conference, after council adjourned. And after they had preached several sermons in the vicinity, Elders Brigham Young, Orson Hyde, and William Smith returned to Kirtland, as witnesses on a cer· tain case wherein President Joseph Smith, Jun., was con· cerned before the county court, in which he righteously triumphed over his enemies.

" 'ORSON HYDE, Clerk.' . . .

"The Presidency, Bishop, and High Council of Zion, hav· ing removed to Kirtland, or gone forth in the vineyard, I Affairs caused it to be published in the June number of of Zion. the *Messenger and Advocate*, that, according to the order of the kingdom ·begun in the last days, to prepare men for the rest of the Lord, the elders in Zion or in her immedi· ate region have no authority or right to meddle with her spiritual affairs, to regulate her concerns, or hold councils for the expulsion of members, in her unorganized condition. The High Council has been expressly organized to adminis· ter in all her spiritual affairs; and the Bishop and his council are set over her temporal matters; so that the elders' acts are null and void. Now, the Lord wants the wheat and tares to grow together; for Zion must be redeemed with judgment, and her converts with righteousness. Every elder that can, after providing for his family (if he has any) and paying his debts, must go forth and clear his skirts from the blood of this generation. While they are in that region, instead of trying members for transgression, or offenses, let every one labor to prepare himself for the vine· yard, sparing a little time to comfort the mourners, to bind up the broken-hearted, to reclaim the backslider, to bring back the wanderer, to reinvite into the kingdom such as have been cut off, by encouraging them to lay to while the day lasts, and work righteousness, and, with one heart and one mind prepare to help to redeem Zion, that goodly land of promise, where the willing and obedient shall be blessed.

"About this time I received an introduction to Mr. Hewitt,

a preacher who had come out from Europe, with his lady, to

Mr. Hewitt. examine this work, and, as he stated, was delegated by his church for this purpose. His interview was short, and he left with the understanding he would call again and renew his investigations. As he did not return according to agreement, and hearing he was at Fairport, the Council of the Presidency sent him the following letter:—

" 'June 14.

" 'To the Rev. Mr. Hewitt.

" '*Sir:*—In consequence of your not returning as we understood you at your introduction to us, it was resolved and approved in council, on the evening of the 14th instant, that the bearer, Oliver Cowdery, one of the Presiding Elders of our church, should proceed to Fairport, and ascertain if possible the cause of your delay; and this is done as one reason that we feel an anxious desire for the salvation of the souls of men, and to satisfy your inquiries concerning the religion we profess. If at Fairport it is the sincere desire of the council that Mr. Hewitt return, that we may satisfy him concerning our religion, and he satisfy us concerning his; for we feel as great a desire for the welfare of his people as he can for ours. With respect, etc.,

" 'W. W. PHELPS, Clerk.'

"Elder Cowdery repaired immediately to Fairport, and on the day following reported to the council that Mr. Hewitt was not in the place; that he left their letter with Mrs. Hewitt, who informed him that her 'husband had frequently spoken of his wish to become further acquainted with the people whom he had come out from Europe to see.' But the next we heard of the Rev. John Hewitt was that he had opened a school in Painesville, Ohio. Mr. Hewitt was elder of the Irvingite Church, in Barnsley, England, and received a delegation from that church, as expressed in a letter from Mr. Shaw, of April 21, to visit the saints in America, and ascertain their faith and principles; and if Mr. Hewitt found them as they expected, the saints in America might expect help from them (the church in Barnsley), as they were rich in temporal things, and had received the gift of tongues in the church.

"Thursday, June 18. Nine hundred and fifty dollars were subscribed for the Temple, by the saints in Kirtland. Great anxiety was manifest to roll on the work.

"'On the 19th, nine of the Traveling High Council met with the church in conference at Pillow Point, New York, and The Twelve resolved that the limits of the conference embrace in the East. all the northern part of the State, to be called the "Black River conference." The elders of this conference had been diligent in their callings. Their manner of teaching, in some respects needed correction, which they gladly received.

"'The church at Pillow Point numbered twenty-one, but did not generally observe the "Word of Wisdom." Sacket's Harbor numbered nineteen; Burville, seven; Champion, six; Ellesburgh, thirty-three; Henderson, four; Alexandria, four; Lyme, four; and two in Orleans, three in Potsdam, and six in Stockholm. . . .

"'Orson Hyde, Clerk.'

"The twenty-first, being Sunday, I preached in Kirtland on the evangelical order.

"Thursday, June 25. There was a meeting in Kirtland to subscribe for the building of the Temple; and $6,232.50 were added to the list. Joseph Smith subscribed $500; Oliver Cowdery $750; W. W. Phelps $500; John Whitmer $500; and F. G. Williams $500; of the above, all of which they paid within one hour, and the people were astonished.

"June 29. Six of the Traveling High Council, viz.: D. W. Patten, H. C. Kimball, Luke Johnson, Orson Pratt, John F. Boynton, and Lyman E. Johnson, assembled in conference with the church in Loborough, Upper Canada. The church in Loborough, composed of twenty-five members, were uninformed in many principles of the new covenant, not having had the same privilege of instruction as the churches in the States. . . .

"Elder Frederick M. Van Leuven was appointed Presiding Elder, and a number were added to the church during our stay.

"On the 3d of July, Michael H. Chandler came to Kirtland to exhibit some Egyptian mummies. There were four human

figures, together with some two or more rolls of papyrus
Mummies. covered with hieroglyphic figures and devices.
As Mr. Chandler had been told I could translate
them, he brought me some of the characters, and I gave him
the interpretation, and like a gentleman, he gave me the following certificate:—

"'KIRTLAND, July 6, 1835.

"'This is to make known to all who may be desirous, concerning the knowledge of Mr. Joseph Smith, Jr., in deci-
phering the ancient Egyptian hieroglyphic characters in my
possession, which I have, in many eminent cities, showed
to the most learned; and, from the information that I could
ever learn, or meet with, I find that of Mr. Joseph Smith,
Jr., to correspond in the most minute matters.

"'MICHAEL H. CHANDLER,
"'Traveling with, and proprietor of,
"'Egyptian mummies.'

" . . . Soon after this some of the saints at Kirtland purchased the mummies and papyrus (a description of which
will appear hereafter), and I, with W. W. Phelps and O.
Cowdery as scribes, commenced the translation of some of
the characters or hieroglyphics, and much to our joy found
that one of the rolls contained the writings of Abraham,
another the writings of Joseph of Egypt, etc., a more full
account of which will appear in their place, as I proceed to
examine or unfold them. Truly can we say, The Lord is
beginning to reveal the abundance of peace and truth. . . .

"'July 17. The Twelve met in conference, agreeably to
The Twelve again. previous appointment, at Saint Johnsbury, Vermont.

"'Resolved: That this State be the limits of this conference, and include the branches in Littleton, Dolton, and
Landaff, in New Hampshire, to be called the "Vermont Conference."

"'The St. Johnsbury branch numbered forty-one members; Danville, twenty-three; Charlton, twenty-one; Jay,
eleven; Dalton, fifteen; Landaff, four; Littleton, ten;
Andover, Vermont, fifteen; Beneeon, seven; and Lewis, New
York, seventeen.

" 'Six of the council addressed the conference on principles of faith and action.

" 'Adjourned to the 18th, when the remaining six enforced the necessity of sending up wise men, and purchasing lands, according to the commandments, which they readily agreed to do.

" 'Sunday, 19. Our public meeting was attended by more than a thousand people, and during our conference nine were baptized.

" 'ORSON HYDE,   } Clerks.' "
" 'WM. E. McLELLIN, }

—*Millennial Star*, vol. 15, pp. 204, 205, 206, 209, 210, 211, 212, 213, 230, 231, 245, 260, 261, 262, 263, 283, 284, 285, 296, and 297.

During this time the *Messenger and Advocate* was published monthly, at Kirtland, Ohio, and gave accounts of the prog-

Progress.

ress of the work as reported by the elders. With the June number it changed editors, Oliver Cowdery retiring, and John Whitmer succeeding him. From a glance over its pages we see reports of work done in the following named places, in the most of which additions were made, and in many of them organizations effected: Green County, Sugar Creek, and Brookville, Indiana; Norfolk, Connecticut; Dover, New Hampshire; Bradford, Dighton, and Wendell, Massachusetts; Lewiston, Gilead, Pleasant Grove, Washington County, Lebanon, Troy, Clinton County, Green County, Canton, Flatbush, and Paris, Illinois; Freedom, Java, Wethersfield, Portage, Grove, Perrysburgh, Laoni, Hanover, Geneseo, and Sacket's Harbor, New York; North Danville, Vermont; Farmington, Maine; Allegheny County, Pennsylvania; Paris, Tennessee; Cincinnati, Cummingsville, Fulton, Batavia, Huntsburgh, Carthage, and Stark County, Ohio; Providence, Rhode Island; and Saco, Maine.

To show the condition of the work and the nature of the opposition we quote the following editorial from the *Messenger and Advocate*, vol. 1, pages 76 and 77:—

"From the foregoing extracts it may be seen how much truth there is in the reports which are circulated by many of all parties and sects. We are confident that there never has been a time since the church commenced that the prospects have been more flattering than they are at present. In all parts of our country multitudes are inquiring after truth. So numerous are the calls that if the number of elders were three to every one they could not supply them. These facts are opening the eyes of some of the worst of our enemies, among whom is A. Campbell, of *Millennial Harbinger* memory. He has recently begun to howl most prodigiously, calling upon the people in great agony to read Mr. Howe's book as a sure antidote against delusion. As this is all that Mr. C. can do, or dare do, we do not wish to deprive him of this privilege. So we say concerning Alexander, Dudley and Company, Let them exert themselves with all their power, for they will find it a harder task to 'kick against the pricks,' than to reform, as they call it, Masons and sectarians; they have undertaken a task too great for them: the arm of Omnipotence is too potent for 'schoolboys,' and this they will find after they have exhausted all their power. The 'black speck' will still 'stain the American character,' for the people will receive the everlasting gospel, nor can men nor devils prevent it. The people may rage and the heathen imagine a vain thing; but He who sits in the heavens will laugh, the Lord will have them in derision, and ere long he will speak to them in his wrath and vex them in his sore displeasure.

"Mr. Campbell has been invited to show himself a man of principle—after repeated insults to the Church of the 'Latter Day Saints,' and to exchange papers and cut a quill like a man; but seeing he dare not do it (for notwithstanding the confidence which his satellites have in him, he knows the weakness of his cause too well to hazard an investigation with an elder of the Church of the 'Latter Day Saints'), we consider this effort of his in the same point of light which we do a whipped spaniel, when he is afraid to face his enemy he turns his hind parts and barks – so bark on, Alexander."

The saints in Missouri remained in about the same condition, harassed to some extent by the opposition and suffering much privation, with no immediate prospect of a restoration to their lands and rights.

CHAPTER 22.

GENERAL ASSEMBLY—DOCTRINE AND COVENANTS - THE WITNESSES
—THE EVIDENCE—JOHN WHITMER ON DOCTRINE AND COVENANTS.

A MONTH passed in Kirtland in regular routine work, with
nothing of peculiar importance transpiring until August 17,

General Assembly. 1835, when the quorums of the church met in General Assembly, the minutes of which are as follows:—

"GENERAL ASSEMBLY.

"At a General Assembly of the Church of the Latter Day
Saints, according to previous notice, held on the 17th of
August, 1835, to take into consideration the labors of a certain
committee which had been appointed by a General
Assembly of September 24, 1834, as follows:—

"'The Assembly being duly organized, and after transacting
certain business of the church, proceeded to appoint a
committee to arrange the items of doctrine of Jesus Christ,
for the government of his church of the Latter Day Saints,
which church was organized and commenced its rise on the
6th day of April, 1830. These items are to be taken from
the Bible, Book of Mormon, and the revelations which have
been given to said church up to this date, or shall be until
such arrangement is made.

"'Elder Samuel H. Smith, for the assembly, moved that
Presiding Elders, Joseph Smith. Jr., Oliver Cowdery, Sidney
Rigdon, and Frederick G. Williams compose said committee.
The nomination was seconded by Elder Hyrum
Smith, whereupon it received the unanimous vote of the
assembly.

"'(Signed)   "'OLIVER COWDERY, } *Clerks.*'
                    "'ORSON HYDE,

"Wherefore O. Cowdery and S. Rigdon, Presidents of the
First Presidency appointed Thomas Burdick, Warren Par-

rish, and Sylvester Smith, clerks, and proceeded to organize the whole assembly, as follows: They organized the High Council of the church at Kirtland, and Presidents W. W. Phelps and J. Whitmer proceeded and organized the High Council of the church in Missouri. Bishop Newel K. Whitney proceeded and organized his counselors of the church in Kirtland, and acting Bishop John Corrill, organized the counselors of the church in Missouri: and also Presidents Leonard Rich, Levi W. Hancock, Sylvester Smith, and Lyman Sherman, organized the Council of the Seventy; and also, Elder John Gould, acting President, organized the traveling elders; and also Ira Ames, acting President, organized the Priests; and also Erastus Babbit, acting President, organized the Teachers; and also William Burgess, acting President, organized the Deacons; and they also, as the assembly was large, appointed Thomas Gates, John Young, William Cowdery, Andrew H. Aldrich, Job L. Lewis, and Oliver Higley, as assistant presidents of the day, to assist in preserving order, etc., in the whole assembly. Elder Levi W. Hancock appointed chorister: a hymn was then sung and the services of the day opened by the prayer of President O. Cowdery, and the solemnities of eternity rested upon the audience. Another hymn was sung: after transacting some business for the church the audience adjourned for one hour.

"Afternoon.—After a hymn was sung, President Cowdery arose and introduced the 'Book of Doctrine and Covenants of the Church of the Latter Day Saints,' in behalf of the committee. He was followed by President Rigdon, who explained the manner by which they intended to obtain the voice of the assembly for or against said book: the other two committee, named above, were absent. According to said arrangement W. W. Phelps bore record that the book presented to the assembly, was true. President John Whitmer also arose and testified that it was true. Elder John Smith, taking the lead of the High Council in Kirtland, bore record that the revelations in said book were true, and that the lectures were judiciously arranged and compiled, and were profitable for doctrine; whereupon the High Council of Kirtland accepted and acknowledged them as the doctrine and covenants of their faith, by a unanimous vote. Elder Levi Jackman, taking the lead of the High Council of the church in Missouri, bore testimony that the revelations in said book were true, and the said High Council of Missouri accepted and acknowledged them as the doctrine and covenants of their faith, by a unanimous vote.

"President W. W. Phelps then read the written testimony of the Twelve, as follow: 'The testimony of the witnesses to the book of the Lord's commandments, which he gave to his church through Joseph Smith, Jr., who was appointed by the voice of the church for this purpose: We therefore feel willing to bear testimony to all the world of mankind, to every creature upon the face of all the earth, and upon the islands of the sea, that the Lord has borne record to our souls, through the Holy Ghost shed forth upon us, that these commandments were given by inspiration of God, and are profitable for all men, and are verily true. We give this testimony unto the world, the Lord being our helper: and it is through the grace of God, the Father, and his Son Jesus Christ, that we are permitted to have this privilege of bearing this testimony unto the world, in the which we rejoice exceedingly, praying the Lord always that the children of men may be profited thereby.' Elder Leonard Rich bore record of the truth of the book and the Council of the Seventy accepted and acknowledged it as the doctrine and covenants of their faith, by a unanimous vote.

"Bishop N. K. Whitney bore record of the truth of the book, and with his counselors accepted and acknowledged it as the doctrine and covenants of their faith, by a unanimous vote.

"Acting Bishop, John Corrill, bore record of the truth of the book, and with his counselors accepted and acknowledged it as the doctrine and covenants of their faith, by a unanimous vote. Acting President, John Gould, gave his testimony in favor of the book, and with the traveling Elders, accepted and acknowledged it as the doctrine and covenants of their faith, by a unanimous vote.

"Ira Ames, acting President of the Priests, gave his testimony in favor of the book, and with the Priests, accepted and acknowledged it as the doctrine and covenants of their faith, by a unanimous vote.

"Erastus Babbit, acting President of the Teachers, gave his testimony in favor of the book, and they accepted and acknowledged it as the doctrine and covenants of their faith, by a unanimous vote.

"William Burgess, acting President of the Deacons, bore record of the truth of the book, and they accepted and acknowledged it as the doctrine and covenants of their faith, by a unanimous vote.

"The venerable Assistant President, Thomas Gates, then bore record of the truth of the book, and with his five silver-headed assistants, and the whole congregation, accepted and acknowledged it as the doctrine and covenants of their faith, by a unanimous vote. The several authorities, and the General Assembly, by a unanimous vote, accepted of the labors of the committee.

"President W. W. Phelps then read an article on Marriage, which was accepted and adopted, and ordered to be printed in said book, by a unanimous vote.[1]

[1]MARRIAGE.

1. According to the custom of all civilized nations, marriage is regulated by laws and ceremonies: therefore we believe, that all marriages in this Church of Christ of Latter Day Saints should be solemnized in a public meeting, or feast, prepared for that purpose: and that the solemnization should be performed by a presiding high priest, high priest, bishop, elder, or priest, not even prohibiting those persons who are desirous to get married, of being married by other authority. We believe that it is not right to prohibit members of this church from marrying out of the church, if it be their determination so to do, but such persons will be considered weak in the faith of our Lord and Savior Jesus Christ.

2. Marriage should be celebrated with prayer and thanksgiving; and at the solemnization, the persons to be married, standing together, the man on the right, and the woman on the left, shall be addressed, by the person officiating, as he shall be directed by the Holy Spirit; and if there be no legal objections, he shall say, calling each by their names: "You both mutually agree to be each other's companion, husband and wife, observing the legal rights belonging to this condition; that is, keeping yourselves wholly for each other, and from all others, during your lives." And when they have answered "Yes," he shall pronounce them "husband and wife" in the name of the Lord Jesus Christ, and by virtue of the laws of the country and authority vested in him: "May God add his blessings and keep you to fulfill your covenants from henceforth and forever. Amen."

3. The clerk of every church should keep a record of all marriages solemnized in his branch.

4. All legal contracts of marriage made before a person is baptized

"President O. Cowdery then read an article on 'governments and laws in general,' which was accepted and adopted,
and ordered to be printed in said book, by a unanimous vote.[2]

into this church, should be held sacred and fulfilled. Inasmuch as this
Church of Christ has been reproached with the crime of fornication,
and polygamy: we declare that we believe that one man should have
one wife; and one woman but one husband, except in case of death,
when either is at liberty to marry again. It is not right to persuade a
woman to be baptized contrary to the will of her husband, neither is it
lawful to influence her to leave her husband. All children are bound by
law to obey their parents; and to influence them to embrace any religious faith, or be baptized, or leave their parents without their consent,
is unlawful and unjust. We believe that husbands, parents, and masters
who exercise control over their wives, children, and servants, and prevent them from embracing the truth, will have to answer for that sin.

[2] OF GOVERNMENTS AND LAWS IN GENERAL.

That our belief, with regard to earthly governments and laws in general, may not be misinterpreted nor misunderstood, we have thought
proper to present, at the close of this volume, our opinion concerning the
same.

1. We believe that Governments were instituted of God for the benefit
of man, and that he holds men accountable for their acts in relation to
them, either in making laws or administering them, for the good and
safety of society.

2. We believe that no Government can exist, in peace, except such
laws are framed and held inviolate as will secure to each individual the
free exercise of conscience, the right and control of property, and the protection of life.

3. We believe that all Governments necessarily require civil officers
and magistrates to enforce the laws of the same, and that such as will
administer the law in equity and justice should be sought for and upheld
by the voice of the people (if a Republic), or the will of the Sovereign.

4. We believe that religion is instituted of God, and that men are
amenable to him and to him only for the exercise of it, unless their
religious opinion prompts them to infringe upon the rights and liberties
of others; but we do not believe that human law has a right to interfere
in prescribing rules of worship to bind the consciences of men, nor dictate forms for public or private devotion; that the civil magistrate should
restrain crime, but never control conscience; should punish guilt, but
never suppress the freedom of the soul.

5. We believe that all men are bound to sustain and uphold the respective Governments in which they reside, while protected in their inherent
and inalienable rights by the laws of such Governments, and that sedition and rebellion are unbecoming every citizen thus protected, and should
be punished accordingly; and that all Governments have a right to enact
such laws as in their own judgments are best calculated to secure the
public interest, at the same time, however, holding sacred the freedom
of conscience.

6. We believe that every man should be honored in his station: rulers
and magistrates as such—being placed for the protection of the innocent
and the punishment of the guilty; and that to the laws all men owe
respect and deference, as without them peace and harmony would be
supplanted by anarchy and terror: human laws being instituted for the
express purpose of regulating our interests as individuals and nations,

"A hymn was then sung. President S. Rigdon returned thanks, after which the assembly was blessed by the Presidency, with uplifted hands, and dismissed. ·

"OLIVER COWDERY, } Presidents.
"SIDNEY RIGDON,

"THOMAS BURDICK,
"WARREN PARRISH, } Clerks."
"SYLVESTER SMITH,

Some comments on the Book of Doctrine and Covenants will be necessary in order to present to the reader the differ-

between man and man, and divine laws, given of heaven, prescribing rules on spiritual concerns, for faith and worship, both to be answered by man to his Maker.

7. We believe that Rulers, States, and Governments have a right, and are bound to enact laws for the protection of all citizens in the free exercise of their religious belief; but we do not believe that they have a right, in justice, to deprive citizens of this privilege, or proscribe them in their opinions, so long as a regard and reverence is shown to the laws, and such religious opinions do not justify sedition nor conspiracy.

8. We believe that the commission of crime should be punished according to the nature of the offense: that murder, treason, robbery, theft, and the breach of the general peace, in all respects, should be punished according to their criminality and their tendency to evil among men, by the laws of that Government in which the offense is committed: and for the public peace and tranquility, all men should step forward and use their ability in bringing offenders, against good laws, to punishment.

9. We do not believe it just to mingle religious influence with civil government, whereby one religious society is fostered and another proscribed in its spiritual privileges, and the individual rights of its members, as citizens, denied.

10. We believe that all religious societies have a right to deal with their members for disorderly conduct according to the rules and regulations of such societies, provided that such dealing be for fellowship and good standing; but we do not believe that any religious society has authority to try men on the right of property or life, to take from them this world's goods, or put them in jeopardy either life or limb, neither to inflict any physical punishment upon them,—they can only excommunicate them from their society and withdraw from their fellowship.

11. We believe that men should appeal to the civil law for redress of all wrongs and grievances, where personal abuse is inflicted, or the right of property or character infringed, where such laws exist as will protect the same; but we believe that all men are justified in defending themselves, their friends and property, and the Government, from the unlawful assaults and encroachments of all persons, in times of exigencies, where immediate appeal cannot be made to the laws, and relief afforded.

12. We believe it just to preach the gospel to the nations of the earth, and warn the righteous to save themselves from the corruption of the world; but we do not believe it right to interfere with bond servants, neither preach the gospel to, nor baptize them, contrary to the will and wish of their masters, nor to meddle with, or influence them in the least to cause them to be dissatisfied with their situations in this life, thereby jeopardizing the lives of men: such interference we believe to be unlawful and unjust, and dangerous to the peace of every Government allowing human beings to be held in servitude.

ence between it and the "Book of Commandments" published
Doctrine   by. W. W. Phelps, at Independence, Missouri,
and Covenants. in 1833.

It is true that the revelations were sent to Zion for publication, by the hands of Oliver Cowdery and John Whitmer.
Some work was done on them but the issue was never completed, the press and office being destroyed while the work
was being done. The most of those that were printed were
destroyed by the mob. Some of them were preserved by
individuals, who picked up the scattered sheets, and a few
copies of the unfinished work are still in existence. The
Book of "Doctrine and Covenants" contains revelations that
the other does not, and parts of some of the revelations
found in both books read differently.

The point as to which is the more reliable wherein they
differ, has been a subject of much discussion. We are not
able to account for how the differences occurred, but we
think the testimony is overwhelmingly in favor of the correctness of the revelations as published in the Doctrine and
Covenants:—

1. The Book of Commandments was never indorsed by
conference, quorum, council, or assembly that we have any
record of. The Book of Doctrine and Covenants was
indorsed by the General Assembly, as the minutes herein
published show; first by the quorums separately, and then
by the assembly as a whole, and that in every instance by
unanimous vote.

2. The Book of Commandments, so far as we know, never
in early days received the indorsement of a leading man of
the church, so far as the correctness of the revelations is
concerned. The Book of Doctrine and Covenants received
The w tnesses.   the indorsement of the committee compiling it;
namely, Joseph Smith, Sidney Rigdon, F. G. Wil-
liams, and Oliver Cowdery;[3] of all the members of the Quo-

---

[3]To the members of the church of the Latter Day Saints—
Dear Brethren:—We deem it to be unnecessary to entertain you with a
lengthy preface to the following volume, but merely to say that it contains in short, the leading items of the religion which we have professed
to believe.
The first part of the book will be found to contain a series of Lectures

rum of Twelve; of Leonard Rich, of the Presidency of Seventy; of W. W. Phelps, John Whitmer, John Smith, for the High Council in Kirtland; of Levi Jackman, for the High Council in Missouri; of Bishops N. K. Whitney, John Corrill; of John Gould, acting President of the Elders; of Ira Ames, acting President of the Priests; of Erastus Babbit, acting President of the Teachers; of William Burgess, acting President of the Deacons; and of the aged Thomas Gates.

To question the correctness of the revelations as published in Doctrine and Covenants is to question the honor of these men, some of whom were with the church from the beginning and knew whereof they affirmed; and among these witnesses is W. W. Phelps, the very man who published the "Book of Commandments."

as delivered before a Theological class in this place, and in consequence of their embracing the important doctrine of salvation, we have arranged them into the following work.

The second part contains items or principles for the regulation of the church, as taken from the revelations which have been given since its organization, as well as from former ones.

There may be an aversion in the minds of some against receiving anything purporting to be articles of religious faith, in consequence of there being so many now extant; but if men believe a system, and profess that it was given by inspiration, certainly, the more intelligibly they can present it, the better. It does not make a principle untrue to *print* it, neither does it make it true not to print it.

The church viewing this subject to be of importance, appointed, through their servants and delegates the High Council, your servants to select and compile this work. Several reasons might be adduced in favor of this move of the Council, but we only add a few words. They knew that the church was evil spoken of in many places—its faith and belief misrepresented, and the way of truth thus subverted. By some it was represented as disbelieving the Bible, by others as being an enemy to all good order and uprightness, and by others as being injurious to the peace of all governments civil and political.

We have, therefore, endeavored to present, though in few words, *our* belief, and when we say this, humbly trust, the faith and principles of this society as a body.

We do not present this little volume with any other expectation than that we are to be called to answer to every principle advanced, in that day when the secrets of all hearts will be revealed, and the reward of every man's labor be given him.

With sentiments of esteem and sincere respect, we subscribe ourselves Your brethren in the bonds of the gospel of our Lord Jesus Christ,

JOSEPH SMITH, JR.
OLIVER COWDERY.
SIDNEY RIGDON.
F. G. WILLIAMS.

KIRTLAND, Ohio, February 17, 1835.

8. No one in those early days ever questioned the correctness of the revelations, as published in the "Doctrine and Covenants," while of the revelations in the Book of Commandments published by W. W. Phelps, and by him also published in the *Evening and Morning Star*, we find the following:—

"There are many typographical errors in both volumes, and especially in the last, which we shall endeavor carefully to correct, as well as principle, if we discover any.
The evidence. It is also proper for us to say, that in the first fourteen numbers, *in the revelations*, are many errors, typographical, and others, occasioned by transcribing manuscript; but as we shall have access to originals, we shall endeavor to make proper corrections."—*Evening and Morning Star*, vol. 2, p. 884.

The first fourteen numbers of the *Star* were published at Independence, Missouri, and edited by W. W. Phelps. When the press was destroyed the publication was transferred to Kirtland, Ohio, and edited by Oliver Cowdery, where also the first fourteen numbers were reprinted.

In the first number of the original issue we find what is now section 17 of the Doctrine and Covenants substantially as it appears in the Book of Commandments; but in the reprint it appears substantially in harmony with the Doctrine and Covenants; and the difference is explained by Oliver Cowdery, as follows:—

"On the revelations we merely say, that we were not a little surprised to find the previous print so different from the original. We have given them a careful comparison, assisted by individuals whose known integrity and ability is uncensurable. Thus saying we cast no reflections upon those who were intrusted with the responsibility of publishing them in Missouri, as our own labors were included in that important service to the church, and it was our unceasing endeavor to have them correspond with the copy furnished us. We believe they are now correct. If not in every word, at least in principle. For the special good of the church we have also added a few items from other revelations. —[*Editor of the*

Latter Day Saints' Messenger and Advocate.]"—*Evening and Morning Star*, vol. 1, p. 16.

This last sentence has been interpreted to mean that "a few items from other revelations" were added to this one, but he evidently intended to say he had added other items in the reprint not found in the first issue of the paper. But these other items are not incorporated with this revelation. Here then is positive evidence that the revelations in the Book of Commandments were found to be wrong when compared with originals. Later this revelation was published the third time, and this time just as it appears in the Doctrine and Covenants. (See *Evening and Morning Star*, volume 2, page 193.)

Of this the Editor, Oliver Cowdery, states:—

"We have again inserted the articles and covenants according to our promise in a previous number, for the benefit of our brethren abroad who have not the first number of the first volume. As there were some errors which had got into them by transcribing, we have since obtained the original copy and made the necessary corrections." — *Evening and Morning Star*, vol. 2, p. 196.

To doubt the correctness of the revelations as they appear in the Doctrine and Covenants is to doubt the veracity of Oliver Cowdery as well as the testimony of all those who testified in the above-mentioned assembly. If we were prepared to do this we would lay down the pen, having no history to write. We feel sure then that we can historically affirm that the revelations contained in the Doctrine and Covenants are substantially in harmony with the originals.

In connection with this point we will cite the testimony of John Whitmer and then leave it with our readers.

In his "Address" when leaving the Editorial chair of the *Messenger and Advocate*, in March, 1836, after bearing testimony to the Book of Mormon, which we have before referred to, he adds:—

"I would do injustice to my own feelings if I did not here notice still further the work of the Lord in these last days: The revelations and commandments given to us are, in my estimation, equally true with the Book of Mormon, and equally necessary for salvation. It is necessary to live by every word that proceedeth from the mouth of God: and I know that the Bible, Book of Mormon, and Book of Doctrine and Covenants of the Church of Christ of Latter Day Saints, contain the revealed will of heaven. I further know that God will continue to reveal himself to his church and people, until he has gathered his elect into his fold, and prepared them to dwell in his presence."—*Messenger and Advocate*, vol. 2, p. 287.

John Whitmer on Doctrine and Covenants.

CHAPTER 28.

1835.

ON August 21, 1835, nine of the Twelve met in conference at Saco, Maine.

On August 23, Joseph Smith returned to Kirtland from his mission to Michigan.

August 28, 1835, the Twelve met at Farmington, Maine, and organized the Maine conference. The same day Joseph preached in Kirtland on the duty of wives.

On September 1, 1835, Joseph wrote the following to
Gathering and John Whitmer, which was published in the *Mes-*
other items. *senger and Advocate.* It will be valuable as showing the attitude of Joseph on the gathering, Zion, and other things.

"To the Elders of the Church of Latter Day Saints:—

"After so long a time, and after so many things having been said, I feel it my duty to drop a few hints, that perhaps the elders traveling through the world to warn the inhabitants of the earth to flee the wrath to come and save themselves from this untoward generation, may be aided in a measure, in doctrine, and in the way of their duty. I have been laboring in this cause for eight years, during which time I have traveled much, and have had much experience. I removed from Seneca County, New York, to Geauga County, Ohio, in February, 1831.

"Having received by an heavenly vision a commandment, in June following, to take my journey to the western boundaries of the State of Missouri, and there designate the very spot which was to be the central spot for the commencement of the gathering together of those who embrace the fullness of the everlasting gospel, I accordingly undertook the journey with certain ones of my brethren; and, after a long and tedious journey, suffering many privations and hardships, I arrived in Jackson County, Missouri; and, after viewing the country, seeking diligently at the hand of God, he manifested himself unto me and designated to me and others the very spot upon which he designed to commence the work of the gathering and the upbuilding of an holy city, which should be called Zion: Zion because it is to be a place of righteousness, and all who build thereon are to worship the true and living God; and all believe in one doctrine, even the doctrine of our Lord and Savior Jesus Christ.

" 'Thy watchmen shall lift up the voice; with the voice together shall they sing: for they shall see eye to eye, when the Lord shall bring again Zion.'—Isaiah 52:8.

"Here we pause for a moment to make a few remarks upon the idea of gathering to this place. It is well known that there were lands belonging to the Government, to be sold to individuals; and it was understood by all, at least we believed so, that we lived in a free country, a land of liberty and of laws, guaranteeing to every man or any company of men the right of purchasing lands and settling and living upon them: therefore we thought·no harm in advising the Latter Day Saints, or Mormons as they are reproachfully called, to gather to this place, inasmuch as it was their duty (and it was well understood so to be), to purchase, *with money*, lands, and live upon them—not infringing upon the civil rights of any individual or community of people; always keeping in view the saying, 'Do unto others as you would wish to have others do unto you.' Following also the good injunction: 'Deal justly, love mercy, and walk humbly with thy God.'

"These were our motives in teaching the people, or Latter Day Saints, to gather together, beginning at this place. And inasmuch as there are those who have had different views from this, we feel that it is a cause of deep regret:

For, be it known unto all men, that our principles concerning this thing have not been such as have been represented by those who, we have every reason to believe, are designing and wicked men, that have said that this was our doctrine: to infringe upon the rights of a people who inhabit our civil and free country, such as to drive the inhabitants of Jackson County from their lands, and take possession thereof unlawfully. Far, yea, far be such a principle from our hearts: it never entered into our mind, and we only say that God shall reward such in that day when he shall come to make up his jewels."—*Messenger and Advocate,* vol. 1, pp. 179, 180.

On September 2, 1835, Joseph Smith and Sidney Rigdon went to New Portage, Ohio, to attend a conference, returning to Kirtland on the 8th.

Historical items.

The High Council was in session on September 14, 1835, when they provided for compensation for Patriarch Joseph Smith, Sen., and for F. G. Williams, his scribe. Oliver Cowdery was appointed "Recorder for the Church," and Emma Smith was appointed to make a selection of sacred hymns to be revised and arranged for printing by W. W. Phelps.

On the 16th the Presidency of the Church appointed David Whitmer and Samuel H. Smith, agents for the "Literary Firm."

Joseph adds a few items of history at this date which are as follows:—

"I labored in obtaining blessings, which were written by Oliver Cowdery. We were thronged with company, so that our labor in this thing was hindered; but we obtained many precious things, and our souls were blessed. O Lord, may thy Holy Spirit be with thy servants forever. Amen.

"September 23. I was at home writing blessings for my most beloved brethren, but was hindered by a multitude of visitors. The Lord has blessed our souls this day, and may God grant to continue his mercies unto my house this night, for Christ's sake. This day my soul has desired the salvation of Brother Ezra Thayre. Also Brother Noah Packard came to my house and loaned the committee one thousand dollars, for building the house of the Lord. O, may God bless him an hundredfold, even of the things of the earth, for this righteous act! My heart is full of desire to-day, to be blessed of the God of Abraham with prosperity, until I will be able to pay all my debts; for it is the delight of my soul to be honest. O Lord, that thou knowest right well. Help me, and I will give to the poor.

"Brothers William, John, and Joseph Tippits started for Missouri, the place designated for Zion, or the saints' gathering place. They came to bid us farewell. The brethren came in to pray with them, and Brother David Whitmer acted as spokesman. He prayed in the Spirit, and a glorious time succeeded his prayer, joy filled our hearts, and we blessed them and bade them Godspeed, and promised them a safe journey, and took them by the hand and bade them farewell for a season. May God grant them long life and good days. These blessings I ask upon them for Christ's sake. Amen.

Some depart for Zion.

"The High Council met at my house on the 24th, to take into consideration the redemption of Zion. And it was the voice of the Spirit of the Lord that we petition the Governor; that is, those who have been driven out should petition to be set back on their own lands next spring, and that we go next season, to live or die on our own lands, which we have purchased in Jackson County, Missouri. We truly had a good time, and covenanted to struggle for this thing, until death shall dissolve the union; and if one falls, that the remainder be not discouraged, but pursue this object until it is accomplished; which may God grant unto us in the name of Jesus Christ our Lord. Also, this day drew up a subscription for enrolling the names of those who are willing to go up to Missouri next spring, and settle; and I ask God in the name of Jesus, that we may obtain eight hundred or one thousand emigrants.

Redemption of Z on.

"I spent the 25th at home.

"This morning the Twelve returned from their mission to the East, and on the same day, the Council of the Presidency of the Church, consisting of Joseph Smith, Jr., Sidney Rigdon, David Whitmer, W. W. Phelps, John Whitmer, Hyrum Smith, and Oliver Cowdery, met to

The Twelve return.

consider the case of the Twelve who had previously been reproved in consequence of certain letters and reports coming to the ears of the Council. First, the items contained [in] Warren A. Cowdery's letter, in connection with certain other reports, derogatory to the character and teaching of the Twelve, were considered; and from the testimony of several witnesses (the Twelve), it was proved before the council, that said complaints originated in the minds of persons who were darkened in consequence of covetousness, or some other cause, rather than the Spirit of truth. Second, one item contained in William E. McLellin's letter to his wife, expressing dissatisfaction with President Rigdon's school. Elder O. Hyde was also designated with him (McLellin) or blamed in the matter, in which they were found to be in the fault, which they frankly confessed, and were forgiven, and all things satisfactorily settled.

"Sunday the 27th. I attended meeting. Elders Thomas B. Marsh, David W. Patten, Brigham Young, and Heber C. Kimball preached and broke bread. The Lord poured out his Spirit and my soul was edified."—*Millennial Star*, vol. 15, pp. 342, 343.

From this date to the close of 1835 the history will be sufficiently explicit to follow the account of Joseph Smith as published in *Millennial Star*, volume 15; and from what we can learn from other records it is approximately correct. It as follows:—

"In the afternoon I waited on most of the Twelve, at my house, and exhibited to them the ancient records, and gave explanations. This day passed off with the blessing of the Lord.

"Sunday, 4. I started early in the morning, with Brother John Corrill, to hold a meeting in Perry. When about a mile from home we discovered two deer playing in the field, which diverted our minds by giving an impetus to our thoughts upon the subject of the creation of God. We conversed on many topics. The day passed off very agreeably, and the Lord blessed our souls. When we arrived at Perry, we were disappointed of a meeting, through misarrangement, but conversed freely with Brother Corrill's relatives, which allayed much prejudice. May the Lord have mercy on their souls.

"Monday, 5. I returned home, being much fatigued from riding in the rain. Spent the remainder of the day in reading, meditation, etc. And in the evening attended a Council of the Twelve Apostles; had a glorious time, and gave them much instruction concerning their duties for time to come; told them that it was the will of God they should take their families to Missouri next season; also this fall to attend the solemn assembly of the first elders, for the organization of the School of the Prophets; and attend to the ordinance of the washing of feet; and to prepare their hearts in all humility for an endowment with power from on high; to which they all agreed with one accord, and seemed to be greatly rejoiced. May God spare the lives of the Twelve, with one accord, to a good old age, for Christ the Redeemer's sake. Amen.

"Tuesday, 6. At home. Elder Stevens came to my house, and loaned F. G. Williams and Company six hundred dollars, which greatly relieved us of our present difficulties. May God bless and preserve his soul forever.

"Afternoon. Called to visit my father, who was very sick with a fever; some better towards evening. Spent the rest of the day in reading and meditation.

"Wednesday, 7. Went to visit my father, found him very low, administered some mild herbs, agreeably to the commandment. May God grant to restore him immediately to health for Christ the Redeemer's sake. Amen.

"Bishop Whitney and Brother Hyrum Smith started by land, in the stage, for Buffalo, New York, to purchase goods to replenish the committee's store. May God grant, in the name of Jesus, that their lives may be spared, and they have a safe journey, and no accident or sickness of the least kind befall them, that they may return in health and in safety to the bosom of their families.

"Thursday, 8. At home. I attended on my father, with great anxiety.

"Friday, 9. At home. Waited on my father.

"Saturday, 10. At home, and visited the house of my father, found him failing very fast.

"Sunday, 11. Waited on my father again, who was very sick. In secret prayer in the morning, the Lord said, 'My servant, thy father shall live.' I waited on him all this day with my heart raised to God in the name of Jesus Christ, that He would restore him to health again, that I might be blessed with his company and advice, esteeming it one of the greatest earthly blessings to be blessed with the society of parents, whose mature years and experience render them capable of administering the most wholesome advice.

Sickness.

"At evening, Brother David Whitmer came in. We called on the Lord in mighty prayer in the name of Jesus Christ, and laid our hands on him, and rebuked the disease. And God heard and answered our prayers: to the great joy and satisfaction of our souls our aged father arose and dressed himself, shouted, and praised the Lord, called Brother William Smith, who had retired to rest, that he might praise the Lord with us, by joining in songs of praise to the Most High.

"Monday, 12. Rode to Willoughby, in company with my wife. . . .

"Tuesday, 13. Visited my father, who was very much recovered from his sickness indeed, which caused us to marvel at the might, power, and condescension of our heavenly Father in answering our prayers in his behalf.

"Wednesday, 14. At home.

"Thursday, 15. Labored in father's orchard, gathering apples.

"Friday, 16. Was called into the printing office to settle some difficulties in that department. At evening I baptized Ebenezer Robinson. The Lord poured out his Spirit upon us, and we had a good time.

"Saturday, 17. Called my family together and arranged my domestic concerns, and dismissed my boarders.

"Sunday, 18. Attended meeting in the chapel, confirmed several that had been baptized, and blessed several children with the blessings of the new and everlasting covenant.

Elder Parley P. Pratt preached in the forenoon, and Elder John F. Boynton in the afternoon.   We had an interesting time.

"Monday, 19. At home. Exhibited the records of antiquity to a number who called to see them.

"Tuesday, 20. At home. Preached at evening, in the schoolhouse.

"Wednesday, 21. At home.

"Thursday, 22.   At home, attending to my domestic concerns.

"Friday, 23. At home. At four o'clock, afternoon, Oliver Cowdery, David Whitmer, Hyrum Smith, John Whitmer, Sidney Rigdon, Samuel H. Smith, Frederick G. Williams, and W. W. Phelps assembled and we united in prayer with one voice before the Lord for the following blessings: That the Lord would give us means sufficient to deliver us from all our afflictions and difficulties wherein we are placed by means of our debts; that He would open the way and deliver Zion in the appointed time, and that without the shedding of blood; that he would hold our lives precious, and grant that we may live to the common age of man, and never fall into the hands nor power of the mob in Missouri, nor in any other place; that he would also preserve our posterity, that none of them fall, even unto the end of time; that he would give us blessings of the earth sufficient to carry us to Zion, and that we may purchase inheritances in that land, even enough to carry on and accomplish the work unto which he has appointed us; and also that he would assist all others who desire, according to his commandments, to go up and purchase inheritances, and all this easily and without perplexity and trouble; and finally, that in the end, he would save us in his celestial kingdom. Amen.

Special prayer.

"Saturday, 24. Mr. Goodrich and lady called to see the ancient records, and also Dr. F. G. Williams to see the mummies. . . .

"Sunday, 25. Attended meeting with Brothers Hawks and Carpenter. President Rigdon preached in the forenoon, Elder Lyman E. Johnson in the afternoon, after which Elder S. Brunson joined Brother William Perry and Sister

Eliza Brown in matrimony, and I blessed them with long life and prosperity in the name of Jesus Christ.

"At evening I attended prayer meeting, opened it, and exhorted the brethren and sisters about one hour. The Lord poured out his Spirit, and some glorious things were spoken in the gift of tongues, and interpreted, concerning the redemption of Zion.

"Monday, 26. Went to Chardon to attend the County Court, in company with Brothers Hyrum, Samuel, and S. H. Smith fined Carlos Smith. Brother Samuel was called in question before this court for not doing military duty, and was fined because we had not our conference minutes with us for testimony to prove that F. G. Williams was clerk to the conference. This testimony we should have carried with us, had it not been for the neglect of our counsel or lawyer, who did not put us in possession of this information. This we felt was a want of fidelity to his client, and we consider it a base insult, practiced upon us on account of our faith, that the ungodly might have unlawful power over us and trample us under their unhallowed feet. And in consequence of this neglect, a fine was imposed upon Brother Samuel, of twenty dollars, including costs, for which he was obliged to sell his cow to defray the expenses of the same. . . .

"Tuesday, 27. In the morning I was called to visit at Brother Samuel Smith's. . . . This evening I preached in the schoolhouse, to a crowded congregation.

"Wednesday, 28. At home, attending to my family concerns.

"Thursday, 29. Brother W. Parrish commenced writing for me, at fifteen dollars per month. I paid him sixteen dollars in advance out of the committee's store. Father and Mother Smith visited us. While we sat writing, Bishop Partridge passed our window, just returned from the East. . . .

"Bishop E. Partridge came in, in company with President Phelps. I was much rejoiced to see him. . . .

"Bishop Whitney and his wife, with his father and mother, called to visit us. His parents having lately arrived here from the East, called to make inquiry concerning the coming forth of the Book of Mormon. Bishop Partridge and some others came in. I then sat down and related to them the history of the coming forth of the book, the administration of the angel to me, the rudiments of the gospel of Christ, etc. They appeared well satisfied, and I expect to baptize them in a few days, though they have made no request of the kind.

"Went to the council. The Presidency arose and adjourned. On my return, Elder Boynton observed that long·debates were bad. I replied that it was generally the case that too much altercation was indulged in on both sides, and their debates protracted to an unprofitable length.

"We were called to supper. While seated at table we indulged in a free interchange of thought, and Bishop Whitney observed to Bishop Partridge that the thought had just occurred to his mind that perhaps in about one year from this time they might be seated together around a table on the land of Zion. My wife observed she hoped it might be the case, that not only they, but the rest of the company present might be seated around her table on that land of promise. The same sentiment was reciprocated from the company around the table, and my heart responded, Amen. God grant it, I ask in the name of Jesus Christ.

"After supper I went to the High Council, in company with my wife, and some others that belonged to my house-
Trouble with William. hold. I was solicited to take a seat with the Presidency, and preside on a trial of Brother Elliot. I did so. My mother was called as testimony, and began to relate circumstances that had been brought before the church and settled. I objected against such testimony. The complainant, Brother William Smith, arose, and accused me of invalidating or doubting my mother's testimony, which I had not done, nor did I desire to do. I told him he was out of place, and asked him to sit down. He refused. I repeated my request. He became enraged. I finally ordered him to sit down. He said he would not, unless I knocked him down. I was agitated in my feelings on account of his stubbornness, and was about to leave the house, but my

father requested me not to do so. I complied, and the house was brought to order after much debate on the subject, and we proceeded to business.

"The decision of the council in the case of Brother Elliot, was, 'that the complaint was not without foundation, yet, the charge has not been fully sustained, but he has acted injudiciously, and brought a disgrace upon himself, his daughter, and upon this church, because he ought to have trained his child in a way that she should not have required the rod at the age of fifteen years.' Brother Elliot made his confession and was forgiven. Sister Elliot confessed her wrong and promised to do so no more, consequently the council forgave her. And they were both restored to fellowship.

"Friday, 30. At home. Mr. Francis Porter, from Jefferson County, New York, a member of the Methodist Church, called to make some inquiry about lands in this place (Kirtland), whether there were any valuable farms for sale, and whether a member of our church could move into this vicinity, and purchase lands, and enjoy his own possessions and property, without making them common stock. He had been requested to do so by some brethren who live in the town of Leroy, New York. I replied that I had a valuable farm joining the Temple Lot I would sell, and that there were other lands for sale in this place, and that we had no common stock business among us; that every man enjoys his own property, or can, if he is disposed, consecrate liberally or illiberally to the support of the poor and needy, or the building up of Zion. He also inquired how many members there were in this church. I told him there were about five or six hundred who commuued at our chapel, and perhaps a thousand in this vicinity.

No common stock.

"At evening I was presented with a letter from Brother William Smith, the purport of which is, that he is censured by the brethren on account of what took place at the council last night, and wishes to have the matter settled to the understanding of all, that he may not be censured unjustly, considering that his cause was a just one, and that he had been materially injured. I replied that I thought we parted with the best of feelings, that I was not

More about William.

LIBRARY OF THE UNIVERSITY

to blame on account of the dissatisfaction of others. I invited him to call and talk with me, and that I would talk with him in the spirit of meekness, and give him all the satisfaction I could. [This reply was by letter.]

"Saturday, 31. In the morning Brother Hyrum Smith came in and said he had been much troubled all night, and had not slept any, that something was wrong. While talking, Brother William Smith came in, according to my request last night. Brother Hyrum said that he must go to the store. I invited him to stay. He said he would go and do his business and return. He did so. While he was gone Brother William introduced the subject of our difficulty at the council. I told him I did not want to converse upon the subject until Hyrum returned. He soon came in. I then proposed to relate the occurrences of the council before-named, and wherein I had been out of the way I would confess it, and ask his forgiveness, and then he should relate his story, and make confession wherein he had done wrong, and then leave it to Brother Hyrum Smith and Brother Parrish to decide the matter between us, and I would agree to the decision, and be satisfied therewith.

"He observed that he had not done wrong, and that I was always determined to carry my points whether right or wrong, and therefore he would not stand an equal chance with me. This was an insult, but I did not reply to him in a harsh manner, knowing his inflammatory disposition, but tried to reason with him and show him the propriety of a compliance with my request. I finally succeeded, with the assistance of Brother Hyrum, in obtaining his assent to the proposition that I had made. I then related my story, and wherein I had been wrong I confessed it, and asked his forgiveness. After I got through he made his statements, justifying himself throughout in transgressing the order of the council, and treating the authority of the Presidency with contempt. After he had got through Brother Hyrum began to make some remarks, in the spirit of meekness. He (William) became enraged. I joined Brother Hyrum in trying to calm his stormy feelings, but to no purpose; he insisted that we intended to add abuse to injury, his passion increased, he arose abruptly, declared that he wanted no more to do with us. He rushed out at the door. We tried to prevail on him to stop, but all to no purpose. He went away in a passion, and soon after sent his license to me. He went home and spread the leaven of iniquity among my brethren, and especially prejudiced the mind of Brother Samuel. I soon learned that he was in the street, exclaiming against me, which no doubt our enemies rejoiced at. And where the matter will end I know not, but I pray God to forgive him and them, and give them humility and repentance.

"The feelings of my heart I cannot express on this occasion, I can only pray my heavenly Father to open their eyes, that they may discover where they stand, that they may extricate themselves from the snare they have fallen into.

"After dinner I rode out in company with my wife and children, Brother Carlos, and some others. We visited Brother Roundy and family, who live near Willoughby. We had an interesting visit. As soon as I returned, I was called upon to baptize Samuel Whitney, and his wife and daughter. After baptism we returned to their house, and offered our thanks in prayer. I obtained a testimony that Brother William would return to the Church, and repair the wrong he had done.

"Sunday morning, November 1, 1835. Verily thus saith the Lord unto me his servant, Joseph Smith, Jr., 'Mine anger is kindled against my servant Reynolds Cahoon, because of his iniquities, his covetous and dishonest principles, in himself and family, and he doth not purge them away, and set his house in order. Therefore, if he repent not, chastisement awaiteth him, even as it seemeth good in my sight, therefore go and declare unto him these words.'

A Prophecy verified.

"I went immediately and delivered this message according as the Lord commanded me. I called him in, and read what the Lord had said concerning him. He acknowledged that it was verily so, and expressed much humility.

"I then went to meeting. Elder Corrill preached a fine discourse.

"In the afternoon President Phelps continued the services of the day by reading the fifth chapter of Matthew, also the laws regulating the High Council, and made some remarks upon them, after which sacrament was administered. I then confirmed a number who had been baptized, and blessed a number of children, in the name of Jesus Christ, with the blessings of the new and everlasting covenant. Notice was then given that the Elders' School would commence on the morrow.

"Monday, 2. I was engaged in regulating the affairs of the school, after which I had my team prepared, and Sidney, Oliver, Frederick, my scribe, and a number of others went to Willoughby to hear Doctor Piexotto deliver a lecture on the theory and practice of physic. Called at Mr. Cushman's, dined, attended the lecture. Was treated with great respect throughout, and returned home.

"Lyman Wight arrived from Zion, also George A. and Lyman Smith returned from a mission, after an absence of
Bookbindery. five months, to the east. The question was agitated whether Frederick G. Williams or Oliver Cowdery should go to New York, to make arrangements respecting a bookbindery. They referred to me for a decision.[1] . . .

"Tuesday, 3. Thus came the word of the Lord unto me concerning the Twelve.[2] . . .

[1] [The following was obtained:—]
It is not my will that my servant Frederick should go to New York, but inasmuch as he wishes to go and visit his relations, that he may warn them to flee the wrath to come, let him go and see them for that purpose, and let that be his only business, and behold. in this thing, he shall be blessed with power to overcome their prejudices; verily thus saith the Lord. Amen.—*Millennial Star*, vol. 15, p. 374.

[2] Behold, they are under condemnation, because they have not been sufficiently humble in my sight, and in consequence of their covetous desires, in that they have not dealt equally with each other in the division of the moneys which came into their hands; nevertheless, some of them dealt equally, therefore they shall be rewarded; but verily I say unto you, they must all humble themselves before me, before they will be accounted worthy to receive an endowment, to go forth in my name unto all nations.
As for my servant William, let the eleven humble themselves in prayer and in faith, and wait on me in patience, and my servant William shall return, and I will yet make him a polished shaft in my quiver, in bringing down the wickedness and abominations of men; and there shall be none mightier than he, in his day and generation, nevertheless. if he repent not speedily he shall be brought low, and shall be chastened

" ... Wednesday, 4. At home in the morning. Attended school during school hours, made rapid progress in our studies. In the evening lectured on grammar, at home. King Follet arrived from Zion this day.

"Thursday, 5. Attended school. Isaac Morley came in from the East.

"This morning I was called to visit Thomas Burdick, who was sick. I took my scribe with me, and we prayed for and laid our hands on him in the name of the Lord Jesus Christ, and rebuked his affliction.

"William E. McLellin and Orson Hyde came in and desired to hear the revelation concerning the Twelve. My scribe read it to them. They expressed some little dissatisfaction, but after examining their own hearts they acknowledged it to be the word of the Lord, and said they were satisfied. After school Brigham Young came in and desired also to hear it read; after hearing it, he appeared perfectly satisfied.

"In the evening I lectured on grammar.

"Friday morning, 6. At home. Attended school during school hours, returned and spent the evening at home. I was this morning introduced to a man from the East. After hearing my name, he remarked that I was nothing but a man, indicating by this expression that he had supposed that a person to whom the Lord should see fit to reveal his will must be something more than a man. He seemed to have forgotten the saying that fell from the lips of St.

---

sorely for all his iniquities he has committed against me; nevertheless the sin which he has sinned against me is not even now more grievous than the sin with which my servant David W. Patten, and my servant Orson Hyde, and my servant William E. McLellin have sinned against me, and the residue are not sufficiently humble before me.

Behold the parable which I spake concerning a man having twelve sons; for what man among you having twelve sons and is no respecter of them, and they serve him obediently, and he saith unto one, Be thou clothed in robes and sit thou here; and to the other, Be thou clothed in rags and sit thou there; and looketh upon his sons and saith, I am just? Ye will answer and say, No man; and ye answer truly; therefore, verily thus saith the Lord your God, I appoint these Twelve that they should be equal in their ministry, and in their portion, and in their evangelical rights; wherefore they have sinned a very grievous sin, inasmuch as they have made themselves unequal, and have not hearkened unto my voice; therefore let them repent speedily and prepare their hearts for the solemn assembly, and for the great day which is to come; verily thus saith the Lord. Amen.—*Millennial Star*, vol. 15, p. 374.

James, that Elias was a man of passions like unto us,
yet he had such power with God that he in answer to his
prayers shut the heavens that they gave no rain for the
space of three years and six months; and again, in answer
to his prayer, the heavens gave forth rain, and the earth
brought forth fruit; and indeed such is the darkness and
ignorance of this generation that they look upon it as
incredible that a man should have any intercourse with his
Maker.

"Saturday, 7. Spent the day at home, attending to my
domestic concerns.

"The word of the Lord came unto me.[*]

"Sunday, 8. Went to meeting in the morning at the usual
hour. . . .

"Monday morning, 9. After breakfast, Mary Whitcher
came in and wished to see me. I granted her request. She
gave a relation of her grievances, which are unfathomable
at present, and if true, sore indeed; and I pray my heavenly
Father, to bring the truth of the case to light, that the
reward due to evil doers may be given them, and that the
afflicted and oppressed may be delivered.

"While sitting in my house, between ten and eleven this
morning, a man came in and introduced himself to me by the
name of 'Joshua, the Jewish Minister.' His appearance was
something singular, having a beard about three inches in
length, quite grey; also his hair was long, and considerably
silvered with age; I thought him about fifty or fifty-five
years old; tall, strait, slender built, of thin visage, blue
eyes, and fair complexion; wore a sea-green frock coat and
pantaloons, black fur hat with narrow brim; and, while
speaking, frequently shut his eyes, with a scowl on his countenance. I made some inquiry after his name, but received
no definite answer. We soon commenced talking on the sub-

---

[*] Behold, I am well pleased with my servant Isaac Morley, and my
servant Edward Partridge, because of the integrity of their hearts in
laboring in my vineyard, for the salvation of the souls of men. Verily I
say unto you, their sins are forgiven them, therefore say unto them, in
my name, that it is my will that they should tarry for a little season,
and attend the school, and also the solemn assembly, for a wise purpose
in me. Even so. Amen.

ject of religion, and, after I had made some remarks concerning the Bible, I commenced giving him a relation of the circumstances connected with the coming forth of the Book of Mormon, as recorded in the former part of this history.

"While I was relating a brief history of the establishment of the Church of Christ in the last days, Joshua seemed to be highly entertained. When I had closed my narration, I observed that the hour of worship and dinner had arrived, and invited him to tarry, to which he consented. After dinner the conversation was resumed, and Joshua proceeded to make some remarks on the prophecies, as follows: He observed that he was aware that I could bear stronger meat than many others, therefore he should open his mind the more freely. . . .

"I told Joshua I did not understand his remarks on the resurrection, and wished him to explain.

"He replied that he did not feel impressed by the Spirit to unfold it further at present, but perhaps he might at some other time.

"I then withdrew to transact some business with a gentleman who had called to see me, when Joshua informed my scribe that he was born in Cambridge, Washington County, New York. He says that all the railroads, canals, and other improvements are performed by the spirits of the resurrection. The silence spoken of by John the Revelator, which is to be in heaven for the space of half an hour, is between 1830 and 1851, during which time the judgments of God will be poured out, after that time there will be peace.

"Curiosity to see a man that was reputed to be a Jew caused many to call during the day, and more particularly in the evening.

"Suspicions were entertained that the said Joshua was the noted Matthias of New York, spoken so much of in the public prints, on account of the trials he endured in that place, before a court of justice, for murder, manslaughter, contempt of court, whipping his daughter, etc.; for the last two crimes he was imprisoned, and came out about four months since. After some equivocating he confessed that he really was Matthias.

"After supper I proposed that he should deliver a lecture to us. He did so, sitting in his chair.

. "He commenced by saying, 'God said, let there be light, and there was light,' which he dwelt upon through his discourse. He made some very excellent remarks, but his mind was evidently filled with darkness.

"After the congregation dispersed, he conversed freely upon the circumstances that transpired at New York. His name is Robert Matthias. He says that Joshua is his priestly name. During all this time I did not contradict his sentiments, wishing to draw out all that I could concerning his faith.

"Mr. Beeman, of New York, came to ask advice of me, whether he had better purchase lands in this vicinity, as he could not arrange his business to go to Missouri next spring. I advised him to come here and settle until he could move to Zion.

"Tuesday, 10. I resumed conversation with Matthias, and desired him to enlighten my mind more on his views respecting the resurrection.

"He said that he possessed the spirit of his fathers, that he was a literal descendant of Matthias the apostle that was chosen in the place of Judas that fell; and that his spirit was resurrected in him; and that this was the way or scheme of eternal life—this transmigration of soul or spirit from father to son.

"I told him that his doctrine was of the Devil, that he was in reality in possession of a wicked and depraved spirit, although he professed to be the Spirit of truth itself; and he said also that he possessed the soul of Christ.

"He tarried until Wednesday, the 11th, after breakfast, when I told him that my God told me that his god was the Devil, and I could not keep him any longer, and he must depart. And so I, for once, cast out the Devil in bodily shape, and I believe a murderer. . . .

"Thursday, 12. Attended school again during school hours, rain and snow still falling, about one inch in depth, and wind very heavy, the weather extremely unpleasant. The laborers who commenced finishing the outside of the chapel, were obliged to break off from their business at the commencement of this storm, on the 11th instant.

"This evening at six o'clock met with the Council of the Twelve, by their request. Nine of them were present. Council opened by singing and prayer. And I made some remarks as follows:—

"'I am happy in the enjoyment of this opportunity of meeting with this council on this occasion. I am satisfied Council with that the Spirit of the Lord is here, and I am satis- the Twelve. fied with all the brethren present; and I need not say that you have my utmost confidence, and that I intend to uphold you to the uttermost, for I am well aware that you have to sustain my character against the vile calumnies and reproaches of this ungodly generation, and that you delight in so doing.

"'Darkness prevails at this time as it was at the time Jesus Christ was about to be crucified. The powers of dark- ness strove to obscure the glorious Sun of righteousness that began to dawn upon the world and was soon to burst in great blessings upon the heads of the faithful; and let me tell you, brethren, that great blessings await us at this time, and will soon be poured out upon us, if we are faithful in all things, for we are even entitled to greater blessings than they were, because they had the person of Christ with them to instruct them in the great plan of salvation. His personal presence we have not, therefore we have need of great faith, on account of our peculiar circumstances; and I am deter- mined to do all that I can to uphold you, although I may do many things inadvertently that are not right in the sight of God.

"'You want to know many things that are before you that you may know how to prepare yourselves for the great things that God is about to bring to pass. But there is one great deficiency or obstruction in the way that deprives us of the greater blessings; and in order to make the foundation of this church complete and permanent we must remove this obstruction, which is, to attend to certain duties that we have not as yet attended to. I supposed I had established this church on a permanent foundation when I went to Missouri, and indeed I did so, for if I had been taken away, it would have been enough, but I yet live, and therefore God requires more at my hands. The item to which I wish the more particularly to call your attention to-night, is the ordinance of washing of feet. This we have not done as yet, but it is necessary now, as much as it was in the days of the Savior; and we must have a place prepared that we may attend to this ordinance aside from the world.

" 'We have not desired much from the hand of the Lord with that faith and obedience that we ought, yet we have enjoyed great blessings, and we are not so sensible of this as we should be. When or where has God suffered one of the witnesses or first elders of this church to fall? Never, nor nowhere. Amidst all the calamities and judgments that have befallen the inhabitants of the earth his almighty arm has sustained us, men and devils have raged, and spent their malice in vain. We must have all things prepared, and call our solemn assembly as the Lord has commanded us, that we may be able to accomplish his great work, and it must be done in God's own way. The house of the Lord must be prepared, and the solemn assembly called and organized in it, according to the order of the house of God; and in it we must attend to the ordinance of washing of feet. It was never intended for any but official members. It is calculated to unite our hearts, that we may be one in feeling and sentiment, and that our faith may be strong, so that Satan cannot overthrow us, nor have any power over us.

" 'The endowment you are so anxious about, you cannot comprehend now, nor could Gabriel explain it to the understanding of your dark minds. But strive to be prepared in your hearts; be faithful in all things, that when we meet in the solemn assembly, that is, such as God shall name out of all the official members will meet, and we must be clean every whit. Let us be faithful and silent, brethren, and if God gives you a manifestation, keep it to yourselves; be watchful and prayerful, and you shall have a prelude of those joys that God will pour out on that day. Do not watch for iniquity in each other, if you do you will not get an endowment, for God will not bestow it on such. But if we are faithful, and live by every word that proceeds forth from the mouth of God, I will venture to prophesy that we shall get a blessing that will be worth remembering, if we should live as long as John the Revelator; our blessings will be such as we have not realized before, nor in this generation. The order of the house of God has been, and ever will be, the same, even after Christ comes; and after the termination of the thousand years it will be the same; and we shall finally roll into the celestial Kingdom of God, and enjoy it forever.

" 'You need an endowment, brethren, in order that you may be prepared and able to overcome all things; and those that reject your testimony will be damned. The sick will be healed, the lame made to walk, the deaf to hear, and the blind to see, through your instrumentality. But let me tell you, that you will not have power, after the endowment, to heal those that have not faith, nor to benefit them, for you might as well expect to benefit a devil in hell as such who are possessed of his spirit, and are willing to keep it; for they are habitations for devils, and only fit for his society. But when you are endowed and prepared to preach the gospel to all nations, kindred, and tongues, in their own languages, you must faithfully warn all, and bind up the testimony, and seal up the law, and the destroying angel will follow close at your heels, and exercise his tremendous mission upon the children of disobedience, and destroy the workers of iniquity, while the saints will be gathered out from among them, and stand in holy places ready to meet the Bridegroom when he comes.

" 'I feel disposed to speak a few words more to you, my brethren, concerning the endowment: All who are prepared, and are sufficiently pure to abide the presence of the Savior, will see him in the solemn assembly.'

"The brethren expressed their gratification for the instruction I had given them. We then closed by prayer, when I returned home and retired to rest.

"Friday, 13. Attended school during school hours; after school, returned home. . . .

"This afternoon, Erastus Holmes, of Newbury, Ohio, called
on me to inquire about the establishment of the
church, and to be instructed in doctrine more
perfectly.

Mr. Holmes.

"I gave him a brief relation of my experience while in my
juvenile years, say from six years old up to the time I
received the first visitation of angels, which was when I was
about fourteen years old; also the revelations that I received
afterwards concerning the Book of Mormon, and a short
account of the rise and progress of the church up to this
date.

"He listened very attentively, and seemed highly gratified,
and intends to unite with the church.

"On Sabbath morning, 15th, he went with me to meeting,
which was held in the schoolhouse, as the chapel was not
finished plastering.

"President Rigdon preached on the subject of men's being
called to preach the gospel, their qualifications, etc. We
had a fine discourse; it was very interesting indeed. Mr.
Holmes was well satisfied, and returned and dined with me.
Said Holmes has been a member of the Methodist Church,
and was excommunicated for receiving the elders of the Latter Day Saints into his house.

"Monday, the 16th. . . .

"In the course of the day Father Beeman, Elder Strong,
and others, called to counsel with me. In the evening a
council was called at my house to counsel with Alva Beeman
on the subject of his moving to Missouri. I had previously
told him that the Lord had said that he had better go to
Missouri next spring; however, he wished a council called.
The council met, and President David Whitmer arose and
said the Spirit manifested to him that it was his duty to go.
Others bore the same testimony.

"The same night I received the word of the Lord on Mr.
Holmes' case. He had desired that I would inquire at the
hand of the Lord whether it was his duty to be baptized
here, or wait until he returned home. The word of the Lord
came unto me, saying, that Mr. Holmes had better not be
baptized here, and that he had better not return by water,

also that there were three men that were seeking his destruction; to beware of his enemies.

"Tuesday, 17. Exhibited the alphabet of the ancient records to Mr. Holmes and some others. Went with him to F. G. Williams' to see the mummies. We then took the parting hand, and he started for home, being strong in the faith of the gospel of Jesus Christ and determined to obey its requirements. I returned home and spent the day in dictating and comparing letters. A fine, pleasant day, although cool.

"This evening at early candle light I preached at the schoolhouse.

"Wednesday, 18. At home in the forenoon until about eleven o'clock. I then went to Preserved Harris' to preach his father's funeral sermon, by the request of his family. I preached on the subject of the resurrection. The congregation were very attentive. My wife, my mother, and my scribe accompanied me to the funeral. Pleasant out, but cool and cloudy on our return. . . .

"At evening Bishop Whitney, his wife, father, mother, and sister-in-law came and invited me and my wife to go with them and visit Father Smith and family. My wife was unwell and could not go, but I and my scribe went.

"When we arrived some of the young elders were about engaging in a debate on the subject of miracles, the question, Was it or was it not the design of Christ to establish his gospel by miracles? After an interesting debate of three hours or more, during which time much talent was displayed, it was decided, by the President of the debate, in the negative, which was a righteous decision.

"I discovered in this debate much warmth displayed, too much zeal for mastery, too much of that enthusiasm that characterizes a lawyer at the bar, who is determined to defend his cause, right or wrong. I therefore availed myself of this favorable opportunity to drop a few words upon this subject, by way of advice, that they might improve their minds and cultivate their powers of intellect in a proper manner, that they might not incur the displeasure of heaven; that they should handle sacred things very sacredly, and with due deference to the opinions of others, and with an eye single to the glory of God.

"Thursday, 19. Went, in company with Dr. Williams and my scribe, to see how the workmen prospered in finishing the house. The masons in the inside had commenced putting on the finishing coat of plastering. On my return I met Lloyd and Lorenzo Lewis, and conversed with them upon the subject or their being disaffected. I found that they were not so, as touching the faith of the church, but with some of the members. I returned home and spent the day in translating the Egyptian records. A warm and pleasant day.

"Friday, 20. At home in the morning. Weather warm and rainy. We spent the day in translating, and made rapid progress.

"At evening President Cowdery returned from New York, bringing with him a quantity of Hebrew books, for the benefit of the school. He presented me with a Hebrew Bible, Lexicon, and Grammar; also a Greek Lexicon, and Webster's English Lexicon. President Cowdery had a prosperous journey, according to the prayers of the Saints in Kirtland.

"Saturday, 21. Spent the day at home, in examining my books, and studying the Hebrew alphabet.

"At evening, met with our Hebrew class, to make some arrangements about a teacher. It was decided, by the voice of the school, to send to New York for a Jew to teach us the language, if we could get released from the engagements we had made with Dr. Piexotto to teach us, having ascertained that he was not qualified to give us the knowledge we wished to acquire of the Hebrew.

"Sunday, 22. Went to meeting at the usual hour. Simeon Carter preached from the seventh of Matthew. President Rigdon's brother-in-law and other relatives were at meeting.

"In the afternoon the meeting was held in the schoolhouse.

"In the evening, a council of high priests and elders was held in the presence of the members of the church, when Mr. Andrew Jackson Squires, who had been an ordained elder in the church, and for a time had preached the gospel successfully, but after a while sent his license to President Smith, in a letter, came before the council and confessed that he had been in temptation and fallen into error, so much as to join the Methodists; yet said he was not in faith with their doctrine. He desired to return to the fellowship of the church, asked forgiveness of the brethren, and restoration of his license. . . .

"President Rigdon showed the folly of fellowshipping any doctrine or spirit aside from that of Christ.

"Mr. Squires arose and said he felt firm in the determination of doing the will of God in all things, or as far as in him lay; was sorry for his faults, and, by the grace of God, would forsake them in future.

"Council and church voted to restore him to fellowship, and the office of elder also, and that the clerk give him a license.

"Monday, 23. Several brethren called to converse with me and see the records. Received a letter from Jared Carter. Spent the day in conversing, and in studying the Hebrew. A stormy day.

"Tuesday, 24. At home. Spent the forenoon instructing those that called to inquire concerning the things of God in the last days.

"In the afternoon we translated some of the Egyptian records.

"I had an invitation to attend a wedding at Brother Hyrum Smith's in the evening; also to solemnize the matrimonial ceremony between Newel Knight and

A marriage.

Lydia Goldthwaite.[4] My wife accompanied me. On our arrival a considerable company had collected. The bridegroom and bride came in, and took their seats, which gave me to understand that they were ready. After prayers I requested them to rise and join hands. I then remarked that marriage was an institution of heaven, instituted in the garden of Eden; that it was necessary it should be solemnized by the authority of the everlasting priesthood. The ceremony was original with me, and in substance as follows:

[4] Lydia Knight in her history, page 30, says this was on the 23d.

You covenant to be each other's companions through life, and discharge the duties of husband and wife in every respect; to which they assented. I then pronounced them husband and wife in the name of God, and also the blessings that the Lord conferred upon Adam and Eve in the garden of Eden, that is, to multiply and replenish the earth, with the addition of long life and prosperity. Dismissed them and returned home. Freezing, some snow on the ground.

"Wednesday, 25. Spent the day in translating. Harvey Redfield and Jesse Hitchcock arrived from Missouri. The latter says that he has no doubt but a dose of poison was administered to him, in a bowl of milk, but God delivered him.

"Thursday, 26. Spent the day in translating Egyptian characters from the papyrus, though severely afflicted with a cold. Robert Rathbone and George Morey arrived from Zion.

"Friday, 27. Much afflicted with my cold, yet I am determined to overcome in the name of the Lord Jesus Christ. Spent the day at home, reading Hebrew. Brother Parrish, my scribe, being afflicted with a cold, asked me to lay my hands on him in the name of the Lord. I did so, and in return I asked him to lay his hands on me. We were both relieved.

"Saturday, 28. Spent the morning in comparing our journal. Elder Josiah Clark, from the State of Kentucky, called on me. Considerably recovered from my cold. Cold and stormy, snow falling, and winter seems fast to be closing in; all nature shrinks before the chilling blasts of rigid winter. Elder Clark, above-mentioned, whose residence is about three miles from Cincinnati, was bitten by a mad dog some three or four years since; has doctored much, and received some benefit, but is much afflicted notwithstanding. He came here that he might be benefited by the prayers of the church. Accordingly we prayed for and laid hands on him in the name of the Lord Jesus Christ, and anointed him with oil, and rebuked his afflictions, praying our heavenly Father to hear and answer our prayers, according to our faith. Cold and snowy.

"Sunday morning, 29. Went to meeting at the usual hour. Elder Morley preached; and in the afternoon, Bishop Partridge. These discourses were well adapted to the times in which we live, and the circumstances under which we are placed. Their words were words of wisdom, like apples of gold in pictures of silver, spoken in the simple accents of a child, yet sublime as the voice of an angel. The saints appeared to be much pleased with the beautiful discourses of these two fathers in Israel. After these services closed three of the Zion brethren came forward and received their blessings, and Solon Foster was ordained an elder. The Lord's Supper was administered. Spent the evening at home. Snow fell about one foot deep. Very cold.

"Monday morning, 30. The snow continues to fall—an uncommon storm for this country, and this season of the year. Spent the day in reviewing and copying the letter I dictated on the 16th, concerning the gathering, for the *Messenger and Advocate*. Henry Capron, an old acquaintance from Manchester, New York, called on me. I showed him the Egyptian records.

"December 1, 1835. At home. Spent the day in writing for the *Messenger and Advocate*. Fine sleighing, and the snow yet falling.

"Wednesday, 2. A fine morning. I started to ride to Painesville, with my family and scribe. When we were passing through Mentor Street, we overtook a team with two men on the sleigh. I politely asked them to let me pass. They granted my request, and as we passed them they bawled out, 'Do you get any revelation lately?' with an addition of blackguard language that I did not understand. This is a fair sample of the character of Mentor Street inhabitants, who are ready to abuse and scandalize men, who never laid a straw in their way; and in fact those whose faces they never saw, and [whom they] cannot bring an accusation against, either of a temporal or spiritual nature, except our firm belief in the fullness of the gospel. . . .

"When we arrived at Painesville we called at Sister Harriet Howe's,[6] and left my wife and family to visit her, while

[6] This is the wife of E. D. Howe, author of "The History of Mormonism."

we rode into town to do some business. Called, and visited H. Kingsbury. Dined with Sister Howe, and returned home. Had a fine ride— sleighing good, weather pleasant.

"Thursday, 3. At home. Wrote a letter to David Dort, Rochester, Michigan; another to Almira Schoby, Liberty, Clay County, Missouri.

"At evening visited with my wife, at Thomas Carrico's. A respectable company waited our arrival. After singing and prayer, I delivered an address on matrimony, and joined in marriage, Warren Parrish and Martha H. Raymond. Closed by singing and prayer. And after refreshment, returned home, having spent the evening very agreeably.

"Friday, 4. In company with Vinson Knight drew three hundred and fifty dollars out of Painesville bank, on three months' credit, for which we gave the names of F. G. Williams and Company, N. K. Whitney, John Johnson, and Vinson Knight. Settled with Brother Hyrum Smith and Vinson Knight, and paid Knight two hundred and forty-five dollars; also have it in my power to pay J. Lewis, for which blessing I feel heartily thankful to my heavenly Father, and ask him in the name of Jesus Christ, to enable us to extricate ourselves from all embarrassments whatever, that we may not be brought into disrepute in any respect, that our enemies may not have any power over us. Spent the day at home, a part of the day studying Hebrew. Warm, with some rain, snow fast melting.

"This evening a Mr. John Hollister, of Portage County, Ohio, called to see me, on the subject of religion, and I spent the evening conversing with him. He tarried over night with me, and acknowledged in the morning, that although he had thought he knew something about religion, he was now sensible that he knew but little, which was the greatest trait of wisdom I could discover in him.

"Saturday, 5. Weather cold and freezing, with a moderate fall of snow. In the forenoon, studying Hebrew with Dr. Williams and President Cowdery. I am laboring under some indisposition of health. . . .

"Sunday, 6. Went to meeting at the usual hour. Gideon Carter preached a splendid discourse. . . .

"Monday, 7. Received a letter from Milton Holmes, and was much rejoiced to hear from him, and of his success in proclaiming the gospel. Wrote him a letter, requesting him to return to Kirtland. Spent the day in reading Hebrew. Mr. John Hollister called to take the parting hand with me, and remarked that he had been in darkness all his days, but had now found the light, and intended to obey it.

"This evening a number of brethren called to see the records, which I exhibited and explained. Fine sleighing.

"Tuesday morning, 8. At home. Read Hebrew in company with Dr. Williams, President Cowdery, Brother Hyrum Smith, and Orson Pratt.

"In the evening preached at the schoolhouse as usual; had great liberty in speaking, congregation attentive. After the services closed, the brethren proposed to draw wood for me.

"Wednesday, 9. At home. . . .

"This afternoon I was called, in company with President David Whitmer, to visit Angeline Works. We found her very sick, and so much deranged that she did not recognize her friends and intimate acquaintances. We prayed for and laid hands on her in the name of Jesus Christ, and commanded her in his name to receive her senses, which were immediately restored. We also prayed that she might be restored to health; and she said she was better. . . .

"The petitions of the people, from all parts of the United States, to the Governor of Missouri to restore the saints to their possessions, were arranged and mailed at Kirtland, this day, for Missouri. The petitions were numerous, and the package large, the postage thereon being five dollars. It was directed to the Governor.

"Friday morning, 11. A fire broke out in a shoemaker's shop owned by Orson Johnson, but the flames were soon extinguished by the active exertions of the brethren. A pleasant morning. Spent the day in reading, and instructing those who called for advice.

"Saturday morning, 12. Spent the forenoon in reading. . . .

"At evening attended a debate at Brother William Smith's, on the following question: Was it necessary for God to reveal himself to man in order for their happiness? I was on the affirmative, and the last to speak on that side of the question, but while listening with interest to the ingenuity displayed on both sides, I was called away to visit Sister Angeline Works, who was supposed to be dangerously sick. Elder Corrill and myself went and prayed for and laid hands on her in the name of Jesus Christ; and leaving her apparently better, returned home.

"Sunday, 13.   At the usual hour, ten a. m.. attended meeting at the schoolhouse on the flats.   Elder Jesse Hitchcock preached a very feeling discourse.

"In the afternoon Elder Peter Whitmer related his experience; after which President F. G. Williams related his also. They both spoke of many things connected with the rise and progress of this church, which were interesting.   After this the Sacrament of the Lord's Supper was administered, under the superintendence of President David Whitmer, after which I made some remarks respecting prayer meetings, and our meeting was closed by invoking the blessing of heaven. I returned home and ordered my horse, and myself and scribe rode to Mr. E. Jenning's, where I joined Ebenezer Robinson and Angeline Works in matrimony, according to previous engagements.   Miss Works had so far recovered from her illness as to be able to sit in her easy chair while I pronounced the marriage ceremony.

"We then rode to Mr. McWithy's, a distance of about three miles from town, where I had been solicited to attend another marriage.   We found a large and respectable number of the friends present.   I had been requested to make some preliminary remarks on the subject of matrimony, touching the design of the Almighty in this institution, also the duties of husbands and wives towards each other.   And after opening our interview with singing and prayer I delivered a lecture of about forty minutes, in which all seemed interested, except one or two individuals, who manifested a spirit of groveling contempt, which I was constrained to reprove and rebuke sharply.   After I had closed my remarks I sealed the matrimonial engagements between Mr. E. Webb and Miss E. A. McWithy, in the name of God, and pronouncing the blessings of heaven upon their heads, closed by returning thanks. A sumptuous feast was then spread, and the company invited to seat themselves at the table by pairs, male and female, commencing with the eldest. The interview was conducted with propriety and decorum, and cheerfulness prevailed. After spending the evening agreeably until nine o'clock, we pronounced a blessing upon the company, and returned home. . . .

"Monday, 14. A number of brethren from New York called to visit me and see the Egyptian records. Also Elder Harris returned from Palmyra, New York, and Brother Francis Eaton of the same place, and Sister Harriet Howe, called to visit us. . . .

"Tuesday, 15. At home, and. as usual, was blessed with much company. Samuel Barnum is very sick, his arm much inflamed.

"This afternoon Elder Orson Hyde handed me a letter, the purport of which was that he was dissatisfied with the

O. Hyde complains.

committee in their dealings with him, in temporal affairs; that is, that they did not deal as liberally with him as they did with Elder William Smith; also requested me to reconcile the revelation given to the Twelve since their return from the East, that unless these things and others named in the letter could be reconciled to his mind, his honor would not stand united with them. This I believe is the amount of the contents of the letter, although much was written.

"My feelings on this occasion were much lacerated, knowing that I had dealt in righteousness with him in all things and endeavored to promote his happiness and well-being as much as lay in my power. And I feel that these reflections are ungrateful, and founded in jealousy, and that the adversary is striving with all his subtle devices and influence to destroy him, by causing a division among the Twelve, whom God has chosen to open the gospel kingdom in all nations. But I pray my heavenly Father in the name of Jesus of Nazareth that he may be delivered from the power of the destroyer, that his faith fail not in this hour of temptation, and prepare him, and all the elders, to receive an endowment in thy house, even according to thine own order from time to time, as thou seest them worthy to be called into thy solemn assembly.

"Wednesday morning, 16. Weather extremely cold. I went to the council room to lay before the Presidency the letter that I received yesterday from Elder Orson Hyde; but when I arrived I found that I had lost said letter; but I laid the substance of it, as far as I could recollect, before the council; but they had not time to attend to it, on account of other business; accordingly adjourned until Monday evening, the 20th instant. Returned home.

"Elders McLellin, B. Young, and J. Carter called and paid me a visit with which I was much gratified. . . .

"This evening, according to adjournment, I went to Brother William Smith's, to take part in the debate that was More trouble commenced on Saturday evening last. After the with William. debate was concluded, and a decision given in favor of the affirmative of the question, some altercation took place upon the impropriety of continuing the school (debate) fearing that it would not result in good. Brother William opposed these measures and insisted on having another question proposed, and at length became much enraged, particularly at me, and used violence upon my person, and also upon Elder J. Carter, and some others, for which I am grieved beyond description, and can only pray God to forgive him inasmuch as he repents of his wickedness and humbles himself before the Lord.

"Thursday morning, 17. At home, quite unwell. Elder Orson Hyde called to see me, and presented me with a copy O. Hyde's of the letter he handed me on Tuesday last, which case. I had lost. The following is a copy:—

"'December 15, 1835.

"'President Smith; Sir:—You may esteem it a novel circumstance to receive a written communication from me at this time. My reasons for writing are the following: I have some things which I wish to communicate to you, and feeling a greater liberty to do it by writing alone by myself, I take this method, and it is generally the case that you are thronged with business and not convenient to spend much time in conversing upon subjects of the following nature.

Therefore let these excuses palliate the novelty of the circumstance, and patiently hear my recital.

" 'After the committee had received their stock of fall and winter goods, I went to Elder Cahoon and told him I was destitute of a cloak, and wanted him to trust me, until spring, for materials to make one. He told me that he would trust me until January, but must then have his pay, as the payments for the goods became due at that time. I told him I knew not from whence the money would come, and I could not promise it so soon. But, in a few weeks after, I unexpectedly obtained the money to buy a cloak, and applied immediately to Elder Cahoon for one, and told him that I had the cash to pay for it; but he said the materials for cloaks were all sold, and that he could not accommodate me; and I will here venture a guess that he has not realized the cash for one cloak pattern.

" 'A few weeks after this I called on Elder Cahoon again and told him that I wanted cloth for some shirts, to the amount of four or five dollars. I told him that I would pay him in the spring, and sooner if I could. He let me have it. Not long after my school was established, and some of the hands who labored on the house attended and wished to pay me at the committee's store for their tuition. I called at the store to see if any negotiation could be made, and ·they take me off where I owed them; but no such negotiation could be made. These, with some other circumstances of a like character, called forth the following reflections: —

" 'In the first place I gave the committee two hundred and seventy-five dollars in cash, besides some more, and during the last season have traveled through the middle and eastern States to support and uphold the store; and in so doing have reduced myself to nothing, in a pecuniary point. Under these circumstances this establishment refused to render me that accommodation which the worldling's establishment gladly would have done; and one, too, which never received a donation from me, or in whose favor I never raised my voice or exerted my influence. But after all this, thought I, it may be right, and I will be still—until, not long since, I ascertained that Elder William Smith could go to the store and get whatever he pleased, and no one to say, Why do ye so? until his account has amounted to seven hundred dollars or thereabouts, and that he was a silent partner in the concern, yet not acknowledged as such, fearing that his creditors would make a haul upon the store.

" 'While we were abroad this last season, we strained every nerve to obtain a little something for our families, and regularly divided the moneys equally for aught I know, not knowing that William had such a fountain at home from whence he drew his support. I then called to mind the revelation in which myself, McLellin, and Patten were chastened; and also the quotation in that revelation of the parable of the twelve sons, as if the original meaning referred directly to the Twelve Apostles of the Church of the Latter Day Saints. I would now ask if each one of the Twelve has not an equal right to the same accommodations from that store, provided they are alike faithful? If not, with such a combination, mine honor be not thou united. If each one has the same right, take the baskets off from our noses, and put one to William's nose; or if this cannot be done, reconcile the parable of the twelve sons with the superior privileges that William has. Pardon me if I speak in parables or parody.

" 'A certain shepherd had twelve sons, and he sent them out one day to go and gather his flock which was scattered upon the mountains and in the valleys afar off. They were all obedient to their father's mandate, and at evening they returned with the flock, and one son received wool enough to make him warm and comfortable, and also received of the flesh and milk of the flock; the other eleven received not so much as one kid to make merry with their friends.

" 'These facts, with some others, have disqualified my mind for studying the Hebrew language, at present; and believing as I do that I must sink or swim, or in other words, take care of myself, I have thought that I should take the most efficient means in my power to get out of debt; and to this end I proposed taking the school; but if I am not thought competent to take the charge of it, or worthy to be placed in that station, I must devise some other means to help myself, although having been ordained to that office under your own hand, with a promise that it should not be taken from me.

" 'The conclusion of the whole matter is such, I am willing to continue and do all I can, provided we can share equal benefits one with the other, and upon no other principle whatever. If one has his support from the "public crib," let them all have it; but if one is pinched, I am willing to be, provided we are all alike. If the principle of impartiality and equity can be observed by all, I think that I will not peep again. If I am damned, it will be for doing what I think is right. There have been two applications made to me to go into business since I talked of taking the school, but it is in the world, and I had rather remain in Kirtland, if I can consistently. All I ask is right.

" 'I am, sir, with respect, your obedient servant,

" 'ORSON HYDE.

" 'To President J. Smith, Jr., Kirtland, etc.'

"Elder O. Hyde read the foregoing copy himself, and I explained upon the objections he had set forth in it, and satisfied his mind upon every point, perfectly. And he observed, after I got through, that he was more than satisfied, and would attend the Hebrew school, and took the parting hand with me with every expression of friendship that a gentleman and a Christian could manifest; which I felt to reciprocate with cheerfulness, and entertain the best of feeling for him, and most cheerfully forgive him the ingratitude which was manifested in his letter, knowing that it was for want of correct information, that his mind was disturbed, as far as his reflections related to me; but on the part of the committee he was not treated right in all things; however, all things are settled amicably, and no hardness exists between us and them.

"I told Elder Cahoon, of the Temple committee, that we must sustain the Twelve, and not let them go down; if we do not, they must go down, for the burden is on them, and is coming on them heavier and heavier. If the Twelve go down, we must go down, and we must sustain them.

"My father and mother called this evening to see me upon the subject of the difficulty that transpired at their house, on

Wednesday evening, between me and my brother William. They were sorely afflicted in mind on account of that occurrence. I conversed with them and convinced them that I was not to blame in taking the course I did, but had acted in righteousness in all things on that occasion. I invited them to come and live with me. They consented to do so, as soon as it was practicable.

William a case again.

"Friday morning, 18. Brother Hyrum Smith called to see me, and read a letter that he received from William, in which he asked forgiveness for the abuse he offered to him [Hyrum] at the debate. He tarried most of the forenoon, and conversed freely with me upon the subject of the difficulty existing between me and Brother William. He said that he was perfectly satisfied with the course I had taken in rebuking him in his wickedness, but he is wounded to the very soul, because of the conduct of William; and although he feels the tender feelings of a brother towards him, yet he can but look upon his conduct as an abomination in the sight of God. And I could pray in my heart that all my brethren were like unto my beloved brother Hyrum, who possesses the mildness of a lamb, and the integrity of a Job, and in short, the meekness and humility of Christ; and I love him with that love that is stronger than death, for I never had occasion to rebuke him, nor he me, which he declared when he left me to day.

"This day, received the following letter from Brother William Smith:—

" 'Brother Joseph:—Though I do not know but I have forfeited all right and title to the word "brother," in consequence of what I have done, (for I consider, myself, that I am unworthy to be called one,) after coming to myself, and considering what I have done, I feel as though it was a duty to make an humble confession to you, for what I have done, or what took place the other evening; but leave this part of the subject at present. I was called to an account, by the Twelve, yesterday, for my conduct; or they desired to know my mind or determination, and what I was going to do. I told them that on reflection upon the many difficulties that I had had with the church, and the much disgrace I had brought upon myself in consequence of these things, and also that my health would not permit me to go to school to make any preparations for the endowment, and that my health was such that I was not able to travel, that it would be better for them to appoint one in the office that would be better able to fill it, and by doing this they would throw me into the hands of the church, and leave me where I was before I was chosen; then I would not be in a situation to bring so much disgrace upon the cause, when I fell into temptation; and perhaps, by this I might obtain salvation. You know my passions, and the danger of falling from so high a station; and thus by withdrawing from the office of the apostleship, while there is salvation for me, and remaining a member in the church—I feel afraid, if I don't do this, it will be worse for me some other day.

" 'And again, my health is poor, and I am not able to travel, and it is necessary the office should not be idle. And again, I say you know my passions, and I am afraid it will be the worse for me by and by. Do so, if the Lord will have mercy on me, and let me remain as a member in the church, and then I can travel and preach when I am able. Do not think I am your enemy for what I have done. Perhaps you may say or ask why I have not remembered the good that you have done to me. When I reflect upon the injury I have done you, I must confess that I do not know what I have been about. I feel sorry for what I have done, and humbly ask your forgiveness. I have not confidence as yet to come and see you, for I feel ashamed of what I have done; and as I feel now, I feel as though all the confessions that I could make, verbally or by writing, would not be· sufficient to atone for the transgression. Be this as it may, I am willing to make all the restitution you shall require. If I can stay in the church as a member, I will try to make all the satisfaction possible. Yours with respect,

" 'WILLIAM SMITH.

" 'Do not cast me off for what I have done, but strive to save me in the church as a member. I do repent of what I have done to you, and ask your forgiveness. I consider the transgression, the other evening, of no small magnitude; but it is done, and I cannot help it now. I know, Brother Joseph, you are always willing to forgive; but I sometimes think, when I reflect upon the many injuries I have done you, I feel as though confession was hardly sufficient. But have mercy on me this once, and I will try to do so no more.

"'The Twelve called a council yesterday, and sent over after me, and I went over. This council, remember, was called together by themselves, and not by me.   w. s.'

"To the foregoing I gave the following answer the same day:—

"'*Brother William:—* Having received your letter I now proceed to answer it, and shall first proceed to give a brief narration of my feelings and motives since the night I first came to the knowledge of your having a debating school, which was at the time I happened in with Bishop Whitney, his father and mother, etc.; and from that time I took an interest in them, and was delighted with it, and formed a determination to attend the school, for the purpose of obtaining information, and with the idea of imparting the same, through the assistance of the Spirit of the Lord, if by any means I should have faith to do so. And with this intent I went to the school on last Wednesday night, not with the idea of breaking up the school, neither did it enter into my heart that there was any wrangling or jealousies in your heart against me. Notwithstanding, previous to my leaving home, there were feelings of solemnity rolling across my breast, which were unaccountable to me; and also these feelings continued by spells to depress my spirits, and seemed to manifest that all was not right, even after the school commenced, and during the debate; yet I strove to believe that all would work together for good. I was pleased with the power of the arguments that were used, and did not feel to cast any reflections upon anyone that had spoken; but I felt it was the duty of old men that sat as Presidents, to be as grave, at least, as young men, and that it was our duty to smile [not] at solid arguments and sound reasonings; and be impressed with solemnity, which should be manifest in our countenances, when folly and that which militates against truth and righteousness rear their head.

" 'Therefore, in the spirit of my calling, and in view of the authority of the Priesthood that has been conferred upon me, it would be my duty to reprove whatever I esteemed to be wrong, fondly hoping in my heart that all parties would consider it right, and therefore humble themselves, that Satan might not take the advantage of us and hinder the progress of our school.

" 'Now, Brother William, I want you should bear with me, notwithstanding my plainness. I would say to you that my feelings were grieved at the interruption you made upon Elder McLellin. I thought you should have considered your relation with him in your apostleship, and not manifest any divison of sentiment between you and him, for a surrounding multitude to take the advantage of you; therefore, by way of entreaty, on the account of the anxiety I had for your influence and welfare, I said unto you, Do not have any feelings; or something to that amount. Why I am thus particular is that if you have misconstrued my feelings towards you, you may be corrected. But to proceed. After the school was closed Brother Hyrum requested the privilege of speaking; you objected; however, you said if he would not abuse the school he might speak, and that you would not allow any man to abuse the school in your house. Now you had no reason to suspect that Hyrum would abuse the school; therefore my feelings were mortified at these unnecessary observations. I undertook to reason with you, but you manifested an inconsiderate and stubborn spirit. I then despaired of benefiting you, on account of the spirit you manifested, which drew from me the expression that you was as ugly as the Devil. Father then commanded silence, and I formed a determination to obey his mandate, and was about to leave the house, with the impression that you was under the influence of a wicked spirit; you replied that you would say what you pleased in your own house. Father said, Say what you please, but let the rest hold their tongues. Then a reflection rushed through my mind, of the anxiety and care I have had for you and your family, in doing what I did in finishing your house, and providing flour for your family, etc.; and also, Father had possession in the house, as well as yourself; and when at any time have I transgressed the commandments of my father, or sold my birthright, that I should not have the privilege of speaking in my father's house, or in other words, in my father's family, or in your house (for so we will call it, and so it shall be) that I should not have the privilege of reproving a younger brother? Therefore I said, I will speak, for I built the house, and it is as much mine as yours; or something to that effect. I should have said that I helped to finish the house. I said it merely to show that it could not be the right spirit that would rise up for trifling matters, and undertake to put me to silence. I saw that your indignation was kindled against me, and you made towards me. I was not then to be moved, and I thought to pull off my loose coat, lest it should tangle me, and you be left to hurt me, but not with the intention of hurting you. But you were too soon for me, and having once fallen into the hands of a mob, and been wounded in my side, and now into the hands of a brother, my side gave way. And after having been rescued from your grasp, I left your house with feelings indescribable—the scenery had changed, and all those expectations that I had cherished, when going to your house, and brotherly kindness, charity, forbearance, and natural affection, that in duty binds us not to make each other offenders for a word. But alas! abuse, anger, malice, hatred, and rage, with a lame side, with marks of violence heaped upon me by a brother, were the reflections of my disappointment; and with these I returned home, not able to sit down or rise up without help; but, through the blessing of God, I am now better.

" 'I received your letter, and perused it with care. I have not entertained a feeling of malice against you. I am older than you, and have endured more suffering, having been marred by mobs. The labors of my calling, a series of persecutions and injuries continually heaped upon me—all serve to debilitate my body; and it may be that I cannot boast of being stronger than you. If I could or could not, would this be an honor or dishonor to me? If I could boast, like David, of slaying a Goliath, who defied the armies of the living God; or, like Paul, of contending with Peter, face to face, with sound arguments, it might be an honor; but to mangle the flesh, or seek revenge upon one who never did you any wrong, cannot be a source of sweet reflection to you nor to me, neither to an honorable father and mother, brothers and sisters. And when we reflect with what care and with what unremitting diligence our parents have striven to watch over us, and how many hours of sorrow and anxiety they have spent over our cradles and bedsides, in times of sickness, how careful we ought to be of their feelings in their old age. It cannot be a source of sweet reflection to us to say or do anything that will bring their gray hairs down with sorrow to the grave. .

" 'In your letter you ask my forgiveness, which I readily grant. But it seems to me, that you still retain an idea that I have given you reasons to be angry or disaffected with me. Grant me the privilege of saying then; that however hasty and harsh I may have spoken at any time to you, it has been done for the express purpose of endeavoring to warn, exhort, admonish, and rescue you from falling into difficulties and sorrows, which I foresaw you plunging into, by giving way to that wicked spirit, which you call your passions, which you should curb and break down, and put under your feet; which if you do not, you never can be saved, in my view, in the Kingdom of God. God requires the will of his creatures to be swallowed up in his will.

" 'You desire to remain in the church, but forsake your apostleship. This is the stratagem of the evil one; when he has gained one advantage, he lays a plan for another. But by maintaining your apostleship, in rising up and making one tremendous effort, you may overcome your passions, and please God. And by forsaking your apostleship, is not to be willing to make that sacrifice that God requires at your hands, and is to incur his displeasure; and without pleasing God we do not think it will be any better for you. When a man falls one step, he must regain that step again, or fall another; he has still more to gain, or eventually all is lost.

" 'I desire, Brother William, that you will humble yourself. I freely forgive you, and you know my unshaken and unchangeable disposition; I kuow in whom I trust; I stand upon the rock; the floods cannot, no, they shall not, overthrow me. You know the doctrine I teach is true, and you know that God has blessed me. I brought salvation to my father's house, as an instrument in the hand of God, when they were in a miserable situation. You know that it is my duty to admonish you, when you do wrong. This liberty I shall always take, and you shall have the same privilege. I take the liberty to admonish you, because of my birthright; and I grant you the privilege, because it is my duty to be humble, and receive rebuke and instruction from a brother, or a friend.

"'As it regards what course you shall pursue hereafter, I do not pretend to say; I leave you in the hands of God and his church. Make your own decision; I will do you good, although you mar me, or slay me. By so doing my garments shall be clear of your sins. And if at any time you should consider me to be an impostor, for heaven's sake leave me in the hands of God and not think to take vengeance on me yourself. Tyranny, usurpation, and to take men's rights, ever has [been] and ever shall be banished from my heart. David sought not to kill Saul, although he was guilty of crimes that never entered my heart.

"'And now may God have mercy upon my father's house; may God take away enmity from between me and thee; and may all blessings be restored, and the past be forgotten forever. May humble repentance bring us both to thee, O God, and to thy power and protection, and a crown, to enjoy the society of Father, Mother, Alvin, Hyrum, Sophronia, Samuel, Catharine, Carlos, Lucy, the saints, and all the sanctified in peace, forever, is the prayer of your brother.

"'JOSEPH SMITH, JR.

" 'To William Smith.'

"Saturday morning, 19. At home. Sent the above letter to Brother William Smith. I have had many solemn feelings this day concerning my brother William, and have prayed in my heart fervently that the Lord will not cast him off, but that he may return to the God of Jacob and magnify his apostleship and calling. May this be his happy lot, for the Lord of glory's sake. Amen.

"Sunday, 20. At home all day. Took solid comfort with my family. Had many serious reflections. Brothers Palmer and Taylor called to see me. I showed them the sacred records, to their joy and satisfaction. O my God have mercy upon these men, and keep them in the way of everlasting life, in the name of Jesus. Amen.

"Monday, 21. Spent this day at home, endeavoring to treasure up knowledge for the benefit of my calling. The day passed off very pleasantly. I thank the Lord for his blessings to my soul, his great mercy over my family in sparing our lives. O continue thy care over me and mine, for Christ's sake.

"Tuesday, 22. At home. Continued my studies. O may God give me learning, even language; and endue me with qualifications to magnify his name while I live.

"I also delivered an address to the church this evening. The Lord blessed my soul. My scribe is unwell. O my God, heal him. And for his kindness to me, O my soul, be thou grateful to him, and bless him. And he shall be blessed of God forever, for I believe him to be a faithful friend to me, therefore my soul delighteth in him. Amen.

"Wednesday, 23. In the forenoon, at home, studying the Greek language. . . .

"Thursday, 24. The forenoon at home. In the afternoon I assisted the commissioner appointed by the court, in surveying a road across my farm.

"Friday, 25. Enjoyed myself at home with my family all day, it being Christmas, the only time I have had this privilege so satisfactorily for a long period. Brother Jonathan Crosby called this eve.

"Saturday, 26. Commenced studying the Hebrew language in company with Brothers Parrish and Williams. In the meantime Brother Lyman Sherman came in, and requested to have the word of the Lord through me; 'for,' said he, 'I have been wrought upon to make known to you my feelings and desires, and was promised that I should have a revelation which should make known my duty.'"[*]

_____

[*] Verily thus saith the Lord unto you, my servant Lyman, your sins are forgiven you, because you have obeyed my voice in coming up

"Sunday morning, 27. At the usual hour attended meeting at the schoolhouse. President Cowdery delivered a very able and interesting discourse.

"In the afternoon Brother Hyrum Smith and Bishop Partridge delivered each a short and interesting lecture, after which sacrament was administered. . . .

"Monday, 28. . . . This day the Council of the Seventy met to render an account of their travels and ministry, since they were ordained to that apostleship. The meeting was interesting indeed, and my heart was made glad while listening to the relation of those that had been laboring in the vineyard of the Lord with such marvelous success. And I pray God to bless them with an increase of faith and power, and keep them all, with the endurance of faith in the name of Jesus Christ to the end.

Seventy's
Council.

"Tuesday, 29. The following charges were preferred:—

" 'To the Honorable Presidency of the Church of Christ of Latter Day Saints, against Elder William Smith.

" '1. Unchristianlike conduct in speaking disrespectfully of President Joseph Smith, Jr., and the revelations and commandments given through him.

Charges against
William Sm th.

" '2. For attempting to inflict personal violence on President Joseph Smith, Jr.'

"At home until about ten o'clock. I then attended a blessing meeting at Oliver Olney's, in company with my wife, and father and mother, who had come to live with me. Also my scribe went with us. A large company assembled, when Father Smith made some appropriate

Pa'riarchal
blessings.

---

hither this morning to receive counsel of him whom I have appointed.
Therefore let your soul be at rest concerning your spiritual standing,
and resist no more my voice; and arise up and be more careful henceforth, in observing your vows which you have made, and do make, and
you shall be blessed with exceeding great blessings. Wait patiently
until the solemn assembly shall be called of my servants, then you shall
be remembered with the first of mine elders, and receive right by ordination with the rest of mine elders, whom I have chosen. Behold, this
is the promise of the Father unto you if you continue faithful; and it
shall be fulfilled upon you in that day that you shall have right to
preach my gospel wheresoever I shall send you from henceforth from
that time. Therefore strengthen your brethren in all your conversation, in all your prayers, and in all your exhortations, and in all your
doings; and behold and lo! I am with you to bless you, and deliver you
forever. Amen.

remarks. A hymn was sung, and he opened the meeting by prayer. About fifteen persons then received a patriarchal blessing under his hands. The services were then concluded as they commenced. A table was then crowned with the bounties of nature; and after invoking the benediction of heaven upon the rich repast, we fared sumptuously; and suffice it to say that we had a glorious meeting throughout, and I was much pleased with the harmony and decorum that existed among the brethren and sisters. We returned home, and at early candle light I preached at the schoolhouse to a crowded congregation, who listened with attention about three hours. I had liberty in speaking. . . .

"Wednesday, 30. Spent the day reading Hebrew at the Council Room, in company with my scribe, which gave me much satisfaction, on account of his recovering health, for I delight in his company.

"Thursday, 31. At home. After attending to the duties of my family, retired to the Council Room to pursue my Council of studies. The Council of the Twelve convened in the Twelve. the upper room in the printing office, directly over the room where we were assembled in our studies. They sent for me, and the Presidency, or a part of them, to receive counsel from us on the subject of the council which is to be held on Saturday next.

"In the afternoon, I attended at the chapel to give directions concerning the upper rooms, and more especially the west room, which I intend occupying for a translating room, which will be prepared this week."—*Millennial Star*, vol. 15, pp. 369, 370, 371, 372, 373, 374, 375, 396, 422, 423, 424, 444, 467, 468, 469, 470, 503, 504, 517, 518, 519, 520, 521, 541, 542, 543, 548, 549.

During this period of time the *Messenger and Advocate* made its regular appearance, edited by John Whitmer. According to accounts given therein much work was Encouraging reports. being done in different parts of the country and many became obedient to the faith. Encouraging reports are found in its pages from Clear Creek, Illinois; Eel River, Indiana; New York; Canada; Vermont; Bradford, Massachusetts; Boston, Massachusetts; Saco and Farmington,

Maine; Jamestown, Smyrna, Chenango, and Amity, New York; Beaver, Fallston, Bridgewater, Pennsylvania; Fulton. Schuyler, and Adams Counties, Illinois; Paris and Clark River, Tennessee; Genesee, Wayne, and Montgomery Counties, New York; Andover, Whitefield, and Franconia, New Hampshire; and Enfield, Vermont.

Sylvester Smith reports the Seventy as follows:—

"At a meeting of the seventy elders held in Kirtland on the 27th of December we were informed of the spread which the mighty work of God has taken by their means the past season. They have traveled, through the assisting grace of God, and preached the fullness of the everlasting gospel in various States, and generally with good success; many have been convinced, and one hundred and seventy-five baptized into the kingdom of Jesus. Notwithstanding many treat the proclamation of the last days with neglect, yet others seem disposed for eternal life, and receive it with a joy which none but the faithful can realize; and when the Lord in accordance with his word pours out the gift of the Holy Ghost upon those who believe and are baptized for the remission of sins, they are enabled to bear a testimony to their neighbors in favor of the work, and so the mighty wheel rolls on like a bright cloud in the heavens, unchecked by the efforts of men."—*Messenger and Advocate*, vol. 2, p. 253.

Thus ended the year 1835 in Kirtland and the East, while in Missouri nothing of particular interest transpired. The saints were peaceably following their several avocations and patiently awaiting the termination of suits which they had planted for damages against the citizens of Jackson County.

BIOGRAPHICAL.

CHAPTER 24.

JOSEPH SMITH THE PROPHET—JOSEPH SMITH THE PATRIARCH—SIDNEY RIGDON—FREDERICK G. WILLIAMS.

IN consequence of its being impracticable to insert biographies in the body of the work, because it would often break into the historical narrative, it is thought best to place short biographical sketches in separate chapters, which we do in the following pages.

JOSEPH SMITH THE PROPHET.

We think it unnecessary to write of Joseph Smith the Prophet, as the history of his early life is given in the body of the work, and the remainder of his life work is interwoven in the history of the church.

JOSEPH SMITH, THE PATRIARCH.

Joseph Smith, the Patriarch, was the first Presiding Patriarch of the Church of Jesus Christ of Latter Day Saints, and the father of Joseph Smith the Prophet.

He was born in Topsfield, Essex County, Massachusetts, July 12, 1771, and was the third child and second son of Asael and Mary (Duty) Smith.

He had six brothers; namely: Jesse, Asael, Samuel, Silas, John, and Stephen; and four sisters; namely: Priscilla, Mary, Susanna, and Sarah.

In 1791 he removed with his father to Tunbridge, Orange County, Vermont.

On January 24, 1796, he married Lucy, daughter of Solomon and Lydia (Gates) Mack, by whom he had ten children; namely:—

Alvin;	born February 11. 1799.
Hyrum;	" " 9. 1800.
Sophronia;	" May 18. 1803.

Joseph;	born December 23, 1805.
Samuel Harrison; "	March 13, 1808.
Ephraim; "	" 13, 1810.
William B.; "	" 13, 1811.
Catharine;[1] "	July 28, 1812.
Don Carlos; "	March 25. 1816.
Lucy; "	July 18, 1821.

At the time of his marriage he owned a farm at Tunbridge, upon this he resided about six years after marriage. In 1802 he rented his farm and moved into the town of Randolph and engaged in merchandising, and soon after invested all he had in buying and shipping ginseng to China. He was swindled out of the entire proceeds by an agent, and consequently had to sell his farm to pay his debts.

After selling the farm he removed to Royalton, Vermont, thence to Sharon, Windsor County, Vermont, where he rented a farm of his father-in-law, which he cultivated in summer, and taught school in winter. After remaining here a few years he returned to Tunbridge, thence to Royalton again.

In 1811 he removed to Lebanon, New Hampshire. Here he was prospered for a time, but again lost what he had accumulated, through sickness and failure of crops.

About 1815 he removed to Palmyra, Wayne County, New York, where he bought a farm and by the assistance of his boys succeeded by hard struggles in partially paying for it, and making comfortable improvements; but they finally lost the farm through unscrupulous, designing swindlers.

He afterwards removed to Manchester, Ontario County, New York, where he procured a small but comfortable home and resided there until he removed to Ohio in 1831.

He was the first to receive the message of his son Joseph after the angel appeared to him, and was closely associated with every important movement of the church until the time of his death. Joseph, his son, wrote of him at the time of his death, as follows:—

"He was the first person who received my testimony after I had seen the angel, and exhorted me to be faithful and dili-

[1] Catharine is still living at Fountain Green, Illinois.

gent to the message I had received. He was baptized April 6, 1830.

"In August, 1830, in company with my brother Don Carlos he took a mission to St. Lawrence County, New York, touching on his route at several of the Canadian ports, where he distributed a few copies of the Book of Mormon, visited his father, brothers, and sister, residing in St. Lawrence County, bore testimony to the truth, which resulted eventually in all the family coming into the church, excepting his brother Jesse and sister Susan.

"He removed with his family to Kirtland in 1831: was ordained Patriarch and President of the High Priesthood, under the hands of Oliver Cowdery, Sidney Rigdon, Frederick G. Williams, and myself, on the 18th of December, 1833; was a member of the First High Council, organized on the 17th of February, 1834, (when he conferred on me and my brother Samuel H., a father's blessing.)

"In 1836 he traveled in company with his brother John two thousand four hundred miles in Ohio, New York, Pennsylvania, Vermont, and New Hampshire, visiting the branches of the church in those states, and bestowing patriarchal blessings on several hundred persons, preaching the gospel to all who would hear, and baptizing many. They arrived at Kirtland on the second of October, 1836.

"During the persecutions in Kirtland in 1837, he was made a prisoner, but fortunately obtained his liberty, and after a very tedious journey in the spring and summer of 1838, he arrived at Far West, Missouri. After I and my brother Hyrum were thrown into the Missouri jails by the mob, he fled from under the exterminating order of Governor Lilburn W. Boggs, and made his escape in midwinter to Quincy, Illinois, from whence he removed to Commerce in the spring of 1839.

"The exposures he suffered brought on consumption, of which he died on this 14th day of September, 1840, aged sixty-nine years, two months, and two days. He was six feet two inches high, was very straight, and remarkably well proportioned. His ordinary weight was about two hundred pounds, and he was very strong and active. In his young

days he was famed as a wrestler, and, Jacob-like, he never
wrestled with but one man whom he could not throw.   He
was one of the most benevolent of men, opening his house to
all who were destitute.   While at Quincy, Illinois, he fed
·hundreds of the poor saints who were flying from the Missouri persecutions, although he had arrived there penni-
less himself."—*Millennial Star*, vol. 18, p. 134.

His funeral took place where he died, at Commerce, afterwards called Nauvoo, Illinois, on September 15, 1840,
when the following address was delivered by Elder R. B.
Thompson:—

"The occasion which has brought us together this day is
one of no ordinary importance, for not only has a single
family to mourn and sorrow on account of the death of the
individual, whose funeral obsequies we this day celebrate;
but a whole society, yes, thousands, will this day have to say,
'A Father in Israel is gone.'   The man whom we have been
accustomed to look up to as a 'Patriarch,' a father, and a
counselor, is no more an inhabitant of mortality; he has
dropped his clay tenement, bidden adieu to terrestrial scenes,
and his spirit, now free and unencumbered, roams and expa-
tiates in that world where the spirits of just men made perfect dwell, and where pain and sickness, tribulation and
death, cannot come.

"The friends we have lost prior to our late venerable and
lamented father were such as rendered life sweet, and in
whose society we took great pleasure, and who shed a luster
in the several walks of life in which they moved, and to
whom we feel endeared by friendship's sacred ties.   Their
virtues and kindnesses will long be remembered by the sor-
rowing widow, the disconsolate husband, the weeping children, the almost distracted and heartbroken parent, and by
a large circle of acquaintances and friends.   These like the
stars in yonder firmament shone in their several spheres and
filled that station in which they had been called by the
providence of God with honor to themselves and to the
church; and we feel to mingle our tears with their surviving
relatives.   But on this occasion we realize that we have suffered more than an ordinary bereavement, and consequently

we feel the more interested. If ever there was a man who
had claims on the affections of community it was our beloved
but now deceased Patriarch, if ever there was an event calculated to raise the feelings of sorrow in the human breast
and cause us to drop the sympathetic tear it certainly is the
present; for truly we can say with the king of Israel, 'A
Prince and a great man has fallen in Israel;' a man endeared
to us by every feeling calculated to entwine around and
adhere to the human heart by almost indissoluble bonds; a
man faithful to his God and to the church in every situation,
and under all circumstances through which he was called to
pass.   Whether in prosperity, surrounded by the comforts
of life, a smiling progeny, and all the enjoyments of the
domestic circle; or when called upon like the patriarchs of
old to leave the land of his nativity, to journey in strange
lands, and become subject to all the trials and persecutions
which have been heaped upon the saints with a liberal hand,
by characters destitute of every principle of morality or
religion, alike regardless of the tender offspring and the
aged sire whose silvery locks and furrowed cheeks ought to
have been a sufficient shield from their cruelty. But like
the Apostle Paul he could exclaim, (and his life and conduct
have fully borne out the sentiment,) 'None of these things
move me, neither count I my life dear, so that I may finish
my course with joy.' The principles of the gospel were too
well established in that breast and had got too sure a foot-
ing there ever to be torn down or prostrated by the fierce
winds of persecution, the blasts of poverty, or the swollen
waves of distress and tribulation. No, thank God, his house
was built upon a *rock*, consequently it stood amid the contending elements, firm and unshaken.

"The life of our departed father has indeed been an eventful one, having to take a conspicuous part in the great work
of the last days; being designated by the ancient prophets,
who once dwelt on this continent, as the father of him whom
the Lord had promised to raise up in the last days to lead
his people Israel; and by a uniform consistent, and virtuous
course for a long series of years, he has proved himself
worthy of such a son, and such a family, by whom he had

the happiness of being surrounded in his dying moments; most of whom had the satisfaction of receiving his dying benediction.

"He was already in the wane of life when the light of truth broke in upon the world, and with pleasure he hailed its benign and enlightening rays, and was chosen by the Almighty to be one of the witnesses to the Book of Mormon. From that time his only aim was the promotion of truth; his soul was taken up with the things of the kingdom, his bowels yearned over the children of men, and it was more than his 'meat and drink' to do the will of his Father which was in heaven.

"By unceasing industry, of himself and family, he had secured a home in the State of New York, where he no doubt expected, with every honest and industrious citizen, to enjoy the blessings of peace and liberty. But when the principles of truth were introduced, and the gospel of Jesus Christ was promulgated by himself and family, friends forsook, enemies raged, and persecution was resorted to by wicked and ungodly men, insomuch so that he was obliged to flee from that place and seek a home in a more hospitable land.

"In Ohio he met with many kind and generous friends and was kindly welcomed by the saints; many of whom continue to this day, and can call to mind the various scenes which there transpired; many of which were of such a nature not to be easily obliterated.

"While the house of the Lord was building he took great interest in its erection, and daily watched its progress, and had the pleasure of taking a part at the opening and seeing it crowded by hundreds of pious worshipers. As the king of Israel longed for and desired to see the completion of the house of the Lord, so did he; and with him he could exclaim, 'O Lord, I love the habitation of thine house, and the place where thine honor dwelleth:' To dwell in the House of the Lord and to inquire in his Temple was his daily delight; and in it he enjoyed many blessings, and spent many hours in sweet communion with his heavenly Father.

"He has trod its secret alleys, solitary and alone from mankind, long before the king of day has guilded the eastern horizon; and he has uttered his aspirations within its walls, when nature's has been asleep. In its holy inclosures have the visions of heaven been opened to his mind, and his soul has feasted on the riches of eternity; and there under his teachings have the meek and humble been instructed, while the widow and the orphan have received his patriarchal blessing.

"There he saw the work spreading far and wide, saw the elders of Israel go forth under his blessing, bore them up by the prayer of faith, and hailed them welcome when they again returned bringing their sheaves with them. There with his aged partner he spent many happy days, in the bosom of his family, whom he loved with all the tenderness of parental affection. Here I might enlarge and expatiate on the 'scenes of joy, and scenes of gladness' which were enjoyed by our beloved patriarch, but shall pass on to an event which was truly painful and trying. The delightful scene soon vanished, the calm was succeeded by a storm, and the frail bark was driven by the tempest and foaming ocean; for many who had once been proud to acknowledge him a father and friend, and who sought counsel at his hands, joined with the enemies of truth, and sought his destruction, and would have rejoiced to see his aged and venerable form immured in a dungeon; but, thank God, this they were not suffered to do; he providentially made his escape, and after evading his enemies for some time, he undertook, and accomplished a journey of a thousand miles, and bore up under the fatigue and suffering necessarily attendant on such a journey, with patient resignation. After a journey of several weeks he arrived in safety at Far West, in the bosom of the church, and was cordially welcomed by the saints; who had found an asylum in the rich and fertile county of Caldwell. There he in common with the rest of the saints hoped to enjoy the privileges and blessings of peace. There, from the fertile soil and flowery meads which well repaid the labor of the husbandman and poured forth abundance for the support of the numerous herds which decked those lovely and widespread prairies he hoped to enjoy uninterrupted the comforts of domestic life. But he

had not long indulged these pleasing anticipations before
the delightful prospect again vanished; the cup of blessing
which he began again to enjoy was dashed from his aged
lips, and the cup of sorrow filled to overflowing was given
him instead; and surely he drank it to the very dregs; for not
only did he see the saints in bondage, treated with cruelty,
and some of them murdered; but the kind and affectionate
parent saw, and ah! how painful was the sight, two of his
sons, to whom he looked up for protection, torn away from
their domestic circles, from their weeping and distracted
families, by monsters in the shape of men, who swore and
threatened to kill them, and who had every disposition to
embrew their hands in their blood! This circumstance was
too much for his agitated and now sinking frame to bear up
under; and although his confidence in his God was great,
and his conduct was that of a Christian and a saint; yet he
felt like a man and a parent. At that time his constitution
received a shock from which it never recovered. Ah! yes;
there were feelings agitated in the bosom of our deceased
friend at that time of no ordinary kind; feelings of painful
anxiety and emotion too great for his earthly tabernacle to
contain without suffering a great and a sensible injury, and
which from that time began to manifest itself.

"It would be unnecessary to trace him and his aged partner
(who shared in all his sorrows and affections) from such a
scene, as many of the saints are knowing to the privations
and sufferings which they in common with the church suffered while moving from that land of oppression. Suffice it
to say he arrived in safety in Illinois, broken down in constitution and in health, and since then he has labored under
severe affliction and pain, while disease has been slowly but
surely undermining his system.

"Whenever he had a short respite from pain he felt a
pleasure in attending to his patriarchal duties, and with
cheerfulness he performed them; and frequently his labors
have been more than his strength would admit of; but having great zeal for the cause of truth, he felt willing to be
spent in the service of his God.

"For some time past he has been confined to his bed, and

the time of his departure was near at hand.   On Saturday evening last an eruption of a blood vessel took place, when he vomited a large portion of blood.   His family were summoned to his bedside, it being now evident that he could not long survive.   On Sunday he called his children and grandchildren around him, and like the ancient patriarchs, gave them his final benediction.   Although his strength was far gone, and he was obliged to rest at intervals, yet his mind was clear, perfectly collected, and calm as the gentle zephyrs.   The love of God was in his heart, the peace of God rested upon him, and his soul was full of compassion and blessing.   All the circumstances connected with his death were calculated to lead the mind back to the time when an Abraham, an Isaac, and a Jacob bade adieu to mortality and entered into rest.   His death like theirs was sweet, and it certainly was a privilege indeed to witness such a scene; and I was forcibly reminded of the sentiment of the Poet:—

" 'The chamber where the good man meets his fate,
Is privileged beyond the common walk of virtuous life.'

"There were no reflections of a misspent life - no fearful forebodings of a gloomy nature in relation to the future, the realities of eternity were dawning, the shades of time were lowering; but there was nothing to terrify, to alarm, or disturb his mind.   No, the principles of the gospel, which 'bring life and immortality to light,' nobly triumphed in nature's final hour.   Those principles so long taught and cherished by our lamented friend were honorably maintained to the last; which is not only a consolation to the immediate relatives; but to the church at large.

"The instructions imparted by him will long be remembered by his numerous progeny, who will undoubtedly profit by the same and strive to render themselves worthy of such a sire; and that the whole church will copy his examples, walk in his footsteps, and emulate his faith and virtuous actions, and commend themselves to his God and to their God.

"Notwithstanding his enemies frequently 'shot at him, yet his bow abode in its strength, and the arms of his hands were made strong by the hands of the mighty God of Jacob;' and his courage and resolution never forsook him.   His anxiety for the spread of truth was great, and he lived to see great and important things accomplished. He saw the commencement of the work, small as a mustard seed, and with attention and deep interest he watched its progress; and he had the satisfaction of beholding thousands on this continent rejoicing in its truths, and heard the glorious tidings that other lands were becoming heirs to its richest blessings. Under these circumstances he could exclaim, like pious Simeon of old, 'Lord, now lettest thou thy servant depart in peace, for mine eyes have seen thy salvation.'

"Although his spirit has taken its flight and his remains will soon mingle with their mother earth, yet his memory will long be cherished by all who had the pleasure of his acquaintance, and will be fresh and blooming when those of his enemies shall be blotted out from under heaven.

"May we, beloved friends, who survive our venerable Patriarch, study to prosecute those things which were so dear to his aged heart, and pray that a double portion of his spirit may be bestowed on us, that we may be the humble instruments in aiding the consummation of the great work which he saw so happily begun; that when we have to stand before the bar of Christ we may with our departed friend, hear the welcome plaudit, 'Come up hither ye blessed of my Father, inherit the kingdom prepared for you from the foundation of the world. Amen."—*Times and Seasons*, vol. 1, pp. 170–173.

SIDNEY RIGDON.

An account of the early life of Sidney Rigdon up to the time of his uniting with the church in 1830 is quite fully given in this volume, on pages 129-142, and it would be unprofitable to repeat it. He entered zealously into the work, and was the means of leading many of his former associates and others to the church. A revelation given in December foreshadowed this by informing him that he had been preparing the way but he knew it not. He was then given a greater commission and promised that he would do a great work.

Having received an ordination to the office of elder under the hands of the missionaries going west, he began to preach the new faith with zeal and convincing power.

After December, 1830, he acted as scribe for Joseph Smith in the translation of the Holy Scriptures, and was a participant in the glorious vision recorded in Doctrine and Covenants, section 76.

It was while engaged in this work that he with Joseph was so severely maltreated by a mob at Hiram, Ohio, on March 25, 1832.

Soon after he visited Missouri, and assisted in dedicating the land of Zion and the Temple Lot.

On March 18, 1833, at the organization of the First Presidency he was ordained First Counselor to President Joseph Smith, the first man occupying that position in this dispensation. Soon afterward he took a mission to Canada in connection with Joseph Smith.

In 1834 he with others took an active part in raising volunteers for Zion's Camp, and when the Camp went to Missouri he remained at Kirtland, taking the active oversight of the church in the absence of President Smith, encouraging and aiding in the erection of the Temple. It is said that he often went upon the unfinished walls by night and plead with God to open the way for the completion of the building while he wet the walls with his tears.

He was an active participant in the scenes through which the church passed in Kirtland. He took part in the dedication of the Temple, and in the General Assembly, and was one of the committee on compiling the Doctrine and Covenants.

In the spring of 1838 he removed to Missouri, locating at Far West, in Caldwell County, and was a participant in the scenes enacted there. He stood faithfully by Joseph Smith and the church when many others wavered and fell.

In October, 1838, he with others was taken prisoner at Far West, by General Lucas, and was one of those sentenced to be shot, and saved by the gallant and heroic conduct of General Doniphan. With others he was then taken to Independence, thence to Richmond, where he was again under sentence of death, but was finally turned over to the civil authorities and had an *exparte* examination before Judge King and committed to Liberty Jail to answer in Caldwell County to a charge of treason, and other counts. He afterwards obtained a release on a writ of *habeas corpus* in the court of Judge Turnham, and went to Illinois.

After the release of his companions in bonds, which occurred some weeks after, he was appointed with Joseph Smith and Elias Higbee to go to Washington City and present the grievances of the saints before the President and Congress. With his associates he started on this mission, but was delayed and finally prevented from participation in the duties of the committee, by sickness.

For a time he was inactive on account of which there was much dissatisfaction. At the October conference of 1843 President Smith expressed his unwillingness to sustain Elder Rigdon because of his "unprofitableness to him as a counselor." Some other charges were brought against him at the time, but on these he was fully vindicated. Upon his promise of renewal of faithfulness and diligence he was sustained in his position and retained his standing until the death of Joseph Smith in 1844.

At the State convention held at Nauvoo in May, 1844, Sidney Rigdon, then a resident of Pennsylvania, was nominated for Vice President of the United States on an independent ticket, on which Joseph Smith was nominated for President.

The head of the ticket being removed by death pending the campaign, his candidacy of course came to an end.

After the death of Joseph Smith he differed from the Twelve on the question of presiding authority, he claiming the superiority by virtue of his being a member of the First Presidency, and the only one living.

His claims were rejected in a meeting held at Nauvoo, August 8, 1844.

He was afterwards cited before the High Council and after what, from accounts, seems to have been a very unfair and partial examination, was expelled from communion with the body under the presidency of the Twelve.

He subsequently formed an organization of which he was himself the president, and Samuel James and Ebenezer Robinson were his counselors. He had a considerable following in 1845, and unto the time of his death and afterwards some adhered to his claims.

After leaving Nauvoo he commenced on October 15, 1844, the publication of a periodical at Pittsburg, Pennsylvania, called *The Latter Day Saints Messenger and Advocate.* This publication continued for a year or more, and in its columns he and others advocated his claims to the Presidency and denounced the plural wife doctrine taught in Nauvoo. In a letter written to J. Gregg, October 15, 1844, by Elder Rigdon, and published in the first issue of his paper, he makes some very damaging charges against the Twelve, which if true, or the half of them true, will account for some of the conflicting testimony regarding polygamy. He died at Friendship, New York, July 14, 1876.

FREDERICK G. WILLIAMS.

Of the early life of Dr. F. G. Williams we have but little information. When the missionaries (Oliver Cowdery, P. P. Pratt, Peter Whitmer, and Ziba Peterson) visited Western Ohio in 1830, they found him there engaged in the practice of medicine. Dr. Williams was among the first to receive the message, and when the elders moved on westward he accompanied them to Western Missouri and into the Indian country.

Returning to Kirtland he took an active and prominent part in the work incident to the establishment of the church.

On March 18, 1833, he was ordained Second Counselor to Joseph Smith, and for some years at least was faithful to his trust.

In November, 1833, Joseph Smith wrote of him as follows: "Brother Frederick G. Williams is one of those men in whom I place the greatest confidence and trust, for I have found him ever full of love and brotherly kindness. He is not a man of many words, but is ever winning, because of his constant mind. He shall ever have place in my heart, and is ever entitled to my confidence. He is perfectly honest and upright, and seeks with all his heart to magnify his presidency in the Church of Christ, but fails in many instances, in consequence of a want of confidence in himself. God grant that he may overcome all evil."—*Times and Seasons,* vol. 6, p. 899.

He went to Missouri with Zion's Camp in 1834.

In the trouble which occurred at Kirtland in 1837, when many became estranged, President Williams was disaffected, and some difference arose between him and Joseph Smith. Notwithstanding this it seems that Joseph was still willing to sustain him, for at a conference held at Kirtland, Ohio, September 3, 1837, Joseph presented him as his counselor. The conference however refused to sustain him. Joseph persisted, however, and at a conference held at Far West, Missouri, November 7, 1837, he again presented Elder Williams as his counselor, but he was again rejected by vote of the conference.

He was expelled from the church at Kirtland, but in 1838 came to Missouri and was rebaptized.

After this he practically dropped out of active life. He was mixed up some way with difficulties in Missouri, but there has been but little recorded concerning him, and so we will not venture to give particulars.

CHAPTER 25.

LYMAN E. JOHNSON—BRIGHAM YOUNG—HEBER C. KIMBALL—ORSON HYDE—DAVID W. PATTEN—LUKE S. JOHNSON—WILLIAM E MC-LELLIN—JOHN F. BOYNTON—ORSON PRATT—WILLIAM SMITH—THOMAS B. MARSH—PARLEY P. PRATT.

WE herein propose to give short sketches of the lives of the Twelve Apostles in the order in which they were chosen.

LYMAN E. JOHNSON.

Lyman E. Johnson, though the youngest of the Twelve chosen in 1835, and for that reason ranked as number twelve in the final arrangement, was the first chosen. He was the son of John and Elsa Johnson, and was born in Pomfret, Windsor County, Vermont, October 24, 1811.

He was baptized in February, 1831, by Sidney Rigdon. In November, 1831, he was mentioned by revelation in connection with his brother Luke, Orson Hyde, and W. E. McLellin, in a commission to preach the gospel and administer its ordinances. (Doctrine and Covenants 68: 1.) He labored as a missionary in Ohio, the Eastern States, and Nova Scotia.

In 1834 he went to Missouri in Zion's Camp. In February, 1835, he was ordained an apostle of the Quorum of Twelve; after that he was constantly engaged in the ministry until the fall of 1836, when partaking of the spirit of speculation then so prevalent in Kirtland, he commenced merchandising.

At a conference held in Kirtland, September 3, 1837, he was rejected as an apostle and suspended from fellowship, for leaving the duties of his calling and engaging in other occupations.

On the 10th he was restored to fellowship and permitted to retain his apostleship. It does not appear, however, that he quit his merchandising at that time.

On the 13th of April, 1838, he was expelled from the church at Far West, Missouri, for what cause does not appear. It is said that he remained friendly to his former associates, and made frequent visits to Nauvoo.

Some time after his expulsion he removed to Davenport, Iowa, and engaged in the practice of law; thence to Keokuk, where he continued the practice.

He met his death December 20, 1856, by being drowned in the Mississippi River at Prairie du Chien, Wisconsin.

We have no information regarding his family.

BRIGHAM YOUNG.

Brigham Young was the second apostle chosen in February, 1835, but ranked third when arranged in the order of their age, on May 2, 1835. He was born in Whitingham, Windham County, Vermont, June 1, 1801. When a boy, his parents moved to Chenango County, New York, where his early years were spent in farming. When twenty years old he united with the Methodist Church, and his early religious training was in the communion of that society.

On October 8, 1824, he married Miss Miriam Works and resided in Cayuga County, New York, until 1829, following the trades of carpenter, glazier, and painter. He then removed to Monroe County, New York, where, in 1830, he first saw a Book of Mormon, brought there by Samuel H. Smith. He was baptized April 14, 1832, by Eleazer Miller. On September 8, 1832, his wife died, leaving two small children. Soon afterward he went to Kirtland, Ohio, and made the acquaintance of the Prophet. The following winter he spent in missionary work in Canada, in company with his brother, Joseph Young. In July, 1833, he removed his family to Kirtland. In February, 1834, he married Miss Mary Ann Angel. In the summer of 1834 he went with Zion's Camp to Missouri.

He was ordained an apostle February, 1835, and afterwards did considerable missionary work in the Eastern States.

He left Kirtland, Ohio, in December, 1837, and arrived at Far West, Missouri, in March, 1838, where he resided until February, 1839, when he removed to Atlas, Pike County, Illinois; thence to Quincy; thence to Commerce; thence to Montrose, Iowa.

In September, 1839, he accompanied others of his quorum on a mission to England, where he did some effectual labor; and at a meeting of the quorum held at Preston, April 14, 1840, he was chosen president of the Twelve.

He returned to Nauvoo, July 1, 1841, and took an active part in church affairs, as well as doing some missionary work in the Eastern States, until the death of Joseph and Hyrum Smith in June, 1844.

On August 8, 1844, the church assembled in Nauvoo voted to support "the Twelve in their calling." (See *Times and Seasons*, volume 5, page 638.) The Twelve, with Elder Young at their head, (William Smith, John E. Page, and Lyman Wight dissenting,) assumed that this vote sustained them as the presiding quorum of the church; and proceeded to act in that capacity for as many as would receive them, until the exodus westward in 1846. He was one of the pioneer company, and reached Salt Lake Valley, July 24, 1847, and returned East after deciding to settle in the Valley.

At Council Bluffs, Iowa, December 5, 1847, a part of his quorum (John Taylor and P. P. Pratt, besides the three mentioned above—William Smith, John E. Page, and Lyman Wight being absent), resolved to elevate Elder Young to the office of President of the Church. This was ratified December 27, 1847, by about one thousand members of the church who assembled at Kanesville, now Council Bluffs, Iowa, out of a total membership of about one hundred and fifty thousand.

In 1848 he emigrated to Utah, where he served as president for those who were willing to accept his leadership, until his death, which occurred on August 29, 1877.

HEBER C. KIMBALL.

Heber C. Kimball was the third apostle chosen, but ranked fourth in the order of age. He was born June 14, 1801, in Sheldon, Franklin County, Vermont. When he was ten years old his parents moved to Ontario County, New York. When nineteen years old he went to Mendon, Monroe County, New York, and learned the trade of potter with his brother Charles, with whom he remained until he was twenty-one years old. In November, 1822, he married Miss Vilate Murray. Immediately afterwards he bought out his brother Charles and followed the potter's trade for over ten years. In April, 1832, he was baptized by Elder Alpheus Gifford, and in September of the same year he accompanied Brigham and Joseph Young to Kirtland.

In 1833 he removed to Kirtland, Ohio, and in 1834 was a member of Zion's Camp.

In February, 1835, he was ordained an apostle, and accompanied his quorum on a tour of the eastern churches, organizing conferences and setting in order the churches.

In the summer of 1837, accompanied by Orson Hyde and others, he went on a mission to England, and opened the work there, having great success. He was absent on this mission about eleven months, during which time he and his colleagues had baptized about fifteen hundred persons.

Soon after returning from England he removed to Far West, Missouri, arriving there July 25, 1838.

He took an active part in the exciting scenes enacted there. His efforts in behalf of his imprisoned brethren were constant and untiring. Through dangers and difficulties his vigilance never wavered, and everything he could do was done for their comfort, safety, and final release.

In September, 1839, he started on his second mission to England, this time associated with the majority of his quorum.

After a little more than a year's labor he returned to America, and was active in church affairs about Nauvoo, and in missionary labor, until the death of Joseph Smith.

In 1844 he stood with Brigham Young and the majority of his quorum in taking control of affairs.

In December, 1847, when Brigham Young assumed the Presidency, Elder Kimball was selected as First Counselor, which place he occupied until his death, which occurred at Salt Lake City, Utah, June 22, 1868.

ORSON HYDE.

Orson Hyde was the fourth chosen of the first Twelve, but when arranged according to age he was the fifth. He was the son of Nathan and Sally Hyde, and was born in Oxford, New Haven County, Connecticut, January 8, 1805. When seven years old his mother died and he was placed under the care of a gentleman by the name of Nathan Wheeler, who when he was fourteen years old took him to Kirtland, Ohio. He remained with Mr. Wheeler until he was eighteen years old. He worked at several occupations, among others clerking for Gilbert and Whitney in Kirtland.

In 1827, during a religious revival, he embraced the Methodist faith and was appointed a class leader. Subsequently, under the preaching of Sidney Rigdon, he became identified with the Disciples. Soon afterward he began preaching this new faith and founded several churches in Lorain and Huron counties, Ohio, and in 1830 was appointed their pastor.

In the latter part of the year the Book of Mormon was presented to his churches. He first opposed it, speaking publicly against it, but subsequently he was converted, and on October 31, 1831, was baptized by Sidney Rigdon. He was soon after ordained a high priest and entered actively into missionary labor. On February 17, 1834, he was chosen a member of the High Council, and in the same year he went with Zion's Camp to Missouri, and in company with Elder P. P. Pratt called on Governor Dunklin. On September 4, 1834, he married Miss Marinda N. Johnson, sister of Apostles Luke S. and Lyman E. Johnson.

In February, 1835, he was ordained an apostle, and with his colleagues traveled extensively, setting in order the churches.

In 1837, in company with H. C. Kimball and others, he assisted in opening the English mission, remaining from America nearly one year; after which he removed to Far West, Missouri, and in October, 1838, just before the mob militia marched on Far West, he and Thomas B. Marsh apostatized, went to Richmond, and by making affidavit to certain questionable things, contributed to incense the public feeling against the church and authorities.

He was suspended May 4, 1839, at Quincy, Illinois.

On June 27, 1839, at Commerce, Illinois, he returned, made

confession of wrongdoing and was restored to fellowship and also to his standing in the Quorum of Twelve.

At the spring conference of 1840, he and Elder John E. Page were appointed a mission to Jerusalem. Elder Page failed to go and Elder Hyde proceeded alone. He visited England, Germany, and Egypt, and after many hardships reached the Holy Land.

On Sunday morning, October 24, 1841, he offered from the Mount of Olives a prayer recorded elsewhere in this work, dedicating the land for the gathering of Israel. He arrived home in December, 1842.

In consequence of his action in Missouri many had lost confidence in him, and did not believe he would fulfill the mission; nor did they believe when he returned that he had done so. Doubts exist unto this day with some, but we know of no sufficient reason for these doubts. From all the circumstances with which we are acquainted we conclude that he performed this mission faithfully.

In 1844 he stood with his quorum, and followed the fortunes of the Utah faction to the time of his death, which occurred at Spring City, Utah, November 28, 1878.

DAVID W. PATTEN.

David W. Patten was the next one of the Twelve in the order of selection, but in the arrangement according to age he was number two. He was born in the State of New York about the year 1800.

He was religiously inclined and in his early life was constantly seeking for truth. He first heard of the Book of Mormon in 1830. On June 15, 1832, he was baptized in Green County, Indiana, by his brother, John Patten, and ordained an elder on the 17th, by Elisha Groves. He entered zealously into missionary labor and was among the most faithful men in the church, doing missionary work in Michigan, Ohio, Pennsylvania, New York, and in the Eastern States; in all of which he was quite successful.

He went to Missouri early in 1834, accompanied by William Pratt, to bear dispatches from the church authorities to the scattered members in Clay County who had recently been expelled from Jackson County. They accomplished this mission after much toil and suffering, arriving in Clay County, March 4, 1834.

In September, 1834, accompanied by Warren Parrish, he started on a mission to Tennessee, where they accomplished some acceptable work, but were subjected to much persecution. He returned to Kirtland sometime the following winter, where in February, 1835, he was chosen and ordained an apostle, and with his quorum traveled through the Eastern States and Canada. He returned to Kirtland in September, 1835, where he remained until after the dedication of the Temple in March, 1836, when he went again to Tennessee on a mission, accompanied by his wife. Here he met Wilford Woodruff, and shortly after they were joined by Warren Parrish. They were harrassed by persecution and by prosecution under color of law, but nothing was established against them.

In September, 1836, he left Tennessee and with his wife journeyed to Far West, Missouri. In 1837, he took a mission east, and the same year returned to Missouri.

On February 10, 1838, at the time David Whitmer, W. W. Phelps, and John Whitmer were deposed, Thomas B. Marsh and David W. Patten were elected Presidents pro tempore of the church in Missouri, and served in that capacity until the arrival of the First Presidency from the East.

On October 25, 1838, Elder Patten received a mortal wound in an engagement with the mob in Caldwell County, Missouri, from which he soon afterwards died. He was buried in Far West, October 27. Of his family we have no account.

Joseph Smith thus wrote of him:—

"Brother David W. Patten was a very worthy man, beloved by all good men who knew him. He was one of the Twelve Apostles, and died as he lived, a man of God, and strong in the faith of a glorious resurrection, in a world where mobs will have no power or place. One of his last expressions to his wife was, 'whatever you do else, O! do not deny the faith.'"—*Millennial Star*, vol. 16, p. 408.

LUKE S. JOHNSON.

Luke S. Johnson was the sixth apostle chosen, but in the arrangement according to age he was the eighth.   He was the son of John and Elsa Johnson, and was born in Pomfret, Windsor County, Vermont, November 3, 1807.   He was baptized by Joseph Smith in June, 1831.   He was soon after ordained a priest by Christian Whitmer, and commenced active work as a missionary.   Subsequently he was ordained a high priest by Joseph Smith, after which he traveled and preached extensively in Ohio, Virginia, and Kentucky.   He was married November 1, 1833, to Miss Susan H. Proteet, in Cabell County, Virginia, whose acquaintance he made on his missionary tour.

At the organization of the High Council, February 17, 1834, he was chosen a member, and the following summer went to Missouri with Zion's Camp.   In February, 1835, at the organization of the Apostles' quorum, he was chosen and ordained a member of that quorum.   With his quorum he visited Canada and the East.   He also partook of the spirit of speculation, neglected the duties of his office, and at a conference held at Kirtland, Ohio, September 3, 1837, he with his brother Lyman, and John F. Boynton, was rejected.   On the 10th they made confession and were received into fellowship, and permitted to retain their apostleship.   He however did not renew his diligence sufficiently to restore confidence, and was subsequently rejected by the church.   He continued friendly to the church during the life of Joseph, and after his death affiliated with the organization under the Twelve and with them went West, where he died in Salt Lake City, Utah, December 9, 1861.

WILLIAM E. M'LELLIN.

William E. McLellin was the seventh of the apostles chosen, but in the final arrangement he was the sixth.   He was born in Tennessee about the year 1806.   In 1831 he heard the gospel preached by some of the elders while they were on their way to Missouri.   As soon as he could arrange his business he followed them to Independence; and was baptized by Hyrum Smith.   He afterwards visited Kirtland,

and did considerable missionary work in different places.

On July 3, 1834, he was chosen a member of the High Council of Zion, in Clay County, Missouri. Soon after he went again to Kirtland, where he was engaged for a time as a teacher in the school of the elders. He was ordained an apostle in February, 1835.

On May 11, 1838, he was expelled from the church at Far West, Missouri, for apostasy; and during the trouble in Missouri he used all his influence against the leaders of the church. In 1845 he was identified with the movement under Rigdon, warmly indorsed his claims, and on April 8 of that year was appointed one of the Twelve Apostles in Rigdon's organization.

In 1847 he with others at Kirtland, Ohio, effected an organization which they claimed was a reorganization of the church, and called on David Whitmer to assume the presidency, claiming that he was ordained by Joseph Smith on the 8th of July, 1834, as his successor. In March, 1847, Elder McLellin, by the authority of this organization, commenced the publication of a paper at Kirtland, called *The Ensign of Liberty*, in which he contended that the proper name of the church was "The Church of Christ," and advocated the claims of David Whitmer as President of the Church. In 1847 Elder McLellin went west, and in September called on David Whitmer, Jacob Whitmer, and Hiram Page, at Richmond, Missouri, who accompanied him to Far West, to visit John Whitmer. The five counseled together, and during their counsel received several communications through David Whitmer. As a result of this counsel and instruction given in these revelations through David Whitmer, Elder McLellin, who had previously been rebaptized at Kirtland, Ohio, rebaptized these four men and reordained them high priests, and also ordained David Whitmer to the Presidency, and John Whitmer to be his counselor.

This organization so far as we know was short lived, and after struggling in vain to perpetuate it, the participants abandoned the effort. Elder McLellin finally settled at Independence, Missouri, where he died on Tuesday, March 13, 1883.

JOHN F. BOYNTON.

J. F. Boynton was the eighth apostle chosen, but in the final arrangement he was the eleventh. He was born September 11, 1811, in Bradford, Essex County, Massachusetts; and was baptized at Kirtland, Ohio, in September, 1832, by Joseph Smith; and soon after was ordained an elder by Sidney Rigdon. Was actively engaged in the ministry until his ordination to the office of apostle, in February, 1835.

He accompanied his quorum on their journey through the Eastern States and Canada, returning to Kirtland in time to fulfill an engagement with Miss Susan Lowell, on January 20, 1836, by which she became his wife. The ceremony was performed by President Joseph Smith. Subsequently, he entered into the mercantile business with Lyman E. Johnson.

On September 3, 1837, he with Luke S. and Lyman E. Johnson was disfellowshiped, and like them he made confession on the 10th, and was restored. In 1838, his quorum refused to sustain him.

For many years he resided at Syracuse, New York, where we understand he died a few years ago, a respected citizen.

He was ever on friendly terms with his former associates, doing nothing against the church, but frequently speaking a word in its favor. He never joined any other church, but was skeptical regarding religion. For many years he traveled through the United States, lecturing on natural history and geology. In 1853 and 1854 he was on a geological surveying expedition to California by appointment of the Government.

ORSON·PRATT.

O. Pratt was the ninth apostle chosen, but in the final arrangement was the tenth. He was the son of Jared and Charity (Dickinson) Pratt, and was born in Hartford, Washington County, New York, September 19, 1811. In his youthful days he was a diligent student, and for his time and the opportunities offered he was a good mathematician and bookkeeper. He also became quite proficient in geography and surveying. These things were of great value to him in after life.

On the day he was nineteen years old he was baptized at Canaan, Columbia County, New York, by his brother Parley P. In October, 1830, he went to Fayette, New York, to visit the Prophet, where a revelation was given concerning him, and he was soon after ordained an elder.

Early in 1831 he went on foot to Kirtland, Ohio, preaching and baptizing by the way. For many years he was among the most able and active missionaries of the church. On February 2, 1832, he was ordained a high priest; and in 1834 he was a member of Zion's Camp in its memorable march to Zion. On July 7, 1834, he was ordained one of the standing High Council of Zion.

He was not present at the time of his selection as an apostle in February, 1835, having not yet returned from Missouri; but he arrived on April 26, and was on the same day ordained. On July 4, 1836, he was married to Miss Sarah M. Bates, whom he had baptized in Sacket's Harbor, New York, the year previous. On July 4, 1839, he assisted his brother Parley and companions to escape from Columbia jail, Missouri.

In the spring of 1840 he with others of his quorum went to Europe, where he labored faithfully in England and Scotland, returning to America in the spring of 1841. He was for a time Professor of Mathematics in Nauvoo University.

In 1844 he stood with the majority of the Twelve, and in 1847 was a participant in the proceedings which sought to elevate Brigham Young to the Presidency. He emigrated westward with that people and the remainder of his life was devoted to their service. He was probably the best scholar among them, and is the author of several works. He died at his home in Salt Lake City, Utah, October 3, 1881.

WILLIAM SMITH.

William Smith was tenth apostle chosen, but in the final arrangement was the ninth. He was the sixth son of Patriarch Joseph Smith and Lucy (Mack) Smith, and brother of Joseph Smith the Prophet. He was born in Royalton, Vermont, March 13, 1811. His early life was of course spent with the family, with the history of which the reader is sufficiently acquainted. He was baptized soon after the organization of the church, by Oliver Cowdery, and was subsequently ordained a teacher. He was an active and zealous missionary during the early days of the church. Subsequently he was ordained an elder; and in June, 1833, he was ordained a high priest. On February 14, 1833, he was married to Miss Caroline Grant, daughter of Joshua Grant, by whom he had two daughters; namely: Mary Jane; born January, 1835; Caroline L.; born August, 1836.

He was ordained an apostle at the organization of that quorum in February, 1835. In the spring of 1838 he removed to Far West, Missouri, and was an active participator in the exciting scenes of the times. On May 4, 1839, he was suspended from exercising the functions of his office, but for what cause we are not informed. On the 25th of the same month he was reinstated by action of his quorum.

When the Twelve went to Europe in 1839 and 1840, he failed to accompany them. This was the occasion of much criticism. He explained his reasons in a letter published in *Times and Seasons*, December 15, 1840, as follows:—

"*D. C. Smith; Dear Brother:*—I improve the opportunity of writing to you, that through the medium of the *Times and Seasons* the brethren may be informed, respecting the discharge of my duty for some time past. I am the more disposed to do so as many have thought my course of conduct strange and have had hard feelings respecting me. I do not wish to exonerate myself from all blame, but merely wish to state the circumstances in which I have been placed, which have been a barrier to my preaching the gospel to the extent which my calling and standing in the church many would suppose it was my duty to do.

"I can assure you that it is not because I have any doubts respecting the work of the last days, or that I have been destitute of the love of God, or a desire that Zion should not flourish; but because my impoverished situation has rendered it necessary for me to use every exertion to support my family. And we read in the New Testament, 'that he who will not provide for his own household is worse than an infidel and hath denied the faith.'

"Unfortunately for me, poverty has been my lot ever since I was called to the ministry; and it has been through much tribulation that I have had to labor in the vineyard since that."—*Times and Seasons*, vol. 2, p. 252.

In the winter of 1842-43 he was a member of the Illinois Legislature elected from Hancock County, and his service, so far as we have learned, gave general satisfaction.

· After the death of his brothers, William Smith never fully agreed with Brigham Young and his colleagues; yet he submitted to be ordained, under their hands, to the office of Patriarch to succeed his brother Hyrum, but without relinquishing his position as a member of the quorum of Twelve. Subsequently, however, he refused to affiliate with them, renounced their claims to the Presidency, and announced his claim to preside over the church temporarily as the guardian of the eldest son of his brother Joseph, who, he contended, was the rightful successor. He had some following for a time, but the organization that he effected gradually declined, and was finally disrupted. After many moves he finally settled at Elkader, Iowa, where he resided many years.

On April 9, 1878, on his request and by action of General Conference, he was received into the Reorganization on his original baptism, and the next day by the same authority his name was enrolled with the High Priests' Quorum. After reuniting with the church he did some missionary work, but his age prevented him from being very active. A certain inaccurate historian has written that he officiated as Patriarch in the Reorganized Church, but this is a mistake. He was connected with the High Priests' Quorum until his death, which occurred November 13, 1893, at his home in Osterdock, Clayton County, Iowa.

THOMAS B. MARSH.

Thomas B. Marsh was the eleventh apostle chosen, but in the final arrangement he was the first. He was born in Acton, Middlesex County, Massachusetts, November 1, 1799. The family removed to New Hampshire, and when he was fourteen years of age he left home and went to Vermont; thence to Albany, New York; and then to New York City.

In the two last named places he worked in hotels. The day he was twenty-one years old he was married to Miss Elizabeth Godkin. After his marriage he entered the mercantile business in New York; thence he went to Boston, Massachusetts, where for seven years he was engaged in a type foundry.

While at Boston, he united with the Methodist Church, but subsequently withdrew from them, and stood aloof from all religious societies, until he united with the Latter Day Saints.

He visited the printing office of E. B. Grandin, at Palmyra, New York, while the Book of Mormon was in press. He obtained some advanced sheets, visited Joseph Smith, Sen., where he met Oliver Cowdery, and from him received an account of the plates and the translation. He returned home taking the sheets with him and presented them with the account to his wife who received it. Mr. Marsh entered at once into correspondence with Oliver Cowdery and Joseph Smith the Prophet, and in September, 1830, he removed to Palmyra, and soon afterward was baptized by David Whitmer. Shortly after he was ordained an elder. In 1831 he removed with the church to Kirtland, Ohio. At the June conference of 1831 he was ordained a high priest.

Soon after, in obedience to revelation, he journeyed to Missouri in company with Selah J. Griffin. He returned to Kirtland in the spring of 1832, and in November of the same year removed to Missouri and located in Jackson County, on the Big Blue. In the troublesome times of 1833 he shared the fate of his brethren in being driven from his home. He spent the winter in Lafayette County, thence removed to Clay County, where on July 7, 1834, he was ordained a member of the High Council in Zion. The following January he returned East and engaged actively in missionary work.

He was not present when he was chosen an Apostle, in February, 1835, but arrived in Kirtland in the April following when he was ordained, and subsequently was elected President of the quorum. The summer of 1835 he accompanied his quorum on their eastern mission, and subsequently he returned to Missouri, where he assisted in the settlement of difficulties in Clay County, and with the church moved to Caldwell County.

On February 10, 1838, he and David W. Patten were appointed presidents pro tem. of the church in Missouri. In October, 1838, as set forth elsewhere he apostatized and made affidavit to some questionable things at Richmond, Missouri, which increased the persecution against the church. He located in Clay County, Missouri; and later in Richmond, Ray County. Of his life there we know but little.

He emigrated to Utah in 1857, having previously united with the organization under Brigham Young. He died at Ogden, Utah, in January, 1866. In the Ogden cemetery a neat marble monument marks his resting place on which is chiseled the following inscription:—

"Thomas B. Marsh, First President of the Twelve Apostles of the Church of Jesus Christ of Latter Day Saints. Born at Acton, Massachusetts, November 1, 1799. Died January, 1866. Erected by his friends, July 17, 1893."—*Saints' Herald*, vol. 42, p. 470.

PARLEY P. PRATT.

Parley P. Pratt was the twelfth apostle chosen, but in the final arrangement he was the seventh. He was the third son of Jared and Charity Pratt. He was born April 12, 1807, in Burlington, Otsego County, New York. In October, 1826, he left his home and friends and journeyed westward, and spent the winter in solitude, in the forest, about thirty miles west of Cleveland, Ohio. In the spring he made some improvements and then returned to his home, where on September 9, 1827, he was united in marriage to Miss Thankful Halsey. In the October following they set out for the wilderness of Ohio, where they succeeded in making a comfortable home.

In 1829 Elder Sidney Rigdon came into the neighborhood preaching, and Mr. Pratt became identified with the movement then becoming so popular under Rigdon, Alexander Campbell, Scott, and others, and began shortly after to preach the new doctrine. In August, 1830, accompanied by his wife, he left their Ohio home and returned to New York, where he first saw the Book of Mormon. After some travel and diligent inquiry he was baptized in Seneca Lake, New York, by Oliver Cowdery, September 1, 1830, and the same evening he was ordained an elder.

In October, 1830, a revelation was given directing Elder Pratt with others to go on a mission to the West; accordingly in the same month, accompanied by Oliver Cowdery, Peter Whitmer, and Ziba Peterson, he started on that eventful mission, an account of which has been recorded in these pages. From this mission he returned alone to report their labor, and in 1831 was ordained a high priest. Again he went up to Missouri, accompanied by his brother Orson.

He afterwards settled in Jackson County, Missouri, and was among those banished from the county in 1833 by the violence of the mob. On July 7, 1834, he was ordained a member of the High Council in Zion, in Clay County, Missouri.

In February, 1835, he was ordained an apostle at Kirtland, Ohio, and in the following summer went with his quorum on its eastern mission. In 1836 he did missionary work in Canada. On March 25, 1837, his wife died at Kirtland, Ohio. In the summer of 1837, when so many turned away from the faith at Kirtland, he was to some extent affected by this spirit of apostasy; but he subsequently recovered from it, and made confession of his wrong. In this year he published from New York the first edition of the "Voice of Warning." Though he afterwards published other works, this was his masterpiece. Sometime during this year, or early in 1838, he was the second time married, espousing Mrs. Mary Ann (Frost) Stearns, widow of Nathan Stearns.

In May, 1838, he settled in Caldwell County, Missouri, and in October of the same year was among those demanded by General Lucas and delivered as prisoners by Colonel Hinkle. With Joseph Smith and his fellow prisoners he was taken to Independence, and thence to Richmond, where they had a mock trial before Judge King; but when others were sent to Liberty he was retained at Richmond. He afterward obtained a change of venue to Boone County and was lodged in jail at Columbia, from whence he escaped on July 4, 1839, making his way to Illinois.

In 1840 he accompanied his quorum on its mission to Europe, and was made editor of the *Millennial Star*, which that year made its first appearance. In 1841 when the rest of his quorum returned to America he was left in charge of the mission. In the autumn of 1842 he returned to America.

In 1844 he indorsed the action of Brigham Young and other members of his quorum, and with them he went West. He was not present at Council Bluffs in 1847 when the action was taken which sought to make Elder Brigham Young President. He with John Taylor of his quorum was in Utah at the time. He, however, continued to associate with Young and his fellows until his death. He was killed about twelve miles north of Van Buren, Arkansas, May 14, 1857, by an enraged man by the name of Hector H. McLean, who was jealous of his wife and Elder Pratt. He was buried about one mile from where the tragedy occurred.

CHAPTER 26.

EDWARD PARTRIDGE—NEWEL K. WHITNEY.

In this chapter we will give Biographies of two of the leading Bishops of the church.

EDWARD PARTRIDGE.

Edward Partridge was the first Bishop of the church. A sketch of his early life quoted from the words of Joseph Smith is published in the body of this work—pages 170, 171. The statement of Elder Pratt, found on page 155 regarding his ordination is a mistake, as he was not baptized until his visit to New York. See page 171.

In a revelation given February 4, 1831, he was called to this office, and of him it was said: "His heart is pure before me, for he is like unto Nathaniel of old, in whom there is no guile." In the summer of 1831, in obedience to revelation, Bishop Partridge journeyed to Missouri in company with Joseph Smith and others.

In May, 1831, while at Kirtland, a revelation was given instructing Bishop Partridge regarding consecration, inheritance of the saints, and other matters; and in July further instruction of the same nature was given him concerning Zion. Independence was pointed out as the place for the building of the City, and the Temple Lot indicated. Instruction was also given for the Bishop and others to be planted in Zion. In harmony with this commandment the Bishop located there as soon as he could arrange to do so. Active measures were at once adopted for the gathering of means to purchase land in Zion, and especially to get title to the Temple Lot. This was successful, and on December 19, 1831, Bishop Partridge bought for the church a tract of land including that lot, which has ever since been known as the Temple Lot.

This transfer was made by Jones H. Flournoy and wife, and is on record in Jackson County.[1] The deed was held by

[1] To all people to whom these presents shall come, Greeting. Know ye that we, Jones H. Flournoy and Clara Flournoy, wife of the said

Bishop Partridge until the time when the church was driven from the State under the exterminating order of Governor Boggs, when the Bishop, not knowing what would befall

Jones, of the county of Jackson, and State of Missouri, for the consideration of one hundred and thirty dollars, received to our full satisfaction, of Edward Partridge of the county and State aforesaid, do give, grant, bargain, sell, and confirm unto the said Edward Partridge, the following described piece or parcel of land; being a part of the southeast Quarter of Section three in township number forty-nine of range number thirty-five in the aforesaid county, bounded and described as follows, to wit: Commencing on the south line of said quarter section forty poles from the southeast corner of said quarter section, at the corner of a certain piece of land sold by said Flournoy and wife to one Lewis Jones, and from thence running west one hundred and twenty poles to the southwest corner of said quarter section. Thence north sixteen poles and ten links, thence north forty degrees east, ten poles, thence north twenty-one degrees east, fourteen poles, thence north fifteen degrees east, twenty poles, thence north forty-two degrees east, thirty-four poles, thence north fifty-five degrees east, thirty poles, thence north sixty-four degrees east, forty poles, thence north seventy degrees east, seventeen poles and fifteen links to the corner of a certain tract of land sold by the said Flournoy and wife to one G. M. Hensley, south one hundred and twenty-two poles and seventeen links to the place of beginning containing sixty-three acres and forty-three one hundred and sixtieths of an acre, be the same more or less. To have and to hold the above granted and bargained premises, with all and singular the rights and privileges thereunto in any wise belonging and appertaining unto him the said Edward Partridge, his heirs and assigns for ever, to his and their own proper use and behoof. And also we the said Jones H. Flournoy and Clara Flournoy, wife of the said Jones, as aforesaid, for ourselves, our heirs, and assigns, that at and until the ensealing of these presents we are well seized of the premises as a good indefeasible, and have good right to bargain and sell the same in manner and form as it is above written and that the same is free from all incumbrances whatsoever. And further more we the said Jones H. Flournoy and Clara Flournoy, wife of the said Jones, as aforesaid, do by these presents bind ourselves, our heirs and assigns, forever, to warrant and defend the above granted and bargained premises to him, the said Edward Partridge his heirs, and assigns, against all lawful claims and demands whatsoever.

In witness whereof we have hereunto set our hands and affixed our seals the nineteenth day of December in the year of our Lord, eighteen hundred and thirty-two [thirty-one].

JONES H. FLOURNOY. Seal.
CLARA FLOURNOY. Seal.

STATE OF MISSOURI, }
County of Jackson. } ss.

Be it remembered that on this nineteenth day of December in the year of our Lord one thousand eight hundred and thirty-one before the undersigned deputy for Samuel C. Owens, Clerk of the Circuit Court for the aforesaid county, personally came Jones H. Flournoy and Clara Flournoy, both personally known to the said undersigned, to be the persons whose names are subscribed to the foregoing instrument of writing as having executed the same and acknowledged said instrument of writing to be their act and deed for the purposes therein mentioned, she, the said Clara Flournoy, being by me first made acquainted with the contents thereof

him or other adults, and supposing that children would be
spared, made a transfer of the property to the minor heirs
of Oliver Cowdery, being careful to state the purpose for
which the property was held.[2]   This title was finally trans-

and examined separately and apart from her husband, whether she executed such deed and relinquished her dower in the lands and tenements
in said deed mentioned, freely, voluntarily, and without compulsion or
undue influence of her said husband, acknowledged and declared that
she executed said deed and relinquishes her dower in the lands and tenements in said deed mentioned, freely, voluntarily, and without compulsion or undue influence of her said husband.

Taken and certified under my hand and the private seal of Samuel C.
Owens, Clerk of the said Circuit Court, there being no official seal at said
office the day and the year above written.

RUSSELL HICKS,

[SEAL]   Deputy for Samuel C. Owens, Clerk C. C. J. C.

STATE OF MISSOURI, }
County of Jackson. } Sct.

I, Samuel C. Owens, Clerk of the Circuit Court, and *ex officio* recorder
within and for the aforesaid county, do hereby certify that the foregoing
deed of bargain and sale from Flournoy to Partridge, was filed in my
office for record on the 19th day of December, 1831, and duly recorded in
my office on the 24th day of May, 1832, in Book B, page 1.

SAMUEL C. OWENS, Clerk.

STATE OF MISSOURI, }
County of Jackson. } ss.

I, R. T. Hinde, Recorder of Deeds, within and for said county of Jackson and State of Missouri, do hereby certify that the foregoing is a full,
true, and complete transcript of the record of the W. D.———Acknowl-
edgement———and note of record thereon indorsed from Jones H. Flournoy and wife to Edward Partridge, as the same now remains of record in
my office in Independence, Missouri,———Book No. B, at page 1, and
following.

In testimony whereof, I have hereunto set my hand, and affixed the
seal of said office, at my office in the city of Independence, in said county,
this 11th day of June, A. D. 1887.

R. T. HINDE, Recorder,
By W. R. HALL, Deputy.

[2]EDWARD PARTRIDGE,
      To
JANE COWDERY, *et al.*

KNOW ALL MEN, that whereas there was money put in my hands, to
wit,—in the hands of Edward Partridge, by Oliver Cowdery, an elder in
the Church of Latter Day Saints, formerly of Kirtland, State of Ohio, for
the purpose of entering lands in the State of Missouri, in the name of,
and for the benefit of said church; and, Whereas, I, Edward Partridge
was Bishop of, and in said church he took said money and funds thus put
in his hands and entered the land in his own name, in the county of
Jackson, State of Missouri, in the name of Edward Partridge, the signer
of this deed,

Now know ye that for the furthering the ends of justice, and as I have to
leave the State of Missouri, by order of Governor Boggs, and with me also
our church, I do for the sum of one thousand dollars, to me in hand paid
by said Oliver Cowdery, do give, grant, bargain, and sell to John Cowdery,

ferred to the Reorganized Church, in the manner described in "Plaintiff's Abstract of Evidence in Temple Lot Suit," page 243, and following pages; to which the reader is referred.

Through the trying scenes in Jackson, Clay, and Caldwell counties, accounts of which are elsewhere given in this book, Bishop Partridge was a patient and faithful participant, being prominently engaged in every measure to

son of Oliver Cowdery, now seven years old; and Jane Cowdery three years, and Joseph Smith Cowdery one year old, all the lands entered in my name in the county of Jackson, in the district of Lexington, in the State of Missouri. Said Edward Partridge the first party and signer of this deed does also sell, alien, and confirm to the aforesaid John Cowdery all real estate and lands he has both entered as aforesaid, and all he owns in his own name by private purchase and holds by deed of gift, being intended for the use of the Church of Latter Day Saints or otherwise. This sale is to embrace all lots of all sizes, situated in Independence, and to embrace the lot known as the Temple Lot, and all other lands of whatever description said Partridge the first party is entitled to in said Jackson county, in the State of Missouri. Said Partridge also agrees to amend this deed to said Oliver Cowdery at any time for the purposes aforesaid.

Given under my hand and seal on the date above written.

E. G. GATES, Witness.　　　　　EDWARD PARTRIDGE. [Seal.]

STATE OF MISSOURI, } ss.
　Caldwell County. }

Be it remembered, that on the 25th day of March, 1839, before me, the undersigned, one of the Justices of the County court in and for said County, came Edward Partridge, who is personally known to me to be the same person whose name is subscribed to the foregoing instrument of writing as party thereto, and did acknowledge the same to be his act and deed for the purposes therein mentioned.

In testimony whereof I have hereunto set my hand and affixed my private seal on the day and year above written.

ELIAS HIGBEE, J. C. C. C.

The foregoing deed with the acknowledgment thereon from Edward Partridge to Jane Cowdery, et al., was filed and duly recorded in my office on the 7th day of February, A. D. 1870.

A. CUMINGO, Recorder,
By H. G. GOODMAN, Deputy.

STATE OF MISSOURI, } ss.
County of Jackson. }

I, R. T. Hinde, Recorder of Deeds within and for said County of Jackson, and State of Missouri, do hereby certify that the foregoing is a full, true, and complete transcript of the record of the Deed————acknowledgment————and note of record thereon endorsed from Edward Partridge to Jane Cowdery et al., as the same now remains on record in my office in Independence, Book No. 73, page 432, and following.

In testimony whereof, I have hereunto set my hand and affixed the seal of said office in the city of Independence, in said County, this 11th day of June, A. D. 1887.

R. T. HINDE, Recorder,
[SEAL.]　　　　　　　By W. R. HALL, Deputy.

advance the interests of the church, to gain redress for her wrongs, or to legally defend her against the encroachments of ungodly and unlawful men. He ever maintained the high character ascribed to him in the revelation of 1831, when he was designated for the office he held. He shared in the expulsion from the State in 1839, and was indefatigable in his efforts to ameliorate the condition of the suffering saints. In Illinois he served in his office diligently, leaving behind him an untarnished record for faithfulness and good works.

He died at Nauvoo, Illinois, May 27, 1840. The June number of the *Times and Seasons*, pays a high tribute of respect to his honor, faithfulness, and unselfishness.[*]

NEWEL K. WHITNEY.

Newel K. Whitney, Bishop of Kirtland, was born in Marlborough, Windham County, Vermont, February 5, 1795.

[*][Communicated.]

DIED—In this place, on the 27th day of May, Bishop Edward Partridge, aged 46 years. In recording the death of this our brother, we record the death of one of our earliest, most faithful, and confidential members. His life was one continual exhibition of the sincerity of his religious belief, and a perpetual evidence of his confidence in a future state of rewards and punishments: in view of which he always acted. His strict regard through life to all the commandments of heaven, and his undeviating obedience to them, are consoling evidences to his friends that if there are any such things as rewards in the future world for well-doing in this, he is certain of enjoying them.

No man had the confidence of the church more than he. His station was highly responsible; large quantities of property ever intrusted to his care. Deeds and conveyances of lands, to a large amount, were put into his hands, for the benefit of the poor, and for church purposes; for all of which the directest account was rendered, to the fullest satisfaction of all concerned. And after he had distributed a handsome property, of his own, for the benefit of the poor; and being driven from his home, found himself reduced to very limited circumstances, still, not one cent of public property would he use to indemnify himself or family; but distributed it all, for the benefit of the widow, the fatherless, and the afflicted; has deceased, leaving his family in very ordinary circumstances.

Had there been one covetous desire in his heart, no man had the opportunity better to gratify it; but he has left a testimony, to be had in everlasting remembrance, that he lived above its influence, and over him it had no control; but in all things, he had respect to the reward of the just.

A life of greater devotedness to the cause of truth, we presume, was never spent on this earth. His religion was his all, for this he spent his life, and for this he laid it down. He lost his life in consequence of the Missouri persecutions, and he is one of that number whose blood will be required at their hands. As a church we deplore our loss, but we rejoice in his gain. He rests where persecutors can assail him no more.

When the missionaries of the church first visited Kirtland, Ohio, in 1830, they found him engaged in the mercantile business as a member of the firm of Gilbert and Whitney. He was among the first to embrace the gospel in that place. When the Prophet Joseph Smith and wife arrived in Kirtland, in January, 1831, Mr. Whitney received them into his house and provided them a home until other provision could be made.

In December, 1831, Newel K. Whitney was called to the office of bishop, to officiate in Kirtland. He was thereafter designated as the Bishop of Kirtland, while Bishop Partridge was known as the Bishop of Zion. The Bishop of Kirtland was made subject to the Bishop in Zion and instructed to report to him.

In April, 1832, Bishop Whitney accompanied Joseph Smith and others to Missouri. On May 6, in company with Joseph Smith, he started to return. In Indiana the Bishop undertook to jump from a stage while the horses were running, and broke his leg. This delayed them about four weeks, Joseph remaining with him, and caring for him. They finally reached Kirtland sometime in June.

In September, 1832, Bishop Whitney was instructed by revelation to travel around among the churches, searching after the poor to administer to their wants; and was also enjoined to visit the cities of New York, Albany, and Boston, and warn the people with the sound of the gospel.

During the fall of this year he visited those cities, to carry out this instruction. He was accompanied by Joseph Smith.

In May, 1833, Bishop Whitney was reproved by revelation for not having his family in order, and warned that if not more diligent they would be removed out of their place. When Zion's Camp went up to Missouri he remained at his post in Kirtland and looked after church affairs in his department. Though there was nothing especially remarkable about the career of Bishop Whitney, he followed the fortunes of the church while President Smith lived, and was faithful in his calling, retaining the office of Bishop. In September, 1844, he presided over the council which tried Sidney Rigdon. The *exparte* manner in which he conducted that council, or suffered it to be conducted, is not very complimentary to his judicial ability or his sense of fairness.   He followed the fortunes of the western exodus under Brigham Young, and died in Salt Lake City, September 23, 1850.

INDEX.

Thompson and Atchison to Phelps, 536: to Hewitt, 567; of Joseph Smith to elders of the church, 583; of Orson Hyde to Joseph Smith, 614; of William Smith to Joseph Smith, 618; of Joseph Smith to William Smith, 620.

Leonard, Abigail, affidavit of, 409.

Leonard, Lyman, mobbed, 409.

Levi, sons of, to offer an offering in righteousness, 38.

Lewis, brothers, not disaffected, 606.

Lewis, Joshua, conference at his residence, 209; messenger to Lexington, 355.

Liberty, public meeting at, 494.

License, instruction concerning, 71.

Likens, Rev., leader of mobs, 352.

Linvill, Thomas, killed, 357.

Loborough, conference at, 568.

Louisville, visited enroute, 244.

Lovelady, Rev., leader of mobs, 352.

Lowry, John, assists the Kirtland messengers, 400.

Lucas, S. D., participates with the mob, 315; failed to obey orders, 423.

Luther, Martin, a forerunner, 2.

Majors, Benjamin, one of the mob committee, 317.

Malachi, quoted by the angel, 13.

Manuscript, date it was received by printers, 81.

Manuscript found, claims concerning, 143, 144; claims untenable, 144, 145.

Marriage, article on, 575: of Joseph Smith and Emma Hale, 17; of Sidney Rigdon and Phebe Brooks, 130; of William Perry and Eliza Brown, 590; of Newel Knight and Lydia Goldthwaite, 607; of Warren Parrish and Martha H. Raymond, 610; of Ebenezer Robinson and Angeline Works, 612; of E. Webb and E. A. McWithey, 612.

Marsh, T. B., another traveling companion for, 199; accompanies Pratt to Lexington, 327; chosen to go to Kirtland, 478; a member of the High Council, 503; chosen an apostle, 538, 541; ordained, 542; biography of, 655.

Marvin, Edward, to travel eastward, 435.

McCarty, Richard, caught in lawless act, 326; complaint of, 329.

McClentic, attends meeting, 243.

McCord, Robert, dies of cholera, 481.

McCoy, Rev., leads a mob, 332, 352.

McIlwain's Bend, revelation received at, 211.

McLellin, W. E., revelation to, 221; attempts to imitate revelations, 224; revelation to, 224; required to leave Jackson County, 317; a prisoner, 358; a member of the High Council, 503; chosen an apostle, 538, 541; ordained, 542; appointed clerk of Twelve, 549; holds discussion, 554; biography of, 650.

Melchisedec priesthood, provision made for, and privileges of, 59; commanded to ordain to, 60; Joseph and Oliver to ordain each other to, 64; two separate ordinations doubtful, 64; ordained to, 77; fullness conferred first time, 192.

Mentor, Ohio, unseemly conduct of inhabitants, 609.

Messenger and Advocate provided for, 372; first number, 525; changes editors, 564.

Messenger and Enquirer published at Liberty, 394.

Messengers dispatched to Jackson County, 372; sent to Zion, 386; sent to Kirtland, 399.

Methodist preacher, repulses Joseph Smith, 10; preachers, leaders of mobs, 352.

Methodists engage in the mob, 243.

Minutes of the organization of the High Council, 429; corrected, 432; President given privilege to correct, 432; of conference at New Portage, 448; of conference at Kirtland, 453; of council, 481; of High Council, 503; of Grand Council, 560; of General Assembly, 572.

Miracle, first performed, 84.

Miracles, not designed to establish the church, 605.

Missionaries aid mob, 304.

Missionaries arrive at Kirtland, 129.

Mission, to the West, 118, 128: among Indians, 179; in Canada, 378; east, 439.

Mitchill, Dr., sanctions the opinion of Anthon, 19.

Mob, destroys a dam, 89; raging with anger, 95; first in Zion, 290;

Presbyterian preachers lead mobs, 352.

Press, in opposition to the truth, 251.

Priesthood, revelation on, 253.

Printing office, in ruins, 353; arrangements concerning, 524; building for, 525.

Printing press, provision for, 217; arrives at Kirtland, 379.

Prior, Rev., on Joseph Smith, 3.

Prisoners released without trial, 331, 358.

Progress in various places, 528, 570.

Propositions, of "Mormons," 474; from Jackson County, 494; of Jackson County rejected, 498; offered by the saints, 499.

Provision made for President of High Priesthood, 245.

Public meeting at Liberty, 494.

Purchase of lands, 213.

Quincy, Josiah, writes of Joseph Smith, 3.

Rathbone, Robert, arrives at Kirtland from Missouri, 608.

Rathbun, Hiram, testimony of, 335.

Rebaptism, instruction on, 79.

Redfield, Harvey, arrives at Kirtland from Missouri, 608.

Reed, Attorney, gives account of Joseph's trials, 101.

Reese, Amos, concurs in Gilbert's letter, 367; attorney for the saints, 389.

Religious revival, 7.

Report of Seventy, 628.

Resolutions, passed by citizens of Jackson County, 312.

Revelation, given by a woman, 175; to gather out of eastern lands, 183; on Zion, 204; on the Sabbath, 209; on returning east, 210; received at McIlwain's Bend, 211; on Zion, 216; to Hyde, Johnson, and McLellin, 224; on the Rebellion, 261; to Enoch, 450; given on Fishing River, 475; to Twelve examined, 597.

Richards, F. D., publishes "Pearl of Great Price," 262.

Rider, Simonds, apostatized, 240; attends meeting, leader of the mob, 242.

Rigdon, Sidney, sketch of, 129, 142; his whereabouts from 1826 to 1831, 145, 152; his reputation, 152;

called on by missionaries, his baptism, 154; his ordination, 155; visits Joseph Smith, 158; revelation to, 158, 188; assists in translating, 160; journeys to Missouri, 201; arrives in Missouri, 204; at dedication of Temple Lot, 209; arrives at St. Louis, 213; goes to Kirtland to settle a difficulty, 220; preaches at Shalersville and Ravenna, 232; mobbed, 236, 241; seriously hurt, 243; starts for Missouri, 243; settles difficulty with Partridge, 244; preaches in Zion, 249; returns to Kirtland, 250; attends conference, 277; called to the Presidency, 280; ordained to the Presidency, 282, 283; organizes high priests, 282; to take a missionary tour, 303; preaches at Chardon, 303; in council at Kirtland, 372; starts to Canada, 373; preaches at Perrysburgh, 377; returns to Kirtland, 378; sent to Strongsville, 435; blessing conferred upon, 447; presides over the church, 518; prefers charges against S. Smith, 520; goes to New Portage, 585; preaches at Kirtland, 604; biography of, 638.

Rights of the people recognized, 61.

Riley, Rev. M., speaks against the saints, 496.

Robinson, Ebenezer, baptized, 589; married, 612.

Rockwell, A., baptized, 79.

Rockwell, Caroline, baptized, 88.

Rockwell, Electa, baptized, 88.

Rockwell, Peter, baptized, 88.

Rose, conference at, 566.

Rudd, Erastus, dies of cholera, 481.

Russel, States Attorney, calls on Joseph Smith, 444.

Ryland, Judge J. F., visited by Pratt and Marsh, 327; letter of, 360; sends sheriff to meet Zion's Camp, 473; writes to Gilbert, 492.

Sabbath, revelation on, 209.

Saco, Maine, conference held at, 521, 583.

Sacrament, manner of administering, 72; instruction on, 115.

Sad change, a, 397.

Sadler, J. C., one of the mob committee, 317.

Sagers, Harrison, appointed to travel, 435.

Saints, arrive from the east, 191;

Strong, Elial, dies of cholera, 481.

Sweet, Northrop, revelation to, 156.

Tanner, Elder, advised, 540.

Tanner, John, seeks instruction, 372.

Temple, (Kirtland,) corner stones laid, 368; erection of, 518; building prosecuted, 523; exertions made to expedite, 523; blessed for work on, 551; amounts subscribed to, 568; progress of, 606.

Temple lot, location revealed, 203; dedicated, 209.

Testimony, of three witnesses, 47; of eight witnesses, 48; nature of, 48.

Thayre. Ezra, revelation to, 156; is delayed, 199; attends conference, 277; appointed to purchase farms, 283; appointed to purchase tannery, 285.

Thompson and Atchison write Phelps, 536.

Thompson, J. T. V., writes to Phelps, 534.

Thornton, J., writes to Governor Dunklin, 488.

Three witnesses, ordain apostles, 538, 541; blessed, 541.

Tippets brothers, start for Missouri, 586.

Tracy, J. M., discusses with McLellin, 555.

Translation delayed, 28; of Jewish Scriptures, 159; to be resumed in Ohio, 165; preparation for, 215; of Scriptures, 220; postponed, 231; commanded to resume, 233; continued, 235, 236; resumed, 251; of Scriptures finished, 303; of New Testament finished, 278; of papyrus, 569.

Trenton, Steamer, passage on, 244.

Turnham, Judge, speaks in behalf of saints, 496.

Twelve apostles, hold conference at St. Johnsbury, 569; at Saco, Maine, and Farmington, Maine, 583; hold council, 539, 547, 552, 559; receive their charge, 542, 547, 559; start on their mission, 562; hold conference at Freedom, 564; at Rose, 566; at Loborough, Canada, 568; at Pillow Point, 568; at Westfield, 563; return from their missions, are heard by the Presidents, 586; visit Joseph Smith, 587; meet in council, 588, 601; must be sustained, 617; in council, 627.

Two personages appear, 9.

Upper Missouri Advertiser suspended, 316.

Urim and Thummim, deposited with the plates, 13; description of 13; not to be shown, 14; by means of translation, 18; taken from Joseph Smith, and again restored, 24, 25.

Van Buren County, saints locate in, 318; take refuge in, 334.

Vision, representing different glories, 235; heavenly, 283.

Volunteers for Zion's Camp, 440.

Wales, ——, stabbed, 496.

Waller, Zachariah, one of the mob committee, 317.

Warren, Company arrive at, 243.

Webb, E., married, 612.

Wells, Attorney General, letter of, 363.

Wesley, John, on ushering in a latter-day dispensation, 2; on spiritual gifts, 89; persecuted, 109.

Western Monitor, mob's resolutions published in, 318; censures the mob, 319.

Westfield, conference at, 297, 563.

Weston, Samuel, engages in a mob, 315; one of the mob committee, 317; declines to issue warrant, 326.

Wheeling, paper purchased at, 244.

Whitcher, Mary, has an interview with the prophet, 598.

Whitlock, Harvey, required to leave Jackson County, 317.

Whitmer, Anne, baptized, 84.

Whitmer, Christian, becomes one of the eight witnesses, 48; baptized, 84; ordained to high priesthood, 371; chosen to go to Missouri, 478.

Whitmer, David, offers assistance, 42; and John and Peter, Jr., become zealous friends, 43; baptized, 44; becomes one of the three witnesses, 46; reaffirms testimony, 50, 54, 55; inscription on tomb of, 54; appointed on committee of instruction, 220; chosen to go to Kirtland, 478; elected President of High Council, 503; appointed agent, 585.

Whitmer, Elizabeth Anne, baptized, 85.

Whitmer, Elizabeth, baptized, 84.

Whitmer family, disturbed, 114.

LIBRARY
OF THE
UNIVERSITY

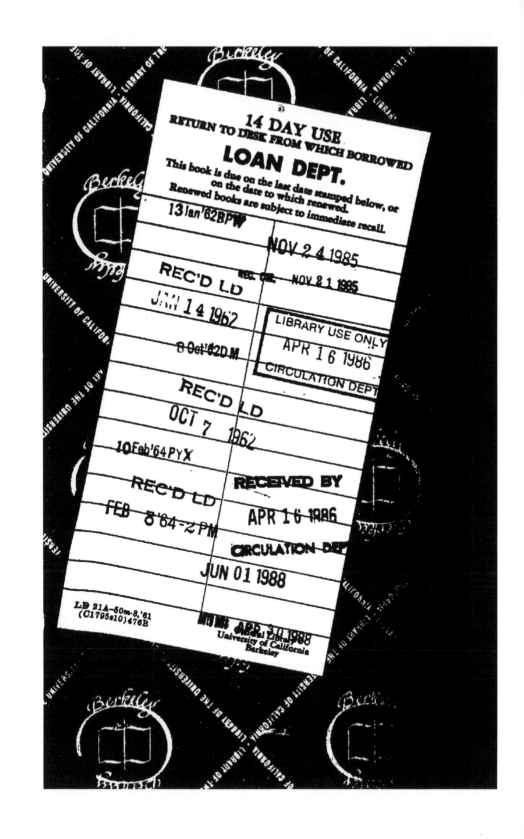

Ingram Content Group UK Ltd.
Milton Keynes UK
UKHW022259080523
421436UK00005B/115